1959   D J Morgana

THE MASS OF THE
ROMAN RITE

✝✝✝

THE MASS OF THE ROMAN RITE

ITS ORIGINS AND DEVELOPMENT
(*Missarum Sollemnia*)

BY

REV. JOSEPH A. JUNGMANN, S.J.
Professor of Theology, University of Innsbruck

TRANSLATED BY

REV. FRANCIS A. BRUNNER, C.SS.R.
Former Professor, St. Joseph's College, Kirkwood, Mo.

REVISED BY

CHARLES K. RIEPE
Collegium Canisianum, Innsbruck

NEW REVISED AND ABRIDGED EDITION IN ONE VOLUME

BENZIGER BROTHERS, INC.

NEW YORK · BOSTON · CINCINNATI · CHICAGO · SAN FRANCISCO

NIHIL OBSTAT
Myles M. Bourke, S.T.D.
Censor Librorum
IMPRIMATUR
† Francis Cardinal Spellman
Archbishop of New York
NEW YORK, MARCH 20, 1959

The Nihil Obstat and Imprimatur are official declarations that a book or pamphlet is free of doctrinal or moral error. No implication is contained therein that those who have granted the Nihil Obstat and Imprimatur agree with the contents, opinions or statements expressed.

Translated from the German Revised Edition of Missarum Sollemnia (1949) and revised in accordance with the latest German edition published by Herder Verlag, Vienna, Austria

THE MASS OF THE ROMAN RITE: ITS ORIGINS AND DEVELOPMENT (MISSARUM SOLLEMNIA), © 1951, 1955, 1959, BY BENZIGER BROTHERS, INC. PRINTED IN THE UNITED STATES OF AMERICA. ALL RIGHTS RESERVED—NO PART OF THIS BOOK MAY BE REPRODUCED IN ANY FORM WITHOUT PERMISSION IN WRITING FROM THE PUBLISHER.
LIBRARY OF CONGRESS CATALOG CARD NUMBER: 59-10312

To the Fathers, Alumni, and Students
of the Collegium Canisianum
Innsbruck, Austria
on the Occasion of Our 100th Anniversary
1858–1958
This Edition of Our Rector's Greatest Work
Is Humbly Dedicated

AUTHOR'S FOREWORD

The present volume is a shortened version of the English translation of my two-volume work *Missarum Sollemnia*. It was during the war years, 1939–1945, that this work came into being. After the removal of the Theological Faculty by Hitler's regime and the closing of the Jesuit College (October 12, 1939), our teaching activity in Innsbruck was brought to an end. But there still remained, apart from actual parish work, the opportunity to serve the Church of God through quiet literary endeavor.

With all my strength, I utilized this opportunity. This was especially made possible through the kindness and care of my superiors, who secured a new home for me in which to pass my exile. This was the home of the School Sisters of St. Pölten in Hainstetten. (This village would hardly be found on any map in America; it is a tiny farming village close to the Danube between Linz and Vienna.) In the years previous, it had been my most cherished task to instruct young seminarians in the liturgy of the Mass. It was certainly a gift of God that in the midst of the noise of war I was able to carry on this task, albeit in a different form. In Hainstetten I was able to work with few worries as on an island of peace.

I was just in the midst of bringing the final pages of the book into shape when the American troops appeared in the vicinity in May of 1945. (To our great terror, they turned the area over to the Russians within a few days.) However, as a consequence of the disturbances of the war, three years had still to pass until the appearance of the book.

In the ten years which have gone by since then, the work has made many friends throughout the world. Still, it seemed to some who were familiar with the book, especially in busy America, that to become closely acquainted with its contents required a great deal of courage indeed! Two volumes of over 450 pages each, complete with apparatus, certainly presented an ominous appearance to the average reader. And so it is that my student, Charles K. Riepe, of the Archdiocese of Baltimore, who was already best prepared for such a task, undertook to correct this situation by cleverly combining the two volumes into one. How he accomplished this, he himself will explain.

May this work continue in its new form to be of service in leading many souls to a deeper understanding of the precious legacy of Our Lord.

Joseph A. Jungmann, S.J.

REVISER'S FOREWORD

This new edition of "The Mass of the Roman Rite" (*Missarum Sollemnia*) was suggested by Benziger Brothers, Inc., who felt that a one-volume edition would be perhaps better suited to the average American reader. Thus, at the suggestion of Father Jungmann, I began the work while in the United States during the summer of 1957.

Those familiar with the two-volume original will notice that the greater part of editing has consisted in the elimination of the apparatus. In addition, each page, some 958 in all, had to be cut, pasted on a larger sheet, and then edited, added to, and occasionally newly translated. The purpose in view was to preserve the substance of the German original but to eliminate what could be sacrificed to expediency. Only occasionally were larger sections omitted, as in the chapter "Præparatio ad Missam." New footnotes were added where it seemed advisable and occasionally other devices were added to facilitate understanding, such as the diagram on the development of the various forms of the Mass. And of course, footnotes from the original which seem essential to illuminate the text as well as those which are simply interesting have been retained. At the same time, care was taken to ensure that this edition is fully up to date and in accord with the fourth German edition which appeared in the late winter of 1958. The chapter on the Rite of Commingling, which Father Jungmann prepared especially for the present edition, is certainly the latest word on that difficult subject.

It is true that because I am a seminarian, I have naturally had an eye open to the needs of my colleagues in the preparation of this edition. But this book is by no means intended solely for seminarians. It is hoped that clergy and laity will be able to profit accordingly. And, too, perhaps this edition could be used as a text for a course in Mass Liturgy if adapted by the individual professor to his own taste and needs. It goes without saying that for scientific research recourse to the original two-volume work is essential.

Finally, I wish to thank Father Jungmann for his kindly patience as well as for checking the manuscript. Not only did he offer suggestions (and find mistakes!) but he also saw to it as my Rector that I did not neglect my theology in the process. I have taken the liberty of dedicating this edition to my Alma Mater, the Canisianum, on the occasion of our 100th anniversary celebrated this year (1958). Perhaps in this way I can express my gratitude for the opportunity to make even a small contribution to the Apostolate of the Liturgy which Pope Pius XII has called "the working of the Holy Spirit in His Church."

INNSBRUCK, JULY 1, 1958   *Charles K. Riepe*

ABBREVIATED BIBLIOGRAPHY

Atchley, E. G. Cuthbert. *A History of the Use of Incense in Divine Worship.*
  (Alcuin Club Collections, 13) London, 1909.

Baumstark, A. *Liturgie comparée. Conférences faites au Prieuré d'Amay.*
  Edition refondu. Chevetogne O. J., 1940.

Bishop, E. *Liturgica historica.* Oxford, 1918.

Bishop Serapion's Prayer Book. With Introduction, Notes, and Indices by J.
  Wordsworth. 2nd ed. revised. S.P.C.K. London, 1923.

Bouyer, L. *Liturgical Piety.* (Liturgical Studies II) Notre Dame, 1955.

Braun, J. *Der christliche Alter in seiner geschichtlichen Entwicklung.* 2 vols.
  Munich, 1924.

Brightman, F. E. *Liturgies Eastern and Western. I. Eastern Liturgies.* Oxford,
  1896.

Connolly, R. H. *The Liturgical Homilies of Narsai.* (Texts and Studies, VIII,
  1) Cambridge, 1909.

Coventry, J. *The Breaking of the Bread.* A Short History of the Mass. New
  York, 1950.

Danielou, J. *The Bible and Liturgy.* (Liturgical Studies III) Notre Dame,
  1956.

DeLubac, H. *The Splendor of the Church,* New York, 1956.

Denzinger H. and Rahner, K. *Enchiridion Symbolorum.* 30th ed. Freiburg,
  1955.

De Puniet, P. *The Roman Pontifical: A History and Commentary.* New York,
  1932.

Dix, G. *The Shape of the Liturgy.* 2nd ed. Westminster, 1945.

——— *The Treatise on the Apostolic Tradition of St. Hippolytus of Rome.*
  London, 1937.

Duchesne, L. *Christian Worship: Its Origin and Evolution.* 5th ed. trans. from
  3rd French ed. by M. McClure. London, 1927.

Ellard, G. *Christian Life and Worship.* Milwaukee, 1950.

——— *The Mass in Transition.* Milwaukee, 1956.

Fortescue, A. *The Mass. A Study of the Roman Liturgy.* London, 1912.

Gihr, N. *The Holy Sacrifice of the Mass.* Rev. trans. St. Louis, 1949.

Jungmann, J. A. *Public Worship*. Trans. C. Howell. Collegeville, 1958.

—— *Liturgical Worship. An Inquiry into Its Fundamental Principles*. New York, 1941.

—— *The Sacrifice of the Church*. Trans. C. Howell. Collegeville, 1957.

Kennedy, V. *The Saints of the Canon of the Mass*. Vatican City, 1938.

Koenker, E. *The Liturgical Renaissance in the Roman Catholic Church*. Chicago.

Lechner-Eisenhofer. *Liturgik des Römischen Ritus*. Freiburg, 1953.

Legg, J. W. *Tracts on the Mass*. (HBS, 27) London, 1904.

Masure, E. *The Sacrifice of the Mystical Body*. London, 1954.

O'Shea, W. *The Worship of the Church*. A Companion to Liturgical Studies. Westminster, Md., 1957.

Parsch, P. *The Liturgy of the Mass*. Trans. and adapted by H. Winstone. St. Louis, 1958.

—— *Study the Mass*. Collegeville, 1953.

Putz, J. *My Mass*. Westminster, Md., 1955.

Quasten, J. *Monumenta eucharistica et liturgica vetutissima*. Bonn, 1935–1936.

Sacraments and Worship. (Sources of Christian Theology I) ed. with commentary by P. Palmer. Westminster, Md., 1955.

Salaville, S. *Eastern Liturgies*. London, 1938.

Trethowan, I. *Christ in the Liturgy*. New York, 1952.

Wilson, H. *The Gelasian Sacramentary*. Oxford, 1894.

Contents

PART TWO

The Nature and Forms of the Mass

PART THREE

The Mass Ceremonies

Part One

THE FORM OF
THE MASS THROUGH
THE CENTURIES

1. Mass in the Primitive Church

The first Holy Mass was said on "the same night in which He was betrayed" (1 Cor. 11:23). Judas' resolution had been taken, the next few steps would bring our Lord to the Mount of Olives where an agony would overtake Him and His enemies seize Him. In this very hour He gives His disciples the Holy Sacrament which for all time would be the offering of the Church. The setting was significant—the paschal meal. Since the withdrawal of the people out of Egypt the paschal lamb had served year after year to prefigure the great expectation. The fulfillment, too, would serve to recall the exodus not only from Egypt but from the land of sin, and the arrival not into a promised land but into God's kingdom. From this hour on it was to continue as a fond reminiscence from generation to generation. But the records of the Last Supper contain few details concerning the ceremonial of the meal, probably because this ceremonial was not meant to be the lasting setting of the celebration.

And still we should like to know more about that first Mass. Attempts have been made, through research into the form of the paschal meal in Christ's time and a thorough study of the New Testament accounts, to reconstruct the events of the Last Supper. Attention must be called to the apparent differences in these accounts—differences even in detailing the form of the words of institution; these differences must arise from the differences in the liturgical practice from which the accounts sprang. In Matthew and Mark the words spoken over the bread are followed by those over the chalice, while in Luke and Paul a more or less large interval elapses, as the Roman rite itself announces: *simili modo postquam cœnatum est*. Seemingly at the Last Supper the presentation of the eucharistic Chalice was separated from the presentation of the sacramental Body. It was the liturgical practice of the primitive Church which first brought them together. The older exegesis, indeed, apparently attempted a justification of the time elements of the text without separating the two consecrations. But the modern interpretation, even of Catholics, is almost unanimous in taking the words at their face value. Besides the natural meaning of the words, another argument is to be found in the ease with which we can thus dovetail the narrative into the paschal rite current in our Lord's time, as research has revealed it.

In Christ's day the paschal meal was surrounded with a very complicated ceremonial. Before the meal proper, at which the Easter lamb was eaten, there was a little preliminary—a serving of bitter herbs and unleavened bread that recalled the want felt during the journey out of Egypt. Both before and after this preludial meal the cup was filled. Then the son of the family or the youngest of those present had to place the question: What did these unusual customs signify? With a prayer of thanks to God, the father of the house then told the story of the ancient days in Egypt and of the liberation from darkness into light, from bondage into freedom (*Haggada*). This closed with the singing of the first part of the *Hallel* (Vulgate, Psalms 112; 113:1–8), in which all those at table joined by answering "Alleluia" after each half verse.

Only after this did the meal proper begin. The father of the house took one of the loaves of unleavened bread, broke it, pronounced over it a little blessing and passed it around. This ceremony of brotherly communion in one bread was the signal for starting the meal. Then the paschal lamb was eaten, with no ritual to hem in the eating and drinking. But after the meal was over the father of the house took the cup, newly filled with wine, and sitting upright he lifted it slightly while he spoke the grace after meal, the real table prayer. Then all drank of it. This was the third cup, called "the cup of the blessing," or "chalice of benediction." All then sang the second and larger part of the *Hallel* (Vulgate, Psalms 113:9–117:29 and 135) and, after a last blessing, drank the fourth ceremonial cup.

Into this arrangement our Lord's Last Supper fits very easily. The consecration of the bread is connected with the blessing before the eating of the lamb, grafted on to the rite of breaking the bread. For this blessing Matthew and Mark employ not the word *eucharistesas*, which contains the idea of thanks, but rather *eulogesas*, which conveys the idea of blessing. This better describes such a prayer. The bread which the father of the house passed around in the preliminary *Haggada* was to be accompanied (according to an old Aramaic formulary) with the words: "See the bread of misery which was eaten by our fathers who passed out of Egypt." Our Lord hands it to His disciples with the weighty words, "This is my body which is to be given for you." The consecration of the chalice is connected with the grace after meal and with the third cup, the cup of the blessing (chalice of benediction), of which all could partake in common, whereas during the rest of the meal each of those at table drank from his own individual cup. For the table prayer a special formula was prescribed; Jesus devised one of His own.

THE MASS OF THE APOSTLES

Our Lord concluded the institution with the command, "Do this for a commemoration of me." How did the Apostles and the primitive Church carry out this order? As the New Testament accounts intimate by their omission of nearly all details of the paschal feast, the setting of the paschal rite was not considered. Its repetition was not only impracticable, because of the surrounding ceremonial, but it was impossible from the standpoint of law, for in the Old Testament law, to which the Apostles still clung, the eating of the paschal lamb was set for only one time of the year. Prominent in the narrative of St. Luke and St. Paul is the placing of the consecration of the chalice after the meal; Matthew and Mark do not take any special notice of this peculiar circumstance. When Matthew and Mark wrote, it must have already been customary in their locality to put the two consecrations together. Does that mean that Paul and his disciple Luke still suppose an actual separation? At least in this case there would be some basis for the related opinion that in the early community the Eucharist was, as a rule, bound up with a meal. But unfortunately we cannot clear up this or any similar question, nor can we recreate the form of the Mass-liturgy up to the middle of the second century except through little vestiges and hints and by deductions from later facts.

The Acts of the Apostles mentions three times the "breaking of bread" in the Christian congregation [1]—mentions it in such a way that it designates not some introductory ceremony at a meal but a complete and self-contained action. In this term "breaking of bread" we have an entirely new, Christian mode of expression, a term alien to both Jewish and classical literature. The term evidently corresponds to a new thing, the holy Bread of the Christian community. The neo-converts of Whitsunday lived in holy happiness; "and continung daily with one accord in the temple . . . , and breaking bread in their houses" (Acts 2:46). Besides the liturgy of the Old Law in which everyone regularly took part, there was also this new celebration, which was referred to only by suggestion, and to which the Christians had to come in smaller groups and in their own dwellings. "And they continued steadfastly in the teaching of the Apostles and in the communion of the breaking of the bread and in the prayers" (Acts 2:42). Reference is made to prayer conjoined to the breaking of bread. We can discover nothing further.

In a later chapter we read that there was an assembly one Sunday night at Troas "for the breaking of bread" (Acts 20:7). A long sermon by

[1] Acts 2:42, 46; 20:7.

St. Paul precedes this "breaking of bread" and partaking of the Eucharist (Acts 20:11). From the words "breaking of bread" we cannot infer anything more. Since the words were not used simply for "to have a meal," we cannot conclude from them alone that the essential sacramental rite, which our Lord had instituted with the breaking of bread, and which was thereafter so spoken of, was always bound up with a real meal.

But several other arguments do lead to this conclusion. When we see the Apostles gathered together after our Saviour's resurrection, it seems to be the common table that brings them together. That could also have been the case after Pentecost. This was then the opportunity at set times to combine with it the memorial meal of the Lord, just as He Himself had combined it with a meal. Every meal was already impressed with a reverential character, since it was always begun and ended with prayer. Especially the Sabbath meal—the meal on Friday night which initiated the Sabbath—possessed a highly religious stamp. An expansion of the table company beyond the family circle was a well-loved practice on this day just as at the Easter meal. Like these Sabbath meals in character were the community banquets which were held on certain occasions for one's circle of friends (*Chaburah*).

One of the ceremonies which appears to have been part and parcel of the practice at such meals was for the master of the house to bless the bread, break it and distribute it. Thus the entire company was drawn together by the blessing and the eating in common. Of course the blessing of the wine would naturally be added. The "cup of the blessing" itself was filled at the end of the meal, right before the saying of grace which concluded the meal. As an invitation to drink of this cup, a prescribed formula was used. At a later period the prayer was composed of four doxologies of which the first two can be traced back to the time before the destruction of Jerusalem, namely, the "Praise of the Meal" and the "Praise of the Land."

Certain it is that this custom (with the proper changes) was continued within the Christian communities. We have striking proof of this in the prayer of the *Didache* near the end of the first century:

> 9. Regarding the Eucharist. Give thanks as follows:
> First concerning the cup:
> "We give Thee thanks, our Father, for the Holy Vine of David Thy servant, which Thou hast made known to us through Jesus, Thy Servant."
> *"To Thee be the glory forevermore."*
>
> Next, concerning the broken bread:
> "We give Thee thanks, our Father, for the life and knowledge which Thou hast made known to us through Jesus, Thy Servant."
> *"To Thee be the glory forevermore."*

"As this broken bread was scattered over the hills and then, when gathered, became one mass, so may Thy Church be gathered from the ends of the earth into Thy Kingdom.'

"For Thine is the glory and the power through Jesus Christ forevermore."

Let no one eat and drink of your Eucharist but those baptized in the name of the Lord; to this, too, the saying of the Lord is applicable: *Do not give to dogs what is sacred.*

10.   After you have taken your fill of food, give thanks as follows:

"We give Thee thanks, O Holy Father, for Thy holy name which Thou hast enshrined in our hearts, and for the knowledge and faith and immortality which Thou hast made known to us through Jesus, Thy Servant."

"To Thee be the glory forevermore."

"Thou, Lord Almighty, hast created all things for the sake of Thy name and hast given food and drink for men to enjoy, that they may give thanks to Thee; but to us Thou hast vouchsafed spiritual food and drink and eternal life through [Jesus,] Thy Servant."

"Above all, we give Thee thanks because Thou art mighty."

"To Thee be the glory forevermore."

"Remember, O Lord, Thy Church: deliver her from all evil, perfect her in Thy love, and from the four winds assemble her, the sanctified, in Thy kingdom which Thou hast prepared for her."

"For Thine is the power and the glory forevermore."

"May grace come, and this world pass away!"

"Hosanna to the God of David!"

"If anyone is holy, let him advance; if anyone is not, let him be converted. *Maranatha!*" "Amen."

But permit the prophets to give thanks as much as they desire.[2]

Much as these prayers have been discussed, little has been achieved in the way of clarifying their precise meaning and import. In every case we have table prayers in the setting of a Christian meal: Blessing of wine and bread, and grace at the end. That the meal included the sacramental Eucharist is hardly likely. The call at the end of the final grace may perhaps relate to the Eucharist. But again it is not clear how it is connected here. At a much later time, after the close of the second century, we learn more about the agapes which the Christian community conducted for the benefit of the poor and to foster the spirit of Christian concord. But these agapes are absolutely separate from the Eucharist. We cannot therefore directly derive anything more from them than the picture of a religion-sponsored meal.

From what has already been said, this only can be deduced with cer-

[2] Tr. J. A. Kleist, S.J., *The Didache* (Ancient Christian Writers, VI; Newman Press, Westminster, Md., 1948), 20–21. Quoted with permission of the publisher.

tainty, that the various forms of table customs taken over by the young Church from Judaism easily led to employing for Christ's institution the setting of a meal even outside the paschal meal. The grace after meals was the given occasion for the consecration of the chalice, no matter whether the consecration of the bread had occurred earlier, at the very start of the meal, or took place here.

To prove that in this early period of the Church the Eucharist was actually bound up with a meal, we have only one corroborating fact in the example of Corinth, as described by St. Paul. The first undoubted fact is that the Corinthians really connected the holy celebration with a great banquet, but certain abuses had crept in which were in glaring contradiction to the spirit of Christ's institution. As might have been expected, the meal was supplied not from a common stock but from the provisions brought by the well-to-do. But instead of spreading out all in common and awaiting the start of the supper, the people divided into little groups and consumed their own supplies with a selfishness that was often climaxed by drunkenness. Under such circumstances the words and the ceremonies of the holy action became a secondary matter, a formality which the officiant could perform at his own table and scarcely be noticed. Add to the scandal the painful situation of those guests who had brought nothing. Denouncing such conduct, St. Paul speaks with solemn seriousness of the content and worth of Christ's institution. It might surprise us that he introduces the phrases about the chalice with the words already noticed, *after he had supped,* and thus has the intervening meal of the community precede. That would hardly make it appear as if he wanted to suppress the meal itself. Rather we have an indication of how Paul wanted it set in order—and it was to be enclosed by the two consecrations! And so he could very correctly speak of the whole thing as a unit under the term "a supper of the Lord."

That we are not making a mistake in this deduction is indicated by another remnant which we meet about the beginning of the third century. In the church regulations of Hippolytus of Rome, a special provision is made for the Easter Mass at which the newly baptized are to receive their first Holy Communion. After the Body of the Lord is given them, they are to receive, besides the consecrated chalice, also two others, one filled with milk and honey and the other with water, and these, it would seem, before the consecrated chalice, which comes at the very end. As new-born children of God they get the children's meal, milk and honey, to strengthen them and to recall to their minds God's promises; they receive, too, the water that suggests that cleansing of soul which they have just experienced. Although the consecration had already for a long time been bound together by a single eucharist, this solemn Communion at Eastertide harks back to a time when the meal was interposed before the consecration of the chalice.

The drawing together of the doubled thanksgiving prayer into one was naturally the concomitant of the drawing together of the two consecrations. And this must have occurred even in apostolic times, when the meal was still connected with the celebration of the Eucharist. If the latter followed the meal, the next step was to take up and enlarge the closing thanksgiving prayer—a solution which the appearance of later liturgies clearly points to. But the eucharistic celebration, along with the prayer of thanksgiving, could also be set first, and there are traces of such a solution too.

On the basis of all these facts we can now attempt to outline the probable development of the eucharistic celebration in the first century of its existence. The Apostles fulfilled the command of our Lord given them at the Last Supper by celebrating regularly in the setting of a meal which was conducted with the ritual forms of a Jewish community meal. The most important point of contact was the grace after meals and the "cup of blessing" (chalice of benediction) connected with it. The grace or prayer of thanks was introduced by an invitation from the host to the guests. This invitation must have fused already in this early period into the double exclamation, *Sursum corda* and *Gratias agamus*, which we find, along with their corresponding answers, practically unaltered in all the succeeding liturgical traditions. The grace or thanksgiving prayer itself, which even in its pre-Christian original had led from gratitude for food and drink into gratitude for the benefits of the grace-filled guidance of God's people, could and did take on Christian features.

This new Christian concept is revealed in the prayers of the *Didache*, which are ever so much more meaningful if they are considered simply as table prayers. Besides, the *Didache* also stresses (10, 7) the improvisation of this prayer of thanks by the "prophets." Certainly if anything in the story of Redemption was to be the occasion for happy remembrance and thanksgiving, it would be this moment of fulfillment in Christ. To build up these thoughts expressly, the example of the Jewish Easter and feast-day Haggada would provide a model, although this was scarcely necessary since the apostolic preaching itself supplied ample material for such memories. Many of the heavenly songs which in St. John's Apocalypse are sung to God and the Lamb can very well be placed in the mouth of an earthly congregation which is gathered with its officiant for the celebration of the Eucharist.

The consecration of the bread which stands at the beginning of the service must have been drawn over to the consecration of the cup of blessing, and this very soon, perhaps even in the first generation, at least in the sense that bringing them together was considered admissible. Our Lord's words of institution used on these two occasions were thus merged into a single two-part account, and the *eulogia—eucharistia* spoken over the bread became then a thanksgiving prayer which introduced or even enclosed the account and the double consecration therein contained. For the words, "For as often as you shall eat this bread and drink the cup, you proclaim the death of the Lord," with which St. Paul continues his narrative of the institution, and even the sense of Jesus' own command, would early have given rise to the practice of expressing these thoughts right after the account itself, as we again actually find it in all the liturgies, namely in the anamnesis.

Since, on the one hand, the prayer of thanks was thus enriched and rounded out and settled in form, and on the other, the growing communities became too large for these domestic table-gatherings, the supper-character of the Christian assembly could and did fall out, and the eucharistic celebration stood out as the proper form of divine worship. The tables disappeared from the room, except for the one at which the presiding official pronounced the eucharist over the bread and wine. The room was broadened into a large hall capable of holding the whole congregation. Only in isolated instances was the connection with a meal continued into the following centuries.[3] And the ideal toward which all energetically strove was to hold in each congregation only one single Eucharist.

It was both the Jewish and hellenistic practice to hold the meal, as a δεῖπνον, at an evening hour, but once the meal disappeared there was nothing to hinder the choice of another time of the day for the celebration. Since Sunday, as the day of the Resurrection, was very early promoted as the day for the celebration, and attention was thus focused on the remembrance of the story of Redemption and especially of its glorious outcome, the next step was easy, namely, to transfer all to the morning hours, since it was in the morning before sunrise that Christ had risen from the dead. The earliest Easter celebration known to us was an evening celebration but it followed the time-schedule mentioned and its climax was not reached till early in the morning at cockcrow. Sunday service, too, would fit nicely into this scheme, for if one began to see in the sunrise a picture of Christ rising from the dead, one would lay considerable store in the notion of greeting Christ himself with the rising of the sun. And besides, as long as Christianity was not publicly acknowledged, the circumstances of the laborer's life would have urged the choosing of an hour outside the usual time of work.

When about 111–113 A.D., Pliny the Younger, Legate of Bithynia, had arrested and examined a number of Christians, he established the fact that they were in the habit of meeting on a certain fixed day before dawn and of singing in alternate verses a song to Christ their God; they bound themselves by solemn oath not to do any wrong; they then dispersed but assembled again at a later hour for a harmless meal. Quite

principal meal

---

[3] One last vestige was still to be found on Holy Thursday.

probably we have in the first-named gathering the celebration of the Eucharist, and in the hymn sung alternately the prayer of thanks which opened with alternate prayer and closed with the Amen of the people and which might even have included the *Sanctus* said in common. The second assembly, which was considered less important and which was discontinued after Pliny intervened, would then be the evening agape as we see it continuing even later on. If these conjectures are right, then we have further in the act of moral obligation bound in with the morning celebration, a distant parallel to the Sunday confession of sins, of which the *Didache* speaks. Although we are completely in the dark as to the form and performance of this act, the general sense of it is doubtless the securing of that state of mind which Paul had already demanded for the Eucharistic celebration and which in one case is looked upon as a contrite confession, in the other as a resolve and sacred promise of amendment. We see later on, time and again, new forms arising from the same root. Besides we can acknowledge that the kiss of peace which we have already supposed as the opening of the holy celebration even in this early period had a similar function.

religious manual of teaching

If we thus see forming in this early period the large outlines of the later mass-liturgy, there still remains the task of pointing out a great many details of a later and even present-day practice, in which, within the Mass celebration, a primitive and apostolic liturgy survives, a liturgy adapted by the Apostles from the usage of the synagogue. Here belongs the common way of starting and ending the prayer: At the beginning came the greeting with *Dominus vobiscum* or a similar formula, the answer to which was the genuinely Hebraic *Et cum spiritu tuo*. The close of the prayer referred in some way to God's boundless dominion, which lasts *in sæcula sæculorum*. The stipulated answer of the people remained, in, fact, untranslated: Amen. Thus with particular reference to the prayer of thanks, the general scheme remained unaltered, no matter how the contents changed. This holds true in every instance for the conclusion just mentioned and likewise for the introductory dialogue of which we spoke earlier. For the opening formula of the prayer of thanks itself, the formula of the customary Jewish *berachah* [4] did not persist; but even the opening with *Vere dignum et justum est* must have been adapted by the primitive congregation from some older tradition. For the further conduct of the prayer of thanks and for the transition into the triple *Sanctus* various hints from the Sabbath service of the synagogue must have been at work for this contained a very expansive

---

[4] The name "Berachah" comes from the opening word of the grace at table, "Praised." The type beginning in this fashion survives, e.g., in the formula of our table prayer, *Benedictus Deus in donis suis* . . . The beginning of the table prayer in the *Didache*, εὐχαριστοῦμέν σοι—also stemming, no doubt, from pre-Christian tradition—we will find again as the start of the eucharistic prayer in Hippolytus.

praise of God for His creation and His provident care of Israel. It could even be that the first phrase of the *Sanctus* stems from this source.

A second stream of adaptation from the primitive judæo-Christian community emerges in the service of readings of the fore-Mass, as we shall meet it in Justin. The tie with the Temple, which (according to the Acts of the Apostles 2:46) the emergent Christian church still maintained along with its own eucharistic gatherings, entailed above all, here as elsewhere, attendance at the synagogue for the Sabbath service, which was primarily a reading of the Scriptures. Only after the break with the synagogue, consequent upon the persecution of the year 44, did the hour of worship devoted to reading take on a specially Christian shape, and gradually combine with the eucharistic celebration as the fore-Mass. This old legacy is also definitely retained in the imitation of the two-fold division of the Law and the Prophets (which is at the basis of several Christian pericope lists) and in the arrangement of the singing in between.

In all these instances we are concerned only with the materials and the ground-plan which were taken over in the new structure of Christian worship. But there was also a new soul by which it was transformed. And what is of greater consequence in this formation and growth is not the age of the materials used in the building, but the building itself, the new architecture of the Mass itself which arose from within. And we dare not overlook the body which the new soul had shaped for itself from the old material and which even in the earliest phases of development had undergone a considerable change of appearance.

From the very start the basic motif was to observe the memorial of our Lord, the remembrance of His redemptive Passion, in the form of a meal. Therefore at first, the framework of a supper remained in the foreground. The faithful sat at table; under cover of simple nourishment they feasted upon the Body and Blood of Him who had laid down His life for us all and who should some day come again to gather His own into His Kingdom. The spoken word would slip easily from the recital of the words of institution and the command therein contained into such thoughts of memory and expectation. Union with our Lord in His glory came as strongly into the consciousness as union amongst themselves came visibly to the eye by means of the meal. But this framework of a meal could not even in the very beginning limit and define the type of eucharistic service. The meal was not an ordinary meal but a sacred banquet, not only hallowed and inspired by the memory which gave it value and which in its course was sacramentalized, but also borne Godwards by the word of the prayer that was added to it. For if, in primitive Christian culture, every meal imported not only various blessings but the prayer of thanks as well, this meal did so *par excellence*.

The mind of a man not blinded by pride will be turned toward God even by a natural meal. Nowhere is it more plainly and visibly seen that man is a receiver, than when he takes nourishment to keep his life powers together. Therefore a meal has always been the incentive to acknowledge one's own creation by means of a prayer of thanks which is bound up with the meal. In Christianity man is a double receiver. Not only is he fitted out with goods of the natural order, but he is gifted beyond measure and beyond his capacity; because it is God who imparts Himself to man. That prayer of thanks is the right echo responding to God's wondrous benefits to man.

Nothing is therefore more natural than that thanksgiving to God should be the very basis of Christian conduct, that thanksgiving in the prayer of the nascent Church should become a mighty sound growing ever stronger, that as the *eucharistia* it should be combined with that holy meal in whose sacramental core God's greatest gift is continually renewed.

Hallowing the meal by means of the Eucharist soon accomplished a result which affected its liturgical appearance very much, namely a gradual ousting of the meal itself. This result corresponds to that spiritualization in matters of worship which is for incipient Christianity—in contrast to the synagogue—very significant. For the conduct or guidance of those who participated, the movement of prayer became—if it had not already been so from the very start—settled and determined. The Eucharist became the basic form and shape of the Mass-liturgy.

The prayer of thanks in the adopted table customs of the judæo-Christian communities was thus combined with our Lord's *giving thanks* to form the starting point of a development which seemed to demand externalization. In the hellenistic surroundings this development found just the soil it needed to grow.

The *Didache* already uses a double phrase, and in reference to Sunday worship combines with the old term "breaking of bread" the newer term "offering thanks." Ignatius of Antioch simply employs *eucharistia* as the name of the Sacrament of the "Eucharist."

2. From Justin to Hippolytus of Rome

Justin, the philosopher and martyr, who wrote his *First Apology* in Rome about 150, preserved to us the first full account of a Christian Mass celebration. The picture is valid in the first instance only for Rome, but surely the features included hold true for the whole Christian world through which Justin had travelled from East to West. After speaking about Christian Baptism, Justin continues . . .

(c. 65) After we have baptized him who professes our belief and associates with us, we lead him into the assembly of those called the Brethren, and we there say prayers in common for ourselves, for the newly-baptized, and for all others all over the world. . . . After finishing the prayers, we greet each other with a kiss. Then bread and a cup of water and wine mixed are brought to the one presiding over the brethren. He takes it, gives praise and glory to the Father of all in the name of the Son and of the Holy Ghost, and gives thanks at length for the gifts that we were worthy to receive from Him. When he has finished the prayers and thanksgiving, the whole crowd standing by cries out in agreement: "Amen." "Amen" is a Hebrew word and means, "So may it be." After the presiding official has said thanks and the people have joined in, the deacons, as they are styled by us, distribute as food for all those present, the bread and the wine-and-water mixed, over which the thanks had been offered, and which they carry to those not present.

(c. 66) And this food itself is known amongst us as the Eucharist. No one may partake of it unless he is convinced of the truth of our teaching and is cleansed in the bath of Baptism. . . .

(c.67) . . . And on that day which is called after the sun, all who are in the towns and in the country gather together for a communal celebration. And then the memoirs of the Apostles or the writings of the Prophets are read, as long as time permits. After the reader has finished his task, the one presiding gives an address, urgently admonishing his hearers to practice these beautiful teachings in their lives. Then all stand up together and recite prayers. After the end of the prayers, as has already been remarked above, the bread and wine mixed with water are brought, and the president offers up prayers and thanksgivings, as much as in him lies. The people chime in with an Amen. Then takes places the distribution, to all attending, of the things over which the thanksgiving had been spoken, and the deacons bring a portion to the absent. Besides, those who are well-to-do give whatever they will. What is gathered is deposited with the one presiding, who therewith helps orphans and widows. . . ." [1]

EUCHARISTIA

The double picture shows precisely that the liturgical appearance of the Mass at this time was essentially defined by the *eucharistia*. Notice, too, the sharp emphasis which Justin puts on the seemingly unimportant matter of the congregation's Amen. The thanksgiving spoken by the one presiding comes from the heart of the whole assembly and is confirmed by all. Justin, who was himself a layman, bears witness by this

[1] Greek text of chapters 61 and 65–67 with explanatory notes, in Quasten, *Monumenta*, 13–21. Cf., Schuster, *The Sacramentary*, I, 59–61.

detail how much value the faithful set on their pronouncing this word. This community spirit, this feeling of oneness which was so immediately expressed when the celebration had the character of a meal, continues thus to put its stamp on the worship. And it was even more strongly impressed in the Communion which by its nature united the entire community.

What was received in Communion was designated the "Thank-you gift," and the Amen was intoned as a *thanksgiving*. In Justin's description of the Mass, the expression of thanks, the very notion of thanks, stand out as the second significant and characteristic feature.

That we really have here an idea which was currently operative in the Christian community can be gathered not only from the fact that *eucharistia* is now generally used as the technical term for the Mass, but even more from the explanation which is given this word. Justin himself says elsewhere that Christ gave us "the bread of the Eucharist" as a memorial of His Passion, and "that through it we might thank God, both for establishing the world and all that is in it for man's sake, and for freeing us from the evil in which we were born and, through Him who had willingly undertaken to suffer, entirely destroying the Powers and Forces." Irenæus also sets it down as a basis for the institution: the disciples of Christ should "not be sterile and ungrateful." Origen maintains: "We are not men with thankless hearts. True, we do not make any offerings, we do not sacrifice in worship things which, far from being of benefit to us, are really our enemies. But toward God, who has showered us with benefits . . . we are ashamed not to be grateful. The token of our gratitude to God is the Bread which we call Eucharist."

One cannot help but notice with what enthusiasm the ecclesiastical writers of this period describe God's benefactions; first of all, those in the order of creation, but more especially those with which the children of the Church have been favored. And with what energy they urge that deep feeling of self-sacrifice and of subservient obedience, from which gratitude proceeds. According to Clement of Alexandria, the Christian owes God a life-long gratitude; this is the expression of true reverence. "The offering of the Church," thus Clement continues, "consists in a prayer in which all our thoughts, given over to God, are wrapped up along with the offering."

The subjectiveness and spirituality of worship and the offering of the heart to God are so emphasized in the Christian sources of this period that one might have supposed that there was an absence of outward offering; before Irenæus (so runs the opinion), no offering was recognized in the Church except that which consisted in thanksgiving. Actually, many pronouncements during this period lend a semblance of verity to this supposition and appear to our ears very exaggerated. Aristides, for example, states that God "does not demand an offering of victim or drink nor of any visible things." He requires "not blood-obla-tions and drink, not the odor of flowers or of incense, since He is the perfect perfume, without want or blemish." Athenagoras pursues the same line of thought by emphasizing that the highest sacrifice one can offer Him is to acknowledge Him and tender Him our spiritual service. The only honor worthy of Him is to put His gifts to use for ourselves and for the poor, and to "be thankful and by our spirit send heavenward songs of praise and hymns of glory for our creation and for every means of prosperity, for the qualities of the different kinds of things, and for the changes of season." For this reason, the apologists explained, the Christians no altar and no temple.

But if one were to decide from such expressions that in the minds of the Christians of the time there was a Eucharist but no eucharistic sacri-fice properly so called, one would be jumping to conclusions. Along with phrases of this sort, meant to emphasize the differences between Christianity and paganism, there are found from the very beginning other phrases which not only declare that the eucharist was pronounced over the bread and wine, but which speak plainly enough of gifts which are sacrificed to God in the Eucharist. Others simply designate the Eucharist as an oblation or presuppose its *sacrificial* character, as both the *Didache* and Ignatius of Antioch bear witness. There are expressions which can be interpreted, without violence, in a broader sense, like the repeated reference to the prophecy of Malachy which is fulfilled in the celebration of the Christian Eucharist.

We are therefore certain from the very start that in the Eucharist not only do prayers of thanksgiving rise from the congregation to God, but that at the same time a gift is offered up to God. How much this thought coincides with the notion of *eucharistia* is manifest from the fact that already in Philo *eucharistia* does not mean only thanksgiving but a sacri-fice for the purpose of rendering thanks. It is another question, however, how the offering of a gift is evaluated in the rite of that period. But remember, it is not necessary that the details of eucharistic theology appear in the rite. Even in the developed Mass-liturgy of today many pertinent points of dogma are entirely omitted. So it is quite understand-able that in a primordial form of the celebration, evolving chiefly either from the memorial of our Lord, or from the prayer of thanks, little would be said about oblation and sacrifice. Such, in fact, is our conduct whenever we present a gift that is due; we do not talk much about the gift we are tendering, preferring instead to concentrate on the labors and merits that occasioned the gift.

But actually we do find in the oldest text of the Eucharist, in Hippo-lytus of Rome, an expression of sacrifice, immediately connected with the anamnesis, right where all later Catholic liturgies employ a similar word: *memores igitur mortis et resurrectionis eius offerimus tibi panem et calicem . . .*[2] It is possible that these words of oblation, or words like them, were included in the prayer of thanks at an earlier stage, perhaps even from the very first.

FIRSTLINGS OF CREATION

On the other hand, many obstacles had to be overcome before the oblation to God—and with it, the sacrificial character of the Eucharist—would be expressed not only in words but in the external appearance of the celebration, and thus stretch out beyond the framework of a prayer of thanks connected with a meal. We have already heard the apologists of the second century who contrast the heathen sacrifice—with its intoxication of the senses and its external pageantry—with the simple and spiritual worship of the Church, a worship that strives only to prove the grateful offering of those hearts asembled before God in Christ. The only outward symbol of this offering added to the words of the prayer, was something exalted high above the offerings of heathen and of Jew— the body of our Lord, which had been obediently sacrificed, and the blood that He shed, manifested to the eye as a piece of bread and a chalice of wine. The New Law does not have an oblation that is a "manmade one." Thus was excluded the notion that a true and genuine oblation to God could be discerned in the gifts of bread and wine which were placed on the table for the Eucharist, or in those things presented by the faithful for the agape or for alms. Justin holds this view quite firmly, while Tertullian has watered it down. But Irenæus plainly takes a new stand. In explaining the Eucharist, he emphasized the fact that we offer the firstlings of creation. At the Last Supper our Lord took "bread growing out of creation" and a "chalice coming from our creation," spoke the words over them, and thus taught His disciples the new oblation of the New Testament. He had therefore commanded the disciples "to offer up to God the firstlings of creatures, not because He needed them, but that they themselves might not be sterile and ungrateful." These words show that for Irenæus no less than for his predecessors, it was the inner intention, the offering of the heart that was decisive before God, and that only the Eucharist of the body and blood of Christ presented the clean oblation of which Malachias had spoken. For only in Christ is all creation gathered together and sacrificed to God, as Irenæus does not tire of repeating.

But in taking a position against the exaggerated spiritualism of the Gnostics, Irenæus appears to be compelled to defend the worth of earthly creation. With clear vision he sees the symbolic meaning of what occurred at our Lord's institution of the Blessed Sacrament, when things of

[2] "We, therefore, recalling His death and resurrection offer to Thee both this bread and cup."

this earth of ours were so exalted that by the word of God they became Christ's flesh and blood and were thus empowered to enter into the clean oblation of the New Covenant.

Once the natural gifts of bread and wine were recognized as symbols of the internal oblation of the heart, nothing stood in the way of developing the ceremony of their presentation into an oblation to God, and so giving a stronger expression to the sacrificial element which was at the center of the Eucharist—not only in words but in the external rite. Since the beginning of the third century there appear accounts of an offering by the faithful preceding the eucharistic prayer. From then on this is liturgically revised in various ways and gradually shaped into a genuine offertory procession which we shall discuss later on. But even so, it is only the broader notion of oblation that receives a liturgical stamp. The narrow idea of a sacrifice in the sense of the changing or destruction of a gift first appears later in the Orient in the Rite of the Slaughtering of the Lamb (*proskomide*) in which the species of bread is divided with the Holy Lance. We get the first inklings of the liturgical development of the rite in question in the church regulations or church order of Hippolytus of Rome. Over this document which brings the history of the Mass-liturgy out of the twilight of scattered accounts into the light of day, we must delay awhile. For in it we find for the first time the complete text of the eucharistic prayer.

3. From Hippolytus to the Separation of Liturgies

The work we are here dealing with was known for a long time under the title *The Egyptian Church Order*.[1] But it was not till recently that its authorship was ascribed to the Roman presbyter, Hippolytus, the skilful controversialist writer of the third century. He had come into sharp conflict with two popes, Zephyrinus (d. 217) and Callistus (d. 222), had in fact set himself up as anti-pope in opposition to the latter, but at last he was reconciled with the Church and died as a martyr (235), as his cultus in Rome bears witness even up to this very hour. He is commemorated on August 13. The name of the work, composed in Greek, is *Apostolic Tradition*. As representative of the conservative wing, Hippolytus had in mind compiling what were esteemed as the "apostolic traditions" in the regulation of ecclesiastical life. The work was probably completed about 215, before the schism which broke out when Callistus was chosen pope. The division that followed, together with the fact that the work

1 No absolutely critical text has so far been published. The most important investigation is G. Dix, *The Treatise on the Apostolic Tradition of St. Hippolytus of Rome* (London, 1937).

was done in Greek, explains why the *Apostolic Tradition*, like so many of the writings of Hippolytus, was almost entirely forgotten in Rome and in the West, while in the Orient, in Egypt as well as in Syria, precisely because it claimed to present the apostolic tradition and because it came from Rome, it had a tremendous success. And that explains why, except for a few tiny fragments, it has survived not in the original text, but in translation—in Coptic, Arabic, Ethiopian and partly in Syrian. Some important fragments of a Latin version have also come down, contained in a collection of oriental legal papers. For our knowledge of ecclesiastical life in Rome in the third century, this document is the most important source. The text begins with the directions for the consecration of a bishop. The newly consecrated is acclaimed with the cry a x i o s, *he is worthy*. Then the deacons bring the gifts. Both the bishop and the assembled presbyters lay their hands over the gifts, but it is the new bishop who proceeds alone with the prayer of thanks:

"The Lord be with you. And with thy spirit. Lift up your hearts. We have them with the Lord. Let us give thanks unto the Lord. It is meet and right. And he shall so proceed: We give thee thanks, O God, through Thy beloved Child, Jesus Christ, Whom Thou didst send us in recent times as Saviour, Redeemer and Messenger of Thy counsel. Who is Thine inseparable Word through whom Thou didst make all things and in Whom Thou was well pleased. Him Whom Thou didst send from heaven into the Virgin's womb, and Who, conceived within her, was made flesh and shown to be Thy Son, being born of the Holy Spirit and a Virgin. And Who, in order to carry out Thy will and acquire for Thee a holy people, stretched forth His hands in suffering that He might release from suffering those who believed in Thee. And when He was delivered up to voluntary suffering that He might abolish death and rend asunder the bonds of the devil and tread upon hell and enlighten the righteous and show forth the resurrection, took bread and giving thanks to Thee, He said: this is My Body which is broken for you. And likewise taking the cup, He said, this is My Blood which is shed for you. When you do this, make memory of me. Making memory therefore of His death and resurrection, we offer to Thee this bread and chalice giving thanks unto Thee for finding us worthy to stand before Thee and to minister unto Thee. And we beseech Thee to send Thy Holy Spirit upon the oblation of Thy Church, to gather into one (body) all thy holy ones who partake of it that they may be filled with the Holy Spirit for the strengthening of their faith in truth, that we may praise and glorify Thee through Thy Child Jesus Christ, through Whom glory be to Thee and honour, to the Father and the Son, with the Holy Spirit in Thy holy Church now and forever. Amen."

At the conclusion the remark is added: If anyone offers oil, or cheese or olives, a similar prayer of thanks may be said over it—and, as an example, a short blessing is appended.[2] After some regulations about the other degrees of orders, and about church offices, there follow precepts for the catechumenate and Baptism. At the conclusion of this last we find—as in Justin—further mention of the Mass. But here there is only the note that the participation of the newly-baptized in the service of the congregation begins with the common prayer and the kiss of peace before the offering of the gifts. There are also regulations for the peculiar usage—already touched upon—of offering at this Mass of the newly-baptized, besides the sacramental Eucharist, also a chalice filled with milk and honey and a third one with water.

It would be a mistake to envision in this text which Hippolytus proposes, *the* Roman Mass of the third century, pure and simple. That would hardly coincide with the stage of liturgical development reached at that period. At this time there is still no fixed formulary for the Mass-liturgy, but only a fixed framework which the celebrant fills out with his own words, as older accounts clearly indicate. Hippolytus presents his text only as a suggestion, and expressly stresses the right freely to extemporize a text as a right which remained long in force. This right Hippolytus himself here laid claim to. Favorite thoughts, favorite turns of expression from his other writings recur time and again.

A TYPE OF THE CONTEMPORARY LITURGY

The Eucharist of Hippolytus does on the whole exhibit a type of the contemporary liturgy, but not the only type then in use. For it is rather surprising that ideas derived from the Old Testament, which play such a major role in most of the later texts, and which one rightly deduces from synagogue traditions, are here entirely absent. No reference is made to the work of creation, nor to God's salvific plan in the pre-Christian era—a point which remained the rule in later Greek liturgies. The *Sanctus*, too, is missing, along with the corresponding introduction. Only the work of Redemption is gratefully delineated, and in such an ingenious way that the account of the Institution is organically conjoined. The prayer therefore gives the impression of a well-rounded completeness. Hippolytus appears to have striven consciously for this completeness in his model formulary, sharply distinguishing it from the forms at hand in which the connection seems somewhat loose. (Perhaps this other type developed from the circumstance that, when the Eucharist was disjoined from the evening agape, it was linked with an already existent

[2] A portion of this came by a very roundabout way into the Roman Pontifical, and here survives within the ceremony for the consecration of the oils on Maundy Thursday, at the close of the canon, as in Hippolytus.

Sunday morning church service.) It was in this above-mentioned service of the synogogue that the readings and praise of God for creation and gracious guidance of His people lived on. And this praise included the mention of the angelic choirs with its threefold *Sanctus* from the vision of Isaias.

But besides the strictly christological type of Hippolytus and the type derived from the synagogue, a third type must also have developed quite early, a type of thanksgiving, or rather of praise, in which the thoughts of the Christian acknowledgment of God were clothed in the phrases of hellenist philosophy. The infinite greatness of God was presented by the repetition of negative attributes, as a rule formed with the privative. For example in the *Anaphora* of Serapion, Bishop of Thmuis, we find, "God non-inchoate, unsearchable, inexpressible, incomprehensible to everything made." Or creation is reviewed, with that feeling for nature that is reawakened in those centuries, and from this is shaped a glorification of God's power and wisdom.

It stands to reason that these types did not ever have independent forms or exist by themselves in a pure state, for the basic Christian and christological motif of the prayer of thanks could indeed wane but never entirely vanish. But they comprise components which formed parts of the eucharistic prayer, or directions toward which it tended—until the word of authority and the official text put a stop to the development. In the sources of the Mass-liturgy surviving from the fourth century, we meet, besides the organic growth of liturgical forms and usages, concrete examples of the types noticed.

From what has been said we are forced to conclude that the liturgical prayer texts were, in the third century, still elastic and continually subject to new influences. But at the same time there is a good deal to show that, for the general course of the liturgy in the Church as a whole, there was a unified order, a network of still flexible regulations stamped with the authority of custom. These statutes regulated the building of the house of God, the time and manner of service, the division of functions, the way prayers were to begin and end, and so forth. The fundamental design of the prayer of thanks—the Eucharist—is everywhere the same: it begins invariably with a short dialogue and closes with the Amen of the people. When in 154 Bishop Polycarp of Smyrna visited Pope Anicetus at Rome, the latter invited him to celebrate the Eucharist in church, an honor for the episcopal guest which the Syrian Didascalia of the third century makes compulsory in analogous instances. There was no fear, therefore, of any disturbing deviation because of the strange liturgies. The same thing is indicated by the transfer of the liturgical formulary of Hippolytus from Rome to distant Egypt and as far away as Ethiopia where it remains even till today, the usual Mass formulary under the title "Anaphora of the Apostles." What was here set down fitted without trouble into the indigenous order of the strange country. We can therefore, in this wider sense, speak of a unified liturgy of the first centuries.

4. The Mass in the Orient after the Fourth Century

With the coming of the fourth century an important differentiation makes its appearance. In the organization of the Church, especially within Greek territory, there grew up, bit by bit, over and above the individual communities with their episcopal overseers, certain preponderant centers, above all Alexandria and Antioch. From these centers and their provincial synods there radiated special legislation that in time gave a particular stamp to the church life of those affected. Thus, too, divergent liturgies gradually acquired their fixed form. This was a necessary development. The speedy spread of congregations, for whom, since Constantine, numberless buildings of often vast proportions had been erected, required a more rigid control of common worship, and demanded a greater carefulness about the text of the prayers that was needed in the smaller groups where the officiant might perhaps on occasion extemporize.

So it became more and more the rule that the text should be set down in writing. And so, too, it became necessary to borrow texts from other churches. The possibility of a strict control was also heightened. In North Africa they were satisfied to issue a warning that this borrowing should not be haphazard, but that the texts should be carefully passed upon by capable brethren (in episcopal office). The result was the gradual standardization of formulas to be used unvaryingly throughout a province.

From the turn of the fourth century, however, there survive two collections of liturgical texts which emanate from the two leading oriental metropolises already mentioned, and the Mass formulas they contain differ considerably from the later authorized forms. From the sphere of Alexandria-Egypt we have the *Euchologion* of Bishop Serapion of Thmuis. From the sphere of Antioch-Syria we have the liturgy in the eighth book of the *Apostolic Constitutions,* also called the Clementine liturgy. A closer inspection of both these documents will be rewarding.

THE EUCHOLOGION OF SERAPION

Serapion, bishop of Thmuis, a little town in lower Egypt, is well-known as a friend of St. Athanasius and of the hermit St. Anthony. He was a bishop between 339 and 362. The *Euchologion* authored by him, first discovered in a monastery on Mt. Athos in 1894, contains amongst other things the liturgy of the Mass, but unfortunately with no explanatory rubrics.[1]

The list of Mass prayers begins with a prayer for a fruitful reading of the Scriptures. There follows a prayer "after standing up from the homily," then a group of formulas for the general prayers for the Church: for the catechumens, for the people, for the sick. To each of these groups is appended a blessing by the bishop—for a good crop, for the church, for the bishop and the Church, and finally a "genuflectional prayer," probably a closing benediction. These prayers—like the eucharistic prayer that follows—display a definitely theologizing trend, and, in their broad unfolding of parallel periods, the ornament of Greek oratory. Remarkable is the uniformly recurring doxology, which is characteristic of the third/fourth century. The doxology is directed to God through Christ in the Holy Ghost. The prayer, for instance, will make mention of our Lord and then continue somewhat in this fashion: Through whom there is to Thee honor and power in the Holy Ghost now and forever!

More important for us is the eucharistic prayer. It begins: "Fit it is, and proper, to praise, to glorify and to exalt Thee, the everlasting Father of the only-begotten, Jesus Christ." Then is lauded the unsearchable being of God, made known to us through the Son. And praise turns to prayer for a right understanding and to the vision of the angelic choirs over whom God reigns:

> *Before thee stand a thousand thousand and ten thousand ten thousand Angels and Archangels, Thrones, Principalities, Dominations, and Powers. Before Thee stand the two six-winged Seraphim, with two wings hiding their face, two their feet, and flying with two, and they praise Thee. With them do Thou accept our praise, as we say: Holy, holy, holy Lord of Sabaoth, heaven and earth are full of His glory.*

Typical of this, as well as of all later Egyptian Mass-liturgies, is the passage from the *Sanctus* to the account of the Institution; peculiar is the interruption of the account with prayers—reminiscent of the usages of the primitive Church.

> *Complete this sacrifice with Thy power and with Thy participation, for it is to Thee we have offered up this living sacrifice, this unbloody gift. To Thee we have offered this Bread, the oblation [ὁμοίωμα] of the body of the Only-begotten. This Bread is the oblation of His holy Body; for on the night . . . [there follows the words over the bread, 1 Cor. 11:23–4.] Therefore we too, ratifying*

[1] Text in Quasten, *Monumenta*, 48–67. The exact arrangement of the prayers is uncertain.

the offering of His death, have offered up the Bread, and we cry out
through this offering: Be merciful to us all and be appeased, O God
of truth! And as this Bread was scattered . . . so gather Thy
Church together . . . into one living Catholic Church. We have
also offered up the chalice, the offering of His Blood; for the Lord
Jesus . . . [Here is inserted the passage from Matt. 26:27 ff.]
Therefore we have also offered up the chalice as the offering of
Blood. May Thy holy Logos, O God of truth, come down upon
this bread, so that it become the Body of the Logos. . . . and grant
that all who partake may receive a medicine of life. . . .

This petition for a fruitful Communion passes over into an intercessory prayer for the dead (presupposing a reading of the names) and
for the living. The prayer then closes with the doxology. Then follows
the breaking of the bread, to the accompaniment of a prayer by the
celebrant, and then the Communion of the clergy, a blessing of the
people, their Communion, and finally a closing thanksgiving prayer
spoken by the celebrant.

APOSTOLIC CONSTITUTIONS

The Mass-liturgy found in the eighth book of the *Apostolic Constitu-*
tions is, in several respects, of a very different stamp. This is often called
the Clementine liturgy because it is contained in the long, eight-book
collection of Church legislation which posed as the work of Pope
Clement I, a pupil of the Apostles. Actually it is a product of the late
fourth century.

The eighth book of the *Apostolic Constitutions* is, in its structure and
its legal regulations, little more in general than a revision of the *Apostolic*
Tradition of Hippolytus. But as regards the Mass-liturgy the traces of
Hippolytus' draft are faint. In its place we have the usage, by now somewhat fixed, of the Syrian capital. But the eucharistic prayer itself is text-
ually a creation of the redactor, a model formulary that could be spun
out to vast proportion, and must therefore be looked upon not as a real
usage but as a suggested source to which the celebrant could turn in
freely composing his prayer. In this liturgy the service of reading is
definitely combined with the sacrificial worship. The Clementine liturgy
begins with the readings which here, as in the case of Hippolytus, precede the consecration of a bishop. It presupposes a fourfold reading.
There is a reading from the Law and from the Prophets—the synagogue
tradition, quite obviously—and then from the Apostles and the Gospels.
Afterwards there is a homily. Then those who are not full members are
dismissed—the catechumens, energumens, candidates for Baptism and the
penitents—each group after an intercessory prayer of the congregation
and a blessing by the bishop. Then there is a two-part prayer for the

faithful. After the kiss of peace and the washing of hands, the gifts are brought in and the eucharistic prayer begins. We will do well to try to visualize at least its outline and sequence. The prayer begins with the introductory dialogue, and continues:

(VIII, 12, 6) Fit indeed it is, and proper, that we praise Thee above all, the true God, who wast before all creation, from whom all paternity in heaven and on earth takes its name, alone without becoming, without beginning, over whom there is no king and no lord, who needest nothing and grantest every good . . .

(7) . . . Thou hast called all things from nothing into being, through Thine only-begotten Son, and Him hast Thou conceived before all times. . . .

(8) . . . Through Him hast Thou created before all else the Cherubim and the Seraphim, the eons and the Dominations, the Virtues and the Powers . . . and then this visible world and all that is in it.

(9) Thou didst build up the sky like a vault and didst stretch it out like a hide. . . .

(10) Thou who didst make the water for drinking and cleansing, the air for breathing and carrying the tone of the voice . . . [praise is meted out for the fire, the sea and its tides, the earth with its changes of wind and rain; finally for man].

(17) Thou hast made him of an immortal soul and a decaying body, the former created from nothing, the latter from the four elements. . . .

(18) Thou, almighty God, hast planted Paradise in Eden towards the east. . . .

(20) [After the trial and fall] hast justly driven him from Paradise, but in Thy goodness didst not despise him who was entirely lost, since he was Thy creature [the stories of Cain and Abel, Abraham, Melchisedech, Job, Isaac, Jacob, Joseph, Moses and Aaron, and the wonders of the Exodus from Egypt are recounted].

(27) For all this, glory to Thee, omnipotent Lord! Thee do the uncounted hosts of angels praise, the archangels . . . who . . . without ceasing and without becoming silent cry out:—*and all the people should say together:*—Holy, holy, holy Lord of Sabbaoth, Heaven and earth are full of Thy glory. Praised forever! Amen.

(28) *And the bishop continues:* (29) Holy indeed art Thou and all-holy, the highest and most exalted in eternity;

(30) But holy, too, is Thine only-begotten Son, our Lord and God, Jesus Christ . . . who did not disdain the race of men, that had perished, but . . . [and another review of the history of Israel and its continued faithlessness] . . . according to Thy pleasure resolved to become man, He the creator of men. . . .

(32) He lived holily and taught justly, and banished every sickness and every weakness from men. . . .

(33) He was turned over to the Governor Pilate, and was judged, He the Judge, and was condemned, He the Saviour, and was nailed to the cross, He who was not subject to suffering, and He died, He the Lord of nature, and was buried, He who gave life, in order to conquer suffering and to tear away from death those for whose sake He had come, and to loose the devil's fetters and free men from his deceit.

(34) And He arose again from the dead, and after spending forty days with His disciples He ascended into heaven and sat down at Thy right hand, O God and Father.

(35) Remembering what He has suffered for us, we give thanks, omnipotent God, not in accordance with our debt but in accordance with our ability, and we fulfill His command.

(36) For on the night in which He was betrayed . . .

After the words of consecration there follows the anamnesis in which, besides the death of our Lord and His resurrection, His second coming is mentioned. The arrangement of the rest of the text is like Hippolytus', with this distinction, that an epiklesis and an intercessory prayer are added:

(38) Recalling . . . we offer Thee, King and God, according to His command, this Bread and this Chalice, by giving Thee thanks for having considered us worthy to stand before Thee and perform our priestly service,

(39) And we beg Thee, look with favor, O God of riches, upon these gifts that lie before Thee, and let them be pleasing to Thee, for the honor of Thy Christ, and deign to send down upon this sacrifice Thy Holy Ghost, the witness of the Passion of Jesus, that He might manifest (ἀποφήνη) this Bread as the Body of Thy Christ and this Chalice as the Blood of Thy Christ, so that all who partake might grow in devotion, obtain the forgiveness of their sins, be freed from the devil and his deceit, and, filled with the Holy Ghost, might be made worthy of Thy Christ and partakers of everlasting life, if thou be merciful to them, almighty Lord.

Then follows the intercessory prayer, the ten sections of which each begin with the phrase, "We ask Thee further." The final doxology ends with the Amen of the people. For the Communion, too, a special liturgical frame is provided. True, the *Pater noster* is still missing, although it is elsewhere—a short time later—mentioned as a Communion prayer, but there is presupposed a long prayer of preparation to be said by the bishop after a litany by the deacon. Then is the cry raised: Τὰ ἅγια Τοῖς ἁγίοις, with the hymnic response of the people. During the Communion of the congregation Psalm 33 is sung. After a preparatory admonition by the deacon, comes the finish, a prayer of thanksgiving and the final benediction of the bishop.

Although the text of the Mass-liturgy in both cases is not yet that which is standardized in the later liturgies of Alexandria and Antioch, still the external outlines of the liturgical usages of the East are clearly discernible. This is especially true in the Clementine liturgy whose prescriptions would soon be established and enlarged by that great preacher of Antioch, St. John Chrysostom. If we compare these fourth-century liturgies with what is seen in the contemporary Roman Mass, we notice in them a longer list of readings and a richer development of the general prayer for the Church which follows. We also notice, in this general prayer for the Church—and elsewhere, too—the prominent role of the deacon, who introduces the celebrant's prayer with a dialogue between himself and the people, and thus insures the latter a closer bond with the course of the sacred action. The eucharistic prayer (preface and canon) has indeed introduced the first suggestion of petitions, but its lines are so firmly drawn that the whole is presented as a large unit. The *Sanctus* and the epiklesis appear in it as two climactic points. The Communion, too, is enriched in its surroundings.

ST. BASIL

The fourth century, especially in the Orient, is still a time of lively development. But the fundamental liturgical texts are already beginning to take on a fixed shape. A new investigation of the Basilian formula of the Byzantine Mass, and of the formularies related to it, permits us to get a clearer view of the manner in which the texts extant at that time were revised and expanded. A Greek redactor—there are good grounds to suggest St. Basil the Great (d. 379)—came upon a prepared eucharistic prayer which was for him apparently too immature although it was not poor in scriptural allusions. He enlarged it, and enriched it with a stronger sifting of quotations from the Bible. The still extant basic text, had this to say, for instance, right after the *Sanctus:* After we had transgressed Thy command in Paradise, "Thou hast not thrust us aside entirely, but hast watched over us through Thy prophets, and didst appear to us in these latter days through Thine only-begotten Son, who took flesh of the holy Virgin and became man and showed us the way of salvation." The redactor weaves into the text, after the mention of the Son, a number of phrases: the praise of His divinity, from Hebrews 1:2 f.; the quotation from Baruch 3:38 about the Wisdom that appeared on earth; the quotation about the nature of a slave, from Philippians 2:6 f.; and then the conquest of sin and of death, to which all had been condemned through Adam, in phrases from Romans 5:12 and 6:29.

It was also Basil who first makes us aware of a new trend which, as it grew, became for all oriental liturgies a fundamental trait. This trend was a growing consciousness of sin and a mounting reverence in the presence of the great mystery—a trend which increased to almost gloomy proportions. Those celebrating the liturgy describe themselves as "Thy lowly and sinful and unworthy slaves" who should be tried "on the day of Thy just judgment." This change in expression coincides clearly with the veering in theological attitude resulting from the struggle with Arianism, a struggle waged over the essential divinity of the Son. The noise of this battle penetrated even into the house of God and is reflected in the wording of prayers. In place of the doxology, customary up to then, which offered praise to the Father "through the Son in the Holy Ghost," Basil favored the new form, which offered praise to the Father "with the Son, at one with the Holy Ghost"—a way of praying and of praising in which our vision is no longer cast upon Christ's humanity, by which He is our intermediary before God, but upon His divinity, in which He is one in nature with God. Emphasis is not on the grace which He brings but in the right that He exercises, His might as a fearsome judge, before whom we ought to tremble and be afraid. And already in Basil the sentiment toward the Eucharist is altered. The pertinent chapter in his *Shorter Rule* is entitled: "With what fear . . . we ought to receive the Body and Blood of Christ." The same attitude toward the Blessed Sacrament, even aside from the thought of communicating, is noticeable in various parts of the eastern world. It is especially strong in Chrysostom, who time and time again talks about "the terrible sacrifice," about the "shuddering hour" when the mystery is accomplished, and about the "terrible and awful table." This attitude left its mark not only on the character of the oriental liturgies, but on the peculiar form of oriental piety. Even Chrysostom gave vent to the complaint that few dared approach the holy table for Communion. The decline in the frequentation of Communion in the East was already remarked by Latin Fathers of the fourth-fifth century.

It is therefore no mere accident that precisely in the Orient the celebration of the mysteries took on an ever greater splendor. The activities at the altar became the object of the awesome gaze and wonder of the assembled congregation. The clergy appear in splendid vestments, lights and incense are introduced into the service, an external ceremonial with bowings and *prostrations* is gradually evolved. Forms broaden out, following the pattern set by the Emperor and his highest officials on festive occasions.[2] The bearing of gifts to the altar and, of course, the procession for their distribution in Holy Communion are turned into solemn parades of the clergy, who appeared like the legions of the heavenly spirits (as the festive hymns expressly declare).

[2] As Prof. Th. Klauser has pointed out, the ceremonial rights were transferred to the bishops already under Constantine when they were raised to the rank of the official hierarchy. Amongst these ceremonial rights were the above mentioned *prostratio* and the right to be preceded by lit torches.

In addition the line of demarcation between the altar-sanctuary and the people became more and more pronounced. The railings which lay between the two grew higher until at last they became the ikonostasis, the picture-wall which fully hides the sanctuary from the gaze of the people. Thus the action at the altar is all the more raised in dignity. It is enveloped in an atmosphere of holy awe. As a further result, the actions before the liturgy—that is, before the readings—are formed into a more important prelude. And so the divine service is noticeably lengthened. Later on, it would seem they strove for more brevity here by having the celebrant say some of his prayers silently, for instance, reading his oration softly even while the deacon is still repeating with the people the litany which was intended as an introduction to the oration.

The details of the evolution in the oriental Mass do not fall within the scope of this book. However, in order to understand the various analogies which a comparative study of the liturgies of Rome and the East must necessarily draw between the two, it is imperative that we give at least a broad outline of the branching out of the eastern liturgies as this occurred since the fourth century.

EASTERN LITURGIES

Up till now we confined our attention exclusively to the liturgies in the Greek tongue, that great cultural language in whose ambit the Apostles themselves trod and within whose limits most of the liturgical evolution of the first centuries occurred. But the liturgy of the primitive Church in Palestine was certainly not Greek but Aramaic. Aramaic—that is, Syriac—was, by force of necessity, also the language of the ecclesiastical liturgy which penetrated to the North and East beyond the bounds of the Roman Empire. The liturgy that thus evolved was the *East-Syrian*.

The East-Syrian liturgy is known also as the *Nestorian*, because of the desertion to Nestorius, or as *Chaldean*, with reference to the groups who returned to communion with Rome. It is still employed by the descendants of these Christian peoples: by the Syrians in Mesopotamia and by the Christians living on the Malabar coast (the most important mission territory of the East-Syrians). The East-Syrian Mass, as recorded in the oldest documents, gives indications of a period of Greek influence, but this soon came to an end as this part of Christendom became gradually isolated. For the sacrifice or anaphora three different formulas are in use.

In the Greek world, as was already noted, there were two outstanding metropolises, Antioch and Alexandria. The former became the center of the *West-Syrian* liturgy, also called the Liturgy of St. James; after the fourth century it was Jerusalem that took the lead in this sphere.

We can get an idea of the radiating power of this liturgy of Jerusalem from the description of the Gallic pilgrim-lady, Ætheria, who had visited the holy places about 390 or (according to other interpretations) 417, and to whose account we will have occasion to return more than once, although it touches on the Mass itself only in passing. However, a lengthy description of the Mass is recorded in the last of the conferences known as the *Mystagogic Catecheses*, ascribed to St. Cyril of Jerusalem (d. 386). From Jerusalem, too, is derived the basic formulary for the sacrifice in the West-Syrian liturgy, the anaphora of St. James. After the Council in Chalcedon (451) the majority of the West-Syrians became Monophysites; their Church is called the Jacobite, after its tireless organizer (Jacobus Baradæus). The non-Monophysite Christians are the Maronites. A growing national consciousness provoked the introduction of Syriac as the liturgical language, although after the suppression of the Syriac by the Arabic, the vernacular Arabic was later adopted for the readings (lessons) and the litanies. The West-Syrian liturgy is distinguished for its numerous anaphora which were composed in the course of centuries after the pattern of that of St. James and of which the older are Greek in origin. There are over sixty, but the present-day Syrians use only a small portion of them.

Parallel to that of the West-Syrian liturgy is the development of the *Egyptian* liturgy known as the Liturgy of St. Mark. In the Patriarchate of Alexandria after the Council of Chalcedon there is the same sort of movement: mass desertion to Monophysitism and the adoption in the liturgy of the ancient national language now called Coptic (and later on, in part, the use of Arabic and, in the Abyssinian highlands, of Ethiopic [Géez]). But, besides the *Euchologion* of Serapion and the papyrus of Der-Balyzeh (containing remnants of a related Greek Mass-liturgy), there survive also some documents of a Greek liturgy of St. Mark. The oldest of these are certain fragments of the basic anaphora of St. Mark, from the fourth-fifth century, distinguished from the rest of the composition by the lack of many amplifications. The Copts possess only three anaphora formularies. The Ethiopian liturgy is known to have seventeen, but not all are in common use. The effect of the Monophysite attitude, which is inclined to view in Christ only His divinity, is noticeable in several anaphoras: the Coptic anaphora of St. Gregory Nazianzen, for instance, directs all prayers straight to Christ; the Ethiopian anaphora of Mary directs all to our Lady.

At the time when the liturgical texts were beginning to be definitely fixed and determined, a third center of Greek liturgy was gradually asserting itself alongside the other two, a center destined to surpass the others in point of influence—Byzantium-Constantinople. All of the East-Slavic countries adhere to the *Byzantine* liturgy, in this case a liturgy vested in the Old Slavonic (Staroslav) tongue. The constant contact with the Eastern Roman imperial court brought about in this liturgy above all, a rich development of forms. Still only two formularies are extant, although these take in not only the anaphora but almost the whole Mass-service. These are the liturgy of St. John Chrysostom and the liturgy already noticed, that of St. Basil. The pronounced unchangeableness of the priest's prayers has had repercussions of some consequence in the multiplication of hymns and other songs which for the most part vary with the Church year, not to mention the readings which, of course, comprise a variable element in all liturgies.

Byzantine and Syrian forms have been combined with primordial materials in the *Armenian* liturgy, the language of which—after a brief Syro-Greek beginning—became and remained the national tongue, classical Armenian. In addition, as a result of the return of the Armenians to union with Rome, the liturgy has been considerably modified by Latin influences; there is Psalm 42 (*Iudica*) at the beginning, and the St. John prologue at the end. For the Mass-sacrifice proper there are extant several anaphoras.

Of all these Eastern liturgies the Byzantine is nowadays by far the most important. For that reason we shall meet with it often in the course of the following study. But for the present we must content ourselves with an outline of its structure, along with a description of some of the peculiarities that set it apart. In that way we shall see that its ground-plan was already to be found in the Antiochene Mass of the fourth century.

The fore-Mass begins with two introductory rites of considerable length, which precede the readings. The first of these rites, developed during the course of the Middle Ages, is the *proskomide* or preparation of the offerings. This takes place at a special table amid many ceremonies at the north or left side of the altar—the churches being regularly oriented. The second is the opening, something like a condensed form of the Lauds in our Office, but supplemented by solemn incensations at the beginning and by a hymn at the end. The readings start with a solemn procession, the Little Entrance of the clergy, carrying the book of the Gospels (which had previously lain on the altar) through the nave of the church and back again to the sanctuary. Several songs with the trisagion (Ἅγιος ὁ Θεός, *O holy God*) at the finish, accompany this procession. There are only two readings, the "Apostle" and the Gospel. The fore-Mass closes with a general prayer for the Church, which passes into a special prayer for the catechumens—who are then dismissed—and a prayer for the faithful; each of these sections consists of a diaconal litany and a prayer by the celebrant—a typical arrangement in the Byzantine liturgy.

The Mass proper begins with the Great Entrance, the beautiful procession in which the offerings are carried from the small table on through the nave of the church and then back to the altar. Meanwhile the Cherubikon or Hymn of the Cherubim is sung. The kiss of peace and the recitation of the Creed follow. After the usual dialogue the great eucharistic prayer begins. The priest says the invariable preface secretly while the choir is singing a prolonged *Dignum et justum est*. He raises his voice at the transition into the *Sanctus*, again at the words of consecration, and lastly after the anamnesis at the words of offering. This is followed at once by the epiklesis and an intercessory prayer, and the reading of the diptychs by the deacon.

The train of thoughts in the eucharistic prayer is quite in line with the primitive tradition. In the liturgy of St. Basil it is much elaborated, in that of St. Chrysostom it remains very concise. The chief ideas of the latter—after the usual introduction and some references to the unfathomable greatness of God—are thanks for the creation and the Redemption:

> Thou hast called us out of nothing into being, and when we were fallen, hast lifted us up again, and hast done everything to lead us to heaven and to give us the Kingdom to come.

Words of thanks to the Triune God carry over into adoration, into an invocation of the heavenly hosts and into the *Sanctus* sung by the people. The priest then takes up the cry: "Holy":

> Holy art Thou, and holy is Thine only-begotten Son and Thy Holy Ghost. . . . Thou hast so loved the world as to give Thine only Son. . . . Who came and consummated the whole work of salvation for our sakes, and on the night when He delivered himself up, He took bread . . .

The eucharistic prayer ends after the mementos with a doxology and the Amen of the people.

The *Pater noster* which follows is said in common by all. It is introduced by a deacon's litany and a prayer of the priest, and ends with the tranitarian doxology, "For Thine is the Kingdom." The priest blesses the people and elevates the sacred Host saying, "Holy things to the holy" (Τὰ ἅγια τοῖς ἁγίοις), the Host is broken and a particle is placed in the chalice and the deacon adds thereto a little warm water. After the priest and the deacon have received Holy Communion, the latter goes to the open doors and invites the faithful to communicate. The choir, which has just sung the *communion hymn*, intones a *closing hymn*. A prayer of thanksgiving and a blessing by the priest—as usual with an introductory litany by the deacon—form the closing portion of the service, but there are added various ceremonies like the distribution of the bread (antidoron). This had been blessed during the *proskomide* but had not been consecrated.

5. *The Latin Mass in Christian Antiquity*

A Latin Christianity makes its first appearance in North Africa about the close of the second century, at a time when in Rome itself Greek was still the standard liturgical language. While for the Greek period of the Roman Mass we possess the valuable descriptions of Justin and Hippolytus, the incipient history of the Latin Mass in Rome, and in the West generally, is until the sixth century dim and uncertain. All we have are a few citations and the scanty light that can be thrown on the period by a reconstruction from later authoritative records. A close parallel can be drawn between the variegated history of oriental liturgies and that of the West; here, too, until well into the Middle Ages, there were various liturgies and therefore also various forms of the Mass. There is this distinction, however: in the West, Latin, which was the sole language of culture, was retained as the only language of the liturgy. Another feature which distinguishes the western liturgies as a whole from the eastern is the constant variation of the formulary—or at least of specific formulas—in the course of the Church year.

From here on, we will consider the liturgies of the West other than the Roman, only in so far as such a consideration is requisite for a more complete exposition of the liturgy of Rome.

TWO FAMILIES

The Mass-liturgies of the West are broadly divisible into two families: the *Roman-African* and the *Gallic*. Although fixed forms were generally preserved, there were in both groups many local differences, consequent upon conditions in earlier times. No complete text of the African Mass has come down to us, but scattered references give us sufficient grounds for believing that in many points it coincided closely with the Roman. The Gallic liturgies are further subdivided into four chief forms: the Gallican (in a narrower sense), the Celtic, the Old Spanish or Mozarabic, and the Milanese or Ambrosian.

The *Milanese* liturgy, still employed in the archdiocese of Milan, was from earliest times permeated with Roman forms, and to be more precise, right in the Mass itself, where the Roman canon was incorporated. But numerous details of pre-Roman usage survive, and even the parts taken over from Rome exhibit, to a degree, older forms than are found in the present Roman Mass.

The *Old Spanish* or *Mozarabic* liturgy is also in use, but only in one place, a chapel of the cathedral of Toledo which the great Cardinal Ximenes had established around 1500 to insure the perpetuation of this rite. The Mass book used here, the so-called *Missale Mixtum*, which

Ximenes had had compiled from the manuscripts then at hand, shows Roman influence in several instances. By using older manuscripts it has since been possible to regain a pure form of the Mozarabic Mass as it appeared before the Moorish invasion (A.D. 711).

The term *Celtic* is applied to the Latin liturgies in use among the Celtic peoples of northwestern Europe, especially the Irish and the Scots. The chief propagators of this rite were the Scotch-Irish monks who in their pilgrimages and missionary journeys travelled through many countries. In the few documents that survive, the liturgy reveals the character of this wandering monasticism. So far as the Mass is concerned, it is a liturgy generally composed of foreign elements: Gallican, Roman, Mozarabic and (not least) oriental patterns were borrowed and in some way or other woven together, so that it is only in a broad sense that we can speak of a distinct liturgy.

In contrast, the *Gallican* liturgy, used in the Frankish realm during the early part of the Middle Ages, shows a magnificent independence and exclusiveness. Although it disappeared by the eighth century, at least the Mass from this liturgy is fairly well known. Amongst the documents that have come down, there is especially the work which originated near the end of the seventh century, the so-called *Missale Gothicum*, a sacramentary which is supposed to have come from the monastery of Gregorienmünster in Alsace. There are also authoritative records of the systematized list of pericopes. In addition there are countless references to various particulars, especially in Gregory of Tours (d. 594), and in the seventh century *Expositio Missæ* at one time ascribed to St. Germanus of Paris.

All the Gallic liturgies can be reduced to a simple basic type, especially in reference to two pecularities in the priest's Mass prayers. These are composed, not as in the Orient—at least for the Mass proper—of a continuous prayer, not even for the anaphora, but of a series of individual prayers, even for the great (or eucharistic) prayer. Furthermore, not only are certain of these prayers subjected to the variations of the church year, but the whole series. Every feast of our Lord and every saint's feast had as a rule a distinctive formulary, although this did not exclude the possibility of having neutral formulas to be used at any time, of which the Masses discovered and published by Mone (the Reichenau fragments) offer fair samples.

CENTER FOR GALLIC LITURGY

One question that up till now has been given no uniform answer is, where this liturgical type had its origin. How could such an important liturgical sphere arise in Western Europe without having the Roman mother-church, whose leadership was commonly accepted, as a center? How opposite to what we saw happening in the Orient, apparently without there being any such center at all. Msgr. Duchesne has suggested a solution [1]: he proposes *Milan* as just such a center. During the fourth century Milan was the residence of the Emperors. In ecclesiastical affairs Milan's influence later extended as far as Spain. Accordingly, if we suppose that one of Milan's bishops who came from the Orient—like the Cappadocian Auxentius (355–374)—had established this liturgical type, then we can explain many of the coincidences with oriental usage, more particularly with Antioch—coincidences which are features of the Gallican liturgies and distinguish them from the Roman. Such points of coincidence are the offertory procession after the fore-Mass, the position of the kiss of peace, the epiklesis. However, a great change must then have taken place even under St. Ambrose, for the canon of the Mass, as Ambrose describes it, is essentially Roman. The opinion advanced by others, that the Gallic liturgy was originally the common liturgy of the West, abandoned later on by Rome and, particularly, by Milan, runs up against one big difficulty, namely, that the Gallic liturgical type itself exhibits a relatively late stage of evolution, so that, with all its complications and enrichments, it could hardly be earlier than the fourth century.

The Gallic liturgy did not last long. In France the lack of any regulating center and the resulting multiplicity of forms brought on a growing distaste for this particular liturgy, so that by the eighth century the Roman rite was being substituted for it. On the British Isles it was the advance of the Anglo-Saxon element that forced the introduction of the Roman Mass. In Spain it was the recapture of the peninsula by the young kingdoms which had, in the interval, adopted the Roman system. We shall later come upon many details of the Gallic rites in our exposition of the Roman Mass. The following survey takes in the condition of the Gallic Mass in its final stage.

GALLIC MASS

The Mass begins with a fourfold song sequence. First there is a psalmody which, like the Roman introit, accompanies the entrance of the clergy. After the bishop has greeted the congregation (*Dominus sit semper vobiscum*) there follows the singing of the trisagion (Ἅγιος ὁ θεός), in Greek and Latin. Then the *Kyrie eleison*, sung by three boys, and finally the canticle *Benedictus* (Luke 1:68–79), which is concluded with an oration. The service of readings consists of three lessons. The first is as a rule taken from the Old Testament, the second from the Acts

[1] Duchesne, *Christian Worship*, 90–95.

or the Epistles, the third from the Gospels. After the first reading, the Canticle of the Three Young Men in the Babylonian furnace, *Benedictus es*, is interposed, along with a responsorial chant. The trisagion is again introduced, both before and after the Gospel. Before the Gospel there is a solemn procession led by seven torch-bearers. Following the reading of the Gospel there is a homily. And the fore-Mass is brought to a conclusion with the general prayer for the Church, which is in two parts: a prayer for the faithful and a prayer for the catechumens (who are then dismissed)—both parts, as in the East, introduced by the dialogue of the deacon in the form of a litany.

The Mass proper begins with a second solemn procession, in which the clergy carry the offering-gifts to the altar—the offering of the gifts by the people had already taken place before Mass. This is the entrance of the triumphant Christ. The procession is accompanied by the chanting of what is called a *sonus*, and is brought to a close with another song. A kind of opening address (*præfatio missæ* or *missa* it is called) expounds in carefully contrived periods the motive and meaning of each particular festivity; an oration follows. Next comes the reading of the diptychs with the names of those who are offering the sacrifice, or for whom the sacrifice is being offered in a particular way. This closes with a prayer; then there is the kiss of peace, and another prayer. After that, at last the eucharistic prayer.

There is the customary introductory dialogue, then the first part or preface—called *immolatio* or *contestatio*, whose basic motif is thanksgiving but which frequently turns to petitions. This leads into the *Sanctus*. After the *Sanctus*, and usually linked to some word of it, comes the *Post Sanctus*, which forms a simple transition to the words of consecration. The next prayer is designated *Post secreta* or *Post mysterium* (in Spain, *Post Pridie*); it comprises mostly both an anamnesis and an epiklesis. What follows, the breaking of the Bread and the arrangement of the particles on the altar, is carefully regulated; an antiphonal chant accompanies the ceremony. A special prayer, variable like all the others, leads into the *Pater noster*; this is said by the entire assembly, and ends in a frequently changing embolism. The culmination and climax of the Gallican Mass comes, at least at a pontifical service, just before Communion, when the deacon invites all to receive the blessing and the blessing is given; there are special collections of the formulas for this blessing, fitted to each changing feast. The Communion itself is accompanied by the chanting of Psalm 33 or appointed selections thereof or some other song; it is concluded with an oration.

Even this rough sketch makes one thing sure. The plan of the Gallican Mass, which reappears with slight changes in all the liturgies of the type, shows a definite leaning toward splendor and ceremonial. Even if we deduct some of the chants, which obviously belong only to the later stages of the liturgy, the trend is still discernible. The same impression is given by the rhetoric employed, ornamental and diffuse, often spinning its message out to such an extent that the form is lost and a prayer becomes an address, and an address becomes a prayer. The theological thought-structure reflects the constant upheavals provoked by christological battles; after all it was not only in Spain that the opposition to Germanic Arianism had an effect on Christian life.

6. *The Roman Mass from the Third to the Sixth Centuries*

The beginnings of the Latin Mass in Rome are wrapped in almost total darkness. The oldest documents to register such a Mass are nearly all the work of diligent Frankish scribes of the eighth and ninth centuries, and even with all the apparatus of literary criticism and textual analysis, we can hardly reconstruct any records back beyond the sixth century, certainly not beyond the fifth. For the most part whatever is here transmitted as the permanent text—especially the canon, but likewise the major portion of the variable prayers of the celebrant, and the readings—is almost identical with present-day usage. We are thus brought face-to-face with a sharp contrast: the Latin Mass as it has been practiced ever since, and the Greek Mass to which Hippolytus attests—and a broad gulf between. In place of the earlier freedom within a given schema, there is now to be found a fast and solid rigidity of forms. Of these forms there is a veritable treasure, their variety conditioned by the course of the church year. Although well within the stiff limitations of the new outline, these forms seem to have explored every possibility of the newer arrangement. There are hundreds and hundreds of variable texts, especially for feasts of martyrs. There are one or two prayers by the celebrant in the fore-Mass, a prayer over the sacrificial gifts, an ever-changing text for the *præfatio* before the *Sanctus*, and a prayer after the Communion. This is the content of the older formularies of the priest's Mass prayers for each day's celebration.

The tendency to diversify the texts is set in bold opposition to the stability of what was later called (in a narrow sense) the canon, the essentially unchanging text of the prayer from the *Te igitur* to the concluding doxology, and its continuation from the *Pater noster* to the dismissal. In contrast to the smooth-flowing eucharistic prayer recorded by Hippolytus, the Roman canon, with its separate members and steps, and its broken-up lists of saints, presents a picture of great complexity. For the new science of liturgy, schooled as it was in philology, here was an alluring problem. The new science, as it developed till the turn of the century, had only the Clementine liturgy of the fourth century as the last link before the appearance of the Roman canon; how to fill in the hiatus, at least by hypotheses, proved an inviting question.

ROMAN CANON

Thus a number of theories were developed to explain the origin of the Roman canon, but as a result of their mutual disagreement little more is left of them now than ruins. One of the boldest of these theorists, Anton Baumstark, not long ago, while making a new examination of the problem, himself summarized it in this very way. That does not mean, however, that there is absolutely no hope of clearing up the history of this development. The only thing that seems doomed to failure is the attempt to gather from here and there bits of text that appear to be similar, and then expect to explain the whole configuration, for such similarities are to be found everywhere. The liturgy of Rome must have developed in Rome itself, although there may have been influences there from outside.

The first thing that was to be done during that interval between the third and the sixth century, was to translate the liturgy from Greek into the Latin tongue, the result, no doubt, of the changed composition of the Roman community. This transition was not a sudden one. The inscriptions on the papal tombs are found in Latin during the second half of the third century, beginning with Pope Cornelius (d. 253) although this inscription does not date precisely from the time of his death. If there were in Rome already before Constantine more than forty churches, it is possible that Latin congregations had existed before Cornelius. Yet even as late as the year 360 the Roman rhetorician Marius Victorinus cites a Greek quotation from the Roman *oratio oblationis* of his day.

While the variable formularies of the Latin Mass book could naturally arise only by a slow process, and even the principle of change and the method of its employment could not have been uniform all at once, there must have been from the start a requirement regarding the formulation of the great eucharistic prayer that could not be rejected. Was this first formulation already our Roman canon? The conjecture has indeed been put forth, and an attempt made to support it. But it is more probable that the change-over from Greek to Latin produced many intermediary forms, particularly since in the third century we have not in general to reckon with any universally fixed texts. Besides, it is hardly like that the sober temper of the Romans, which speaks so plainly even in the prayer-language of the canon, would have penetrated through and through immediately after such a transition.

On the other hand, at least the core of the Roman canon must have existed by the end of the fourth century. In an anonymous writing of this period a phrase is cited from the *Supra quæ;* the unknown author remarks in connection with his rather remarkable opinion that Melchisedech was the Holy Ghost:

> And likewise, the Holy Spirit sent as the High Priest (i.e., Melchisedech) was called priest of the most high God, not most high priest of God as we say in our oblation.

The words of the canon that immediately adjoin these, namely the words which designate Melchisedech's gift as a sacrifice, are attested for the middle of the fifth century by the *Liber Pontificalis* which gives an account—here more trustworthy—of Pope Leo the Great's insertion *intra actionem sacrificii* of the words *sanctum sacrificium et cetera.* Further, Jerome seems to play on the words of introduction to the Lord's Prayer, *audemus dicere.* But it is above all St. Ambrose who, in his instructions to the newly-baptized, gives us an extensive excerpt from the Mass prayers, which differs very little from the respective prayers of the present Roman canon. He is trying to show his listeners that it is Christ's creative word which turns the earthly gifts into the Lord's Body and Blood:

> Hear the words which the priest says: "Make for us," he says, "an approved, a spiritual, and an acceptable oblation which is the figure of the Body and Blood of Our Lord Jesus Christ. Who, on the day before He suffered, took bread into His holy hands, looked up to heaven to Thee, holy Father, almighty and eternal God, and giving thanks, He blessed, broke, and having broken it, He delivered it to His apostles and His disciples saying: All take and eat of this, for this is my body which shall be broken for many. And He likewise took the chalice after He had supped on the day before He suffered, and looked up to heaven to Thee, holy Father, almighty and eternal God, and giving thanks He blessed it and delivered it to His apostles and His disciples saying: All take and drink of this, for this is my blood.

> Notice what He says: as often as you shall do this, you shall make memory of me until I shall come again. And the priest says: "Making memory therefore of His most glorious passion and resurrection from the dead and ascension into heaven, we offer to Thee this immaculate host, this spiritual host, this unblooody host, this holy bread and chalice of eternal life; and we beseech and pray that Thou wouldst receive it on Thy altar on high through the hands of Thine angels, as Thou didst deign to receive the gifts of Thy just

servant Abel and the sacrifice of our patriarch Abraham and that
which the high priest Melchisedech offered to Thee.[2]

Certain details of this text will engage us elsewhere. Right now we
must accept this as certain: *the core of our Mass canon, from the* Quam
oblationem *on, including the sacrificial prayer after the consecration,
was already in existence by the end of the fourth century.* We do not
know for sure whether the slight differences in wording are to be traced
to a divergent older text or are to be charged to the episcopal orator
who, to be sure, was really concerned only with the words of consecration. At least the first words, which have no real connection with anything preceding, would be a free rendering of the sense, since the prayer
for the changing of the gifts, as thus introduced, is presumably the con-
tination of a previous presentation of the material gifts. This fourth-
century canon exhibits, by comparison with the eucharistic prayer of
the third, only these new elements: a more pronounced expression of the
prayer that the gifts will be graciously accepted, and the explicit prayer
for a change in these gifts.

We might ask, are the intercessory prayers contained in our Roman
canon, particularly the doubled *Memento*, part of the fourth-century
contents? We saw how in the Orient these intercessary prayers, which
had their roots in an earlier stage of the eucharistic prayer, had actually
become part of it during the fourth century, and in part precisely in
conjunction with the enumeration of the names.

Another striking allusion to the Roman canon is to be found in the
remark by which Ambrose introduces the quotation already given;
everything, he says, that precedes the efficacious words of transubstantiation, is but human utterance: "The rest, which are said in order, are
said by the priest, praises are offered to God. Prayer is sought for the
people, for kings, for others."

This could refer to prayers of intercession which would be inserted

---

[2] *Accipe, quæ sunt verba. Dicit sacerdos: Fac nobis, inquit, hanc oblationem scriptam,
rationabilem, acceptabilem, quod est figura corporis et sanguinis Domini nostri Jesu
Christi. Qui pridie quam pateretur, in sanctis manibus suis accepit panem, respexit in
cœlum ad te, sancte Pater omnipotens æterne, Deus, gratias agens benedixit, fregit frac-
tumque apostolis suis et discipulis suis tradidit dicens: Accipe et edite ex hoc omnes, hoc
est enim corpus meum, quod pro multis confringetur. Similiter etiam calicem, postquam
cœnatum est, pridie quam pateretur, accepit, respexit in cœlum ad te, sancte Pater omnipotens æterne Deus, gratias agens benedixit, apostolis suis et discipulis suis tradidit dicens:
Accipe et bibite ex hoc omnes, hic est enim sanguis meus.*
*Vide quid dicat: Quotiescunque hoc feceritis, toties commemorationem mei facietis,
donec iterum adveniam. Et sacerdos dicit: Ergo memores gloriosissimæ eius passionis et
ab inferis resurrectionis et in cœlum ascensionis offerimus tibi hanc immaculatam hostiam,
rationabilem hostiam, incruentam hostiam, hunc panem sanctum et calicem vitæ æternæ;
et petimus et precamur ut hanc oblationem suscipias in sublimi altari tuo per manus
angelorum tuorum, sicut suscipere dignatus es munera pueri tui iusti Abel et sacrificium
patriarchæ nostri Abrahæ et quod tibi obtulit summus sacerdos Melchisedech.*

after the preface. Still the intercessory prayers mentioned are such as the people would be invited to make, and that is certainly unusual within the canon. Ambrose is probably telling off the prayers in reverse order, from the consecration backwards. His mind would recall the arrangement in which the general prayer for the Church preceded the Mass proper, the arrangement which was continued in the Gallican liturgies.

The question of arranging the diptychs was one that was at that very time much discussed so far as the Roman liturgy was concerned. In the year 416, Bishop Decentius of the Apennine town of Gubbio had consulted Pope Innocent I on this very point of usage. The bishop had been wont to have the names read (by the deacon) before the celebrant, by his prayer, commended the gifts to God. But now some openly objected to this arrangement. Innocent's reply to Decentius is not clear. Nevertheless, this much seems sure: according to Pope Innocent the reading of the names (on the diptychs) should not take place till after the gifts have been commended to God. This commendation has been understood by some liturgists to refer to the *secreta*. But the words that follow in the letter of Innocent indicate a recitation within the eucharistic prayer or canon, perhaps after a prayer corresponding to our *Te igitur.*

That the continuation of the *Te igitur* was also in existence at this time, we can gather from papal letters of the years immediately following, which speak of a remembrance of the Emperor *inter ipsa mysteria,*[3] *oblatis sacrificiis.*[4]

We thus account for at least three formulas in the canon (before the consecration) at the start of the fifth century: *To igitur* (with the continuation: *in primis quæ tibi offerimus*), *Memento Domine* (or some such formula for introducing the listing of names), and *Quam oblationem.* It is striking that the Spanish *Liber ordinum*, which in several other places contains a mixture of old Roman materials, actually exhibits a Mass prayer which welds precisely these three elements into one.[5] Thus it would seem that these three prayers at one time actually existed alone, and the question then arises, whether the independent *Memento* had been from the beginning bound up with both the others.

Only the following parts of our Roman canon could not be found at the beginning of the fifth century: *Communicantes, Hanc igitur,* and

---

[3] "During the very celebration of the mysteries." Boniface I (418–422).

[4] "After the oblation (i.e. commendation) of the sacrifice." Celestine I (422–432).

[5] It runs: *Per quem te petimus et rogamus, omnipotens Pater, ut accepta habeas et benedicere digneris hæc munera et hæc sacrificia inlibata, quæ tibi in primis offerimus pro tua sancta Ecclesia catholica, quam pacificare digneris per universum orbem terrarum in tua pace diffusam. Memorare etiam, quæsumus Domine, servorum tuorum qui tibi in honore sanctorum tuorum illorum reddunt vota sua Deo vivo ac vero pro remissione suorum omnium delictorum. Quorum oblationem benedictam, ratam rationabilemque facere digneris, quæ est imago et similitudo corporis et sanguinis Jesu Christi Filii tui ac Redemptoris nostri.*

after the consecration, *Memento etiam* and *Nobis quoque*. However, these formulas too (with the exception of the *Memento* of the dead), are to be found in the oldest extant manuscripts of the Roman canon, in a form that must at all events belong to the sixth century. During the interval all these prayers came into being; and the others took on, where they differed, the form they have at present. The authentic version goes back possibly to Pope Gelasius I (492–496), to whom the finished canon of the so-called Stowe Missal is ascribed, and to whom many other references point.

But there is something distinctive even about the more ancient shorter version, in which the prayers mentioned above are missing. If we join to this version the preface and the *Sanctus*, and compare it then with the anaphoras of the Orient, we will notice the vast difference. Of course the difference is not so great but that in many spots a glimmer of the most antique tradition peers through, displaying again and again the resemblances to peculiarities of the Egyptian liturgy. We have here to do with traditional material from a period when the congregations of Rome and Alexandria were linked not only by an intense sea commerce, but by the ties of a common language and culture, a period when there were still no fixed texts but a living custom that sought uniformity with friendly sister-churches.

In an effort piously to preserve such traditions, someone in the fourth century must have worked out the basic text of the Roman canon. That this text, compared with the great eucharistic prayer of other liturgies, incorporated the lineaments of a greater antiquity, has already been demonstrated more than once. To try to name the author would be a thankless undertaking. But it will be well to point out a few of the author's stylistic peculiarities. He has a preference for word-doubles (the coupling of synonyms or related expressions): "we pray and beseech; to receive and bless; Catholic and apostolic faith; whose faith and devotion are known to Thee; holy and venerable hands; etc., etc." Even in the prelude to the *Pater noster*, that same trait is dominant: admonished by saving commands, following divine directions. Sometimes he employs a three-member phrase, and in the petition for the consecration (epiklesis) and in the prayer of blessing before the closing doxology there are even five members: bless, consecrate . . . , and create, sanctify . . .

MASS ALTERED AND SIMPLIFIED

In the same era in which the canon got its final shape, other portions of the Roman Mass must likewise have been altered and amplified. The oldest sources of the Latin Mass of Rome exhibit, in every single Mass formula, along with the current expansion of the canon, by way of the preface, a regular tripling (or even quadrupling) of the priest's orations, as is still the rule: one (or two) at the beginning, one over the sacrificial offerings, one after the communion. Thus the communion obtained a conclusion in prayer, and the offering of the gifts, as its counterpart, is made grander in such wise that the gifts of the people are accented and emphasized. This latter is a peculiarity of the Roman liturgy. The valuation of the material gifts already insisted on by Irenæus has thus discovered a corresponding expression in ritual and prayer, more pronounced than in other liturgies. Besides these, there is also, just as nowadays, an oration before the readings.

The documents of the fourth century still show the Mass beginning abruptly with the lessons, and these are followed—as in the oriental and Gallic liturgies of the following centuries—by the general prayer for the Church. With regard to both of these items the Roman Mass made changes.

The general prayer for the Church was still a part of the Roman rite under Pope Felix (483–492), and precisely with a division into prayer for the catechumens and prayer for the faithful. After that there are no further records of it, and the oldest sources of the Latin Mass show it to have disappeared. On the other hand an oration has appeared just before the lessons. This can be explained only as a part of some already existing introductory act, like those subsequently developed in other liturgies. The adopting of such an introductory act, with the opening oration just spoken of, must be as old as the oldest examples of the Mass formularies which are regularly fitted out with such an oration. Now these reach back at least as far as the middle of the fifth century. The introductory act was then filled out further with song and prayer. There is much to be said in favor of the view that it was under Felix II's successor, Pope Gelasius I (492–496), whose liturgical activity is celebrated in the *Liber Pontificalis*, that here and elsewhere many important changes were introduced into the Roman Mass. It must have been Gelasius who introduced the *Kyrie*-litany, thus providing for the oration a preliminary dialogue after the oriental fashion, the prayer traditionally styled *deprecatio Gelasii*. Note, however, that the list of petitions in this litany coincides rather closely with the themes of the general prayer for the Church as it is to be found in Rome prior to Gelasius. *We are justified in concluding that Gelasius had removed the general prayer for the Church, and had substituted the* Kyrie-*litany*. A concomitant factor in deciding to make this exchange might have been the thought that intercessory petitions had now been included in the canon—it might even have been Gelasius who gave them greater prominence—and the further consideration that, since circumstances had voided the custom of separating catechumens from the faithful, there was no longer any reason for continuing a series of prayers, the apparent basis for which was gone.

This then is the conclusion to be drawn from all the facts we have established: *the framework of the Roman Mass must have been essentially determined by the turn of the fifth century, at least as regards the public utterance of prescribed prayers by the priest.* Later on, in the course of our study of various Mass-elements, we will encounter only a few modifications by Gregory the Great (590–604)—chiefly in the *Kyrie, Pater noster*, preface and *Hanc igitur;* but these are for the most part a return to older simpler forms.

As far as the time of establishment or fixation is concerned, what was said about the arrangements for the prayers holds true similarly for the singing which served as an added embellishment to the prayers and readings. Not indeed that the texts were fixed this early, but the type had been determined and the scheme planned out. This is certain in regard to the old simple chants between the lessons, and probable in regard to the processional chants at the beginning, at the offertory and Communion. A more minute study will be provided later on in the chapters devoted to the particular chants. In any case, however, at this early period before the sixth century, we have to reckon only with a very unpretentious type of singing, still affected by that timid attitude toward the musical arts which caused the Church to ban every instrument from divine service.

The fifth century was for Rome a time of great calamity indeed, but the following century, with its Gothic threat and its Lombard invasion, was one long succession of disasters and oppressions. Yet it was in this very period that Roman worship unfolded into ever-increasing splendor. This development is closely linked with the extraordinary esteem in which papacy and Church were held in the Eternal City during these years. The papacy had become the one only glory and pride of the Roman population. As the pope became more and more the only support of the afflicted city, and finally found himself burdened with the cares of civil administration, the papal church-service became the prime expression of civic life.

Gradually, along with the simple services held Sundays and feast days in the many titular churches of the city for the people attending, there arose also a community service, conducted by the pope himself in the church privileged as the day's *statio*, and attended not only by members of the court but by people from every quarter of Rome. A trace of this is still to be found today during Lent (under the name *stazione*) as an evening penitential procession at the church marked in the missal as the stational church of the day. People and clergy from all parts of the city participate. Stational worship of a similar sort is mentioned also in connection with other episcopal churches of the early Middle Ages. These services must necessarily have been more modest in character. It was Rome that produced the most extensive results in setting down in writing this new type of service. Two factors contributed: the greater splendor of the Christian capitol, and the Roman's native sense of order. The effect was not only to fix forms, but to fix them in such wise that they were regulated for the whole course of the year—*per circulum anni*, as the caption puts it. With this we come to the books of the Roman Mass over which we will tarry long enough to get to understand the references made to them in our later elucidations.

7. *The Oldest Books of the Roman Mass*

What we get to know from the books of the old Roman liturgy is, as has been said, first of all the great festival services. This follows from the very character of the books themselves. They are divided according to the persons or groups performing the prescribed actions. For the celebrating priest or bishop there is the *liber sacramentorum* or *sacramentarium*, which contains the orations and prefaces that vary from feast to feast. Only in later times were the ordinary or fixed parts included, and among these the canon of the Mass, for the latter was anteriorly to be found on a special tablet or was presumed to have been memorized by the celebrant. For the lessons (readings), which were of course recited by two different readers, two separate books were prepared, the *apostolus* for the reader of the Epistle, and the *evangelium* for the deacon who read the Gospel. Further, a book was required containing the texts for the group of singers that now appear, the *schola cantorum* who had to accompany the processions at the entrance, the offertory and the communion with their antiphonal singing. There was also a special book, the *cantatorium,* for the individual singer who took the lead in singing the old traditional responsorial chants between the lessons. And not to be overlooked, finally, there was the book of directions to help regulate the functions, in view of the great array of liturgical factors, especially for the rites that occur only on certain days of the year. This book even took into account the ordinary celebration of the stational services which took place each time at a different place and partly under diverse surroundings. The books which were composed for this purpose were the *ordines,* rubric-books for the cleric whose function it was to act as a sort of master of ceremonies in directing the celebration. These older liturgical books are thus laid out like the actors' parts in a secred play, as the share of each individual in a community performance. The oriental Churches to this day employ only liturgical books of this sort, while in the West, the liturgical books are ordinarily organized—for reasons which we shall consider later on—not on the basis of the participants but on the basis of the acts performed. The result is that everything for Mass is found in the missal, just as everything for the Office is bound into a breviary and everything for the dispensing of the sacraments is contained in the ritual.

THE SACRAMENTARIES

Of the Roman Sacramentary, three different versions have come down to us, giving us three different plans for the priest's part of the liturgy, and thus furnishing us with another proof that, as the period of Christian antiquity came to a close, there was little thought of a form for the Mass prayers that would be once and for all fixed and firm. These three sacramentaries—which were manifestly preceded by smaller collections of Mass formularies in various *libelli*—were rather arbitrarily named, by the liturgists of the last centuries, after the three popes to whom they were ascribed, an assignment which proves to be at least partially confirmed.

The Leonine Sacramentary, *Sacramentarium Leonianum*, preserved in a single manuscript of the seventh century, is a collection of Mass formularies arranged according to the Church year, and apparently finished about 540. The first part, from Christmas to the middle of April, is missing. The Roman origin of the book is manifest in several places. The compiler seems to have drawn on every source at his disposal. Thus there are fourteen Masses for the feast of St. Lawrence, twenty-eight for SS. Peter and Paul. The Leonine is generally considered a private venture, and rightly, for some of the formularies are put together in part very casually, and some of the texts have a strikingly personal tone, two things hardly compatible with a Mass book intended for general use. In fact one may well wonder whether at the time under consideration, namely the middle of the sixth century, a Mass book that would be the obligatory standard text was even possible. Conversely, it is quite thinkable that this compilation did have some official standing as an orderly arrangement of available liturgical materials. Not a few texts—174 by actual count—have found their way from the Leonine Sacramentary into our present-day missal, and three of them are used daily in the Ordinary (*Aufer a nobis; Deus qui humanæ substantiæ; Quod ore sumpsimus*).

The Gelasian Sacramentary (*Sacramentarium Gelasianum*) is a real and proper Mass book. Two different forms of it have to be distinguished, an older and a later. The older form, *the* Gelasian, preserved entire in only one manuscript, a text of the early eighth century which probably comes from St. Denis, contains Mass formularies arranged in three books: the first book has the formularies for the Christmas and Easter cycles; the second for saints' feasts of the entire year from January to December, and, as a supplement, formularies for Advent-tide and the Advent Ember-week; the third book has a list of Sunday Masses and a selection of Votive Masses for the most diverse occasions and contingencies. The Gelasian is indeed a Roman Mass book in all essentials. But the special Roman local coloring is obscured by the fact that stational notices are missing and a large number of non-Roman saints' feasts are incorporated. Gallican materials are interspersed in several places—some prayers, some saints' names in the canon. The Good Friday oration for the Emperor has the wording, "Look graciously upon the rule of the Romans or Franks." And completely Gallican is the section devoted to minor orders (I, 95, 96), the texts of which crept into the Roman Pontifical, just as much of the other material of this sacramentary survives in our Roman Missal.

The Roman materials in the Gelasian Sacramentary, either in the form of a complete book or in small collections, got into France at the very latest in the first half of the seventh century. Previously, in the sixth century, the corresponding formularies must have been in use at Rome. That the book goes back to Pope Gelasius I (492–496) is impossible since it can be proved that a considerable number of the matching sections were taken from those parts of the Leonianum which have Vigilius (537–555) as their author. From the materials in this Gelasian Sacramentary, and from other liturgical materials meanwhile imported chiefly from Rome, another type of Mass book was composed in France around the first half of the eighth century, the later or Frankish Gelasian. This sacramentary, often called the eighth-century Gelasian, is preserved in several manuscripts, the best known of which was written about 800 at St. Gall. In this sacramentary the movable and immovable cycles are not separated but are confusedly intermingled.

The same is the case in regard to the third type of sacramentary, the *Sacramentarium Gregorianum* which brings us back once more to Rome. It is true the manuscripts are for the most part Frankish, and—except for some fragments—no earlier than the ninth century. But a comparative study has enabled us to reconstruct the exemplar sent by Pope Hadrian I to Charlemagne in the year 785–786. It is even possible to suggest the oldest attainable form of the sacramentary, as it appeared in the time of Honorius I (625–638) or just a little later. In fact, during the last few decades the conviction has grown that Gregory the Great actually produced this Mass book. Again, many of the prayer-texts still in use today stem from Gregory, as, for example, the prefaces of Easter and Ascension.

The work was not thought of primarily as a book for the ordinary parish services; it was a papal feast-day and stational missal. That explains many of the omissions in the book—the customary Sunday service, for instance, which the Gelasian Sacramentary is so careful to provide. However, a second edition must have been put out for the use of the titular churches, although we have only indirect knowledge of such an issue. Because the sacramentary sent to Charlemagne was incomplete—the Sunday Masses, amongst others, were missing—a supplement was added by Alcuin containing the requisite materials for parochial services and also mixing many Gallican traditions with the Roman. In its further development, more and more material of the supplement—like so much of the

Gelasian—was transferred to the sacramentary itself. And so a new type of the Roman Mass book was produced.

For the liturgical lessons it was customary till far into the Middle Ages to use not some special reading texts, but simply the Holy Scriptures, from which were read the excerpts which had already been appointed for a long time. Later on we find lesson-indexes or catalogues, which marked the pertinent passages (chapters or *capitula*); hence they are called capitularies. These are the most extensive sources for our knowledge of the old system which governed the liturgical readings, particularly the lessons of the Roman Mass. But even at an early period, there were special texts prepared for divine service, called lectionaries or *comes* or (in accordance with their contents) *epistolarium, evangeliarium*. The most ancient lectionary of the Roman Church containing Epistles and Gospels is the *Comes* of Würzburg, whose contents indicate the seventh century. Still such lectionaries are the exception until well beyond the year 1000.

The arrangement of the readings within the Mass from the earliest sources which make them known, has undergone fewer alterations than the prayer of the celebrant as transmitted in the sacramentary. However, certain definite degrees of development, or types, can be distinguished, particularly as regards the changes of the calendar. Through the work of Theodore Klauser, the arrangement of the Gospel readings in the Roman Church has been fixed for the years 645, 740, 755, and an arrangement which was expanded in Frankish territory has been dated 750. The last named arrangement indicates a final stage and it is, in all essentials, the order which survives in the Roman Missal. For the Epistle readings, besides the *Comes* of Würzburg and a *comes* worked on by Alcuin, the most remarkable table is that of Murbach, whose Church year is based on that of the later Gelasian, and which remained (along with the latter) more or less definitive.

A text book of some sort for the singing of the *schola cantorum* was a requisite from the very foundation of such an organization. Consequently, fragmentary remnants survive from even pre-Georgian days. But what comes to us as a complete work is a book that can also be traced to Gregory the Great, but which survives only in manuscripts of the Carolingian period, the *liber antiphonarius* or the antiphonal. But by a process of collation, especially by the excision of formularies for newer feasts, we can arrive at the form of the Mass songbook in the time of Honorius I (625–638). In these oldest manuscripts no melodies are given. It is not till the tenth century that we find the first witness to the melodies written in neums. Before this time the songs must have been handed down by tradition in actual performance. That St. Gregory busied himself with ecclesiastical chant is a tradition which had wide vogue even in the early Middle Ages. Precisely in what his reform consisted we can only guess, but this much is certain: the attribution of the "Gregorian Chant" to him is not groundless.

The antiphonal (antiphonary) which, properly speaking, contained only the antiphonal chants of the *schola cantorum*, was at this early period distinguished from the *cantatorium*, which contained the songs traditionally assigned to the soloist who intoned them from the ambo. The people answered with a short verse of response—the songs called the gradual, the alleluia chant and the tract. Only a few such *cantatoria* have survived. When the performance of these chants was turned over to a *schola* divided into soli and chorus, the text was likewise incorporated into the choir's antiphonal, so that, because of its new contents, the latter was also called a gradual.

The content of the *Roman Ordines* is the rubrics for the papal stational service. They were first brought to light by John Mabillon who in 1689 published fifteen of them extending into the late Middle Ages. Since then, their number has increased through new discoveries. For the older *Ordines* (up to the tenth century) there is now available—complete for the Mass-liturgy—the critical edition of Michael Andrieu which employs all the manuscript material which has been handed down to us. Thus we not only have now a certified text of these books of ceremonies, but also a new basis on which to judge them. As far as the Mass-liturgy goes, only the First Roman *Ordo* (*Ordo Romanus Primus*) can be considered a pure source for the city of Rome. Of this Ordo, there is only one older and one somewhat younger expanded edition extant, both of which stem from the seventh century. We see in them a thorough picture of the papal services with the inclusions of the preparations that go with it. Information from it will serve as a starting point for more than one place in our explanation of the Mass-liturgy.

Just as for this *Ordo* the written tradition goes back exclusively to Frankish scriptoriums, so too the *Ordines* of the Roman Mass-liturgy which belong to the following centuries are generally products of the Franks. They stand in connection with the acceptance of the Roman liturgy in Frankish territory in the middle of the eighth century, the period at which the Roman liturgy had entered its decisive stage. We shall examine this more closely later on. Thus it happened that enthusiasts for the Roman liturgy adapted the already existing order found in the *Ordo Romanus Primus* either by leaving out only the peculiarities of the service of the papal court, or by undertaking at the same time a new version of the text and, at varying degrees, introducing into it customs of the Gallican liturgy which, it was felt, should continue within the Roman liturgy. All this was done without acknowledging the fact that what was being presented was not indeed a "Roman" *Ordo*. By way of exception, Roman usages could have crept in which did not come from the *Ordo Romanus Primus*. Of such is the *Capitulare ecclesiastici ordinis* from the second half of the eighth century. This is a freely formulated, only slightly Gallican sounding offshoot from the *Ordo Romanus Primus* that is followed by a second more strongly gallicanized Mass Order with its appended *Instructio Ecclesiastici Ordinis* which is chiefly concerned with the Church year. This is likewise true of the monastic adaptation of the same material, the *Breviarium Ecclesiastici Ordinis*, also of the eighth century. Of similar character as the *Capitulare* and *Instructio* is the *Ordo* of St. Amand from the end of the eighth century.

From a somewhat earlier period, there are three *Ordines* for the Mass-liturgy which likewise stem from the first Roman *Ordo*. These no longer show the liturgy of Rome, but pointedly show a Mass order for episcopal services in Frankish lands according to the Roman rite. The first of these is the second Roman *Ordo* of Mabillon, numbered by Andrieu as five, and designated in the manuscripts as *Ordo "secundum Romanos,"* a name we shall use to avoid confusing the numbers. Its origin is attributed to shortly before 900 somewhere in the Rhineland. The other two *Ordines* of the episcopal Mass are expanded from this *Ordo*. Of these last two, the first which begins "in primis" must have originated somewhere about 900 in south-west Germany. The other which expands on it still further has the beginning "Postquam" and probably came from Mainz before the middle of the tenth century. Of a related type is also the *Ordo* "Qualiter quaedam orationes et cruces in Te igitur agendae sunt." It is a section from the Gregorian sacramentary that a Frankish cleric in the ninth century, probably in Metz or Besançon, supplied with rubrics which he took generously from the *Ordo Romanus Primus*. These rubrics mention the pope but take Frankish circumstances into consideration at the same time. The younger version of this *Ordo* which begins the canon with the *Te igitur* and to which the above-mentioned name belongs, originated in the tenth century and found the greatest acceptance.

Finally, we must mention the *Ordo Romanus Antiquus*, which originated as a part of the Romano-German Pontifical around 950 in a monastery in Mainz. There are also younger *Ordines* which are important for the history of the development of the Mass-liturgy.

8. The Roman Stational Services in the Seventh Century

The grand Roman stational worship, as it was developed up to about the eighth century, is especially important for the further history of the Mass-liturgy, and this for two reasons. For one thing, the service achieved a moment of stability, when all its component elements were set down in writing—as all codification entails a fixed arrangement, at least for some time. A certain interval must have ensued before the lineaments of such a form were again broken here or there. And secondly, by the very fact that this solemn service was written down in a definite and determined form and thus could easily be transmitted to other territories—by that very fact it became the model and standard for further shaping and forming the Mass generally. The effect of this example would be felt in the divine service of every village church and would even touch the ceremonial of low Mass.

On this account we must now glance at the stational services at least in their broad outlines.

POPE'S ARRIVAL

The pope comes mounted from his *patriarchium* on the Lateran to the appointed stational church. In a later stage of development, in the eighth century, this trip has become a stately procession in which the entire papal court takes part: first a group of acolytes on foot, and the *defensores* (the legal administrators of church properties in the whole city), then on horseback the seven deacons from the city's seven regions which they managed for the care of the poor, each with his appointed regional subdeacon. Behind the pope, and likewise on horseback, come the chief dignitaries of the Apostolic Palace, the *vicedominus, vestiarius, nomenclator,* and *saccellarius.* At the entrance to the appointed church the pope is met by those in charge of the place. The rest of the clergy have already taken their places on the benches which run the length of the semi-circle in the *presbyterium* (sanctuary) and around the altar, like the later choir-stalls. In the middle, that is, at the vertex of the apse, is the slightly-raised *cathedra* or throne for the pope. At the right sit the six suburbicarian bishops, to the left the presbyters of the titular churches. The altar, a simple table, stands about the center of the semi-circle. Since there is no superstructure, it does not hinder the view from the back. The nave of the basilica has already filled with a large crowd, which has come in seven processions from the seven regions of Rome, each with its silver processional cross at the head.

The pope is first led to the *secretarium* which is built close to the entrance of the basilica. Here he is vested with the liturgical *paramenta,* a rather considerable number: *linea* (our alb), *cingulum,* shoulder cloth or scarf, *linea dalmatica* (our tunicle), and *major dalmatica,* finally the *planeta,* the bell-shaped chasuble worn by all the clerics, even the acolytes. The last vestment put on by the pope is the pallium. Now the Gospel book is opened; it is held by an acolyte, not bare-handed but over the ruffled *planeta;* accompanied by a subdeacon he carries it to the altar, and meanwhile all stand up. The paraphonist then presents himself to the pope to announce which of the regional subdeacons will sing the Epistle and what choir soloist will sing the responsorial chants between the readings; one of the deacons has already been appointed for the Gospel.

When all is ready the pope reaches for his maniple and waves it as a signal.[1] The clerics who have been waiting in front of the *secretarium* with tapers and incense receive their command: *Accendite!* [2] And the singers who have lined up in a double row to right and left at the entrance of the *presbyterium* receive theirs: *Domni iubete!* The introit is intoned and the procession is on its way.

The signs of reverence which are given to the pope as he makes his entrance for divine service are noteworthy. It is evident that the incense and the seven torches of the acolytes are in his honor; it is a reverence to which the emperor and the higher state officials had been entitled. The pope reaches out his hands to the two deacons accompanying him; they kiss them and continue to assist him in walking—another custom which must derive from the ancient and originally oriental court ceremonial. Incidentally, among noble Austrian families it was still customary even in our century to meet a member of the imperial house at the door with two burning candles (or, according to another communication, a servant stood at the foot of the steps with a candelabrum).

The cortege pauses as two acolytes approach to show the pope an opened casket (*capsæ*) in which is reserved a particle of the Holy Eucharist. The pope adores, making a low bow. When the procession reaches the place where the *schola* has its station, between the nave and the sanctuary, the torch-bearers part, four to the right and three to the left. The pope goes up before the altar, bows, makes a sign of the Cross on his forehead, and exchanges the kiss of peace with one of the bishops who has approached from his seat, as well as with one of the priests and the assembled deacons.

MASS BEGINS

At a sign from the pope, the *prior scholæ* brings the introit to an end with the *Gloria Patri* and the repetition of the antiphon. Meanwhile a carpet is spread out and the pope prostrates himself in prayer, in silent homage to God—a rite with which divine service is opened even now on Good Friday and Holy Saturday. After a moment he rises, kisses the Gospel book and the altar. Meanwhile, during the interval of silent prayer, the deacons have come up to the sides of the altar two-by-two and kissed it. While the choir sings the *Kyrie eleison*, the pope goes to

---

[1] This gesture appears to be connected with the taking up of the maniple (*mappula*): the pope picks it up in order to give the signal with it, just as in ancient Rome the consul used the *mappa* to give the signal for starting the games.

[2] It is interesting to note that this initiating *Accendite* was still to be heard a thousand years later in French cathedrals on feast days. At Angers it was sung in polyphony.

the *cathedra*, but remains standing with his face to the East, in an attitude of prayer. Again he gives the signal to stop the singing of the *Kyrie eleison*, which is nothing more than the continuous repetition of the same unchanging strain. Then, if the day's festival appoints it, he intones the *Gloria in excelsis Deo*, and since it is an invitation and an address to the people, he momentarily turns to them (if he is not already facing them) but at once faces eastward again in the attitude of prayer. At the end of the chant he greets the throng with *Pax vobis* and sings the oration to which all answer *Amen*.

This over, all in the half-circle of the sanctuary—the only place where there are seats—sit down. A subdeacon goes into a pulpit (ambo) and reads the Epistle. When he descends, a singer goes up into the ambo with his *cantatorium* and sings the gradual alternately with the *schola*, and (as the occasion demands) the alleluia or the tract. The chanting of the Gospel is attended by a flourish of ceremony. First the deacon goes up to the *cathedra* and kisses the foot of the pontiff, who then pronounces a blessing over him. The deacon then takes the Gospel book from the altar, kisses it, and preceded by two subdeacons—one carrying a censer—and two acolytes with torches, he marches to the ambo from which he reads the sacred text. Then the papal subdeacon takes the book, holding it with the ruffled *planeta*, reaches it to every one in the Sanctuary to be kissed, and then hands it to an acolyte who immediately carries it back to the Lateran.

No sermon is considered. Nor is there any further mention of dismissal of the catechumens. With the disappearance of heathendom, the forms of an exclusion of those under instruction were no longer usable, and, except in the Orient, actually disappeared.

The pope again greets the throng with *Dominus vobiscum* and intones *Oremus*—but there is no prayer immediately following. Now the external preparations for the Mass-sacrifice begin. First there is the covering of the altar which up till now has stood there, a stately but empty table, decorated only with a costly cloth that hung from the edges—the forerunner of the antependium. An acolyte approaches with a chalice over which he has laid the folded corporal. A deacon takes the latter, lays it on the right side of the altar and throws the open end to the second deacon at the other side in order to spread it over the entire top. Then the offertory begins with the offering of the gifts of the people. The pope starts proceedings by receiving the bread-offerings of the nobility, while the archdeacon accepts their offerings of wine. The other members of the clergy continue accepting the offerings, while the pope returns to his throne. After the people have presented their gifts, the archdeacon, at a signal from the pope, goes to the altar and, with the help of a subdeacon, arranges the breads that are to be consecrated. The chalice is placed on the altar and water is added to the wine by one of the members of the singing choir. After all this is done the pontiff leaves his place and kisses the altar and then himself receives the oblation of the assisting clerics. Lastly he lays his own oblation (two small loaves brought for this purpose from the Lateran) on the altar. The *schola* has meanwhile accompanied the offertory with singing, but now a signal is given to stop so that the single offertory prayer—the prayer nowadays called secret—can be said.

Then begins the canon, taking the word in the comprehensive meaning it then had. Each one has taken his appointed place. Normally that would mean that the pope, coming from his *cathedra*, would stand behind the altar facing the people—for the church usually was not oriented in our sense, but "occidented," the entrance towards the East. Behind the pope, and forming a row in the axis of the church back toward the throne, stand the bishops and perhaps the priests also. To the right and left of the pope and in front of the bishops, the deacons are ranged, and behind them the acolytes. The subdeacons are on the other side of the altar opposite the pontiff. During the canon there is no further change externally.

The pope begins the prayer in a loud voice. The subdeacons respond to the introductory versicles and take up the singing of the *Sanctus*. The pope alone stands once more erect and continues the prayer, while the others remain bowed. The words of consecration, like all the other parts of the canon, are said audibly; otherwise there is nothing distinctive about them. At the *Nobis quoque* the subdeacons straighten up and make ready for the ceremony of breaking the Bread; the paten for this has already been brought up to the altar at the start of the canon. At the *Per quem hæc omnia* the archdeacon too straightens up; when the pope elevates the Host in the sight of all and recites the final doxology, it is the archdeacon's duty to take the chalice by the handles—holding it with a cloth called the *offertorium*—and to lift it, too, on high. The canon is therefore quite simple and free of any other display. The "action," as it is termed, simply presents the pontiff's sacramental word, with no ornament other than his prayers. Even the succeeding *Pater noster*, with its appended embolism, does not break into the picture, at least since Gregory the Great had fixed it immediately after the canon.

External activity does not commence again until the *Pax Domini*, the signal for the mutual greeting with the kiss of peace, which the archdeacon gives first to one of the bishops and which the people, too, exchange. The pope initiates the breaking of the Bread, detaching a portion and laying it on a paten that is handed to him. Then he returns to his throne. The archdeacon advances to the altar while the *defensores* and the notaries take their station beside him to right and left like a guard of honor. First the archdeacon hands over the chalice with the Precious Blood to a subdeacon standing at the right side of the altar; this is a safety measure. Next he places the consecrated breads in the small linen bags held by the acolytes. They are then taken to the bishops and the presbyters, who continue the *fractio* while the *schola* intones the *Agnus Dei*.

In the meantime, very inconspicuously, a more profane activity is going on, in reference to the papal court. The *nomenclator* and two other officials approach the pontiff to get the names of those who are to be invited to his table or to that of the *vicedominus*. They at once relay his invitations.

Then the paten with the Sacrament is carried to the throne. The pope communicates, but leaves a small particle which he places in the chalice, handed him by the archdeacon, meanwhile saying the words of commingling. Then he receives the Precious Blood, the archdeacon supporting the large chalice (*confirmatur ab archidiacano*). Since those not communicating could now depart, the archdeacon first makes the announcements regarding service on the succeeding days.

Then follows the Communion of the clergy and people. The procedure is an almost exact duplicate of the reception of the gifts at the offertory. The pope and the archdeacon begin the distribution, others carry on. For the Communion of the chalice, a number of large vessels (*scyphi*) are used, filled with wine into which a few drops of the consecrated Blood from the pope's chalice have been poured. Meantime the *schola* is singing a Communion psalm. The Communion over, the pope goes once again to the altar and recites the postcommunion. Then a deacon appointed for this duty by the archdeacon, having received a nod from the pope, sings the *Ita missa est*, to which the answer is given, *Deo gratias*. The procession then forms for the return to the *secretarium*.

MAGNIFICENT COMPLETENESS

If we mull over this description in its entirety, we will get the strongest impression of a magnificent completeness. A great community exercise, heir of a thousand years' culture, had produced its final form in the church, lending to the divine service the splendor of its noble tradition. The person of the papal liturgist is surrounded by a court of many members. The ceremonial has absorbed courtly elements and has been filled out to the smallest detail. And still, through all this luxuriant growth, the bold outlines of the Christian eucharistic solemnity stand out clearly in all their essentials: the gorgeous pomp is suddenly quieted when the canon begins, and does not burst forth again until it is concluded. The old communal feeling, it is true, is no longer so strongly and immediately involved. The people apparently no longer answer the prayers, no longer take part in the singing, which has become the art-function of a small group, but the choir is not a profane intrusion into the texture of the service, but rather a connecting link joining the people to the altar.

Prayer and song still sound in the language of the masses, and the people still have an important role in the action through their offering of gifts and their reception of Communion.

As new practices in the proper course of the liturgy, mention should be made of the commingling of the bread and wine before Communion and the introduction of the *Agnus Dei* chant in connection with the enriched build-up of the *fractio* rite. Both these elements the Roman liturgy derived from the Orient, the result of the constant flow during the seventh and eighth centuries of clerics from the East into places of importance in the Church of Rome—even to the papal throne.

The Greek influence, which for two centuries had also been felt in the Byzantine domain in Italy, forms at the beginning of the Middle Ages an important factor in the development of the Roman Mass. Even at an early period the *Kyrie eleison* and certain names of oriental martyrs in the canon—Cosmas and Damian, Anastasia—had already been introduced. The Roman Antiphonal shows a great many chants which were created at this time from Greek models, and not seldom—according to the evidence of various *ordines* and also several manuscripts—songs in the West were sung in Greek. The readings at a solemn papal Mass are still today sung in both Latin and Greek, following an old tradition. Even greater was the influence of the Orient in other spheres of the liturgy, especially on the festival calendar. It was not without solid grounds that the statement was made that the Roman liturgy in the eighth century was seriously in danger of being intrinsically orientalized.

But against this danger a counter-influence was at work in the very same period. The liturgy, which until then—except for the Anglo-Saxon missionaries—was in force only in Rome and its environs and claimed nothing more, soon rose up as the liturgy of a large kingdom.

9. The Roman Mass in France

Even before the eighth century some individual bishops of France must have been seeking a liturgical "annexation" to Rome. It was significant that St. Boniface, coming from the Anglo-Saxon Church, also strove for the same thing in his continental mission field. After 754, the year Pepin must have decreed the acceptance of the Roman liturgy, the political power likewise appeared on the scene, and from then on great progress was made in taking over Roman forms. Thus the Roman liturgy acquired a new home, a hothouse for a further growth that would be determined for more than two hundred years essentially on Franco-German soil.

Because of the difficulty of travel, one had to rely chiefly on books to achieve this transplanting of the Roman liturgy to its new ground, books which were obtained, not without trouble, from Rome. Only in the very slightest degree was there any additional help from clerics who traveled to Rome to see with their own eyes how the services were conducted there. Amalar, the first great commentator on the Roman liturgy in the Carolingian kingdom, who made a trip to Rome in the year 831, prefaces the third edition of his work *De ecclesiasticis officiis* with a foreword in which he points out a great many differences which he remarked between the liturgical praxis of Roman clerics and the practice as it had developed meantime in the North. The fact, then, that books were practically the only means employed in transplanting this foreign liturgy, brought along as a matter of course the danger of misunderstanding; we will encounter such mistaken interpretations in not a few places in the Mass-liturgy.

One of the big disadvantages in this system was that the books to be had from Rome, although they contained directions that went into the minutest details, really dealt only with the solemn form of the liturgy, the liturgy of the papal stational services. Of course in eighth-century Rome divine service was also conducted in another fashion. In the titular churches of the city and in the country towns of the vicinity, which as a rule had only one presbyter and one or the other extra cleric, the arrangement was necessarily quite different; the Mass was the Mass of a simple priest, not that of a bishop. As a rule it was neither necessary nor possible to have a trained choir. And it is quite doubtful that the songs of the antiphonal, with their variable texts—even prescinding from the melodies—were generally in use. In any case it was only at the turn of the seventh century that there was any obligation to begin every Mass—in town or country, Sundays and weekdays—with an introit, and to join to every Communion a psalm with *Gloria Patri* and an antiphon.

ROMAN TEXTS ON FRANKISH SOIL

Although filling out the lacunæ in the books sent from Rome, especially the Gregorian Sacramentary, and adapting and supplementing them as Alcuin had undertaken to do was hardly avoidable, it is nevertheless astonishing how devotedly the new texts were forthwith adopted in all other things. The Frankish sacramentaries which were now produced embodied many feasts of Roman martyrs whose very names must have been almost entirely unknown. All the native saints' feasts were displaced except Martin who was also in the Roman books. They kept even the notations regarding the Roman stations wherever they were found in the captions of the Mass formularies, even though they obviously had a practical meaning only for Rome. Only a few Mass formularies, recognized as being post-Gregorian, would Alcuin allow the copyists to omit from the transcription. With similar fidelity the directions of the first Roman *Ordo*, directions which had in view Roman circumstances and presupposed the pope as celebrant, were copied and made the basis of local liturgical practice. It was not till the ninth century that anyone dared to work out a conscious revision and expansion of the Roman rubric book.

Unconsciously, of course, but nonetheless surely, profound alterations were made from the very outset in the Roman liturgy, especially in the Roman Mass—in fact, fundamental transformations. The exotic seedling, when planted in a new soil and in a new climate, was still pliant enough to be reshaped and modified by these influences. Still it was not primarily a Germanic world that it came face to face with, but rather a Romanized Celtic world, which had created for itself in the Gallican liturgy a religious mode of life all its own. The features which bring the Celt into bold contrast with the clear logical orderliness of the Roman, with his laconic brevity and stark realism, are hardly to be distinguished from the features we are wont to emphasize in the German. The restlessness and agitation, the strong passionate estheticism which mark the German character, must have been the Celt's too, but only in greater measure, and so were found already well suited to the Gallican liturgy. This liturgy continued in force and did not give way before the Roman till it had communicated to it something of its own stamp.

Going into the peculiarities which must have been anchored in the very temperament of the new people, we find two especially which had an effectual bearing on what we are considering: a predilection for the dramatic and a delight in endlessly long prayers. In both of these features the Gallic tradition is closer to the oriental mode than to the Roman; in some cases, in truth, we come across traces of direct oriental influence.

Take as an instance the *dramatic* build-up of the Mass-liturgy. Even in the first adaptations of the *Ordo Romanus Primus* in Frankish territory, directions are inserted in which varying positions are laid down for the seven candle bearers who accompanied the bishop at his entrance: they should be in one place at the beginning of Mass, at another during the readings, and at still another after them. Whereas the Roman system had a carrying of the censer only for the entrance of the pope and for the procession before the reading of the Gospel, the high Mass in the Gallic area introduced a number of incensations. With censer swinging, the altar was encircled according to an elaborate and fixed plan, first at the beginning of the Mass proper, soon also at the beginning of the fore-Mass. For the reading of the Gospel it was not enough that the incense envelop the book, but in conformity with a practice in vogue for quite a time, it was carried out into the midst of the assembled people, necessitating soon a multiplication of censers. Then the parade to the Gospel-singing became Christ's triumphal march: to Christ resounds the *Gloria tibi Domine,* of which until then the Roman Mass knew nothing. The heightened dignity of the Gospel is further emphasized by the place in which the reading is done; the top of the ambo is reserved for it alone, while the Epistle and the intervening chants, particularly the gradual, must be satisfied with the steps (*gradus*). The appearance at this spot in the Mass of a poetic element, the sequence, was a related phenomenon.

The second basic change, the *multiplying of prayers,* was first of all noticeable in this, that, along with the one oration of the Roman tradition —we are concerned for the present with the collect before the Epistle— several others are introduced. Even strict upholders of the Roman manner do not seem to fret at this as long as the number seven is not overstepped. Again, at the high Mass of a bishop the solemn pontifical blessing, of Gallic tradition, is retained. And in a number of places in the Mass the private praying of the celebrant in a low voice is extended, with more and more texts appearing as the next few centuries go by.

The prayers which serve for this last-mentioned purpose are mostly couched in the singular, unless some older specimens are utilized. No longer is it "we" but "I" that dominates. In phrasing and styling too they are far removed from the form of the Roman oration. The Sacramentary of Amiens, which originated in the ninth century, contains in addition to the Roman textual contents a great variety of such prayers. A long series is placed even before the commencement of the Mass. Then again several prayers for the offertory, five of them beginning with *Suscipe sancta Trinitas,* and the last the *Orate fratres.* Then prayers for Communion, including already the text *Domine Jesu Christe, Fili Dei vivi.* And finally the *Placeat* and a prayer while unvesting. A large body of these prayers is already wholly or partly identical with the prayers still in use. There we find, besides the examples cited, several of the present-day vesting prayers and the *Quod ore sumpsimus.*

That all this silent praying was alien to the tenor of the old Roman scheme is noticeable even today in the external deportment of the priest while saying the prayers, for he stands not with arms outstretched, like the *orans* of the religious culture of antiquity, but with hands folded, a posture matching the usage of the northern countries.[1]

APOLOGIAE

While most of the sacramentary manuscripts of the tenth century still display but few of these new accessions, they are to be found in bewildering profusion in the eleventh. What we have at the present is but a

---

[1] This usage, with its symbolism expressive of submissiveness, of the resignation of one's own power to a higher one, is traced back to Teutonic culture. It is akin to the custom by which a vassal or liegeman vowed homage and fealty by placing his hand in that of his lord.

fraction of what was then developing. If there is one element in which this accretion of quiet prayers of a private stamp was made especially and emphatically prominent, and by which it showed most clearly how far removed it was from the spirit of the older Roman liturgy, that element is the *apologiæ*. These are the personal avowals of guilt and unworthiness[2] on the part of the celebrant, mostly of considerable length. Usually they are conjoined to a prayer begging God's merciful favor. They appear earliest in various documents of the Gallican liturgy and have their parallels in the contemporary and later sources of oriental liturgies. Already in the ninth century they break into the Romano-Frankish liturgy, and by the eleventh century reach an ultimate of power and extent, then disappear as at a blow, with only a small remnant surviving, amongst others especially our *Confiteor* and the oratio *S. Ambrosii* in the preparation prayers of the Roman Missal.

The zenith in the development of the *apologiæ* is evinced in the Mass *ordo* which had its origin about 1030 and which Flacius Illyricus, the historian amongst the Reformers, published in 1557 from an old manuscript as an example of a Mass in use (he thought) about 700—before the Romish Mass!—in which there was no acknowledgment of the Real Presence; hence it is generally styled *Missa Illyrica* for short. This Mass order, which assembles practically all the prayer formulas to be gotten anywhere at that time, contains *apologiæ* after vesting, before entering the house of God, a lengthy series after the kissing of the altar, one during the *Gloria*, again a long list during the chants between the readings, and another group during the offertory singing, during the preparation of the gift-offerings, after the *Orate fratres*, during the *Sanctus*, and during the Communion of the people. A phenomenon akin to this is the tenth-century sacramentary from St. Thierry near Reims, which has seven formularies for a *Missa generalis*, each of which consists of collects, *Super oblata* (our Secret), preface, *Hanc igitur* and *Ad complendum*—all having the form and mood of *apologiæ*, put in the plural.

It is not easy to comprehend the world of thought in which so remarkable a crop could be produced, a world which speaks to us in almost frightening fashion of the consciousness of sin and its attendant miseries.[3] Besides a popular factor which we cannot well grasp, there are two things we must take notice of. On the one hand, there was the

---

[2] The word *apologia* has here a meaning analogous to the English "apology," an acknowledgment of guilt in a spirit of regret.

[3] As an example of an unnaturally extended self-accusation this shorter formula, which in the *Missa Illryica* is said after kissing the altar, will do: "*Suscipe confessionem meam, unica spes salutis meæ, Domine Deus meus, Jesu Christe, quia gula, ebrietate, fornicatione, libidine, tristitia, acidia, somnolentia, negligentia, ira, cupiditate, invidia, malitia, odio, detractione, periurio, falsitate, mendacio, vana gloria, levitate et superbia perditus sum et omnino cogitatione, locutione, actione atque omnibus malis extinctus sum; qui iustificas impios et vivificas mortuos, iustifica me et resuscita me, Domine Deus meus. Qui vivis.*"

Gallic tendency to confusing God and Christ, which obscured the concept of saving grace. On the other, the fact that up into the eleventh century sacramental penance was customary only once a year even in monastic institutions. But for an acknowledgment or confession as such, there was claimed an extraordinary power of forgiveness because of the humbling of self that went with it. The disappearance of the *apologiæ* is bound up with the clarification of the notions of forgiveness and the growth of the practice of more frequent sacramental confession.

If there is here a *tie-in with the history of dogma*, the case is even clearer with regard to the apparently insignificant text-change which not a few of the variable prayer formulas of the Roman Mass underwent, a change which became more and more a determinative standard for the texts newly incorporated. The orations of the Roman Sacramentary were so constructed that they concluded, without exception, in a "through," that is to say, they were directed to God the Father and could come to a close with the well-known mediation formula. Not a few of these orations, wherever they offered the opportunity, now acquired the conclusion "Who livest," that is, they were now considered as being addressed to the Son even if they perchance had the introductory greeting "God Who." The inclination to make such a change derived from the style of prayer in the Gallican liturgy, whose earliest development in the atmosphere of the anti-Arian struggle had led to a similar rejection of this mediation formula and a similar stressing of the essential equality of the three divine Persons, just as the oriental liturgies have done. A connected element, the Gallican emphasis on the Trinity, has had visible effect even on our present Ordinary of the Mass, in the two prayers addressed to the Holy Trinity, *Suscipe sancta Trinitas* and *Placeat tibi*. The same grounds have been effective in annexing to the liturgy the *Credo* which originated amidst the doctrinal battles of the East.

LITURGICAL LANGUAGE

More profound and more enduring has been the effect of another circumstance on the basic character of the Roman Mass. When the Roman liturgy was brought into France it invaded an area where only a small layer of society—principally the clergy—knew the language of the liturgy. True, the Gallican liturgy was also a Latin one, but it was not till after its disappearance that the Romance popular dialect became so remote from the basic Latin that it was no longer possible for one not specially educated to understand. But Latin was the universal literary language and consequently the only language considered for divine service. Even a translation of the Scriptures into the vernacular—whether Romance or one of the German dialects—so that the vernacular would actually become a "literary" language, and so capable of becoming a liturgical language, was at that time unthought of. And because even amongst the laity the leaders were so impressed by things Roman that they recognized and acknowledged therein the highest culture, there was therefore no wish or demand for the use of their own language.

Quite different was the course of affairs a short while later amongst the Slavs, where Sts. Cyril and Methodius from the very beginning conducted services—and at least by the death of St. Cyril (869) even the Roman Mass—in the Slavic tongue. German clerics were their bitterest opponents, alleging that they dared conduct divine worship in a "barbarous language," whereas in accordance with the inscription on the Cross, this should be done only in Hebrew, Greek, and Latin. One could reply that Slavic was not a "barbarous language," since there were versions of Holy Scripture in that tongue and in at least a portion of Slavic territory the Roman liturgy has survived to this day in the Old Slavic, the Glagolitic, language.

Thus in the Carolingian empire the Mass-liturgy, so far as understanding its language was concerned, became a clerical reserve. A new kind of discipline of the secret had developed, a concealment of things holy, not from the heathen—there were none—but from the Christian people themselves.

At the time the situation was not conceived of as a problem. Aside from the consideration that religion is always concerned with mysteries, and concealment and secrecy have ever been associated with mysteries—aside from this, the development also encountered a theological notion which led to the same conclusion from two different angles.

In the concept of the Church, the foreground was no longer, as in earlier times, the communion of the redeemed bound together with a glorious Christ in one Mystical Body. In Spain and France the fight against Arianism had caused the thought of the glorified God-man, mediator and highpriest, to be brushed aside in favor of a stronger accentuation of His divine prerogative. One necessarily became more clearly aware of the external earthly Church, its hierarchical structure of clergy and laity. The social position of the clergy—who were far and wide the governing class in society and practically alone in possession of a higher education—contributed no little to estranging them, lifting them above the people.

In addition a change had been taking place in the *concept of the Eucharist.* In the earlier periods of liturgical life we saw the emphasis placed on the Mass as a *eucharistia,* as a prayer of thanks from the congregation who were invited to participate by a *Gratias agamus,* and whose gifts, in the course of the Mass, were elevated by the word of the priest into a heavenly sacrificial offering. But now an opposite view was taking precedence in men's minds, swayed as they were especially by the teaching of Isidore of Seville. The Eucharist is the *bona gratia*, which God grants us, and which at the climactic moment of the Mass, the consecration, descends to us. Soon scholars were earnestly at work trying to discover when, precisely, in the Mass-liturgy this descent took place. According to St. Isidore it was the *sixth oration*, that group of prayers in the Gallic liturgy which began with the *Post Sanctus* and to which the *Post Pridie* belonged.

A VEIL OF MYSTERIOUS ISOLATION

Transferring this to the Roman liturgy, it is the series of prayers from the *Te igitur* to the doxology just before the *Pater noster*. By grasping suggestions that apparently led to this way of thinking, this portion of the Mass is explained as the canon in the sense of Isidore's *sixth oration*, to which the preface serves as a solemn but important introduction. And this section is now enveloped in a second veil of mysterious isolation, being now spoken by the priest in a soft, low tone. The priest alone is to enter this inmost sanctum, while the people stand praying without, as once they did when Zachary burned incense in the Temple sanctuary.

The idea is extended and developed with conscious tenacity. At a spot where it was still thought that changes could be made, a new rite was introduced during the eighth century. When the priest has laid out and prepared the gift-offerings, before he steps into the sanctum of the canon he turns around once more at the altar and begs the bystanders for their prayers that he—as one commentator puts it—might be made worthy to offer up to God the oblation of the whole congregation. Even in the text of the canon a slight emendation was permitted. If one thought about it, it seemed rather surprising that the *Memento* for the living should speak about the faithful as people *who offer to Thee this sacrifice of praise*. Although no one in general dared to cross out these words, nonetheless an addition was introduced, to make certain of the leading role of the priest; in the recension of the Gregorian Sacramentary emanating from Alcuin are prefaced the words *for whom we offer to Thee*.

The line of separation between altar and people, between clergy and laity, between those whose duty it was to perform the sacramental action and those who formed the celebrating congregation was now made into a broad line of demarcation, not to say a wall of division. Yet this was a separation which was always taken for granted as essential to the Church's constitution and which was never really forgotten. This had its effect even on *church architecture*. The altar was moved back to the rear wall of the apse. In cathedrals, that necessitated transferring the bishop's throne; it is now generally placed at the side of the altar. The choir-stalls of the assistants, which in the old arrangement formed a half-circle around the altar, following the line of the apse, are now set in two rows facing each other in front of the altar. The way was open for a further development, the rood-gallery or choir which somewhat later became in many places a real wall separating the sanctuary from the nave of the church.

The function of the priest, by whose action the *Eucharistic Presence* was effected, and the reality of this Presence itself were brought more sharply into focus than heretofore. Even theoretically such questions were studied more thoroughly. About the middle of the ninth century (after 831) a controversy was waged in which Ratramnus maintained, against Paschasius Radbertus, that the Body of Christ was present in the Sacrament in all reality, not, however, in His earthly appearance but only in substance. Into the background recedes that interest in the symbolism of the Sacrament in which Augustine laid such great—perhaps too great—stock, and which is exhibited in the prayers of the Roman Sacramentaries, particularly in the post-communions. Forgotten is the relationship between the sacramental Body—the "mystical" Body, as it was then often termed—and the Body of Christ which is the church. The same is true for the connection between the Sacrament and the death of Christ. And so, too, the conscious participation of the community in the oblation of Christ is lost sight of, and with it that approach of the community towards God to which the Sacrament in its fulness is a summons or invitation. Instead the Mass becomes all the more the mystery of God's coming to man, a mystery one must adoringly wonder at and contemplate from afar. The approach to the Holy Table of the Lord in Communion is no longer the rule even on feast days; already the Eucharist had not been our daily bread for a long time.

Closely connected with such extinguishing of the Sacrament throughout all phases of every-day life was the change which took place about this time in the type of *bread* used, the change to unleavened bread. Alcuin and his pupil Rabanus Maurus are the first indisputable witnesses to this new practice, which spread only very slowly. The increased reverence for the Sacrament probably helped to introduce the use of the pure white wafers which could be so much more easily broken without worry about crumbs.

The change in the type of bread brought in its train a whole series of further changes in the Mass-liturgy. The *offertory procession* is relegated to specified feast-days and by slow degrees becomes an offering of money. Likewise there was a gradual diminishing in the importance of the breaking of the bread within the Mass. The *Agnus Dei*, which had just been introduced in the seventh century as a song to accompany the ceremony of breaking the Bread, appears at the beginning of the ninth century in some of the Carolingian sources as a Communion song, or a song at the *Pax*. The ceremony which had previously

been so carefully built up now disappears, either because the breaking
has been taken care of beforehand (since with unleavened bread there
was no longer any fear of a too-quick drying-up) or because the particles intended for the Communion of the faithful were already prepared
in the desired shape and size—a thing which was not the rule till the
eleventh century.

Then, too, there is a transformation in the *paten* hitherto in use. Some
sort of large platter-like dish had been required for breaking the Bread
into, and for distributing it. But now that type falls out of use and
instead the paten becomes a tiny plate fitting over the cup of the chalice
and used for the priest's host alone, while for the particles intended for
the Communion of the faithful the container employed is a chalice-like
ciborium. In the manner of distributing Communion, opportunities arise
for giving in to the desire for a more reverent handling. The particles
are no longer handed to the faithful (the particles are hardly suited to
this), but are laid at once on the tongue, a thing more difficult in the case
of the brittle pieces of leavened bread. The next step—which, however,
took quite a long time—was for the faithful to receive kneeling. And this,
in turn, had a final effect on the church building: the low communion
rail was introduced, a feature of which ancient church architecture
knew nothing.

Still, despite all these features calculated to broaden the moat between
the faithful and the sanctuary, during the Carolingian period there was
at work an earnest endeavor to bring about an efficacious religious renewal in the whole population. This included a correspondingly *organized participation* of the faithful in divine service and especially in Holy
Mass. Various prescriptions aimed at this very thing. The people were
urged to join in singing the *Kyrie* and the *Sanctus*, and even the *Gloria
Patri*—obviously the doxology which concluded the chants of the *schola*.
They were also encouraged, it seems, to respond to the greeting and
the prayers of the priest. The faithful were likewise admonished to take
part in the offertory procession and in the kiss of peace. And an attempt
must even have been made to acquaint the faithful with the contents of
the priest's prayers, those at least that were spoken aloud and that recurred time and again during the Mass. The Carolingian clergy were not
only to know the liturgy themselves—to guarantee this there was a yearly
examination in the liturgy, prescribed since 742—but they were also to
disclose it to the faithful. As a matter of fact, amongst the explanations
of the Mass that appeared around the turn of the eighth-ninth century,
there is one which is concerned only with the texts spoken aloud, and
handles them with remarkable minuteness and detail. After a short
survey of the fore-Mass, it takes up the words and phrases from *Dominus
vobiscum* and *Sursum corda* to *Hosanna in excelsis;* then it skips over
the canon and continues with *Præceptis salutaribus moniti.*

ALLEGORICAL INTERPRETATION

Since, in this case, the pronouncement on the instruction of the faithful reveals that the inaudible prayers—especially the canon—are missing, a new and different sort of explanation soon evolves. It is developed entirely from the viewpoint of the faithful and is generally concerned not with the words of the Mass—they are spoken in a strange tongue—but rather with the forms and external actions that are perceptible to the eye. This is the allegorical interpretation of the Mass. It was known even in pre-Carolingian France. The seventh century "Exposition" of the Gallican Mass already mentioned is dominated by it, and even earlier yet it was common in the Orient. Just as in pre-Christian times the olden myths of the gods were explained as meaning something else than what their immediate sense indicated, and just as Philo of Alexandria had begun in a grand style to give a philosophical turn to the accounts of primitive biblical history, so too in Christendom it early became the practice to put an allegorical interpretation on sacred texts whenever they appeared mystifying. At first it was the Old Testament, where actual types were at hand to suggest the possibility of extending such prefigurements. Then, as liturgical life began to become fixed and standard, and thence to become obscure, the liturgy, too, received this treatment. A preparatory step and condition for the introduction of allegorization was a delight in symbolism. Rites were in use that had been consciously introduced into the liturgy as indications of deeper things, like the washing of hands and the kiss of peace; there were others which had indeed a different origin but whose significance easily obtruded, like the mixing of water with the wine. Allegory went a step further and sought no longer for any apparent and actual signification.

One of the first to champion this liturgical allegorization at the start of the sixth century was Pseudo-Dionysius, whose neo-Platonic thinking inspired not only the method but, to a degree, also the content of his interpretation of the liturgy. However, he uses the allegorical system to explain only isolated moments in the Mass, as when he interprets the priest's coming from the altar to distribute Communion as an image of the Incarnation. Before him others had already gone much further: Theodore of Mopsuestia (d. 428) and the Syrian Narsai (d. about 502), who understand, for instance, the carrying of the gift-offerings to the altar as the burial of Jesus, the transubstantiation as His Resurrection, and the breaking of the consecrated bread as the appearance of the risen Saviour. Of a different sort are Sophronius (d. 638) and Maximus Confessor (d. 662), of whom the former finds in the Mass-liturgy representations of our Lord's life (the Annunciation, the Nativity, the Revelation on the banks of the Jordan, the Transfiguration) and especially of His Passion, while the latter perceives images of the relationships and activities of the spiritual life.

In regard to the Roman liturgy, it was seemingly Alcuin who first applied the allegorical method. But it was his pupil Amalar who made the most extensive and thorough use of it. Although it was nothing new, still the type of explanation as handled by Amalar with such thorough logic appeared unwonted and strange. Pressed by one of Amalar's opponents, the deacon Florus of Lyons, the interpretation was condemned at the Synod of Quiercy in 838, the allegation being that shadows and images might perhaps suit the Old Testament but certainly not the New, which claimed a "reasonable offering" without superstitions or nebulous fancies. But this judgment was unable to halt the triumphal progress of Amalar's allegorical method, or to hinder the constant spread of his writings. The following centuries do, however, exhibit expositions of the Mass that give scarcely any space to allegory.

AMALAR

But in the years that followed it was not these attempts that proved determinative, but rather Amalar's work, especially his chief opus, *De ecclesiasticis officiis*. Because of its heaping up of allegorical meanings, this book had given its opponents many opportunities for attack. Everything receives a significance—persons, vestments, church vessels and utensils, dates, actions and motions. Different types of signification are employed: ethical admonitions (moral allegory), fulfillments of the Old Testament (typological allegory), events in the economy of salvation (rememorative allegory) or allusions to the consummation at the end of time (eschatological or anagogic allegory). The shoulder-cloth of clerics signifies the mortification of one's speech (II, 17); the seven torches carried by the acolytes signify the seven gifts of the Holy Ghost (III, 7); the two lights that go before the Gospel refer to the Law and the Prophets because these, too, preceded the Gospel (III, 18); when the bishop mounts his throne he images Christ sitting at the right hand of God the Father (III, 10). It was the rememorative meaning, however, which was predominant in Amalar.

This appears almost exclusively in Amalar's shorter *Expositio* (813–814). A good view of the whole scheme is presented by the author himself in the summary of contents with which he prefaces the work:

> The *introit* alludes to the choir of the Prophets [who announced the advent of Christ just as the singers announce the advent of the bishop] . . . , the *Kyrie eleison* alludes to the Prophets at the time of Christ's coming, Zachary and his son John among them; the

Gloria in excelsis Deo, points to the throng of angels who proclaimed to the shepherds the joyous tidings of our Lord's birth [and
indeed in this manner, that first one spoke and the others joined in,
just as in the Mass the bishop intones and the whole church joins
in]; the [first collect] refers to what our Lord did in His twelfth
year . . . ; the Epistle alludes to the preaching of John, the *respon-*
sorium to the readiness of the Apostles when our Lord called them
and they followed Him; the Alleluia to their joy of heart when they
heard His promises or saw the miracles He wrought . . . , the
Gospel to His preaching . . . The rest of what happens in the Mass
refers to the time from Sunday on, when the disciples drew close to
Him [along with the multitude—shown in the Mass by the procession of the faithful making their gift-offerings], up to His Ascension
or to Pentecost. The prayer which the priest says from the *secreta*
to the *Nobis quoque peccatoribus* signifies the prayer of Jesus on
Mount Olivet. What occurs later signifies the time during which
Christ lay in the grave. When the bread is immersed in the wine,
this means the return of Christ's soul to His body. The next action
signifies the greetings offered by Christ to His Apostles. And the
breaking of the offerings signifies the breaking of bread performed
by the Lord before the two at Emmaus.

Not all the points, but the more important, occur again in Amalar's
greater work: the choir of Prophets, the sermon of Christ, the parade of
the multitude, the prayer on the Mount of Olives, the breaking of bread
in Emmaus. For the Mass proper, where the shorter work of 813–814
contains only the summary signification already quoted, the later Amalar
proffers a whole series of supplementary details. Many of these additions
by the later Amalar were not retained in the allegorical explanations of
later years, e.g., the meaning of *Sursum corda* as the summons to enter
into the cenacle, the preface as a reference to our Lord's speeches, and
His prayer of thanks at the Last Supper, the communion antiphon as
imaging the mutual encouragement of the disciples at Emmaus and the
Apostles when apprised of Christ's Resurrection (III, 33). Others, at
least in main outline, become part and parcel of the standard Mass
allegorization during the following centuries: The assistants stand bowed
from the *Te igitur* till they hear the final petition of the Our Father, the
Sed libera nos a malo, to signify the sorrow of the disciples over the
suffering of Christ till they hear the news of His deliverance from
the power of death (c. 23).

The deacons who stand behind the celebrant are a type of the
Apostles who hid themselves in fear. The subdeacons who stand opposite the celebrant on the other side of the open altar are types of the
holy women who remained standing near the Cross (*ibid.*). The prayer
after the consecration signifies the Passion of our Lord on the Cross.
When the priest bows down (at the *Supplices*), our Lord bows His

head and dies (c. 25). The slight lifting of the voice at *Nobis quoque* refers to the centurion's loud profession at the death of Jesus (c. 26). The deacons at this point straighten up and begin to busy themselves with the Body of the Lord, to signify the steadfast courage which seized the women and their work at the grave (*ibid.*). At the concluding doxology the celebrant and the deacon elevate the Host and the Chalice and then set them down again, to signify Nicodemus' and Joseph of Arimathea's taking down our Lord's corpse from the Cross (*ibid.*). The seven petitions of the Our Father typify the rest and quiet of the seventh day, that is, Holy Saturday (c. 28), while the division of the formula into three parts, introduction, prayer and subsequent embolism, typifies the three days our Lord lay in the tomb (c. 29). The division of the Host into three parts refers to the threefold Body of Christ (c. 35). The commingling of the species refers to the reunion of Christ's soul and body at the Resurrection, the *Pax Domini* to the peace which the Resurrection brought to mankind (c. 31). The last blessing and the dismissal remind us of our Lord's last blessing of the disciples on the Mount of Olives and of His departure from this world (c. 36).

In these allusions and references there is revealed a fancy that is without doubt remarkably perceptive. The transparency of the meanings, be it admitted, is often spoiled by the fact already pointed out that several methods of allegorizing are used side by side, as when at the offertory and the *Hosanna* the multitude represent Old Testament prefigurements, the altar is the sacrificial altar for burnt offerings on which we should offer up the mortification of the flesh and our good works, while the altar cloth is a symbol of the soul's purity, and the censer is the presentation of Christ's body through which we hope for God's grace (c. 19). But this juxtaposition is not meaningless. In one part of the moral allegories there is clearly disclosed the important notion that the Mass involves not only the oblation of Christ but at the same time the oblation of the Church. Therefore, Amalar maintains, the fore-Mass means the preaching of Christ and also the preaching of His followers to the end of the world, and the rest fo the Mass means the Passion and glorification of Christ and also the sacrifice and glorification of His followers. Therefore the altar is the Cross in reference to the mysteries of Christ, it is the altar for burnt offerings in reference to our own self-oblation. Both meanings should be kept in mind.

On the whole, then, this way of explaining the Mass, as practiced by Amalar, marked out the trend for the future. The share of the Church was perhaps less prominently mentioned, but in other matters the majority of commentators, as we shall see, followed in Amalar's footsteps.

It can thus be seen that the transplanting of the Roman liturgy into Frankish lands was associated with many profound changes. These changes clearly bear witness to the intense spiritual life with which the

Carolingian epoch was filled, a spiritual life which sparkled especially in the monasteries and in the cathedrals, whose clergy were organized in conventual life by means of chapters. It is to be noted that, in spite of difficulties of travel, distance put hardly a barrier in the way of mutual exchange and mutual stimulation. Thus at St. Denis they were studying Greek culture, rewriting a life of St. Dionysius from Greek sources and adapting liturgical texts from the Antiochene liturgy. Liturgical creativeness is to be traced at several points within the confines of the Frankish empire. At the outset of the period of accepting the Roman liturgy, the German monasteries—like St. Gall, Reichenau, Rheinau—stand out above all as the native places of more important liturgical manuscripts. But from the ninth century on, we can detect, through the manuscripts, a shift in the centers of Carolingian culture, first to places in the heart of French territory, like Tours, Corbie, Paris, Reims, but then also to some on the periphery, like Arles, Verona, Regensburg, Fulda or the episcopal cities of Normandy.

10. The Romano-Frankish Mass as a New Basic Type, and Its Differentiation

Out of all this shaping and shifting of liturgical forms in the Carolingian area a new Mass rite of the Romano-Frankish type was produced. It was at once rich and sharply outlined and soon had won wide acceptance. The evidences are scattered over broadly separated parts of a Carolingian realm which had meanwhile disintegrated. The episcopal city of Séez in Normandy, and Minden on the Weser (which is considered the place of origin of the *Missa Illyrica*), the monastery of Gregorienmünster in Alsace, and St. Lawrence in Liége—these are the principal places where this Ordinary was to be found. It appears in various settings and was soon transferred also to Italy.

The nearest thing to a basic form of this Ordinary is in general apparently the Mass *ordo* of Séez; accordingly—perhaps we could speak about a Séez group. However, it cannot be the basic form itself since—to instance one point—the *apologiæ* which are inserted here are replaced in the other manuscripts by different *apologiæ*. The basic form must have developed somewhere in Franco-German territory before the year 1000, since there are extant several derivatives to be dated about this period.

In the meantime, a young Flemish researcher, Boniface Luykx, O.Praem., has undertaken a study of the numerous and widely spread out manuscripts. The first published part of his findings has shown that for the origin of the basic form we must rather look to the Rhineland. For this reason, it is now better to speak of a Rhinish Mass Ordo.

Among the many peculiarities of this Rhinish Mass Ordo is the mention of psalm prayers. While the sacramentary of Amiens adds Psalm 50 right before vesting, this Ordinary includes along with a fully developed series of vesting prayers, an independent group of prayers, the kernel of which is composed of Psalms 83, 84, and 85, with the versicles and the oration *Aures tuæ pietatis*. Here, too, Psalm 42 appears for the first time, to be said upon entering the House of God; it begins with the antiphon *Introibo ad altare Dei,* and concludes with the oration *Aufer a nobis,* and only after that follow the avowals of sinfulness or, *apologiæ,* which are different in the various redactions. At a high Mass, at least, these continue all through the fore-Mass. Only one short, oration-like *apologia, Omnipotens (sempiterne) Deus qui me peccatorem,* seems to belong to the original form of this group of prayers, recurring as it does in the same form in all the manuscripts. Just before bringing the gift-offerings to the altar, there are a number of sacerdotal oblation prayers, of the Gallican type *Suscipe sancta Trinitas,* like those that already appear in the sacramentary of Amiens. The offertory itself is accompanied by some new texts. At the mixing of the water with the wine the formula *Deus qui humanæ substantiæ* is used. The incensing that follows is accompanied by all the prayers still in use today. The assisting clergy respond to the bidding *Orate fratres* with a prayer which is taken up again after the *Sanctus,* a whole series of appropriate psalms being said in common; thus the quiet of the canon is again undermined. The communion series is composed of most of the prayers still in use. A psalm prayer—namely the canticle of the Three Young Men, with Psalm 150 and corresponding conclusion—follows at the end, on the return to the sacristy. The obligation to say this final series—just as with the entrance prayers—was far less strict than the obligation with regard to the other parts of the Mass.

As can be seen, in this Mass Ordinary which hails from Franco-German territory, there are not a few elements that are still to be found in today's Roman Mass or at least appear as preparation and thanksgiving.

THE RETURN TO ITALY

Soon after its origination, this Ordinary was on its way to Italy where its further development was again decided. In many Italian Mass books of the eleventh and twelfth centuries we find not only the elements still retained at present but also other peculiarities, some of them trivial, which have since disappeared. Some of the items of this *ordo,* like Psalm 42 and its oration, or the prayer for incensing, appear from this time on in all the Italian Mass books. We could refer particularly to some manuscript witnesses which either present us with the complete *ordo* unaltered, as does Codex Chigi, or at least give us the greater part with more or fewer additions. Among these latter are especially two Mass books of the eleventh century, from the Benedictine center of Camaldoli, a somewhat later book from Monte Cassino, another Benedictine sacramentary from the vicinity of Verona, the sacramentary of Modina which was finished before 1174, and two pontificals of the eleventh and twelfth centuries.

Thus we come to that episode which proved to be of such incalculable importance for the entire subsequent history of the Roman liturgy. About the middle of the tenth century the Roman liturgy began to return in force from Franco-Germanic lands to Italy and to Rome, but it is a liturgy which meanwhile had undergone radical changes and a great development. This importation entailed supplanting the local form of the Roman liturgy by its Gallicized version, even at the very center of Christendom. A Romano-Germanic pontifical compiled at Mainz about 950—the basic model of today's *Pontificale Romanum*—at that time found its way to Lucca and to Rome, as we learn from manuscripts which were written about this period at both the places mentioned. It was likely the frequent journeys to Rome of Otto the Great, in whose company a large number of German clerics made the trips, that brought the book into Italy. The earliest copies of the pontifical contained the so-called *Ordo Romanus VI* which provides an arrangement for the bishop's Mass that is in extraction and content very similar to our own Ordinary. Some usages had already got to Rome from the North at an earlier period. A great many others were soon to follow, as northern liturgical books replaced those locally in use and thus crowded out the customs hitherto obtaining.

At the time, this displacement was unfortunately not very difficult. In matters liturgical (as in other matters) the tenth century was for Rome an era of collapse and demoralization. It would seem that at that time new manuscripts were simply not being produced. In the scriptoria of the North, on the contrary, there was bustling activity; in particular there flourished at the time in German monasteries the art of manuscript illumination. It is worthy of note that Pope Gregory V made an agreement in 998 with the abbey of Reichenau, stipulating that in return for certain privileges accorded on the occasion of the blessing of a new abbot, the monks were to send, amongst other things, a new sacramentary. It goes without saying that this would mean only the style of Mass book then current in the North.

Of course there were many different ways in which this revamped Mass book from Carolingian territory, with its new *ordo*, could get to Italy. In the instance cited in the last paragraph the path led from a German monastery directly into the Lateran. But in other cases it could be easily the road from one monastery to another. Amongst the examples of places on Italian soil where this new Mass *ordo* clearly made its appearance, the Benedictine share looms very prominent. Even Codex Chigi, one of the earliest witnesses, is of Benedictine origin. Recall the early shift of the Cluniac reform to Italy. Abbot Odo (c. 942) was able to draw into the reform a great number of monasteries of Rome and its environs, and even Monte Cassino. In 1000 Abbot Odilo was at Ravenna to meet St. Romuald, founder of the Camaldolese, from whose ranks we already mentioned two witnesses of the new Mass *ordo*. On the other side, Cluny also had won great power and influence in France even during the tenth century, so extensive that it came into contact with the new Mass *ordo* at many points and could thus become its "carrier."

The chief factor for ensuring the penetration, through and through, of this new fashion in Roman liturgy and its arrangement of the Mass, was *the political power of the Romano-German empire*. Although this influence was indirect it was considerable, for since Otto the Great, the Emperor had interfered in the affairs of Rome and Italy and had time and again put his own candidates in the chief positions. In one case, in fact, we are told of a direct interference by a German ruler in the shaping of the liturgy of Rome; when Henry II came to the Eternal City for his imperial coronation in 1014, he asked as a favor that at Rome also the *Credo* be sung at Mass as was long the case in the North.

So, for a second time in the West, liturgical unity was achieved but this time it was not the members that yielded to the head, but rather the head accommodated itself more and more to members grown meanwhile strong and wilful. The refined clarity of the old forms was no longer present in the newer growth, nor were latent there the inner forces that might have reformed it in the olden spirit.

Fundamentally the new Mass *ordo* from the North was only one type out of many. Open suggestions were offered therein for new elements in the Mass-liturgy as demanded by the trend of the times, but none of these had any real binding force. Such elements were left on principle to local or at most regional regulations. Indeed the new silent prayers, which formed a goodly part of the recent acquisition, could be changed or even extended by the priest himself, since they were purely the expression of private devotion. Many details of external deportment, especially in a non-solemn Mass, such for instance as the manner of preparing the chalice, and the precise moment of the Mass that this was to be done, were left more or less free, since the rubrics were concerned only with a high Mass where many assistants took part. Thus we find throughout the later Middle Ages a great variation in all those parts of the Mass-liturgy which were not fixed as a heritage of the ancient Roman sacramentaries—variation not only from country to country but from church to church, in fact, from Mass book to Mass book. Amongst the Mass books from the latter half of the Middle Ages which are still in existence —there are thousands of them—there are seldom (to judge from descriptions at hand) two Mass books that agree to such an extent that the later copy does not add a prayer text or a rubric, or leave one out, or consciously alter it.

A special case, all through the Middle Ages, is the variation in the wording of many prayers, particularly the shorter ones. The shorter the formula, the greater the diversity. The formula for the distribution of Communion, the text accompanying the offering of host and chalice, or the *Suscipiat*—only with great trouble can one arrive at a fixed basic text. A phrase is enlarged here or there, it is doubled, it is enhanced with emotional highlights, or it is even changed to something else or left out entirely. This is understandable, for such texts were mostly handed down, not in writing, but by word of mouth, and were spoken by heart till such time as they were again taken down, somewhere, somehow, in writing. In many Mass books they were not to be found at all, or they were inserted only as an appendix. They were on the very verge between official prayers and private prayers. And so there was sometimes no hesitation in inserting absolutely private prayers in the course of the Mass, as did a certain twelfth century Bishop Gondulph of Rochester, who daily said a second Mass in the presence of his monks, and after the Gospel, while the choir-boys sang the offertory, he sat down and gave himself over entirely to his devotions, and sighed and wept.

DIVERGENCE OF CUSTOMS

The direction of all this lay as a matter of principle in the hands of the metropolitan. But there was no stopping the continual procurement of books (and consequently of ritual customs) from other church provinces, if the books were not obtainable from one's own. Nor was there any special aversion to a conscious difference of usage. Over and over during medieval times the phrase of St. Gregory is reiterated sometimes word for word, sometimes only in substance: "as long as the Church preserves one faith, there is nothing inconsistent about a divergence of customs."

It was the monasteries that first introduced a more rigid discipline. The customs of the larger reformed abbeys, which were written down chiefly since the eleventh century, contain in good measure prescriptions for divine worship and, among these, exact and detailed regulations of the Mass *ordo*. This is true, first of all, of the catalog of the customs of Cluny as set down in the middle of the eleventh century by the monk Bernard, and in a stricter arrangement around 1080 by the monk Udalrich. Therein everything is carefully regulated that concerns the handling of the Eucharist, from the preparation of host-bread to the ablution after reception, for which a series of new regulations is introduced.

The new branches of the *Benedictines*, too, soon after their establishment, prescribed fixed liturgical arrangements for their churches. Among these was also a peculiar regulation of the Mass *ordo* which was afterward altered very little. A concomitant factor was—as in similar cases—the local tradition of the home diocese of the mother-house. Take the case of the Cistercians whose rite was regulated in the *Liber usuum* shortly after 1119, incorporating the usage of Chalon-sur-Saône. As regards singing and architectural appointments, the Cistercian service is very simple, a conscious contrast to Cluny. For an external portrayal of this special rite—outside Castile—which was given up in 1618, the most significant point was this: almost nothing except the preface and canon was said at the center of the altar; the *Gloria* and the greeting that followed were said on the Epistle side, the *Credo* and the secret on the Gospel side.

The liturgical arrangement for the *Carthusians* was compiled in the *Statuta antiqua* just shortly before 1259, but it belongs substantially to the twelfth century. The Savoyard origin of the first Carthusians explains the similarities to the rite of Lyons. The Mass ceremonial, in use even today, is distinguished by its archaic character. In this rite the Mass still concludes with the *Ite missa est*. The liturgy of the Premonstratensians was also put in order by the twelfth century. But the ancient form of the *Liber ordinarius* which was then compiled, unlike the corresponding books of the Cistercians or the Dominicans, was altered in the course of years, until in the seventeenth century the Missal of Pius V was finally adopted.

If the old orders, living on the basic principle of *stabilitas loci*, found it necessary to secure uniformity in liturgical regulation, this was true in a higher degree even with regard to the itinerant orders of the thirteenth century. The *Dominicans* had their first Mass book determined even before 1244. This was fixed by the "Ordinary according to the Rite of the Sacred Order of Friars Preachers," and was produced under the General, Humbert de Romans, and enacted into law in 1256. As far as the rite of the Mass is concerned—there was a special chapter on the private Mass—this extremely careful regulating had its repercussions far beyond the confines of the order itself. Various monastic groups, like the Teutonic Knights, adopted the Dominican rite. The Mass ceremonial of the *Liber ordinarius* of the Benedictine abbey of St. James in Liége, which in its turn had an extensive influence, was nothing else than a slight modification of the Dominican. The same is true of the ceremonial established by the Carmelites in the General Chapter of 1312, a ceremonial still used by the Calced Carmelites. It was also taken over and celebrated by parts of the Armenian Union, and even in this century there were four Armenian Churches in Siebenbürgen (Czechoslovakia) which used the Dominican Rite in Armenian. While the Dominican rite in some details displays certain antique traits, as for instance the shortness of the prayers at the foot of the altar, in others it exhibits an energetic progress and development. Thus, for the first time, the repetition at the gradual is underlined, the customary ablution rite makes its first appearance, and likewise the St. John Gospel at the end of the Mass. The dramatic moments are visibly high-lighted—the extension of the arms after the consecration, and the signing of the chalice at the end of the canon.

Even more extensive in its effect on the history of the Mass-liturgy was the conduct of the other mendicant order, the *Franciscans*. They too at first took up the liturgical usage of the order's native place, but afterwards, prompted by the many diversities of the Mass-liturgy which they met with in their early wanderings, they chose for themselves the "Missal according to the Rite of the Roman Curia." The papal curia, which already by that time had grown into an organization of quite considerable range, had formed for itself, out of the various designs of the contemporary city liturgy, especially along the lines of the old patriarchal basilicas, a special type of Roman Mass book. This was done chiefly, it appears, under Innocent III. This type is characterized by a sanctoral calendar cataloging many old popes, and by a Mass *ordo* that is really simple, as the unsettled life of the papal court at that time indeed required. The new enlargement by multifarious greetings and blessings and petitions, versicles and responses, as we find them in the Mass books of Northern lands, especially in the compass of the offertory and the communion, are omitted, and continue to be omitted during the succeeding centuries. In fact in some places there is a noticeable attempt at simplification. Here especially the change from sacramentary to missal which we will investigate in a moment, had been comparatively swift.

This missal the sons of St. Francis made their own, but without renouncing the right to make changes—the trend of the time. But from this period on, the Franciscan missal and the *Missale secundum consuetudinem Romanæ curiæ* (also called *Missale Romanum* for short) are almost identical. This missal type was carried all over the world by the wandering mendicant Friars. It was soon the predominant type of Mass book in Christendom. And after the inauguration of printing it won public prevalence in the whole Latin Church. It paved the way for the reform under Pius V.

Also in other churches of the later Middle Ages were found special rites clearly designed. This was true of solemn pontifical service in the cathedrals; several *ordines* of such churches, especially in France, give us further knowledge of them. For a non-solemn Mass, however, there was seldom if ever any written regulation, and in fact the tendency was toward utter simplicity. Local tradition and living custom had to suffice. However, certain centers were the exception, among them the churches of Lyons in France and Braga in Portugal, which developed their own definite rite and have retained it, with some modifications and restrictions, to this very day.

In England, too, where since William the Conqueror liturgical life had been determined to a great extent by that of Normandy, the rite of Salisbury or Sarum was gradually developed as a distinct and, up to the Reformation, an essentially conservative and fixed arrangement, both for the entire service and more especially for the Mass. It was the standard not only in a great portion of the English Church but also here and there on the Continent.

In general, however, the right to regulate and supervise the liturgy by dioceses and ecclesiastical provinces appears to have produced very little. In German territory it was rather the literary work of one liturgist that produced big results in directing, coordinating, and simplifying the liturgy. This work was the *Micrologus* written about 1085 by Bernold of Constance, a champion of the reform of Pope Gregory VII, who had traveled much in Italy. His short explanation of the Mass, distinguished by its calm clarity, contained a special chapter (c. 23) with the text of the *Ordo Missæ* which he considered correct. While the psalmodic prayer of the *Præparatio Missæ* and at the end of the Song of the Three Young Men, with the pertinent prayers, form a single series with the other parts of the Mass *ordo*, still, as regards adopting the prayers within the Mass that had long been in circulation, a great amount of discretion and conservativeness is exercised. For instance, both the prayers at the offering of host and chalice are missing. Between *Agnus Dei* and communion only one prayer, *Domine Jesu Christe Fili*, was adopted. Bernold expressly states (c. 12) that in the canon nothing was allowed to be added, not even the names of saints.

Thus out of the great amount of prayer material that had grown up, a fixed core was lifted out, to become the basis, at least in Germany, for further development. In Hungary about 1100, the bishops, by explicit decree, prescribed the arrangement laid out in the *Micrologus* as the obligatory norm.

A similar importance for France, if not a similarly extensive influence, might be attached to the short and predominantly rubrical portrayal of the Mass which Bishop John of Avranches, who died in 1079 as Archbishop of Rouen, offers in his explanation of the liturgy.

11. The Gothic Period

Someone has said, and rightly, that Gothic is in a special degree not only an art style (*Kunststil*) but a period style (*Zeitstil*). Because up till now the younger peoples of the North had studied zealously in the school of the older order of things, propriety and proportion, as they appeared in Romanesque, could become the expression of their life. But their growing powers were beginning to spring the old grooves on all sides, seeking newer designs. The individual and subjective, seeing and feeling on one's own personal activity and personal capability—these came to the fore, and led to a stressing of the concrete and realistic, and consequently to a multiplicity of forms which could be kept together and coherent only by a renewed desired for organization. This new spirit did not call a halt even with regard to divine service; the arrangement of the Mass felt its influence in a most profound manner. Already there was talk of that multiplicity of forms which had developed after the year 1000, but an effort was also made to codify the new forms; we can see in this a parallel to an attempt at mastering the heaped-up resources of knowledge by means of the *summas* which have been ranged side by side with the daring architecture of the Gothic cathedrals.

At least in the eleventh-century community, forces still held the balance of power in ecclesiastical life and the life of divine worship. Beside the cathedral chapter there was in every large place, and often also in the country, a collegiate chapter in which clerics under the leadership of a provost or dean led a life in common, and above all conducted a community service of worship. In contrast to them the clerics who were individually in the service of the nobility remained absolutely in shadow, especially since most of them lacked any higher education. For these capitular churches, and for Roman church architecture in general, a characteristic was the roomy choir with its stalls, no longer set in a half-circle around the altar but arranged in several parallel rows between altar and people. The daily conventual Mass, which was celebrated, as in the monasteries, in the presence of the assembled clerical community, formed the crown of choir prayer and the very climax of divine service. In the Mass regulations and in the rubrics of the liturgical books this community service is almost the only one considered; there the celebrant appears nearly always accompanied by deacon and subdeacon, even though private celebration is not unknown. Above all, however, the entire setting of the liturgical texts is still always predicated on the cooperation of a plurality of officials and ministers. The priest needs only the sacramentary. Lectionary and antiphonary continue to be separate books for the use of those who are to read or sing. This situation continues to prevail till about the start of the twelfth century.

NEW ARRANGEMENT OF LITURGICAL BOOKS

But then a new arrangement of the liturgical books breaks into the picture; on the strength of this the priest can take over the roles of lector and chanter and thus discharge the duties of his office independently of them. The ties of the individual are thus loosed in the liturgy, just as in this same period the organization of the canonries had slackened or even dissolved with the trend toward personal prebends and separate residences. In the thirteenth century the *Missale Plenum* displaces the sacramentary. Presages of this new arrangement were the many silent prayers which, as we have seen, had begun to appear in the sacramentaries, at first (since the ninth century) only here and there, but since the eleventh almost universally. These prayers the priest did not have to perform with the community, but softly by himself.

There are isolated instances, especially within the confines of monasticism, where even at an earlier period the priest's Mass book was fitted out with the lessons, so that the service of a lector could be dispensed with. Such books were very likely intended for the convenience of wandering monks, as may also be judged, in the case of the Missal of Bobbio, from the smallness of the book. In the church of Milan too, the oldest sacramentaries almost all incorporate the readings. Since the ninth century there appeared at various places sacramentaries in which, appendix fashion, a number of Masses with readings are inserted, sometimes also with the chant-texts. As a rule, in fact, the Masses of the *commune* and the *Missæ diversæ*, along with the Votive Masses, including the Masses for the Dead, were thus distinguished. Votive Masses and Masses for the Dead were employed essentially in the interests of individual families and persons, and especially if they followed each other in rapid succession, were held in the simplest form, often without the lector whose presence was, as a rule, still presumed.

But cases occur at least as often, in which the song-texts are inserted all through the sacramentary. Frequently all that was done was to indicate the first words on the margin—in an age that knew all the psalms by heart this was more than sufficient. In other instances an antiphonary was bound up in one volume with the sacramentary. Especially since the eleventh century, Mass books which contain the song-texts but (outside of the *commune* and the Votive Masses) not the readings, occur more often. There again the first thought must have been private celebration, in which the notion of the *Capitulare ecclesiastici ordinis* prevailed, that these texts were never to be left out. They had to be in the Mass books even when the lessons were left out, because a lector always co-operated, reading the Epistle and perhaps sometimes the Gospel also, if he did not have to hand the evangeliary to the priest or if the priest did not have the pertinent Gospel pericope in his own Mass book.

Since the thirteenth century simple sacramentaries were very seldom produced. The *Missale Plenum* or complete missal, which had at first predominated only in monasteries, has become the rule. The cleric to read the Epistle disappears from private Mass. If there are no deacon and subdeacon, both readings are done by the priest himself, and are therefore indispensable in the Mass book, just as the chant-texts, too, cannot be omitted from it.

At high Mass the chant-texts are to be read by the celebrant (and the assistants); this we find stipulated for the first time in 1140 in regard to the introit, and the prayers the priest intones, *Gloria, Credo, Sanctus* and *Agnus Dei.* This is expressly ordered for all the chant-texts for the first time, about the middle of the thirteenth century, although a similar rule for the readings is not yet prescribed. Here in this approach to the private Mass we find a sensitive loosening of the liturgical texture, corresponding in general to the centrifugal tendency of the Gothic period. The priest makes himself, to a certain extent, independent of the singing choir. What the latter is doing is no longer considered as a complementary part of the community celebration. Thus the trend to secular song instead of ecclesiastical can grow all the more powerful. But another factor may have had some influence with regard to the priest himself. Right into the twelfth century it had been customary for the celebrant to fill every pause in his prayers at high Mass with *apologiæ.* Were people finally getting tired of them? It was at any rate a step forward to admit that it would be much more fitting if the priest would replace those endless self-accusations with the biblical texts which were being sung by the choir.

The complete Missal is not therefore the product of the *predominance* of the private Mass (which had long been in use), but it is at least the result of the general extension and increased acceptance of that form of worship.

For the participation of the faithful, the Sung Mass celebrated with or without sacred ministers, with its Latin chanting and its mystery-filled ceremonies, continued during the years to follow as the standard form. The manner of explaining also remained the same, namely allegory, as we saw in Amalar. The Mass is looked upon as a holy drama, a play performed before the eyes of the participants. But meanwhile the graphic ceremonial has been enriched. The signs of the Cross in the canon, most of them of pre-Frankish origin, were multiplied till far into the eleventh and twelfth centuries—at the *Supplices* and at the closing doxology. In addition there were in many churches signings with the Cross, and corresponding blessing formulas at the offertory, after the presentation of the gifts; and the priest blessed himself a number of times, especially at the Gospel. The Gothic principle of cumulation, the repetition of the same detail, the heaping up of ornament, had its effect on the kissing of the altar. Although up to the twelfth century, this was customary—in line with tradition—only when first approaching the altar and again when leaving, since the end of the thirteenth century it was performed every time the celebrant turned around at the altar. The kiss at high Mass when handing the celebrant any object, and the kiss of greeting for the celebrant are also added at various places. The extension of the hands after the consecration became, since the thirteenth century, a vivid imitation of the outstretched arms of the Crucified. For a time, too, the ceremonial was built up further; the priest at the anamnesis, on recalling the Resurrection and Ascension of our Lord, was supposed to mimic these movements with his hands. Bowing the head at the end of the *Memento* of the dead, and striking the breast while saying *Nobis quoque* in a loud voice— these actions appear to have been introduced as a vivid presentation of our Lord's death and the impression it made on the bystanders. Ceremonies of this sort of imitative symbolism were developed in great number, as is well known. And they often turned into something quite playful, as (for instance) when the boy-abbot in the monastery schools was summarily shoved from his chair at Vespers on the Feast of the Holy Innocents at the words "deposuit potentes de sede." The same dramatic instinct was at work here that produced the mystery plays.

And the dramatization of the readings took a new turn since Ivo of Chartres (d. 1117); where there was no single ambo to determine the place for the readings, older memories were recalled and so the Gospel was read at the right side (reckoned from the viewpoint of the ancient position of the episcopal throne) and the Epistle at the left. This led to the distinction between the Gospel side (church or altar) and the Epistle side.

All these usages, making a bid for the curious and fascinated eyes of the Christian people, obtained an allegorical significance. *Less and less did the spoken word project its own contents; one concentrated rather on the alternation between the loud and the soft tones of prayer.* The meaning of ceremonies was often a synthetic one, abstracting entirely from the course of the sacred action, and giving a fixed significance to each repeated ceremony just as a fixed significance was given to the visible appurtenances. Ever since Amalar the priestly vesture had been treated allegorically,[1] and in the years that followed this treatment was extended to the church building.

THE MASS A DRAMATIC REPRESENTATION

In the same way, the ceremonies that were oft repeated acquired a fixed meaning, with little thought given to their particular status here and now in the liturgical action. Often enough, besides the picture which presents itself, the number of repetitions offered a solution. Thus the

[1] Perhaps it would be more correct to say "symbolically," since, to be exact, the vesture does not of itself express or signify anything and therefore it cannot rightly be said to "say something else." But in reality we are dealing here not with any original symbolism (the sort of thing found, for instance, in the washing of hands), but only with a secondary symbolism subsequently connected with it—which is hardly to be distinguished from allegory.

triple silence in the Mass proper—at the secrets, during the canon and after the *Pater noster*—represents the three days our Lord rested in the tomb. The fivefold turning of the priest toward the people refers to the five appearances of our Lord after the Resurrection. Similarly the number of crosses made over the *oblata* received by preference a numerological meaning. The three crosses after the *Te igitur* typify the three times our Lord was mocked before the high priests and Herod and Pilate, the five crosses in the *Unde et memores* typify the five wounds, and so forth. The signs of the Cross within the canon are, since the eleventh century, the main theme for instructing the people about the Mass. A didactic poem of this period outlines the minimum that each priest must know about the Mass; what is the sacrifice, and what the altar and chalice, water and wine, and the crosses signify.

With few exceptions—among them the straightforward and objective exposition by the Parisian doctor, Jean Beleth (d. about 1165), deserves a prominent place—the explanation and interpretation of the Mass remains strictly within the bounds initiated by Amalar. The Mass is understood as a dramatic presentation of an action in the divine economy, especially of the suffering, death and resurrection of Christ, beginning with the longings and sighs of the patriarchs and prophets and concluding with our Saviour's ascension into heaven.

The newly developed and newly added ceremonies had also to be considered in this allegorizing. Keeping the book at the altar and moving it from Epistle side to Gospel side—this did not fit easily into the plans heretofore in vogue. It led, as a consequence, not only to an architectonic enlargement of the measurements of the altar, up to now rather modest,[2] but also to a revamping of the Mass-allegory. Even the first sure evidence of the term "Gospel side"—in Ivo of Chartres—refers to it as the *sinistra pars ecclesiæ* and the author is then faced with the riddle, why the Gospel should be given the less honorable side; he solves it by explaining that this signifies how when the Jews refused the faith, the apostles turned to the Gentiles (Acts 13:46). Thus in the rememorative allegory of the Mass the preaching to the Jews—in contrast to Amalar's plan—had to come before the reading of the Gospel. The collects, too, since they preceded, had to get a new interpretation. Ivo explains them as typical of how our Lord taught His disciples, especially how He taught them to pray. The Epistle then signifies the mission of the disciples. The intervening chants refer to the joyous response of those who were well disposed.

The same interpreter, taking a cue from older projects, sketches for

[2] Until the 11th century the altar tables were rarely more than 3 or 4 feet square. (But by the 15th it was not unusual to find them 12 feet long.) At this time, too, the altar began to be built up beyond the simple *mensa;* not only temporary and occasional reliquaries were placed over it, but permanent altar-pieces as well—the start of the immense reredoses of a later date.

the first time a well-rounded explanation of the canon and its silence as a fulfillment of Old Testament prefigurements. His is therefore a typological allegory intermixed with rememorative elements. Like the high-priest on the great day of Atonement, so the celebrant walks alone into the Holy of Holies, carrying the memorial of the Blood of Christ, and on his breast the names of the twelve patriarchs (the naming of the twelve Apostles), and with the Blood of the Saviour he sprinkles it. When he returns, the scapegoat is chased into the wilderness in the *Jube haec perferri*. Then, instead of changing his garments, he changes his voice and speaks the *Pater noster* aloud. This attempt at an explanation was carried on by later interpreters and deepened theologically, ultimately to the better understanding of the sacrificial character of the Mass.

New images of Old Testament origin were introduced into the allegorizing of the Mass by Honorius of Autun (d. about 1125). In the Mass the exodus from Egypt, the revelation of the commandments, the conquest of Amalec at the prayers of Moses pleading with arms outstretched, the entrance into the Promised Land under the leadership of "Jesu"—all these are re-enacted in a new manner. The bishop, accoutred in his sacred garments as in the armor of war, is the general; the lector is the herald, bells and chants are the fanfare of battle. Even the struggle between David and Goliath is rehearsed in the Mass. Since Honorius adds other pictures, includes audacious number-symbolism, and embraces also much of the traditional allegory of Christ's Passion, the result is a bewildering wealth of variegated meanings, to which one could scarcely apply the title of an explanation. Sicard of Cremona (d. 1215) wanders along the same pathway, but adds to the confusion with a plethora of quotations.

In general, however, the work of the medieval Mass commentators is wedded to the extension of the rememorative type of allegory. Rupert von Deutz (d. 1135) expands it to include the sacerdotal vestments, in which he perceives the person of Christ outlined; the humeral reminds one of the concealment of Christ's divinity by His humanity; the alb, of His purity; the stole, of His obedience unto death; the chasuble, of His raiment which is the Church.

A healthy reaction to this increased overloading of the interpretation of the Mass with so many diverse elements, and at the same time a high point of rememorative allegory is found in the work composed by Innocent III, at that time still Cardinal Lothar, just before his election as Pope (1198). Except for an abundantly practical number-symbolism, he restricts himself almost entirely to the traditional meanings derived from Christ's life and Passion, which he presents distinctly in simple words. His work, therefore, became the basis for the Mass interpretations of the later Middle Ages, which are often content to repeat the words of the great Pope, either cutting them down or broadening them out.

COLORS, VESTMENTS, ALTARS

The great compiler of medieval allegory, William Durandus (d. 1296), acknowledges that he took Innocent III as his guide for the explanation of the Mass. We shall find ourselves returning time and time again to his work *Rationale divinorum officiorum* because of its appropriate mention of the rites then in use.

In Innocent we find for the first time a determination of liturgical colors for specified days, along with the respective significance thereof. His rules are more or less those still in force today: white as the festive color (and he tries to discover a reason for the white—even in the white of the clouds on Ascension Day!), red for martyrs' days and Pentecost, black for days of penance and for Masses for the Dead, green for days without a festal character. The sensuous interest in colors and the zeal in explaining their significance were alike manifestations of the spirit of the Gothic period.

A new trend is manifest also in the understanding and meaning of the various liturgical vestments. Innocent himself finds chiefly a moral meaning like that which Amalar offered; in particular, he is familiar with the spiritual battle (I. 64), although this is better developed in other writers. But Innocent also avails himself of a christological explanation somewhat similar to Rupert von Deutz who saw relationships between the priestly garments and the properties and attributes of Christ's person. But by the middle of the thirteenth century this had turned to a form of rememorative allegory, which here too perceived symbols of the Passion of Christ.

Development is also to be found in practical paramentics. The Gothic chasuble is still broad and mantle-like, but the two ornamental stripes falling down from the shoulder and joined as a line down the middle became in time a forked cross and this in turn became (on the back of the chasuble) a regular cross with horizontal cross-beam. This development means that the allegorical presentation of the Crucified could be imaged even in the external figuration, but it also led not only to a richer and richer ornamentation but also, because of the need for a stiff surface, to the later misshaping of the garment. Similar forces were at work in changing the shape of the altar. The altar screens (polyptych retables or "wing-altars") offer us the very best in Gothic from the viewpoint of artistic performance, but from the viewpoint of the liturgy they were definitely an aberration.

The allegorical method of contemplating and explaining the liturgy had to face a *crisis* in the thirteenth century, and it is really a matter of wonder that it was able to weather the storm and that the old method should survive unscathed in the period to follow. In a century when medieval Scholasticism reached a peak, the very basis of all allegory was naturally called into question. For allegory is founded entirely on a con-

ception of the world which is interested in the sensible and visible phenomena only insofar as they are mirrors and symbols of an invisible,
intangible higher world. Even in the book of nature, attention was
focused not on the forms of individual things, not on the shapes of the
"letters," but only on the hidden meaning which, one thought, could be
read therein. It is the spirit within the writing, the spirit within the
liturgy—especially in its space-visible appearance—that is sought, every
effort being made to grub out the thought that must lie hid there. Art in
this period, whether concerned with animals and plants, or the attributes
of the saints, or geometrical patterns, seeks principally to enlarge and
explain this world of symbols. This is nothing more, really, than the logical consequence of carrying through Plato's theory of knowledge, with
its sharp separation of the world of sense and the world of ideas. But with
the switch to Aristotle and the new basis for a theory of knowledge—
Cognitio incipit a sensibus—the world of sense, and the concrete phenomena of forms in divine worship along with it, at once appears in a new
light. It deserves to be studied and appreciated for its own sake.

LITURGY AND THE SCHOLASTICS

Albertus Magnus was the pathfinder who led the Scholastics along the
new way of explaining Holy Mass. First of all, he presents an enlightened
and theologically grounded explanation of the course of that Mass that is
for the most part derived from the text of the Mass *ordo*. Besides he
makes repeated thrusts at the allegorical exposition, especially at the
rememorative. He says it is *mirabile* to refer the silence of the Mass
proper to events in the story of our Lord's Passion—things in no way
touched upon in the text of the Mass. In fact, in reference to the explanation that the kissing of the altar at the *Supplices* signified Judas' traitor-
ous kiss, and the signs of the Cross that follow signify the bonds and
ropes by which our Saviour was led to Annas, he says scornfully: *omnino
profanum est et omnibus fidelibus abominandum*. The different signification attached to the signs of the Cross at the *Quam oblationem* he termed:
deliramenta et hominum illiteratorum. But Albertus' objections made
little headway. Allegory continued to hold the field. Even St. Thomas'
Summa Theologica contained an interpretation of the Mass that made
many concessions to allegory.[3]

One result of Scholastic thought must be acknowledged, the consideration given to the organization of the Mass into parts following one after
the other. Allegorical thought was concerned mostly with a series of pictures, and either took their order for granted or considered the division
a mere external. Now, however, intrinsic and theological viewpoints

---

[3] Thomas Aquinas, *Summa theol.* III, 83.5.

became paramount. Albertus Magnus had distinguished three parts: *introitus* (up to the collects inclusive), *instructio* (up to the *Credo* inclusive), and *oblatio*, with appropriate subdivisions for the last. This division recurs in the *Expositio missæ* of Nicholas Stoer, written about 1412. Hugh of St. Cher, O.P. (d. 1263), like so many medieval authors, takes the Augustinian interpretation of the words of St. Paul, *obsecrationes, orationes, postulationes, gratiarum actiones*, and applies them to the Mass, thus distinguishing four parts, of which the first embraces everything up to the *Sanctus*, the second takes in the canon, the third begins with the *Pater noster* and the fourth with the post-communion.

In these new attempts at a division of the Mass, the segment before the Epistle, as is remarked more than once, is (even today) instructive. But the weakest point in the outline is the placing of the preface. Since the Mass is viewed chiefly from the standpoint of the consecration and the canon is reckoned as beginning with the *Te igitur*, the prayer of thanks, which had such great importance in the ancient Church, no longer presents a problem. Albertus Magnus, and also Alexander of Hales and his school, considered the preface a part of the offertory, a sort of conclusion to it. According to Beleth, the second of the four Augustinian portions begins with the *secreta;* the preface is thus drawn closer to the canon, but makes of it a very secondary member in the series. Others take a middle course—like Hugh of St. Cher—by placing the preface in the first part of the Mass without further ado, and thus it becomes accidentally one of the preparatory acts for the consecration.

That is about all that Scholastic thought effected in the interpretation of the Mass. As for the development of the Mass-liturgy, or for all that, the development of an understanding of the Mass-liturgy, Scholasticism left scarcely a trace—a rather surprising thing. The *Rationale* of Durandus which is constructed entirely on the basis of allegory, continued to be the liturgical handbook for the late Middle Ages and beyond. And the later interpreters, whose number is not without weight, follow more or less along the same paths.

PRESENTATION OF CHRIST'S SUFFERING

A further evolution was gradually effected. The vestments which the priest wore to the altar had been interpreted as signifying Christ's Passion. The next step was certain—to conceive of the Mass, not only from the canon but from the beginning on, as a presentation of Christ's suffering. An anonymous interpreter of the fifteenth century does just that. According to him, when the priest goes to the altar our Lord is taken away captive, at the *Confiteor* he stands before Annas and Caiphas, etc. A more pronounced extension of this type of consideration does not however come to notice till the post-medieval Mass expositions. A broadening-out of the allegory of Christ's Passion resulted also from the elevation of the species at the consecration, a custom which grew, as we will see, from the thirteenth century on. This ceremony naturally suggested the raising of Christ on the Cross.

Besides, allegorical interpretation of the Mass again went awry in the late medieval period. Elements of different types of explanation were thrown together. The oft-changing explanation of the sign of the Cross did not fit well into the course of the Mass. In the last analysis, all that was needed was a little imagination to invent more arbitrary explanations for the various liturgical details which were already explained quite arbitrarily. So, besides the exclusive Passion interpretation there were other plans—seeing exemplified in the Mass the forty *opera* of Christ's life, or his thirty-three years. With the eclectic methods then in vogue this could lead only to further confusion.

That is precisely what happened, and since no one seemed able to manage any other form of devotion or interpretation, attempts were again made towards the end of the Middle Ages to bring order into the allegorizing by trying to establish a clear and neat series built up on a time basis. Of this sort are the explanations of Simon van Venlo and Franz Titelmans (d. 1537). The latter makes some new suggestions that fit nicely into the full picture: the priest's sitting silently during the singing of the interposed chants after the Epistle is related to Christ's stay in the wilderness; the praise of God in the preface is related to the meal at Bethany, when the whole house was filled with the fragrance of the ointment.

Despite this vacillation, the fundamental theme of all Mass allegory was the suffering, or at least the life and suffering of Jesus. Our Lord's command, "Do this for a commemoration of me," was never lost sight of even in the plain and simple devotion of these centuries; rather it had been fulfilled in a sort of figurative fashion. Significant in this respect is the picture of St. Gregory's Mass, a theme repeatedly utilized by artists of the late Middle Ages. While Gregory is at Mass our Lord appears to him above the altar as a man of suffering, with the instruments of His Passion. On the other hand, the notion of sacrifice as such, and of the sacrifice which is here consummated and which the Church here co-offers—that stays surprisingly in the background, even though the theologians hand on the traditional doctrine. How little and how seldom the idea of sacrifice entered into the liturgical thought of the twelfth century is seen rather pointedly in the reasons given for daily Mass in Honorius of Autun, daily Mass is celebrated, he says, so that (1) the laborers in the vineyard—that is, the priests only—might be able to communicate; (2) that neophytes might be included in the Body of Christ (by the Baptismal Communion); and (3) that the *memoria passionis* might remain alive amongst the faithful.

THE FAITHFUL "LIKE SPECTATORS"

The offertory procession is still the practice on many occasions, but in the various explanations of the Mass there is hardly any mention of the fact that the assembled people have a part in the oblation or at least participate in praising and honoring God. By the gifts which the faithful present at the offertory they purchase and make available to themselves the sufferings of Christ and the merits of His Passion which is commemorated in the Mass. The Mass is viewed almost exclusively as an action of God. In the liturgical unfolding of the celebration of Mass, the action of the Church, its prayer of thanks, and its gift-offerings are no longer perceived as in former ages; only the work, the redeeming work of God. The priest alone is active. The faithful, viewing what he is performing, are like spectators looking on at a mystery-filled drama of our Lord's Way of the Cross. It is no accident, then, that Calderón in his *autos sacramentales* should employ the traditional medieval allegory to present a drama in which the whole economy of salvation, from Paradise to world's end, is hinged to the Mass; and yet never a word, either at the offertory or at the Communion, of the active participation of the laity. The *eucharistia* has become an *epiphania*, an advent of God who appears amongst men and dispenses His graces. To gain a share in these graces, we are gathered before the altar, in an attitude of wondering contemplation that bespeaks our longing to take part in the Mass as often as possible.

It is no wonder that the allegorical method which reigned supreme through so many centuries should leave its traces on the Mass-liturgy which has come down to us. The Middle Ages inserted certain rites to make the sacred drama more potent. Amongst these, as we shall see, is the ceremony of hiding the paten under the corporal at the offertory—to signify our Lord's self-abasement and the hiding of His divinity in His Passion; the bowing of the head at the end of the *Memento* of the Dead—to signify our Saviour's death; the lifting of the voice at *Nobis quoque*—to signify the cry of the captain of the guard; the five crosses at the doxology concluding the canon—to signify the five wounds; the anticipation of the commingling—as symbol of the Resurrection—so that the greeting *Pax Domini* might appear as the greeting of the risen Saviour; the lifting of hands and eyes before the last blessing—after the model of our Lord before the Ascension.

This consideration of the Mass as an epiphany, although brought to the fore by the allegorizing pattern, received, at one point at least, a further impetus and enforcement when, at the turn of the twelfth century, the practice of elevating host and chalice after the consecration came into being. All our bodily eyes can see of Christ in the Eucharist is the sacramental covering and wrapping beneath which His Body and Blood are concealed, but medieval man was so eager to view even this, that various devices were employed to render possible this perception of the Sacrament.

TRENDS IN EUCHARISTIC THOUGHT

Out of the distant past, eucharistic thought had gradually taken a new turn, so that from the time of Isidore and the controversies of the ninth century it began little by little to look upon the Sacrament (omitting its symbolism) almost entirely from the viewpoint of the Real Presence. This Presence and the mode of its achievement were the topics on which theologians focused their attention more and more. Since Anselm of Laon (d. 1117) and William of Champeaux (d. 1121) theological teaching had become more clear and precise, namely that in the Sacrament not only were the Body or the Blood of Christ present, but the whole Christ, *totus Christus*, was present. Thus a formula was attained which blended well with the popular eagerness, nursed by allegory, to look at the Eucharist. The people had learnt that at Holy Mass the Blessed Sacrament was not so much a *thing*, Christ's Body and Blood as sacrificial gift and sacrificial meal, to be offered up prayerfully and received devoutly, but rather a *person*, the person of the Lord, to be accompanied thoughtfully on His path of redemption. Thus the contemplation of the Christ of history and His earthly-ethical appearance (thoughts which had grown more and more prominent in the popular consciousness since the time of St. Bernard) could mingle with the contemplation of the Eucharist, and strengthen interest therein.

A like trend was produced by the defense against heretical agitation during the same period. The heresy of Berengarius of Tours (d. 1088), whose rationalistic explaining-away of the Real Presence had been condemned by various synods, was only a remote attack. The controversy raised by him had hardly gone beyond theological or clerical circles. Here, in any case, and especially in the monasteries, the greatest care was from this time on devoted to the forms with which the Sacrament was surrounded; prescriptions about the choice and preparation of the materials, the custom of keeping the fingers together which—after a special cleansing—had touched the Sacrament, the detailed rules for the ablution of the fingers and of the vessels after Communion.

But in the wider ranks of the people a deep impact was first caused after the rise of the neo-Manichean heresy of the twelfth century which had been aroused over the wealth of a Church become a feudal institution. The heresy had grown particularly conspicuous and rank as Albigensianism. Along with its almost complete denial of the hierarchy and of the sacraments, it had rejected belief in the Eucharist. Here indeed was a struggle for the souls of men! The very word for heretic in German, *Ketzer* (Cathari), which originated at the time, suggests this very pointedly. The new teaching, with its ideal of a poor church and the primitive simplicity of its statements, was indeed alluring. It explained the Blessed Sacrament outright as simply bread, *purum panem;* it regarded its own blessing of bread as an equivalent substitute for the Eucharist.

On the Catholic side, however, even in the twelfth century, we begin to hear accounts of eucharistic miracles. In place of the species of bread, our Lord was seen in His own human appearance. Even if these accounts cannot withstand critical examination, still they are professions of faith all the more emphatic because they are couched in the realistic language of the people. Here again is a clear expression of that longing to see what is concealed in the Sacrament. Even if the ordinary Christian acknowledges his unworthiness to be favored by the visible appearance of the Redeemer, he will at least want to see the outward veil beneath which He lies hid. That was for him, at the same time a substitute for sacramental communion which was then seldom permitted him.

For such a view of the host the first opportunity was offered by an old traditional rite, when at the words *accepit panem* the priest took the bread in his hands, as once our Lord himself had done, and lifted it slightly. Urged by the desire of the people, the priests emphasized and augmented the rite. But since the interest of the people was centered not only on the outward act of oblation but on the presence of our Lord (which was not yet at this moment actual), many bishops were greatly concerned lest the people adore the bread, and so about 1210 a decree of the Bishop of Paris introduced the regulation which determined everywhere that the priest should elevate the Host only after the words of consecration, and so high then that all might see and adore.

"SEE THE CELESTIAL MYSTERY"

Thus the Mass acquired a new center, a new focal point, and the devotion of the people acquired an object which corresponded to their understanding and to which they thenceforth clung tenaciously. To see the celestial mystery—that is the climax of the Grail-legend in which the religious longing of the Middle Ages found its poetic expression. And, as in the legend of the Grail, one naturally expected the same Grace-filled results from the sight of the Mystery at Mass. Esteem for this opportunity to look upon the Host went to such lengths that it was placed side by side with Holy Communion, and the question was asked, would sinners commit a new mortal sin by looking at the sacred Host? [4]

[4] The question was answered by theologians in the negative. Still those who were under excommunication or interdict were sometimes expressly forbidden even to look at the Eucharist; it was to get around this prohibition that now and then the persons concerned made holes in the church walls.

To look at the sacred Host at the elevation became for many in the later Middle Ages the be-all and end-all of Mass devotion. See the Body of Christ at the consecration and be satisfied! In the cities people ran from church to church, to see the elevated Host as often as possible, since rich rewards could be expected from such a practice.[5] People even started lawsuits to ensure their getting a favorable view of the altar.[6] There are examples of congregations where the majority of the faithful waited for the sance-bell signalling the approach of the consecration before they entered the church and then after the elevation they rushed out as quickly as they had come in.

"LONGER SHOWINGS"

Of course such abuses were discountenanced, but the underlying usage itself gradually obtained ecclesiastical approval. Great preachers knew how best to inculcate the right attitude. Berthold of Regensburg in one of his sermons on the Mass cried out: "At the elevation of the Sacrament the priest seems to be saying three things to you: See the Son of God who, for your sakes, shows His wounds to the Heavenly Father; see the Son of God who, for your sakes, was thus lifted on the Cross; see the Son of God who will come to judge the living and the dead." For this reason some wanted the elevation of the sacred Host at this spot to be not a mere momentary lifting but an actual "showing" lasting some time, so that the congregation could greet and worship the Body of the Lord in prayerful song. The ceremony might even be repeated at other places in the Mass—at the end of the canon or after the Agnus Dei—and it was not to be omitted even on Good Friday, a practice that was retained until the Holy Week Reform of 1955. On the other hand, naturally, warnings about moderation had to be given, since some priests seemed to know no bounds, and there were even those who took a stipend for these longer "showings."

However, it was not long before this "showing" was freed from its connection with the Mass, and, with the introduction of the monstrance, was transferred to other occasions. From the beginning of the fourteenth century it became customary to carry the Blessed Sacrament, unconcealed, in solemn procession through the streets on the feast of Corpus Christi, a feast which had come to the fore since 1246 as a result of the new movement. Then, during the high Mass that followed, It was allowed to remain on the altar; this was continued through the entire octave, and sometimes the solemn exposition was extended through the

[5] A Graz MS. of the 15th century indicates that on that day, among other things, one will not lose one's eyesight, will not starve, will not meet a sudden death; that heedless words will be forgiven, etc.

[6] It could happen—as it did in England—that if the celebrant did not elevate the host high enough, the people would cry out: "Hold up, Sir John, hold up. Heave it a little higher." Fortescue, *The Mass*, 341 f.

whole period of the choral office in this festival season. During this same fourteenth century it even became customary to leave the Blessed Sacrament exposed on other feast-days of the year, espcially on Maundy Thursday, in connection with the Votive Mass of the Blessed Sacrament.[7]

Mass before the Blessed Sacrament exposed became customary and, after the Reformation, along with the rest of the exposition cult—again as a protest against heresy—was given a new impetus. This was from then on the most striking expression of the fact that in the whole course of the Mass-liturgy interest and understanding was still centered mostly on the moment of consecration. There was still a desire that this moment and the corresponding elevation of the Host might be stretched out through the whole Mass. Roman legislation had always held aloof from these efforts which had, in the years to follow, grown to great proportions particularly in the south; for such things Rome allowed very little leeway.

Towards the end of the Middle Ages there arose, out of the same zeal for honoring the Blessed Sacrament, a rite which penetrated everywhere and changed the outward picture of the Mass-liturgy between consecration and Communion, ornamenting and enlivening it in remarkable fashion—the genuflection before and after every touching of the Blessed Sacrament. This was not known before the fourteenth century. Thus at this very late date there was transferred to the Blessed Sacrament a token of honor which—like the use of lights and incense, and throne and canopy—originated in princely ceremonial and from thence had long ago been taken over into the liturgy as an honor to persons.

A clear parallel to the conception and presentation of the Mass-liturgy as a dramatic play which appeals primarily to the eyes of the onlooker was to be found in the efforts made to enrich also the audible side of the liturgical action.

GREGORIAN CHANT

Gregorian Chant had already achieved a great height in the eighth century, especially in Rome itself. Not a few Frankish and Anglo-Saxon clerics, coming to Rome, had taken the trouble to procure from Rome books and teachers of the ecclesiastical chant. It was an *art-song* rich in melodies, demanding a *schola* properly trained, but—save for the accompaniment of boy voices singing an octave higher—strictly built on the principle of unison. But even in the last years of the Carolingian period the first waves of ornamental enrichment had risen. At that, it affected chiefly only the text.

[7] There are to this day parishes in the Alpine countries were every day there is celebrated either a Requiem or a "*Segenmesse*," that is, a German *Singmesse* before the Sacrament exposed.

The long melismas or series of notes, often built upon a single syllable, seemed to have had little appeal to Germanic tastes. So new texts were created in which each syllable corresponded to a note of the given melody. This is the original form of the so-called *tropes*. They were sung as decorative covering by one part of the choir, while the rest of the singers sang the foundation text to the same melody. In the tenth century they had spread everywhere, on festive occasions accompanying first the Proper parts of the Mass, later on also the Ordinary, from introit and *Kyrie* right through to the end of the Mass, sometimes including also the *Ite missa est*. At the same time, corresponding phrases were inserted in the traditional melody along with the corresponding text, or—especially in the introit—introductory phrases preceded the melody. A very special case was the sequence which arose out of the many-toned melodies of the alleluia. It then acquired an independent existence, was developed far and wide during the Middle Ages, and produced thousands of poems. It is noteworthy that Rome and Italy, which showed the greatest reserve towards Gothic art, were also very reluctant to admit the sequences which were the very first metrical productions to be introduced into the Mass. Since as a rule only new texts were under consideration, this enrichment of the liturgy was generally of value only to clerics who understood Latin.

But new melodies too, were composed, especially after the year 1000, melodies for those texts which were repeated at every Mass, the texts of the Ordinary. Up to this time the chants of the Ordinary had the same simple recitative character as the altar chants of the priest; in fact, they were often only continuations of these, and it is to this class that the Gregorian Mass numbered XVIII in the *Kyriale* belongs. It is still used at present on Ferias in Advent and Lent and, with changes, at Requiems. The acclamations and responses also possessed this character and differed from the chants of the Ordinary only in length. Actually, not only the *Kyrie*, but also the *Sanctus, Benedictus,* and *Agnus Dei* have an acclamatory quality at least in a wider sense, and even the Gloria is composed in good part of acclamatory material. They were little more than elevated speech, relieved by certain cadences. Everyone could therefore take part in them.

A corroboration of what has been said is found in the fact that only by way of exception is the *schola cantorum* mentioned as carrying these melodies. It is true that even in the Carolingian period they were not as a rule sung by the people—excepting perhaps the *Sanctus*—but they were at least at this time and, in general, also in the twelfth and thirteenth centuries, reserved for the clerics in the sanctuary who formed the choir. The trained singers who sang the chants of the *Proprium* would naturally take the lead here, and as the chants of the Ordinary grew more ornate, gradually take over. This was the case with the *Kyrie* as early as the tenth and eleventh centuries. The songs of the fore-Mass thus assumed a greater importance than those of the Mass proper. Richer melodies for the *Sanctus* and the *Agnus Dei* were not created until somewhat later. The *Gloria* and the *Credo* retained a simple, psalmodic-recitative character even in the new forms they now acquired. Still the musical ornamentation of the chants of the Ordinary had become so elaborate by the time of St. Bernard (d. 1153) that, under the reform of church music begun with his cooperation, it was thought these forms would have to be banned from use in churches of his order. At that time the chants of the Ordinary were not conceived as units. The oldest example of a chant Mass comprehending all its parts as a unit is one originating about the end of the thirteenth century, a Mass still frequently sung, the *Missa de Angelis*.

OTHER FORMS OF CHURCH MUSIC

Gradually *chorus* begins to mean something new. It turns into a choir of singers separated from the clergy, often composed of lay people, and independent even as regards its place in the church. First it rambled to the rood-loft, the high reading- and singing-gallery often found in Gothic structures in place of the sanctuary enclosure between the choir and the nave, and elevated in its entire width. Later it finally wandered to the upper gallery which was built at the back of the church.

Polyphony begins to take on some importance in Church music. The first attempts at counterpoint, starting in the ninth century, affected only the songs of the *Proprium*. These attempts resulted from the use of a second voice singing an accompaniment to the main melody at the interval of a fourth or fifth. The text might be with a trope or without. And the accompanying voice—*vox organalis*—might be an instrument. In the twelfth century it is the cathedral of Notre Dame in Paris that takes the lead. On festive occasions the gradual or alleluia was sung not to the chant melody alone, but a second or even a third or fourth voice was added here and there in a free independent movement. And sometimes, where an over-elaborate melisma presented the opportunity, a special text, often even one in the vernacular, was added to the proper one. Of a similar sort, but of course not so high in rank was the song art of the travelling singers who, we are told, were wont to sing their verses at Mass *super Sanctus et Agnus Dei*. Such music seemed to suit the time which liked this type of light embellishment. But it was a dangerous road to take. So warning voices were raised to safeguard the seriousness of the traditional ecclesiastical chant and even to induce the ecclesiastical authority to take a definite stand.

As a matter of fact the art of Church music did again confine itself to stricter bounds during the last centuries of the Middle Ages. It was satisfied especially in Germany to accompany at Holy Day services the Gregorian chant melodies of the Proper and later especially of the Ordinary with a form of *falso bordone*.[8] This had been the practice in psalmody and still is in some places. By the fourteenth century the organ had been perfected enough to make its entrance everywhere in the larger churches, provided no stricter principles stood in the way, and could perform a like duty. About this same time in France the first example of Mass composition in our modern sense begins to appear—compositions in which all the parts of the Ordinary of the Mass, from *Kyrie* to *Agnus Dei* are set to polyphony and are no longer bound down to the Gregorian Chant, even though chant melodies are used as a *canto fermo* or are interwoven with the harmony. When, in 1377, the papal court returned with Pope Gregory XI from Avignon to Rome, the papal singers brought the art of polyphony with them to Italy. Slowly the new art spread to other countries. It did not get the same joyous reception everywhere; thus Swiss monasteries were very reserved in their attitude, and at St. Gall it was banned from divine service even as late as 1560. But all in all a new period had begun in the history of Church music and in the history of the external embellishment of the liturgy.

During the years that followed, the chants of the *Proprium*, whose texts were built up on the lyrical materials of the psalms and which had been knowingly inserted into the "rest" periods of the service as an artistic element, retained the archaic simplicity of their ancient traditional Gregorian melodies. But the unassuming acclamatory phrases, in which originally the people were able to frame their cries of prayer and praise, or in which at any rate, represented by the clergy, they professedly resumed and continued the altar chants of the priest—these were fitted out in the pomp of polyphony. With the exception perhaps of the Credo, which arose out of the doctrinal struggle of the east and whose recitation was at least in part quite prosaic, these acclamatory phrases proved favorable to an artistic handling because of the vigor of their words. Indeed, their content was not at all ill suited for musical development. Still it was precisely this artistic elevation above the ordinary plane that put them beyond the reach of the people who were called upon to cooperate, and so to a certain extent the texts departed from their proper function.

In view of the foreign language of the liturgy, the only possible pathway was again the stressing of the *Ordinarium*, since there was no question, in general, of creating new texts. Through the development of these various choral Masses, a road was opened to getting away from the traditional melodies. The texts were always the same, and their meaning could easily be explained even to people not knowing Latin; hence these texts

[8] A choral melody or psalm tone sung in four part harmony. The Sulpicians have had great success with this in the U.S.

lent support to the propagation or spread which came about through their new musical setting. Their constant repetition made their performance rather easy. And if the *Sanctus* and *Benedictus* especially filled in with their sound the vacancy left in the canon, this was a compensation to the hearing of the congregation for whom the basic tone of the *eucharistia* was thus once more rightfully restored where it had been barred by the silence of the canon and, fundamentally, by the insertion of the intercessory prayers.

12. *The Close of the Middle Ages and the Tridentine Reform*

The designation of the fourteenth and fifteenth centuries as the "autumn of the Middle Ages" (Huizinga) proved to be exceptionally apt in the history of the liturgy and not least in that of the Mass. There is indeed a rich and manifold growth, as we have just seen exemplified in Church music. New forms, new inferences are continually being developed. But the inferences are developed only from what is already at hand. There is no cutting back to the living roots, no springing forth of new, healthy growths. Scholastic theology produced nothing for the liturgy of the Mass or for a better understanding of it. So the forms appear over-ripe, the growth becomes dry and withered.

But all this does not hold so true for the text of the Mass *ordo*. Even though here too, especially outside Italy, the preparatory prayers, the versicles and invocations of the prayers at the foot of the altar, the blessings at the offertory, the hymnic greetings before the Communion have become prevalent, still, since they are all the silent prayers of the priest, this is all more or less in the background. However, within the ambit of the Ordinary there were some things that fit more surely into the description we have given—the musical expansion mentioned in the last chapter and the increase in the forms by which the Sacrament is venerated.

Reverence for the Sacrament led to a change in policy regarding the handling of the sacred Host by lay people. No lay hand was allowed to touch it, even if that meant depriving a dying person of Viaticum. It was a very special favor when Popes of the fourteenth century gave to princes in certain instances the permission to touch the chalice on Communion days with their bare hands. In the late Middle Ages the corporal was often shown honor that amounted to superstition. For the washing of the corporal special prayers were composed. In this same connection we might note that the chapters on the *pericula* or *defectus* which might occur in the Mass grew larger and larger. The early medieval period had already considered certain contingencies, like spilling the chalice or dropping a particle, and had prescribed stern punishments for them. Now pertinent mistakes and defects are discussed and decided with reference to theology and from the practical viewpoint of what to do so that due reverence will be shown towards the Sacrament in every instance. Innocent III had considered certain cases at some length and St. Thomas devotes an Article of his *Summa* to them. But new *pericula* were constantly being discovered—even such as: what if the Lord should appear in *specie carnis vel pueri!*—and for each, corresponding instructions were given.

LACK OF PROPORTION

Of course here it was often only a lack of proportion—too much of a good thing! But considerable consequences were to be feared from the one-sided discussions and the unenlightened and isolated popularizing of another phase in the teaching of the Mass, the phase of the effects of the Mass. That the Mass not only offers God due honor but also redounds to the welfare of living and dead was already a conviction of Christian antiquity. But now this side of the sacrifice comes to the fore. In the declining Middle Ages it becomes the main theme of sermons on the Mass. Formal enumerations of the fruits of the Mass are compiled, especially of those fruits which derive from a devout hearing of Holy Mass. Such enumerations first appear in the thirteenth century. People were satisfied then with four or five or six points, with the spiritual effects foremost. But soon it became ten fruits, finally twelve. The editor of a German version of them made the remark that "the formulas for the fruits of the Mass take on a more gross appearance the nearer they stand to the end of the Middle Ages." For each of the spiritual effects a Father of the Church is cited in support—no matter how incredible the effect may sound.[1] Although contemporary theology did not approve such exaggerations, still they were able to flourish unimpeded in the homiletic and devotional literature of the day. That meant the people were encouraged to zealous attendance at Holy Mass, but also they were lulled into a false security, as though the salvation of their souls could be assured by merely hearing Mass.

With this exaggerated description of the effects of the Mass, another fact is intimately connected, the Votive Mass. Towards the end of the Middle Ages there appear numerous new formularies. To those already at hand are added formularies of Masses against various sicknesses, against

---

[1] Thus Augustine is saddled with the statement that during the time one hears Mass one does not grow older; Franz, 51; cf. 57. Other fruits are these: after hearing Mass one's food tastes better; one will not die a sudden death; the souls in Purgatory will not have to suffer while one is hearing Mass for them, etc.

dangers to right and property, against attacks by an enemy, and especially formularies in honor of those saints who were honored as patrons and protectors in these various situations. And they are arranged in marked and defined series, the particular order of the Masses being thought to obtain certain specified results. The start of this custom of a series of Masses is traced to the *Dialogues* of St. Gregory the Great, where we read—though without a particular significance being attached to the numbers—that Mass was said for a deceased person in one case for seven days in a row, in another for thirty. This example had successors all through the medieval period. But it was not till the last few centuries that any arrangement was decided upon and carefully planned out. Series are stipulated for 3, 5, 6, 7, 9 and 30 Masses, even for 41, 44 or 45, for the benefit of the dead and also for the wishes and intentions of the living. For each Mass a specified formula, independent of the day's Mass, is prescribed; sometimes, too, a specified number of candles and a specified number of alms-gifts are stipulated. What was really questionable in this practice of Mass series and Votive Masses was the assurance—recurring time and again—of unfailing results. Such assurance could even be seen in Mass books: "If anyone finds himself in a case of extreme necessity and celebrates these thirty Masses—or has them celebrated for him by a priest—his problem will be solved without delay."

It is hardly to be wondered at that the faithful seized upon an easy means like this which coincided with their own mania for miracles. And so there arose during the last centuries of the Middle Ages an unnatural multiplication of Masses and, along with it, an unnatural increase in clergy of whom a part, at least, derived their entire income from Masses either through endowments (foundations or chantries) or by way of Mass stipends. For the most part they celebrated Votive Masses or Masses for the Dead, since these the people wanted most.

This multiplicity of Masses had its effect on the rites and ceremonies. Some of the Masses were celebrated with chant. But since in churches only one Mass could be sung, a solution was worked out by which several such Masses could be celebrated in close succession. These were the so-called "Boxed Masses" which followed each other in this way: one Mass was sung to the offertory or to the *Sanctus*, then continued as a low Mass while at another altar a second Mass was begun. But the most pronounced result of the multiplying of Masses was the increase in low Masses, since most of them were for private requests and had no public character. This trend to the private and the subjective, to an independence from the grand order of things was also displayed in another abuse, namely, setting aside the arrangement of the ecclesiastical year and confining oneself to Votive Masses either chosen at will or arranged according to the rules of the Mass series.

Even while these various conditions were setting in, Peter Cantor

(d. 1197) was inveighing against the evil he saw coming; there would have to be fewer churches, fewer altars, fewer and better priests. Several later German mystics spoke in a similar vein. John Gerson comes out publicly against the nuisance. He says: Preachers who attach extravagant promises to the Mass are misleading the people into Judaism and promoting superstition. In Germany too, voices were raised in like denunciation. Nicholas of Cusa gave the example of practical reform. As Bishop of Brixen, he ordered in 1453 and 1455 that all Mass books in his diocese should be assembled at certain centers, Stams, Wilten, Neustift and Innichen, and corrected according to one stipulated unobjectionable exemplar. The use of uncorrected books was sternly forbidden. Unfortunately men of such energy were not to be found elsewhere. In general, the evil continued to flourish. The holiest of the Church's possessions remained, it is true, the center of genuine piety. But alas, the clouds and shadows surrounding this center brought matters to such a pass that the Institution of Jesus, that well of life from which the Church had drawn for fifteen-hundred years, became an object of scorn and ridicule and was repudiated as a horrible idolatry by entire peoples.

The complaints raised by the Reformers, especially by Luther, were aimed accurately and quite relentlessly against questionable points in ecclesiastical praxis regarding the Mass; the fruits of the Mass, the Votive Masses with their various values, the commerce in stipends. But the complaints went far beyond that. Taking as his principle the Bible alone, Luther denied the sacrificial character of the Mass and thought in this way to have reached the root of the trouble. The Eucharist was only a "testament," a bequest and benefit handed us, and as such—this is Luther's rash conclusion—in no wise a "*bene-fit*" or good work that we can offer God in order to "merit" from Him something for ourselves or epecially for others. Therefore, the Mass cannot be read either for the living or for the dead. All prayers in the Mass-liturgy in which there is any mention of this, particularly of sacrifice—like the canon—are bad human additions and must be dropped. A special work of Luther's deals with "the abomination of the low Mass called the canon." Very effective were the charges made that Masses, especially Masses for the Poor Souls, were a means of fleecing the people. The result was felt even in sections of Europe which remained staunchly Catholic, so that as early as 1528 we are told that in the church of Salzburg a hundred *gratiani* (priests who lived on stipends) could formerly be maintained more easily than now even a single one.

The reference to self-interest and superstition had made an impression. And considering the low state of religious training, this adverse criticism threatened to destroy in people's minds not only the excess foliage but the very branch and root. The Mass was disregarded, despised. And nothing was done about it. The Council of Trent did indeed accomplish one thing; in its doctrinal definition the Council clearly distinguished between truth and error and declared the objective character of the Sacrifice of the Mass as something more than a mere reminder of the Sacrifice of the Cross or a mere Communion rite. Thus the foundations of Catholic liturgy were secured. But a reform was also needed, a reform which would attack the ecclesiastical praxis of the celebration of Mass and, not least, take cognizance of the Mass books which had in many ways become a jungle.

According to the law then in force, the diocesan and ecclesiastical provinces were called upon to undertake such a reform provided only they did not touch the ancient traditional Roman core of the Mass book, particularly the canon. Thus the provincial synod of Trier in 1549 commanded that in all the dioceses of the province the diocesan missal alone should be standard, or if there was none, the Trier missal should. Something similar was prescribed in Mainz, along with the demand that every diocese have its missal checked and corrected by experts, so that some common arrangement might be reached in the whole province. But neither here nor in any other church province was a program, so carefully circumscribed, ever put through. The demand for the reform of the Mass book itself was expressed in the German Reichstag at Speyer in 1526, long before any synod even thought of it. The demand could not be refused.

About the same time there was hue and cry for a unified missal in which only the special diocesan saints' Masses would be added as a sort of appendix. The first such recommendation was made in Italy in 1546, and then later, more strenuously, in Spain and Portugal. But the idea was not shared everywhere. The proposals sent to the Council from France preferred internal regulation within each country, and the attitude of England during the brief period of Mary Tudor was much the same. But in the last analysis, as previous experiences had demonstrated, some sort of initiative on the part of the Church as a whole was quite indispensable.

REFORM

So the Council of Trent took up the matter. In 1546–1547, while considering the use and misuse of Holy Scriptures, it had touched on the question of the Mass book. And in 1562, in connection with the discussions regarding the doctrine of the Sacrifice of the Mass, the subject was finally taken up. A special commission was to assemble the *abusus missæ*. This task was not difficult, since sore points had been constantly marked out not only by the innovators but by the Council itself, by synods, in memorials and reform programs. Saints' sequences and prefaces with legendary content, prayers for peace, prayers in need, and various chants after the consecration, new Mass formularies of questionable origin, especially the abuses regarding Votive Masses, Mass series, and the setting aside of the order for Sundays and the Church year in favor of privately chosen formularies—these were all pointed out. Add to the list the great variety of Mass rites which, as Cardinal Hosius charged, sometimes went so far that, to the surprise and bewilderment of the people, not even in the same Church did all follow the same rite. The confusion grew all the more with the start of the Reformation era, since many priests took it upon themselves to start their own reforms. In Austria many priests even left out the canon.

The commission did not neglect any of this and even added to its collection, which was "the most comprehensive accumulation of reform ideas," a long list of minutiæ which, because they were theologically controvertible, would have to be examined and tested. They included certain expressions like *Hostia immaculata, calix salutaris* at the offertory, the crosses after the consecration, the prayers at the commingling which in Italian Mass books began with *Fiat commixtio,* the offertory of Masses for the Dead. Likewise the custom of saying private Masses in church while high Mass was going on, and the practice of saying private Masses without at least two participants present were placed amongst the disputable points. Without imposing a complete uniformity, the commission desired chiefly for the secular clergy a certain consistency, at least for the beginning and conclusion of Mass, where the greatest differences were to be found, and a certain consistency in the rubrics, especially in external ceremonial.

It stands to reason that the Council, already assembled overly long, could hardly discuss details of this sort, about which there could be many opinions. The plan of the commission had to be drawn in a second, a third and finally a fourth draught, each one shorter and more likely to obtain general acceptance. The *Decretum de observandis et evitandis in celebratione missæ,* which was passed on September 17, 1562, in the twenty-second session, as a supplement to the teaching and the canons regarding the Sacrifice of the Mass, is concerned only with the most obvious abuses and evil conditions which could be lined up under the notions of avarice, irreverence, and superstitution. The bishops should be vigilant about stipends. Mass should be celebrated only in consecrated places. Disturbing and irreverent conduct and frivolous music must be banished. The capriciousness of priests regarding rites and prayers at Mass, and the superstitious observance of numbers for fixed Masses would have to cease. There was no mention of the reform of the missal. By a decree in the twenty-fifth session this was left—along with the reform of the breviary—to the pope.

Pius IV at once (apparently in 1564) set about carrying out this decree by creating for this purpose a commission which his successor, Pius V, enlarged. Unfortunately there are no detailed reports of what the commission did. Only the product of their activity, *Missale Romanum ex decreto ss. Concilii Tridentini restitutum, Pii V. Pont. Max. iussu editum* which by a Bull of July 14, 1570, was made binding, with certain reservations, on the whole Western Church, gives us some ideas, for by comparing this composition with what was then in existence, and adding the few occasional remarks that have been handed down, we can learn something of the work done and of the aims that directed it.

The task of reform was not therefore solved by a number of ordinances and decisions by which the abuses were branded and the proper lines for creating new missals pointed out. One of the proposals sent to the Council had suggested that the regional differences in the Roman Mass and the episcopal right to regulate them be left unrestricted. But the commission took another course, by establishing the wished-for uniform missal. This uniform missal was in truth a Roman Missal, for as its basis they chose the Missal "according to the use of the Roman Curia," which already had the greatest vogue. However, this choice could not have been taken for granted, since not only was Pius V a Dominican, but members of the Dominican order, which had its own well-integrated rite, had been in the commission even before this Pope ascended the throne.

As far as the calendar and the collects and Gospels of each Mass were concerned, the new missal agreed very closely with the *Breviarium Romanum* which the same commission had produced and published just two years before—an agreement hardly to be found in previous books. For the exact rules about the choice and arrangement of each Mass formula and for the directions regarding the ritualistic aspect of the Mass, the *Rubricæ Generales Missalis* and the *Ritus servandus in celebratione Missæ* were prefaced to the new Mass book. These were taken almost bodily from the *Ordo Missæ* of the papal master of ceremonies, John Burchard of Strassburg, a work which appeared in 1502 and had meanwhile circulated widely. By this means Votive Masses were restricted to proper limits. Besides, only a few of these Masses were retained, a small selection of formularies where the danger of superstition was less likely, mostly those for each day of the week, Sundays excepted. The fear that greed might induce abuses prompted the dropping of the offertory procession which was still provided for in Burchard's *Ordo*. One practical innovation was a *Commune Sanctorum* in which not only a number of texts were included for introit, collect, etc., but complete Mass formularies were provided.

Other viewpoints which guided the reform come to light in the study of the festal calendar of the new missal. First of all, the Church year is freed somewhat from the overburden of saints' feasts which in the later

Middle Ages had increased immensely. The new missal had, in round numbers, 150 days free of feasts, not counting octaves. This was achieved by retaining only those feasts which were kept in Rome itself up to the eleventh century. Of the countless feasts later introduced, especially under the influence of the Franciscans, only a small number were preserved, and few of these of saints outside Italy.

The commission's ideal, therefore, was a return to the liturgy of the city of Rome, and indeed, the liturgy of that city as it was in former times. With this coincides the stern opposition the commission showed toward the sequences which abounded in other Mass books and amongst which—even apart from the four kept—there were genuine pearls which might have heightened the splendor of many a solemnity. But they were a modern growth and had never taken hold in Rome or Italy. Besides, their unclassical rhythm might not have suited the humanist taste of the era.

MISSAL OF PIUS V

In many places there was the intention of putting through a real reform in the sense of disengaging the basic "form" from all distorting accretion. This can be seen from the fact that already in 1563, when the correction of the missal was still being taken up by the Council, a Vatican manuscript of the Gregorian Sacramentary was sent from Rome to Trent. This was not a solitary instance. The commission, too, had investigated the ancient sources. In the Bull of July 14, 1570, introducing the new missal, Pope Pius V expressly attests that the scholars on the commission had discharged their work diligently and with the utmost care and had thus brought about the missal *ad pristinam sanctorum patrum normam ac ritum*.[2] The self-evident idea, that the development which had taken place meanwhile, separating the present from the *pristina sanctorum Patrum norma* should not be put aside as long as it did not disturb the ground-plan but rather unfolded it—that idea was never once expressed.

No one need be surprised that this high aim should have been attained only in a very limited way. Even if there had been further sources for research, one could not expect a commission composed of a few men and entrusted with a practical job, to anticipate in two years the liturgico-historical knowledge which would be attained only by the continued efforts of many students during several centuries. So much in the Mass book and in the Mass *ordo* remained unaltered and perhaps even unexamined—much that during the Franco-German period had been overlaid inartistically upon the austere form of the Mass of the city of Rome, or that had during the Gothic period found a place in the Mass books

2 "In conformity with the original norms and rite laid down by the holy Fathers."

secundum usum Romanæ Curiæ. The Mass book of this type, and therefore the traditional practice in Italy, remained the standard, in general,
for the *Ordo Missæ.* But whatever could be done with the tools of the
period, was done substantially. In particular the humanistic period had
an opportunity to leave its own trace on the work. The newer appraise-
ment of the Church Fathers was shown in the fact that, besides the
memorial days of the four Latin Fathers who were alone acknowledged
in the Middle Ages, those of the Greeks were also included. Here and
there in the literary style the humanist touch was added. Besides the
whole task of purifying the Mass book of disturbing accessories was
itself in line with the "love of humanism for the clean, the unadulterated
form." This work of purification was accomplished with remarkable
energy. The members of the commission were not held back from doing
away with added trimmings which the pious mind considered untouch-
able, like the already traditional Marian insertions in the *Gloria in
excelsis.* Finally, it was because of the humanist artistic spirit that the
Council did nothing to hinder the polyphonic Church music which
meanwhile had become strong and flourishing, and so left the road open
for the great masterpieces of Church music.

To have gone farther and deeper, say in the direction of a restoration
of a stronger communion between priest and people, would have demanded different spiritual conditions among the faithful. It was understandable that a preference was felt for things which even in their
traditional form had a meaning and a solid foundation, and not for
exorbitant and often heretical pretensions of reformational polemics,
particularly since their supporters had refused to take part in the Council. Clear limits were here the thing that was essential. One exception
was made in the case of the chalice for the laity; the experiences were
not favorable. For that reason the dogmatic chapters of the Council did
not confine themselves to putting down errors. They tried to focus
attention once more on the grand outlines of the Christian sacrificial
celebration, even to the point where they recommended that the faithful
receive Communion each time they came to Mass, a notion far removed
from the practice of the day.

The greatest and most consequential innovation of the Mass book of
Pius V was the enactment, clearly expressed in the Bull of introduction,
that this book was to be, from then on, the standard in every church
and that no changes were to be made therein. Only churches which
could demonstrate a two-hundred years' custom for their own usage,
were permitted to retain that usage. This was the case with the ancient
orders which since the eleventh century had produced their own variants of the Romano-Frankish Mass-liturgy and which have kept them,
for the most part, till the present. Many dioceses also took advantage
of this stipulation, among them—besides Milan and the remnant of the

Mozarabic rite—Trier, Cologne, Liége, Braga and Lyons, of which only the last two have kept their own rite until now.

CONGREGATION OF RITES

Such a broad and sweeping unification could never have been completely accomplished before the day of the printing press. Even as things stood, there were bound to be many doubts and problems resulting from such widely diverse conditions and local customs, not to speak of the difficulties of making the change. To handle these doubts and problems, Pope Sixtus V, by the Constitution "Immensa" of January 22, 1588, founded the Congregation of Rites. Its charge was to see to it that everywhere in the Latin Church the prescribed manner of celebrating Mass and performing the other functions of the liturgy were carefully followed. It had to settle doubts, to give out dispensations and privileges, and, since there was always a chance of introducing new feasts, it had to provide the proper formularies for them. On the other hand it was not in the ordinary power of the Congregation to change the rubrics or alter the wording of prayers. Thus the Congregation of Rites was not to be an organ for liturgical evolution. In so far as such a development might occur within the narrow limits left for it, the Congregation was to act as a regulator, charged with the duty of seeing that the status of things established by the Missal of Pius V be in no way altered or endangered. To regulate new questions in accordance with existing ordinances, that was the task fulfilled by the decrees of the Sacred Congregation of Rites which have appeared since 1588. Almost half of these have to do with the Mass-liturgy and its requisite concomitants. Few of these decrees, however, provide any new regulations for the rites of the Mass itself. The chief ones are the stipulation of certain reverences, the decree that the chalice be covered after the Communion just as it was at the start of the Mass, the casuistic regulation of the order in which various saints are to be mentioned in the oration *A cunctis*, and who is the *antistes* to be named in the canon.

A greater number of the decisions dealt with the various circumstances around the Mass; the proper hour for celebrating it, consideration of locale in choosing the formulary, the *applicatio pro populo*, bination, removal of defects. Many decrees refer to special questions about high Mass or pontifical Mass, or to peculiarities incident to services with celebrants of various ranks, or to the reverence to be made when handing the celebrant the sprinkler (*aspergillum*), or when offering the Gospel book to be kissed, or at the incensings or at the *pax*. Or they refer to the function of the assistant priest and other assistants, or to the choir rules at a conventual Mass, or to the limitations regarding the use of chant and organ. Many are devoted to the various kinds of Votive

Masses and to the Requiem and how the conflicting wishes of those who set up the foundation or ordered the Masses might be reconciled with the arrangements of the Church year. And finally, the changes in the Mass rite occasioned by the course of the Church year. Very many of the decrees settle an open abuse or decide an anxious question with the simple reply: *serventur rubricae.*

Some real changes since the sixteenth century in the rubrics and in the text of the Missal of Pius V have resulted in certain instances from papal orders. For instance, in the new edition of the missal under Clement VIII (1604), the biblical chant pieces, which in some printings had been arbitrarily changed in favor of the new Vulgate, were restored to their original state, and new regulations were made regarding the final blessing. In another new edition of the Mass book under Urban VIII (1634), the wording of the rubrics was greatly improved and the revision of the hymns already accomplished in the breviary was carried out also in the few hymns of the missal. No new edition with any notable changes came out till that of 1920 which contained the revisions based on the reform of Pope Pius X. For the rest, excepting the increase in saints' feasts, very little was done to affect the arrangement of the Mass. Pope Clement XIII prescribed the Preface of the Holy Trinity for Sundays, and Pope Leo XIII ordered the prayers said after low Mass.

On the other hand, despite the force of general regulation, some rubrics, under pressure of custom, have dropped out of practice—the use of the *Sanctus* candle, for instance, and the rule that at the distribution of Communion each communicant should partake of the *purificatio.* (*Ritus servandus,* X, 6, 9.)

All in all, the changes thus made within the Mass-liturgy are very few indeed. After fifteen hundred years of unbroken development in the rite of the Roman Mass, after the rushing and the streaming from every height and out of every valley, the Missal of Pius V was indeed a powerful dam holding back the waters or permitting them to flow through only in firm, well-built canals. At one blow all arbitrary meandering to one side or another was cut off, all floods prevented, and a safe, regular and useful flow assured. But the price paid was this, that the beautiful river valley now lay barren and the forces of further evolution were often channeled into the narrow bed of a very inadequate devotional life instead of gathering strength for new forms of liturgical expression.

13. The Mass in the Baroque Period, the Enlightenment and the Restoration

Due to the reform of 1570, the divine worship of the Church became refined and purified. Since the new Mass book was not only declared binding everywhere, but also withdrawn from all regional initiative, the Roman Mass entered into a condition of rigidity and fixation, even though this stiffening was not set down as necessarily permanent. To take the place of a development of existing things, prominence was given to the juristic and casuistic discussion of established norms. A special branch of knowledge was developed for this purpose, the science of rubrics. In fact someone has styled this period of liturgical history beginning with Pius V as the epoch of inactivity or of rubrics!

However, it is hard to say whether in the period to follow, this circumstance was good fortune or bad. What would have happened to the Roman liturgy if the various irenic tendencies had taken a path of development closer to that trodden by Protestant worship? Or if the creative spirit of the Baroque had been allowed to tamper with the rite of the Mass as fully as did the Middle Ages, handling it according to its own conceptions of sacrament, sacrifice and solemnity?

In reality, *the Baroque period was but little concerned with the liturgical form of the celebration of Mass.* The contrast between the Baroque spirit and that of the traditional liturgy was so great that they were two vastly different worlds. The new life-spirit which would wrap earth and heaven in one whirling tempest—how different from the quiet dignity of the old Roman orations. More than this: theological and religious thought, caught up in the swirl of the Counter-Reformation, was as different from the old Roman tradition as it is possible to be, granted the basis of the same Catholic faith. No one who learns to know the intellectual situation of the time will make it a matter of reproach that the period had found no closer tie to the liturgy.

Through the controversy with the Reformers, the whole stress of thought on the Eucharist was directed to and bound down to the Real Presence, almost to the neglect of other aspects. Even for the scientific treatment of the liturgy which now began, how much the defense of the eucharistic mysteries stood in the foreground is seen in the fact that Muratori, who issued a careful edition of the older sacramentaries, devoted the greater part of the introductory study to a discussion of this dogma as revealed in the liturgical texts. A detailed re-evaluation of the sacrificial character of the Eucharist resulted from the efforts of a new blossoming of Scholastic study. But these studies were likewise aroused by the Protestants' impugning of the dogma and consequently more or less determined by it. Since the greatest concern was Christ's oblation which is constantly realized and re-realized without hurt to the singleness of the Christian sacrifice, and since no interest was felt for the offering through the Church, of which the prayers of the Roman Mass speak, these studies too merely skirted the edge of the liturgy. Thus the spirit of the times forced into the background any notion that the faithful had a part to play in the prayer of the priest or that they should co-offer in closer union with him. For, since the Reformers had denied a special priesthood, it seemed necessary to stress not what was common and connective between priest and people, but rather what was distinctive and separative. This was certainly the case in the Society of Jesus whose theologians were leaders in the intellectual movement of this period; its members had no close contact with the liturgy and did nothing towards a pastoral development of liturgical possibilities. True, the Ignatian *Exercises*, with their definite theocentricity and their conscious alliance to Christ, appeared to harmonize most favorably with liturgical prayer and thought, but the circumstances of the time did not permit this germ to bud forth—in fact, they acted quite the contrary.

But an important step toward realizing what the Mass had to offer was taken in the French Oratory of Cardinal Pierre de Bérulle (d. 1629). On the basis of meditation on the Word made flesh and of His complete lifelong dedication to the Father, worship was established from the start as the center of piety. Private prayer was deliberately allied to public liturgy. In fact participation in the oblation of Christ gradually became the fundamental concept of piety in the school of Bérulle, of Condren (d. 1641) and of Olier (d. 1657). Thus in regard to the Mass, the sacrifice of the Church and with it the liturgical side of the sacrifice became more prominent. During this period, one of the best explanations of the Mass came from the circle of the Oratory. The invitation was given to the people to draw closer to the priest's action. Similar attempts, be it said in passing, were not absolutely lacking in Germany.

But efforts of this sort did not at the time gain a favorable reception. Apparently fearing that an effort was being made to introduce the vernacular into the Mass, Alexander VII had in 1661 condemned a translation of the Roman Missal into French and had forbidden any further translations under pain of excommunication. The strict idea which had already obtained in the Middle Ages was thus increased. Rome took, and continued to take, the stand that the Latin Mass prayers were not to be given to the faithful in any way, although nowhere was this formulated in a general Church law. In harmony with such a misconception, was another fundamental notion, that the faithful would reverence the liturgy of the Mass more if the veil of mystery were kept around it. The old idea of the canon as a sanctuary which only the priest could enter thus survived and was in fact extended to the whole Mass. There was therefore little chance of encouraging a closer participation in the priest's celebration, and in any case this approach was left to the devotion of each individual. All these endeavors made hardly any impression on the general picture of the divine service at this time.

On the other hand, it is the heritage of the Middle Ages, purified and refined by the Tridentine reform, which really determines the religious picture of the Baroque period as well as the picture of its religious service. The great abuses have all disappeared. But still the Mass remains a service in which only the priest and his assistants have an active role. The faithful follow the divine action only from a distance. As in the late Middle Ages, an effort is made to foster their devotion by bringing certain more general features of the Mass closer to them—its worth, its fruits, its imaging of the Passion of Christ. The old themes are thus the standard.

THEOLOGICAL DEEPENING

But there are plain traces of a deepening effected by the theology of Trent. The essence is more distinctly laid in the sacrifice and by preference unfolded on the basis of the four aims of sacrifice. The fruits of the Mass are spiritualized and the representation of our Lord's life and sufferings is no longer culled from the individual ceremonies but connected with the celebration only in their great phases. Allegorizing is not yet dead, but in an age already nearing empiricism and scientific study it has lost most of its strength. No longer does it satisfy the people. It can no longer so shackle the minds of the faithful that they are able to follow the action in silence. Those who during the Counter-Reformation attempted to rebuild religious life had to look for other ways and means to enable the faithful to participate in a devout manner. Of course, judging from what we have said, these ways and means could only be stopgap measures, filling in what the Middle Ages had to offer, since there were too many obstacles in the way of a closer approach to the priest's prayer.

Amongst these ways and means was *the prayer book* which, after the advent of the printing press, had gained in importance at least for people with some education. It is true there is at first only a slight inducement to any participation in Holy Mass, since the prayer book originated chiefly from the Book of Hours with its extra-eucharistic prayer material. In the early stage it generally appears in the form of one of the traditional allegorical explanations of the Mass, but formulated prayers are also offered. Aside from the elevation of the species at the consecration, these prayers for the most part follow the course of the Mass along very general lines, and even when the prayers are more or less faithful to the missal text, the fundamental rule still holds that the canon must be excluded.

The masses, however, were not reached by the prayer book. A genuine interest in souls, however, did hit upon a plan of overcoming the estrangement of those who attended Mass without really taking part in it—namely, common prayers and singing. This method had often been chosen since the beginning of the eighteenth century, especially during the popular missions of the Jesuits. Thus they started, in certain instances even on the occasion of a common celebration, to have a low Mass but accompanied by prayers said out loud. In the prayer texts employed in such cases, one cannot expect any closer approach to the liturgy than was to be found in the prayer books. Quite often, it appears, the rosary was used, with or without additions. Inadequate as such an attendance at Mass might seem to us in the light of our own superior methods, it must be conceded that, in common with the allegorizing of the Mass, it offered the contemplation of the mysteries of Redemption, and offered it, moreover, in a way comprehensible to the people, and with the advantages of congregational participation.

There is somewhat more consideration of the course of the liturgy in the *German Mass-songs* which begin to gain in significance about this time. In their beginning in the Middle Ages, these songs did not manifest any close regard for the liturgy; a continued series of verses unfolded the meaning of the Mass as a memorial of the Passion and as a sacrifice, and interspersed appropriate petitions. A short time later the custom appears of singing a song at the *Credo* and at the sermon, and of inserting into the sequence strophes in the German tongue. The cultivation of German ecclesiastical song by the Reformers could not remain without its repercussions on the Catholic side. Canisius continually spoke out warmly for German church song. In the sixteenth century we again find not only the song at the sermon but likewise (since the sequence had practically disappeared) a song in the vernacular at the gradual. Besides these, there was also a song at the offertory and at the communion, or one after the *Sanctus* or after the consecration. These do not appear to be anything but pre-Reformation growths which at that time sprang up into stronger life and spread out over a wider area.

The Cantual of Mainz (1605) contains a fixed plan for singing in German in churches in which non-Latin song had long been customary. The Cantual first makes a reference which is very significant for the changes in men's minds, namely, that many of the laity had a greater desire to sing than to meditate on Christ's Passion, as they did of old, by praying from their prayer books or on their rosaries; and because it often happens that there are not enough singers for the chant, the Cantual goes on to outline a plan for the sung-Mass (*Singampt*). According to this arrangement, German hymns could be inserted even at a Latin Mass, especially in place of the chants of the Proper, namely, instead of the gradual, the offertory, and likewise after the *Agnus Dei* and also during the Communion. Besides, one could also insert a hymn in honor of the Blessed Sacrament after the consecration. The Cantual also gives directions for singing German hymns during a low Mass: The singing should stop at the Gospel, at the elevation, and at the final blessing. From then on, these directions are repeated in various places.

If certain starts were thus given to a communal celebration of Mass that reached down to the people, still in all these instances, as can be plainly seen, there was little thought of following the course of the Mass except within very modest limits. The liturgy of the Mass stands before the faithful in all its splendor, but it is a splendor whose greatness is self-contained and whose arrangement is as immutable as it is puzzling; and in the midst shines the blessed Sacrament, a precious pewel for which this traditional setting appeared just, right, and necessary.

MASS AND BAROQUE CULTURE

Indeed, the Mass was actually treated as self-contained even where it appeared in its festive form and where a Baroque culture could share with it its own riches. The mighty Baroque sermon was extended before the Mass whenever it did not lay claims to its own hours as it might rightfully have. And when it did find its way into the Mass, it seemed to burst beyond its limits, so that it seldom had any connection with the Gospel. Since the Middle Ages the site of the pulpit had gradually been altered, moved generally away from the altar and further into the nave. Like the sermon, it grew independent. The Communion of the faithful took place as a rule *after* the Mass, and *not* after the parochial Mass but rather—because of the law of fasting—after one of the early Masses. As far as frequency went, this was once more on the increase. But Communion was an independent, self-contained exercise, looked upon not as a participation in the sacrifice but simply as a reception of our Lord present continually in the Sacrament.

What has been said holds true also for church music at this time. Here, too, the Mass was treated as self-contained. Music spread its gorgeous mantle over the whole Mass, so that the other details of the rite scarcely had any significance. Encouraged by the moderate attitude of the Council of Trent, it had developed into mighty proportions. The seventeenth and eighteenth centuries are marked by a plethora of new musical forms. Besides the organ, there were accompaniments by other instruments, growing ever richer, more gorgeous. And often a single many-voiced choir was not sufficient, but use was made of several choirs either answering each other or even blending together. The history of music, therefore, makes mention of a particular "splendid" style which was formed during this period. The victorious temper of the post-Tridentine age, which once more felt the courage to absorb the entire wealth of the contemporary culture into the Catholic cosmos—that temper found its triumphal voice in this music.

It is significant that the princely courts, both great and small, were the first places where this type of church music was cultivated and where it reached its splendor. Because of the religio-cultural situation it sometimes happened that this church music, which had fallen more and more into the hands of laymen, forgot that it was meant to subserve the liturgical action. As a result of this, the music often fitted very poorly into the liturgical setting. And since this latter was but little understood, and because esthetic consideration began to hold sway, the liturgy was not only submerged under this ever-growing art but actually suppressed, so that even at this time there were festive occasions which might best be described as "church concerts with liturgical accompaniment." Even the connection with a text was taken very ill by music such as this. Texts which could be chosen at random—as was permitted after the elevation—were transferred to other places in the Mass, and the Proper especially was replaced by some such songs. On the other side, the celebrant often tried to continue with the offertory even while the choir was still singing the *Credo*, or to restrict the singing of the preface and *Pater noster* to the initial words so as to leave the rest for the music and the organ. Thus singing, too, had freed itself from the liturgical bonds and achieved independence.

The place taken by the choir corresponds to this new situation—not in the *choir* from which it derives its name, but far away, on the boundary between the world and the church, in the organ-loft.

The development in the field of music made it really possible to "hear" the Mass. In fact on festival occasions the hearing of polyphonic pieces—which demanded no activity whatever on the part of the congregation—cast all other sensations into shadow. But in ecclesiastical Baroque the eye, too, was satisfied. Looking at the Host at the consecration no longer possessed the attraction and significance that it had towards the end of the Middle Ages. The new age sought not the sight of the holy, but the sight of the beautiful in art and universe. And so the church became a great hall, its walls shimmering with marble and gold. The paintings on the ceilings, which grew right out of the plaster of the entablature, made the room appear to fade away into heavenly glory. The *presbyterium* is hardly any longer distinct from the nave, and along with the latter it mounts upwards, by force of the cupola or dome, into a higher unity. At its base the glance falls on the mighty structure of the high altar in which the design of the Gothic altar-piece has been reconstructed architecturally. The prominent thing in this structure is the altar-piece itself, perhaps also the exposition throne for the Blessed Sacrament, and finally the tabernacle which has become part and parcel of the plan. By contrast, what really makes the altar an altar, the *mensa*, is not given the prominence it deserves. Its significance appears to have suffered, just as in Baroque polyphony the liturgical action suffered. The interior of the church has become a great hall filled with sensuous life. Even the galleries and boxes are there. And the liturgy itself is conceived of as a play, to be looked at and listened to. But it is no longer—as it was in the Middle Ages—the Mass itself with its succession of ceremonies which bears this dramatic character. Only the adoration of our Lord at the consecration retains its position as the dominating climax. Indeed, the adoration and glorification of the Sacrament, which had been so outrageously attacked by the Reformers, now stands so prominently in the foreground that one is almost bound to look upon the Mass in general chiefly from this point of view. The catechism of J. M. Kettler which appeared at Würzburg in 1734 treats the Mass as one of the five ways in which to worship Christ in the Sacrament. It is no wonder, then, that eucharistic devotion, especially the Forty Hours and the grand processions, vied with the Mass in splendor and in the fervor of attendance, and that in many countries it became the rule more and more to expose the Blessed Sacrament during Mass as an enhancement of the celebration, especially on feast days. This type of piety achieved at this very time its highest artistic manifestation and, at the same time, the proof of its power in the *autos sacramentales* of Spanish poetry.

REACTION

That the manner of celebrating Mass in the post-Tridentine era did not correspond in every respect to the deep mystery and especially to the faithfully guarded form of its Roman vesture could not even then remain hidden from everyone. The advent of the Reformers had not only awakened a theology of controversy but had also necessitated a closer and deeper study of the writings of the Fathers and of the life of the ancient Church. Along with the writings of the Fathers the old liturgical texts came to light—the sacramentaries, the *ordines*—and with them a picture of a divine service which, far and wide, had embraced the entire Christian people in the community of celebration. This picture easily became a pattern and model. Knowledge became a spur to make some attempt—on one's own initiative—in the direction which was deemed, or at least poetically painted, as the ideal. There were few restraints in the way of this attempt, at least where the relationship to the government of the Church Universal had become slack either because of dogmatic differences as in the circles of Jansenism, or because of canonical and legal disagreements as in Gallicanism, or finally because of a novel view of Christendom which de-emphasized the supernatural in favor of the natural, as in the Enlightenment. So various attempts were made at improvement, but even in the good and worthwhile things that they contained they were burdened by this double difficulty, that they worked on their own and that they were stimulated by questionable motives, so that they were from the outset bound inevitably to fail.

It was not a good omen when one of the first to take up the slogan that simple people were not to be deprived of the consolation of lifting their voices in union with the voice of the entire Church, was Pasquier

Quesnel. Soon after his appearance the endeavor was made in France to have the canon prayed aloud, but an episcopal prohibition was passed against this for the first time in 1698. In a new printing of the Missal of Meaux in the year 1709 there suddenly appeared in the canon and in some other places a red-printed *R* just before the Amen; the people were thus expected to respond to each prayer section, and this presupposed that the praying was done aloud. A lengthy battle ensued regarding this inconspicuous but yet not unimportant innovation. The ominous letter had to disappear. In the year 1736 a Missal of Troyes carried this notice regarding the praying of the canon: *submissa voce;* it sought thus to retain the rubric in a mitigated form. According to the same authority, the prayers before the distribution of Communion, from the *Confiteor* to the *Domine non sum dignus*—which had formerly been said in the Mass—were to be left out. And the priest was no longer obliged to repeat softly to himself the chants and readings which had formerly been performed aloud. There were also in this Mass book as in the Paris Mass book of 1684, attempts along another path, to substitute biblical texts for the non-biblical song texts. The former directions had to be rescinded, in accordance with a governmental decree which the then archbishop of Sens obtained in 1738. But editions of the missal which made changes in the texts of the *Proprium* continued to appear and, following the example of Paris, were finally adopted in more than fifty dioceses.

DISSATISFACTION

Later, but more pretentiously, the feeling of dissatisfaction with the traditional forms of the divine service found expression elsewhere. It was especially in Germany, where the baroque had had its greatest development in ecclesiastical life, that the reaction was strongest after the development had lost its strength. This occurred during the Enlightenment. The desire was to get free from all excess of emotions, free from all surfeit of forms; to get back again to "noble simplicity." As in contemporary art, where the model for this was sought in antiquity and attained in classicism, so in ecclesiastical life the model was perceived in the life of the ancient Church. And so a sort of Catholic classicism was arrived at, a sudden enthusiasm for the liturgical forms of primitive Christianity, forms which in many cases one believed could be taken over bodily, despite the interval of a thousand years and more, and despite the fact that one was far removed from the spirit of that age.

One group of liturgists in the Enlightenment absolutely misjudged the essence of the liturgy and wanted to make of divine service a human service designed for instruction and moral admonition. Others desired only to set aside disturbing non-essentials and to bring into prominence an outline of the celebration of the Mass which would consolidate the congregation. The whole community should assemble in the parish church; here one Mass, and only one Mass should be celebrated. After the Gospel there was to be a sermon, and after the priest's Communion the Communion of the faithful. Instrumental music was not to be allowed, or at most only on great feast-days. As much as possible the people themselves were to accompany the sacred ceremony with singing in the vernacular or even with prayer, which, however, should correspond to that of the priest. The common recitation of the rosary during Mass was censured. These demands are repeated in the pastoral theology of the period with almost wearisome uniformity. They are demands in which one would hardly say an ecclesiastical spirit was wanting. Other wishes which often reappear are for an increase in the frequency of Communion, for a decrease in altars, for the turning of the altar towards the people, for greater restraint in the exposition of the Blessed Sacrament. The offertory procession, the kiss of peace, and concelebration are also proposed as the objects of reform.

ATTEMPTS AT POPULAR PARTICIPATION

In all of these desires for change, one point plainly recurs time and again, and that is that the participation of the faithful had reached a certain critical stage. The faithful ought not only to be present at Mass but ought to be able to follow along. Concern over this matter was practically as old as the split between the vernacular and the liturgical language. The solution adopted for many centuries, the allegorical interpretation, is no longer considered; it is not even mentioned. The ornamentation of the Mass with rousing music is hardly a more practical remedy than the common praying of the rosary, which appears to have become quite extensive at the daily celebration of Mass. So new ways had to be sought. One substitute would be the thorough instruction of the faithful. Prayer books would have to be distributed in which the Mass prayers are offered in faithful translation. For a similar reason, praying and singing in common should be practiced. But ultimately one had to acknowledge that for a closer coordination between the people and the liturgy the language was the great stumbling-block. This was a time when Latin, which had already for a long time ceased to be the means of communication between the cultured, no longer served as the language of learned literature. Therefore the desire was expressed time after time for a more or less extensive use of the vernacular, especially where the priest turns to the people. A reference to 1 Cor. 14:16 f.[1] often recurs. Still no one was blind to the value of Latin, any more than to the

---

[1] "Else if thou givest praise with the spirit alone, how shall he who fills the place of the uninstructed say 'amen' to thy thanksgiving? For he does not know what thou sayest."

limits of the advantages which a language change could produce. Indeed there were continual warnings against any arbitrary procedure and a demand for deference to ecclesiastical superiors.

While other points in the program of the liturgists of the Enlightenment left no traces in the devotional life of the subsequent period, their work in one field was crowned with lasting success, namely, in the field of German church-song. As we have already seen, it had been customary even in the previous centuries under certain circumstances to accompany the celebration of Mass with singing in the vernacular. But now there was inaugurated a certain systematic promotion of popular church singing, which led eventually to the formation of the German *Singmesse*. German songs replaced not only the variable chants of the Proper but also those of the Ordinary which up till now had continued current here and there in their Latin text and with their ancient chant melodies even amongst the people. The Paderborn Hymnal of 1726 contains German songs for the *Gloria, Sanctus, Agnus Dei*; finally the Speyer Hymnal of 1770 contains a *Singmesse* with German selections for all parts of the Ordinary. The best known example from this period is the *Singmesse "Hier liegt vor deiner Majestat"* (Here before thy majesty lies), which appears with a first melody in the Landshut Hymnal of 1777 and which, after acquiring a new set of melodies by Michael Haydn (d. 1806) continues in use even today.

Just as the first attempts to introduce German singing into the Mass-liturgy dealt with a service in which the priest continued to sing his part at the altar, so also in the eighteenth century no one had any misgivings about combining the new *Singmesse* with a chanted Mass as well as with a low Mass. That is plainly to be seen especially from the prefaces in the hymnals. A circumstance which might have urged some such solution was the situation in which country choirs found themselves at that time— a situation even now not entirely overcome. The many-voiced church music performed at the court churches and the large city churches had become the fashion, a fashion which was followed even in the country, although with inadequate resources. Therefore a simple song in the vernacular actually appeared to deserve the preference, more especially since the ecclesiastical prescriptions regarding the language of the accompanying singing were not then so precise and the liturgical books generally left the question quite open. Thus a German high Mass came into common use and as a result of a custom already in vogue it remained in use, especially in North German dioceses, all through the nineteenth century and right down to the present.

This type of service employed at sung Mass appears to have been carried over to the low Mass only secondarily. As a matter of fact the German *Singmesse*—the term was now by preference applied to this latter case—gave somewhat the impression of a one-sided conversation, for not only the orations but the readings (or at least the Epistle) and the preface and *Pater noster*, none of them unimportant parts in the structure of the Mass, do not receive any kind of expression. That there was no mention of any of the changeable chants of the *Proprium* was again a carry-over from the high Mass that was then current and is to a great extent still current. But, this much must be conceded, that in the German *Singmesse* a form of celebrating the Mass had been found which was both popular and dignified, a form moreover which was nowhere in contradiction to existing legal prescriptions; for with regard to the method of accompanying a *missa lecta* with prayer and song the fullest liberty reigned, and still reigns. It was a form by which the people could not only understand the action of the priest but also to a certain extent actively follow. It was a form in which, through singing in common, the community consciousness was aroused, and indeed imbued with a certain degree of solemnity. No wonder that in many dioceses the German *Singmesse* gradually won great popularity. That this did not occur more quickly was due in part to the violent methods by which its introduction was effected in many places, in part also to the weaknesses of content which the creations of the period of Enlightenment so frequently displayed.

RESTORATION

The weaknesses and mistakes with which the Enlightenment proved to be burdened, in other fields more plainly perhaps than in the liturgy, turned out to be the reason why a reaction was bound to set in, a return to the complete affirmation of dogma and the supernatural, to a respect for the hierarchic structure of the Church and for tradition. A Catholic *Restoration* was bound to come. The excessive enthusiasm for reform reached an end. The older arrangements were once more honored, including the arrangement of the celebration of Mass, just as a former generation had found it, with all its excellencies and, to a great extent with all its deficiencies. No one wanted to listen to critical voices. Even the healthy reform aims of the older period—many of which were to be taken up, a century later, by the highest authority in the Church—were looked upon with suspicion because they had emanated from the epoch of the Enlightenment.

Still by teaching respect for the existing liturgy, this period of Catholic Restoration did begin the necessary preparation for a healthier and more blessed resumption of these former strivings at a later time. The beauty of the Latin prayers, the dignity of the ceremonies, the harmony of the whole conglomerate—all these were extolled. Enthusiasm developed once more for Gregorian Chant and for all vocal art based on the chant after the manner of Palestrina.

It was in the field of church music that the Restoration set to work most visibly to remodel the divine service. The works of the Baroque period which had found in the liturgy only an occasion for unfolding a musical splendor that was all too worldly and which often bore no relationship to the seriousness of the liturgical text and the liturgical mystery —from these one turned aside. An effort was made to bring the unabbreviated words of the sacred songs into their rightful place. War was declared on the amalgamation of songs in the vernacular with the Latin service, which now frequently returned in its pure unadulterated form. The Cæcilian movement made the relevant demands and principles common property of the widest circles, and succeeded in introducing even in country churches many-voiced Latin singing in place of the German Mass-songs.[2]

But this movement had one drawback; the people at Mass were once more—and this time more consciously than ever—reduced to the role of spectators, and the attempt to reveal the Latin liturgy to the faithful was turned aside partly as a matter of principle. The Mass-liturgy was, for the leaders who espoused this tendency, a monument, finished and fixed once and for all, a monument which in its mystery-filled objectivity not only did not take the faithful into consideration but even shut off their every approach. Therefore the liturgy is praised as a finished art-product, as a wondrous work of the Holy Spirit, and it is almost forgotten that in the service of this higher master, human hands had been at work through the centuries, probing and fumbling and not always very happily, endeavoring to make the eternally incomplete as fit for its purpose as they possibly could.

In such a treatment of the liturgy we recognize the expression of a time grown tired, a time which is accustomed, with every technical skill, to measure the tasks of intellectual culture, not by an independent judgment of things themselves but by comparison with certain finished patterns which thus passed muster as an unalterable canon. This was the age which started out in classicism, following the traces of classical antiquity, an age which in matters ecclesiastical considered Gothic the ideal in architecture, Raffaele and Perugino in painting, and Palestrina in music. It is an age in which our churches began to be filled with imitations and in which the liturgy of the Mass, by and large unquestionably wonderful, was crystallized in a framework that was utterly unworthy of it.

The intellectual backgrounds of this phase of evolution will be made more plainly visible by a consideration of the parallel phenomena in the French area. In Abbot Prosper Guéranger, founder of Solesmes (1833)

2 For the decision of the Third Plenary Council of Baltimore (1884) regarding Chant, and for other early evidences of an American "liturgical movement" see Wm. Busch, "The Voice of a Plenary Council," *Orate Fratres*, XXI (1946–47), 452–458.

and renovator of the monastic ideal, there arose an implacable adversary of the so-called neo-Gallican liturgies, or to speak more exactly, of the arbitrary changes introduced into the Roman Missal and Breviary. He demanded an uncompromising return to the books of the pure Roman liturgy, and was so successful in carrying this out all along the line that in many dioceses even the Propers which were ancient and traditional were swept by the board. By 1860 the Roman Missal and the Roman Breviary without any additions had once more been reintroduced nearly everywhere.

Here, too, it is the spirit of the Catholic Restoration which stands behind the movement. At the same time, however, the opposition to the previous generation's deification of reason took on, in one strong group, the form of traditionalism. This became the teaching that, in general, man can achieve all higher knowledge, not through the labor of his own reason, but only from tradition, and in the last analysis from an original revelation. Tradition and authority, as opposed to every individual project and all private initiative, thus acquired an unconscionably great importance. This attitude was prominent already in the case of Joseph de Maistre. And young Guéranger, too, paid homage to this spirit. He had picked it up in the circle of Lamennais and in his work with him. After Lamennais' condemnation Guéranger definitely broke with him, but the unsparing fight against the liturgical independence of the French bishops which he had opened up in Lamennais' publication, he continued to the end in the same spirit in which he had started it. Guéranger therefore stood squarely for the persistence of the existing Roman liturgy and a veneration for it that set aside any critical consideration. In spite of his great work on the Church year he did not favor an unrestricted elucidation of liturgical texts and practices for the people; for the Christian multitude the liturgy should instead remain wrapped under a veil of mystery.

14. The Mass since Pius X

Notwithstanding the shadows that envelop even a figure like Dom Prosper Guéranger, it was from him and from what he established that the most momentous impulses proceeded for that intense rapprochement of the liturgy to the people and for that far-reaching reorganization of divine service which we witness today. Reverent and loving submersion in actualities has at last proved to be a blessing, thanks to the wealth that lies buried deep in the liturgy. *It led to a knowledge of the ways and means to bridge, at least in some scant manner, the thousand-year old cleft between the Mass-liturgy and the people, without using allegory and also without any fundamental changes.*

First of all, the *opus Dei* as performed in the new centers of monasticism, dignified, replete with the spirit of adoration, became a drama in the best sense of the word, drawing to itself the eyes of all. The products of Beuronese art soon gave it a visible background. Gregorian Chant, too, was refurbished. There were many differences to be found in the various editions and even at Rome there was no obligatory norm regarding the use and execution of the chant, but at Solesmes it was made the object of learned study, so that its true form in the flourishing period, as discovered in the manuscripts, was once more re-established. These studies received the highest recognition under Pius X, who had already in early life been influenced by the Benedictine movement for the renewal of chant, and who, as Pope, utilized the results of the labors of Solesmes as the basis of his efforts for the restoration of chant and for the new authentic editions of the chant books (*Editio Vaticana*). The chants of the *Ordinarium missæ* appeared in 1905, the complete *Graduale* by 1907. Already in the very first year of his pontificate, on November 22, 1903, the *Motu Proprio* on church music had appeared, calling attention to the dignity of Gregorian Chant, encouraging the participation of the people in its rendition, but also developing the norms for a polyphony and a harmonized music that is ready to serve in the sacred celebration.

ENDEAVORS OF PIUS X

Under Pius X, too, other endeavors, which in the nineteenth century had resulted in a deeper search into the treasures of the Church's heritage, began to bear fruit in the life of Christian worship. Not in vain had the life of the ancient Church been lifted out of the darkness of the catacombs. Not in vain had a more intense study of patristic literature been inaugurated. Not in vain had a revival of Scholasticism brought honor once more to an uncurtailed affirmation of dogma and of the Sacrament. Since the middle of the nineteenth century voices had been raised more and more confidently to seek for a return of the practice of the ancient Church regarding Communion, and to point to the natural conclusion of the Mass in the Communion of the faithful. Thus the ground was somewhat prepared for the decree *On frequent and even daily Communion* which appeared in 1905, marking a milestone in liturgical history even more important than the decrees of the same pope which were more directly liturgical.

At first glance the decree seemed to have little relation to liturgical affairs. It had indeed in its very first words (*Sacra Tridentina synodus*) alluded to the wish of the Council of Trent that the faithful receive Communion at Mass not only spiritually but also sacramentally. But for the rest, it had not gone into the connection between Mass and Communion at all, but had restricted itself to setting forth and analyzing the value and the conditions of frequent Communion. If you read through the religious periodicals in the years following the publication of the decree, conning the articles that urged frequent Communion, you will see that at first the liturgical connection hardly played any role at all in their arguments. For generations men had been accustomed to regard Communion as an exercise complete in itself, and everywhere, in town and country, in the convent and in the parish church, Communion was distributed each day, perhaps, but always before or after Mass. After a few years had passed, however, the realization began to grow that this Communion movement could last only if Communion were fitted into some larger entity and became fully integrated in the organization of Christian life—if it took its rightful and natural place within the Mass.

Here it was, then, that the *Communion movement came into contact with the liturgical movement*, a decade or so after the appearance of the decree. And the latter kept making these facts plainer and more manifest: the offering to God in the sacrifice is the proper preparation for Holy Communion; the sacrificial meal belongs to the sacrifice, God invites us to it; all the prayers of the Mass lead up to it; and this meal is at the same time the meal of the Christian community. The Eucharist once more appears in a new light. The ancient and more complete symbolism gradually creeps back into Christian consciousness; the simple cult of adoration, already shaken by the decree on Communion loses its dominance. After another decade these realizations begin to have an effect on parochial life: Communion once more stands in its natural liturgical relationship as a conscious participation in the Holy Sacrifice. From the viewpoint of liturgical history that was a very important step, and it was not the only one.

LITURGICAL MOVEMENT

The liturgical movement, which, especially in its first beginnings was almost entirely a movement promoting the Mass, had come closer to the Mystery of the altar also from another angle. When the movement—a closed movement embracing wider circles—suddenly came into being in Belgium only to spread at once into Germany and other countries, it made itself manifest, above all, by a new way of participating in the celebration of Mass. Growing out of the intellectual movement of the past decade, it had still to overcome many obstacles. The first thing that demanded solution, even if it was not formally expressed, was the question whether the separation between people and celebrating priest, maintained for more than a thousand years, was to be continued. It was certainly continued in law by the prohibition to translate the Mass books. Efforts had been made to shake this prohibition, but even as late as 1857 the prohibition to translate the Ordinary of the Mass was renewed by Pius IX, although, to be sure, its enforcement was no longer seriously urged. However, it was not openly and definitely rescinded until near the end of the century. In the revision of the *Index of Forbidden Books*, issued under Leo XIII in 1897, the prohibition was no longer mentioned. After that the spread of the Roman Missal in the vernacular took on greater and greater proportions. Ever-widening circles of the laity began to read the prayers of the Mass along with the priest. And thus the separation between people and priest was closed in at least one definite point: in their prayer the faithful used the same words as the priest at the altar.

But now a new wish stirred, to do collectively and in common what many were already doing by themselves individually, and with this wish the liturgical movement brushed against the picture of divine worship which had prevailed up till now. Thus arose the problem of the community Mass—or as it is called in some places, the *missa dialogata* or *missa recitata*. The argument ran something like this: If reading along with the priest was to be something more than reading from a textbook, as is customary at the opera or at the production of an oratorio, there must be, in some measure at least, an external speaking along with the priest, especially since the rubrics of the missal in several places seem to expect some such response from the *circumstantes*. The first steps in this direction were taken in academic circles, and then by societies of young students. It was only later that parochial worship followed suit. At first there was no clear norm. But in the German area the threatening disorder was held off in some places by private projects. And finally, in 1929, a uniform text of all the prayers to be read in common was agreed on for Germany and this was used as a basis by most publishers.

Gradually the various principles on which the dialogue Mass is to be based became clearer. It is a fact that the history of liturgy must take into account, that at the beginning of the twentieth century the low Mass had gained such a great preponderance over the various forms of high Mass that without further ado it was used as the groundwork for the development of the dialogue Mass. No one seemed to notice that in this sort of Mass the alternation of functions between priest, lector, singing choir and people had been leveled off to a uniform speaking by the priest alone, and this more or less quiet. Now it was recognized that in essentials the high Mass had to set the norm, and that therefore at a *missa recitata* the people would answer and pray along in those parts that had been taken over by the choir, thus to some extent recovering these parts for themselves, while the old chants of the *schola*, the readings, and the prayers spoken aloud by the priest would be read aloud in the vernacular by a special reader or leader. In Germany the development reached a certain definite shape when in 1940 the whole problem of the liturgical movement, and along with it the question of the dialogue Mass, was taken over by the assembled episcopate [1] and thus brought to some kind of clarification. In many dioceses, therefore, directions for the celebration of the dialogue Mass—which left no little room for variations—were published.

A most significant variant of the dialogue Mass grew out of the inclusion in it of elements proper to the German *Singmesse*. The so-called *Betsingmesse*—"Pray and sing" Mass—has very quickly gained recognition since its first trial use at the Vienna Catholic Day in 1933, and since it is at once liturgically inspired, popular, and solemn, not only has it often replaced the simple *Singmesse,* but it is even being used with increasing frequency as the Sunday parish Mass.

A similar development was taking place about the same time in places where French is spoken, and elsewhere it is still in process.

In all of these changes—some of them not unimportant—*not one letter of the* Missale Romanum *was touched, not a word, not a rubric;* for in no case was there any tampering with the priest's performance of the Mass for which the norms of the *missa lecta* continued to serve always as unimpaired principles. All these changes had to do only with the participation of the people, for which there were nowhere any exact regulations. Therefore no objections were raised by the highest authority in the Church, especially since the new forms match the fundamental instructions of the popes with regard to the active participation of the faithful in the liturgy. And yet something very important was achieved. In this setting—even though in a still imperfect form—our celebration of the Mass was assured, at least to some extent, an advantage which the liturgy of the Eastern Church appears to have retained all along by means of its accompanying interchange of prayers between deacon and people. The old distance between altar and people was to a great extent broken down at the opportune moment. From the dialogue Mass the faithful gain a living knowledge of the actual course of the Mass and so they can follow the low Mass as well as the solemn Mass with an entirely new understanding. To have been deprived of such an understanding much longer would not have been tolerable even to the masses in this age of advanced education and enhanced self-consciousness. But what is even more important, now that the faithful answer the priest and concur in his prayers, sacrifice with him and communicate with him, they become properly conscious for the first time of their dignity as Christians and at the same time they achieve an awareness that they are the Church, that they stand in corporate relationship to all those whom God has graciously drawn to Himself in Christ. If in this way a start has been given to a broad and comprehensive cure of souls fed on the very basic forces

[1] In the U. S. inspiration came not only from individual bishops but from the Sodality of our Lady and the Liturgical Conference (see Ellard, *The Mass of the Future,* 202–210).

of the Church, it is not hard to estimate what weight all this will have not only for the individual's confirmation in faith and for his mode of life, but also for the stabilization of the Church at a time when nearly all external props have fallen down.

The community or dialogue Mass achieves its goal by superimposing its own form like a shell over the fixed, permanent structure of the *missa lecta* or low Mass. The price it must pay is high, namely that the first *liturgus*, the priest, is wholly in the background during the audible part of the Mass, the greetings and summonings excepted. For this reason, the Mass which is adorned with the altar songs of the priest—the *missa cantata*—must and will take the first place. The questions about the proper form of the celebration of Mass all come back to this, and chiefly to the priest's celebration. The ideal which Pius V had in view, to give the Mass a purity and clarity such as it possessed in the time of the Fathers (*ad pristinam sanctorum Patrum normam ac ritum*) will always stand before the Church. Not, indeed, as though ancient forms should be or could be merely brought back—even the church architecture of the last century does not simply revive the ancient basilica—but in the sense that in the celebration of the Christian mysteries the inner wealth of the Church comes to light as of old and the children of the Church constantly renew their joy and gladness because of their possessions and their blessings.

LATIN

The monumental greatness of the Roman Mass lies in its antiquity which reaches back to the Church of the martyrs, and in its spread which, with its Latin language, spans so many nations. Nowhere else is it so plain that the Church is both apostolic and catholic. But this double advantage of the Roman Mass also involves weaknesses. The Latin tongue has nowadays become more and more unfamiliar even to cultured people. Will there ever be any relaxing in this matter in the setting of the Mass? As a matter of fact, Latin is by no means the only liturgical language within the Catholic Church, even abstracting from the diocesan rituals in which the vernacular already occupies a large space. The Catholic Mass is celebrated not only in the ancient languages of the Orient and of the Slavic peoples, but also in several modern languages. Even within the Roman Mass tendencies in this direction are to be found: in Glagolitic congregations the Old Slavonic has been in use for centuries. When at the beginning of the seventeenth century the Chinese missions began to flourish, the question was very seriously posed, whether the language of the liturgy should not be Chinese, for, unlike the early medieval mission to the Germans, here a people was being dealt with who already had a literary language of its own.

The Latin language is only one of the peculiarities of the Roman liturgy that, due to its venerable age, has to some extent become a problem. As we already saw in the exposition so far, each succeeding cultural epoch has overlaid the original plan of the Mass-liturgy with its own layer. Not always has this been a harmonious, progressive, organic growth. In our explanation of the various parts of the Mass we shall have to point out continually how in the process of development, displacements, intermixtures, contractions occurred which sometimes left nothing more than a remnant of the expression of the original idea. In other cases the basic idea itself has become strange to us.

Thus in the present shape of the Roman Mass, forms and practices have been retained which are no longer comprehensible to the ordinary onlooker and for which an adequate explanation can sometimes be found only after a tiresome search into history. And when this does not concern some inconspicuous, subordinate rite, it is really very irritating. Still this venerable heritage, which took centuries to produce, should not be discarded lightly. Even so, it is clear that at a time when one unified missal is appointed for nearly all Christendom, it is no longer possible— as it was possible, perhaps, and self-evident in the era of manuscript missals—to make the changes that one recognizes ought to be made, or to make them all at once. A great deal of patient waiting is certainly needed.

And yet, because the Church is eternally young, it will not shrink back from a task however big. When Pius X determinedly undertook the revision of the psalter in the breviary, he remarked that he was thereby taking only the first step towards a correction and reform of breviary and missal. When at the same time he revamped the position of the Sunday Masses and the weekdays in Lent, he was already beginning that very reform. This has been carried still further by the decree on the simplification of the rubrics in 1955 in which the principle *one oration* was again emphasized. The same process was continued in the reform of the Holy Week liturgy which began in 1951 and culminated in the Restored Holy Week Ordo of 1955. Here too, the same general reform is in evidence, as for example the new form of the Ordo Missae which we will certainly be seeing more of as time goes on. And we may not forget to include in these plans the permission for evening Masses and the new ordering of the laws of fasting (1957). This renewal of the pastoral idea in the liturgy has and will continue to characterize the general reform. It was most forcefully brought out and emphasized at the First International Congress of Pastoral Liturgy at Assisi-Rome in September of 1956. In the last analysis, the revival of elementary liturgical thinking, as it was ushered in, in such a magnificent fashion, by the encyclical letter of Pope Pius XII, *Mediator Dei* of November 20, 1947, is the foundation—supporting but also necessary—for any and every renovation in the matter of external forms.

Part Two

THE NATURE

AND FORMS

OF THE MASS

1. *Names of the Mass*

The names by which the eucharistic celebration has been designated at various times do not give us an idea of its essence. They do not even suggest what that essence was thought to consist in. But they do show us certain aspects, whether purely on the surface or deeply intrinsic, by which the Mass was principally known to the faithful. These names are like a shadowy outline which permits certain characteristics of the essence to appear.

The earliest names we meet with are taken from outstanding details in the rite. The Acts of the Apostles uses the term "the breaking of (the) bread," referring thereby to the act by which the presiding person, following the ancient custom and the example of our Lord Himself at the Last Supper, opened the meal. But perhaps the idea behind the "breaking of bread" was not the material meal which was associated with the ceremony, but rather the sacramental bread itself: "Is not the bread we break a participation in Christ's body" (1 Cor. 10:16)? This is all the more certain if—as seems probable—the consecration of the bread was bound up with this rite of breaking. St. Paul himself calls the celebration "the Lord's Supper," Κυριακὸν δεῖπνον (1 Cor. 11:20) and thus places its character as a meal all the more plainly in the foreground.

Since the turn of the first century the term "Eucharist" has been employed, and thus is brought into prominence a spiritualizing word which had been connected with the meal from the outset. Eucharistia is first of all the prayer of thanks with which, after the manner of our Lord himself, the sacred action was surrounded. The word was used by Catholic writers as well as by the Gnostic groups from which the apocryphal histories of the Apostles stemmed. In the Fathers of the second century this is the word which suggests a precise phase of the celebration; it is a celebration in which the thanks of the redeemed rises up to God. In the *Didache* (9, 5.) at least by inference, and plainly in

Justin the consecrated gifts themselves are called "Eucharistia." And in this last meaning especially, the word is adopted by Tertullian and Cyprian as part of the vocabularly of the Latin Church, and has so remained till the present.

As we saw, the celebration of the Eucharist was very early designated as on *offering* or *sacrifice*. And the designation became a name then and there. In the Latin area there appeared, in this sense, the words *oblatio* and *sacrificium*, respectively from *offerre* and *sacrificari*—again first of all in the writings of the two Africans already mentioned. In Africa the word *sacrificium* appears to have prevailed as the usual name. Cyprian and Augustine use it regularly for the celebration of Mass. How strongly it was impressed on the literary usage of the Middle Ages we can learn from the fact that in the penitential books offenses against the eucharistic species are denominated as offenses against the *sacrificium*.

But in other sections of the Church the word *oblatio* prevailed. Thus the pilgrim lady Aetheria, whenever she refers to the celebration of Mass on her pilgrimage, regularly uses *oblatio* and *offerre*. Until the sixth century *oblatio* continued to be the usual name for the Mass. To describe the action, *offerre* (even without an object) continued in use even later; *sacerdotem oportet offerre* is what the bishop still says at ordination.

In the Greek Orient the corresponding word *Prosphora* was used only in passing. A word of similar import, *anaphora* was generally employed only in the narrow sense of the Mass proper, and to designate the formulary used therein. On the other hand, the Syrians, both East and West, commonly used the word *Kurbono* or *Kurbana*, "gift" as the name for the Mass. The Armenians, too, use a word that means offering.

We need not be surprised that, besides those names which go to the very core of the matter, other words are to be met with which—in accordance with a rule of sacral speech—designate the sacred action only with a certain reserve, as though from a distance. Several denominations of this sort are to be found.

Thus the West Syrians use, besides the word already referred to, another which expresses only the reverential and awe-filled "approach" to God, *Korobho*. It is gnerally used not for the whole Mass, but only for the Mass proper—the anaphora—and for the variable anaphora formulas. Elsewhere the Mass is called simply "the Holy," *sacrum*, just as we use it in modern Latin.

Another name originated by considering the personal source from which the sacredness of the celebration springs—Christ our Lord. So the Mass is called *dominicum*, "the Lord's," a name which was current in North Africa and Rome around the third and fourth centuries. This formation of a name which calls the Mass the celebration of Christ is parallel to that which calls Sunday the day of Christ (*dominica*, κυριακή), and the Christian place of worship the house of Christ, the house of the κύριος (κυριακόν = church). Nor is the creation of either term far apart in time.

In other instances, the name for the Mass is derived from the fact that it is a *service* which those who are invested with the fulness of the Church's power perform for the believing congregation. That is, as we know, the sense of the word λειτουργία, liturgy, which in church terminology designates primarily ecclesiastical functioning in general, then secondarily divine worship, and, amongst the Greeks since the ninth century, simply the Mass. Even outside the Greek-speaking area of the Byzantine rite—especially amongst the Slavic peoples and the Roumanians—the same Greek word is in use as a name for the Mass.

There are other instances of a similar practice elsewhere. In German, for example, the solemn Mass is called *Amt* and *Hochamt* (service and high service, respectively), the latter corresponding to the Latin *summum officium* of the decadent medieval period. In the closing years of Christian antiquity the common terms in Latin were *actio*, and the related *agere*. In Ambrose the expression for "to celebrate Mass" was either *agere* or *offerre*. This expression designates the "consummation" of the sacred action. This is brought out by the fact that later the word *actio* is taken in the narrow sense of the sacrifice proper, the canon, which is designated the *canon actionis*. The word *agenda* is also used, so that the full expression for "celebrating Mass" was *agere agendam*.

While in these designations the point of view is the activity of the spiritual officiants, Christian antiquity also recognized names which view the celebration of Mass as an assembly of the Christian people—an assembly that was centered on the mysteries of the Eucharist. A Latin appellation of this kind was actually used for the Mass—the word *collecta*—but its use was only passing. Since it was soon employed in the liturgy in another sense, the word did not endure. But it was different with regard to a Greek word having the same meaning, the word *synaxis* which from the fourth century on was for a long time the prevailing name until it was displaced by the term *liturgia*. However, it still lives in modern Latin as a substitute for Eucharist: *sacra synaxis*. A word of the same type was also developed among the Syrians.

MISSA

That the celebration of the Eucharist which Augustine lauded as *signum unitatis* should have taken its name from a *coming together* is something we could very well understand. But it is puzzling indeed that, as a matter of fact, it has been designated by a *separating*, a *going apart*. Such, however, appears to be the case in regard to the word which both

in Latin and in the modern languages of the West has practically supplanted all other names, the word *missa*, "Mass." For today there is no
doubt at all as to the original and basic meaning of the word: *missa* =
missio = *dimissio*. It meant, in late Latin, a dismissal, the breaking up or
departure after an audience or public gathering. Thus too in the language of the Christian liturgy, it was used both to announce the closing
of the assembly in the *Ite missa est* and to designate what preceded this
close. In this latter signification the word emerges around the end of
the fourth century.

This closing did not consist simply in a mere prosaic announcement,
as we have it in the phrase *Ite missa est*. It regularly comprehended
(whether at Mass or at some other service) a definite ecclesiastico-
religious act, a dismissal in which the Church once more drew her children to herself with motherly affection before sending them on their
way with her blessing. That is the way it was even in the early Church.
Already in the church order of Hippolytus the catechumens are sent
away each time with a laying-on of hands. And thus it continued for
centuries both in the Mass and outside. In a different form this arrangement has remained alive, even today. Nor need that surprise us. For the
arrangement is found in the very essence of the Church, which, as the
holy Church, is for her members essentially a refuge of grace and blessing. Just as the word *missa*, when we first encounter it as a name for the
close of divine service, often implies the blessing just mentioned, so also
the word *missa* became a designation for the concluding blessing, and
then for the blessing in general.

In a more modern extension of the meaning, a custom grew up of calling every divine service as a unit a *missa*, because it included a blessing,
much as we today style every evening devotion briefly as a benediction.
This usage had already appeared about 400. Soon there was talk of a
missa nocturna, of *missæ vespertinæ* and *matutinæ*. The celebration of
Mass, too, was such a *missa*. The usage took hold all the more easily because the same posture of body—standing bowed—which was perceived
when the priest or bishop stretched out his hands in blessing was to be
seen frequently also at the high points in the various functions—at the
priest's orations and especially at the preface and in the canon of the
Mass. In a sense the priestly praying was always a sort of *missa*, for it
always drew down God's favor and blessing upon all who bowed down
before Him in adoration; but especially was this true where Christ's
Body and Blood became present through the word of the priest. So the
name *missa* was gradually appropriated to the Eucharist, not (for a long
time) exclusively, but at least by preference. Since the middle of the
fifth century, examples are to be found in the most widely separated
parts of the Latin area—Italy, Gaul, North Africa—examples in which

missa is used univocally for the Mass celebration. The oldest extant example is in a decretal of Leo the Great in the year 445, in which he inveighs against certain instances in which divine service was held only once on Sundays.

At the outset, the word used in this narrower sense was employed mostly in the plural, *missæ*, or with some addition, *missarum sollemnia*. Only by exception, however, was there any adjective appended like *sanctæ missæ*. Even today in the official language of the Church such adjectives are as a rule left out; it is simply *fit missa* or *celebratur missa*. It is as though the word *missa* has in it so much splendor that it can well do without extra ornament. At the time of origin and development it must have approached, in content and mood, the Græco-Coptic *hagiasmos*, for it is *the* celebration in which the world is sanctified.

2. Meaning of the Mass. The Mass and the Church

If we put together such meanings as we derive from the names of the Mass we get nothing more than a very superficial sketch. The Mass is a celebration for which the Church assembles, a celebration which occupies the center of her charge and service, a celebration which is dedicated to the Lord. It is a celebration which presents God with a thanksgiving, an offering, indeed a sacrifice. And it is a celebration which reacts with blessings upon those who gather for it. Other essential features have been revealed to us by the course of history, for we have learnt the various aspects which were given special prominence as time went by. But we must now inquire what the Church herself has said in her formal pronouncements, whether by direct teaching or in theological discussion, regarding the meaning and the essence of this celebration.

It will not be out of place to present this question in a book which has as its primary subject-matter the variety of forms that the Christian celebration possesses. For the discussion should serve not only to establish or prove this variety but also to understand it in its development and growth from its roots, from the very core of its nature. So it is necessary, first of all, to have this essential core before our eyes to see what it is. Naturally it is not our task to excerpt and to rewrite the pertinent treatise in dogmatic theology as an isolated and self-contained chapter or even one related to the full-rounded theological structure or more particularly to the doctrine of the Sacraments. We must rather realize the liturgical connotations of the problem, and try to pose the questions and construct the answers with an eye to religious life and ecclesiastical service.

Let us first orient ourselves with regard to the liturgical facts hitherto established, making them the starting point for a broader excursion into the field of theology. These facts show that we cannot make the notion of sacrifice a basis absolutely and exclusively, otherwise we would leave no room for many other important and essential features. We must start off from one of the broader and more general ideas which find an application in an examination of the essence of the Mass solemnity. Such a notion is the one by which our Lord himself indicated the meaning of what He instituted: "Do this for a commemoration of me." The Mass is a solemnity dedicated to the memory of Christ; it is *dominicum*. And further, it is not merely a remembrance of His person, but a recollection of His work—according to the word of the Apostle: "For as often as you shall eat this bread and drink the cup, you proclaim the death of the Lord, until he comes" (1 Cor. 11:25).

THE MYSTERY

The consideration of the Mass must therefore commence with the mystery of our Lord's Passion and death. This is what is continually being made present and actual—in the institution of the Last Supper. However, neither can this mystery be exhausted with one simple idea. In this mystery our Lord sealed with His blood His testimony to truth (John 18:37), to the Kingdom of God which had come in His own person, and thus had "borne witness to the great claim" (1 Tim. 6:13). With a heroic obedience that was steadfast even to the death of the Cross (Philippians 2:8), He had in this mystery fulfilled the will of His Father against whom the first Adam had set himself with defiant disobedience. With free resolve our Lord had put himself into the hands of His enemies, silently, making no use of His wondrous might, and had offered up His life as "a ransom for many" (Mark 10:45). He had taken up the warfare against the invisible enemy who held mankind imprisoned in sin, and as one who is stronger still, He had been victorious (Luke 11: 22): He had cast out the prince of this world (John 12:31). He took His place at the head of mankind, striding forward through suffering and death, thus entering into His glory (Luke 24:26). As high priest He has offered up in the Holy Spirit the perfect sacrifice; with His own blood He has entered the sanctuary and set a seal upon the new and eternal covenant (Heb. 9:11 ff.). He himself became the Paschal Lamb, whose blood procured our ransom out of the land of bondage, whose slaughter inaugurated our joyous Easter feast (1 Cor. 5:7 ff.), the Lamb that was slain and yet lives, the Lamb for whose wedding feast the bride has clothed herself (Apoc. 5:6 ff.; 19:7 ff.).

By all these notions, by all these pictures the attempt is made in the writings of the New Testament to circumscribe and to illustrate the

great occurrence by means of which Jesus Christ effected the re-estab-
lishment of mankind.

All that is characteristic of the redeeming death of Jesus is clearly contained in some way in the institution of the Last Supper. There, in a
manner that is full of mystery, this suffering is made present, this suffering that is at once testimony and obedience and atonement and struggle
and victory and stainless sacrifice. It is made present under the signs of
bread and wine, the elements of a simple meal, which are transformed
by the hallowing words into Jesus' Body and Blood, and thus changed,
are enjoyed by all who partake of them. But what is the more precise
meaning of the Presence that is consummated day after day in a hundred
thousand places? Does that meaning rest in the very Presence as such?

When Christ on the Cross cried out His *Consummatum est*, few were
the men who noticed it, fewer still the men who perceived that this
phrase announced a turning-point for mankind, that this death opened
into everlasting life gates through which, from that moment on, all the
peoples of earth would pass. Now, to meet the expectant longing of
mankind, this great event is arrested and, through Christ's institution,
held fast for these coming generations so that they might be conscious
witnesses of that event even in the latest centuries and amongst the re-
motest nations, and might look up to it in holy rapture.

The Middle Ages actually did turn to this side of the eucharistic mystery with special predilection. What takes place on the altar is above all
the *memoria passionis*. The suffering of Christ was seen represented in
the breaking of the bread, in its distribution to the faithful, in the partaking of the Chalice whereby the Blood of the Lord is poured into the
mouth of the faithful. From this obvious symbolism the step to an allegorical interpretation of the whole rite was easily made; particularly
after the ninth century the whole Mass was explained as a comprehensive representation of the Passion of Jesus. In the action of the assisting
clerics, who step back at the start of the preface, is seen the flight of the
disciples. In the celebrant's extended hands our Lord is seen agonizing
on the Cross with arms outstretched. In the commingling of the species
is seen His glorious Resurrection. In fact, the whole life of Christ, the
whole history of Redemption is seen represented in the Mass. The sacred
action of the altar becomes a play, in which drama and reality are intermixed most mysteriously. How strong an impression this viewpoint
made can perhaps be gauged by the fact that even today we use the
expression "to hear Mass," as if we were an audience.

We must perceive that even in these explanations of the medieval
interpreters, a primary essential trait of Christ's institution is given expression; this institution is a memorial ceremony, a sacred action which
recalls into the midst of the congregation a redemptive work which
occurred long ago, a "mystery-action."

THE LORD'S TABLE

Another aspect of Christ's institution which was prominent from the very outset and which in earlier times was made visible through its liturgical form, was the fact that a holy meal was being held—a meal and a memorial. The Eucharist is a memorial instituted by our Lord for a remembrance of Himself. A table is set; it is the Lord's table. For a long time Christian speech avoided—or at least refrained from using—the term for altar derived from pre-Christian religion and even today still employs the simple name *mensa* (table).

At this table the faithful community is gathered in holy society. Here the Lord himself is given them as nourishment, His Body and His Blood handed to them under the species of bread and wine, as a spiritual food, a spiritual drink (cf. 1 Cor. 10:3 ff.).

Thus the eucharistic institution does more than commemorate our Saviour. In it the communion and society of the faithful with their Lord is continually renewed. The meal is a sufficiently striking proof of that. And we can therefore safely say that, aside from the external activity, the meal is still in our own time the basic form of the eucharistic celebration. However, even in the biblical sources, this meal is distinguished as a sacrificial meal. The table of the Lord which is prepared in the church in Corinth is contrasted to the tables of the demons, the tables at which the meat offered up to the heathen gods is eaten. Already in the primitive Church it was recognized that in the celebration of the Eucharist a sacrifice was offered up, and that therein was fulfilled the prophecy of Malachias who foretold a clean oblation which would be offered up in all places. The thought of a sacrifice, of an oblation to God, taking place in the Eucharist, occurs time after time in the works of the Fathers. That thought has definitely figured in every text of the eucharistic celebration which is known to us.

The Middle Ages, too, whose devotion to the celebration of the Mass had drawn the remembrance of the Passion so much into the foreground, did not on that account lose sight of the idea of oblation and sacrifice. In fact the later medieval period did so much to emphasize the sacrificial aspect and stressed in so many forms and fashions the value of the Mass for gaining God's grace and favor for the living and the dead, that not only did the Reformation find herein a subject for its immoderate indictment but even Church authorities, both before and after the storm, found reasons for making certain corrections.

The Council of Trent, therefore, was careful to clarify this very phase of the eucharistic mystery. The Council stressed the doctrine that the Mass is not a mere meal nor only a memorial service recalling a sacrifice that had taken place of yore, but is itself a sacrifice possessing its own power of atonement and petition. Christ had offered this sacrifice at the Last Supper and had given His Apostles and their successors the commission to offer it. Indeed He himself makes the offering through their ministry. Thus He left to His beloved spouse, the Church, a visible sacrifice. The Mass is therefore a sacrifice which is made by Christ and at the same time by the recipients of His commission; it is the *sacrifice of Christ* and the *sacrifice of the Church*. In our liturgical study we may not treat the sacrifice of the Church as a matter of secondary moment.

SACRIFICE OF THE CHURCH

In the theological controversies of the Reformation period and in subsequent theology, the sacrificial notion did indeed stand out as central, but the Church's sacrifice played only a minor role. For the main concern was over a much deeper presupposition, whether the Mass was a sacrifice at all, and—opposing Calvin especially—whether believing that it was contradicted the teaching of the Epistle to the Hebrews regarding the *one* sacrifice of Christ. Thus, above all else, the Mass had to be safeguarded as the sacrifice of Christ.

But when apologetic interests receded and the question once more arose as to what is the meaning and the purpose of the Mass in the organization of ecclesiastical life, it was precisely this point, the sacrifice of the Church, which came to the fore. The liturgies themselves are quite emphatic in the matter. One has only to scan the text of the Roman Mass, or of any other Mass-liturgy for that matter, to see that there is nothing plainer than the thought that in the Mass the Church, the people of Christ, the congregation here assembled, offers up the sacrifice to Almighty God. What is happening at the altar is called, in one of the most venerable texts of our liturgy, an *oblatio servitutis nostræ, sed et cunctæ familiæ tuæ*. And, corresponding exactly to this, there are the phrases to be read right after the words of consecration, at the very climax of the whole action: *nos famuli tui, sed et plebs tua sancta . . . offerimus præclaræ maiestati tuæ*—and the gift mentioned is the *hostia pura*, the sacred Bread and the Chalice of salvation. The same notion finds expression in a phrase incorporated into the Mass some thousand years later, when the priest speaks of *Meum ac vestrum sacrificium* which should be acceptable to God. That the Mass is also the sacrifice of Christ is, in the Roman Mass *ordo*, only assumed, but never directly expressed.

There is actually a definite contrast between this language of the liturgy and the language we are used to nowadays in sermons, catechisms, and other religious writings. We prefer to insist on the fact that on our altars Christ renews His Passion and death in an unbloody manner. We talk about the renewal of the sacrifice of the Cross, about an oblation in which Christ gives himself to His heavenly Father. But it is only in very general terms that we mention the sacrifice of the Church,[1] and for this reason even our theological textbooks in discussing the ensuing problem as to precisely where Christ consummates His sacrifice, refer without much reflection to His presence in the sacred Host.

If, by way of contrast, we skim through the pertinent writings of the Fathers even casually, we are surprised to note that they use similar terms in reference to Christ's oblation in the Eucharist and in reference to our own. They emphasize with equal stress the fact that we (or the Church or the priest) offer up the Passion of the Lord, indeed that we offer up Christ himself.[2] This is likewise true of the pre-Scholastic Middle Ages. Seldom, it is true, do they use words of their own to express the traditional teaching, but when they do they are especially clear in pointing out that it is the priest at the altar, who, in place of Christ, offers up our Lord's Body, that in so doing he is the *coadiutor Redemptionis* and *vicarius eius*. And at the same time they declare that the Church offers up the sacrifice through the ministry of the priest. Even the theologians of earlier Scholasticism and the great teachers of the flourishing schools of the thirteenth century use the same language, without, however, going into any deeper discussion of the topic. Only Duns Scotus lays any great emphasis on the sacrifice of the Church. The Eucharist, he says, is accepted by God, not because Christ is contained in it, but because He is offered up in it, offered up by the Church. The theologians of the declining Middle Ages stress the activity of the Church with such one-sidedness and partiality that the sacerdotal function of Christ himself is to some extent obscured.

Even the Council of Trent itself pointed out, as we already remarked, that it was our Lord's intention at the Last Supper to leave "to His beloved Spouse, the Church, as human nature requires, a visible sacrifice." The Church, therefore, was to have this sacrifice, and through it was to be able to satisfy the desire of human nature to honor God by means of sacrifice. For any theological view which would also do justice to liturgical reality, this statement of fact is fundamental.

Our next question therefore follows along this direction. We want to

---

[1] The New Baltimore is somewhat vague on this point ("Christ gives us His own body and blood . . . to be offered. . . . ," q. 356) and equally one-sided ("The Mass is the sacrifice of the New Law in which Christ, through the ministry of the priest, offers Himself to God in an unbloody manner under the appearances of bread and wine." Q. 357).

[2] Some examples:

Irenaeus, *Adv. haer.*, IV, 18, 4: "only the Church offers this pure oblation to her founder."

Athanasium, *Ep. heort.*, 2, 9: "We offer up not a material lamb but the true Lamb that was already offered, Our Lord Jesus Christ."

Augustine, *Ep.* 98, 9: "Was not Christ Himself once offered and is He not nonetheless immolated by the people in the sacrament not only during the Paschal season but indeed each day?"

know *how* Christ's institution is to be understood as a sacrifice of the Church, in what relation it stands to the life of the Church in all its fulness, and especially what principles of liturgical formation are taken for granted in it.

To be more precise, how is this sacrifice which the Church is supposed to offer up brought about? By the fact that the Church joins in the sacrifice of her Lord and Master, so that His oblation becomes her oblation. Therefore, in the Mass the one sacrifice of Christ, the one oblation of Golgotha by which He redeemed the world, is in mysterious fashion made present. Because of St. Paul's letter to the Hebrews, the oneness of the sacrifice of Christ is a matter which cannot be assailed. (Hebr. 9:24; 10:18.)

But how is this presence of the sacrifice of Christ to be understood? There must be something more here than just a representation of the oblation that took place once upon a time, something more than the *memoria passionis* as we see it commonly exhibited by the separate presentation of the Body and the Blood of Christ. On the altar a sacrifice truly takes place, but it is a sacrifice which in many respects coincides with the sacrifice of the Cross. For the Council of Trent says of it: "There is the same oblation, and the same Person who now makes the oblation through the ministry of the priests and who once had made an oblation of himself on the Cross. Only the manner of offering is different." It is here that the speculations of theologians take their start; the result has been a variety of explanations which, since the sixteenth century, have continued to multiply.

The simplest solution seems to be one that was not proposed till our own day. According to this explanation the *memoria passionis* is intensified into an objective remembrance in the sense of a mystical presence. In the celebration of the Eucharist not only Christ himself but His one-time act of redemption are made present under cloak of the rite, "in the mystery." [3] The past happening, Christ's Passion and Resurrection, is re-enacted in time, not indeed in its historical course but "in the Sacrament." So, from the very nature of the case, there is present an oblation—the same oblation which once took place. This, however, is a supposition which is not found in tradition in the precise form it here takes, but is rather the result of reasoning from tradition, a deduction which must enlist the aid of certain hypotheses which are themselves quite questionable. According to this theory the one oblation of Christ achieves simply a new presence by means of the consecration. The disparity of the actual oblation would thus be reduced to the barest possible minimum, so small

---

[3] The concept is presented by O. Casel in countless publications. Prominent are "Das Mysteriengedächtnis der Messliturgie," *Jahrbuch für Liturgiewissenschaft*, VI (1926), 113–204, and his later article, which sets out his position fully, "Glaube, Gnosis und Mysterium," XV (1941), 155–305.

that it is hard to see how there could be any new "reason to offer" or how the Eucharist could still be called *our* sacrifice, or how we would be linked to Christ's oblation in any relationship except a very external one.

The older explanations, on the contrary, generally sought to find the new and "different" manner of offering, of which the Council speaks, in the act of consecration itself. By means of the consecration, the Body immolated on the Cross and the Blood shed thereon are presented to the Father once again at this point of time and space. In this re-presentation which Christ fulfills through the priest—*ministerio sacerdotum*, says Trent—we have the oblation in which, according to the testimony of Christian tradition, the great high-priest offers himself at every Mass. This new offering is necessarily also a sacrifice in its own right, but not one that has independent redemptive value, since it is nothing else than a sacramental extension of the one and only redemptive sacrifice on Calvary which the Epistle to the Hebrews had in view.[4]

There appeared to be only one difficulty. This re-presentation is indeed some sort of offering (*offerre*), but is not properly a sacrificial offering (*sacrificari*), an *immolation*. Pre-Tridentine theology was not at all agitated over this distinction, the sacrificial character of the Mass being supplied by the *oblatio* which took place in it. But the pressure of controversy seemed to demand a search for the precise sacrificial act within the Mass. And especially in view of the sacrifices of the Old Testament, it seemed necessary to acknowledge that a destruction of the gift was essentially required, so that, in the case of a living thing it had to be killed (destruction theory), just as Christ himself consummated His redemptive sacrifice by His death. The post-Tridentine Mass theories are concerned for the most part with demonstrating this "destructive" sacrificial activity in the Mass. However, no agreement over the solution has ever been reached.

Many theologians, however, consider it sufficient to say that Christ renews His one Sacrifice before God and this is expressed in an outward sign.

Christ does, indeed, make the presentation of His one-time sacrifice before the face of God in an externally perceptible action, namely in the consecration which He performs through His priests. The consecration not only stems from Christ, in so far as the commission and powers are derived from Him, but it is in its very performance His work in the first degree, a work of His priestly office. And it is a work which—unlike the other sacraments, aimed in the first place at the sanctification of souls—is directed immediately to the glorification of the Father. It is a presentation or offering to the heavenly Father in the very here and now, in an

[4] The above formulation is the result of numerous discussions I have had with a confrere of mine, the Rev. Karl Rahner, S.J.

act which enshrines in itself the core of every sacrificial activity: *dedication.*

This dedication is consummated upon a thing which is still profane, still the world, is in fact the world and human life in the intensest sense, since men prolong their life through it; but it is altered and transformed into the holiest thing between heaven and earth, into the sacrificial gift offered up on Golgotha, an image of which is set forth in the species after the transubstantiation. In the "holy and venerable" hands of the Lord the earthly gift has become a heavenly gift in the very act of giving.[5] Thus the oblation of Christ is again on our altars, and as an oblation which He himself preforms anew before our very eyes. But He does not perform it in order to present us a drama, but in order to include us and His Church everywhere on earth and in every century in His *pascha,* His passage out of this world to His Father. His sacrifice becomes each time *the sacrifice of the Church.*

Our Lord offered up the sacrifice on the Cross not for its own sake but that He might therein give His life as "a ransom for many" (Matt. 20: 28). In this way He concluded for us that everlasting covenant with God which was promised in the prophets (Is. 61:8; Jer. 33:20 f.; Bar. 2:35) that covenant by which God receives mankind into His favor so that He no longer remembers their misdeeds (Jer. 31:31–34; cf. 33:8), but rather wishes them every good (Jer. 32:40), in the hope that the destined heirs obtain, forever, their promised inheritance (Heb. 9:15). But because it is a covenant, a compact, obedience and fidelity are expected also on our part. It was at the very time of its institution, at the Last Supper, that Christ spoke of the covenant. He speaks of His body "which is to be

---

[5] That there should be a distinction between the gift as it is alienated by men and the gift as it is determined for God's service, that the point of expropriation and appropriation should not exactly coincide, is seen even in pre-Christian sacrifices, for instance, the presentation of the smoke of sacrifice which is common in ancient heathendom as well as in the Old Testament (Gen. 8:21, et al.) The eucharistic sacrifice, too, was so instituted by Christ that it should start as bread and wine and not till afterwards become the gift properly so-called.

The favorite argument, that the reference of the sacrificial action exclusively to Christ fits the wording of the Tridentinum (*eadem hostia*) better, really proves nothing; for the conception explained above in no way contradicts it, any more than the inclusion of the sacrifice of the Church contradicts the words of the Council about *idem sacerdos.* Since no problem regarding these ideas had been proposed to the Council, there was no call for a more precise statement.

Please notice, however, that in the above demonstration we are not saying that the core of the sacrificial action is the fact that bread and wine are consecrated; what we claim is that the core of the sacrifice is to be found in the fact that, by the consecration, Christ once more presents to His Father the gift of the body and blood He had already sacrificed to Him. But this in no way hinders our perceiving in the sacrifice actually instituted by Christ a further symbolism in the consecration of earthly gifts; for Christ did not institute just any kind of sacrifice, but a determined sacrifice rich in many relationships, the sacrifice of His Passion as the sacrifice of the Church.

given up for you" (1 Cor. 11:24; Lk. 22:19). He designates His blood as "my blood of the new Testament, which is to be shed for many" (Mark 14:24; Matt. 26:28), and points to the chalice as "the new testament in my blood" (1 Cor. 11:25; Lk. 22:20). As if to say, this institution has a special meaning within that testament, and in the commission to do this perpetually as a memorial, something more is intended than merely a theoretical commemoration in connection with the repetition of this transubstantiation. Much more is accomplished than that. In it is created an opportunity for all the faithful of all times to ratify in conscious manner this covenant which He had concluded in their name. At Baptism we are already taken up into this covenant and its goods are portioned out to us, without our having to do anything except receive them. In the Eucharist, Christ sets before us the Passion by means of which He inaugurated this covenant; now it is up to us to step forward with a willing "yes" to protest our adherence to the law of Christendom. His sacrifice should become our sacrifice, the Church's sacrifice, so that it might be offered up in her hands "from the rising of the sun to its going down" and the name of the Lord of hosts "be made great amongst all the peoples" (Mal. 1:10 ff.).

The Church received a sacrifice from Christ because it is in man's very nature to honor God by sacrifice. More especially is this true where all religion is not to be limited to the inwardness of the individual, that is to say in a social union like the Church, in the divine service of the community. Here the need to glorify God by outward gift, by the visible emblem of an interior subjection or an internal giving of oneself to God —this need naturally arises of its own accord. The inner thought has to be the starting-point and the driving force of every sacrificial service if this service is not to be turned to mere pharisaism, for sacrifice is and must always remain only the symbol and sign of something else, an indication of what the soul intends.

But why could not a simpler gift suffice to express this intention? Because this intention, this inner sentiment towards God, is in Christianity a species all its own, at least as an ideal to which our striving is constantly pointed. The Sermon on the Mount, the Gospels, all the books of the New Testament speak of it. It is plainly put in St. Paul's "Have this mind in you which was also in Christ Jesus" (Philippians 2:5). It means entering into the thoughts of Jesus, rising to His mind and sentiment. In the life of our Lord himself the peak and triumph of that sentiment was reached on the Cross—a Cross which was erected as the wood of shame, and which our Lord willingly embraced in order to give himself wholly to His Father and at the same time to stretch out His arms over all the world and mercifully bring it back to the grace of God. The great commandment on which the Law depends and the Prophets, to love God with one's whole heart and soul and strength, and one's neighbor as one's self, this commandment of which He gave the living model, He also exemplified in death. That is the height to which He beckons His disciples. That is the fulness, the maturity of Christ to which they must grow.

So it is understandable—and yet remains a mystery!—that our Lord should choose as the token of His followers' glorification of God the very last and greatest thing that He himself had to give God the Father— His body that was offered and His blood that was shed. But this sacrificial gift is presented in such a way that each time it actually grows out of His followers' own gift, out of the produce of their own clay and sweat, out of a tiny piece of bread and a sip of wine by which they live. And it actually grows out thus by their own doing, by the words of consecration which someone from their midst is empowered to utter. So the Church is able not only to join in some extrinsic fashion in Christ's oblation which is made present in her midst, but she actually offers it as her own gift, as a gift which, in its natural state, is expressive of her own life and leads that life back to God, along with all that God's creative hand apportions to it along the way. This gift in its supernatural state manifests and confesses what the Church has become by God's grace and what she knows she is called to be. Thus the Church is enabled truly to offer up her very self; as St. Augustine says, she learns to sacrifice herself in His sacrifice.[6] This self-oblation of the Church is the precise object which the eucharistic mystery serves. Never is the Church so closely bound to her Master, never is she so completely Christ's spouse as when, together with Him, she offers God this sacrifice.

By the term "Church" is here meant—as everything we have said goes to show—not only the Church Universal and the priest representing her at the altar, but likewise the assembly of the faithful gathered around the priest at each celebration of the Mass. That the faithful offer the sacrifice was taken for granted in the more ancient theological tradition. *Plebs tua* explicitly stands in juxtaposition to *servi tui* in the Roman canon. Now, as an understanding of the priesthood of the faithful reawakens, the thought once more comes consciously to the fore. It is announced with complete clarity in the great encyclicals of Pope Pius XII.[7]

And now, looking at it more closely, how is this self-oblation of the Church accomplished? The action which brings this about precisely is— again—the consecration. The same act which realizes the sacrifice of Christ also realizes the sacrifice of the Church, but with this difference, that the Church's sacrifice begins to take shape from the very start of the Mass and then receives the divine seal and acceptance when at the consecration Christ takes it in hand and, after richly ennobling it, offers it to His heavenly Father as His own. For the priest who performs the conse-

[6] Augustine, *De civitate Dei*, 10, 20.
[7] "Mystici Corporis," (1943) and with even greater emphasis in "Mediator Dei," (1947).

cration in Christ's name and with Christ's power is always at the same time acting on commission from the Church. This commission he received at his ordination, for it was the Church that appointed him and ordained him as a priest of Christ. And he receives this commission for this precise situation by his office or at least by the fact that, in his celebration of the Eucharist, he fits himself into the Church's pattern and thus places himself at the head of the faithful who, as a portion of the Church Universal, have here and now gathered round him. As their representative he stands at the altar. He consecrates the bread and the chalice to present Golgotha's sacrifice to almighty God as their own. And since all through the course of the Mass he acts and speaks not simply in his own name but on commission from the Church, this authorization does not cease at the moment of transubstantiation merely because Christ's commission is superimposed, for it is the Church that calls on him to accept this second commission so that she, as the Bride of Christ, might once more enter into His sacrifice.

This sacrifice is present on the altar under the form of gifts which are emblems of our life-support and are at the same time *manifestations of unity, of the combining of many into one.* The ancient Church was vitally conscious of this symbolism of the eucharist species to which even St. Paul had already alluded: "As this broken bread was scattered upon the mountain tops and then, being harvested, became one," as the wine has flowed out of many grapes into this chalice, so the faithful should, through this sacrament, become one in Christ.

Another thing. This oblation was instituted with the express determination that the participants be fed with it: "Take and eat." The sacrificial meal is not something plainly included in the notion of sacrifice. There were sacrifices in the Old Testament which were entirely consumed in the fire, with nothing remaining for the offerers to eat—the sin-offerings, for instance; the offerers were not worthy to enter into so close a community with God. But the sacrifice of the New Covenant is essentially constituted as a meal, so that the offerers might gather around the sacrificial table, the table of the Lord, to eat. They are in communion with Christ who had undergone His sufferings and is now exalted; they become anew one body with Him.

This element of the symbolism of the species, which is emphasized in the words of consecration—this element above all must be taken in earnest. Every sacrament serves to develop in us the image of Christ according to a specified pattern which the sacramental sign indicates. Here the pattern is plainly shown in the double formation of the Eucharist; we are to be drawn into the sacrifice of our Lord on the Cross. We are to take part in His dying, and through His dying are to merit a share in His life. What we here find anchored fast in the deepest center of the Mass-sacrifice is nothing else than that ideal of moral conduct to which the teaching of Christ in the Gospel soars; the challenge to an imitation of Him that does not shrink at sight of the Cross: a following after Him that is ready to lose its life in order to win it: the challenge to follow Him even, if need be, in His agony of suffering and His path of death, which are here in this mystery so manifestly set before us.

If the Church's gift of homage to God is thus changed by the priest's words into the immolated Body and the spilled Blood of our Lord, and if the Church, firm and unafraid, then offers it to God, she thereby stamps her "yes" upon the chalice which her Master has drunk and upon the baptism which He experienced. And by that same oblation which she bears in her hands, she is dedicated and sealed for the same road that He traveled on His entrance into glory (Luke 24:26). The sacrifice of Christ is renewed sacramentally not only *in* His Church but *upon* the Church, and is renewed daily because it is daily demanded of her (Luke 9:23). The Mass-sacrifice is not only a presentation of the redemptive Passion and, with it, of the whole collection of Christian doctrine on salvation. It is also an epitome of Christian life and conduct. The height on which Christ lived and died comes before our gaze each time as an ideal, admonishing and alluring, as a towering peak which we can only reach by tremendous trying, along the ascent of Christian asceticism. All this puts Communion in a new light. Communion, too, is stamped with the Cross and the death of the Lord.

At the consecration, the Church as a society affirms the oblation of Christ and makes it her very own, but the individual Christian might feel satisfied to follow from afar, more of an onlooker than an actor in the sacred drama. In Communion, however, it is the individual participant who really wants to co-celebrate the Mass—it is his word that counts. Everyone must be seized with the impulse to be swallowed up in the mystery of Christ's Passion. Thus and only thus can the partakers hope to meet Him who had already entered into His glory; thus and only thus can they be embraced by Him and hallowed by the fire of His godhead.

Just as the participation of the Church in Christ's oblation at the consecration is a sacramental proceeding, so too the completed incorporation of the individual in Communion is a sacramental proceeding. The recipients of the Eucharist become participants in the oblation *ex opere operato*. But it is somewhat different with sacrifice as such. Since this is a moral activity, a free and humble homage before God, a genuine and essential consummation of the sacrifice cannot be produced in the mere reception of a divine operation, as is the case with the sacraments in which God sanctifies man. Therefore the sacrifice, in so far as it is the oblation of the Church, is not completely concluded with an *opus operatum*; the *opus operantis* must join in, and not merely as an addition to the completed work, but as a requisite belonging to the very structure at least as an integrating part. True, Mass is not simply man's good work—as Luther pretended to explain Catholic teaching on the subject—but neither is it simply the result of God's activity, as, for instance, Baptism is. The Church is not drawn into Christ's Passion under compulsion, but enters into it freely, consciously, deliberately. That is the Mass.

In a higher measure and in another way than in the sacraments, therefore, there is required beside the passive moment also an active one. Were Mass only the *mysterium* of Christ's Passion or only a memorial meal, then—with the addition perhaps of a consentient anamnesis to cast a glance at the redeeming sufferings—the account of the Last Supper, with the consecrating words over bread and wine, and the reception of the Sacrament would suffice. Mass, however, is also and primarily an immolation to God, an expression of the self-offering of the Church. The Church does not wait for the redemptive grace that pours down on her anew; having long ago obtained the favor of her Lord, she takes the initiative, she sets out on her own to offer God her gift, a gift which, at the height of her ascent, is changed for her into the oblation of Christ.

We therefore find that it is a common phenomenon in the history of the Mass-liturgies that some action of the Church precedes the consecration, a movement toward God which gains its essential utterance in the great prayer of thanksgiving but which is also expressed in many customs that, even during the preparation of the elements, suggest the presentation, the *oblatio*, the gift, just as they continue to express the same thoughts after the transubstantiation. According to its essence, therefore, Mass-liturgy is accomplished in three steps—not very sharply defined: the submissive and laudatory approach to God, the sacramental performance of Christ's sacrifice, and the reception of the sanctified gift.

The institution of Christ thus once more implies that the Church realizes this active moment of the sacrificial proceeding not only in her official representative who stands at the altar but also in the participating congregation. The "we" in the priest's prayers and the spatial assemblage of the participants around the officiating priest already tend in this direction. It follows that an interior immolation is required of the participants, at least to the extent of readiness to obey the law of God in its seriously obligatory commandments, unless this participation is to be nothing more than an outward appearance. A participation that is right and justified in its essentials should, of course, involve the desire to tread again the pathway of the Master and to make progress on it. To such an interior attitude, however, corresponds an exterior expression which exhibits a connection with the essentially significant sacrificial proceedings by means of tokens or words that have the presence of the participants as their starting point. All the liturgies have developed for this a wealth of expressive elements, but of these only a portion have stayed in living practice. The ideal condition would be if the sacred activity conducted by the priest would evolve from the ordered activity of the congregation and all its members, just as it does evolve from their will.

Since the Mass is a sacrifice of the Church, it normally presumes a larger or smaller assembly of the people. The different types of this assembly gave rise, in the course of history, to a principle of formation; it will be our task in the next few chapters to study the development of this principle more closely. In its most complete development we have the assembly of all the people in the place; in early times this occurred mostly under the leadership of the bishop, while later on the priest, especially the pastor, was appointed for this. The bishop's Mass and the priest's Mass, therefore, form two of the basic tyes of the Mass. But the assembly can also shrink to just a few persons, and finally—as an irreducible limit—to the single person of the celebrating priest, who, indeed, can also offer up the Mass in his own name. However, we find the Church constantly trying to avoid this extreme case, to such an extent in fact that in none of the rites, either East or West, did any form of Mass develop in which at least the external outlines of community participation were left out. The forms of private Mass are always only diluted forms of public celebration.

3. *From the Episcopal Collective Service to the* Missa Sollemnis

The primitive and original form of Mass celebration is that in which the bishop surrounded by his clergy offers up the sacrifice in the presence of the congregation. Nearly all the accounts of the Mass which we have from the end of the first century until well into the fourth presuppose this arrangement. This sort of thing was to be expected from the fact that Christianity was then predominantly an urban religion. Ignatius of Antioch is quite pointed in his reference to this common service: "Take care, then, to partake of one Eucharist; for one is the Flesh of our Lord Jesus Christ, and one the cup to unite us with His Blood, and one altar, just as there is one bishop assisted by the presbytery and the deacons, my fellow servants." The Roman *ordines*, too, give the same picture in regard to papal services. In fact in Rome, as also in other localities, there is a further development in so far as the principle of a roving assembly-place makes it possible even in a large city to retain, at least in its fundamental outlines, the system of gathering the whole community together. Since the Roman *ordines* became for centuries the norm for regulating the episcopal services in almost the whole West, this arrangement remained in vogue elsewhere. Thus the ideal form for uniting the whole community of the episcopal see in one service and promoting the complete self-oblation of the community remained alive for long in the consciousness of the occidental Church. In the Orient this is still the case even today.

CONCELEBRATION

The position taken by the clerics, particularly the priests, in this common service is expressed in the principle of *concelebration*. This principle implies, for all the participants, a proper share in the community service, but not necessarily a co-consecration on the part of the priests present.[1] For priests as well as for the rest of the faithful—to whom even late medieval sources quite unabashedly ascribe a *celebrare missam*, a concelebration—the essential thing in this participation was to answer the chief celebrant, to join him in prayer at certain stated times, and to receive with him the Holy Sacrament. Still the dignity of the service demanded that suitable recognition be given each hierarchic rank. The presbyters took their place in the *presbyterium* along with the other clerics; they wore the liturgical garment proper to them—in early medieval Rome this was the *planeta*. At the papal stational Masses they also assisted in receiving the gift-offerings, in breaking the species and distributing Holy Communion. Naturally this assistance was subject to variations in degree. In the Oriental rites the incensings are distributed among the concelebrants. Quite early we meet the custom of dividing the various orations, outside the canon, among the participating priests or bishops. There is mention, too, of pronouncing certain texts, even the preface, together, so that it was but a slight step to the joint pronouncing of the words of consecration as in the present-day rite of ordination.[2]

However, in the Western Church the genuine remnants of ancient Christian concelebration are not to be found in the ordination Mass, but rather in the Mass on Holy Thursday with its priests' Communion, and in the regulation for the last day of Holy Week that all private Masses

[1] Since the allocution of Pope Pius XII to the Assisi Congress in September, 1956, and the Decree of the Holy Office of May 23, 1957, there has been no doubt that a co-consecration is only possible through a common recital of the words of consecration. Without this, the concelebration is only ceremonial and not sacramental. At such a ceremonial concelebration, the priests present, with the exception of the celebrant, do not make full use of their priestly powers. Cf. *Acta Ap. Sedis* 48 (1956), 718; 49 (1957) 370.

[2] In our present-day rite of concelebration at the ordination Mass, the most striking thing is the fact that the newly ordained disregard the architectonics of the Mass, saying all the prayers right through with the bishop, even those otherwise said quietly. Here is an indication that this joint utterance had a different basis than the concelebration otherwise attested in the history of liturgy, for the latter patently sought only a proper arrangement and disposition of all the participants according to hierarchical rank. In the case of ordination the fundamental idea obviously was to put the order just awarded to practical proof, in the same way that the foregoing ordinations were put into practice. The respective rubric, without the prescription of kneeling, is found in the Pontifical of the Roman Curia since the 13th century.

are to be omitted and that the assembled clergy are to participate, informally, with the rest of the faithful in the one public celebration. Another trace of it is the *Ordo ad synodum* of the Roman Pontifical which presupposes that the bishop alone goes up to the altar and that the assembled clergy receive Communion at his hands. A similar prescript holds for the cardinals gathered for the papal election. For the first thousand years, such a method was taken for granted in all cases where a number of priests were assembled and where they individually had no other religious duties—an arrangement which is still today normal in the Orient. When St. Paulinus of Nola (d. 431) on his deathbed was visited by two bishops, he begged that he might commend his soul to the Lord by offering Mass with them. For a long time the custom obtained in the monasteries, especially on feast days, for the whole community, including the priests, to gather together not only for the conventual Mass but for a general Communion. Amongst the Carthusians this is still the rule on Christmas, Easter and Pentecost. St. Francis of Assisi spoke in very general terms when he expressed the wish "that the brethren in their foundations celebrate only one Mass a day, as is the custom in Holy Church. And if there are several priests at home, for the love of God let one be satisfied to assist at the celebration of the other."

For the rest this arrangement was maintained longest in the case of the sacred ministers at high Mass. What had previously been taken for granted was prescribed at least for them on certain occasions, and the arrangement was thus kept up for a long time during the later Middle Ages. In the eleventh century the rule is cited more than once that one or even two of the particles into which the Host was broken should serve for the Communion of deacon and subdeacon. Subsequently, Communion each time for deacon and subdeacon was stipulated only at the Mass of the bishop and of the abbot, or for high Mass on Sundays and holy days, or for the first day of the weekly duty of the respective sacred ministers, or finally in monasteries for the days when Communion was prescribed for all. Only in isolated instances did the later Middle Ages continue the usage of Communion for both sacred ministers at every Mass (outside of Mass for the Dead). The Council of Trent contented itself with making a warm recommendation to this effect.

PAPAL AND EPISCOPAL MASSES

The direct descendant of the bishops' collective service is the pontifical service, especially in its most elaborate form, the papal Mass, although it is true that in these cases the participation of the people has become a matter of fact rather than of principle. Even the solemn high Mass of a simple priest, which one might well have expected would be explained as an elaborated growth of the presbyter Mass, proves rather to be a late simplification of the pontifical service. For that reason the difference between a pontifical Mass and the sacerdotal high Mass in the Roman liturgy is today comparatively slight. This fact is closely connected with the circumstances under which the Roman liturgy was taken over by the Frankish Church, for at that time the only directions in the *ordines* for the external solemnization of the service were the rubrics for a pontifical rite. In consequence, not only were these used in cathedrals, but they had to serve as the basis elsewhere, too. The first Roman *ordo* itself offered a handy pretext for this very thing. In fact, one Roman insertion suggests that bishops should perform everything the Pope does, and that the bishop who replaces the Pope at the Roman stational service has only a few changes to make. This latter direction, it goes on to say, also holds good for a presbyter who offers the stational Mass, aside from the rule that he might not intone the *Gloria* except on Easter. It did not require any bold exegesis to turn this slight suggestion into a definite direction for every case when a priest had to conduct a solemn service in larger surroundings like those to be found (in the centuries to follow) not only in monasteries but also in numerous other capitular churches.

In any case this was the principle that was presently followed. Ample proof is to be found in the arrangement for Mass as outlined in an eighth century *Breviarium ecclesiastici ordinis* adapted to the circumstances of a Frankish Scots monastery; compare this with the prescriptions in the *Capitulare ecclesiastici ordinis*, which describes a papal stational Mass. Aside from the papal court—which is not prominent in the *Capitulare* either—and the rite of *sustentatio* which is proper for the Pope, nearly everything of ritual splendor has been transferred to the monastic *sacerdos*: he is surrounded by priests (*sacerdotes*), deacons, subdeacons, and clerics; the seven candles and the censer are carried before him; he steps up to the altar amid the same greetings as the Pope; like the Pope he employs the *Pax vobis;* during the whole fore-Mass he remains at his place *retro altare* and washes his hands before the offertory, although at that time this was no peculiarity of the papal or episcopal rite.

The same sort of solemn Mass is encountered in Frankish sources of the ninth and tenth centuries. Most of the time it is distinguished as a bishop's Mass, but sometimes the presbyter appears explicitly as the celebrant. Then, too, the new Mass arrangement which is noticed about the year 1000 in the documents of the Séez group is drawn up first of all for the bishop's Mass, but is soon allotted to the priest also.

The outlines of the present-day form of the *missa sollemnis* become distinct and clear after the tenth or eleventh century. Whereas before—and sometimes also later—there is mention of a number of deacons and subdeacons, now there appear only one deacon and one subdeacon to accompany the priest as he proceeds to the altar and to perform their duties there. Amongst the first indisputable testimonies of this arrangement is the writing of John of Avranches which dates about 1065. It still includes for the priest certain details from the episcopal rite which today are no longer retained, but it definitely states that the bishop's *cathedra* is to be more prominent. The conventual Mass at Cluny at the same time also displays the same type of Mass with deacon and subdeacon.

In general the rite of high Mass has not changed much since the eleventh century, if we except the peculiar usages of certain regions and certain monasteries. In the twelfth century there appear, in addition to the other reverences, numerous kissings when handing over or receiving things—kisses which are still prescribed. About this time likewise occurs the rule that the celebrant (and his assistants with him) were to read softly the texts sung by others. The careful description of the priestly high Mass which is presented in the 1256 *Ordinarium* of the Dominicans reveals in all essentials the present-day arrangement, and also the same differences from the arrangement of the pontifical service as it was finally fixed in the *Ceremoniale episcoporum* of 1600. The solemn vesting program is dropped, two to four candles are found sufficient, and they stand on the altar. The priest no longer employs the phrase *Pax vobis* but only *Dominus vobiscum*, he says the oration, and likewise the *Gloria* and the *Credo*, at the altar, and washes his hands only after the incensing. The most impressive distinction, which for years had marked the pontifical service in northern countries, was the solemn pontifical blessing after the canon, which endured all through the Middle Ages and which the priest never dared to assume. Likewise the *presbyter assistens*, substitute for the older college of priests, who was still clearly in the foreground in the twelfth century, has now by universal law been reserved to the pontifical rite.

Many peculiarities of the medieval high Mass and pontifical Mass which were of a more technical sort have since disappeared [3] or have survived only in monastic rites.

FREQUENCY OF SOLEMN MASS

The greatest change in solemn high Mass since the Middle Ages is in regard to its frequency. For centuries the high Mass was the prevailing form of public worship in those churches which held the leadership in liturgical life—and these were, besides the cathedrals, the monastic churches and the capitular churches, that is, the churches of collegiate chapters which were organized on a monastic pattern. In all these churches the daily conventual Mass sung after Terce, with deacon and subdeacon, was part of the fixed order of the day. From this time on, it formed the climax of the liturgical office. Indeed, at Cluny and in its

[3] For example, the deacon was to have a fan handy during the insect season to safeguard priest and offerings.

orbit already since the eleventh century, a second conventual Mass had been said each day, a *missa matutinalis* in addition to the *missa maior*. And at this second Mass there were a deacon and subdeacon. But it was distinguished from the other by a slight diminishing of solemnity; the altar was incensed at the offertory but not at the beginning of Mass, the interposed chants were shortened, and the *Credo* was regularly dropped. On days that had no special feast the formulary of the Mass for the Dead was chosen, since this second Mass was for the benefit of the souls of deceased benefactors for whom Cluny had developed an extended solicitude.

A similar arrangement became customary amongst the Premonstratensians, and was soon adopted elsewhere. In France at the time of Honorius III there appeared a tendency to be satisfied with the daily service for the dead, especially since it had some advantage as regards time, and so the Mass which was due "by reason of the day or feast" was omitted. This was the occasion of a decree issued by this pope in 1217, in which the fulfillment of one obligation as well as the other was required. From this decree many canonists drew the conclusion that all collegiate chapters and even monasteries were bound to the double conventual Mass, so that the frequency of solemn Mass was, where possible, still further increased.[4] In an effort to stem the swell of Masses for the Dead, and to promote as much as possible a correspondence between Office and Mass, the Missal of Pius V took this legislation as the basis for its regulations for cathedrals and collegiate churches regarding the double Mass, of which in the cases given one was to be of the ferial day, the other of the feast, and also for the rules regarding the substitution of Votive Masses and Masses for the Dead. In general the double conventual Mass has in modern times been restricted to days of a double liturgical character (in the sense just indicated). And more often it has been reduced in solemnity so that, outside of Sundays and Feast-days, it is no longer a *missa sollemnis* but a *missa cantata*—this latter probably the form of the monastic Sunday Mass in the beginning.

The real high Mass has again become rarer, the result of various concurring forces. In the cities the collegiate chapters, whose first occupation was solemn divine service, have long since been dissolved. In cathedrals and to some extent also in the surviving monastic establishments, other activities have loomed larger. The independent life of clerical communities, a cloistered and Godward life as it flourished in the later Middle Ages, is rarely possible since the secularization of the past few hundreds years. Its outward expression in the daily high Mass has therefore disappeared with the disappearance of that life.

[4] It has been shown that in reality the ecclesiastical obligation to a conventual Mass for religious with choir did not exist till Pius X. This was the last stage in the development of the principle that Mass is part of the obligation of choir.

There is another point to notice. This Mass was no longer the collective act of worship of a congregation like the old Roman stational Mass from which it derived. As a rule it took place at a choir altar, situated in a chapter choir or sanctuary that had gradually gotten farther away from the nave and had become almost an independent clerical church, and so even from this viewpoint the Mass was truncated and withered-looking. But more than this, in monastic churches the people had been absolutely excluded since the early Middle Ages. "Public masses" were generally not allowed, so that the monastery would not unnecessarily mix into the hurly-burly of the world, and the people, on the other hand, would not be drawn away from their parish churches. The very architecture of the older monastic churches is proof of this—as a rule an immense choir and a very small nave.

In modern times, the interests of the care of souls once more became a focal point in worship and therefore the congregation once more came to the fore. In fact the new orders in the sixteenth century showed a decided opposition to solemn services of the late medieval type, since the liturgical duties left hardly any time for other pastoral tasks which were then growing so urgent. The materialistic and prosaic intellectuality which had become more and more widespread since the eighteenth century, and the increasing independence of the masses had dampened that joy in princely splendor with which the high Mass encompasses the celebrant as the successor of a pope who had become something of a secular ruler and had been surrounded with the pomp of secular courts. The high Mass has been retained only for great feast days when, enriched with musical values that spring from a cultural level very close to us, it continues to function as the expression of highest festive joy and as the self-assertion of a Church happy in its possession.

4. *From the Presbyter Mass to the* Missa Cantata

Besides the episcopal collective service, even Christian antiquity found another type of Mass necessary, since in the territory of each individual bishop there were many churches with their own clergy. This was the Mass of the presbyter, which we must look upon as a second original basic type for the celebration of Mass, a type which survives in the *missa cantata,* the simple sung Mass. Although this second basic type must even then have been much more frequent than the grand stational service, there are practically no accounts of its existence. Perhaps precisely because of its frequent recurrence and because of its greater simplicity, there was no special call to put its description in writing. We can, however, reconstruct it in general outline. We grasp its essential form when we realize that at such a service, besides the congregation, only the presbyter and a second cleric were present as a rule.

The second cleric was generally a deacon. Chrysostom speaks on one occasion of wealthy Christians who possess entire villages but who do not build any churches; he demands that they erect churches and provide for a *priest* and a *deacon* so that divine service might be conducted and Sunday Mass might be celebrated. In the Orient the deacon as a general rule stands next to the priest even today. This was also the case to some extent in the West well into the Middle Ages. Cyprian presupposes that the presbyters who sought out and visited the imprisoned Christians in order to celebrate the Eucharist with them, were each time accompanied by a deacon. In the correspondence of St. Gregory the Great mention is often made of the need to ordain presbyters and deacons for orphaned churches which had no bishop.

ROLE OF THE CLERIC

However, in the Roman liturgy a cleric of a lesser rank took the place of the deacon at a very early period. This was all the easier since the deacon's proper functions were but little in demand even at a bishop's Mass, for his duty as prayer-leader for the people was never much developed and the various invitations to prayer and to the kiss of peace were proclaimed by the celebrant himself. In the city of Rome there was an additional reason, for the number of deacons was limited, as it was in other towns too, to the biblical number of seven (Acts 6:3). Thus it appears that at the titular churches in olden times a lector usually served at the altar, and later usually an acolyte. He went with the priest to the altar. He took over at least one of he readings. The priest probably, even in earlier times, retained the Gospel for himself, no doubt in order to indicate its higher dignity. The assistant helped at the offertory procession of the faithful and at the arranging of the gift-offerings, at the breaking of the bread and at the distribution of Communion. The larger outlines of the liturgical function remained the same. The text of the sacramentary was used in its entirety. But, because a special choir was demanded only for pontifical services, the chants of the *schola* dropped out, that is, besides the introit (which, from the situation itself, was unnecessary), also the offertory and communion. Thus the more ancient arrangement survived, somewhat in general like the arrangement nowadays on Holy Saturday. If it was necessary because of a lack of other assistance, the cleric sang the psalmody between the lessons, to which the congregation responded; that is to say, he took over the duties of the *psalmista*. The responses to the altar chants of the priest were, of course, the right of the congregation, and likewise the chants of the Ordinary— of which, till the sixth century, only the *Sanctus* existed.

Some such Mass celebration must have fitted most naturally into the circumstances of the early medieval monasteries. As long as the individual monks were not as a rule ordained, it was the type that was taken for granted. But even the conservative branches of the Benedictine order in the eleventh century had a conventual Mass in which the basic type of the presbyter Mass can be recognized. The liturgy of the Carthusians, for example, does not even today have a subdeacon as a special functionary; only the deacon assists the priest.[1] For the singing of the Epistle a monk especially appointed steps out of the choir. A similar usage occurred, and occurs even nowadays, amongst the Cistercians, at least for the ferial rite of the conventual Mass and perhaps elsewhere too.

This same manner of celebrating Mass was the only one possible in country churches and in churches on large estates. But that Mass was actually performed in this way, and especially that a cleric served at it— of these things the traces in the older sources are not very clear; there are traces, however. The ninth century *Admonitio synodalis* orders: "Every presbyter should have a cleric or a pupil to read the epistle or readings to answer him at Mass, and to sing the psalms with him." Plainly what is meant here in the first place is the parochial service, a Mass celebrated with chant. The word "answer" seems to suppose that even in parish churches the people no longer themselves gave the answers in a loud voice. Besides, of course, no such responses were needed as yet at the prayers at the foot of the altar, although they were probably at the *Orate fratres*. There is express mention of divine service in rural parishes in a Mainz synod of 1310 which censures the abuse of priests celebrating because of lack of assistants. Against this custom, the synod legislates that even in rural places the priest should not celebrate without the cooperation of some responsible persons who could read and sing. Here, in case of necessity, the assistance of a capable layman is declared sufficient, but even the present-day missal considers it quite normal that, at a Mass celebration without sacred ministers, a lector in surplice should read the Epistle.

So the missa cantata, *which in most dioceses today is the predominant form of parish service, is seen to be the unbroken continuation of the presbyter Mass of Christian antiquity.*

It, too, has been subjected to the trend of borrowing as much as possible from the episcopal service. For one thing, since the sacramentaries intended for the episcopal service were generally also standard for the titular churches, the opening rite of *Kyrie* and oration before the readings must have become customary in the presbyter Mass even in Christian antiquity. Soon, too, at a very early period the antiphonal chants

[1] It is interesting to notice that the so-called *Missa cum diacono* is now in use again, especially in various monastic congregations. At Maria Laach, for example, it is the standard form for the conventual Mass. Aside from monastic use, the new Ordinationes et declarationes for Holy Week (Feb. 1, 1957) make provision that where the simple rite is used, a deacon or second priest acting as a deacon can perform the diaconal functions of the solemn rite. This is certainly an important step in renewing a *presbyterian* liturgy.

were included, but this can only mean that the texts were spoken by the priest, since any musical performance—if the priest himself did not undertake it—was in most instances impossible and even today is still in most instances impossible. And also during these centuries of the Middle Ages the presbyter Mass must have shared in the whole development of the Mass-liturgy: the inclusion of the *Gloria, Credo, Agnus Dei,* the silent prayers, the incensing, and finally the *pax*-usages. It could really not be otherwise, because Church law demanded that all churches conform, in the *institutiones missarum,* to the pattern of the cathedral or the metropolitan church.

Even the more solemn ceremonies of these latter were copied by the smaller churches; especially in the later Middle Ages the services in the larger parishes were very similar to those in the chapter churches. The common choir prayer of the clergy was combined with the repeated celebration of public Mass. Of these a daily *summum officium* was distinguished, a Mass like the *missa maior* of the chapters, marking the climax of the morning service and capable of many varying degrees, reaching a high-point in a solemn Mass with deacon and subdeacon and an introductory procession of the clergy carrying relics of the saints. Taking over polyphonic music in city and country churches was the last step in this development.

5. From Domestic Eucharist to Private Mass

HOUSE MASS

Even though in the early days of the Church it was a fundamental principle that the Eucharist was to be celebrated only for the sake of the faithful and not as a personal devotion of one endowed with the powers of priesthood, still it was not seldom the case in this era when "they broke bread in this house or that" (Acts 2:20), that only a small domestic group gathered around the holy table. *This domestic celebration of the Eucharist in the primitive Church was the forerunner of its later celebration in more or less private circles, and finally also of the private Mass.* Aside from the texts of the *Didache* which have always been taken in this sense, other unmistakable evidences of this usage are to be traced, all of them also of the second century. In the various apocryphal histories of the Apostles we find, along with many vulgar and heretical additions, indubitable testimonies regarding the ecclesiastical customs in this matter, an array of examples where the legends picture the Apostles as "breaking bread" before a small group, of "giving thanks" over bread and wine in the presence of only a few participants. Tertullian includes in his account of the era of persecution the celebration of the *dominica sollemnia* at which only three persons were present. In Cyprian, too, there is mention not only of a morning Mass in the presence of the congregation, but also of an evening Eucharist for a small circle. Basil speaks of priests who, because of a fault, are permitted to perform their priestly office only in private homes. Gregory of Nazianzen cites the eucharistic celebration in his sister's home. However, in the Orient in the fourth century, the Synod of Laodicea issued a general prohibition against such celebrations of the Eucharist. In other places it is simply required that for this the bishop's permission be asked; this was the case in the Byzantine area, where in the ninth/tenth centuries every family in easy circumstances had its house chapel, which was used especially for memorial Masses for the Dead.

At an earlier date in North Africa the second Synod of Carthage (about 390) was content to demand an episcopal permission. This fits in with what Augustine has to tell about one of his priests who was once called to the country estate of a former Roman officer, Hesperius. Here the slaves and cattle were suffering from demoniacal molestations, but the priest offered up the sacrifice of Christ's Body, and the molestations ceased.

In Rome, too, the house Mass was not unusual. Here in many places since the beginning of the third century there were domestic oratories dedicated to the memory of certain martyrs. It might have been in one such oratory that St. Ambrose, at the invitation of a prominent Roman lady, once offered up the sacrifice. It is told of Melania the Younger that she had Mass said daily by her chaplain Gerontius, at her cloister-like home on the precipice of the Mount of Olives, "as was the custom of the Church of Rome." Paulinus of Nola, as we saw above, offered up the holy sacrifice with the visiting bishops in his own sick-room. Gregory the Great admonishes the Bishop of Syracuse to allow Mass to be celebrated in the house of a certain Venantius.

In Frankish territory and later on generally throughout the northern lands, where the manorial estates of the nobles were scattered wide over the country, the house chapels, with their Masses celebrated by the house chaplain or manor priest, became permanent institutions. But it was not easy to legislate against the abuses, which could hardly be avoided under the circumstances.[1] At first, stress was laid on the obligation of attending the bishop's church or the parish church on all higher feasts, but later on this was reduced to just the feast of Easter. The Carolingian reform sought to reaffirm the canon of Laodicea forbidding all divine service in the home, but eventually had to tolerate a practice

---

[1] Archbp. Agobard of Lyons (d. 840) complained that there was hardly a moneyed man who did not have a palace chaplain whom he then employed sometimes as a table-waiter, sometimes as a stablegroom.

less strict. A capitulary of Haito of Basel (807–827) permitted Mass to be said in the homes of the sick. But finally, after much hesitation and change of policy in medieval legislation, the Council of Trent forbade Mass in private dwellings.

PRIVATE MASSES

From these Masses said in private homes, on an estate or at a grave-side where at least a group of people, however small, attends the service, we must carefully distinguish the *private* Mass strictly so called. This we understand as a Mass celebrated for its own sake, with no thought of anyone participating, a Mass where only the prescribed server is in attendance, or even where no one is present, as was once the case in the so-called *Missa solitaria*. These are the Masses—contrasted to the conventual Mass and the parochial Mass—which are most generally referred to in medieval documents as "private Masses or special or particular Masses."

Without doubt there is no intrinsic contradiction in such a performance of the Christian sacrifice. Apart from any consideration of parallels outside revealed religion, the very first sacrifice cited in Holy Writ is one which two individuals, Abel and Cain, offered up, each by himself. Further, in the levitical cult the possibility was not excluded that at a sacrifice requested by someone absent, the priestly officiant alone should be present. Both cases are conceivable also in the New Covenant, all the more when the consciousness grew that in the Eucharist all the sacrifices of former times find their fulfillment and consummation, even those which the individual was wont to offer up or to have offered up. In other words, the sacrifice of the New Testament was not only a Eucharist of the redeemed community, but an oblation which one could present as a prayer or as an expiation in certain difficulties. In this sense the Council of Trent defined the propitiatory character of the Mass sacrifice. Since a public celebration at which the congregation assembled was at first provided only on Sundays and the infrequent feast-days, it was quite easy to assume that a bishop or priest might, on one of the other days, offer up the sacrifice in his own name, urged on by personal gratitude and petition. He could then say Mass at his own home in much the same way as he would say it elsewhere when asked to do so.

Evidences of such Masses survive from at least the sixth century. Gregory the Great says that Cassius, Bishop of Narni, was accustomed to offer God the holy sacrifice every day. John the Almoner (d. 620) reprimands the people who were less zealous, saying that he could just as well have offered Mass at home for himself as in the public Church.

Personal devotion must likewise have induced the individual priest-monks to say private Masses in their monasteries. Although St. Benedict himself showed no inclination to countenance having a number of priests in his convents, St. Gregory the Great already appears to favor the ordination of monks, and the Roman Synod of 610 under Boniface IV, which approved the ordaining of monks, seems to have marked the turning-point. From that time on, the number of priests in monasteries begins to grow. Even if this did not itself give the first impetus to the desire for personal celebration, the latter did soon follow more or less frequently. An indication of this is the increase in the number of altars in the monasteries; at first they are erected, one apiece in all the oratories of the monastery, later on they are all brought together in the main church as side-altars. In eighth-century accounts of the lives of various holy monks mention is made time after time of their celebrating Mass almost daily, and in the ninth century this is already accepted as a permanent rule.

VOTIVES, REQUIEMS

The personal devotion of the celebrant was not, however, whether in the monasteries or elsewhere, the only source of this increase in private Mass, nor was it even the strongest source. Stronger by far was the desire of the faithful for Votive Masses; that is to say, for Masses which took care of their earnest concerns (*vota*), not the least important of which was regard for the dead. The domestic celebration of the Eucharist had also in great measure served such interests. And as these Masses which were devoted to special interests were detached from the domestic congregation and were transferred to the oratories connected with the church or monastery, the occasions when the priest stood at the altar alone were multiplied. Thus from this angle too, impetus was given the private Mass.

A great importance attached even in ancient times to the Mass for the Dead. As early as 170 there is evidence from the apocryphal Acts of St. John that in Asia Minor a eucharistic memorial for the dead was conducted on the third day after burial; this took place at the grave. The anniversary commemoration is no more recent. In the fourth century the commemoration on the seventh day and on the thirtieth day became known; elsewhere it is the ninth day and the fortieth day that are observed. All of these fixed days for the memorial of the dead, along with the ritual solemnization of the day of burial, derive from pre-Christian tradition, with the celebration of the Eucharist taking the place of ancient sacrifice for the dead and sometimes perhaps of the *refrigerium* too.[2]

It was precisely this *refrigerium* or memorial meal, eaten at the

---

[2] A memorial meal for the dead.

grave-side of deceased person, probably without reference to any particular day, and attested in the third/fourth century even for the burial sites of the Apostles Peter and Paul, that could be replaced by Mass when the Church began to take an adverse stand because of abuses that crept in—Mass in the sense of Votive Masses at the graves of Apostles and martyrs, and intercessory Masses for the Dead at the graves of relations.

About the turn of the sixth century it was not unusual for a priest to read Mass for a dead person on a series of days one after the other, with no one participating. This can be deduced from a story of St. Gregory the Great about the priest John, who wanted to give his attendant at the public baths two offering breads, whereupon the latter made himself known as a soul doing penance and asked the priest rather to offer up the sacrifice for him, which the priest John therefore did daily for a whole week. Towards the end of the seventh century there developed various prayer confraternities pledged to offer suffrages from church to church and monastery to monastery, and especially a number of Masses for the Dead. At the Synod of Attigny (762) the attending bishops and abbots bound themselves to say, among other things, a hundred Masses for each of the group who would die. A cooperative agreement entered into in 800 between St. Gall and Reichenau stipulated, *inter alia*, that for each deceased monk every priest was to say three Masses on three successive days after the report of the death was received, and also another Mass on the thirtieth day; at the beginning of each month, after the Office for the dead of the convent, each priest was again to read a Mass; and finally every year on November 14 a general commemoration of the dead was to be held, again with three Masses by each priest. From this time on, private Masses for the Dead is an established arrangement, especially in monasteries.[3]

Votive Masses for other purposes and in favor of individual persons or groups were also initiated in Christian antiquity. About 370 a Roman writer tells of repeated eucharistic celebrations for "strangers as well as residents of the city." Augustine pities the ladies and maidens who had fallen into the hands of barbarians because they do not have the eucharistic sacrifice and, in consequence, they themselves can neither take part in the public celebration nor have Mass said for them. The *Leonianum* contains a great number of formularies which obviously have in view the private petitions either of the priest himself or of other offerers: among others are those marked "after an illness" and several against the menace of evil tongues. The Votive Masses in the older *Gelasianum* are

---

[3] As far as ritual was concerned, the Mass for the Dead was at that time not as differentiated from other Masses as is the case nowadays, even aside from the color of the vestments.

fully developed; they form the main contents of the third of the three books of which the sacramentary is composed. They have reference to private concerns like a journey, unjust threats, sickness, various afflictions, wedding, childlessness, birthday, anniversary of ordination, growth in charity, and we might add the Masses for the Dead; and likewise public concerns like mortality, plague, drought, good weather, war and peace, the welfare of the king, and such. The low state of medicine and hygiene and in general the small knowledge of natural remedies, as well as the widespread uncertainty of legal rights in the early medieval states, to some extent explain the large number of external petitions in these Votive Masses and the strong appeal they had for the people.

Of Gallic Mass books, the Missal of Bobbio is especially rich in Votive Masses, here fitted out with readings.

The high tide for Votive Masses is the Carolingian period. Alcuin himself had not only prepared from older sources an important assortment of Votive Masses for his supplement to the Gregorian Sacramentary, but he had compiled a special collection which has come down to us as a *liber sacramentorum*. Here for the first time we find Masses expressly assigned to certain days of the week, three formularies for each day. Of these, the first is concerned with a particular theme from the Christian economy of salvation appropriated to each day of the week; this section more or less approaches the Proper Masses of the Church year. The second group regards, as a rule, the greater ascetical needs; the formula for Thursday, to instance one case, is headed "Prayer against evil thoughts." The third group called the *Missa s. Augustini*, is written in a tone of penitence and plea for pardon. A considerable part of them was composed by Alcuin himself. From this time on, the Mass books contain a superabundance of Votive Masses. In the Sacramentary of Fulda there are more than a hundred.

In many cases the very topic theme or subject of the prayers shows that the celebrant alone was busy with the sacrifice. Typical in this regard is the formula of a "Mass which the priest should say for himself." Masses of this sort appear already in the Missal of Bobbio around 700 and after that with ever-increasing regularity in the Mass books of the Gallo-Carolingian area, sometimes in several variant forms. These formularies concentrate exclusively on the celebrant's own salvation and therefore all prayers—orations, preface and *Hanc igitur*—are written in the singular. But Masses for the concerns of others also begin to be contrived in such a fashion that the presence of the faithful would be at most incidental. This must have been the case when, in some monasteries, a "daily Mass for the king," became usual or when synods of the tenth and eleventh centuries bound priests, on short notice, to ten or thirty Masses for king and kingdom.

INCREASE OF MASSES

The ninth century is the time in which the celebration of Mass takes on an increase. Many celebrate two or three times a day, and the report is circulated—as an encouragement and comfort—that Pope Leo III occasionally offered the sacrifice seven and nine times in a day. Daily celebration by each individual priest seems to have become at this time if not (by far) the general rule, at least the prevailing one. On Sundays and feasts it is said for the congregation, just as even today the "application for the people" is demanded of the pastor on these days. On weekdays it seems to have been, by and large, a Votive Mass for his own intention or that of others, even though the formulary chosen is one specified for the day, as later on this was actually demanded. This meant a momentous augment in the frequency of celebration. The appropriation of the sacrifice to the diverse concerns of the faithful had really aroused the desire of the faithful and so led to a multiplication of the celebration. This is made manifest in the fact that everywhere that a number of priests were together—not only in monasteries, that is, but also in cathedral churches and in the larger centers—altars started to increase in number. In the whole of Christian antiquity every church had possessed but one altar. In North Africa this continued so till the fall of Christianity in the seventh century, and in the Orient, at least in churches of the Byzantine rite, it is still the rule. At Rome about the sixth century, oratories in honor of the Apostles and martyrs, along with the altars pertaining to them—hitherto scattered all over the city—were erected inside the churches. But we come across this increase of altars on a larger scale in Gaul, where Bishop Palladius of Saintes about 590 had 13 altars constructed in one church. Similar instances are not uncommon after that.

From the ninth century on, side altars are part of the structure of every larger church. A contributing factor was the worship of saints and their relics; it was thought that this could be done best in connection with a special altar. Another factor was the desire on the part of both faithful and priest for Votive Masses for which the path was now free and which could take place inside one's own church. Finally a third element entered in, this one a limitation; it was the practice to celebrate but once each day at any one altar and more especially it was forbidden that a priest should use an altar which had been used by the bishop previously on the same day.

About the era of the Ottos, however, the dark side of this all too frequent celebration began to be remarked. Episcopal and synodal decrees gradually permitted only a triple celebration on any one day. Others even forbade bination outside the case of necessity, as did Alexander II in 1065 and Innocent III even more positively in 1206; since then it has continued as the general norm. As a consequence the number of altars in churches newly built since then, shrinks back to more reasonable proportion.

But in the thirteenth century *a new increase in private Masses sets in,* this time not through the plural celebration of the same priest but rather as the result of the growth of the clergy in larger cities, an element that contributed in no small way to the ecclesiastical crisis of the sixteenth century. This increase was naturally accompanied by a new increase in the number of altars. Churches with thirty-five to forty-five altars were no rarity. The church of St. Mary at Danzig and the cathedral at Magdeburg each had forty-eight of them around 1500.

Meanwhile church architecture had been successfully endeavoring to fit the side-altars into the building properly, worthily. In France the Romanesque period had already created the circle of chapels surrounding the choir of the church, and in the Gothic period this was taken up also in other countries. In other cases Gothic produced a number of altar niches in the aisle of the nave by making use of the buttresses as part of the inner structure; this solution corresponds to the double row of chapels opening onto either side of the nave, which Baroque architecture employed. But that was hardly enough to supply the demand for side-altars which in the late Middle Ages served as church symbols of the guilds and the richer patrician families. In the age of the ecclesiastical reform, when limitations were again set on private Masses and a greater part of the formularies developed for this purpose were reduced to shrunken existence amongst the *orationes diversæ*, St. Charles Borromeo ordered the removal of all altars which had been built near the organ loft or next to the pulpit, in front of the columns and pillars, and many other churches in the course of time followed his example.

In this swaying back and forth one can trace the problem that the private Mass gives rise to. In its favor is the acknowledgment that the holy sacrifice is an offering of impetration and propitiation, and in this sense has a special value for the anxieties and desires of individuals; as the well-known formula puts it, it is offered for the living and the dead. On the other hand, however, society also has its high worth. The ideal of a single Eucharistia embracing all, once uttered by Ignatius the Martyr, should not be needlessly disowned or enfeebled. We saw how in the monasteries of the early Middle Ages (and later too) the stipulation of worship in common was continued. This included the common Communion of priests on Communion days. For a long time private Mass was not generally required, but only tolerated within certain limits.

MISSA SOLITARIA

Thus a distinct form for the private Mass was evolved only slowly and gradually. In the first period, comprising the eighth and ninth cen-

turies, there was a tendency to force the private character of the celebration even to extremes. At this time the so-called *missa solitaria*,
without any server, was formed. The exclusive singular in the prayers
of several Mass formulas bears this out. If the ground-plan of the Roman
Mass and particularly of the canon had not been regarded by tradition
as beyond the reach of change, we would, in the ninth century, surely
have experienced in the Roman liturgy what actually almost happened
to the Gallic liturgy (which has no fixed canon); that is, the entire
wording would have been rewritten in the "I" manner.

Luckily this result did not really occur. On the contrary, in the ninth
century there is some new legislation aimed directly at stopping priests
from celebrating alone. For how can a priest say *Dominus vobiscum* or
Sursum corda when no one else is there? Others refer to *Oremus* or
Orate pro me or to the mention of *circumadstantes*—all of which would
be meaningless if no one but the priest were present. More than once
the demand is made that, besides the priest, at least *two* persons must be
present since he does say: *Dominus vobiscum*. More precisely, mention
is made of "assistants" of *cooperatores* who should be on hand. But the
emphasis is not on the function of serving. Walafried Strabo calls it a
"legitimate Mass" if, besides the priest, there are present "someone to
respond, offer and communicate." The minimum required in the case is
therefore not so much that someone cooperates at the altar in the capacity of a serving deacon, but rather that someone is present as a co-
celebrant, so that the social, plural character which is so distinctly
revealed in the liturgy we actually have, and which in some way or other
issues from the very essence of the New Testament sacrifice, might be
safeguarded. This is the direction taken in all the attempts to vindicate
the position assumed; that the *Dominus vobiscum* might be able to be
understood as a greeting of all Christendom, with whom the priest
knows himself to be conjoined, and so on.

Since the thirteenth century, however, there are extant other statutes
in which *one cleric* is demanded also for private Mass, a demand which
was no longer made in the Missal of Pius V but which was repeated
in many diocesan decrees in the sixteenth century.

The requirement of having a cleric present could only be considered
an ideal, especially after the sacerdotal recruits were derived chiefly
from the Tridentine seminaries, and it was an ideal that even earlier
could not be everywhere realized even for public Mass. The monasteries
could most easily make some corresponding provision. At Cluny in the
eleventh century a lay-brother was summoned to serve any priest-monk
who wanted to celebrate. But there is mention also of the *puer*, which
probably refers to the young oblates. If a cleric was at hand, he was
allowed to exercise the duties of his order, that is, read the Epistle if he

was in orders, and prepare the chalice and purify it after Communion. Amongst the Cistercians the priest was supposed to have two Mass-servers, a cleric to serve him and answer the prayers, and a layman to present the water and light the candles.

Whereas in most monastic constitutions there is only passing reference to serving, in the Dominican *Ordinarium* of 1256 the *servitor* at a private Mass is given greater attention. The pertinent rubrics are still found—naturally somewhat developed—compiled in a special chapter of the Dominican Missal.

In the *Ordinarium* of 1256 these rules for the server belonged to a special chapter which also contains more detailed directions for the priest at private Mass. Of these a noteworthy one is the rule that the sequence, otherwise so frequent, should be dropped at private Mass. Other regulations for the priest, in so far as they did not regard the special Dominican usages, were already extant, scattered in older statutes. Thus it was almost a general custom that the priest vested at his respective side-altar. Nor was the warning that he was to speak only in a medium loud voice anything new. To it corresponds, in the prescriptions of Cluny, the obviously necessary direction that the priest should read the song portions *in directum* but that he certainly should not sing them. Thus out of the private Mass grew the read Mass—the *low* Mass.

That the Mass is only read and not sung has at last become in the Roman liturgy the most prominent particular, in fact, the only actual difference to distinguish the rite of the private Mass from that of the public Mass, if we except the vernacular prayers which have recently been added to the conclusion. Wherever in the oriental rites, as a consequence of union, the private Mass has become usual, the differences are essentially greater.

With us the private Mass has, in the last analysis, almost completely doffed its private character, gaining public recognition and in fact becoming simply *the* Mass. Not only do rubricists nowadays consider it the basis of any presentment of the external actions of the Mass, but even the Roman Missal itself, departing from a custom in vogue till late in the Middle Ages, presents the rite of the *missa lecta* as the basic form, describing the special ceremonies of the solemn high Mass as a sort of appendix and devoting only a short notice to the peculiarities of the simple sung Mass.

This strange phenomenon is on a par with the fact that at the beginning of the modern period the older solemn forms suddenly begin to lose some of the stateliness and the simplified forms partly replace them. Besides a low interest in liturgy which this seems to show, another factor behind this is the unfamiliarity of the faithful in regard to the Latin, the strangeness of which was felt with growing keenness and the loud use of which, in prayers and readings, except in so far as it added to the splendor of the proceedings, was less and less appreciated. Thus it became increasingly easy to discontinue the singing at the altar. The read Mass became the ground form. And if it was found undesirable to follow the Mass in quiet devotion or if, at a larger gathering, it was thought agreeable to emphasize the social side of the celebration, the solution was more frequently in common prayer or song in the vernacular, accompanying the low Mass. And finally, in our own century, a form of community Mass, the dialogue Mass, was devised, built up on the *missa lecta* but recapturing in great part some of the simple beauty of the *missa cantata* and combining therewith the advantage of the vernacular.

To this development another circumstance contributed no little, namely the fact that less and less stress was laid on the demand that the faithful take part on Sunday in a public celebration. The obligation had already been broken down somewhat during the later Middle Ages and was finally set aside entirely. Thus the low Mass, whether with singing in the vernacular or without, could be the Sunday Mass even in parish churches and it could thus easily attain that position of authority at the high altar which it had surely not enjoyed in previous years.

The rubrical convergence of the two forms of celebration to the point where the only distinction lay in the singing or speaking of the text was therefore only the consequence of a legal assimilation. However, this rubrical convergence was not the result only of the fact that the private Mass retained as much as possible of the high Mass, but also that the latter gave up many of its privileges. Already in the twelfth and thirteenth centuries the priest at a high Mass began to read from the Mass book the texts which were handled by others, just as he did at a private Mass. Other privileges, while continuing as rubrics, are practically abandoned. Scarcely ever does one see a cleric in attendance to read the Epistle, or the special server who tends the book and, if a cleric, brings the chalice to the altar, and after Communion covers it and carries it back. At most there is a second server who shares the duties of the first.

The problem of the server is today identical for both sung Mass and private Mass. Whereas in the early Middle Ages a cleric was ordered for the former but not for the private Mass, we see that later a cleric was demanded for both and finally in either case a layman was permitted.[4] The practical solution, in fact, follows what was doubtless the tradition of former clerical schools in monasteries and chapters, and chooses young boys whose innocence can, in a measure, substitute for the clerical character. Still that spiritual character cannot be entirely lacking if, in addition to the technical training, there is a spiritual commitment and,

---

[4] The active assistance of servers was taken into account and prescribed for the first time in a liturgical document in the restored Easter Vigil and later in the general reform of Holy Week in 1955.

under favorable circumstances, even formal enrollment, as is actually being done in many places nowadays under orders of the bishop.

The fact that the boundaries between private Mass and public Mass have gradually disappeared is connected also with the fact that in the last few centuries daily celebration by every priest has been taken more and more for granted. On the one hand, this daily celebration by the priest himself has become, along with the breviary, part and parcel of his spiritual life. The ground for this is the consideration that personal celebration, even from the viewpoint of one's own religious life, has greater value than participation in another's Mass. On the other hand, this personal desire of the priest coincides with the good of the cure of souls. The people are thus offered opportunities to attend Holy Mass every day in churches and chapels, and in large churches, especially on Sundays, also at various hours. At the altar not only the *festa fori* but also the *festa chori*, the individual saints' feasts, are celebrated. Thus the personal and public factors go hand in hand, leading in many cases to a regular semi-public celebration of the Mass.

MASS STIPENDS

There is still another influence at work, one that was efficacious already in Christian antiquity and which continually gives rise to the private Mass properly so called. There should be some way of satisfying the demands of the faithful who request the priest to offer the sacrifice for their special wants and who tender him the offering for this in the form of a stipend. That these offerings form, for a large number of the clergy, an important part of their income, especially at a time when richly endowed foundations are a thing of the past, cannot be denied. But that there is also peril here is equally beyond doubt. Church legislation, as the result of sad experiences which it has had in the course of history, seeks to counter it. Of course the legitimacy of celebration on this title is not at all questionable. In fact, although the votive formularies do not—and rightly—play the same role as of yore, still the Votive Mass, or the sacrifice which is appropriated to a person or a family for their special intention, exhibits that title of private Mass which gives it most obviously the right and power to be, especially since it is anchored in the tradition of the Church since earliest times. But the personal factor which binds the offerer with such a celebration ought to be restrengthened as much as possible. The faithful who request a Mass must be conscious of the fact that they ought to participate as co-celebrants at such a Mass. And besides care must be taken that such a votive celebration does nothing to hinder the development of public worship which must always be our first concern.

We might, then, sum up the last three sections with the following diagram showing the *historical evolution* of the various forms of the Mass as we know them today:

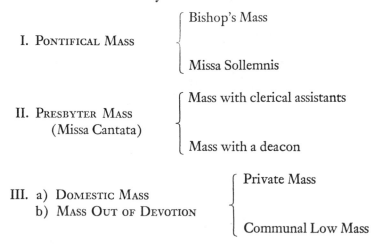

I. PONTIFICAL MASS	{	Bishop's Mass
		Missa Sollemnis
II. PRESBYTER MASS (Missa Cantata)	{	Mass with clerical assistants
		Mass with a deacon
III. a) DOMESTIC MASS b) MASS OUT OF DEVOTION	{	Private Mass
		Communal Low Mass

6. Forms of Popular Participation

The picture of divine worship in Christian antiquity, with the faithful crowded around the altar, offering up the sacrifice together with the priest and joining in the prayers and singing, is familiar to everyone nowadays. In fact the present arrangement of the Mass can be understandably explained at many points only by reference to that primitive picture.

From what has been said above, much can be seen of the many vicissitudes that popular participation at Mass underwent—its ebb and flow in so far as it has been impressed on various periods of liturgical history. Numerous particulars will be called to our attention later in our study of the various parts of the Mass-liturgy. Here we will endeavor to put together in a short sketch the most important factors, complement them with evidence of a more general nature, and, out of the see-saw of history, let certain supratemporal viewpoints come to the fore.

One fundamental condition for the formation of important types of general participation in the Mass celebration was that the assembled faithful should form a community tied together by the same faith and the same love. In the centuries of Christian antiquity that was to a great extent the case. Only at the fore-Mass was an outer circle of guests or candidates to the society admitted, but in the consciousness of the congregation these people were clearly distinguished from the narrower circle of fully authorized members. We thus encounter forms which were composed for their dismissal at the end of the Mass of the Catechumens. Far into the Middle Ages these rites for dismissing the catechumens were used for the children during Lent in the weeks of preparation for Baptism. Even to the very threshold of modern times those who, as public sinners, were no longer worthy to take part in the worship of the community were expelled on Ash Wednesday. The ex-communicated, too, were very strictly excluded all through the Middle Ages. But aside from these very unusual cases the Middle Ages had no recognized outsiders. Just as in church building the old-time atrium and the parts in between became simply the open portion of the church, and the doorway was like an invitation to the whole town to come into the holy place, so all forms of banishment and dismissal fell into disuse. All the townspeople were Christians and all Christians were children of the house.

It was precisely the obviousness of the open doors to the Church, standing unlocked to all, that hindered a return to a more ancient sever-ity when, at the start of modern times, circumstances grew so funda-mentally different. For decades larger portions of the people wavered between the old Church and New Learning. In the hope of winning them back it was necessary not to turn them away at the door. And the suggestion that was brought up at the Council of Trent, to ban public sinners (prostitutes, concubinaries, usurers *et al.*) from the Church or at least to order them out after the Gospel, was recognized as imprac-ticable. Thus for our own time a situation has arisen which would have been incomprehensible to Christian antiquity, even aside from the laws of the "discipline of the secret"—a situation where at our divine service every sharp boundary between Church and world is broken down, so that Jew and heathen can press right up to the steps of the altar and can stand in the very midst of the faithful at the most sacred moment. Such a situation is possible and tolerable so long as the faithful are only on-lookers and listeners at a sacred drama, and it will be substantially and actually overcome whenever and in so far as they take up a more active role.

COMING AND GOING

One of the first forms of expression by which a closed society reveals itself is a fixed order of coming and going; everyone gets there on time and no one leaves until the meeting is adjourned. A noteworthy severity with regard to late-comers was displayed in the fifth century Syrian *Testamentum Domini*. The deacons were directed to keep the doors locked when the sacrifice was being offered. If some of the faithful came late and knocked at the door they were not to be admitted; but for these tardy brethren a special prayer was included, that God might give them greater zeal and love. At the end of the meeting we find in all the liturgies a formal dismissal. It happened of course that some individuals, even communicants, did not wait for this. Little by little a special order became necessary for those who did not communicate, who already, towards the end of the ancient period, formed the greater proportion by far.

As we will see more in detail later, it was the practice in the city of Rome as well as in Gaul to let them depart before the distribution of Communion and this departure of many was not only countenanced but was even taken into account in the setting up of the liturgy; at Rome the announcements for the following week were made at this point, and in Gaul those who were going to leave were given a solemn blessing right after the *Pater noster*. The faithful were thus implicitly admonished to stay at least until then. For already in the sixth century many were under the impression that they had fulfilled their obligation if they heard the readings. Therefore Cæsarius of Arles makes clear to his audience that the minimum required to fulfill one's Christian duty is to be present at the *consecratio Corporis et Sanguinis*, the *oratio dominica* and the *benedictio*.

In the Carolingian reform, too, following the lead of tradition, the blessing is considered the conclusion prior to which no one was allowed to leave; but now it is the blessing of the newly introduced Roman liturgy that is meant, which is given in some form or other at the end of Mass. The prevalent rareness of the reception of Holy Communion had perhaps forced such a change of attitude. Therefore, Amalar, taking up a question often asked by the "uneducated," at what parts of the Mass must one be definitely present, answers: from the offertory to the *Ite missa est*, for here the sacrifice is being offered. Later moral theology also included the fore-Mass, whose independence was perceived less and less. But Church legislation, whether during the Middle Ages or later, did not make any special declaration regarding these precise limits.

PARTICIPATION OF THE PEOPLE

In the liturgical action the participation of the people was manifested especially by the fact that they did not merely listen to the prayers of the priest in silence but ratified them by their acclamations. The custom of using such acclamations was inherted by the Church from the Synagogue; the very style and language in part betrays this: *Et cum spiritu tuo, Amen*. That the people in Christian antiquity actually spoke these answers is obvious from the occasional remarks of the Fathers. Even Justin testified to it. Jerome mentioned one time that the Amen in the Roman basilicas reverberated like a heavenly thunder. Augustine in his sermons and writings often made reference to the responses of the people.

The only question is, how long during the Middle Ages did the practice continue. Cæsarius of Arles still takes it for granted. It is also otherwise ascertained for the Gallican liturgy of the sixth and seventh centuries. Even in the early medieval liturgy of the city of Rome, which had become quite pretentious as the result of the added *schola* and the presence of a numerous clergy, there was still a constant mention of the responses by the people.

The Carolingian reform appears to have insisted on this with a certain doggedness. In Charlemagne's *Admonitio generalis* of 789 there is a decree regarding the people's part. Amalar advises those who do not understand the Latin Gospel lesson, at least to pronounce the *Gloria tibi Domine* with the rest. Other Carolingian authors talk about these responses as something taken for granted.

In his penitential lists, Burchard of Worms (d. 1025) mentions the neglect to respond as an example of unbecoming behavior in church. And even later the responses are referred to as at least the ideal requirement. After that, however, the practice falls into such oblivion that in our own century the right of the people to make these responses has had actually to be proved.

Besides these short acclamations, the people's share in the Mass since earliest times also included a certain ever-increasing number of hymnic texts. The most venerable of them is the *Sanctus* along with the *Benedictus*, which also remained the people's song the longest. Of a similarly venerable age was the refrain in the responsorial chants, namely, in the Roman liturgy, the chants between the readings; but these, with their ever-varying texts, were at an early period turned over to the *schola* in their entirety. Similar in character to the refrain was the *Kyrie eleison* in the introductory litany which came substantially later. After that the *Agnus Dei* was added. The two larger chants, the *Gloria* and the *Credo* (which appeared quite early in the northern countries), were perhaps intended principally for the clergy assembled around the altar. The individual fortunes of all these songs will occupy our attention in connection with the detailed explanation to come. Taken together—aside from the refrains of the interposed chants—they form the chants of the so-called Ordinary of the Mass which, along with the ancient acclamation, were taken over from the people by the choir of clerics and finally by the church choirs.

Besides the words by which the participation of the people in the celebration was made manifest, we have to add also some activity, *doing* something. The "Partaking," (*Koinonia*), which consists in receiving the Sacrament, gradually disappears, its early bloom shrivelled into well-defined and all too few occasions. This receptive participation stands in contrast to the contributive, the upsurging motion of the offertory procession which grew increasingly strong near the end of the ancient period and remained a living practice for over a thousand years. As an introduction either to the Mass proper or to the reception of Communion, we have the kiss of peace, already known to the primitive Church and still remaining at the present in a residue of stylized forms. We will also come across traces of a transient handwashing by the people.

BODILY POSTURE

Most especially, however, the inner participation of the faithful at the holy action has to be exhibited in a suitable bodily posture. The principal posture (aside from the early period with its meal celebration) has always been a posture of standing. Before the higher Being whom he wishes to honor, a person stands erect, particularly when he realizes his obligation of service. Just as the priest at the altar stands before God in reverential readiness, so also the faithful; they are the *circumstantes*. In line with this, it was an understood norm in olden times that the people followed the motions of the bishop or the priest when he said the prayers and, in general, in all the rest of his deportment, so that like him they stood with hands uplifted and facing east.[1] Standing was the ordinary posture of prayer even among ancient peoples, in fact, standing with uplifted hands and with eyes fixed in the direction of the rising sun. This posture of prayer was continued by the Christians, both people and *liturgi* together, with only this variant: they saw in the orient sun which they faced, an image of the Risen Christ. Only when the celebrant pronounced a blessing over the congregation, to whom he turned standing erect, was there any change in the bearing of the congregation; now it differed from his in accordance with the shouted command, *Humiliate capita vestra Deo*—they stood with heads bowed.

But later in the Middle Ages the bodily posture of the faithful grew more and more unlike that of the priest. The bow of the head, as at the blessing, gradually became a sign of the congregation's humility in the sight of God, and was used during the orations and especially during the canon. On the other hand, kneeling was still generally limited during the first millenary to days without festive character and even here it was limited to the fore-Mass. First, kneeling was proclaimed by the deacon's *Flectamus genua* for the people's meditative prayer which introduced the orations. Then, for the people, kneeling was transferred to the respective orations themselves, and on non-festive days the bowed

---

[1] Apparently the turning to the East was expected, no matter what the position of the church building. But we may suppose that this orientation at a prayer had something to do with the subsequent change in the method of construction, having the apse to the East instead of the front of the building (which was the more ancient fashion), so that when the *liturgus* prayed the faithful did not have to turn their back to him and the altar.

but standing posture, hitherto in vogue during the canon and other orations, was also soon changed to kneeling. Already by 813 the Synod of Tours represents this attitude as the fundamental characteristic posture of the faithful (always, of course, excepting the days when, in honor of Christ's Resurrection, one prayed standing). On Sundays and feast-days (taking this latter word in its widest sense) the standing position was retained. It was not till the eucharistic movement of the thirteenth century that any inroad was made here, namely, by kneeling at the consecration. The *Ordo missæ* of John Burchard which appeared in 1502 still directed the participants at a Mass celebrated with singing to use the standing posture as a general rule; the only variations were kneeling at the *Confiteor* in the prayers at the foot of the altar, and at the consecration; there was no longer any mention of bowing.

Sitting, as a posture for the faithful, was hardly thought of seriously in the churches of the Middle Ages, since there was no provision made for seats. Only for the choir of clerics in capitular and monastic churches were choir stalls erected and for this narrower circle of participants new choir rules were devised. Established on the same basis as that which held for the faithful, these rules became constantly more detailed and began to include sitting, just as the bishop and *presbyter* had been doing previously in accordance with the oldest Roman *ordines*. The choir sat at the Epistle and, provided the whole group did not sing, also during the following chants. But it was not till near the end of the Middle Ages that any localities began to consider the possibility of the people's sitting down. But now in many countries it is regularly taken into account in the erection of churches, especially when, as a consequence of the Reformers' agitation, the sermon began to take on greater importance.

The benches of pews used in church also made provision for kneeling. This ties in with the ever-increasing importance of low Mass and the rules set down for it. It would seem that in the later Middle Ages the rules for posture at low Mass and at Masses conducted with less solemnity were basically the rules which held outside of feast-days and festal seasons. That means, as a rule, kneeling at the orations and during the canon, to which must be added kneeling during the *Confiteor* at the beginning. Standing was expressly required only during the Gospel. To retain these regulations regarding kneeling and standing and at the same time to avoid a frequent and, in last analysis, disturbing change of posture during the short space of a low Mass, some simple rule had to be devised for low Mass, namely, that aside from the Gospel one would kneel all the way through. This rule, however, was never very strictly insisted on.

The forms of external participation, however, fulfill their meaning and purpose only when they are props and stays for an interior concurrence on the part of the faithful. The different forms of bodily demeanor are indeed an index to the distinction between prayer and reading, and even in prayer they bring the important thing to the fore. The acclamations help to accentuate this fact. If the faithful of the earlier Middle Ages took part in the offertory procession, sang the *Sanctus* and the *Agnus Dei*, received the Sacrament or at least the *pax*, it is obvious that the grand lineaments of the sacred ceremony must have to some degree continually entered their consciousness. They could not, it is true, follow the wording of prayers and lessons when the language was different from their own, and this was a disadvantage, but it was by no means an absolute hindrance to devout participation. That the faithful were to pray silently by themselves during the sacrifice was also insisted on from early times.

The natural pattern was, of course, for this inward devotion to adjust itself to the actual course of the liturgical function insofar as this was attainable, and to accompany the priest at least at a distance. This ideal had evidently inspired those who, in the Carolingian reform and even later in the Middle Ages, strove for the observance of the olden forms of outward participation. The prayer book of Charles the Bald presents prayer-texts of offering at the offertory, of intercession when the priest asks for prayer for himself, and of preparation for Communion; they are texts which square thoroughly with those of the priest. An English prayer book from the thirteenth century also sets great store on the liturgical collaboration of whoever used it. Joining with the prayers of the priest occurs in many places, often, it may be, quite extrinsically. Just on the threshold of modern times Burchard of Strassburg, in a similar vein, makes a rather comprehensive remark regarding the faithful's participation: Even if people do not understand the priest's words or the Latin tongue, they should not say any other prayers but should pay attention to what the priest is saying and doing and should in spirit offer up, supplicate and plead along with him except during the time when the Sacrament is adored, and at that place in the canon where he (at the *Memento*) prays softly by himself; then one could likewise freely pray for oneself and for all those whom one wishes to commend to God. It is this same Burchard who wanted to inaugurate once more the responses by the *interessentes*, i.e., congregation.

In the period of humanism such extravagant proposals might possibly have been suggested for educated groups. But for the broad masses of the faithful the simplest premises for such plans were entirely lacking, particularly the ability to learn the priest's prayers or even the Ordinary of the Mass. Following the prayers of the priest was, and continued to be, beyond the reach of the average Catholic, and so the external forms of participation were long ago lost. The great stress of popular liturgical leadership has therefore gone in other directions since the ninth century, as we saw. It was enough to point out to the faithful what they could follow with their eyes and to explain the details of these sensible images as representations of Christ's redemptive Passion, extracting as far as possible every last meaning out of our Lord's institution. Allegory dominates the scene till well into modern times.[2] A long intellectual preparation was required, and many intermediate steps had to be taken before it became possible once more to establish a closer spiritual bond with the praying and sacrificing at the altar, and thus to go back again to more ancient forms of expression. It was only after chant and the *Singmesse* and the spread among the laity of the use of the missal paved the road, that an opening was gradually made for a fuller participation in the celebration and offering of the Holy Sacrifice.

7. *The Time of the Celebration of Mass*

As we turn to inquire about the time arrangements made for the celebration of Mass we must be careful to keep our eyes mainly on its public celebration, especially in the centuries in which there was a clear distinction between private Mass and public Mass.

The day for the community celebration of the Eucharist was Sunday, even in the primitive Church. On a Sunday, Paul was with his congregation at Troas where he at night "broke bread." Sunday is unequivocally designated in the *Didache* and in Justin.

What was till then more or less a matter of course, was at the beginning of the fourth century formulated as a sanctioned command at the Council of Elvira. After that, the precept of Sunday Mass was often repeated, both in the East and in the West. From the decrees of the Synod of Agde (506) it was copied into the general law of the Church. Still in the carrying out of the obligation, especially in country places, there were many difficulties that had to be contended with all through the Middle Ages.

OTHER DAYS OF PUBLIC WORSHIP

Besides Sundays, other days began to be reckoned as days of public worship on which one counted on the attendance of the congregation or even demanded it; these were the feast days, including the martyr feasts

[2] In the *Mediator Dei* of Pope Pius XII the Holy Father develops at length the idea that in holy Mass the people offer together with the priest, and bases his teaching on that of the great theologians and above all on the Mass prayers themselves. The pertinent sections (paragraphs 80–111, on "Participation of the Faithful in the Eucharistic Sacrifice") are a wonderful step to a fuller appreciation of the part the faithful must play, in heart and body, in offering the sacrifice. Cf. G. Ellard, "At Mass with My Encyclical," *Orate Fratres*, XXII (1947–48), 241–246.

of the respective church, and also the days after a great festival, especially Easter week, and the days of preparation for such festivals, especially Lent. During Lent daily attendance at divine service was considered of obligation for many centuries from Carolingian times on, and was so enjoined in the penitential books. Besides it was the custom since the fourth century in nearly all Christendom on the stational days, Wednesday and Friday, to conclude the fast in the afternoon with a prayer-meeting. Except in Egypt and probably also in Rome, this was nearly everywhere joined to the celebration of Mass. In Rome the same rule was followed, at any rate during the ember weeks, the Mass formulas for which have been preserved till our own days. And even in Rome it became customary after the outset of the Middle Ages, to celebrate Mass publicly at least on Wednesdays each week, as we are bound to conclude from the Scripture lessons appointed for this purpose. Each Ember week ended in the night between Saturday and Sunday with a long vigil, and the Mass of this vigil counted for the Sunday. However, about the seventh century a special Mass was formulated for this Sunday and the vigil Mass was moved back to Saturday morning so that Saturday too, at least in Ember week, received a distinction like that of Wednesday and Friday.

In the Orient, ever since the fourth century, Saturday had gradually been invested with the privilege of public Mass week after week, but for entirely different reasons. As a defensive parry against Manichean doctrine, Saturday, the day when creation had ended, was in time looked upon as "Sunday's brother" and was therefore fitted out in like manner with divine service.

A daily celebration of Mass with the character of a public service must, however, have remained unknown to the ancient Church until well in the fourth century. More comprehensive expressions are to be understood either of a private celebration or even merely of Communion at home. But in the time of St. Augustine a daily Mass to which all the faithful could come must have been very widespread, at least in Africa. When it became the prevailing rule to transfer Votive Masses to the public church, the sharp distinction between public and private celebration began to disappear in the churches of the West and there arose some transitional forms. The faithful were now able to attend Mass in church daily.

HOUR OF MASS

Still, public Mass on Sundays and feast days continued to retain its special prerogatives. All through the Middles Ages it had its appointed hour. And since the Church was free and (after renouncing the evening meal) no longer bound to choose an early morning hour, a time was set for common worship that appeared to be fitting for such a momentous task. On Sundays and feast days it was the third hour,[1] which was designated at Rome about 530, as well as in Gaul, and this hour it is which consistently recurs in the writings of both the liturgists and the canonists. Since the Middle Ages it was regularly preceded by Terce, not only in monastery and chapter churches but also as far as possible even in parish churches, and Sext usually followed. Therefore, in the still extant directions for ringing the church bells a special peal—rung two or even three times—was provided. The arrangement developed for Sundays and feasts was shifted also to week days when daily conventual Mass became common in monastery and chapter churches. But it must also have been adopted at quite an early period as the order of worship in parish churches. "Mass time" was an unambiguous time-designation all through the Middle Ages and even after, and it meant the third hour of the day.

Already in Ambrose there is evidence of an evening celebration of Mass, but only on fast days. In the Carolingian era a Mass at the ninth hour on fast days was as much a matter-of-course as the Mass at the third hour on other days. This remained the custom in the centuries to follow, especially for Lent. On other days that were midway between strict fasting days and feasts properly so called, a middle course was taken from the eleventh century on, with Mass at the sixth hour. It was not till near the end of the Middle Ages that any tendency was shown to push these later hours ahead by saying Mass as usual right after Sext or None, but anticipating these hours before noon. Taking a cue from this, John Burchard, in his *Ordo missæ* (1502), expanded the existing tradition and thus developed the more exact regulations that were then taken over into the *Rubricæ generales* of our Mass book. Its most important stipulation is that the "solemn Conventual Mass" on Sundays and feasts (semi-duplex and upward) ought to take place "in choir after Terse" on simple feasts and ferial days "after Sext," and on days of penance "after None"; that is, the Mass on feast days could, like the meals, continue to be attached to its usual hour of the day: it always takes place at the "third hour."

However, this holding to an appointed time for public worship has quite generally lost its importance since the later Middle Ages. That fact is connected with what we have already seen regarding the gradual breakdown of the distinction between public and private Mass. For a long time no particular hour was stipulated for private Mass, and therefore no connection with a canonical hour. True, the faithful, in accord-

---

[1] The "third hour" did not, of course, coincide precisely with our "nine o'clock," for the older reckoning was based on an apportionment of daylight into twelve parts from sunup to sundown; in winter these portions started later, were necessarily shorter; in summer they began earlier and were lengthened out. For that reason the Synod of Cambria (1586) stipulated: in summer at 8 o'clock, in winter at 9.

ance with ancient law, were not so free to attend the "private Masses" on Sundays and holy days as to be drawn away from public Mass; in fact, the faithful were obliged to fulfill their Sunday obligations not just in any public church but precisely in their own parish church. But with the coming of the Mendicants this law was slowly relaxed even though synod after synod took a firm stand in opposition. In the fifteenth century it had become in many places a right sanctioned by usage that the Sunday duty could be fulfilled in any church of one's choosing and, in consequence, at any Mass of one's choosing and this right soon obtained papal approbation, beginning in 1517 with a decree of Leo X.

Thus on Sundays we continue to have, at the customary hour, a service which we usually style the main service, but besides this, service has long since been conducted also at other hours, particularly in cities. Of these the early hours with their Communion Mass, at which there is a homily, are from the pastoral viewpoint as important as the main service, though this latter is perhaps richer at least musically. Even if the social aspect—the idea of community—is thus somewhat obscured, there is some compensation in the fact that so many of the faithful are offered the opportunity to take part in Sunday Mass, a viewpoint which was not entirely absent even in Christian antiquity. And likewise service on weekdays has not for a long time been conducted along the pattern of a monastic community that is independent and self-contained and can therefore follow the old rhythm of the Office hours, but the determining factor has been rather the people's work day.

Considerations of a similar sort under the conditions of World War II prompted the extensive approbation of evening Masses,[2] and this exclusively as public Masses, celebrated in the interests of the faithful but without being confined to Sundays and holy days. This is no unqualified innovation, even apart from the primitive Church, and even when we have only divine service of a festal nature in view. For far into the medieval period the services for Easter and Pentecost and for the Ember Sundays were conducted on the eve or vigil at a late evening hour; even in modern times an analogous custom regarding the Christmas midnight Mass, which had its origin in Venice, became quite widespread.

Besides the public Masses on Sundays and holy days with the corresponding assemblage—at least successively—of all the members of the congregation, attendance at weekday Mass also has been on the increase. In the early Church the only ones who attended weekday Mass were as a rule those for whose benefit the sacrifice was being offered. The celebration of Mass on the stational days must, no doubt, have gathered a larger crowd of the faithful. In North Africa where daily celebration was customary earliest of all, Augustine gives us to understand that this

2 By the Motu Proprio of Pius XII of March 19, 1957, daily evening Masses were made possible. Cf. p. 167.

was very necessary for the faithful in days of peril, that they might be able to continue steadfast. However, this is no evidence of a daily Mass attendance by a wider circle.

It was not till the late Carolingian era, in the writings of Regino of Prüm, that there are any traces of the faithful attending daily Mass. Daily attendance at Mass in the castle chapel was part of the order of the day amongst the Norman nobility of twelfth-century England; elsewhere too, the knights appear to have followed a similar practice. The people were encouraged in sermons to attend Mass daily, even in the days before the widespread desire to see our Lord which went to such excesses during the late Middle Ages. As a matter of fact daily attendance at Mass was a prevalent practice amongst all ranks of the people in the later Middle Ages.

8. *Accommodations of Space*

One of the wonderful manifestations of the inner strength, power, and extent of Christian worship is the fact that it is so spiritualized that it seems to be almost indifferent to conditions of space and yet it has produced, in every century, masterpieces of architecture and the other structural arts such as no other of man's ideas has been able to produce. We cannot here go into very great detail in showing, as we have done with other questions, how the construction of buildings and other spatial accessories has developed as an outer frame surrounding the celebration of Mass. All we can do is sketch a general outline and lay bare certain underlying trends that are closely connected with the celebration, pointing out especially the genetic line of these tendencies.

One of the most revolutionary innovations which Christianity produced was the departure from a cultus of place-worship connected with certain localities—holy mountains, mystic groves, even the sacred Temple in Jerusalem. Worship can take place wherever a holy people are gathered before God, for this people is the true Temple of the Lord (2 Cor. 6:16; 1 Cor. 3:16). Therefore in every place, from the rising of the sun to its going down, the new sacrifice is offered up (Mal. 1:11). The true sanctuary is to be found neither in Garizim nor in Jerusalem, but in every place where true adorers worship God in spirit and in truth (John 4:21 ff.).

PLACE OF WORSHIP

If, therefore, in the first centuries of Christianity there is but little mention of the place for divine worship and even that little is only inci-

dental, the reason is to be sought in something more than just the circumstances of the persecutions. People asembled for their Sunday celebration wherever some member of the congregation could manage to set
up the room for its performance. But the Eucharist was also celebrated
in the burial places of the dead [1] and even in the prisons of those held
captive. This basic freedom and mobility of divine service has been
retained all through the succeeding centuries right down to the present.
Today, too, whenever it is necessary, that sacrifice can be offered under
the open sky or in any suitable place, and no other barricade against the
profane world is exacted excepting the altarstone on which the sacred
species can rest; and even this requirement is in our days set aside with
the permission to use instead an *antimensium* like that traditional in the
Eastern Church. But two things continue to be indispensable for service:
a resting place for the sacred species and a place for the assembling of
the people. And thus, as soon as circumstances allowed Christianity to
unfold and develop with less restraint, the history of church architecture
and church art, already in embryo before Constantine's time, began its
marvellous course.

It is significant that in the Romance languages the prevalent word
used to designate the church building is the one which signifies an assembly, *ecclesia*, while in other languages, on the contrary, the word which
is primarily intended for the church building, χυριαχόν, "church," has
been transferred to the assembly. As a matter of fact the building is
nothing else than the material surrounding of the living temple of God,
a substantial shell which has formed and will continue to form even
though human foolishness or the forces of nature may have destroyed it.
For that reason it seems in its design to mirror the idea and structure of
the living temple. Just as the Church of God is built up of people and
clergy, so too the presbytery or choir, in whose vertex stands the
cathedra of the bishop, is separated from the nave of the church. Just as
the ecclesiastical assembly, following ancient custom, was wont to pray
facing East, toward the Orient from on high, so too the ecclesiastical
building is turned into a "ship" (nave = *navis*) voyaging towards the
East, and the orientation of the church is in fact carried out in such a
way (first in the East and later also in the West) that the apse is to the
East, and so the direction which the praying congregation faces coincides with the *lie* of the building.

*Finally, the consecration of the living temple is, in a way, carried over
to the material structure;* church and altar are consecrated and themselves become holy. There is something to be learnt from the fact that
in this consecration ceremony—the old Gallican rite, revitalized with
Roman traditions and still retained in today's *Pontificale Romanum*—

---

[1] But the catacombs were not used for regular community worship, as Sunday Mass, etc.

church and altar are "baptized" and "confirmed" almost like human beings; they are sprinkled on all sides with holy water and are anointed with holy oil; only after that is the first Eucharist celebrated.

The heart of the church, the focal point at which all lines converge, is the place of the sacrifice, the altar. We nowadays take such a thing for granted, but actually a certain development lies back of this. In the church of Christian antiquity the personal element in the assembled congregation was so much to the fore that it was the seat of the bishop or rather the bishop himself who was the central figure; he is the *liturgus* who offers up the Eucharist to God. The material side of the gifts is, if anything, hidden rather than emphasized. The table on which they lie is looked upon merely as a technical aid. It is, you might say, not an altar at all, in the sense of pre-Christian religions where the gift is hallowed and dedicated to God only when it touches the altar; our Gift is intrinsically holy, dedicated to God by its very nature and in the last analysis does not really require an altar. All the references we possess from the third and fourth centuries agree in their account of the altar; they regard the altar not as a part of the permanent structure of the church but only as a simple wooden table which is carried into position by the deacons as occasion dictates. But the new appreciation for the material gift by which the sacrifice of the New Testament extends beyond this earthly space and hallows it, and the deeper rooting of the Church in this world of time, were the cause, or at least the occasion, for the altar's assuming a more fixed form. Often in the fourth century— and regularly thereafter—it is made of stone. But it remained a plain simple table. Even today its name in the Orient is still *the holy table*.

MASS FACING THE PEOPLE

To this table the *liturgus* came at the beginning of the Mass proper, the sacrificial offering. On which side should he take his place—facing the people or facing away? History indicates that both practices were in use from the very start, at least in the vicinity of Rome. Even today they are both countenanced in the *Missale Romanum* (*Ritus serv.* V, 3). One way, the priest stands turned towards the altar facing in the same direction as the people; this is at present the general rule both East and West, and appears to have always been the rule in the East. The other way, he stands on the side opposite, facing the people, and this is the position presupposed in some of the older Roman churches. However, this latter position appears to have been chosen only where there was some special reason for it, as, for example, if the altar was linked to a martyr's grave (confessio), the side facing the people had to be open to give them access to the grave. The rule which grew ever more important, that at prayer all should look to the East—and naturally this included the celebrant first of all—led even in the early Middle Ages to the priest's assuming a place almost without exception like the one he assumes today, on the side of the altar nearest the people, for he is the leader of the people in their prayer and at their head offers up to God their prayer and sacrifice.

Orientation at prayer and the symbolism it entails has lost much of its meaning for us. But the basic principle that at prayer all—including even the celebrant—should take a God-ward stance, could easily be at work here too, in establishing the celebrant's position at the altar. If Mass were only a service of instruction or a Communion celebration, the other position, facing the people, would be more natural. But it is different if the Mass is an immolation and homage to God. If today the altar *versus populum* is frequently chosen, this is the result of other considerations that come into play—considerations which are rated as of paramount importance particularly as a reaction to earlier conditions. It serves to narrow down the distance between priest and congregation and to highlight the instructive items contained in the prayer and the rite. In certain circumstances—like the services for young people—these reasons appear to be well-founded.

THE ALTAR AND ITS POSITION

The same basic relationship is the reason for the position which the altar occupies in the space of the church. It is a striking fact that in the history of Christian church architecture the axial type appears in various localities, but that even here the altar is hardly ever placed in the center; both in oriental churches (with cupola and shaped like a Greek cross) and in the circular churches of the West (a style frequently used during the Baroque period), the altar stands in a niche or apse which was added to the circular structure, as a rule toward the East. But during ancient times an effort was always made to set up the altar in such a way that it seemed to belong both to the nave and to the choir, being placed at the intersection of the two or even brought out a little into the nave itself.

Then in the early Middle Ages a new movement set in, which gradually moved the altar into the background in the rear of the choir. This is but the architectonic expression of an intellectual movement which stressed more and more the sacredness and aloofness of the mystery and restricted immediate access to it to the clergy. In the Orient the altar stands free and open in the sanctuary but, by means of the ikonostasis, it is withdrawn from the people's gaze. In the West, the altar itself was moved closer to the rear wall of the sanctuary and at the same time the sanctuary or choir in Romanesque architecture was vastly increased in size; in monastic and capitular churches it became a formal clerical chapel, specially designed for the clerical services which continually became more richly developed. Here too, the railing which marked the limits of the choir often turned into a dividing wall, although intended to separate the clergy, rather than the altar, from the people. Therefore, a second main altar (often called the "rood altar") was sometimes built in the church in front of this (choir) screen, to serve the people. But when the chapters began to disappear the screen likewise disappeared, first from the leading churches and then soon everywhere. Baroque architecture restored the unity of place without, however, making any changes regarding the placement of the altar.

The altar, too, saw a great development from the simple table of olden times to the elaborate forms of recent centuries; but a clear idea of the purpose of the altar was not always kept in view. As the place where the sacred mystery was celebrated, it was fitting that the altar should receive every mark of respect possible. Even in the pre-Constantine era people were conscious of this. The altar was decked and decorated like a table; precious cloths were spread over it. Chrysostom had to give a warning about an excess of zeal in this matter that left other tasks undone. The frontals (*antependia*) of our day which now cover usually the front of the altar only, are the last vestiges of this sort of reverence. The next move was to add railings and steps. The altar of the church in Tyre which was dedicated in 314 was surrounded by an artistically wrought railing. The elevated position of the altar, standing as it did in a sanctuary which was raised somewhat above the level of the church, already lent special significance to the altar, but, in the Western Church, special steps were constructed in front of the altar itself, though this did not become a general rule till the eleventh century and after. But the most prominent of the marks of distinction given the altar was the special shelter or canopy which surmounted it either by way of a *baldachin* or *testa* or by way of a fixed *civory* (*ciborium*). This covering over the altar served to emphasize the special character of the table.

The closer the altar was put to the rear wall, the more necessary it became that this wall itself should be connected with it in significance and importance. The wall of the apse had long been specially ornamented. Preferably they were decorations that expressed those matters which formed the core and kernel of Christian consciousness, very much as the thanksgiving prayer of the Mass did by means of words—the glorified Cross, the Lamb triumphant, the Good Shepherd, or finally Christ enthroned and surrounded by the saints or by the Apostles or by the ancients of the Apocalypse. Later the representation of the Crucified was more often substituted for these others. Even in places where a decorative wall-painting was introduced over the altar, as was frequently the case in the Gothic period, the choice dictated by the old tradition fell by preference on a crucifixion group either as the only representation or at least as the principal one.

But about the eleventh century quite other rules were formed as the result of the introduction of a decorative structure ornamented with paintings, built either on the altar-table itself or immediately behind it, the so-called retable. In the choice of subjects for these pictures the widest variety prevailed; all of Christian iconography was brought into play. Strikingly enough, it is seldom the mystery of Redemption depicted in any shape or form. Where the crucifix did appear it was generally a quite realistic representation, with a host of strange figures around it. Completely forgotten was the essential notion that a picture over the altar is not a pictorial record of the past but primarily an instrument for professing our Catholic faith and acknowledging our Christian hope.[2] Most often the picture was one of the saint in whose honor the church was dedicated and whose relics—according to ancient principle— were buried there. Next to this, figures of other saints were frequently placed. Here is the key to the understanding of the iconographic phenomenon alluded to. It is explained, in the last analysis, by the connection which the altar had during the early Middle Ages with the grave of the martyr to which the devotion of Christian people had turned quite early with great zeal. The tension and strain which was naturally bound to develop between the shrines of the martyrs and the churches destined for congregational worship was thus finally eased when the relics of martyrs (in a broad sense) were brought into the congregational churches and the latter then became martyr-shrines in their own right. By the sixth/seventh century these relics were dismembered and inclosed in the altar itself, just as is prescribed for every altar today.

The high honor paid to the relics led to another step in the ninth century, namely, that something was permitted on the altar which was not required for the performance of the Eucharist—a thing unthinkable previously, and still avoided in the East. For at this time an exception was made in favor of reliquaries or relic-shrines. Again, as a result, the altar was built up, just as had happened in the case of the saints' pictures. The way was opened to the development of the massive structures we have come to know, the Gothic polyptych altars and the Baroque architectural masses, in which the *mensa* or table often seems to sink into the insignificance of a mere appendage. But there was some compensation to be found for the splitting of the idea of the altar which was thus introduced, when in the eleventh century the crucifix was brought to the altar, a prescription of law still maintained in our own day.

[2] For a more extensive treatment of the subject of liturgical art, cf. the Author's essay "Church Art," in *Worship*, XXIX, 68–82. (Jan. 1955).—REVISER.

Part Three

THE MASS CEREMONIES

IN DETAIL

I. THE OPENING OR ENTRANCE RITE

1. Fore-Mass and Opening as a Unit

The eucharistic celebration could have started with the preparation of the sacrificial offerings and the prayer of thanksgiving. But at the very outset it had become an inviolable rule to have an introductory section composed of readings. First of all an atmosphere of faith had to be created before the great mystery of faith was performed. This introductory section is called the fore-Mass in contradistinction to the Mass proper or the sacrifice-Mass. The terms "Mass of the catechumens" and "Mass of the faithful" are also used to designate these parts respectively, but these expressions did not come into use till the 11th century. Florus in his *De actione missarum*, in the 9th century, still uses both expressions, *missa catechumenorum* and *missa fidelium*, in their original sense of dismissal of catechumens and faithful.

It must be noted in passing that the implications of the phrase "Mass of the catechumens" do not coincide exactly with those of "fore-Mass," for the catechumens were not allowed to stay till the very start of the Mass-sacrifice. The readings were followed by common prayers for the various wants of the Church and its several classes of members. The last part of this was the prayer of the faithful, but before its start the catechumens were told to withdraw if they had not already done so. Indeed at Rome, from about the sixth century it became the custom to send the catechumens away even before the Gospel, because the Gospel was considered as much a matter of the "discipline of the secret" as the Our Father and the Creed.

As we shall see more in detail later, the fore-Mass—or, more precisely, the older portion thereof which began with the lessons—was originally an independent liturgical entity. The consciousness of a certain independence of this older fore-Mass remained alive for a long time. For it other regulations held than for the eucharistic service in the narrow sense. Sometimes the fore-Mass was conducted in one church, the Mass proper in another; this was the custom in Jerusalem at the turn of the fourth century, and also in North Africa. There is, for example, an account of the monastery of St. Sabbas (Mar Saba) in the vale of Cedron, where monks of different nationality, Georgians, Syrians and Latins, lived together; they first performed the introductory service of readings and prayers in separate oratories and in their own vernacular, and then assembled for the sacrifice at which Greek was used. Even today the independence of the fore-Mass is intimated in our pontifical service, for here during the fore-Mass the service hinges not around the altar, but around the *cathedra* of the bishop.

In olden times the fore-Mass began abruptly with the lessons or readings. This was certainly the case in the Orient, and must also have been true in the West until far into the fifth century. St. Augustine gives us an account of the beginning of the Mass on a certain Easter day which was signalized by an unusual event. Before service began, a sick man who had been praying in the *cancelli* of St. Stephen was suddenly cured. There was a great deal of excitement amongst the people already assembled, loud cries of thanks and joy filled the house of God. Augustine, who was in the sacristy, ready to make his entrance into the church, was informed. But what is of real interest to us is that when the tumult had gradually died down, the bishop greeted the people and then without further ado began the reading of the lessons. At that time, therefore—the story comes from the year 426—the fore-Mass began with the readings without any preliminaries. Even in the present-day Roman liturgy there is still one instance of an abbreviated fore-Mass starting with the readings, namely on Good Friday, although it is true no sacrifice-Mass follows, but only the reverencing of the cross and a Communion service; worship on this day begins with a lesson from Osee, after which there are two other readings, followed by the great intercessory prayers.

Further details regarding the course of this more ancient fore-Mass in all liturgies included, as a rule, the following items. The individual readings were generally followed by a song of some sort, usually derived from one of the lyrical passages of Scripture. The last reading was a portion of the Gospels. And finally the series of readings concluded with a prayer. This fore-Mass was therefore nothing else than a Bible lesson, in which the words of Holy Writ were followed by some sort of scriptural echo and in which the last section was always a prayer.

BYZANTINE FORE-MASS

The part preceding the lessons is the result of a less ancient development which ran more or less parallel in the various ecclesiastical provinces, but without following any common ground-plan. However, some sort of common basic idea was everywhere at work. This was the notion that the lessons should have a preliminary, an introduction. But the introduction did not come into full being at a stroke; rather it is here precisely that many different stages can be distinguished in the growing structure. There is one archway after the other, one ante-room after the other, each tacked on as the zeal and reverence of successive centuries dictated. The oriental liturgies have generally evolved a preliminary whose proportions far exceed those of our Roman liturgy. For not only do they interpose at the start, before the readings, some type of entrance ceremonial, but they preface this with a formal hour of canonical office, and in fact the Byzantine Mass even ushers this latter in with the *proskomide* during which the sacrificial gifts are prepared and pre-hallowed at a special offertory table—the *prothesis*—with a whirl of ceremonies and prayers that are in turn wonderfully rich and extensive.

The one peculiarity that the oriental fore-Masses have in common is the preparatory prayer hour which is always incorporated in it; in the East Syrian it is a variant of Vespers, in the other liturgies a creation corresponding to our Lauds. This is the prayer ceremony which Ætheria, in Jerusalem about 390, came to recognize as the first morning service on Sundays. After the bishop had entered the Church of the Resurrection, a priest, a deacon, and another cleric, each in turn, intoned a psalm, to each verse of which the people responded with a refrain; the psalm was followed in each case by an oration. This plan of prayer is most plainly evident today in the Byzantine Mass.

This forms the heart of the so-called ἔναρξις, or Opening. Here we find, one right after the other, three antiphonal songs composed mostly from the psalms (the three "antiphons"), to each of which is attached an oration by the priest along with the deacon's *ektene*. It is not till after this prayer-act that (in the Byzantine Mass) the so-called Little Entrance follows. The clergy participating in the liturgy form a procession, marching from the sanctuary through a side door of the ikonostasis or picture-wall into the nave of the church, and back again through the center door into the sanctuary. This is the entrance with the Gospel-book, to be distinguished from a later procession, the Great Entrance, with the sacrificial offerings. The introit of the Roman Mass corresponds to this first entrance, for in an earlier stage of development the clergy used to make their entry into the house of God in procession. Even in the liturgical formation of this entrance the analogy to the Roman type cannot be mistaken. For this Little Entrance is accompanied by a special chant (εἰσοδικόν = *introitus*), which is usually followed, depending on the festival, by some other hymns (*troparia*) and finally by the *trisagion*, the same that the Roman liturgy also has on Good Friday. Both at the entrance and at the *trisagion* the priest softly recites a lengthy prayer; the lessons begin after that.

ROMAN ENTRANCE RITE

Turning now to the Roman entrance rite, the thing that strikes us about the whole ceremonial, from the prayers at the foot of the altar to the collect, is its lack of coherence; we do not get the impression of something unified. For that reason interpreters of the Mass scarcely ever treat it under one title. Each individual portion, prayers at the foot of the altar, *Kyrie, Gloria,* collects—each has its own individual explanation without much connection with the others. And precisely for that reason *we must try to consider the whole section as a unit*, in order to gain the right background for the various component parts.

Usually the collect is the part selected as a hub for the several connecting lines. But hardly anything could show more clearly than this how much in the dark we are regarding the whole subject. Some have suggested that the oration belongs by right to the reading service; originally its place was after the first reading and not till later was it shifted, owing perhaps to the influence of the introit psalm. Others explain that the oration was originally a part of a special assembling ceremony which preceded the Mass. The reference here is to the old Roman custom of gathering at a different church; after all had convened, ready to start the procession to the church where Mass was to be celebrated, an oration was said over the assembled congregation. After this practice was abandoned, the oration was transferred to the church of the Mass, and placed after the processional litany which still survives in the *Kyrie.*

Such opinions rest on the assumption that otherwise there is no reason for the oration being where it is. Is that really so?

With good cause other commentators maintain that the *Kyrie*, at least in its original form as a litany, required a priestly oration as its conclusion, just as the oriental *ektene* shows today; putting it another way, the oration in the Roman Mass has the character of a conclusion, and must therefore represent in this connection a stopping point after the litany already mentioned.

As a matter of fact *there can hardly be any doubt that the oration and the* Kyrie *belong together*. This becomes all the clearer when we take cognizance of liturgical prayer outside of Mass. For the prayers of the congregation, the litany type, with its petitions intoned by a deacon and with its *Kyrie eleison* as the response of the people, has been the characteristic form since the fourth century. But the ancient Church was conscious of the fact that the litany demanded a concluding prayer by the priest. This manner of concluding with prayer which Ætheria, the Pilgrim lady, noticed was in the congregation of Jerusalem, especially amongst the monks, and for this reason a priest or deacon was always present at their common prayer to recite the oration at the end. In particular, the litany at Vespers was concluded by the bishop with an oration.[1] In our own Office, too, each hour even now closes with the oration.

To be sure the *Gloria*, which is so often interposed between *Kyrie* and oration, and seemingly to no purpose, seems to put this whole matter of a connection between the two once more in serious doubt. For a grasp of the basic plan, however, this can really have very little significance, because originally the *Gloria* was inserted only by way of exception, and even later only on those feasts on which the *Kyrie* appeared to invite a more joyous supplement. Besides, it is not unheard of that some further popular prayers or even hymns were added to the litany and, in general, to all the alternating prayers of the congregation. In the *preces* of the breviary the *Kyrie* is followed by a long series of prayers and psalm verses and on some days even by a formal hymn (namely, the *Sanctus Deus*), and only after that is there a conclusion with the oration. Something of the kind can have happened in the case of the *Gloria*. Moreover, the *Gloria* does not interfere with the *Kyrie's* concluding in an oration, for it too seems to demand such a conclusion. The story is told that when Leo III and Charlemagne met in the year 799, the pope intoned the *Gloria* which was taken up by the entire clergy, whereupon the pope recited a prayer. *We are forced, therefore, to conclude that* Kyrie, Gloria, *and oration are part of a unified plan which is patterned on an ascending scale, the oration forming the high point.* But how does it happen that the Mass is opened with such a schema of prayer? This question leads to still another: What about the prayers that precede, that is, the prayers at the foot of the altar, and the introit?

First *the introit*. Our introit, as everyone knows, is an entrance song, a processional, and to appreciate its meaning and form we must transport ourselves to one of the larger basilicas of Rome for the splendid and solemn ceremonial of a papal Mass, with its numerous clergy and its specially trained choral group. Here we are confronted for the first time by a picture that we shall meet again in two other places in the Roman Mass: an external event which is sufficiently important to warrant some external expression. The people participating do not say a prayer, but the choral group, who are ready precisely for this occasion, sing a psalm, an entrance psalm, exactly as they afterwards sing the offertory psalm and the communion psalm. This external event is concluded with a prayer, as is proper in an assembly gathered for worship. As the *secreta* is said after the offertory, and the *post communio* after the communion, so here the collect (but in this instance with the people's *Kyrie* and *Gloria* intervening). In other words, the act or prayer is introduced by

[1] This close connection between the prayer of the congregation and the oration seems to rule out the suggestion put forth by Dix, *The Shape of the Liturgy*, 452–458, who would trace the introduction of the oration at Rome to an Egyptian model, and the introduction of *Kyrie* and *Gloria* to a later Syro-Byzantine one. The connection itself is vainly contested by Dix, p. 479.

a procession into the basilica. This procession ought not only to be enhanced by the chanting, but it ought also to be distinguished as a movement to prayer, as an approach to God's majesty, as is done when the assembled congregation shouts out the petitions and the priest takes these up, and brings the proceeding to a conclusion with an oration. As a matter of fact, Amalar in the ninth century actually connected the introit and the oration in this manner. Rupert of Deutz, too, includes all the proceedings up to the collects under one heading as "the beginning called Introitus," and we have found the same thing even in Albertus Magnus and other commentators of the period.

What is left to explain now is the group of *prayers at the foot of the altar*, a thing of much later date. But this is a very secondary structure added to the already completed fabric as a further embellishment.[2] It thus happens that the entire complex of prayers and rites antecedent to the readings, in particular the prayers following the introit, are all governed by the entrance procession. We can therefore rightly speak of an entrance or opening rite.

A confirmation of this reconstruction is to be found in parallel phenomena of the Roman liturgy. Take the *Ordo* of St. Amand, which reproduces the customs of the Roman church after 800. In it are presented the practices usual at a *collecta*, that is, at a penitential procession of the Roman community under the leadership of the pope, with which it was customary to introduce the stational services on certain days. These *collecta* took place in the following manner. The people gathered at a conveniently located church, generally St. Adrian's at the Forum, and from there marched to the church at which Mass was to be celebrated. The procedure was this: The pope and his attendant deacons, vested in dark *planetæ*, waited in the sacristy (which was usually near what we call the rear of the church). When it was time to start, the *schola* intoned the *antiphona ad introitum*. While the psalm was being sung, the pope and his deacons proceeded through the church up to the altar. As the pope passed the *schola* he gave a signal to skip to the end of the psalm and sing the *Gloria Patri*. Arriving at the altar, he bowed low in silent prayer. Then he kissed the altar, the deacons following his example. After the antiphon had been repeated in the usual fashion, the pope spoke the greeting, *Dominus vobiscum* and, after the *Flectamus genua* of the deacon, recited an oration. Then everyone left the church and set out in the penitential procession. *Here we have the Roman rite of opening a service clearly separate and carried out for its own sake.* The only thing missing from the comparable portion of the fore-Mass is the *Kyrie* before the oration.

But it is significant that the scribe felt called upon to make a special

[2] It is worthy of note that the prayers at the foot of the altar are omitted on Palm Sunday and at the Easter Vigil in the restored Holy Week of 1955.

note regarding the missing part: "When the antiphon at the close of the introit has been sung to the end, the *schola* does not sing the *Kyrie*." The *Kyrie* therefore normally belongs to this rite. The reason it is left out here is obvious; it is intoned at the very beginning of the penitential procession. This procession is likewise the reason for the insertion of *Flectamus genua*. Almost the same procedure is repeated at every church visited on the way, and lastly at the stational church itself.

One could therefore, in a way, talk about a *rite of visiting churches*. The present-day *Pontificale Romanum* presumes this arrangement in all essentials when a visiting prelate is to be received ceremoniously in a church. Accompanied by singing he marches into the church and kneels down to pray before the main altar. While the versicle in honor of the patron of the church is chanted, he kisses the altar at the middle and then recites the pertinent oration at the Epistle side. Here, too, the entry into the church, the visiting of a church, has been given a liturgical form. In the case of the Mass-liturgy, the visiting of the church has been transformed into an entrance or opening ceremonial.

Although we have used the procedures of the *collecta* to explain the fore-Mass, we must yet take issue with a certain common misconception of the relationship between the two. Some interpreters have been too prone to draw a connection between the litany chant accompanying the procession on its way and into the stational church, and the *Kyrie* of the Mass, as if the latter was derived from the former. In like manner— something we have already touched on—the oration of the Mass, often called the *collecta*, is often derived from the oration recited at the church where the *collecta* took place. Both notions are untenable. The *collecta* as a gathering of the Roman community was not a stable and constituent part of the stational service, but only the *prelude* of a penitential procession which took place before the stational service *on certain days*—in olden times not very frequent—especially in Lent and the ember-tides, but never on Sundays or feasts. The *Kyrie* could not therefore have intruded into the Sunday or feast-day service in this wise. As for calling the first oration *collecta*, we shall see further on that the term had a very different origin, and really means a gathering together, by the priest, of the preceding petitions of the people.

In this sense the term *collecta* is quite appropriate for this first oration of the Mass, for it seems to blend together all that has gone before. The congregational praying and singing and even the entry with its accompanying chant serves only to draw us nearer to God to honor Him in the holy sacrifice. Since the lessons are meant to be introduced before the beginning of the sacrifice, it would appear only proper to indicate the meaning of this common approach by means of a preliminary solemn prayer in much the same way as the Roman congregation did when it assembled at some church for the start of a penitential procession, or when it stopped in at a church on the way. "We come to pray," is the basic motto of this first part of the Mass.

Nowadays, however, this notion is no longer so apparent. The rite of entry has to a great extent lost its meaning, owing in the main to the fate which the entry has suffered in the course of centuries. Up till about 1000 it continued to be a fully-developed ceremonial, and so it was easy to survey the liturgical transformation which it was undergoing. Not only in the Roman stational service but even in the Frankish Church, the entrance of the clergy had been a ceremony of capital importance, and in the descriptions and the allegorical explanations of Carolingian interpreters of the liturgy it assumed a formidable amount of space. But in the years that followed a change set in. John Beleth (d. about 1165), in explaining the introit, had to make the remark that the bishop on feast days sometimes vested outside the choir. In harmony with this, Durandus too felt compelled to note that the bishop—in whose regard, to be sure, every effort must have been made to retain the more solemn formalities—might take up the vestments either "away from the altar" or "next to the altar." All the more quickly, then, would the vesting of the priest be transferred to the sanctuary or its environs.

This change is easily explained by the medieval evolution of choir prayer and the development of the fixed regulation that the conventual service, which for centuries simply meant the Mass, should each day immediately follow Terce or the other corresponding hour, for which the clergy were already assembled. An entrance procession was therefore superfluous. Often the celebrant and his assistants were already clothed in the Mass vestments, as, for instance, when in monastic churches of the eleventh and twelfth centuries all priest members of the choir wore alb, maniple, and stole. Usually, it is true, the vesting in the Mass vestments or—when choir dress and Mass dress were once more distinguished—the putting on of the vestments was transferred to the sacristy.

But in Romanesque structures the sacristy was not built near the entrance of the church but somewhere close to the choir. In these cases the entry called for in the ancient Mass regulations could be reinaugurated. Sometimes, in fact, it was consciously revived and given a greater development by marching the long way through the nave of the church (as was done in the late Middle Ages on great feast days), or at least a procession down the aisle on Sundays in the course of blessing with holy water, as was customary all through the Middle Ages and still is in some residual form. The liturgical reform of the sixteenth century permitted only the bishop to vest at the altar and this both as a privilege and as a prescription, perhaps because the various formalities which had developed meanwhile gave it the character of a dramatic introduction to the pontifical service. The natural consequence of all this evolution was a change in the role of the introit; the introit would have to be sung, but not as an accompaniment to the few steps which as a rule were all that had to be taken to reach the altar. Instead of a processional, the introit became an introductory chant which in Rome already in the fourteenth century was not begun till the priest had reached the altar steps.

The decline of the entrance ceremony entailed some other transformations at which we ought to look briefly. The lights which had previously been carried in procession and then placed next to the altar were now more frequently set on the altar from the very start. Since Carolingian times there was no longer any hesitancy about putting on the altar things other than those required for the sacramental celebration; so in the new circumstances it was taken for granted that when no procession was held the candles should stand on the altar even before Mass and should stay there. Their previous significance as an honor to the celebrant—in the first instance a bishop—was lost (so long as the other attendants at the more solemn feasts were not, in their turn, accompanied by candles). In place of honoring the celebrant was thus substituted a very becoming honor to the mystery that was consummated on the altar. A similar change took place with regard to the censer. It is not used so much as formerly, on the way to the altar or in the procession to read the Gospel, but at the altar itself which is incensed.

Finally the psalm *Iudica*, which about the year 1000 was introduced into pontifical services as a part of the entrance procession, was definitely transferred to the foot of the altar, after a very diversified career; sometimes its few short verses had been said on the way to the altar, sometimes during the vesting, sometimes at the altar—and often not at all.

2. Putting on the Liturgical Vestments [1]

Besides the inner preparation there is also an outer one. Before going to the altar the priest must vest himself in the liturgical garments. The natural feeling that we ought to put on better clothing for the celebration of divine worship was something the faithful had learnt long ago. A similar sentiment of reverence had led, even before the end of Christian antiquity, to a special liturgical vesture for the celebrating priest. At first it was merely more costly, more precious than the ordinary holiday clothing of the townspeople. It was not till city fashion ordained a new shorter costume that liturgical dress began to be distinguished from ordinary dress, for our liturgical vesture is nothing else than a stylized form of the holiday attire of the old imperial days of Rome.

---

[1] For a more detailed study of what follows see a series of articles by Dom Raymund James, O.S.B., "The Dress of the Liturgy," *Orate Fratres*, X (1935–6), 28 to 12, and XI (1937–8), 545.

In the alb, held together by a cincture, we have a survival of the ancient tunic. To this is joined the amice (*humerale*, shawl or shoulder covering), the neckcloth or scarf of old, which went by various names. As an outer garment there is the chasuble, the Mass garment proper, which by its very name (*casula*, "little house") is reminiscent of an older shape that completely shielded the body. This shape suggests clearly its origin in the old Roman *pænula*, which almost entirely replaced the Roman toga in the late imperial period. It was not till the thirteenth century that the ample folds of the ancient bell-shaped *casula* were reduced so that less material—now in various colors—had to be used, and the vestment finally attained its present shape by cutting down the sides. What might first have been induced by the Gothic temper, since the oval outlines suited the style of the period, was eventually pushed to an extreme in the interests of Baroque, which seemed to prefer using heavy, stiff brocades.

The original character of the garment was thus lost, but in the last few years efforts have been made to return to the older shape. As signs of honor and distinction the priest wears two other vestments, both the color of the chasuble, namely, the maniple and the stole. The origin of the stole is not clearly known, but in the maniple we can recognize the fashionable handkerchief of Roman times, called *mappa* or *mappula*, which was carried in the hand—hence the later name *manipulus*—or fastened to the arm.

Since Carolingian times the act of vesting in the liturgical garments gradually became a liturgical act fitted out with prayer. It is usually, but not always, preceded by a washing of the hands. This too is accompanied by a short prayer. The formula which we at present connect with the handwashing, *Da Domine virtutem manibus meis ad abstergendam omnem maculam* does not appear in this connection until later. Where it does appear earlier, it usually concludes with *Per* and as an addition to the oration *Largire*, it accompanies the drying of the fingers. The preparation of the outer man was apparently a very serious concern. In the tenth century and after, there is frequent mention of the comb which the priest uses to arrange his hair, a reference no doubt to the medieval mode of longish hair-cuts.

In medieval sources we find the washing of the hands is preceded, as in present-day pontifical rites, by the ritual putting off of the outer clothing (accompanied by proper prayers) and in the older period also by the putting on of special footwear. At private Mass it was the custom in many medieval churches to prepare the paten and chalice with the offerings right after washing the hands, and to mix the water and wine to the accompaniment of the usual words. After this, followed the vesting.

Vesting did not always occur in the precise order now followed. The amice, for instance, was not put on till after the alb, as would be natural with a scarf or neck-cloth; this usage is still retained in the liturgies of Milan and Lyons. Nor was the manner of putting it on always the same as today's. One practice, which makes its appearance in northern countries about the turn of the ninth century, was to place the amice over the head like a hood and to leave it thus till the other vestments had been donned. For an explanation of the origin of this mode of wearing the amice it might be good to note that the first liturgists who speak of it are the same ones who mention the comb, the work of which would be nullified when putting on the alb and chasuble unless some means were employed to prevent disarranging the hair. This manner of wearing the amice was universally followed in the thirteenth century and so the orders that stem from this time, Franciscans, Dominicans, Trinitarians and Servites, have continued it to the present, while for the rest it disappeared about the same time that the style of hair-cut changed. There were some differences about when the amice thus worn should be pushed back off the head; some removed it right after putting on the chasuble; in the French churches it was customary to keep it on the head till the *secreta* or even till the start of the canon. It is to be noticed, moreover, that the prayer we say at present while putting on the amice, still designates it as a helmet.

The maniple, too, was not in olden times put on as we do it now, right after girdling the alb. It was not taken up till all the other vestments had been donned. And it had to be thus as long as it was customary to carry it in the hand—that is, up till the eleventh/twelfth century. As soon as the fashion set in of fastening it to the arm, the practice changed and finally shifted to our present use. Only the bishop continues the older manner but with this variation, which became quite general since the thirteenth century, that he takes the maniple only after the *Confiteor*.

RITUAL OF VESTING

There was a great simplification in the ritual of vesting, at least in the eleventh and twelfth centuries, when—as was the practice in various Benedictine monasteries—all the monks on feast days wore albs and maniples during the choir prayer that preceded the Mass. Doubtless the priests in this case regularly wore also a stole since it had been made obligatory by ninth and tenth century legislation to wear the stole at all times, both at home and while traveling. As a matter of fact, in the preparation for both private and conventual Mass the Customs of Cluny make mention only of putting on the chasuble.

The prayers which, since Carolingian times, have been said while vesting are extremely diverse. It is hardly an exaggeration to say, as someone actually did, *Quot missalia tot sensus*. There is even a trend to forego any special texts. The diversity of these vesting prayers is in part connected with their half-private nature, but perhaps the most important reason for it is the symbolic interpretation of the vestments, which was based upon various details and continued to produce numerous new formulas in accordance with the changes of thought.

Actually, of course, there is a certain symbolism inherent in the liturgical vestments. The fact that the priest wears garments that are not only better but really quite special, distinct from the garments of ordinary civil life, enhanced where possible by the preciousness of the material and by decoration—all this can have but one meaning: that the priest in a sense leaves this earth and enters another world, the shimmer of which is mirrored in his vesture. But medieval interpreters were not content with such a general explanation; they had to find in each piece of clothing a particular relation to that other world. In one period they directed their attention principally to the moral and ethical order to which the priest must conform; in a second period they kept in view the person of Christ whose place the priest takes; and in the third, Christ's Passion which is commemorated in the celebration.

The concepts in the prayers for vesting are created for the most part out of the explanations of the first period, since they nearly all arose in that period. In these prayers—unlike the prayers at the accession or those at the foot of the altar, with which they share both their derivation and their original obligation—there is not to be found any planned progression in the priest's preparation. The individual garments are not explained on the basis of any conscious essential function which is theirs when worn, but it is rather only some ascetical thought, some handy reference to a scriptural text around which the prayer is composed. Thus the external act is raised, easily and without trouble, to the spiritual sphere. For that reason the individual forms are not spread abroad as a rule in a single unit but they are chosen on their own particular merit as taste dictates. Some Mass books since the eleventh century seek to give the prayers a certain rounding off by concluding not only some but all the prayers where possible with *Per Christum Dominum Nostrum*.

Putting on the vestments, even after the prayers were enjoined, was not always connected with the other preparations of the priest. Although in some instances it precedes the accession prayers which are then included in the liturgy proper as parts of equal worth, at other times it is transferred to the altar, and sometimes even the donning of the last vestments is joined to the very beginning of Mass. A survival of this practice is possibly to be found in the custom which is to be noticed since the thirteenth century and is still followed today, the custom of handing the bishop his maniple only after the *Confiteor*.

According to the Missal of Westminster the priest had first to vest with the stole, then prepare the chalice and say the prayer for the mingling of the water; only after that did he don the chasuble. In French churches it was customary towards the end of the Middle Ages and thereafter, to recite the psalm *Iudica* and the other prayers that went with it during the vesting. This arrangement is given more in detail in the Missal of the monastery of Bec (probably thirteenth century); after girding himself with the cincture, the priest says Psalm 42 and the conjoined prayer *Aufer*, then he puts on the maniple, stole, and chasuble. In other places the maniple and stole were put on before saying the psalm, which was recited while holding the chasuble lying on the altar. Sometimes, too, the *Confiteor* was said without the chasuble. In this way the preparatory and semi-private character of these prayers was more plainly emphasized. In fact, the psalm *Iudica*, as we shall see, was at that time said as a rule on the way to the altar. True, in almost all these arrangements the reference is to private Masses. But amongst the Carthusians in the thirteenth century it was the custom for the priest to put on the chasuble at the altar also in conventual Masses except on the very highest feast days. Even at a later time it was the practice in Orleans to say the psalm *Iudica* in the sacristy, vested in alb and stole, and this before high Mass. So it is not improbable that the same line of thought suggested that at the pontifical Mass the last of the vestments, the maniple—at that time it was really the last of the decorative garments to be donned—should not be handed to the bishop until after the psalm *Iudica*—as the bishop of Minde strikingly testifies with regard to France, the homeland of this special order of vesting—or after the *Confiteor*, as it became customary in Rome later on.

3. The Prayers at the Foot of the Altar as a Unit

When we investigate the beginnings of the prayers at the foot of the altar, we find the seed in the pre-Frankish era not in any definite prayer but rather in the actions which correspond to the two parts of our present-day prayers, the progress towards the altar, all planned in definite forms, and the silent reverence of the celebrant as he bows in front of the altar. The expression "prayers at the foot of the altar" is based on conditions which existed only after the year 1000, because before the 11th century there were, as a rule, no steps up to the altar, no platform even. Only the sanctuary as a unit was raised above the level of the nave. In the solemn services of the Roman basilicas the approach to the altar was turned into a procession of the clergy, during which the singers chanted the introit. In the churches of the Frankish Kingdom, according to a law of procedure which was then in force, the clergy themselves, or at least the celebrant, would have to say some prayers even in such circumstances. And from the first, *apologiæ* were considered above all as suited to this spot. Already in the ninth century such prayers had been inserted here, and until the eleventh century the space they thus occupied at the beginning of Mass grew and grew immensely.

But even before the end of the tenth century a new arrangement made its appearance, an arrangement which was retained in the Rhenish Mass *ordo* and which in the time to come was more or less adhered to.

On the way to the altar, Psalm 42 was spoken in common, and upon arrival at the altar two orations were added in conclusion, one of which is our *Aufer a nobis*. In the witnesses to this particular arrangement of the entry there are found in addition various *apologiæ*, forerunners of our *Confiteor*, included in a variety of ways and in an assortment of forms. They are either added at the beginning or inserted somewhere in the middle or subjoined at the end. This arrangement quickly took the lead over other plans of a similar kind.

By the middle of the eleventh century another step was taken in Normandy, at a time when this land was in the forefront of liturgical reform. From these *apologiæ* a formal *Confiteor*, along with the response begging forgiveness, was composed and introduced between the psalm and the oration. This new plan seems to have spread by way of the Cluniac reform into Italy and even into Germany. It prevailed, however, only to this extent that a formal *Confiteor* in some setting or other, along with the corresponding response and the succeeding oration *Aufer a nobis*, became a part of the established design of every Mass *ordo* since the twelfth century. On the other hand the psalm *Iudica* did not gain an entrance into countless Mass arrangements all through the later Middle Ages and after. It will be enough to refer to the monastic liturgies of the Carthusians, the Calced Carmelites and the Dominicans; from all of these the psalm is missing even at present, since, in accordance with the fluctuations of usage, it was not inserted when their Mass arrangements were established during the thirteenth century. Even at the first general chapter of the Society of Jesus, held in 1558, when a unified rite was to be established within the order, it was decided that the psalm be left out. The Missal of Pius V, following the example of most of the Italian Mass books, and particularly the Missal of the Roman curia where it had long had a permanent place, made it a general prescript.

PSALM 42

There can be no doubt about the appropriateness of Psalm 42; if any prayer was to be chosen to be said on the way to the altar, this was certainly apt. The fourth verse actually made reference to the very act which was occurring: *Introibo ad altare Dei, ad Deum qui lætificat iuventutem meam.* For one special occasion, the entrance of the newly baptized into the church, this verse must have been incorporated in the Milan liturgy even in the time of St. Ambrose. When it came to inserting the text in the Mass, at first it was only this single verse, just as for the incensing the psalm text is confined to a single verse, *Dirigatur, Domine, oratio mea* . . . , and at the washing of the hands to the words *Lavabo* . . . But to secure a certain richness, the other verses were added whenever their use here made some sense; in this case the whole psalm was included. But the dominant tone is given by this one verse which from the very start was selected as the antiphon: I shall go in to the altar of God, to the God who was the joy of my youth. This approach unto God, which the psalmist longed for, has become fully possible in a proper sense only in the New Covenant; for we gain entrance to God only through Christ "who gives us all confidence, bids us come forward, emboldened by our faith in Him" (Eph. 3:12; cf. Rom. 5:2). The altar of the New Covenant is the place where this meeting with God can be best accomplished this side of heaven. How strikingly pertinent it is, that the Syrians call the Mass simply *Kurobho*, that is, "approach."

But not only is the approach accomplished here, but the situation, too, in which the psalmist finds himself in his longing for God assumes the nature of a type. When we desire to draw near God, the way is always blocked somehow by the *homo iniquus*. We therefore cry out to Him who is our strength that He may illumine us with His light and sustain us with His faithfulness and guide us in *montem sanctum*, that height upon which the sacrifice of Golgotha will be renewed. The psalmist closes with shouts of joy and jubilation that anticipate the *eucharistia*, the prayer of thanksgiving.

The rule established in the tenth-century rubric already referred to continued in force throughout the Middle Ages: Psalm 42 was said on the way to the altar in the same way as the canticle *Benedicite* was recited on the way back to the sacristy (as we still do today). In fact, until the Missal of Pius V, this was expressly stated in the rubrics in many cases. Very seldom was there any clear transfer of the psalm to the altar steps. Often this transfer occurred because the chasuble was put on at the altar, as was the custom especially at private Mass. In other cases the rubric was left indefinite. This diversity of practice corresponded to the variety in spatial arrangements. Often the distance from sacristy to altar was very short. In order not to prevent the psalm's being said with proper care and to lend it greater importance, it was not begun until the steps were reached. This must have been the origin of the arrangement now found in the Missal of Pius V.

As early as the eleventh century the characteristic or thematic antiphon was introduced before the start of the psalm. In our present-day manner of handling it, however, the verse is treated not precisely as an antiphon but as a versicle, so that the second half, *Ad Deum qui lætificat* serves as a response. This treatment will be best understood in some situation where a middle way was sought between using the psalm and leaving it out entirely and being satisfied with the one verse which set the tone. With this single verse other versicles could then be joined. This middle way was taken in the Benedictine *Liber ordinarius* of Liége, which in this matter followed the rite of Liége used at that time. The prayers at the foot of the altar began with three verses, *Introibo, Confitemini, Dignare;* in each case the response was supplied by the second half of the verse; the *Confiteor* followed. A similar thing is done in the contemporary Roman Masses in those instances in which Psalm 42 is left out;[1] the confession of faults is preceded by two verses, *Introibo* and *Adiutorium nostrum*. When these verses were joined to the psalm their treatment as versicles was naturally transferred, too; however, this transfer was not by any means a universal practice.

In our present-day Mass the very first words, even before the *Introibo*, are the words of blessing which accompany the sign of the Cross, words which form a Trinitarian gateway to the whole Mass—*In nomine Patris et Filii et Spiritus Sancti. Amen*. As used here, the formula, taken from our Lord's command to preach and baptize, can be traced here and there in the fourteenth century but not any earlier. It had been used as a blessing frequently in the early Middle Ages, and even appears in the Mass itself quite a bit earlier as the characteristic blessing formula. That it should appear at the beginning of Mass as a blessing text—just as it has more recently appeared at the beginning of our other prayers—is probably to be explained by the fact that the sign of "blessing," the *"signum" crucis* is connected with it; we begin the holy action in the power that comes from the triune God through the Cross of Christ. At the same time, in the use of this formula here, we can perceive a bridge between the two great sacraments of Baptism and Eucharist.

Late medieval Mass arrangements often made of this petition for God's blessing a special act of prayer during which the priest knelt at the altar. It was frequently the custom to kneel down first for a few moments' prayer. The psalm *Iudica* was sometimes given a special conclusion, a prayer being said to reaffirm its meaning. In the Norman-English ambit, where such a conclusion was almost universally in use, the *Kyrie* and *Pater noster* were said. A further development of the custom involved going up to the steps of the altar at the conclusion of the

---

[1] The reason why the Missal of Pius V omits Psalm 42 during Passiontide and at Requiem Masses is to be discovered in the feeling that the words *Quare tristis es anima mea* are singularly incongruous on such days of sorrow. Perhaps the fact that on Passion Sunday the psalm occurs as the Introit of the Mass gave occasion for setting precisely this date as the first for omitting it from the prayers at the foot of the altar.

Pater noster (*Et ne nos*), and continuing the prayer with *Confitemini* and *Confiteor*.

4. Confiteor

The *Confiteor*, along with its attendant prayers, forms the second portion of the prayers at the foot of the altar. Its beginnings are to be found in the silent worship to which the pope gave himself when, in the course of the stational services of Rome, he came to the altar. But for this quiet prayer words were soon inserted when the Roman Mass reached Frankish territory. The tendency is manifested, for instance, in the change of the seventh-century Roman rubric, "lying prostrate on the ground"; the Frankish revision of the eighth century makes the addition: "pouring forth prayers for himself or for the sins of the people." Thus the theme of the apologies is sounded.

The prayer in which lowly man humbles himself before the great God is restricted to the expression particularly of man's incapacity and man's unworthiness. Already in the late Carolingian period, prayer of this sort had accompanied the walk to the altar; here at the altar steps it found its proper setting.

In the *Confiteor* the prayer becomes a dialogue spoken by several. The celebrant acknowledges his sinfulness not only before God and heaven but also before his brethren around him and begs their mediation, which is offered him at once in the form of a response to his confession. The distinctive transition to this new form was completed within the Mass in the first third of the eleventh century, and soon it was imitated quite generally. It consisted in making one's confession of faults in the same manner as was customary since the ninth century at daily Prime and Compline—a mutual confession of daily faults made two-by-two. This method was now introduced at the beginning of Mass, at first (usually) the priest and deacon alone confessing to each other, later (more generally) the priest and a number of those in attendance.

ACCOMPANYING NOTIONS

The surprising thing is that not only the *Misereatur* (a companion piece to the *Confiteor* which even the layman was permitted to say as the intercessory response to the confession of faults) but also the *Indulgentiam* (or, as often, beginning with the second word *Absolutionem*) was included in this shift from the very start, for the latter was at this time, and continued to be for several centuries, the regular expression of the priests' sacramental absolution. This was, however, nothing else than a feature of the period. It was right around the year 1000 that (as divers witnesses tell us) the custom came into vogue. Shortly before, it had become a general practice to have the absolution follow immediately upon the sacramental confession. The same pattern was therefore followed in the monasteries where it had long been customary to go to confession to one's spiritual father weekly or even oftener; the sacramental absolution was appended to the *Misereatur*.

The *Confiteor* had thus undergone some development before it was ushered into the Mass prayers at the foot of the altar. From the ninth century on, a number of versions are extant which were intended for use in sacramental confession.

The situation we have here outlined helps to explain how it is that the prayer not only makes acknowledgment before God and his priest, but ends with a petition begging the latter to give counsel and judgment and also to act as an intercessor before God. Intercession of the Church, or more particularly of the priest, was, for the first millenary, the form in which the sacramental power of penance was exercised. This petition for intercessory prayer could well be retained in the confession of lay people and it was also retained in the confession which the celebrating priest made to his assistants. Another standard element in the early *Confiteor* formula was the mention of the saints, and, in the more ancient texts, an additional mention of the altar was also made. This points to the fact that the formula was used with some eagerness whenever the monastic custom then in vogue was followed, of making the rounds from altar to altar, praying at each one.

The oldest *Confiteor* formulas which were inserted into the Mass were satisfied to follow the fundamental lines just indicated. About 1080 the following version was used at Cluny: *Confiteor Deo et omnibus sanctis eius et vobis, pater, quia peccavi in cogitatione, locutione et opere, mea culpa. Precor vos, orate pro me.* A thing to notice here is something that holds also for later formulas of the *Confiteor:* the acknowledgment in the first part is made first of all to God and the Church in heaven, while the intercession in the second part is asked at once of the Church on earth. It is well to remark that even in the eleventh century lengthier formulas had already put in an appearance.

As time went on a general augmentation may be noted. At the General Chapter of the Cistercians in 1184 it was decreed that the Mother of God should be named before all the other saints: *Confiteor Deo et beatæ Mariæ et omnibus sanctis.* The pious devotion of a St. Bernard is patently at work here. The later Middle Ages continued to add further names to the list usually, however, only in the second part of the *Confiteor* so that they appear as intercessors. This penitential prayer was in danger of becoming a very externalized devotion. The Third Council of Ravenna (1314) decreed that aside from Mary, only Michael, John the Baptist and the Apostles Peter and Paul were to be named. These are names calculated to recall to mind the sin-free glory and holiness of the triumphant Church.

Elsewhere there was often a long listing and detailing of faults that often turned into an acknowledgment of sins *in specie* just as was general and usual at choir Office in many localities. The interpreters of the liturgy voice a disapproval of this, alleging rightly that there is question here not of secret confession but of public. An intensification of the utterance of sorrow is manifested when the subject is described at the beginning: "I sinner, wretched and unhappy" or "I guilty priest confess" and other similar phrases.

As to the external rite, we find from the very outset that the *Confiteor* was recited with body bowed profoundly. But kneeling too must have been rather widespread. Striking the breast at the words *mea culpa* is mentioned quite early. This gesture, copied from the Bible story (Luke 18:13) was so familiar to St. Augustine's audience and so intimately connected with the acknowledgment of sin that the saint had to caution them against beating their breasts every time the word *confiteor* was called out.

MISEREATUR

According to an old tradition the *Confiteor* of the priest was answered by the deacon or by one of the assistants with the prayer *Misereatur* which corresponded to the final plea of the *Confiteor*. The formulation of the *Misereatur* was just as multiform as that of the *Confiteor*. The ground text which by and large remained in the Mass is to be seen probably in a version which is found in various places in the ninth/tenth century. However, it is only proper to record that the older Mass books mention this *Misereatur* of the assistants or of the deacon or of the Mass server as infrequently as they do the *Confiteor* that follows. The fact that these two formulas had to follow, was taken as much for granted as the fact that the texts would be almost identical with the priest's. Besides it was hardly necessary to write the formulas down, for not only every cleric but every properly instructed Christian had to know them by heart in some form or other, almost as he did the Lord's Prayer. Still it appears that often the priest used for his *Misereatur* a much more solemn form in which a special phrase was prefixed like, "By the prayers and merits of the holy Mother of God, the Virgin Mary, and all His saints." Or he might use a phrase which changed with the Church year; or several of these phrases together—an opportunity for giving the celebrant's devotion ample play. Even though these additions to the intercessory prayer were very meaningful and suggestive of the whole economy of salvation, they were after all—excepting the first of them—embellishments proposed by the Gothic spirit and were in con-sequence not accepted everywhere, nor were they admitted into the Missal of Pius V. Sufficient that the prayer expressed the wish and hope that God would forgive the faults confessed.

In content the wish expressed in the *Misereatur* differs in nothing ex-cept emphasis from the wish expressed in the priest's *Indulgentiam*. The formula, which had gone through no little development long before being taken into the Mass, had even been shortened in various ways. It was only in a few individual instances that it received an augmentation as did its companion piece *Misereatur*.

INDULGENTIAM

As already hinted, the *Indulgentiam* had become since the year 1000 a favorite form for absolution in the sacrament of penance—a depreca-tive or, more properly, optative form. In what sense was it now incor-porated into the Mass, in the prayers at the foot of the altar? For the sacrament certain conditions appear to be missing. Contrition might be present, provided the *Confiteor* is said with proper intention, for if we stand before God as sinners and if we see the glance of all heaven directed towards us, we become sufficiently aware of the heinousness of sin and turn away from it. That is perhaps the motive for contrition which is closest to us and therefore also most effectual, even if it is not the highest. But the confession was not at all extensive enough since it was essentially very general. Besides the *Indulgentiam* was spoken only by the priest over the assistants, and not in reverse even when these latter was priests, a surprising thing since it was primarily the celebrant who required the purifying action of the sacrament. However, we must remember that the development we are considering belongs to a period which had not yet experienced the clarification of its penance theories through Scholasticism. This was the high tide of sacramental general absolutions regarding which, nevertheless, even then the fact was empha-sized that the general acknowledgment which was connected with them did not suffice for grave sins. But there was a constant effort to despoil the *Confiteor* formula of its general character by inserting specific refer-ences, and doubtless it was not seldom that a personal confession was—by abuse—combined with it. But if the priest does include himself (*tribuat nobis*), he was surely aware that the formula could have, in his regard, only the value of a petition, which did not however rob it in any way of a more extensive power with regard to others.

It is certain that efforts were made to emphasize the formula by means of ceremonial. According to the use of Cluny the priest at a private Mass, while answering the lay-brother with the *Misereatur*, put on the stole which up to then he had carried in his hand, and then recited the

Indulgentiam. In other places a special versicle was inserted between *Misereatur* and *Indulgentiam,* or the *Indulgentiam* was introduced by the word *Oremus. The sign of the Cross* which accompanied the formula here as elsewhere, and which itself developed out of the laying on of hands by means of which penance and reconciliation were once administered, has survived until the present.

The original conception of this absolution as a sacramental formula will serve to explain the fact that a penance was not infrequently imposed just as we will find was done at the "Open Confession" which took place after the sermon. The faithful, too, were sometimes drawn into this penitential act. In many churches of Normandy the priest turned towards the people while he spoke the *Indulgentiam.* The nuns at Fontevrauld used to say a *Confiteor* of their own after the priest said his; the introit was not started until after the *Indulgentiam.* According to South-German Mass books of the late Middle Ages, the priest kissed the altar and then turned to the people and pronounced an absolution, using a second formula of the type which was then otherwise employed when administering sacramental forgiveness.

Of these various formations which are in essence—if not in actual time —pre-Scholastic, only the absolution formula *Indulgentiam* has survived. The Church's penitential practice had followed the lead of Scholastic theory and had begun to limit the use of sacramental powers to very definite conditions. As a result, sacramental absolution was neither considered here nor given, and so the pentitential act which began with the *Confiteor,* even in spite of the formula mentioned, continued to have only that meaning which the confession of faults had in the period of monastic lay confession when this formula was not in use. Of course even the confession of faults had long ago assumed a merely formal character; nevertheless it remains an humble acknowledgment of our sinfulness and a worthy expression of our contriteness, and with these the intercession of the Church will continue to be connected as it has been since the beginning.

VERSICLES

Not counting the oration *Aufer a nobis* which had formed the conclusion of the entrance rite (and before which the *Confiteor* was inserted), the liturgical mind of the Middle Ages added a further framework to the ceremony surrounding the *Confiteor.*

A versicle or two was introduced before the *Confiteor,* and it made no difference whether the psalm *Iudica* preceded or not. From a time, perhaps, when it was still customary to make a concrete confession of faults, comes the use of the verse (Psalm 140:3): "Lord, post a guard on my mouth . . ." Since the thirteenth century there was an almost general use, chiefly outside Italy, of the verse "Give thanks to the Lord; the Lord is gracious." (Ps. 117:1). This original meaning of the psalm verse was twisted into a summons to make a confession of faults to God because He is merciful. In Italy the verse (Ps. 123:8), "Our help is in the name of the Lord" had already been used in this same spot in the eleventh century. In the Roman liturgy this last verse was used to introduce not only all blessings but also other liturgical acts, particularly also the *Confiteor* in the Office. The admission which it implies, that in matters of salvation we are helpless without that help from above which —as the accompanying sign of the Cross indicates—is disclosed in the Cross of Christ, here fulfills the function of an epiklesis to introduce the act of penance. It is therefore very understandable that in several localities it became customary—and still is today—to pronounce the same little phrase when leaving the sacristy.

A number of versicles were also inserted after the act of penance as a sort of transition to the old oration *Aufer a nobis*. These versicles, which appear quite early, serve a purpose similar to the *preces* before the oration in the Office; the similarity is emphasized by the bowed position the priest assumes while saying them. Even though these are prayers of a semi-private nature, the structural rules for liturgical prayer are carefully observed. They alternate between priest and deacon or at most the closer assistants, for the brethren in choir are busy singing the introit and *Kyrie*. The versicles that appear here are seldom newly composed from Holy Writ. Generally they are taken from the verses used earlier at the close of the accession prayers. Thus we find here in Italian Mass books of the end of the twelfth century a portion of the versicle which two centuries before had belonged to the oldest accession arrangements and had then disappeared. Amongst these are also the versicles we still use: *Deus tu conversus* and *Ostende*, with which the basic theme of Psalm 84, and therefore of the accession prayers *in toto*, is reviewed in a brief but striking way. It is the same theme which is sounded in Psalm 42: We can gain joy and new life from the well-springs of God; He wants to manifest to us His protection and His saving power. The series of verses in the missal used in the papal chapels about 1290 is confined exclusively to the verses mentioned. But in other places this same group is merely the foundation to which other verses are added. Then after the general petition *Domine exaudi*, which otherwise almost always and even in an earlier period follows the series of versicles, and after the greeting *Dominus vobiscum*, which is not omitted even for this small group of people, the oration *Aufer a nobis* is said. *This is the oldest element in the prayers at the foot of the altar*, and even after these prayers had been more fully developed, continued to serve as the closing oration. Its glance is turned backward, back toward the sins we must leave behind, and also forward, toward the sanctuary, the holy of holies that we must enter. The oration derives from ancient Roman tradition. It was used at the beginning of the Easter celebration and later was also said when entering a shrine from which the relics were taken for the consecration of a Church. Now it is used while mounting the steps to the altar, and since the later Middle Ages it is said in a low tone, a practice which spread from England and which seems apparently to have been stimulated by the silence of the canon and the reasons which suggested the latter.

5. *Greetings. Kissing the Altar*

In the solemn functions of the seventh century, the first thing that occurred when the pope reached the altar was a series of greetings—kisses, according to ancient custom. There was a greeting for the co-liturgists and also for the two objects most intimately connected with the liturgy, objects which represented Christ, the Gospel book and the altar. Of these only the kissing of the altar has been retained in the universal Mass rite. The greeting of the co-liturgists is also to be found at present in solemn papal Masses; three cardinal priests greet the pope with the kiss of peace when he comes to the altar. In France a similar practice is to be noted in many churches all through the Middle Ages. Here it was done later on—very significantly—right after the *Confiteor*. In the English use of Sarum this was the spot selected for the kiss of greeting for deacon and subdeacon at every high Mass, even at the Mass of a priest. The priest pronounced the phrase which we will meet again elsewhere at the kiss of peace before Communion: "Receive the kiss of peace . . ."

The kissing of the Gospel book was kept in general practice a longer time, and it still takes place in a pontifical service; when the bishop reaches the altar, he kisses the book which the subdeacon presents to him, opened at the beginning of the day's Gospel. Usually the Gospel book was on the altar; so the kissing of the altar followed that of the book, seldom the other way round. Sometimes, in fact, the kissing of the book counted for both.

Since the twelfth century a new object of these greetings was added, the *crucifix*, now generally standing on the altar. Till far into the sixteenth century it was but loosely connected with its stand, so that it could be easily lifted out. Thus, by placing it on a proper shaft, it was also used as a processional cross. It, too, is given a reverential kiss. But towards the end of the Middle Ages the kiss is gradually transferred from the sculptured crucifix on the altar to the miniature image found in the Missal at the beginning of the canon or elsewhere, so that sometimes the veneration of this image counts also for the veneration of the Gospel book or even of the altar. A typical sample of the Gothic mind is displayed in two fourteenth- and fifteenth-century Mass books of Seckau which stipulate that the same honor (with words of the accompanying prayer) be shown to the images of Mary and John that are connected with the figure of the Cross.

However, these ceremonies of greeting were quite secondary and entailed the danger of disturbing the principal lines of the liturgy and so they disappeared from many of the late medieval Mass arrangements for ordinary Masses and finally vanished altogether from the Missal of Pius V. The only thing remaining is the kissing of the altar, the only thing that was there from the start—a fine example of a return to original forms.

KISSING THE ALTAR

In the first Roman *Ordo* the reverential kiss of the altar on arrival at the beginning of Mass is the only such kiss of the altar during the Mass mentioned expressly. The priest today, after mounting the steps, kisses the altar, just as he does often during the course of the Mass, in accordance with present-day practice; but this first kiss has a very special meaning. It is, as we have already indicated, the salutation of the place where the holy mystery will be consummated.

This ceremony is borrowed from ancient culture. In antiquity it was a natural practice to honor the temple by kissing the threshold. But it was also customary to greet the images of the gods by means of a kiss or to throw them a kiss from a distance, as the pagan Cæcilius, mentioned by Minucius Felix, did when he noticed the statue of Serapis while passing by. In like manner, the ancient altar was greeted with a kiss. And it seems that the family table, as a place enshrined by a religious dedication, was often similarly honored at the start of the meal. It was therefore to be expected that the custom of greeting holy places with a kiss should be continued in Christendom, with only a change of object. And since the practice taken over into Christianity was at bottom a civic custom, though indeed a civic custom in a religious milieu, there was no conflict with the attitude then prevailing against admitting religious practices derived from heathen worship. As early as the end of the fourth century the saluting of the altar with a kiss makes its appearance as a popular practice. The salutation must have been in use in the ecclesiastical liturgy at about the same time. A confirmation of this inference is to be found in the fact that the salutation of the altar at the start of Mass is a custom also in the West Syrian, the Armenian and the Byzantine liturgies.

The kiss is intended first of all simply for the altar, the *mensa Domini*. But subsequently the meaning of the kiss was enlarged by the idea that the altar built of stone represented Christ Himself, the cornerstone, the spiritual rock. Thus the kiss could include Him, too. With the growth of the cult of martyrs, it gradually became a rule from the beginning of the Middle Ages on, that even public churches serving for the assembly of the faithful should have their martyr's grave, and finally that every altar must enclose a "sepulcher" or little reliquary. Thus the kissing of the altar is transformed into a greeting of the martyr and, through him, of the whole Church triumphant. Innocent III therefore explains the bishop's kissing of the altar as representing Christ saluting his spouse.

In the prayer said nowadays while kissing the altar, the memory of the martyrs is combined with a longing for purification from sin reminiscent of the prayers at the foot of the altar: *Oramus te, Domine.* This formula appears for the first time in the eleventh century, and with the rubric, *dum osculatur altare.* The formula is a private and personal prayer of the priest to accompany the kiss; for that reason it is without the conclusion *Per Christum D. N.,* with which the *Aufer a nobis* ends. Other texts also occur, touching on the forgiveness of sin, and in some particular instances a formal oration is found or an apology is connected with the kiss. The kiss of salutation also survives at the beginning of other functions but without any accompanying text and, in consequence, its original significance is more easily recognizable; thus it is found before the blessing of candles on Candlemas day. Even at the beginning of Mass it is found without any accompanying words in some sources of the declining Middle Ages.

As late as 1240 the altar kiss in the Mass was customary at Rome only on coming in for Mass and on departing, and at one place—not specified —in the canon. A century later, and it had become the prevailing practice to kiss the altar in every instance mentioned in the present-day missal; it was done every time the priest turned around at the altar in salutation, and at the beginning of the canon and at the *Supplices.*

It is not surprising that modern interpreters of the Mass who went into the matter of the kissing of the altar at so many different parts of the Mass were rather uncertain how to explain it, and even found the constant repetition somewhat ample, perhaps excessive. According to one interpretation, the kiss is referred above all to the saints, with whom the priest confirms his communion before he begins the sacrifice and also whenever he salutes the Church on earth. According to another, the priest first receives the kiss of peace from the altar and from Christ in order to pass it on to the rest. Still another interpretation envisions the kiss simply as a symbolic renewal of the bond and union with Christ. All these things may be true as an extension of the meaning. *But primarily the kiss, especially at the beginning and the end of Mass, is a proper reverence and honor to the sacredness of the altar, and the same may be said even about the kiss that precedes the greeting of the people.*

6. The Incensing of the Altar

At a solemn service the kissing of the altar is followed by the incensing. From the fact that in our present-day rite this action is restricted to the festive form of the Mass, it is plain that incensation is above all a means of heightening the solemnity. Like the flowers and candles, like the beauty of the vestments and the sound of the organ, the clouds of incense rising to the ceiling and filling the whole church with their sweet smell are intended to aid the senses in grasping the greatness of the feast. In ancient times frankincense in its many forms, as the East supplies them, was highly esteemed. In civil life, in better homes, its perfume was in demand. It was used profusely at burials. But above all it played a large part in heathen cult. For Christians, this last circumstance—added to the general objection to any and every materilization of divine service —served rather to exclude incensation from divine worship.

But after the disappearance of paganism it did find its way from profane use into the Christian liturgy. About the year 390 the pilgrim Ætheria noted that incense was carried in at the Sunday service in Jerusalem, so that the Church of the Resurrection was completely filled with its perfume. And the baptistery of the Lateran possessed a *thymiamaterium* of pure gold, the gift of the Emperor Constantine. In the procession at the papel services described in the first Roman *Ordo* seven torch-bearers and a subdeacon with the *thymiamaterium* preceded the pope, a survival from the Roman court ceremonial.

If incense was thus used quite early in religious assembly it was because its special quality lent itself to *religious symbolism*. The psalmist used the smoke of incense billowing upwards as an image of prayer rising to God (Ps. 140:2), and in the Apocalypse the golden bowls of incense represented the prayers of the saints. Thus incense could easily express the religious sentiments of the Christian community—the lifting of the heart in prayer, the elevation of the soul to God; and just as easily was it capable of itself becoming a sacred object, a bearer of divine blessing, after the benediction of the Church was pronounced over it. This definitely religious signification and a corresponding intensification of the use of incense, as it had already developed quite some time in the Orient, is met with in the Roman liturgy for the first time in the Frankish area. Amalar mentions the change from Roman practice in the use of incense at the offertory.

INCENSE AT MASS

By the ninth century, incense was definitely used at the *start of Mass*. After the celebrant had made his confession of faults and saluted those

around him, in many churches a cleric came to the altar and offered incense. The Sacramentary of Amiens presents two prayers for the pertinent *benedictio incensi,* of which the second at least had its origin in the
East—an inkling as to the origin of the custom. A formal incensation of
the altar is mentioned as early as the eleventh century.

The incensation at the beginning of the fore-Mass is even now less
richly developed than the incensation at the beginning of the Mass
proper; in the Middle Ages too, it was only in exceptional cases that it
was further expanded. The incense was blessed, of course, just as is done
elsewhere, and various formulas for this appear, including the one we
use nowadays. But, just as at present, no special prayer was connected
with the incensation.

The external action is also mostly very simple. Besides the incensation
of the altar there is mention in the later Middle Ages also of the incensation at this place of the celebrant by the deacon. The post-Tridentine
Missal carried through the more detailed regulation in this matter by
putting in an incensation of the altar cross and the relics as the first items.

We will have occasion later to pay greater attention to the transition
to the incensing of persons, since it is really from this that the incensing
of objects gets its meaning. In the incensing of the altar, the meaning
that stood in the foreground was the purification and protection that the
incense implied; this became, in turn, a sign of honor. From here the
next step was obvious; it could be carried over generally to all sacred
objects—and to the most sacred of all, the Blessed Sacrament, where it
does today actually find its favorite use.

*Thus the incensation at the start of the Mass is manifestly a true open-
ing rite which is repeated at the beginning of the Mass proper;* the locale
of the sacred action and the *liturgus* himself are removed from this sin-
tainted world in a special manner and transported into an atmosphere of
sanctity. In the last analysis a biblical example could have had some influence. It was a law in Old Testament worship (Lev. 16:12) that the service of the high priest must not begin without incense. Since Carolingian
times it became a favorite interest to discover parallels in the Old Testament and to put them into actual use; this might have had an effect
here too.

7. *The Introit Chant*

After the priest has venerated the altar by means of a kiss and, in
given cases, by incensation, he turns to read from the missal the text of
the introit which the choir had intoned for the procession of the clergy.
This is the practice nowadays. In our modern churches, where the

sacristy is built quite close to the sanctuary, it is impossible to have a real procession even on feast days unless in some way a circuitous route is deliberately introduced. There could hardly have been any thought of a formal procession in the ruder buildings of primitive Christianity, or even in the modest confines of the average basilica. But when, on the contrary, we view today the colossal ecclesiastical structures which have arisen since the fourth century at prominent points of the Eternal City, and when we notice that the *secretarium* in which the ministers made ready for divine service was at that time situated mostly near the entrance of the basilica, that is, at the end opposite the apse, and when we take into consideration the numerous clergy who, according to the oldest *ordines*, took part in papal worship, it becomes quite clear that the procession of the clergy from entrance to altar was an act of great importance and significance.

Such a procession could hardly have been tolerable if it had been conducted in absolute silence. And since there was no organ and instruments were generally proscribed in the ancient Church, it was left entirely to the singing to give musical color to this entrance procession. We will probably get the best notion of the temper of this chant by thinking of the one genuine introit which is still current in our present-day liturgy, namely the *Ecce sacerdos* to the sound of which the bishop makes his entrance into the gayly decorated church on important occasions. Even in the Roman liturgy of later antiquity this entrance chant, the *introitus* —at a later period also called *officium*—was already arranged as an art-chant performed by a special group of singers, just like the songs for the collecting of the offerings and for Communion, and like these—and like the orations and readings—the introit varied according to the festivity. The texts for these songs were taken essentially from the psalter. By the time that our processional chants were composed, the older hymn creations—from which we derived the *Gloria in excelsis Deo*—had lost the prestige they had once possessed and were reduced to very sparse remnants. The new hymnody, composed on the principles of meter and strophe, which was introduced about the time of St. Ambrose, was not admitted to the Roman Mass for over five hundred years. At Rome a strict rule was observed in the face of the wild and crafty song-propaganda of Manichean and Gnostic groups: We use only the songs dictated by the Spirit of God Himself.

THE ANTIPHON

These chants were performed antiphonally, that is, the psalm was sung by two choruses, alternating verse by verse. Already in an early period in ecclesiastical singing, antiphony involved the introduction of a prefatory verse which announced the melody of the following verse, the psalm.

This prefatory verse, which we today style an antiphon, appears to have been introduced as the result of a musical exigency; in order to assure a proper intonation it seems to have been the practice in ancient times to play a short prelude on an instrument. But since musical instruments were forbidden in Christian worship as heathenish, the function had to be taken over by the human voice. This would lead to a creation such as we have in the antiphon. The firt place in which antiphonal song was employed was Antioch where it rode on the swell of a young Catholic movement. When about 350 the leaders of the Catholic monks, Flavian and Diodoros (later bishops), began to gather the people around them and to argue openly against an overmighty Arianism then at its height, they introduced this method of singing at their prayer-meetings in the shrines of the martyrs. From this start antiphonal singing spread everywhere, being carried abroad by the monks, who possessed not only the means of cultivating chant, but also the necessary knowledge of the psalms. The city cathedrals followed, in which special singing groups were formed, the *schola cantorum*.

According to a narrative that has often been repeated, antiphony was introduced into Rome by Pope Celestine I (d. 432), and introduced precisely as a song for the introit, as the *Liber pontificalis* recounts. Unfortunately the account cannot be relied on as an historical report. However, it does give us this much information, that at the time this section of the book was written, prior to the middle of the sixth century, the introit chant composed of psalm texts had long been in use.[1] In the first description of the papal Mass, a description going back to the seventh century, we come across the introit as a chant of the *schola*. When the pope stands in the *secretarium* ready to make his entry, he beckons to the proper cleric, making a sign *ut psallant*; the latter in turn passes the signal on to the director of the *schola*, which stands ready by the passageway to the altar, in two double rows to left and right (corresponding to the two half-choruses), the boys on the inside, the men on the outside. At once the leader begins the antiphon. The psalmody is continued until the clergy have passed the rows of singers and reached the altar. After the pope has saluted his assistants with the kiss of peace, he gives a signal to start the *Gloria (Patri)*. At the *Sicut erat* the deacons rise, two by two, to kiss the altar. The pope meanwhile remains kneeling in prayer "until the repetition of the verse," meaning obviously the antiphon. The antiphon was therefore repeated at the end of the psalm. Whether it was also repeated after each single verse of the psalm, cannot be determined so far as the city of Rome itself is concerned. In fact the phrase cited above seems to prove the contrary, for it does not say:

[1] That all the people originally took part in this is only a later element even in the historical writing of this period; the words *antephanatim ex omnibus* are missing in the older recensions of the text.

"until the last repetition of the verse." But this may well be one of the alterations which were made in the Roman chant when it reached Frankish domains, apparently as the result of Gallican traditions.

The oldest manuscripts of the Roman Mass-chant books, the antiphonaries, surviving from about the year 800, contain only the song-text without the neums; these books do not indicate any explicit shortening of the psalm. This reduction seems to have occurred with varying rapidity in different places. In some places as late as 1000 mention is still made of the nod or gesture to signal for the closing of the psalmody with *Gloria Patri*, or the second (or a second) verse of the psalm is expressly indicated. In other places the psalm was curtailed to the first verse apparently as early as the eighth century. In this abbreviation of the text we have the result, no doubt, partly of a development of the musical forms which had gone on apace, musical forms which we find in the tenth century fully written out, the same melodies that have been once more restored to us in the *Editio Vaticana* of the Roman *Graduale*. Sung thus in solemn fashion, the antiphon itself and its repetition took up no little time in performance.

But a more important factor in producing this reduction of the psalm was the fact that in the more modest circumstances of extra-Roman episcopal and capitular churches there was hardly any room for a lengthy procession like that in the papal liturgy. Moreover, a regular formal procession of this sort was not taken into consideration in the planning of new churches and the distance to the altar was shortened to only a fraction of its former length. True, the time at the altar was stretched out by the expansion of the prayers at the foot of the altar and by the introduction of the incensation, so that the shortening of the introit was somewhat counterbalanced. But in any case the introit was no longer the song accompanying a grand procession. Reduced to its essential elements, it became an independent preludial chant, opening up the celebration of Mass. There was even some doubt about the right moment to start it, whether it should be sung in good part before the celebrant and the assistants appeared, or begin only when the clergy have arrived at the foot of the altar, as the later *ordines* usually demanded. The hope that the introit would once more assume its original character as a processional chant seems to have dictated the rubric in the 1907 *Editio Vaticana* of the songs of the Mass; here the regulation is clear, that the introit is to be intoned "as the priest approaches the altar." And of course the Reformed Holy Week of 1955 has not only adopted the old terminology *antiphona ad Introitum* but even directs (on Holy Thursday) that it is to be sung during the procession "through the church to the altar."

Of the original antiphonal character of the chant—the sort of thing which grew so important in the psalmody of the Office—only a very slight residue is still to be found in the introit. One survival is the sand-

wiching of the psalm verse between the antiphon and its repetition.
Surviving, too, is a recollection of the double chorus: soloists and choir
divide the two halves of the psalm verse between them, and the two
verses of the doxology. And the liturgical books still employ the sign
"Ps." for the beginning of the psalm verse, not the "V." which indicates
the part assigned to the soloist in the responsorial chants.

Besides this curtailment of the introit, we have to consider also the
very remarkable fact that other trends led to more than one enlargement
—to an enlargement and an enlivening. For one thing, the Carolingian
reform had sought to have the *Gloria Patri* sung by the people, in line
with the original character of this doxology. A hundred years later the
prescription was still enjoined. Soon after the Roman liturgy had found
its way to the Frankish area we come upon another extension of the
introit through the practice, already touched upon, of repeating the antiphon after each verse of the psalm, as was customary also in the
psalmody of the Orient under certain conditions. Alongside this there is
the puzzling creation of a "verse to repeat" which is actually found in
some of the oldest manuscript antiphonaries. In these books not only are
the antiphon and psalm noted down for the introit—and likewise for the
communion—but there is an additional verse of the psalm under the
superscription "to repeat." Both of these phenomena perhaps belong to
the same general plan, as we shall see in more detail in a later chapter.

About the twelfth century *two other ways of enriching the introit*
received further attention. They are both mentioned by Beleth (d.
1165). The first method of amplification, followed on feast days, consisted in repeating the antiphon in whole or in part, even before the
Gloria Patri, so that it was sung three times altogether. This was customary in many places north of the Alps, though not general. The practice was followed from the eleventh century on, and is still in use
amongst the Premonstratensians and the Carmelites. The other method
consisted in enlarging the text of the introit by means of tropes. In regard
to the introit the favorite device was the introduction of a preliminary
phrase.

The Missal of Pius V eliminated all these tropes as parasitic. But in
our time the tendency has been manifested more than once to restore the
introit to a fuller form, at least on festive occasions, by substituting the
original full psalm in place of its vestigial single verse. Thus at the coronation Mass of Pope Pius XI in 1922 the entire *Introitus* psalm was sung.

THE PSALM

*In an earlier stage of the introit chant the psalm must have been the
more important by far.* This can be traced quite plainly in the Mass
formularies for feast days. A psalm was picked which, taken as a unit

(in the sense of the allegorizing psalm-exegesis of the period), could best fit the occasion. The only psalm verse left in our present-day introit—as a rule the first verse, or, if the first verse served as antiphon, the one immediately following—often shows absolutely no connection with the *motif* for the day, whereas the idea is actually conveyed by the continuation of the psalm. Take the Wednesday in the Advent Ember week or the fourth Sunday of Advent; the psalm verse beginning "The heavens proclaim the glory of God" conveys no particular impression of Advent. But the psalm from which this verse is derived contains those phrases so often cited in this season with reference to Christ's coming like the orient sun: "He comes as a bridegroom from his bed" (Ps. 18:6). In the third Mass of Christmas the introit verse is one that has certainly only a very general meaning: "Sing to the Lord a new song"; but it is the beginning of Psalm 97 which serves as a Christmas psalm because of the words: "The Lord has given proof of his saving power and has vindicated his just dealings for all nations to see" (vv. 2f.). In the introit for Epiphany we find the verse: "Grant to the king, O God, thy own skill in judgment" from Psalm 71, but a fuller meaning is extracted from what follows, wherein "the Lords of Tharsis" and the "kings of Arabia," etc. appear. On the Feast of Holy Bishops we read the introit verse: "In David's reckoning, Lord, let not his patient care be forgotten" (Ps. 131); it is not till further in the psalm we find the connection with the theme of the day: "Let thy priests go clad in the vestments of innocence" and later "I will clothe her priests in the vesture of triumph" (v. 9; cf. v. 16). In other cases this characteristic verse is at least given prominence by being selected as the antiphon, but of this more later.

GLORIA PATRI

Besides the initial verse of the psalm, the concluding verse has also been retained, namely the *Gloria Patri*. This verse, known as the Little Doxology, has accompanied antiphonal psalm chant as the regular ending of every psalm, joining it in its cradle at Antioch and staying with it in its travels over the world, although not everywhere accepted at once. The opposition to Antiochene Arianism had aided in its introduction. The Arians used as their battle-cry and watch-word the unexceptionable but ambiguous formula, "Glory be to the Father *through* the Son *in* the Holy Ghost," seeing in it the expression of the belief they maintained, of the Son's subordination to the Father. In the Catholic camp the leaders, the very ones who introduced and propagated the new antiphonal chant, set up an opposing formula which had long been traditional amongst the Syrians, "Glory be to the Father *and* to the Son *and* to the Holy Ghost," a formula derived from the baptismal formula

(Matt. 28, 19) which gave unequivocal expression to the essential equality of the three divine Persons. In this way every psalm spoken by the new people of God ended with a shout of praise in honor of the triune God. The succeeding verse is, in its present form, proper to the West, although equivalent phrases are to be found quite early also in the Orient, especially in Egypt. At the Synod of Vaison (529), which is the first to mention it, it is directed against the heretics who denied the eternity of the Son, and therefore likewise against the Arians. The "was in the beginning" was the thing that was to be stressed, especially in relation to the Son (and to the Holy Ghost). According to the wording this additional phrase declares that we ascribe to the triune God that glorification which has been God's from the beginning and will ever be.

Why is the *Gloria Patri* omitted during Passiontide? As early as Durandus the reason given was: sorrow and grief. That would be the reason why the phrase is similarly omitted at Requiem Masses. But this is not really the reason. Actually we have here the working of the old "law of retaining the ancient in seasons of high liturgical worth," in other words, we have the residue of an older system. This means, Rome accepted the antiphonal chant without the *Gloria Patri;* later the verse was added at other times of the year, but not during this season. The same principle is at work—only with greater efficacy—at the high point of the Easter service, the Holy Saturday Mass; here the introit chant, along with the other antiphonal chants, offertory and communion, is entirely absent. And on Good Friday, the entire opening rite, including *Kyrie* and oration, was not accepted.

THE MUSICAL NOTE, THE PSYCHOLOGICAL MOOD

From the viewpoint of music the antiphon is the most important part of the introit. And even as to contents the opportunity was here presented to accentuate the tone or temper with which the celebration was to begin. Thus the antiphon established the tone in a double sense, the musical note, the psychological mood. This latter was done often by selecting for the antiphon a psalm verse that seemed to fit the celebration. Thus for the Christmas midnight Mass Psalm 2 is sung at the introit, and verse 7 is chosen as the antiphon: "Mine to proclaim the Lord's edict; how he told me Thou art my son." An introit of this sort was called in the Middle Ages *regularis*, while others, where the antiphon was not derived from the psalm, were styled *irregulares*. It is understandable that feast days and festal seasons did much to break through this schema of the *Introitus regularis* in order to give free vent to the expression of the mystery of the day. For the most part texts from the Scripture were used. Thus the introit antiphon for the third Christmas Mass proclaims, with the Prophet Isaias, the good news of the Nativity: "For our sakes a child is born, to our race a son is given." And the antiphon for Whitsunday plays upon the Pentecostal miracle with words from the Book of Wisdom: "The spirit of the Lord fills the whole world." A remarkable fact is this, that the text of the antiphon is frequently derived from the Epistle of the day, as, for example, the third Sunday of Advent, *Gaudete*. However, here and there the Bible is sidestepped entirely. On certain saints' days there is a simple invitation to partake of the joy of the feast: "Let us all rejoice in the Lord as we celebrate the feast day . . . ," a text which probably comes from St. Gregory the Great, who is said to have written it for the dedication of St. Agatha's in 592. One of the Masses of the Blessed Virgin begins with the happy greeting of the poet Sedulius: *Salve, sancta parens*.

Thus, by means as simple as they are masterly, the antiphon of the introit set the tone that should dominate the liturgical assembly. In some examples it is hard to mistake the fact that the text selected had in view both the procession itself and the image of a higher reality from the day's celebration which the procession typified. Thus on Epiphany we read: "Behold the Lord of Lords has come." And in Easter week, the crowd of newly baptized who have entered the Church are greeted on Saturday with: "He has led his people in exultation, alleluia, and his chosen ones in joy," and on Monday: "The Lord has brought you into a land flowing with milk and honey," and on Wednesday: "Come, you blessed of my Father."

But on the other hand there are days—like the Sundays after Pentecost —for which there is no special theme to which the introit antiphon might lead. Then the chant master takes up his psalter and chooses one of the psalms that in some way expresses the relationship of the Christian community to God: trust, praise, petition. It is to be noted that the psalter is gone through straight, starting with Psalm 12 on the first Sunday after Pentecost and moving on, Sunday for Sunday, till Psalm 118 is reached on the seventeenth Sunday. Let us remark here at once that the same rule for the Sundays after Pentecost holds for the other antiphonal chants, offertory and communion, and likewise for the alleluia-verse, but not for the gradual. But it is noteworthy that the choice for the various formularies does not generally fall on the same psalms for any two chants of the day.

The arrangement, as far as the succession of the psalms is concerned, is the same today as it was a thousand years ago. The succession of the psalms in each row and the divergence between the rows shows that there was no concerted attempt to hold in each case to one specified theme for all four of the chants. Instead, the Book of Psalms was conned from cover to cover, a bit chosen here, a bit chosen there, whatever appeared to suit the fancy of the praying congregation.

FROM SOLEMN MASS TO EVERY MASS

Although in its origin at least, the introit is essentially a part of the solemn high Mass, it soon found its way also into every Mass, even the private low Mass. This last transition can be seen in full detail in a document of the seventh/eighth century, The *Capitulare ecclesiastici ordinis*. It is in general quite jejune and sober. But in the very midst of its exposition it seems to consider it quite important that the introit should be made a general practice. Twice the author pauses to stress the rule: Every priest at every Mass, in the monastery, in the country, even on weekdays, and even when he celebrates alone, must say the introit with the psalm (-verse) and *Gloria Patri*. That is the arrangement of the *sedes sancti Petri*. Whoever knowingly omits it "does not offer in the proper manner, but barbarously." In the later Middle Ages the rule that the priest had to read the introit at every Mass was transferred also to the solemn Mass in which the choir had already sung it.

Holy Saturday, as we noted, has nevertheless remained without an introit, and also without an offertory or communion. The procession of the clergy from the baptistery is accompanied on this occasion by the singing of the litany. Several of the ancient manuscript antiphonaries have a rubric for this day and also for the vigil of Pentecost: "the litany at the entrance (introitum)." There are also other instances of the *Kyrie*-litany substituting for the introit. In the Roman *Ordo* of St. Amand, when a church is visited on the way during the procession of the *litania maior*, the church is entered to the accompaniment of the singing of the litany, which had been started while approaching the church, and at the end the pope says an oration.

The introit is the first text amongst the variable parts of the Mass, and the first text in general touching the congregation. The first words of the introit therefore often serve as a designation of the formulary or even of the respective day. We speak of *Lætare* Sunday, or of the *Rorate* Mass and the *Requiem*. The introductory character of the introit is emphasized in our present-day rubrics by the fact that the priest, when he starts to read the introit from the missal, blesses himself with the sign of the Cross, just as he does at the beginning of the prayers at the foot of the altar. But, in contrast to the latter, there is no accompanying formula. This is the present Roman practice although it was often different in the Mass ordinaries of the late Middle Ages. Sometimes *In nomine Patris* . . . was used, sometimes the pair of versicles *Adiutorium nostrum* and *Sit nomen Domini*, sometimes both together, or finally some other words were employed. Another indication of the merely private character of all that precedes the introit is given in some later medieval ordinaries where the preparation of the chalice was inserted before the introit as a final preparation for Mass.

The introit is read by the priest at the Epistle side of the altar. Just as the bishop during the fore-Mass takes his place at his *cathedra*, so one who does not use a *cathedra* should take his place at the right side of the altar, according to an old rule that goes back to the old Roman stational arrangements. Here he should stay till the choir finishes singing the introit, and even for everything which he himself sings or says right up to the Epistle. The exception, which came in only gradually, was the practice of transferring *Kyrie*, *Gloria* and *Dominus vobiscum* to the center of the altar.

8. Kyrie Eleison

We have already seen in the *Kyrie eleison* a prayer of the people to which the priest's oration is related. Thus considered, there is in this cry for mercy little that is fundamentally puzzling. But looked at more closely the tiny phrase gives grounds for a whole series of questions: Why this repeated cry, and why precisely a ninefold repetition? What is the derivation of this simple cry, so indeterminate in contents? Why in Greek? And who was originally the petitioner?

The Greek form takes us back to the earliest years of the Church. Not that the *Kyrie* is a vestige of that period in the Roman liturgy when the members of the Church in Rome themselves used Greek for the most part, and the language of worship was Greek, as it was till about the middle of the third century. No, the *Kyrie* was not taken into Rome from the Greek liturgy till much later. In the Orient, too, the non-Greek liturgies—the Coptic, the Ethiopian, and the West Syrian—have either borrowed or retained the *Kyrie eleison* untranslated. *The* Kyrie *did not get to Rome earlier than the fifth century*. And when it was taken over, it was as part of the litany which is traceable in the Orient since the fourth century and which has continued in use even today in the liturgies of the Orient as the so-called *ektenes*.

EARLY BEGINNINGS

However, the beginnings of the *Kyrie eleison* reach much farther back than that. The petition *eleison* taken by itself, with or without vocative, must surely have been very familiar to the early Christians, even from pre-Christian traditions. As late as the fifth century a preacher in

Alexandria felt compelled to denounce the habit many Christians had kept of bowing to the rising sun and crying out *eleison himas* (have mercy on us). Even the formal *Kyrie eleison* (κύριε ἐλέησον), directed to the divinity, is traced to heathen times, and the repetition of the cry a given number of times was also not unknown to antiquity. But no need to appeal to pagan custom; Holy Scripture offered examples in plenty of the cry of *eleison* directed to God, or, in the Gospels, to Jesus, especially in the book that served as the Church's first prayer book, the Book of Psalms. The Septuagint presented phrases like: *eleison me Kyrie* (have mercy on me, O Lord) (Ps. 6:3, *et al.*). True, none of these have the precise form of our *Kyrie eleison,* but the divergence was not so great it could not have been bridged by someone in prayer.

The proper history of our petition within Christian worship begins for us about the fourth century. The Gallic pilgrim lady Ætheria tells us, about 390, how at Jerusalem at the end of Vespers one of the deacons read a list of petitions and "as he spoke each of the names, a crowd of boys stood there and answered him each time, *Kyrie eleison,* as we say, Lord have mercy (*miserere Domine*); their cry is without end." Corresponding to the mode of pronunciation already then in vogue, Ætheria gives us the transcription *eleison* instead of the *eleeson* we might have expected. At the other hours the bishop himself prays these petitions; this appears to have been the more ancient practice.

From Antioch at about the same time there comes to us the very wording of such petitions which the deacon spoke when, for instance, after the Gospel of the Mass the catechumens were dismissed. And the explicit rubric is appended: "At each of these petitions which the deacon pronounces, the people should say *Kyrie eleison,* especially the children." The list of petitions varies from case to case. As a rule there are prayers for the whole Church, for the clergy, for the people and the ruler, for those on a journey and for the sick, for the benefactors of the Church and for the poor, and for peace. This type of prayer, which was called a *litania,* was soon transplanted to the West, perhaps by pilgrims to Jerusalem, and soon came into use everywhere, either in translation or in some free revision. The petition κύριε ἐλέησον is sometimes retained without alteration, sometimes translated, sometimes expanded or otherwise changed to forms like those which still survive in the older part of our Litany of the Saints: *Libera nos, Domine: Te rogamus, audi nos.*

The place where this litany was inserted was sometimes the same one it generally had in the East, namely, at the prayer that followed the lessons. But in the Milanese liturgy—although now restricted to the Sundays of Lent—it is still to be found at the beginning of Mass between the *Ingressa* (introit) and the oration, and therefore exactly where our Roman *Kyrie* is. In the Milanese version the response is made in Latin: *Domine miserere,* but at the end *Kyrie eleison* is repeated three times in succession. *Such a litany in a similar part of the Mass must have been proper also to the Roman liturgy in the fifth century and after.* That some form of *Kyrie*-prayer was customary in Rome by the start of the sixth century is unmistakably clear from Canon 3 of the Synod of Vaison (529), which purposed to incorporate this practice in Matins, Mass and Vespers, and appealed to the usage of the Apostolic See where the *Kyrie eleison* was often repeated. But from the remarks of St. Gregory the Great it is clear that even in his time there were two ways of performing the prayer; one a simple repetition of the cry *Kyrie,* the other, combining a further text with the *Kyrie.* This second way must be the litany, in which the *Kyrie* forms the response. However, in the sacramentaries which otherwise permit us to gather a picture of the Mass as it was in the sixth century, no text is presented. The Gregorianum does remark innocently, that the Mass begins with the introit, *deinde Kyrie eleison.* But we need not be amazed, for the celebrant did not intone the litany, and the sacramentary was intended only for his use. There are good reasons for suspecting that the old Roman *Kyrie*-litany survives in the so-called *Deprecatio Gelasii.* For there are various signs to suggest that this prayer had its origin in Rome and that the Pope Gelasius (492–496) named in the title was the redactor. It might seem improbable that the Roman liturgy should have had the *Kyrie*-litany at a time when the General Prayer for the Church, which is so akin to the litany in content and form, was still said after the readings. But it is quite likely that the *introduction of this* Kyrie-*litany coincided with the correction or revision of the General Prayer for the Church and with the amplification of the intercessory prayers of the canon,* which occurred about this time, so that it would have been only one part of a thoroughgoing reform of the Mass-liturgy undertaken by Pope Gelasius. Following is the text of this *Deprecatio Gelasii:* [1]

"Deprecatio" Which Pope Gelasius Ordered Sung
by the Universal Church
 Let us all say: Hear us, O Lord, and have mercy upon us.
 We call with faithful hearts upon the Father of the Only-begotten and upon the Son of the God Who is Creator from all eternity and upon God the Holy Spirit. Kyrie eleison.
  I. We beseech Thee for an abundance of divine goodness upon the spotless Church of the living God set up throughout the world. Kyrie eleison.
  II. We entreat Thee, Christ Our Lord, for the holy priests of God the all-powerful, for the ministers of the sacred altar, and for all people who worship before the true God. Kyrie eleison.

[1] In this translation, the Latin idiom, etc., has been sacrificed to provide what might be considered a *usable* English rendition. A more accurate version could also be provided from the viewpoint of liturgical science.—Rev.

III. Especially do we beg the manifold wisdom of Him Who is the Word of God for all who are right bearers of the word of truth. Kyrie eleison.

IV. We beseech the Giver of spiritual gifts for all those who mortify themselves in mind and body for the kingdom of heaven and busy themselves with the work of spiritual things. Kyrie eleison.

V. We call down the might of the Lord upon holy rulers who hold in high esteem justice and right judgment and also upon all the armies in their service. Kyrie eleison.

VI. We entreat the Lord and Governor of the world for the comfort of good weather and suitable rains, for the careful tending of the vital winds and the favorable course of the several seasons. Kyrie eleison.

VII. We beg the mercy of almighty God for those who by virtue of their initial acknowledgment of the Christian faith are now numbered among us and in whose hearts has been enkindled the burning desire for heavenly grace. Kyrie eleison.

VIII. We implore the mercy of our Redeemer for those caught in the weakness of human infirmity, who rejoice in spiritual sloth or in any other worldly error. Kyrie eleison.

IX. We pray the Lord Our Saviour for those undertaking long journeys or whom wicked powers have oppressed or the hardships of hostility have afflicted. Kyrie eleison.

X. We beseech the Lord of truth for those deceived by Jewish error . . . or heretical perversity or steeped in pagan superstition. Kyrie eleison.

XI. We entreat the Lord of mercies for the doers of pious works, who out of fraternal charity care for the needs of the sick. Kyrie eleison.

XII. We invoke the Lord of glory for all who enter this holy house of the Lord and who gather here with religious fervor and suppliant devotion. Kyrie eleison.

XIII. We beg the most merciful Lord for the strength of our souls and bodies and for the forgiveness of all our sins. Kyrie eleison.

XIV. We entreat the Lord of spirits and the Judge of all flesh for the repose of the faithful departed and especially for those holy priests of the Lord who have been in charge of this Catholic church.

XV. That our flesh may be free of blemish and our souls living in faith, Hear us, Lord, hear us. (Lit. *praesta, Domine, praesta*).

XVI. That we may have holy fear and true love, Hear us, Lord, hear us.

XVII. That our life in this world may be peaceful and our goal in the next assured, Hear us, Lord, hear us.

XVIII. Grant us, O Lord, the Angel of peace and the solace of the saints, Hear us, Lord, hear us. We commend to His mercy and the judgment of providence both ourselves and all that we have. For we acknowledge that we have received all these things from the Lord Who is their Author and we beg to retain them under His loving care. O Lord, have mercy on us.

This litany or one like it, with the *Kyrie* attached, must have become quite popular in Rome and its environs. Inserting it into the Mass was only one of its uses. In the Rule of St. Benedict the *litania* or the *supplicatio litaniæ id est Kyrie eleison* was part of the ending of every hour, introducing the *Pater noster* (here used as an oration). In Lauds and Vespers, where there is a more detailed mention of *litania*, the reference is apparently to a fuller text, like that in the *Deprecatio*, while in the other hours only the repeated *Kyrie eleison* seems to have been considered. In the older Gelasianum the litany is mentioned in the rite of the major ordinations; after the candidates have been summoned and the invitation to make objection has been issued, the rubric follows: "and soon after a brief pause, all begin the *Kyrie eleison* with the litany." From Gregory of Tours (d. 594) we get an account of a penitential procession which Pope Gregory the Great had ordered shortly after his election in the year 590, while pestilence raged in Rome. Seven processions were to assemble at seven Roman basilicas and, with a group of priests in each, were to start for St. Mary Major's in order to beg God's mercy by a "sevenfold litany." The one who told the story to our Frankish historian was himself an eyewitness of the event, and testified how the crowds marched praying through the city crying out *Kyrie eleison*. It is plain that this *Kyrie eleison* was not the entire text, that it was the answer of the throng of people to the invocations spoken by the groups of priests. This manner of saying the litany was retained later and (within limits) even today for the Rogation procession which itself obtained the name of *litania*.

AT MASS

The litany at the beginning of Mass had at any rate undergone a change at the time of Gregory the Great, perhaps partly through his work. In a letter to Bishop John of Syracuse, Gregory took pains to deny that he had been introducing Greek practices into Rome. In this connection he refers also to the *Kyrie*. Gregory stresses the differences from the Greek manner, which must have been very familiar to him from his stay in Byzantium. The differences are chiefly these: Amongst the Greeks all answer *Kyrie eleison* together, both clergy and people, whereas in Rome the clergy sing and then the people respond. Moreover, the Greeks have only the invocation *Kyrie eleison* whereas in Rome the *Christe eleison* is also used, being said as often as the *Kyrie*.

Finally Gregory remarks that on ordinary days they leave out whatever is usually said besides the *Kyrie eleison* and *Christe eleison*, in order to linger longer on these two invocations.

What was omitted on ordinary days can only have been the invocations of the litany. On solemn services, therefore, they were still in use, but the manner of rendering included a pre-intonation of the *Kyrie* or *Christe;* the chanters or the *schola* included the *Kyrie* and *Christe* in the invocation, and they were then repeated by the people. In line with this was the practice which lasted far into the Middle Ages—as late as the twelfth century—of omitting the *Kyrie* at Mass on days when the *collecta* with its protracted litany preceded the *statio*. The same thing happened at the major ordinations, since the litany followed. Even at present the litany (with its *Kyrie*) which is said on Holy Saturday counts for the *Kyrie* of the Mass. *In all these instances there is a survival of the original form of the* Kyrie *as part of a larger, more complete form of prayer.*

OTHER USES

A short invocation of this type, using only a word or two to express our beggary, implied, by its very brevity, a tendency to independence and to iteration. This tendency would be all the more pronounced if the *Kyrie eleison* had been known already in pre-Christian antiquity as an independent formula, as a cry repeated many times over, as an acclamation. Actually the *Kyrie eleison*, freed from any ties with other prayer-forms and repeated over and over again, is found in the liturgical prayer of the Orient as an ancient traditional usage. And time-honored numbers play a part here: a twelvefold *Kyrie eleison* at the opening of every hour in the Byzantine liturgy, a fortyfold *Kyrie* at the close of every little hour. The fervent *ektene* after the Gospel in a Byzantine Mass has a threefold *Kyrie eleison* after each invocation. The threefold *Kyrie* also appears elsewhere, especially near the end of the *ektene*, and also independent of such a litany. Aurelian of Arles (d. 550) had his monks begin and end the psalmody at every hour of the Office with a *Kyrie* said three times. The Lauds of the Milanese liturgy still contains a threefold *Kyrie* and, near the end, a twelvefold *Kyrie*. Likewise our present-day litanies still have a threefold *Kyrie eleison, Christe eleison, Kyrie eleison* at the beginning and at the end. A parallel to this independence and iteration of a response is to be seen in the history of the alleluia, which served first of all as a refrain which the people sang as they joined in at each verse of the responsorial psalm-chants. It soon turned into a cry of jubilee which could be repeated as long and as loud as you please. The Roman Breviary also has a threefold alleluia on occasion after occasion, and before Pius X it had a ninefold alleluia on the *Dominica in albis*.

We come upon this independent *Kyrie* in the first Roman *Ordo*, even though the service described is a festive one. According to this arrangement, the petition—a song now—is repeated until the pope, after saluting the altar and going to his *cathedra*, turns to the east and gives a signal. But not long afterwards—in fact, still in the eighth century—a specified arrangement for this signal is found, as we learn from other *ordines*, which give us further details about the *Kyrie*-chant. The *schola* sings *Kyrie eleison*, which is repeated three times—that is, most likely, till the number three has been reached. (Custom had thus consecrated the number three.) Then the pope gave a signal for the *Christe eleison*, which was repeated three times in like manner; then another signal for the triple repetition of the *Kyrie*, and so the end of the chant.

This arrangement based on threes corresponds to a primitive sacral usage, found even in pre-Christian worship. In Christian worship itself, there was introduced the idea of the Mystery of the Trinity which stood very much in the foreground in the Gallican liturgies because of the battle against Arianism. But it is noteworthy that Amalar makes no use of this idea in his older writings, but only later comes around to the Trinitarian meaning of the nine invocations of the *Kyrie*. The same meaning is impressed on us in all our prayer books and Mass interpretations and Mass devotions, right up to the present: God the Father is invoked three times, God the Son three times, and God the Holy Ghost three times. There is the appearance of truth in the fact that the second group uses the word *Christus*. But in reality the *Kyrie* groups, too, are directed to Christ. That is the Pauline and primitive Christian usage, where *kurios* is generally applied to Christ. And it corresponds to the whole tradition in which the *Kyrie eleison* itself arose. True, in some instances in the early period the connection with the Godhead is clear. At other times the meaning of *kurios* is undetermined, and it might well be, considering its use as a simple invocation. But in most cases, especially within the Eastern diaconal litanies, where the *Kyrie eleison* is indigenous, the whole construction of the various invocations of the deacon makes it more or less clear that the *kurie* has reference to Christ. The same is true in the Western litanies; in the oldest versions all the invocations from beginning to *Agnus Dei*, are addressed exclusively to Christ; the invocations of the saints are later insertions.

This ninefold invocation of Christos, the Kyrios, serves even at present as a kind of prelude leading very suitably to the priest's oration—an oration which gathers up the prayer of the Church and brings it, through Christ, to the throne of God.

ARRANGEMENT FOR THE KYRIE

Although we find that in Gregory the Great the arrangement for the *Kyrie* is still: "said by the clerics, answered by the people," in the first

Roman *Ordo,* the *schola* appears as the only performer. It is the job of the *schola* to sing the *Kyrie*—or perhaps more correctly, to intone it and sing the first part. There is no express statement that no one else participates in the singing, but the directions are all given to the *schola;* it is the *prior scholæ* who has to watch out for the pope's signal to conclude the singing. The Roman *Ordo* of St. Amand confirms this description and adds the detail, that the repetition of the song intoned by the *schola* is the duty of the *regionarii,* that is, of the subdeacons who were organized in Rome according to regions. The people no longer participate, at least in these grander pontifical services. Of course the possibility is not excluded that, in simpler surroundings and under other conditions, the *Kyrie* still remained the people's song. This was surely true in the lands of the North, where *Kyrioleis* was used as a refrain in folk-songs for many centuries, and the "Leise" (Fr. *lais*) represented a special class of spiritual folk-songs.

But at the beginning of Mass, the clergy forming the choir took over the singing of the *Kyrie,* at least in the larger churches where the clergy were numerous—and it is about such churches that most of the accounts are written. We need not necessarily think that the intonation and first-singing was done by a *schola cantorum;* in fact, as a part of the clergy, it was not very carefully distinguished from the rest. Instead the singers, it seems, were divided into two semi-choruses, and thus the tradition that the *Kyrie* was an antiphonal chant was retained. At first the nine invocations of one chorus were, as we have seen, repeated by the other; later the two choirs divided the nine invocations between them. It was but a step to have the first of each of the three sung by one choir and then repeated twice by the other choir, a mode of rendition many propose at the present. But even in the twelfth century it was customary for the choirs simply to alternate, exactly as the priest and the Mass-server alternate while saying the prayer.

The plain litany-quality of the old *Kyrie* chants is still recognizable in the Gregorian melody assigned to it in the Requiem Mass where the same simple tune recurs eight times and only in the ninth is there any embellishment. But the process of enhancing the musical form of the *Kyrie* made quick progress, right from the time its performance was given over to the *schola,* as we have seen indicated in the first Roman *Ordo.* When Gregorian chant flourished anew, in the tenth and succeeding centuries, many of the elaborate *Kyrie* melodies of the Roman *Kyriale* were composed. The titles which they bear give us a hint of another remarkable and colorful development in the evolution of the simple *Kyrie* text, the so-called *trope.* Amalar already suggests a forerunner of this type of troping, for he has the singers chant a fuller text (he is, indeed, merely paraphrasing the contents of their song): *Kyrie eleison, Domine Pater, miserere; Christe eleison, miserere qui nos rede-*

misti sanguine tuo; Kyrie eleison, Domine, Spiritus Sancte, miserere. But from this time on, from the ninth to the sixteenth century, a full literature of *Kyrie* tropes is developed. Every church possessed a dozen or so, some purely local, others spread far and wide. The collection in the *Analecta hymnica* covers 158 complete numbers. Every one of the nine invocations was amplified into a full verse line in such a way that the notes of the melismas were distributed over the complete text. In rendering this chant one choir would often take up the trope while the other sang the original *Kyrie* with its melismas, till both came together on the word *eleison*. It is from the first lines of these tropes that we derive the labels which many of the melodies of the *Kyriale* bear: *Lux et origo; Kyrie Deus sempiterne; Cunctipotens genitor Deus; Cum iubilo; Alme pater; Orbis factor; Pater cuncta*. As an example let us look at the trope of the first Gregorian Mass; its rhythm follows the melody simply, although several others employ definite verse forms like the hexameter.

1

a.	b.	c.
Lux et origo	*In cuius nutu*	*Qui solus potes*
lucis, summe Deus,	*constant cuncta, clemens*	*misereri, nobis*
eleison; Kyrie eleison.	*eleison; Kyrie eleison.*	*eleison; Kyrie eleison.*

2

a.	b.	c.
O mundi redemptor	*Per crucem redemptis*	*Qui es verbum Patris,*
salus et humana	*a morte perenni,*	*verbum caro factum,*
rex pie, Christe,	*spes nostra, Christe,*	*lux vera, Christe,*
eleison; Christe eleison.	*eleison; Christe eleison.*	*eleison; Christe eleison.*

3

a.	b.	c.
Adonai, Domine,	*Qui machinam gubernas*	*Quem solum laus et honor*
Deus, iuste iudex,	*rerum, alme Pater,*	*decet, nunc et semper*
eleison; Kyrie eleison.	*eleison; Kyrie eleison.*	*eleison; Kyrie eleison.*

It is clear that such artistic productions could be performed only by a skilled choir. For some of the tropes even many-voiced melodies appear in the thirteenth century. The tropes themselves were not included in the Missal of Pius V, thanks to the stricter tastes of his century. The monumental *Kyrie* was thus freed of overgrowth. But at the same time polyphonic music set to work to give this ninefold plea of mankind to the *Kyrios* a full musical expression.

Originally the celebrating priest took no part in the *Kyrie*. For that reason it is not mentioned in most Mass Ordinaries, not even in those that contain all the texts of the prayers at the foot of the altar, or of the offertory. This held true for all Masses celebrated with singing, right down to the late Middle Ages. It was not till the thirteenth century, when the general principle was formulated that the priest had to read the variable texts from the missal, that a like prescription was made in regard to the *Kyrie;* the celebrant says the *Kyrie* together with his assistant (or assistants). But this novelty did not take everywhere at once. The 1290 Mass *Ordo* of the papal chapels, although it stipulates that the priest should read the introit, says nothing of the sort for the *Kyrie;* but a few centuries later the papal chapels also followed the general custom.

For private Mass, on the other hand, even the eighth-century "*Capitulare ecclesiastici Ordinis*" included the *Kyrie eleison*, along with the introit, in the prayers for the priest; he is to say it nine times, bowing low all the while. There is no explicit mention here—nor for some time later—of any participation by the server. Even at solemn service, where the assistants are mentioned as taking part, it seems that the nine invocations were said by all together, since there is no indication of any apportionment. If later on the alternation of the nine between priest and those around him became common, the cause is to be traced to the example of the sung *Kyrie* with its double choir. There is record, however, of another manner of distributing the invocations, the priest taking the first three *Kyries,* the serving cleric the three *Christes,* and the priest the last three *Kyries.*

The priest used often to say the *Kyrie,* as he does the introit, on the Epistle side of the altar. This is still the practice of the Carthusians, the Carmelites and the Dominicans, and we also do the same at a solemn high Mass. It has been suggested that the change to the center was influenced by the wish to stress the prayer-quality of the *Kyrie;* the priest therefore stands facing the image of his crucified Lord, to whom he directs his appeal.

9. Gloria in excelsis

The *Gloria,* like the *Kyrie,* was not created originally for the liturgy of the Mass. It is an heirloom from the treasure of ancient Church hymns, a precious remnant of a literature now almost buried but once certainly very rich, a literature of songs for divine service written in the early Church in imitation of the biblical lyrics, especially the psalms. These lyrics were called *psalmi idiotici,* psalms by private persons in contrast to those of Holy Scripture. They are, for the most part, rude creations, and like the biblical psalms and canticles are not constructed on rhythmic and metrical principles. In their literary expression, too, they hold pretty close to their biblical models, and yet in them the religious inspiration of those centuries lives on perceptibly. The line begun in the New Testament with the *Magnificat* and Zachary's song of praise and the canticle of aged Simeon, is continued in these works. Few, however, have remained in use to the present, among them the Φῶς ἱλαρόν, already mentioned by Basil, which is still used in the Byzantine liturgy, the *Te decet laus*, which is in use in the monastic liturgy, and the *Te Deum* and the *Gloria* which survive in our Roman liturgy. This last, often called the Greater Doxology, was already so highly esteemed even in the ancient Church that it outlived the fate that overtook so many songs which perished as the result of an adverse attitude towards church hymns created merely *humano studio*.

"TEXTUAL TRADITION"

In the textual tradition of the *Gloria* three principal versions can be distinguished: (1) the Greek version from the *Apostolic Constitutions;* (2) the Syrian version from the Nestorian liturgy; and (3) the Greek version from the Byzantine liturgy, which is found already in the *Codex Alexandrinus* of the New Testament and which coincides in all essentials with our Western version. The first mentioned text is the first attested, since the *Apostolic Constitution* already existed around the year 380. But Abbot Capelle has shown that the noteworthy aspects of this text, namely the extraordinary manner in which Christ is subordinated to the Father and the omission of the address to Christ in the second part, are the work of an editor who takes the occasion to introduce his Arian ideas and expressions. If we abstract from this editor's additions, we have almost the exact text of the *Codex Alexandrinus* which served as his point of departure, i.e., the text into which he inserted his own Arian ideas. Of lesser importance is the Syrian edition, whose peculiarities show it to be the result of later expansion rather than the original wording.

Thus the *Codex Alexandrinus* remains the witness for us of the early form of our hymn. Its differences from the text of the *Missale Romanum* are no greater than those for the oldest Latin text, which is the Antiphonal of Bangor (690). We may then set the two texts side by side.

| *Codex Alexandrinus* | *Bangor* |
MORNING HYMN	FOR EVENING AND FOR MORNING
1. Glory to God in the highest, and peace on earth, may his good will dwell among men.	1. Glory to God in the highest, and on earth peace to men of good will.
2. We praise thee, we bless thee, we adore thee, we glorify thee.	2. We praise thee; we bless thee; we adore thee; we glorify thee; we magnify thee.
3. We give thee thanks for thy great glory, Lord, heavenly King, God Father, Pantocrator.	3. We give thee thanks because of thy great mercy, Lord, heavenly King, God Father, almighty.
4. Lord, only begotten Son, Jesus Christ, and Holy Spirit.	4. Lord, only-begotten Son, Jesus Christ, Holy Spirit of God. And we all say Amen.

5. Lord, God, Lamb of God, Son of the Father, Thou who takest away the sins of the world, have mercy on us.

6. Thou who takest away the sins of the world, have mercy on us, receive our supplications, Thou who sittest at the right hand of the Father, have mercy on us.

7. For Thou alone art holy, Thou alone art the Lord, Jesus Christ, to the glory of God the Father. Amen.

5. Lord, Son of God the Father, Lamb of God, who takest away the sin of the world, have mercy on us.

6. Receive our prayer; who sittest at the right hand of God the Father, have mercy on us.

7. For Thou alone art holy, Thou alone Lord, Thou alone glorious with the Holy Spirit in the glory of God the Father. Amen.

In the structure of the *Gloria* three sections are plainly discernible; (1) the song of the angels on the night of the Nativity; (2) the praise of God; and (3) the invoking of Christ.

First there is the song of the angels as recorded by St. Luke (2:14). The use of a biblical phrase as the theme at the start of a poem is also found elsewhere in ancient Christian hymns. For instance, the evening hymn which compares with the *Gloria*, a morning hymn, opens with an analogous word of praise utilizing the first verse of Psalm 112: "Praise the Lord, you that are his servants, praise the name of the Lord together." The same verse is used as the opening of the *Te Deum* in the version found in the Antiphonary of Bangor. And in particular this song of the angels was used as an introduction to prayer.

In all the versions the second section is a praise of God. This consists in a simple accumulation of phrases expressing our activity, and of names for the godhead. In the oldest witnesses of the version we are concerned with, this portion has obtained a certain exclusiveness and independence by making the address to all three divine Persons. The same thing is noticed even earlier in the Syrian version. In the effort to call God by all His grand names it was but a step to rise to the mystery of the Trinity, which had been made known by revelation. There is an exact parallel to be seen in the *Te Deum* where the praise of God also ends in address to the Trinity: *Patrem immensæ maiestatis, venerandum tuum verum et unicum Filium, Sanctum quoque Paraclitum Spiritum.*

KERYGMATIC UNFOLDING

And just as in the *Te Deum*, the next section in our present text, clearly distinct from what precedes, is a christological portion; *Domine, Fili unigenite.* God and Christ—that is not an arbitrary addition nor an unfinished enumeration of the three divine Persons (as some commentators seem to imagine when they make excuses for the fact that the Holy Ghost is mentioned only at the very end, and then only in passing). No, God and Christ are the pillars of the Christian order of the universe: God, the beginning and the end of all things, towards whom all religious seeking is bent and all prayer eventually is turned; but in the Christian order also Christ, the way, the road on which all our God-seeking must be directed. Therefore in St. Paul's letters we find this duality of God and Christ not only in the introductory salutation, but time and time again throughout the writing. And if at times St. Paul rounds out the duality and completes it in the Trinity, this is done not so much to acknowledge the three divine Persons themselves, as rather to mark more distinctly the structure of the Christian order of salvation, in which our ascent to God is vouchsafed through Christ in the Holy Spirit. To this notion the construction of the *Gloria* in its present version corresponds in a very extraordinary way, although the musical compositions of the hymn seldom if ever take note of it. We might add that the two main parts of the hymn are in a way allied to the two members of the introductory biblical motto: To God, glory—we join our voices to the angelic choirs in praising God; to men, peace—we turn to Him in whom the peace of heaven was brought to earth, begging Him to fulfill His work in us.

And now let us get down to details.

The oriental liturgies employ the song of the angels as a triple phrase. This is the form adopted by Luther and the King James Bible: on earth peace, good will towards men. But from the viewpoint of textual criticism the form εὐδοχία in Luke (2:14) is considered untenable; the reading must be *eudokias*. This betokens a double phrase in the original text, just as our version has it. But there is another thing to notice. Our ordinary rendering, "Peace on earth to men of good will," does not quite give us the original sense. *Eudokia* is not the good will of men but the good will of God, God's pleasure, God's favor and grace. The *men of good will* are therefore men of God's grace and selection, men to whom the news of God's kingdom has been proclaimed. According to the wording of the text, therefore, there is a limitation in this message of peace: *hominibus bonæ voluntatis*—to those whom God has chosen. But since all men are invited into the kingdom, the only thing clearly enunciated here is that "the children of His kingdom" partake of this peace not because of a turn of fortune's wheel, but because of God's free, merciful decree (cf. Eph. 1:5). The entrance of the Redeemer among the race of men spelt out two things, the glory of God and "peace" for men. Christ's coming to earth really meant the start of Redemption. In this sense it is possible that the angels' song contained not a wish but the expression of a fact, not an optative but a declarative: *Glory is given to God and peace to men!* It is the same thing that our Lord spoke of at the Last Supper in His great sacerdotal prayer, the only difference being the degree of development: "I have exalted thy glory on earth, by achieving the task which thou gavest me to do." But precisely because the glorification of God and the salvation of mankind was not "achieved" in its fullness till the sacrifice of Christ's Passion, and even then its fruits had still to ripen, and to continue to ripen till the end of time, it is correct to view the angelic song as proclaiming not the work that had already been completed, but the plan and purpose that was yet to be done, step by step: May God be given glory in the highest and may men in His grace find peace! *Gloria sit in excelsis Deo.* And if this were true of the song when the angels sang it, it is truer still when we on earth repeat it. Every day that the Church lives, every time the Church gathers her children in prayer, and particularly when she assembles them for the Eucharist, a new light flashes across the world and the Church beholds, with mingled joy and longing, the approach of the Kingdom of God, the advent, in spite of every obstacle, of the consummation of the great plan: that glory will come to God, and to men of God's choice, peace and salvation.

In the eastern liturgies which do not use the Greater Doxology at Mass, the opening scriptural words at least are often used, either at the start of the celebration, or at the preparation of the offerings, or at the kiss of peace, or before Communion.

The praises of God, which now follow are plain and clear. We simply list them, inadequate as they are: We praise thee, we bless thee, we glorify thee. The parallels in both of the older versions evidence the fact that the accent is not on the precise and distinctive meaning of each word but on the common basic concept of acclaiming and extolling the greatness of God. If we then construe the next clause, "we give thanks," in the same fashion, the pendent phrase, "because of thy great glory," is not so surprising. Still it seems better to take the words at their fullest meaning, for we can really thank God "for His great glory." In the new order of the world, built on grace and love, in which God has given us all things along with His Son (Rom. 8:32), God's kingdom has almost become our kingdom, and the revelation of His glory has become for us an overflowing grace and the beginning of our glory. Still this point of grace must not be overstressed. The magnificent thing about the hymn, and the thing that at the same time makes it so liberal, is the fact that it does not pay God tribute in exact ratio to man's indebtedness, nor does it thank Him only in acknowledgment of benefits received. Love does not recognize any scrupulous distinction; with the pardonable pride of children of God, we direct our glance wholly to God's glory, God's grandeur. We are happy to be allowed to praise His glory. For that reason a song such as this has such wonderful power to free men from any egoistic narrowness and to bring them all together on a higher plane.

The list of God's names which comes next also serves to praise God. These titles follow each other in a distinct gradation; Lord, King of heaven, God, Father, Almighty. The designation, *Deus, Pater omnipotens*, which is also found in the Apostles' Creed, shows again the venerable age of the hymn.

Immediately after this list of God's titles there comes an address to Christ, written in much the same style. It introduces the christological section. The transition is so imperceptible that it goes almost unheeded and we are scarcely aware that something new has started. This can be explained, from the viewpoint of the history of the text, by comparing it with the older versions where an address to the Trinity closed this first section, just as it does in the *Te Deum;* the mention of God the Father was therefore followed by that of the Son and of the Holy Ghost, and at once a new turn of thought set in with an apostrophe to Christ. There is really no doubt about where this section starts. On the other hand, there is no reason for considering this as the beginning of a new theme. Our grateful glance toward God's glory moves naturally on toward Christ, in whom that glory was revealed to us. In this christological section we can distinguish the following framework: (1) the laudatory salutation; (2) the litany-like invocations; (3) the triple predication, *Tu Solus;* and (4) the trinitarian conclusion.

First of all there is a list of names, all of them ancient. They are the same as those found in the oriental creed, in the profession of belief in Christ: Lord, only-begotten Son, Jesus Christ. At the top of the list is the word "Lord," with the connotation of the Pauline κύριος, which is made clear near the end of the hymn in *Tu solus Dominus.* The term "only-begotten Son" also had been highly esteemed in the ancient Church as a special name for Christ. In the *Euchologion* of Serapion the word (the Only-begotten) was often used all by itself as a usual title for Christ.[1] There is a second group of three names, and once again the Kyrios-term *Domine* comes first, in our present-day text amplified to *Domine Deus,* to indicate, no doubt, the essential equality of Father and Son. In the earlier versions this was followed by *Filius Patris,* now transferred to third place obviously because of its special importance. It is a name which appears to say nothing and yet says everything, and it definitely acknowledges our human inability to comprehend the mystery, for Christ is naught else than the radiance of His Father's splendor (Heb. 1:3). Then follows the term *Agnus Dei,* the sacrificial Lamb come from God, a title which refers to Christ's redemptive work. It is no accident that the title "Lamb of God," which recalls our Lord's great mercy, was connected from time immemorial with the cry for mercy in our litanies. Here, too, the term "Lamb of God" is followed by a short litany, likewise composed of three members. But in this case there is a mixture of hymnic predication and pleading. Taking up the

---

[1] I, 1; II, 1, 3; etc. (Quasten, *Mon.,* 49 ff.).

words of the Baptist, we remind our Lord of that voluntary abasement to which He, as Lamb of God, subjected Himself; we remind Him of that atoning Passion by which He "took away" the sins of the world; remind Him also of His triumph as He sits, exalted, "at the right hand of the Father," and there, as Lamb of God, hears the bridal songs of the elect. Thus it is that the same cry breaks forth which was heard in the *Kyrie:* "Have mercy on us, receive our prayer." In order to avoid misunderstanding as much as possible, the Church hesitates to call upon the Saviour to intercede for us, although there is no theological difficulty in doing so. It is He through whom she offers her prayers, and of whom it is said that He lives always to make intercession for us. It seems to suit our reverence and our joy in acknowledging His greatness merely to beg His mercy, for we do not want it to appear even for a moment that He cannot help us through His own power. Still the phrase *suscipe deprecationem nostram* does in some way imply Christ's mediatorship, that office of His which was accented so in older forms of the *Gloria:* Let us lay our pleadings in Thy hands, and carry them up before Thy Father's throne!

By means of a spanning *Quoniam*, the litany once more turns into a word of praise: "For Thou alone art the Holy One, Thou alone art the Lord, thou alone the Most High." In the period when our hymn originated, such expressions very vividly outlined the sharp antithesis between our Catholic worship and heathen worship with its many loosely-given attributes of divinity, its many *lords*, and its emperor-worship. Above and beyond all these creations of human fancy stands Jesus Christ, radiant and grand, the sole and only Lord. Our own day has great appreciation of this sublime contrast. Taking this as a background there is no need to reflect that the epithets mentioned can also attach to any of the three divine Persons, for if we refer them to Christ, they must also by that very fact be claimed for the triune God.

Next follows, as the final chord of this great hymn, a mighty act of homage to the Trinity; the name of Christ blossoms out into a naming of the three; "Jesus Christ—with the Holy Ghost—in the glory of God the Father." Again there is no question here of a mere roll-call of the divine Persons. The image of the God-man remains—of Him to whom we have raised our pleading, of Him who is exalted and glorified, who lives on eternally in that glory which He had with the Father before the world began (John 17:5).

The hymn started with the praise of God. It ends with the praise of Christ, in whom God's glory is disclosed to us. This praise of Christ employs terms which we also meet elsewhere in the ancient Christian liturgy. When the priest before Communion showed the blessed Body of Christ he cried out *Holy things to holy ones* and the people answered *Only One is holy, Jesus Christ, dwelling in the glory of God the Father.* Here the same acclamation is enlarged, and modified to a form of address: "Thou alone art the Holy, Thou alone the Lord," and in our Latin rendering another clause is added to the text, a clause from Psalm 82:19, "Thou alone art the most high," which was likewise understood as referring to Christ.

USE OF THE GLORIA

In the Latin Church the *Gloria* was not at first intended for the Mass. Its position must have been somewhat similar to that now occupied by the *Te Deum.* It was a song of thanksgiving, a festival song. And in this role it was sometimes included in the Mass at Rome on occasions especially festive. The account written in the *Liber Pontificalis* in 530 reports Pope Telesphorus (d. 136) as ordering for the nighttime Christmas Mass "as we begin the Sacrifice of the Mass the hymn of the angels should be said." This shows that by the beginning of the sixth century the *Gloria* had long had a place in the Mass at Rome.[2] Another account from the same source (more trustworthy, because closer in time to the matter reported) relates that Pope Symmachus (d. 514) had permitted the *Gloria* to be used on Sundays and the feasts of martyrs, but only at the Masses of bishops. The rubric in the *Sacramentarium Gregorianum* matches this; after the *Kyrie* it decrees: "The *Gloria in excelsis* is likewise said, if the celebrant be a bishop, on Sundays and feast days, but it may be said by a priest on Easter only." According to the *Ordo* of St. Amand, the priest was allowed to intone it during Easter night, and also on the day of his ordination if he was installed in his titular church and there celebrated his first Mass. Even as late as the eleventh century the carping question was asked, why cannot a priest use the *Gloria* at least on Christmas night, when it certainly is in place. But by the end of the same century the distinction between bishop and priest seems to have fallen out, and the present-day rule became universal: The *Gloria* is said in all Masses of a festive character.

Unlike the *Kyrie,* the *Gloria* was from the very outset a song, but it was the song of the congregation, not of a special choir. But it was soon transferred to the clergy gathered in the sanctuary. In contrast to the *Kyrie,* the *Gloria* had the unique distinction of being intoned by the pope himself. He stood at his *cathedra,* facing east; after the *Kyrie* was finished, he turned to the people and intoned the first words, just as is done nowadays. The priest, when he intoned the *Gloria,* stayed originally in the place he took after kissing the altar, namely at the Epistle

---

[2] Since the assignment to Telesphorus is pure fiction, it is enough to admit, with older commentators, that Telesphorus meant only the text of Luke 2:14, since the entire hymn seemingly came to the West only with Hilary.

side, as the Carthusians still do. It was not till the twelfth century that the intonation was transferred to the center of the altar, and then finally the *Gloria* was said through to the end at the same spot. Two things perhaps brought this about, first, symbolism,[3] and second, the desire to underline the importance of the hymn. On feasts of our Lord in the later Middle Ages the *Gloria* was given extra significance also by a special ceremonial in which one of the singers invited the celebrant to intone the hymn.

The fact that the bishop when intoning the *Gloria* formerly turned to the people, just as he does at the *Dominus vobiscum* or *Pax vobis*, is an indication that originally the entire congregation was called upon to sing this hymn. The musical setting corresponded to this disposition of the hymn. As Wagner emphasizes, the oldest melodies that are noted down have "the character of a syllabic recitation; it was more like a declamation performed with voice uplifted than a song," obviously because the hymn was to be sung not by a group of trained singers but by the congregation. Even Radulph de Rivo (d. 1403) still refers to the simplicity of the *Gloria* (and of the *Sanctus*) when he writes: "In the *Graduale* of Blessed Gregory of Rome, there are few notes." However, the oldest sources are absolutely silent about any real participation of the faithful. This is understandable, considering the limited use of the *Gloria* only at pontifical services where only an ever-changing segment of the people could gather and where there was always a preference for a more festive and a more artistic accompaniment, so that the singing of the people was hardly favored. But when use of the *Gloria* spread beyond the limits of pontifical Mass, we do learn—through Sicard of Cremona—of the actual singing by the people. In smaller surroundings and especially in the Romance countries, this did most likely become the custom. But the accounts that survive deal for the most part with the cathedral and monastery churches and here the performers of the *Gloria* are almost without exception the chorus, that is, the clerics assembled at the service. They either sang the *Gloria* straight through, or alternately in two semichoruses, as in the *Kyrie*. At Rome in 1140 the *Gloria* is expressly mentioned as the special concern of the *schola cantorum*, but that is an understandable exception in this, the oldest place where Church music was fostered.

But at this time and even quite a bit earlier there are traces of a greater musical development of the *Gloria*. The melodies increase in number. And since the ninth century there appear the farced *Gloria* or *Gloria*-tropes which we have come to recognize as the bases for a melodic amplification of these tropes. Clement Blume edited 51 independent

---

[3] Hugh of St. Cher presents as the reason for intoning the *Gloria* in the center (*in medio altaris*) the fact that the angel who appeared at Bethlehem stood *in medio eorum*.

texts, not counting those not written in metrical or rhythmical forms.[4] The reform under Pius V banned the tropes, but grave free rein to the musical composition which the *Gloria* seems to invite.

10. The Collect. The Inclusion of the Congregation Assembled

Keeping in mind the original plan of the Roman Mass, we perceive that the oration is the first place—and, until the so-called *secreta*, the only place—in which the celebrating priest himself steps before the assembly to speak. All the other things are singing and reading which— aside from the intonation of the *Gloria*—are carried on by others, or they are prayers inserted later on which the priest says quietly to himself. Here is a clue to the fact that we have reached the first climax in the course of the Mass. The ceremony of entry reaches a peak in the oration of the priest, in the same way that the presentation of the offerings and the reception of Communion come to a fitting conclusion with an oration. Consequently, in the oration the very essence of liturgical prayer is expressed with especial clarity. "Oration" is the name by which the priestly prayer is most often called in the Roman liturgy, even in the oldest Roman *Ordines*. It is a prayer which has, to a certain extent, the character of a public discourse (*Oratio*); it is as spokesman for the people, that the priest speaks it, and for that reason the people themselves are first summoned to pray. In the same sense the term *collecta* is used at present as a designation for the prayer, particularly (as we shall use it in the following discussion) for the first of the three orations of the Mass which here concerns us, the oration which at Rome was distinguished from the *oratio super oblata* and the *oratio ad complendum* by being called the *oratio prima*. The term *collecta* or *collectio* was native to the Gallican liturgy. The ancient Roman liturgy recognized the word

---

[4] In these tropes the *Gloria* is divided into a variety of small sections (as high as 20), with the tropings inserted between the sections. These were written mostly in a given verse form, often hexameters or distichs, in such a way that in each opening a (double-) verse appeared. Frequently there is but little connection with the basic text. This is especially the case when the trope is fitted to a special festival. A favorite was the trope used on our Lady's feasts, popular all over the west: . . . *Filius Patris, promogenitus Mariæ virginis. . . . Suscipe deprecationem nostram, ad Mariæ gloriam. . . . Quoniam tu solus sanctus, Mariam sanctificans, Tu solus Dominus, Mariam gubernans, Tu solus altissimus, Mariam coronans. . . .* The special popularity of this farcing for our Lady's feasts accounts for the rubric in the Missal of 1570 expressly banning this trope: *Sic dicitur Gloria in excelsis, etiam in missis beatæ Mariæ, quando dicendum est.* (This rubric was still found in the Ordinary of the Mass in the Missal of Leo XIII, but has apparently been dropped since.) At the Council of Trent there was mention of this trope among the *abusus missæ*.

collecta as the designation for an assembly, especially for the assembly that preceded the penitential processions in the stational services. When the interpreters of the Romano-Frankish liturgy employ the word in the meaning of oration, this linguistic usage derives manifestly from Gallican tradition. Despite some vacillation in the use of the words in the Roman sources at hand, the knowledge of the only meaning of the word which is here in question was kept intact, especially in Walafrid Strabo who says, "we say *collectas*" because "we collect, i.e., gather together" our petitions.

DOMINUS VOBISCUM

The oration is, as a matter of fact, the prayer in which the priest "collects" the preceding prayers of the people and presents them to God. This fact explains certain peculiarities in its make-up and in the way it is introduced. Before the priest begins the oration, he summons the congregation to prayer: *Oremus*, Let us pray. And before he gives this summons, he turns around to them with a *Dominus vobiscum*. Older commentators usually cling to a consideration only of the content of this greeting, stressing the fitness of the wish that the Lord might be near and God's favor accompany their praying, as he, the priest, offers up to God the prayer of all. But the form of the salutation, this direct address to the people, is not explored. For why does the priest just here turn to greet the people? It will not be easy to answer this if we examine only our present concept of divine worship. Such a consideration will not explain why the one saying the prayer should first of all greet the congregation, much less why he should repeat the greeting several times in the course of the prayer-meeting. Yet he does just that. The *Dominus vobiscum* recurs every time the congregation receives an invitation or a special announcement: the summons to join in prayer at the *oratio* and the *gratiarum actio*, or the announcement of the close with the *Ite missa est* or *Benedicamus Domino*. It is omitted only when there is question of continuing an activity already started. Obviously the formula which introduces the reading of the Gospel, *sequentia sancti evangelii*, is intended as an announcement and is therefore preceded by the same greeting. Another gesture is to be noticed in this connection. Aside from the beginning of the preface, when the priest already stands at the gates of the Holy of Holies, and aside from the Gospel, the priest always kisses the altar before he turns to the people with his greeting. In the medieval high Mass the deacon always turned around with the priest, and in the monastic rite the practice is still observed today.

The *Dominus vobiscum* thus has a clear relation to the action that follows; it serves to focus our attention. We might render its monition somewhat prosaically by the use of the vocative: Brethren in Christ, we are going to pray. Devout Christians, listen to today's Gospel. The *Dominus vobiscum* is then, in the first instance, an address to the people and, without overstressing its content (which of course is more than merely an address), it serves to arouse the attention and to denote, each time, an important moment in the course of the liturgy. In other words, we might formulate more exactly the rule for the *Dominus vobiscum* at Mass as follows: It introduces the sacerdotal prayer in each of four main sections: at the opening, at the reading service, at the thanksgiving and in the Communion section. Besides these, it also ushers in both of the proclamations of the deacon, namely the reading of the Gospel and the dismissal. But it is, of course, a matter of only secondary development that it also precedes the oration at the end of the prayers at the foot of the altar, and that it precedes the last Gospel, for both of these are texts audible only to the assistants around the altar. Besides, the use of a greeting form enables the congregation to return the greeting, and so, through this religious setting of reciprocal salutation, the feeling of God's nearness is intensified.

Both the greeting and the reply are ancient, their origins hid in pre-Christian times. In the Book of Ruth (2:4) Booz greets his reapers with *Dominus vobiscum*. The salutation was thus a part of everyday life. It is met with several times in Holy Scripture.[1] The reply of the reapers to Booz's greeting was: *Benedicat tibi Dominus*. We employ in its place a phrase which means almost the same thing: *Et cum spiritu tuo*, a formula which betrays its Hebrew origin and has many parallels in St. Paul.[2] We render its full meaning by saying simply, "And with you too."[3]

Since the greeting is Old Testament, the *Dominus* originally meant merely God: God be with you. But there is no difficulty about referring

---

[1] Luke 1:28; cf. Judg. 6:12; 2 Chron. 15:2; 2 Thess. 3:16.

[2] Tim. 4:22 (Vulg.): *Dominus (J. Chr.) cum spiritu tuo*; cf. Philem. 25; Gal. 6:18; also Phil. 4:23.

[3] This is a Semitism: *spiritus tuus* = your person = you.

Still it is to be remarked that even Chrysostom, *In II. Tim. hom.*, 10, 3 (PG, LXII, 659 f.), had already referred "thy spirit" to the indwelling Holy Spirit. In fact, in his first Whitsun sermon, n. 4 (PG, L, 458 f.) he sees in the word "spirit" in this counter-greeting an allusion to the fact that the bishop performs the sacrifice in the power of the Holy Spirit. That is the reason the *Dominus vobiscum* was even at an early age restricted to those endowed with major orders, bishops, priests and deacons, and not given to sub-deacons, who were numbered among the higher orders only since the 13th century. It is quite possible that the reason for kissing the altar each time the people were greeted stems from the idea that by the kissing, the priest received the "Pax" from Christ through the altar and then transmitted it to the people. The reference to Christ is employed in a different way in the recent edition of the *Rituale Rom.* (IX, 5, 5) where the *Dominus vobiscum* is omitted between the *Panem de cœlo* and the oration that precede the eucharistic benediction. (This had already been odered by a decree of the Sacred Congregation of Rites, June 16, 1663; Gardellini, *Decreta*, n. 2223, 7); the reason that seems to have prevailed was this, that the desire that God might be with his people finds its expression in the eucharistic blessing itself. However, this principle was not carried through in all instances; cf. *Rituale Rom.* IV, 4, 24-26.

the indeterminate *Dominus* to Christ, and this is more consonant with Christian worship. Take it in the sense of Christ's own promise (the wording is reminiscent anyway): "*Ecce ego vobiscum sum*" (Matt. 28:20), or that other assurance whose conditions are certainly fulfilled in the liturgical gathering: "Where two or three are gathered in my name, I am there in the midst of them" (Matt. 18:20). Actually this is the sense in which the *Dominus vobiscum* is usually interpreted in modern times. But it would be practically the same thing to say, more exactly, that the liturgy leaves the word *Dominus* indefinite; in the greeting the wish is made that "the Lord" may be with the congregation, but we know implicitly that the Lord God does come to us in Christ who is our Emmanuel.

This christological sense is more plainly expressed in the salutation *Pax vobis*, the greeting of the Risen Lord to his Apostles, used by the bishop before the collect. In the Orient, outside Egypt, this formula has taken the place of the *Dominus vobiscum* since the fourth century. There is early testimony regarding its use in North Africa. In Spain in the sixth century it challenged the position of *Dominus vobiscum*, and was forbidden by the second Synod of Braga (563) even as the greeting of a bishop. However, it became firmly established in the West, but under certain conditions; the bishop was to use *Pax vobis* only as his first greeting of the people, and only on days when the *Gloria* had been sung, a rule which is still binding. After the song of peace sung by the angels, the salute of peace is tendered to the people by those who, as successors of the Apostles, are in a special way entrusted with this greeting.

The greeting is spoken by the bishop in the same way as the priest; at the center of the altar he turns toward the people and stretches out his hands. This gesture, which in its basic form implies great vivacity and a natural pleasure in bodily expression, deepens once more the utterance of a desire to be united with the congregation and to draw them together into the prayer which is about to begin. This can be recognized even in the form we have today.

In the *response* the congregation for its part also confirms this community of desire, this will to be united. Do we have here only an acclamation in a wider sense? [4] We will surely have to picture these responses in ancient times as acclamations somewhat stormy and unregulated. And it is certain, too, that for centuries the entire people considered this shout, this call as their very own. *We can best understand the* Et cum spiritu tuo *as a popular consensus in the work of the priest*, not that the

---

[4] Acclamations in the strict sense were, in later ancient times, the shouts of a crowd which disclosed the will of the people: veneration when a ruler or his vicar appeared, assent to propositions and resolutions, congratulation, demand and desire. One such is still retained in the consecration of a bishop: *Ad multos annos.*

congregation here gives the priest authority or power to act in its stead, but that the congregation once more acknowledges him as the speaker under whose leadership the united group will approach almighty God. Thus in the greeting and its response we have the same double note that reappears at the end of the oration; the *Dominus vobiscum* seems to anticipate the *per Christum* of the close of the oration, and the *Et cum spiritu tuo* is a forerunner of the people's agreement expressed in the Amen. How sadly we must admit that, just when we try to recall this simple salutation to its original vitality, we realize how difficult it is for us moderns to make this formality our own in all its former import, even in such surroundings as the "dialogue" Mass presents, when the outer form is present fully and beyond quibble.

OREMUS AND ACCOMPANYING ACTIONS

In its chief function as an address, the greeting, as we said, introduces the summons to prayer. This summons in the Roman Mass consists in one single word, *Oremus*. In the oriental liturgies the formula, spoken here mostly by the deacon, is much less concise. Thus in the Byzantine Mass you have: "Let us ask the Lord," "Let us ask the Lord again and again in peace," and then the deacon begins the litany. In Egypt the cry is sometimes quite simple: "Pray" or "Stand for prayer," but sometimes the object of the prayer is mentioned: "Pray for the emperor," "Pray for the bishop"; in fact sometimes the object is cited in detailed formulas, particularly at the prayer of the faithful after the Gospel, and in the intercessory prayers which are inserted in the canon. In the West this invitation to prayer was especially amplified in the Gallican liturgy. The formula, called a *præfatio*, precedes various prayers and series of prayers, both within the Mass and without; its form is sometimes reminiscent of a little homily. A remarkable thing in regard to the invitation to prayer in the oriental liturgies is this, that the summonses already quoted are usually followed by the prayer of the people put in words. In the Alexandrine liturgy, for example, the people respond to the simple summons with a triple or at least with a single one, and even the more detailed summonses of the deacon are thus answered, and meanwhile the priest begins the oration.

The Roman liturgy has always been more restrained than the liturgies of the Orient in all that concerns the participation of the people. And yet even here we do find in certain instances an extra effort to enlist the cooperation of the people. At the *orationes sollemnes* of Good Friday— amongst the oldest in the liturgy—the Oremus is expanded into a longer phrase, like: *Oremus, dilectissimi nobis, pro Ecclesia sancta Dei.* . . .

At the *orationes sollemnes* of Good Friday the invitation is followed by the deacon's imperative, *Flectamus genua*, that is, with the order to kneel down for silent prayer till the deacon himself—later, the subdea-con [5]—gives the further signal, *Levate*, stand up again. The same com-mand is heard on Ember days and on some other occasions, preceded by a simple *Oremus*. Here we are face to face with a custom which pos-sessed a much greater importance in the ancient Church, both West and East, than it does in our own time.

The question naturally comes up, why this command, which appears here in the ordinary Mass *ordo*, should in the Roman Mass be restricted to certain extraordinary occasions. The most important source for this restriction is mentioned in Canon 20 of the Council of Nicea (325), which ordered that kneeling be omitted during Eastertide and on Sun-days. This arrangement for Easter and Sundays very quickly spread to the feasts (which were already on the increase) and even to saints' days; the only days left were the *dies quotidiani*, and finally only the days which had definite penitential character, and even these were further reduced to the merest remnant, with the loss of the entire Lenten season and all days which did not have two proper orations before the Epistle. And even on the days that remained, kneeling was restricted to the prayer before the real start of the Mass. For even the celebration of the Eucharist, which took place for a long time only on Sundays and feast days, seemed to bear an Easter character.

FLECTAMUS GENUA

The only problem was to establish just when precisely the Mass really began. A rule of the high Middle Ages fixed this start at the *Gloria*. Thus the orations which preceded the *Gloria*, that is, those which preceded the proper collect, and only those, remained under the law regarding kneeling. Or to put it more exactly, only these were subject to the diminished rules of *Flectamus genua*; for in addition kneeling was pre-scribed for those assisting in choir, and continues to be so prescribed, at all the orations during Advent, Lent, the Embertides, most of the vigils and the Mass for the Dead.

Thus a new thing had appeared, or rather, a substitution: kneeling not *before* the oration but *during* the oration. This change concurred with the gradual contraction of the pause which the *Flectamus genua* implied. The *Ordo Romanus antiquus* (about 950) offers a transitional aspect; in the introduction to the *orationes sollemnes* of Good Friday it includes the ancient prescription after the *Flectamus genua*, namely, "he pauses for a short while in silent prayer" (*et orat diutissime*) (whereupon the *Levate* would have followed), but in the text of the orations it indicates a different order: *Oremus. Flectamus genua. Omnipotens æterne Deus*

[5] And since 1955, the deacon again.

. . . *Levate. Per eumdem.* . . . Thus the pause during which the congregation was to pray was filled by the priest's oration.

It is self-evident that the Nicene rule for Easter and Sundays was intended to eliminate not the prayer before the priest's oration, but only kneeling during that prayer. This is evident in the oriental liturgies, in which the litanies of the deacon are still customary, unchanged, even on Easter and on Sundays. *We must therefore come to the conclusion that the elimination of the* Flectamus genua *after our* Oremus *did not purport to eliminate the pause for prayer which this command ordinarily signalized, but that at least a moment's quiet meditation was still retained.*

But just as the pause after the *Flectamus genua* disappeared, leaving only a simple hurried genuflection, so the same fate was bound to overtake the pause after *Oremus* when no *Flectamus* intervened, and even more quickly. After all, the elimination of the pause could be tolerated here more easily, since in the *Kyrie* and the *Gloria* which preceded the *Oremus* the opportunity for prayer was offered, for, although the people did not perform these, yet the clergy assisting in choir did, even in later times. A small vestige of the olden *Oremus* pause is still to be seen in a little notice of Durandus, who records with some emphasis that the priest spoke the *Oremus* before the collect and the post-communion at the middle of the altar and only then went to the right side of the altar to finish the oration. The pause will be seen in full strength and remarkable extent at the *secreta.*

POSTURE DURING THE ORATION

The effort to draw the congregation into the prayer of the priest also found another mode of expression. Carolingian sources of the tenth century contain the prescription that at the *Oremus* of the priest the people were to bow and were to remain in this position until the end of the oration. In the Gallican liturgy the practice had already been several centuries old. And in the choir rules of many monastic groups the custom was retained for some time, and is, in fact, still retained but with this modification, that the bow is stipulated only for the first oration, not for the commemorations that follow. But elsewhere this rather uncomfortable posture was soon changed either to the usual upright stance—this mostly for festival worship—or to an out-and-out kneeling—this on days of penance. In other words, the old regulation of the *Flectamus genua* before the oration has been replaced more and more—at least since the twelfth century—by kneeling during the oration.

While the priest says the oration, he stands with hands upraised. Until far into the Middle Ages weight was attached to the rule that he stand facing east, and originally the faithful, too, stood facing east and with arms lifted up. Although this orientation lost much of its importance, and the posture of the faithful underwent many changes, the priest still remains standing and his hands are still upraised. For after all, this standing posture has a double purport so far as the priest is concerned, since he is the one who leads the congregation in prayer, since he is the *liturgus*. The raising of the arms heavenward is a fitting accompaniment to the prayer that rises to Him who dwells in heaven.

But even this raising of the hands could undergo some alteration, corresponding to the expression of the prayer; sensitive men of antiquity saw how this pose could imply reverential appeal or even passionate demand. Hence even at an early date we hear the admonition, to lift both hands and glance only moderately and modestly. At the same time the apologists perceive in this posture an image of the Crucified in whose name the Christian appears before God, a thought which recurs again in the commentators of the Middle Ages, who make much of it particularly as regards the posture during the canon of the Mass. In the Roman Mass both during the orations and during the canon this moderate and somewhat stylized raising and stretching out of the hands has become a prescription of law for the priest. However, the priest assumes this posture only in those prayers which have been his since olden times and which he says as speaker for the congregation (the orations, the preface, the canon and the *Pater noster*), but not in those prayers which are only the expression of personal piety and which were given him only later, especially as a contribution from the Frankish Church. For these latter prayers the attitude is one derived from Germanic tradition: praying with hands folded. Thus in the posture of the priest the various strata of prayers, the distinctions between the ancient deposits and the later ones, are made visible to the eye even today.

11. *The Collect: Form and Content*

The nucleus of that collection of Roman orations which we meet for the first time in the sacramentaries must have been formed in the period from the third to the sixth centuries, that is to say, from the time that the Roman Church completed the transfer from Greek to Latin. The formulation of the prayer material was for long left to the *liturgus*, to extemporize freely perhaps, as he did in his admonitions to the people in the homily, or to recite a text previously fixed and written down by himself or by another. St. Augustine bears witness to both methods of composition. In his booklet on *The First Catechetical Instruction* (*De catechizandis rudibus*) he remarks as an aside that candidates for admission to the catechumenate, if they are well educated or come from schools of rhetoric, ought to be warned not to mock when some bishops or ministers of the Church either fall into barbarisms and solecisms while calling upon almighty God or do not understand or nonsensically separate the words which they are pronouncing; not (he adds) that such faults should not be corrected, so that the people may plainly understand what they are saying "Amen" to, but that at an ecclesiastical *benedictio* the *bona dictio* is not the important thing it is in the forum. But from the territory of the same Augustine we have conciliar resolutions proposing that at divine service only texts which have been approved should be used. Still even in Rome as late as the sixth century some orations show clearly that they were composed for a certain special occasion.[1]

Even for this freely formed prayer, however, a certain style was definitely adopted even from the very beginning of the Latin liturgy. Its external outlines were already conditioned by the laconic spirit of the Roman and his preference for conciseness and clarity. This did not exclude lengthy prayer-formulas. The extended ordination prefaces of the Roman Pontifical (like those for the consecration of bishops and the ordination of priests and deacons) are in substance a part of the most ancient Roman sacramentaries. The Mass-liturgy, too, contains besides the three terse orations which begin with *Oremus* also the rather protracted prayer of thanks introduced with *Gratias agamus*. But when compared with the prayer language of oriental or even of Gallic liturgies, the Roman character is still distinctly recognizable even in these longer prayer-formulas. Take just the opening address; in the oriental and Gallic liturgies there is usually an accumulation of divine titles and predicates, arranged in solemn groups of positives and negatives, whereas in the Roman there is seldom more than a single, simple term. But it was in the oration that this Roman mode found its perfect outlet. In its few phrases liturgical prayer was reduced to the most succinct formula, and yet within that small compass there was room for the most dignified development and the greatest variety.

These orations have the character of petitions. This is not something self-evident, fundamentally, for according to Origen the normal course of every properly adjusted prayer—and surely this holds most especially

---

[1] Thus that oration in the *Leonianum* (Muratori, I, 371) in which God is thanked for having granted us, "freed from the furious foes, to receive the paschal sacrament with peaceful mind," takes us back to the year 538 when the long siege of Vitiges was raised just before Easter. Cf. also in this connection H. Ashworth, "The Influence of the Lombard Invasions on the Gregorian Sacramentary." Reprinted from the "Bulletin of the John Rylands Library," 36, 2. The author shows how political circumstances had their effect on the prayers of the time, many of which have come down to us in the Missal of Pius V. Thus, phrases such as *contra omnia adversa . . . dexteram tuae majestatis extende . . . ad defensionem nostram . . .* take on added meaning when we realize that at the time of their composition, Rome was being besieged.—REV.

for public prayer—should begin by praising God through Christ in the Holy Ghost; should then pass on to thanksgiving and an acknowledgment of our weakness; and only after that would it be fitting to make petitions, and these, petitions "for great and heavenly things"; and lastly it should close with the doxology repeated over again. But the Roman oration is restricted almost wholly to the petition. The other elements are heard only in the address and in the closing formula. Since the very core of the Mass is entirely circumscribed by the prayer of thanksgiving, it seemed to be enough if the close of the three liturgical complexes which are appended to this core should be confined to petition. This is what actually happened in the orations. They consist of a single main clause or at most of a double clause in which the petition is formulated more plainly in a second phrase connected with the first by *et*.

Coming now to details, we have to distinguish two types of Roman orations. The *simple type* contains basically nothing except the barest ingredients of the petition, as when a child asks its father: Father, give me bread. Thus there is nothing more than the address and the designation of what we want God to do for us. The expression can be either imperative or subjunctive, and the word order can be varied (schematized: Bread give unto me, Father. Give me, Father, bread). This is simple, direct praying, without ornaments or extras. This type is preserved in substance even when there is an additional clause (*ut . . .*) to describe the object petitioned. But there is a second type, the *amplified type*, in which the address to God is enlarged by a phrase praising Him, the so-called *relative predication: Deus, qui. . . .* This is a definitely literary device, the work of rhetorical art, the sort of oratorical craft one would expect on the occasion of a solemn assembly of the faithful.

The striking thing is that this second type generally does not appear in the secret or post-communion but only in the collect. In the secret and the post-communion, the type commonly used is the simple type, since the object of the petition is already made abundantly clear in the presentation of the offerings and in the reception of Communion. The appearance of this amplified type in the collect is not governed by any strict rule, but we can say that this relative predication is generally found only on days of special solemnity, namely, days of commemoration. It is especially frequent on feast days; in fact, for modern saints' feasts it is a fixed part of the collects, as already indicated in the schema of the *Commune Sanctorum:* "God, who bids us rejoice at the solemnity of Blessed N., Confessor, grant. . . ." Relative predication is not the only method of incorporating the thought suggested by the feast into the petition, but it is certainly the handiest. This relative clause, which emphasizes the concepts of praise and thanksgiving, thus plays within the priest's oration a part comparable to that which the *Gloria* plays in the preceding prayer of the people. Putting it another way, the *Gloria*, which on festive occasions follows the *Kyrie,* resounds again in this relative clause.

In these and similar ways the festal thoughts have been able to slip into the narrow space of the orations. But by so doing it was almost impossible to avoid burdening, and even overburdening, the traditional schemas. It is, for instance, only right, and indicative of a feeling for the hierarchy of the Christian economy of salvation, that the saint of the day be inserted by asking God's help "through the intercession of Blessed N." But it is more than the schema can bear when chunks of the saint's biography are introduced into that pliant form, or lengthy theological reflections are projected into it.[2] Still we must never lose sight of the fact that we are dealing with liturgical, communal prayer which always has a tendency to pass from the simple prayer of inspired feeling to the more rational manner of a profession of faith and the utterance of many thoughts. The classical form of the oration, with its beautiful balance between praying and thinking—this we will always be able to admire in the collects of the Sundays after Pentecost.

Before we turn to the study of the theology and contents of these collects, we must take one further glance at their literary design. The striking feature of the old Roman orations has always been their majestic flow, their rhythm. It is evident that there is here a survival of the rhetorical art of dying antiquity; undoubtedly the earliest writers of these collects had studied in the schools of classical rhetoric. What is the secret of this rhythm? The attempt has been made to show that the ancient orations are still guided primarily by the quantitative meters of the classical era. The orations are composed, as a rule, of several members, all more or less of the same length, and these metrical elements are so repeated (not indeed with the regularity of a verse but with a certain freedom) that the opening phrase and the close are brought close together.

It could well be that these metrical laws of classical poetry did have an influence, unsought perhaps, on the elevated prose of the period of the Empire's decline, but in our case the proof is not easy. But the chief factor in achieving this agreeable harmony in the Roman orations was the *cursus,* the rules for which were followed in Latin artistic prose from the fourth/fifth century on. By *cursus* is meant the rhythm of the cadences produced by arranging the accents in the last syllables of a literary period or clause according to certain fixed rules. In the sermons of St. Peter Chrysologus and in the sermons and letters of Pope Leo the Great the rules of the *cursus* are observed with meticulous care, with such care, in fact, that the absence of the *cursus* has been used as a clue

---

[2] Thus, for the former, the collect of St. Jane Frances de Chantal, and for the latter the oration on the feast of Our Lady of Sorrows.

to the spuriousness of some of the pieces ascribed to the latter. We have already discovered on other grounds that the orations of these earliest levels of our liturgy are compositions of the era of Pope Leo the Great and may even be the work of his hands.

Since the collect is a prayer which is supposed to represent within the limits of the introduction to divine service our approach to God, and since, save for an occasional solemnity, no special theme is proposed for it, its content is necessarily very general. It is, in fact, even more general than the nature of a priestly *collectio* demands, even though this *collectio* as such could incorporate only what is general and transsubjective. The Church approaches God in all that indigence and need that must be a part of her in this earthly pilgrimage. Many formulas do not mention any specified object, but merely ask to be heard—for all the desires in the hearts of the assembled petitioners. Or perhaps one or the other constant and ever-recurring desire is mentioned: Help of divine power, overthrow of error and overcoming of danger, inclination to good, forgiveness of sin, attainment of salvation. At the same time, however, these prayers often mirror the powers that stand opposed to each other in the spiritual combat, especially in the form of pairs of contrasting ideas, a literary device which matched the notorious fondness for antithetical phrasing: Corporal and spiritual, thinking and doing, burden of one's own effort and the heavenly intercession of the saints, abstaining from nourishment and fasting from sin, freedom from oppression and devotion to good works, profession and imitation, faith and reality, earthly life and eternal blessedness. Very often we meet that profound and comprehensive antithesis of external action, temporal service, faithful devotion on the one hand, and internal achievement, eternal welfare, and lasting reality on the other, somewhat as it is expressed for example in the collect of the twenty-second Sunday after Pentecost: what we ask with faith, we may some day obtain in reality.

KERYGMATIC STRUCTURE

Above all, however, the collect makes visible to us the grand outlines of that spiritual universe in which our prayer lives and moves and is; it arises in the communion of holy Church and ascends through Christ to God on high. The oration turns to God in an address which, by its very brevity, appears to disclaim all ability to make comprehensible the nature of the unfathomable: *Deus, Domine, Omnipotens Deus*, or at most, *Omnipotens sempiterne Deus*. Even on saints' feasts, and where some special patronage might put us in mind of a particular helper, the oration is still directed to God Himself, begging Him, through the intercession of this saint—presupposing therefore, that he is invoked in the personal prayers of the faithful—to grant us protection and aid. Even the direct address to Christ within the Mass was not permitted in the ancient Church. At the Council of Hippo (393), an explicit decree was written precisely on this point, apparently directed against certain new trends: "Let no one substitute in the prayers the Father for the Son or the Son for the Father. And when at the altar, prayer should always be directed to the Father." In the Roman liturgy, which never wavered in its profession of the divinity of Christ, this law, that within the Mass the prayers were to be addressed to God the Father, was kept without exception right down to the year 1000. Till that time not even one collect—nor, for that matter, one secret or one post-communion—can be found to have infringed this rule. It was not till about the end of the millenary, when the native Roman liturgy gave way before the Gallicized form which returned from the north, that any forms of address to Christ Himself appear, as they had previously appeared in the Orient and as they had developed in the Gallic liturgy.[3] In private prayer, in the prayer of the people, in hymns, and in fact wherever prayer could be more free and not cramped by the need to keep the divine order of the world in full view, prayer to Christ had always been customary; it is attested even in the days of the Apostles. But in the oration, which is the official prayer of the priest, it has always been exceptional.

And still it is evident that Christ also must be mentioned in the official prayer of the Christian community. As a matter of fact His name does appear, and has appeared for ages, in the closing formula. And it appears there in such a way that a much deeper insight is granted into the whole structure of the Christian economy than would be vouchsafed by a prayer addressed simply to Christ even though this latter seems at first glance to be eminently suitable to a Christian assembly. The Roman oration suggests pointedly: We offer up our prayer through our Lord Jesus Christ, Thy Son. This method of prayer or variations of it, already seen in the writings of the New Testament,[4] prevails in the whole Christian service till the fourth century. The expression "through Christ" appears especially as a member of the doxology which usually concludes the prayer: we offer our praise to God through Jesus Christ, or (as sources in the second/third century put it) through our high-priest Jesus Christ. The Roman manner, however, which avoids the doxology

---

[3] This change was made in the spirit of the Gallic liturgical tradition with its strong anti-Arian bias, wherein, in consequence of the struggle against the Arians who disputed the essential unity of the Son with the Father, the ambiguous *Per Christum* was restricted, and the address to Christ freely exchanged with that to God and thus permitted to appear on a par with it. But even on Frankish soil this change within the Roman liturgy did not go unchallenged.

[4] Rom. 1:8; 16:27; 2 Cor. 1:20; Heb. 12:15; 1 Pet. 2:5; 4:11; Jude 25.

except at the end of the canon, builds up the thought of Christ's mediatorship in a different way, which it has retained to the present. Note especially that the *per Christum* does not mean a mere *adiuratio* as some older authors thought, as though we begged a hearing "*by* Christ," for His sake, in virtue of His merits. Nor does it signify that the gifts we ask *be handed* us through Christ. It must be understood rather as a progressive movement, a mounting upwards. For we declare that we offer up our petitions to God *through the mediation* of Christ, who (as St. Paul says) "lives on still to make intercession on our behalf" (Hebr. 7:25). This kind of prayer is familiar to the Roman Mass, and therefore the concluding formula of the oration must actually be taken in this sense, so that the completed form would read something like: "this we ask through Our Lord Jesus Christ." Corroboration is seen clearly in the phrase in the canon: *Te igitur . . . per Jesum Christum . . . supplices rogamus ac petimus*, and from allied phrases in other consecratory prayers. We bring our prayer before God "through our eternal high-priest," as the expression is sometimes expanded in medieval Latin texts.

This approach to someone "through" the intervention of someone else was familiar to men in olden times not only in the relationship of attorney or proctor, who represented his client at a legal suit or in a petition for a favor, but perhaps even more in the current version of the greeting in a letter, which at that time could reach its destination only by messenger: "through the bearer I greet you." Just as here a friend is kept in view, so in our case it is God, but in both instances the direct approach is to him who stands in his presence and who speaks to him in our name. It is important to notice that two attributes are attached to the name of Jesus in our formula, two attributes which bring out this connection to both parties: *Dominus noster* and *Filius tuus*. He is our Master; we belong to Him since He has bought us with His blood. And He is God's Son, related by the closest ties and one with Him in the unity of the divine essence.

Such words would, of course, be quite strange and alien to vital prayer unless in our consciousness there was actually the immovable background that made such prayer a matter of course, perhaps not under all circumstances but at least during the solemn prayer of the Church. But such was really the case in the world in which a conclusion to prayer such as this was used for the first time. When this type of conclusion was incorporated into the daily prayer of the Church, this background must have been thoroughly established in the soul of the faithful community—I mean the thought that the earthly Church had its Head in heaven, Jesus Christ, the Lord, who in His glorified body returned to the Father as the first-born of many brethren, as King of His holy people, which is bound to Him in the Holy Ghost. It was out of this consciousness that the Roman mediator-formula got its further amplification—a second phrase which is this time an irremovable relative clause referring to Christ: who with Thee liveth and reigneth in the unity of the Holy Ghost,[5] God, world without end.[6]

Here the glory of the Church triumphant shines forth resplendent, to balance the Church terrestrial assembled and made visible in the community at prayer. And this is the third notion with which the spiritual world of liturgical prayer is rounded out in the oration. It is the Church that prays: "Thy Church, Thy people, Thy servants, Thy faithful"—these are the terms by which the oration designates the petitioners and the recipients of God's gifts. In every instance the prayer is worded in the plural, "we": *quæsumus, rogamus, deprecamur*. However, the Church is included here not only conceptually, but actually. In liturgical prayer there is—there must be—in fullest reality a communion in which all those participate who join with the priest as he performs the service, who are represented expressly by the greeting and its answer and by the comprehensive *Oremus*. Even in a small group of faithful, with the priest standing at the altar at their head, not only is there present a number of Christians, but the Church itself is there in its hierarchic structure—God's people of the New Covenant in the order and arrangement given them by Christ.

Short and summary though the Roman orations might be, in every one of them the new creation is marked out with monumental lines, and it seems to encompass us most forcefully when the priest, at the head of his congregation, looking up to Christ, approaches God with his pleading prayer.

In the Amen the people are once again called upon to confirm the prayer of their speaker. The word remains untranslated in all the liturgies. Justin renders it by γένοιτο; so be it, and that is obviously the meaning it has here, for it expresses the assent of the people to the priest's praying and pleading. For this purpose it is not the only expression used, but it is by far the most prevalent.

[5] *In unitate Spiritus Sancti* = in the unity which the Spirit founds; cf. Eph. 4:3. The unity may be considered in the concrete as the Communion of Saints, particularly (in the present instance) the triumphant Church in whose midst the glorified Christ lives and reigns.

[6] The expression *per omnia sæcula sæculorum* is a heritage from the service of the primitive Church (cf. Apoc. 1:6; 5:13, etc.). It is found in all liturgies and means simply "forever, till eternity" (cf. Hebrews 7:24, etc.). This intensified form was already in use in the synagogue service. In the context of the closing formula, the *per omnia sæcula sæculorum* refers to the life and reign of Christ, *Qui vivit et regnat*. It follows, then, that the English version "world without end" must be taken to mean "through all eternity" and must not be referred simply to the preceding word "God" which did not belong in the primitive text.

COMMEMORATIONS

The present-day Mass usually has several collects. It was not always thus. The Roman Mass for a thousand years had only one oration. Amalar took the occasion of his visit to Rome in 830 to ask the clerics of St. Peter's about this, and he sets down the results of his inquiry with some emphasis in a special preface to his work. Even in cases (he says) where in the sacramentaries two Mass formularies are stipulated for one and the same day, because a feast coincides with a Sunday or two feasts fall due the same day, they told him that they have only one oration: *unam tantum*. And Amalar tries to assure his readers that this will suffice even where special reasons intervene; if someone wants to pray for the forgiveness of sin, there is opportunity during the offering of gifts; if someone seeks to enlist the cooperation of the angels, the opportunity is found at the end of the preface; if he wishes to plead for peace, the plea is found in the canon (*pacificare digneris*), etc. But for cases where the same priest wants to fulfill two offices, he suggests the possibility of saying a Mass for each one in particular, that is, several Masses on one day. This possibility was often taken advantage of at the time, until for very good reasons it was finally prohibited. There was another solution which many made use of, namely, to append the fore-Mass of one celebration to the fore-Mass of another, and only then to continue with the Mass proper (*missa bifaciata*, resp. *trifaciata*), but since this latter would then contain the corresponding number of formulas for the *secreta* and the post-communion the arrangement was rejected as a "monstrous mixture." However one other way remained open: the *missa sicca*.[7] The text of one Mass was tacked on to the other in this fashion: after the (post-) communion the priest removed the chasuble and then, standing at the Epistle side of the altar, he read the second Mass formulary, starting with the introit, but skipping from the offertory-verse to the communion-verse; and thus coming to a conclusion. Everyone was aware that this was but a *nudum missæ officium*, and for that reason it was plainly separated from the real celebration. It was a commemorative rite, a devotion which later on acquired an independent existence, being used on various occasions particularly as an extra-eucharistic service till, after the Council of Trent, it was replaced by the Benediction service.[8]

[7] The term *missa sicca* was derived originally from a rite which was customary at the Communion of the sick; even here in the sick-room the Mass formulary was read, skipping however from the fore-Mass (this might even reach to the *Sanctus*) to the *Pater noster*, and then giving Communion in the usual way, but only under the form of bread (hence the *sicca*).

[8] The classic example of a "dry Mass" was the one still to be found in the Blessing of Palms on Palm-Sunday before 1955. Even the rubric to be found here, not to turn to the people at *Dominus vobiscum*, belongs to this rite.

However, besides such a commemoration which comprised all the proper texts, the other type already discovered (and disapproved) by Amalar continued in use. Here for the commemoration of the extra Office or of some other special exigency only the respective orations (collect, secret, and post-communion) were appended. Traces of a tendency to use this expedient are found in the Frankish area quite early. Still the effort was made to work out a scheme whereby both themes would be incorporated in one formula. A hundred years before Amalar, the older *Gelasianum* contains a formulary in which the orations (and the *Hanc igitur* formula) express a double purpose, the remembrance of a holy martyr and a service for the dead. But the *Gregorianum* of Hadrian, in the second Christmas Mass, displays the other expedient, a second oration added for the second theme (St. Anastasia). By the ninth century the second oration appears as an independent formula in many other liturgical texts. Still, as late as the turn of the eleventh century we hear a voice raised to re-establish the old rule that at each Mass, just as there is one introit and one Gospel, there should be but one oration and at the same time it lauds those who, when adding extra orations, but seldom overstep the number seven. It is quite possible to see in this trend towards a multiplication of orations the same influence at work that produced the long, wordy prayers of the Gallic liturgies.

As time went on the stress was entirely on this rule, that the number seven should not be exceeded, and that the last should not be an oration *pro defunctis*. Besides there was a new regulation, emphasizing that the number of orations should be uneven—seven or five or three or one.[9]

Moreover we will have to point out another development in this growth of orations. The collect (and with it, the secret and the post-communion) has acquired a second function along with the original one. Since the disappearance of the Prayer of the Faithful and the curtailment of the *Kyrie*-litany, these orations have become the most obvious place to put into words the special wants of the Church and the needs of the time. To be sure, this was almost entirely the part of the priest and not of the people, so that in very modern times a new substitute was devised, namely the prayers said with the people after Mass. The liturgical practice of older religious orders still gives some indication of the effort to make the oration of the day more prominent and to let the other added orations recede into the shadows; the demeanor in choir manifests the distinction, for it is only during the first oration that the clergy are bowed, showing that this is the priestly prayer they make their own. A similar point is made by a regulation we occasionally meet with, according to which the celebrant says only the first oration out

[9] See above, page 255.

loud, the other being recited *secrete*. This method has been revived by some in the conduct of the "dialogue" Mass. The present rubric that the first oration end with its own concluding formula is apparently derived from the same line of thinking.

LAUDES GALLICANÆ

Today the Epistle follows right after the orations. At a high Mass this is read by the subdeacon; at a less solemn Mass it is the priest himself who reads it, and he does so at once, without changing his position. As a result, especially in the latter case, we do not get the impression that something new is starting, and that here we have a clear line of separation cutting off the introductory or opening rite from the readings. In the Middle Ages the consciousness of this transition was still alive. This consciousness betrayed itself, for instance, in an abuse which the Roman Council of 743 had to denounce, namely, that many bishops and priests conducted only the procession and said the oration and left the rest of the Mass to another. Many divisions of the Mass in Scholastic times take cognizance of this separation. In greater pontifical functions, too, this spot was singled out for the development of those acclamations which, because of their derivation, are called *laudes gallicanæ*. They are still customary at this very place even today, above all at the coronation of the pope. In France until modern times they were a constituent part of the pontifical Mass. After the oration, two (or elsewhere six) knights stood forth, or, in their place, an equal number of clerics; they began: *Christus vincit, Christus regnat, Christus imperat.* The choir repeated. Then the song became a declaration of fealty and homage: *Summo Pontifici et universali Papæ vita!* and then it became a plea to Christ, *Exaudi, Christe,* and to a series of saints, *Sancte Petre . . . ,* and after each of the invocations the choir responded: *Tu illum adiuva.* The cry of allegiance to the pope is followed by similar acclamations in honor of the emperor or king, of his wife, of the bishop, of the army, and in each instance the plea *Exaudi, Christe* is inserted along with a series of selected saints. If the bishop who was named was present, the whole assembly arose, and the special singers who were chanting the acclamations mounted the steps of his throne, kissed his hand and received his blessing. The *Laudes* closed with a repetition of *Christus vincit;* a doxological ending, calling upon Christ, the victor over all enemies, was often connected with this close, or sometimes a *Kyrie eleison.* In the course of time the acclamations were much altered, place and situation motivating the adaptations.

It is quite obvious that here in the pontifical liturgy a special finale has been added to the introductory rite, and this with apparent good reason. But this pledge of allegiance to the bishop who has just entered his cathedral could not fittingly take place until after the bishop him-self, by means of the oration, had made his own homage and pledge of loyalty to almighty God. This custom is a continuation of a custom stemming from ancient times, of acclaiming the ruler when he ascended his throne or also when he was solemnly received. In the form of prayers now prevalent we have the Christian adaptation of the ancient acclaim.

II. THE SERVICE OF READINGS

1. Origin and Plan of the Service of Readings

The service of readings forms the second section of the Mass-liturgy. The reading of Holy Scripture represents the proper content of the fore-Mass in much the same way as the Sacrament forms the heart of the Mass proper; they are both precious treasures which the Church safeguards for mankind. Just as our Lord himself first taught, and only after this foundation was laid did He erect His kingdom, so now too the word of God should first fill our soul before the mystery of the New Covenant is realized amongst us anew. Since the service of readings was at one time an independent entity, it was able to exist even without the continuation in the Mass proper. But since, like every Bible lesson, it demanded some sort of conclusion, we must inquire whether even in the present liturgy its plan stretches out beyond the readings, or at least helps to mould some of the forms now found in the Mass proper. At least the second alternative is plainly verified. And in the oriental liturgies the first is quite apparent; the readings are followed by prayer as is the custom otherwise and the last of the prayers is the Prayer of the Faithful. The same picture is presented in the most important sources of ancient Christian liturgy.

So it is an a priori probability (and the detailed facts will bring this out) that in the Roman Mass too the *Oremus* which follows the readings and the oration which really belongs to it (the so-called secret), if viewed formally, are still part of the reading rite, even if the material shape of the oration and the interval between it and the *Oremus* are concerned with the preparation of the offerings and thus belongs to the opening of the Mass proper. So it is with all the greater right that we speak of a *service* of readings or of lessons.

The beginnings of this service go back, as we have already seen, to the practice in the synagogue, with whose arrangement the Apostles and the Christians of the primitive Church had been acquainted as they grew up. We must, therefore, next turn our attention to the synagogue service.

The very nature of the religion of the Old Testament, as a religion of revelation, implied a heavy leaning on the reading of the sacred Books. This reading took place not in the Temple at Jerusalem but in the many synagogues which were built everywhere after the Exile. Here, on appointed days, above all on the Sabbath, the community was assembled. The reading was disposed in such a way that two passages were read at each meeting, one passage from the "Law" and the other from the "Prophets." The lection from the "Law" (Torah) was first. It was continued from one meeting to the next as a *lectio continua*, so that the whole was finished during a stipulated period and the series started all over again. A fixed cycle, with a certain number of definitely outlined passages (*parashoth*) arranged for each Sabbath, is not traced until the time of the Talmud. The reading of the Law in the Palestinian synagogues was also signalized by the fact that it was not done by one reader but was distributed amongst several, usually at least seven, each of whom read a number of verses. Of the remaining Books, the "Prophets" (*Nebiim*), a passage was usually chosen at will. This formed the conclusion of the service and was therefore called *haphtarah*, "conclusion." Added to the readings was a homily. According to the New Testament accounts (Luke 4:16–20; Acts 12:15 f.) this followed the prophetic reading, but the customary arrangement appears to have been to insert the homily after the first reading, which was the more important one.

The assembly was opened with the *shema*, a kind of profession of faith made up of passages from Holy Writ. Every assembly also had a congregational prayer, spoken by one of the members of the group appointed by the ruler of the synagogue; it was introduced with the words "Praise the Lord." However, just how it was done in the time of the Apostles and just where it was inserted, is not clear, since exact and detailed accounts are wanting. Still the groundwork for the *Shemoneh Esreh*, which was developed after the destruction of Jerusalem, can be traced back prior to this. The assembly was concluded with the blessing of a priest, if there was one present, or else with some corresponding prayer.

The elements of this arrangement can be found quite unmistakably in the service of the Christian congregations at an early date. According to Justin the readings on Sundays were followed by a homily (spoken by the one presiding) and by the common prayer of the congregation—two elements which continue to be constituent parts of the fore-Mass. The chants or songs which are generally connected with the readings in the Christian liturgies must also go back to some common primitive Christian source. The psalmodic form of the songs carries us back to the synagogue. The *Apostolic Constitutions* of the fourth century makes mention of a singer's psalming the hymns of David after the first of the two readings, and of the people's responding to it. But even two hundred years or so before this, Tertullian makes a cursory reference to the psalmody which follows the readings. Writing as a Montanist, he gives an account of a prophetess who "during the Sunday services" regularly fell into ecstasy "as the Scriptures are read or psalms sung or during the address or while the petitions are being made." Since he alludes to an "address" (*allocutiones*), it is more or less plain that the narrative deals with an occurrence during a public assembly for reading —obviously the fore-Mass.

The arrangement here to be seen, therefore, is the same as that which, in the oldest sources both East and West, prevailed also in the extra-eucharistic service of the Church, the same that is still in use in the Roman Breviary as the second part of every canonical hour. The series is this: reading, responsorial singing of the assembled congregation, prayer. The only thing added to this plan, as occasion demanded, was the homily.

2. The Choice of Readings

Regarding the number and the selection of the readings a great variety has prevailed and still prevails amongst the Christian liturgies. The only agreement is the rule that there should be at least two lessons, of which the last in all cases is to be taken from the Gospels. And the lessons have all been biblical; aside from the primitive era when the various community letters were read, the lessons were gradually restricted to readings from the Scriptures, although there was some variation here and there. That besides the Old Testament lessons there should be readings from the New Testament—and these even by preference— was to be taken for granted, and was, in fact, explicitly urged in the regulations of St. Paul (1 Thess. 5:27; Col. 4:16). For the rest, the various arrangements can be best understood if we contemplate them in their first beginnings, already indicated in the previous chapter, the arrangement of lessons in the synagogue. But we will be amazed to see how strongly Christian principles of choice gradually took over.

It is not surprising that during this festive season of the Church year, when the mystery of our Redemption stands out so plainly, there should be a tendency to restrict the readings from the Old Testament in favor of those from the New. The connection with the eucharistic celebration must have tended in the same direction insofar as there was any consciousness of the Easter character of that celebration. Thus in the Egyptian liturgies we find a fourfold lesson, probably in the beginning an attempt to compromise with readings from both Testaments, but now (in both the Coptic and the Ethiopian liturgies) actually taken from the New Testament only: the Epistle of St. Paul, the Catholic Epistles, the Acts and the Gospels. The Byzantine liturgy, too, since about the seventh century, has only two lessons at Mass, both from the New Testament, the "Apostle" and the Gospel.

The Roman liturgy underwent the same evolution to a degree at least. Here, too, the Mass must once have had three lessons regularly, as it still has on certain of the older liturgical days,[1] and the usual arrangement must have included—in part at least—one reading from the Old Testament and two from the New. But later the Old Testament reading disappeared from the permanent plan of the Mass-liturgy. For on all Sundays the first of the two lessons is always taken from one of the Letters of the Apostles—an "Epistle," therefore, in the strict sense— and all through Paschaltide it is either from the Letters or from the Acts of the Apostles. Outside this season the pre-Gospel reading at the ferial Masses is, as a rule, from the Old Testament, but for feast days, especially for the feasts of saints, no definite rule can be set down.

But it is plain that wherever the Old Testament appears in the readings of the fore-Mass, it is not for its own sake, nor simply to have some spiritual text for reading, but it is chosen for its prophetic worth and its value as an illustration of the New Testament. This is unmistakable in the prophecies of Holy Saturday; here, with gaze fixed on Baptism, the Old Testament illustrations proclaim the new creation, the new people of God, the triumph over death, the new life and the renovating power of God's spirit. It is equally apparent in the Old Testament readings which here and there appear on feast days, as when on Epiphany the Prophet Isaias views the peoples streaming into the new Kingdom of God, or on feasts of the Blessed Virgin the Son of Sirach praises the divine Wisdom which has built itself a house on earth. Nor is it much different in regard to the Old Testament readings in the ferial formularies for Lent. They illustrate certain relationships in the New Testament economy of salvation or in the ecclesiastical discipline of the Lenten season: forty days of prayer and penance, the call to repentance, Baptism and its effects, the Law of God; or they present little sidelights to the story of the Gospel or to the life of the stational saint; or they suggest some other association with the peculiarities of the stational church.

But we would misunderstand the position of even the New Testament texts and accounts in their liturgical associations if we were to take

[1] Ember-Wednesday, Wednesday of the 4th week of Lent, Wednesday and Friday of Holy Week. The longer series of readings on the Saturdays of Ember-week, on the other hand, is the remains of an ancient vigil service. The ancient tradition had on these days 12 lessons, like those which were customary on Holy Saturday before 1955. The formularies on these days are therefore regularly given the following headings in the liturgical books of the earlier Middle Ages: *Sabbato in duodecim lectionibus*.

them solely as primitive accounts of the time of their origin, as mere witnesses of things past, from which we gain no other edification than we might gain from the rest of the testimonials of Christian living. For the words of the Apostles and the accounts of the Evangelists are given a new meaning by being proclaimed anew by the Church to this assembly of Christian men. They must be regarded entirely in the perspective of the present, for they are themselves bearers of the grace-laden message which God gives to men through His Church. The word of God in Holy Writ sounds with renewed vigor, waking in the congregation the consciousness of the foundation on which it is built, the spiritual world in which it lives and the home to which its path is directed. It has a message for this very hour, to arouse the congregation to find a Christian solution for the problems which face each of us today.

LECTIO CONTINUA

It is well known that in the service of the ancient Church the various books of Holy Scripture were read straight through, in the manner of a *lectio continua*. The most manifest voucher for this is found in the voluminous commentaries to whole books of both New and Old Testament which various Fathers have left us—commentaries which are nothing else than the homilies which they delivered at the end of the reading at worship. In fact the relationship to this reading is quite often very obvious.

This continuous reading of the Scriptures was broken into, as might have been expected, first of all by the greater feast days. For such days a pertinent pericope was selected. For the feasts of martyrs, too, this was done, as Augustine already testifies. It was but natural that the passages in question should be used again each year. Still this practice could not have been very extensive even by the end of the fourth century. For the Aquitanian pilgrim lady seemed never to weary of pointing out, as a peculiarity of divine service at Jerusalem, that the lessons and the psalms and antiphons here used on Epiphany or on the days of Holy Week and Easter week were always "suited to the day." But to the Gallic Church of the fifth century belong the first unmistakable evidences of a system of pericopes. On the other hand the festal seasons, even at an early period were already given special consideration by selecting certain more relevant books of the Bible for the reading. Thus at Antioch in the fourth century the Mosaic books were read during the weeks before Easter. Elsewhere during Holy Week first Job and then Jonas were read, in reference to Christ's suffering and Resurrection. After Easter the reading of the Acts of the Apostles is affirmed quite early in more than one region. So for the Scripture readings of the fore-Mass an arrangement was established much like that which still holds good today in the *scriptura occurrens* of our Roman Breviary.

In the Orient the continuous reading of certain books has remained the normal form in the Nestorian and the Jacobite liturgies, and even in modern times it is scarcely ever interrupted. In the Byzantine liturgy for the most part the readings, at least for the Gospels, have continued in so-called serials, just as we have them in the *scriptura occurrens* of our breviary; only selected passages of the respective book are read but the readings are so arranged that the selections follow the course of the text. Thus after Pentecost, Matthew is started and continued for seventeen Sundays (with some few pericopes now displaced from their proper order); then sixteen Sundays follow with readings from St. Luke. There are also shorter series of readings from Mark and John.

Vestiges of such a progressive reading of the Scriptures are also to be found in our Roman liturgy. The Gospels of the last weeks before Easter, for instance, are taken from St. John and the same is true of the Sundays after Easter. True, the pericopes follow the biblical order only in part, but still the original intent peers through. One other point, noteworthy enough, must be stressed, the fact that at least the title of this continuous type of reading has been retained, for every Gospel is announced with *Sequentia sancti evangelii*—the continuation of the reading of the Gospel.

More evident and incontestable are the traces in the Epistles. The Epistles of the Sundays after Pentecost still form a series of pericopes in which the Letters of St. Paul are covered with almost no disturbance of the order of the Scripture canon. Because of the many saints' days which have replaced the weekdays, and which have either special readings or readings taken from the *Commune Sanctorum*, we fail today to recognize such a plan. Actually there are documentary evidences to enable us to trace this plan back to the height of the Middle Ages where it is found to have an even more remarkable extent. The so-called Würzburg *Comes*, the oldest of the documents in question, offers (in addition to the Epistle for specified occasions during the Church year and those for votive Masses) forty-two further readings not stipulated for any precise liturgical function. These forty-two pericopes are taken from the Letters of St. Paul, starting with Romans 5:6–11 and continuing in the order of the accepted canon down to Hebrews 13:17–21. The collected Sunday Epistles of that period, insofar as they follow the canonical arrangement, are contained in this group. Of the rest of the pericopes in this Würzburg index, some are found in various reading lists, either as Sunday Epistles, or partly as Epistles appointed for Wednesdays.

That the reading begins with the Catholic Epistles is in accordance with an older arrangement of the canon, in which the Catholic Epistles were placed first immediately after the Acts of the Apostles.

The obvious system of having the weekday readings continue the Sunday ones is followed on only five Wednesdays. The other Wednesdays form an independent series using the material left over from the Sunday series. It is to be noted that the readings from Romans which, break off at Romans 8:17, are actually continued in our present-day Roman arrangement on the second to the fourth Sundays after Epiphany. In the course of the Middle Ages other systems for the Epistles were constructed, incorporating Wednesdays and sometimes even Fridays; but these lists never had other than local importance.

We also possess a clear idea of *the early medieval Roman arrangement for the Gospel*. This, too, agrees fairly well with the arrangement followed today insofar as the same liturgical days come into question. Here, too, weekdays were taken into account, in this case not only Wednesday but Friday, and, as often as not, Saturday also. This involves us in the religious life of the ancient Church, in which the "stational days" as well as the Sundays were taken into account. To the fasting which was an old tradition on these days, was added a prayer-meeting with readings, and gradually—first on Wednesdays, as many evidences indicate—also a eucharistic service. The system of readings which was developed for these services continued to be used throughout the Middle Ages in various places, particularly (it seems) in monastic churches. Some of the references are as late as the sixteenth century. What is not a little surprising is that this system of pericopes, although extended to two or three days a week, nowhere gives any signs of any continued series of lessons, not to mention a *lectio continua*. The pericope is chosen very freely, with no regard for previous or succeeding passages. For feast days, those of our Lord and of the saints, the thought of the feast naturally dictated the choice of both Epistle and Gospel. The same thing was true to a rather wide extent also for festive seasons. We have already cited the Sundays after Easter. The choice for Advent was plainly decided by the catch word: the coming of our Lord, the approach of his Kingdom. The Gospels for Sundays after Epiphany are similarly selected on the basis of a catch-word (especially if we take into account some older Gospel references which no longer obtain): this is the revelation of the wisdom and miraculous might of the God-man who had appeared on earth. In the period from Septuagesima to Easter the theme for both Epistle and Gospel is founded on the prospect of the grand festival and on concern for a proper preparation of the congregation and—to a certain extent—of the candidates for Baptism and the penitents. Above all, however, it is the Roman stational churches with their martyr graves and local reminiscences that offer the key in many cases to an understanding of the choice of a pericope. Least satisfactory is the search for a motive in the choice of the Gospels for the Sundays after Pentecost. In some instances the proximity of the feast of a great saint honored in the Roman Church appears to have influenced the choice.[2] The other passages, we must conclude, are in substance a group of synoptic passages which were not considered in the lists previously made up, but which seemed to have special value for religious instruction.

When the stational days lost their importance and saints' days (with their own readings) began to appear in ever-increasing numbers, the weekday pericopes in the old Roman lesson-system lost their significance. So by the dawn of modern times they were almost entirely forgotten. But about this very time the Council of Trent heard the plea for an expansion of the system of readings, and the suggestion was made that for each week three unused Pauline and Gospel passages be selected for ferial Masses, to be inserted in the formulary of the preceding Sunday. The plan, however, never came up for consideration and so nothing was done.

3. The Liturgical Setting of the Lessons

The reverence which the Church pays to the written word of God in no way blinds the Church to her task of breaking the bread of God's word to the people. Her consciousness of this duty is revealed in the very fact that some passages are chosen rather than others, and that given passages are used to illustrate certain Church days and feasts. There are even instances in which a passage is put together by omitting some intervening portions of the text,[1] a practice which was widespread in the ancient Gallican liturgy and led to the custom of centonization [2] and to the harmonization of the Gospel accounts.

From the Church the various pericopes have received their setting. First of all a title telling the origin of the passage: *Lectio libri* . . . , *Lectio epistolæ* . . . , or announcing whether the passage is the beginning, *Initium*, or a continuation, *Sequentia*, of a certain passage. Then there is an introductory word, either the word of address, *Fratres* (in St. Paul's congregational letters), *Carissime* (in his pastoral letters), *Carissimi* (in the Catholic Epistles), or a phrase suggesting the prophetic

[2] Thus the pericope of the great catch of fish (Luke 5:1-11; 4th Sunday) was induced by the feast of the Princes of the Apostles; the pericope of the wise steward (Luke 16: 1-9; 8th Sunday) and the Ephphetha pericope (Mark 7:31-37; 11th Sunday) by the feast of St. Lawrence, and at least the pericope of the healing of the lame man (Matt. 9:1-8; 18th Sunday) by the feast of the sainted physicians Cosmas and Damian.

[1] Thus on the Wednesday of Passion week the Epistle reading is derived from Lev. 19: 1-2, 11-19, 25. This is often the case in regard to Old Testament readings, as can be seen easily in the new edition of the Roman Missal where the exact citation is noted in each instance.

[2] *Cento* = "patchwork," a text made up of pieces of various provenience.

character of the reading: *Hæc dicit Dominus*, or a reference to the time of the story, *In diebus illis, In illo tempore, (dixit Jesus . . .)*. Sometimes there is a closing formula corresponding to this introduction, but in the Mass this has not become the rule as it did, for example, in our Matins. Only at the closing of the reading of the prophecies is there always a regular concluding formula, *dicit Dominus omnipotens*. In some of the readings from St. Paul there is also a tacked-on phrase, the words reminiscent of the very theme of all Pauline concepts: *in Christo Jesu Domino nostro*.

The setting of the holy texts in the oriental liturgies is much the same; it has been especially developed in the Coptic.

Besides this immediate setting, the readings also generally have an introduction designed to arouse the attention of the audience. The people are addressed, just as they are before the priestly oration, with the salutation *Dominus vobiscum*, to which the people respond. In the Roman Mass this salutation is in use only before the Gospel, whose higher worth is also emphasized by the extra richness of the liturgical framework. In the Milanese liturgy the same greeting precedes the Epistle also, and in the Mozarabic Mass it is found before each of the three readings and the people answer Amen at the close of each.

In the summons to the people to be attentive, there is revealed a wish that *the faithful might really understand the readings*. But the big obstacle to this is the fact that the liturgical language retained from ancient times has become incomprehensible to the people. Sometimes, however, we find that in such cases an actual shift was made to the current vernacular; thus amongst the Maronites and other groups of Syrians a switch was made from the Syrian, which the people no longer understood, to Arabic. Even in the Roman liturgy (which at a papal Mass has at least a symbolic bilingualism in the readings), a similar change was made, only in the territory where the Croatian language is spoken. In these places use is made of the "*Schiavetto*," a collection of Sunday and feast-day Epistles and Gospels translated into "Slavic," that is, modern Croatian. From this book the lessons are produced, whether the Mass is sung in Old Slavic or in Latin. Amongst the Copts every lesson is read first in Coptic and then in Arabic. This has its parallel in our own Roman Mass, when, after the reading of the Latin Gospel, there follows a reading (of Epistle and Gospel) in the vernacular, but with this difference, that the reading in the vernacular is viewed by the general law of the Church only as an introduction to (or a substitution for) the sermon and is left devoid of any liturgical framing.

Examples of a bilingual reading of the Scriptures are known also from more ancient times. But in these instances the basis is usually to be found in the bilingual character of the congregation. Thus we learn from our Aquitanian pilgrim lady that the readings in Jerusalem at the end of the fourth century were in Greek, but that they were also presented in Syrian. Similar arrangements are likewise mentioned in other historical sources. It would, indeed, seem that these methods go back to traditions from Apostolic times, to surroundings in which, for the texts in question, no authentic translations into the vernaculars were as yet available for use. We have already made reference to the solution of the problem of a congregation of mixed language, where the service of readings was conducted in groups separated according to language.

It is here in the matter of the lessons that we can see most plainly the great rift that exists—a rift growing wider with the centuries—between *the holy text in its traditional sacred language and the natural objective of being understood by the audience.* From time to time some sort of decision was inevitable. Sometimes the solution is made in favor of understanding the text; this is done especially where the reading at divine services (by means of a planned catechesis or a sermon) is the only form of religious instruction, as in many oriental countries. In other places, where there were other opportunities for religious teaching, reverence for tradition was too strong to permit such a change. The liturgical lesson then became merely a symbolic presentation of God's word. But even then, whenever a new tide of liturgical thought set in, the reading felt the brunt of the forces that sought a more intelligible form of divine service and desired the use in the lesson of a language which the congregation could understand.

Still the liturgical reading cannot long remain on the level of a prosaic presentation that looks only to the congregation's practical understanding of the text. The performance must be stylized, much in the same way as we have found in the case of the priestly oration. The reader must never inject his own sentiments into the sacred text, but must always present it with strict objectivity, with holy reverence, as on a platter of gold. He must recite the text. This can be done by avoiding every change of pitch—the *tonus rectus.* As a matter of fact the Roman *tonus ferialis* has no modulation whatsoever, outside the questions. But in addition there have been, since time immemorial, many forms of elevated performance with certain cadences, little melodic figures which are indicated by punctuation marks. They serve especially to signalize the Gospel above the other readings. Augustine makes mention of a "solemn form" for the reading of the Passion on Good Friday. The Epistles, too, were fitted out more richly than the prophetic lessons. In the ninth century we hear of a festive tone for the lessons which was used at Rome for the reading of St. Paul's Epistles on Sundays. However, the readings in the fore-Mass were consciously kept free of melodic overgrowth. Compared with the Office lessons on feast days, the readings at Mass even now display a great severity, which is, however, well suited to the dignity of the sacrifice.

THE LECTOR

Early in the Church's history a special reader was appointed for the performance of the readings—always someone other than the leader of the divine service, as we see already in Justin. There is a certain amount of drama in this; the word which comes from God is spoken by a different person than the word which rises from the Church to God. Even if Justin does not actually present the office of lector, that office does certainly appear in the second century as a special position; the lector is the oldest of the lesser degrees of ordination. It is clear that the lector has to have, or to receive, a certain amount of education. But this was not the only thing kept in view in choosing him. It is a remarkable fact that since the fourth century in the West—especially in Rome—boys appear preponderantly as lectors. In many places these youthful lectors live under ecclesiastical tutelage in special communities, which thus become the foremost seed-beds for promotion to the higher degrees of spiritual office. Childish innocence was considered best suited to lift the word of God from the sacred Book and to offer it, unadulterated, to the congregation. But at the same time an effort was made to lay greater stress on the Gospel reading by turning it over to someone in higher orders. While in the Orient the position of the lector was not disturbed by this shift, in the West the reading of the Epistle in the Roman stational services of the seventh/eighth century had become the work of the subdeacon, and so it has remained at high Mass even now. On the other hand, the service of a lector or of some other cleric to read the Epistle continued to be put to use for hundreds of years at the celebration of the pastor in his parish. Even in private Mass the reading of the Epistle by a Mass-server is mentioned a number of times as late as the thirteenth century. And even now in the Roman Mass the desirable thing at a *missa cantata* is to have the Epistle sung not by the celebrant but by a lector in surplice (*Missale Rom., Rit. serv.,* VI, 8).

When the reader performed his duty, this was made visible in the older Roman liturgy by the way he wore his official garb. He is now definitely "in service" and should not seem to be hindered by his garments. This vesture was—as with all clerics—the bell-shaped *planeta* or *casula*. But the deacon and subdeacon wore this tucked up in front, so that their hands were free, and the subdeacon's formed a sort of envelope or pocket so that he could pick things up and carry them around not with bare hands but holding them through the garment. So when the deacon got ready to read the Gospel he arranged the *planeta* in such a way that it lay tightly folded over his left shoulder and fell across his breast at an angle. Thus he kept it all through his service till after the Communion. But the subdeacon or other cleric, when getting prepared for the reading, took the *planeta* off. Thus the gradation of office was kept somewhat in a recognizable form. This practice, which appears about the ninth century, is still retained in broad outline at high Masses which take place during Lent or on other days of similar dignity; the deacon and subdeacon make use of the *planeta* (since replaced by dalmatic and tunicle), but the deacon, before the reading, substitutes the broad stole, and the subdeacon takes off his outer vestment before he reads the Epistle.[3]

PLACE FOR THE READINGS

For the presentation of the sacred text the reader also chooses a special place. To be better understood he will turn to the listeners, perhaps—if possible—take an elevated place, as Esdras did, and as the Roman Pontifical actually prescribes for the lector. As early as the third and fourth centuries there is mention of an elevated place where the reading-desk stood or where the lector stood even without a desk. Later this was turned into an ambo or pulpit, a podium fitted out with a balustrade and lectern, set up at some convenient spot between sanctuary and nave, and either standing free or else built into the choir railing or into the side-railings of the enclosure, which, in many basilicas, surrounded the space for the *schola cantorum*. The ambo also served—as we will see later in greater detail—for the singer in the responsorial chant. Frequently the preaching was done from here. In the Orient the deacon ascended—and still ascends—the ambo to lead the prayer of the people in the *ektene*, but it was especially intended for the reader who presented the Sacred Scriptures. This is indicated, *inter alia*, by the names it has: *lectrinum, lectionarium, analogium*. Frequently it was very richly adorned with mosaics, sculpture and the like.

But now the Roman Mass contains hardly a trace of an arrangement which seemed so well suited to making the reading as understandable as possible. As far as the people are concerned, the readings have, during the past thousand years, become a mere symbol. The subdeacon who reads the Epistle stands at his accustomed place, facing the altar and therefore with his back to the people. The deacon who sings the Gospel should indeed turn *contra altare versus populum*, but the latter direction, *versus populum*, seems to be countermanded by the first, *contra altare*.[4] So, for a practical suggestion as to the position to be taken by

---

[3] *Missale Rom., Rubr. gen.,* XIX, 6.

The "broad stole" (*stola latior*) is really a stylized folded chasuble—a limp chasuble that was folded over the shoulder and pinned there; eventually the folds were sewed in and the cloth cut down to its present nondescript shape.

[4] The most reasonable explanation for the *contra altare* seems to be that of Th. Schnitzler, *Die Messe in der Betrachtung* II, Freiburg, 1957, 81 f. who suggests that it refers not to the direction faced by the reader in question but rather the *place* where he is to stand. Thus the reading or singing of the Epistle facing the people is by no means excluded. This is borne out by the *Cæremoniale episcoporum* II, 8, 15.

deacon, the rubric from the pontifical Mass is usually given, since it is plainer: the deacon turns in that direction which corresponds to the north side of an oriented church. Or recourse is had simply to local custom, which is actually diversified.

On the contrary there are no differences of opinion regarding the further rule, that the Epistle is read on the south side of the sanctuary, the Gospel on the north—a rule which the priest himself must observe at the altar even at the simplest private Mass. In addition, a more detailed regulation regarding the Gospel is this, that he does not face straight ahead but towards the corner of the altar, that is, in an oriented church he turns just a bit to the north. This is almost the same rule as that for the deacon at solemn Mass. From the standpoint of the ordinary participant, this means that the Epistle is said at the right side, the Gospel at the left. Further it means that at every Mass the book has to be carried over from one side to the other. The difference in the locale of the readings and the accompanying conduct of the Mass-server are some of the peculiarities of the external Mass rite which make the strongest impression. "Epistle side" and "Gospel side" are phrases that even poorly instructed Catholics are acquainted with. It is therefore very much in place to go into greater detail regarding this regulation.

The north side as the place for the Gospel is specifically mentioned for the first time in the commentary of Remigius of Auxerre (d. c. 908); the north, he says, is the region of the devil whom the word of God must contend with. And Ivo of Chartres (d. c. 1117) continues the line of thought, remarking that the Gospel is proclaimed against paganism, which is represented by the northern part of the world, and in which the coldness of unbelief had so long prevailed. And Ivo does not mean merely the direction of the body which the reader assumes in the ambo, but the actual position on the north side of the sanctuary, for he speaks of the passage of the levite or of the priest "to the left side of the church" in order to read the Gospel. And that too has a meaning, for it represents the transfer of preaching from the Jews to the Gentiles. The suspicion is forced upon one that these are but later attempts to explain by allegory a practice which was long in use and no longer understood, a practice which did not concern north and south at all, but had an entirely different viewpoint.

An inkling of this is to be found in the author of the *Micrologus*, a work almost contemporaneous with Ivo. The author writes that it is almost a general custom that the deacon reading the Gospel turn toward the north. But he takes exception to this, not only because the north side is the side for the women, and it is therefore unbecoming that the deacon turn that way, but also because it is plainly *contra Romanum ordinem*, according to which the deacon stands on the ambo turned to the south, that is, the side of the men. He explains the variant practice, which had already become fixed and rooted, as a conscious imitation of the movement and position of the priest who, when saying Mass without a deacon, does really have to say the Gospel at the north side of the altar in order to leave the other side free for the sacrificial activity, and who thus could give the appearance of actually turning towards the north. But this explanation, suggesting the private Mass as the origin of the practice, although it has been repeated in our own day, is presented only for lack of something better.

Just what is to be said about this "Roman order" which Bernold had in view? He is thinking, one might say, of Mabillon's second Roman *Ordo,* but this order he could not have known since it was not compiled till the tenth century and in Franco-German territory. The real Roman arrangement was not as precise as Bernold supposes. We can reconstruct it as it actually was, better perhaps from archeological evidences than from literary sources.

The spot from which the deacon at a solemn function could read the Gospel most conveniently and fittingly had to be chosen in such a way that on the one hand the reader had the people before him, and on the other he did not turn his back on the bishop and the clergy surrounding him. In the basilicas of the dying ancient period, where the *cathedra* of the bishop stood in the apse, he would therefore have to stand to the side, in the forward part of the choir, to the right of the presiding bishop (for all the ranks of honor were reckoned with the *cathedra* of the bishop as the point of departure). He would thus face either north or south depending on the position of the apse and the *cathedra*, whether to the west, as they were in the older Roman structures, or to the east, as later became customary. As a matter of fact we find the ambo is arranged in many places in accordance with these notions. In the latter case, where the apse is towards the east, the deacon who wanted to talk to the people turned towards the south. This position is evinced both by the placement of ambos and by literary documents; this is the position which Bernold wanted observed (Fig. 1). In the Roman churches of the older type, which had the apse toward the west, the deacon would, under the same circumstances, assume a position facing north, and many Roman basilicas actually indicate this layout (Fig. 2) (e.g., S. Clemente).

It is this latter position, set free of its natural foundation, that continued to be the fixed norm in the conception of the medieval liturgists and still survives in the rubrics of the *Cæremoniale episcoporum.* But in the transfer to the oriented churches two possibilities remained open. The deacon could place himself to the left of the *cathedra* (still standing at the center of the apse) and thus speak from the south side of the church, facing the nave and the north (Fig. 3); again there are actual examples (S. Maria in Cosmedin). But it was hardly possible to tolerate for long the reading of the Gospel at the left of the *cathedra* and with

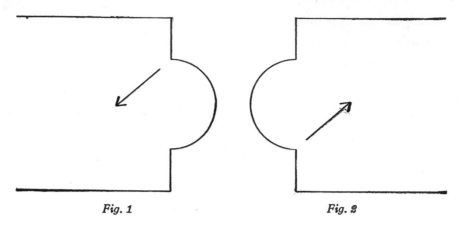

Fig. 1   Fig. 2

face towards the women's side of the church. So the second possibility came to mind; the deacon could stand to the right and still face northwards, too—as we are accustomed to seeing it done (Fig. 4).

This last solution is basically in complete correspondence with the intellectual and cultural condition of the Middle Ages. It seemed more important to hold on to the symbolism of the northward direction (since this had a message for the symbol-hungry eyes of the people of that era) than to turn to the people (since the contents of the Latin lesson were not grasped by them anyway). This arrangement then became a norm for the priest in reading the Gospel at the altar. Thus, besides this symbolical northward direction both at solemn and simple Masses another rule remained in force, that the Gospel should be read at the right side (reckoning from the viewpoint of the bishop's *cathedra*). The opposite side was then the Epistle side, but this only at a comparatively late date. Beleth in 1160 objects that the priest generally reads the Gospel at the altar instead of at a special lectern. It appears that up to that time the norm mostly followed was a very practical one, to keep the right side of the altar—our Epistle side—free for the gift-offerings at least from the offertory on.

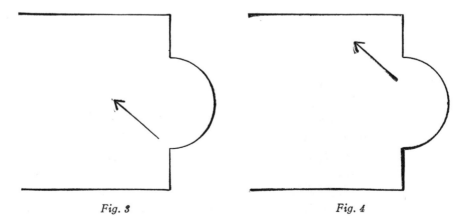

Fig. 3   Fig. 4

Interest in a gradation amongst the readings was early at work in the choice of readers, as we have seen. But in localizing the reading the process was slower. Even in the early Middle Ages there was, as a rule, but one ambo, which served for all the lessons. Amalar is the first to mention a "higher place" (*excellentior locus*) at which the Gospel was read. The *Ordo Romanus II*, which originated in the north in the tenth century, directs the subdeacon who reads the Epistle to mount the ambo, "not to the higher step which only he should ascend who is to read the Gospel," a rule which is often repeated later on. At the same time we hear of a specially built desk for the reading of the Gospel; it had the form of an eagle with wings outspread.

In the church architecture of the later Middle Ages the ambo is no longer considered, or, to be more precise, it is moved away from the *cancelli* farther into the nave of the church where it becomes a pulpit. Obviously the smaller churches did not possess an ambo even in earlier times. The Gospel thus retained the place it got either by tradition or by symbolic interpretation—a place on the level of the choir (sanctuary), on the north side. The subdeacon became the bearer of the Gospel book, replacing the lectern or desk—a new honor for the Gospel. But the Epistle later obtained its place on the opposite side, with the subdeacon reading toward the altar, and himself holding the book. Thus the "Epistle side" of the altar was evolved. Ivo of Chartres seems to stipulate some such thing, although in many other places, even at a much later date, there is still no fixed rule. In an intervening period, when the division of readings to right and left was recognized and still at the same time the need was felt for an ambo, two ambos were sometimes constructed, one more ornamental on the Gospel side, the other more modest on the Epistle side. In our modern buildings we sometimes see this plan followed, since the regulations in force at the present time leave room for such an arrangement.

4. The Epistle

The first of the two readings of the Roman Mass is called simply "the Epistle" although it is not always taken from the Letters of the Apostles. This usage, which the *Missale Romanum* retains, existed even in the twelfth century. The reading was also called "*lectio*," corresponding to the designation by which the title of the book being read is introduced: *lectio Isaiæ prophetæ, lectio epistolæ*. . . . Since enough was already said previously about the selection of the Epistle, the choice of a reader and his position in the sanctuary, it is only necessary to state that in our Roman liturgy it seems that the principle of the highest simplicity has been followed in the framing of the Epistle itself at high Mass. Consequently there is no address to the people and no reply on their part, no blessing of the reader (as is customary otherwise even in the Office before the longer readings at Matins) and no prayer by the reader for purification, no solemn escort to the ambo (in recent times only the accompaniment of an acolyte has been allowed). Even the melody to which it is sung is kept much simpler than at the Gospel.

This sobriety was evidently intentional, in order to let the Gospel stand out more strongly. Putting it more exactly, it was retained when the richer fitting-out of the Gospel was begun. In general an older manner in the fitting-out of the lection still survives in the Epistle. Here, too, the role of the lector is still acknowledged at least in part—which agrees with what we have said. To sit during the Epistle was also one of those olden reading practices. On the other hand, this sobriety is not quite so pronounced as at the readings which bear the stamp of greatest antiquity —those of Good Friday and Holy Saturday. About these the rubric still remarks that they are read *sine titulo* and the answer *Deo gratias* is omitted at the end—two elaborations which have nevertheless been accorded the Epistle.

DEO GRATIAS

The *Deo gratias* at the end is not necessarily proper to the Epistle only. It is repeated at the end of the last Gospel, just as it follows at the lessons of the Office, and also at the *Ite missa est*. In truth only in the last case does the response bear the marks of primitiveness, since it is made by the choir and not by the servers.

It is without doubt sensible and very becoming for one to thank God after being permitted to receive His word. But it is questionable whether the *Deo gratias* is here intended as a spoken thanks. Primarily its function seems to be quite different. In this *Deo gratias* we have a formal shout which was much used outside of divine service especially in the North African Church, e.g., as an acclamation in the sense of approval, and as a greeting of Christians on meeting each other. The *Deo gratias* seems to have come from North Africa into the Arabian liturgy, where it is used along with *Amen* as a response after the reading. We find also that it was a part of the Roman liturgy at an early period. At the stational service in the eighth century when the deacon made the announcement of the next station, right after the Communion of the Pope, the people answered, *Deo gratias*. The sense in which the formula is here used is plain. The only purpose is to express the fact that the hearers have understood the announcement. It is the same situation as that predicated in the rule of St. Benedict where the gate-keeper is told to answer *Deo gratias* whenever anyone knocks at the monastery doors. Surely he is not shouting his gratitude for any benefit received; he is merely indicating that he has heard the summons. But he does use a formula which goes down deep into Christian concepts, a formula which has become so much a part of everyday life that it can serve as a simple signal. It is in this sense that we must understand the *Deo gratias* which is said after the *Ite missa est* and on other occasions in the Roman liturgy, especially after the Epistle and the lessons. We can trace here the prevailing tone that dominates the Roman liturgy, the strong, religiously accented consciousness of the community, the realization that after the proclamation made to all, after the presentation of God's word, no doubt should be left about its reception. The proclamation has been heard, the reading has been received, and the reply that resounds from the people is one which the Christian should use in every challenging situation in life: *Deo gratias*, Thanks be to God.

5. *The Intervenient Chants*

It is in the very nature of things that the grace-laden message which God proclaims to men would awaken an echo of song. In the chant which is linked with the readings we have the most ancient song of the Christian liturgy, and in particular of the Roman liturgy. In contrast to the more modern strata of the Mass chants: introit, offertory and communion, which were antiphonal in design and so demanded a special singing group for performance, the gradual and alleluia still show plainly the traits of the older responsorial method which dominated the field till at least the fourth century. For this type of music only one trained singer was required, with the people all answering together. Only this solo singer had any continuous text to reproduce; the people answered by repeating after each passage the unchanging verse, the refrain or *responsum*. This is a very simple procedure, but for a vital participation of the people a procedure suitable in the highest measure, since neither any special preparation nor a written text were necessary for the people. This responding of the people was customary both in the singing of the races of the ancient Orient and in the divine service of the Old Covenant. But in the pre-Christian and primitive Christian eras there was in the texts scarcely any distinction between song and prayer, nor was there any definite singing tune for use only in the performance of the psalms, since certain recitatives and even formal melodies were customary also for the other books of the Bible. But responsory itself was to some extent inherent in the very text of the psalms. It was a legacy which the synagogue inherited from the services in the Temple. And thence it passed to the primitive Church where it is found in full practice.

RESPONSORIAL SINGING

According to the arrangement of the agape outlined by Hippolytus of Rome, the faithful were to say "alleluia" when the psalms were read at the beginning of the agape. The reference is to the alleluia psalms in which the biblical text already contains the entry, "alleluia," either at the beginning or at the end, as an indication that the word was to be inserted as a response after every verse. St. Athanasius on one occasion mentioned the deacon's reciting a psalm before the entire people, while the people responded repeatedly: "for his mercy is eternal," just as we find it sketched in Psalm 135.

Since the third century, contemporaneous with the vanishing of the vogue of privately composed hymns, the use of the Scriptural psalms became more pronounced. And the opposition to these hymns probably led to a greater stressing of the musical character of the psalms. In the fourth century there is explicit evidence of the use of psalm chant in the reading service of the fore-Mass, and its performance followed the method of responsorial song already in vogue. In this process the alleluia gained considerable importance. It is, at any rate, a phenomenon worth remarking, that nearly all the liturgies both East and West still display the alleluia in the Mass in some form or other. And usually the alleluia follows the second-last reading, either immediately or (as in the Roman liturgy too) mediately, so that it looks like a prelude to the Gospel; but sometimes it does not appear till after the last lesson.

In the sermons of St. Augustine we are introduced to the fully developed form of the responsorial psalming as it was done between the lessons. He speaks of a psalm "which we heard sung and to which we responded." Augustine himself was wont to select the psalm. Even lengthier psalms were sung right through without curtailment. The refrain seems always to have consisted of an entire verse of the respective psalm. It could be taken either from the beginning of the psalm or from the context. The first alternative we see exemplified in Psalm 29, where the response is: "Praise to thee, Lord, thou hast taken me under thy protection, and balked my enemies of their will." Due to their constant recurrence these refrains were quite familiar to the people. Like Augustine, another preacher, St. Chrysostom, takes occasion time and time again to refer to these refrains as a starting point for a deeper study of the contents of the psalms. St. Leo the Great, too, makes reference to this community singing of the psalms with the people.

It is really remarkable that now only a few remnants remain of this responsorial singing which was once so flourishing. Quite early it invaded the domain of art. In the Oriental Church the refrain was first expanded into a strophe, the *heirmos*, then further verses were intercalated for the repetition of the refrain, and these groups of strophes, called a "canon," entwine around the psalm or canticle of the singer like an ivy-vine. These canons were performed by a choir, or by two choirs. The next step in the evolution was to drop most of the psalm at a solemn Office, retaining a few verses which were hymnically interwoven in the manner indicated. Finally in the canticles the basic text disappeared entirely and all that was left was an elaborate store of hymn poetry, redolent of the biblical songs upon which they had been founded.

In the Roman liturgy, too, this curtailment of responsorial song has been allowed a free hand, and not one single chant has retained the original type unimpaired. Aside from the ferial formularies, in which only one responsorial chant follows the Epistle, as is also the case after the several lessons of the vigil Masses on Ember Saturdays—aside from these instances the full form of the Sunday and feast-day formularies includes two songs, the gradual and the alleluia (*resp.* Tract), and in addition the more recently composed sequences also belong in this grouping. There are various indications that tend to show that the gradual originally followed the first of the three readings (which disappeared very early). That is manifested even at present on the few days that have three readings; one of the chants follows the first reading, one the second. Similarly in the Milan liturgy the *psalmellus* follows the first of the three readings, and the alleluia chant follows the second. In fact, even in the Roman liturgy a fragment of a Mass book has recently come to light which regularly has the gradual follow the first of its three lections, and the alleluia the second.

When the first reading disappeared, it was hard to sacrifice either the gradual or the alleluia, probably because both had become by that time— the sixth century—jewels of the Roman Mass; perhaps, too, because by that time the alleluia was more and more considered an Easter piece admirably suited to the eucharistic celebration especially on Sundays and feast days. And then it was no longer regarded simply as an echo of the Epistle but a presentiment of the joyous Gospel message, as the later interpreters regularly explain it.

All the more, then, must the texts of the two chants be shortened, and all the more thoroughly in proportion to the melodic elaboration which by this time they had gained. If in the Orient it was poetics that proved to be the enemy of the ancient responsorial technique, in the Western world it was musical art. Already in St. Augustine's time the singers displayed the tendency more and more to enhance the chant with richer melodies. The external beauty of God's house had been enhanced, the service increased in splendor; it was but natural that the music should follow suit. The formation of the elaborate melismas must have been accomplished in the solo singing of the psalmist long before a similar development could be inaugurated in the *schola cantorum.* This hypothesis is confirmed by the fact that even later melodies of the responsorial songs, compared with those of the antiphonal songs of the *schola*, show an unevenly greater embellishment. This can be seen to best advantage only since the *Graduale Romanum* has been republished with the fuller ancient melodies. The richness of the solo chant must have had a reaction also in the *responsum* of the people. Gradually this response slipped away from the congregation and into the ranks of the singers, that is, the *schola*. With this new development another fact was closely related, namely that even the most ancient books containing the texts for the Roman chants between the readings—with a few exceptions that were fast disappearing—indicate for both gradual and alleluia only a single verse instead of the full psalm. This is what we are accustomed to at present, and so the responsorial design of these songs is scarcely ever noticed.

Still this abbreviation of the texts did not make such progress in other parts of our liturgy. In these places it came to a halt. Thus in the invitatory in Matins we have an example of the original form of responsorial singing.

GRADUAL

In the gradual almost nothing of the original responsory character is retained, though the older sources did keep the names *responsorium* or *responsorium graduale*. Still the second half of the text is designated as versus ($\mathbb{V}$.). This verse takes the place of the once complete psalm sung by the precentor. Even now all of it except the final cadence is performed (according to rule) by one or two soloists. But the preceding portion of the text which corresponds to the older response of the people is now begun by the soloist(s) and continued by the choir. This method of performance, of which there are evidences even at an earlier period, is a substitute for the more ancient plan according to which the *responsum* was first preintoned by the precentor and then repeated by all. The further repetition of the *responsum* after the verse was still customary in the thirteenth century, and in many places even later. As a rule it was at first omitted only in those instances in which another chant, the alleluia or a tract, followed, but in most churches it soon disappeared entirely. In order to avoid an unsatisfactory ending it then became the practice to have the entire choir join in during the closing cadence of the verse, as usually happens today. But in the new edition of the *Graduale Romanum* (1908), the original plan was also permitted, that namely of repeating the *responsum* after the verse.

In Holy Week two graduals are retained which even today show several verses instead of the usual one.[1] The repetition of the response after

[1] On Wednesday: *Domine, exaudi orationem meam,* with five verses; on Good Friday: *Domine, audivi,* with four verses.

the individual verses which was still customary in the Carolingian period and even later has disappeared, it is true, so that the chants are no longer to be distinguished from the *tractus;* indeed they have actually taken this title from the latter form. In Easter Week also a lengthy section of the Easter psalm *Confitemini*, with a constant repetition of the refrain, "This is the day the Lord hath made, let us be glad and rejoice thereon," long survived. But as time went on the verses of the psalm were distributed throughout the week. Just as here in the Easter octave a store of antique responsorial song is to be found, so (to cite another example) in the second Christmas Mass, too. The head-piece of the gradual, "Blessed is He who comes in the name of the Lord, the Lord God has manifested Himself unto us," was the song which the Christian people in the fourth century repeated tirelessly during the Christmas procession from Bethlehem to Jerusalem.

If in the gradual only a rudiment of the ancient responsorial singing has been retained, in the *alleluia*, as it is presented now, the original design still peeps through. The singer chants alleluia, just as he usually intones the refrain. The congregation repeats it. The singer begins the psalm, that is, he sings the verse which replaces the psalm. The choir again repeats the alleluia. In Eastertide, from Low Sunday to Whitsunday, where a double alleluia is inserted in place of the gradual and alleluia, a second verse follows and then the alleluia once more.

The present-day manner of executing the alleluia really corresponds in substance to this description: the first alleluia is sung by one or two soloists and then, with the *jubilus* added, is repeated by the choir; the verse again is the soloist's; and in the repetition after the verse the choir joins in once more at least with the *jubilus*.

The tendency to drop the repetitions, particularly the repetition after the verse, was also manifested in the alleluia, but, excepting the days of lesser solemnity, the tendency was overcome. The nearness of the joyous message of the Gospel probably helped to produce this result.

In the *jubilus* of the alleluia Gregorian chant achieved its highest expression, and, no doubt, in the ages before people were spoiled by the charms of harmony, the untiring reiteration of the melismatic melodies with their endless rise and fall must have been a wonderful experience for the devout congregation.

In penitential periods the *tractus* takes the place of the alleluia. Its one big peculiarity today is the fact that it consists of a lengthy series of psalm verse, each marked with the designation ℣ (*ersus*). The tract for Palm Sunday, for instance, embraces the greater part of Psalm 21, that of the first Sunday of Lent the complete Psalm 90. The Carolingian liturgist thought the chief distinction between tract and gradual was the lack of a response (refrain) after the verses in the former, where it was still customary in the latter. Musically the distinctive mark is the scantier store of melody. This in fact may possibly be the derivation of the name: *tractus*, a typical melody, which recurs according to fixed rules in the course of the piece. Medieval interpreters sought the derivation in the "drawn-out" method of singing, a style appointed for penitence and grief; but this was hardly the original notion of these chants, for amongst them are found several that begin with *Jubilate, laudate Dominum.* Wagner has good grounds for his opinion that in the tract we have simply graduals—perhaps we ought to say responsorial chants—of the fourth/fifth century, chants which, in their melodic design and partly in the range of their text, stem from the more ancient period of Roman solo-psalmody and so reflect the condition of the chants before the art of the singer had succeeded in embellishing it and thus led to the shortening of the psalm. This traditionally simpler manner was later used more and more exclusively for fast-day Masses, in which we generally find the older forms retained, especially in the last days of Lent. Later the tract was given a certain animation by being divided amongst the whole choir in alternate fashion, as is the rule now.

It was really an important moment in the liturgy when, at the Roman stational service of the seventh century, right after the Epistle the singers ascended the ambo, first the one who intoned the *responsorium* and after him the one who did the alleluia. For these songs were not like those of the *schola*, intended merely to fill out a pause, nor were they, like the latter, broken off at the signal of the celebrant. They were independent, self-sufficient members inserted between the readings like a moment of pious meditation, like a lyrical rejoicing after the word of God had reached the ears of men. The name of the singer like that of the reader of the Epistle had to be made known to the pope at the beginning of the service. Previous to Gregory the Great these chants were done by deacons, but St. Gregory forbade this, since he wanted to avert the possibility of a beautiful voice counting in the promotion to diaconate. So the duty fell to the subdeacon's lot. When the singer mounted the ambo, he was not allowed to stand at the top—at least this was true later, in the territory of the Romano-Frankish liturgy. This platform was reserved to the Gospel. Instead, like the reader of the Epistle, he had to be satisfied with one of the steps (*gradus*) of the stairway. Hence the chant took the name "*graduale.*" And his vesture, too, was that of the reader of the Epistle—that is, he first took off the *planeta.*

TEXT OF THE CHANT

For the text of the chant the singers of the responsorial songs looked to a special book which is called, in the Roman *Ordines*, simply *cantatorium.* This he carried along to the desk. Amongst the six oldest manuscripts which give us the Mass chants, only one is devoted entirely to the solo-songs. All the others combine these in one book with the antiphonal chants of the *schola;* this shows that by the ninth century the singer had become simply a member of the ensemble, and the latter, in turn, had long since taken over the response and therefore needed to have the text in view. Nor was the singer separated from the choir in space, particularly when the ambo gradually disappeared from the plan of the church. About the same time the soloist was replaced by two or three singers; soon even four were mentioned. In other places the boy singers appeared as performers of the solo chants, apparently as a continuation of the arrangement followed in the Gallic liturgies—an arrangement which must have been carried over into the Roman liturgy only after encountering great opposition.

The text of these chants is derived, as a rule, from the psalms and canticles; after all, this matches their origin as psalmodic chants. But where two songs follow each other, they are totally independent and the choice of one in no way influences the choice of the others. The tracts follow the rule strictly and are taken, without exception, from the psalms. For the gradual and the alleluia chant, texts not taken from the psalter are very infrequent in the pre-Carolingian Roman liturgy. They do appear now and then on feast days, when the remarkable art which was able to adapt the psalm verses to the occasion did not seem able to achieve its aim. On Sundays no effort was made to draw a particular connection between the chants and the readings; the effort would probably have been fruitless anyhow. But on feasts there is a certain agreement between them. Thus on the feast of St. Stephen, after the account of the hearing before the High Council, the gradual continues with Psalm 118:23: "Closeted together, princes plot against me." And on Epiphany the closing sentence of the lesson is simply taken up and amplified: "All shall come out of Saba." Indeed there is even an instance where the chant is an actual continuation of the reading, namely on Ember Saturday when the lesson from Daniel concludes with the canticle.

For the alleluia verse in the Sunday formularies there was from the very start no fast connection with certain psalms. But Amalar does advise choosing those verses which would most appropriately lead to the repetition of the alleluia, those (in other words) which gave expression to the joy of the Church or the praise of God. The antiphonaries often contained a list of suitable alleluia verses to be chosen at will. It is therefore evident that later on, after the various churches had settled on a certain alleluia verse for each formula there should be very little uniformity on this matter amongst the Mass books. And this also explains why the present *Missale Romanum* should contain amongst these verses such a great number of non-psalmodic and even non-Biblical texts, for the connection with the original psalm-chanting had meanwhile been loosened even more.

In medieval liturgical practice the alleluia obviously received greater attention than the gradual. The gradual was allegorically interpreted only as a re-echoing of the penitential preaching of John the Baptist and at best as a transition from the Old Testament to the New, and therefore, despite its content and its musical form, it was often accounted penitential in character. But the alleluia was the first of the Mass chants to be treated with troping. The alleluia verses which were performed by a soloist were the very first texts of the Mass to be set to multi-voiced compositions. But in general, the stress was put not on the verse but on the alleluia itself. On its final vowel tune was piled upon tune, florid melodies called *jubili* or, to follow medieval precedent, *sequentiæ*.

SEQUENCE

Singers found it no easy task to memorize these long intricate tonal figures. But since about the middle of the ninth century certain texts begin to make an appearance in Normandy and then in St. Gall—texts intended to support the melodies and at the same time (and perhaps even primarily) to render the melodies more agreeable to the musical sensibilities of the northern peoples to whom up to now the melismatic chant was strange. Soon this new art was also extended to newer and more protracted melodies. It is the same routine that was later repeated in the tropes, but with this difference that in the latter case brief texts already in existence were expanded. Notker Balbulus, a monk of St. Gall (d. 912), set to work to supply texts on the principle of one note to a syllable. This text was then itself called *sequentia*. They were written in a free rhythmic style, a kind of elevated prose, and were therefore also called "proses," a term which is still used in French for church hymns. But since each of the musical phrases or strophes of the complete melody was repeated with a different text, the result was a series of paired strophes which were then usually performed by alternate choirs. However, the first and last strophes—the introduction and the conclusion—were not usually paired.

After the year 1000 a new type of sequence began to develop, a type founded on rhythmical principles and, in general, composed of even verses and strophes; they also make use of rhyme. This is the flourishing period in the composition of sequences, the most famous writer of which was Adam of St. Victor (d. about 1192). Some 5000 sequences have been collected from the manuscripts; they form an important branch of literature in the Middle Ages.

In northern countries the Mass books of the later Middle Ages contain a sequence for almost every feast day, or even (you might say) for every Mass formula that uses the alleluia. A Cologne missal of 1487 has 73 of them, the Augsburg missal of 1555 has 98. But elsewhere, above all in Rome, their reception was very cool, or at least (in line with their origin) they were not used at low Mass. In the reform of the Mass books under Pius V, out of all the luxuriant crop only four were retained—the same, approximately, as those which are encountered earlier here and there in Italian Mass books. The Italian tradition and the humanist attitude were probably both at work in bringing this result about.

The fact that here the swift course of the Mass seemed to reach a point of rest, a breathing spot before the triumphal entry of the divine word in the Gospel, was early manifested in the possibility of making various insertions here. In contrast to a more ancient arrangement, which placed the ordinations (without any fore-Mass) immediately before the start of the Mass proper, it was customary at Rome as early as 600 to insert the conferring of the major Orders before the Gospel, or more precisely, between gradual and alleluia, *resp.* tract. This has remained the rule even today, at least for ordination to priesthood and episcopacy. Like the consecration of abbots and virgins and the crowning of kings, these are introduced before the alleluia or, as the case may be, before the last verse of the sequence or the tract.

In the later Middle Ages it became customary at a high Mass to start the preparation of the offerings during these interposed chants before the Gospel. This custom was then taken over here and there into the less solemn Mass. At the same time we hear occasionally that during these chants and preparations the celebrant was to say certain *apologiæ* quietly to himself, or at least that he could do so; in fact some Mass books of the eleventh and twelfth centuries offer a large store of them in this place. It is hard to say whether this is the expression of an exaggerated sin-consciousness or of a remarkable *horror vacui* which could not tolerate a pause not filled with vocal prayer. Both practices disappeared in the course of time.

6. The Gospel

It is a strict rule which holds true in all liturgies, that the last of the readings should consist of a passage from the Gospels, but this is not something self-explanatory. If the order of the biblical canon or the time sequence of the events were the norm, the Acts of the Apostles would, at least on occasion, come last. But obviously there had to be some order of precedence, and there was never any doubt that the Gospels hold the highest rank; they contain the "good tidings," the fulfillment of all the past, and the point from which all future ages radiate. And just as in a procession of the clergy the highest in rank comes last, so too in the series of readings.

How highly the Gospels were regarded is seen in the care and the wealth that was expended on the manuscripts containing them. The Gospels were long written in stately uncials even after these had otherwise gone out of use. Not a few manuscripts were prepared in gold or silver script upon a purple ground, or they were richly decorated with miniatures. What Christian antiquity had begun in this regard, was even surpassed in the Carolingian era. Not seldom was the binding of the evangeliary covered with ivory and pure gold or silver. The Gospel book alone was permitted on the altar which otherwise bore only the Blessed Sacrament, a conception which survives in the Greek Church down to the very present.

ACCOMPANYING CEREMONIES

In the liturgy itself the effort was made from earliest times to enhance and stress the *evangelium* as much as possible. It was to be read not by a lector but by a deacon or a priest. On feast days perhaps the bishop himself read the Gospel; in Jerusalem this was the case every Sunday. In the West the delivery of the Gospel was the deacon's duty from earliest times, for he was the first cleric amongst all those assisting. On Christmas night it became the privilege of the Roman emperor to stand forth in full regalia to deliver the Gospel: "There went forth a decree from Caesar Augustus."

In the latter part of the ancient Christian period the question was agitated, whether the Gospel was not too sacred to be heard by the profane ears of the catechumens. The Roman baptismal rite as revised in the sixth century at all events puts the sharing of the Gospel on a par with the sharing of the confession of faith and the Our Father which were always regarded as restricted by the *disciplina arcani*. And as a matter of fact the catechumens—as a rule children who were subjected to the forms of adult baptism—were dismissed before the Gospel at the Scrutiny-Masses. Similar endeavors must have made themselves felt in Gaul even earlier, for the Council of Orange in 441 had occasion to insist that the catechumens were also to hear the Gospel. This latter attitude paralleled the counsel of our Lord: Preach the Gospel to the whole of creation (Mark 16:15), and was always the standard in the Church as long as the catechumenate continued to be a vital institution for the instruction of candidates for Baptism. The word of the Gospel should resound throughout the world—this idea sometimes found (and finds) a special symbolical expression in the practice of reciting the Gospel-pericope on festive occasions in several languages.

The deportment of the deacon, too, as he walked to the place where the Gospel was to be read, was built up gradually into a formal procession. The beginnings of such a ceremonial are already to be seen in the first Roman *Ordo;* the deacon kisses the feet of the pope, who pronounces over him the words: "The Lord be in thy heart and on thy lips." Then he goes to the altar where the Gospel book has been lying since the beginning of the service (having been placed there ceremoniously by a deacon, accompanied by an acolyte). He kisses it and picks it up. As he betakes himself to the ambo, he is accompanied by two acolytes with torches, and by two subdeacons, one of whom carries a censer.

In the Gallican liturgy of this period we come upon somewhat the same picture as that at Rome, but heightened a little. The well-known commentary on this ancient liturgy—a work of the seventh century—sees in the solemn entry of the *evangelium* (which is accompanied by the chanting of the *Trisagion* and at which seven torches are carried) a representation of Christ's triumphal coming. We can also include as parallel the Little Entry of the oriental liturgies, although this is placed at the very beginning of the reading service. Its center, too, is the Gospel book—if not exclusively, at least predominantly. A procession which apparently centers on the Gospel book is also found in the Coptic liturgy. The procession is formed immediately before the reading of the Gospel; lights are carried in front of the book, and the altar is circled.

As seems plain from what has been said, the carrying of tapers before the Gospel tallies with an ancient Christian practice that must have been common to all the liturgies. In fact St. Jerome testifies that it was customary in all the churches of the Orient to light lights when the Gospel was to be read, and this on the brightest day; in this way an air of joy could be lent to the gathering. More precisely, however, the practice was palpably an honor paid to the holy book. The Roman *Notitia dignitatum* of the fifth century, amongst the official insignia of the various dignitaries of the Roman State which are there illustrated, shows for the *præfectus prætorio* a picture in which a book stands opened on a covered table between two burning candles—a book whose cover bears a likeness of the emperor on a ground of gold; it is the *liber mandatorum* which contains the powers granted to this official by the emperor. We can also recall the custom of carrying lights and incense before the bishop at a solemn entry—one of the honors which, since the time of Constantine, was transferred from the higher civil officials to Church dignitaries. It is but a step to explain the carrying of lights and incense before the Gospel book on the basis of the personal honor paid to the bishop; in the Gospel book, which contains Christ's word, Christ Himself is honored and His entry solemnized. This custom is on a level with the practice of erecting a throne at synods and placing the Gospel book thereon to show that Christ is presiding, or with that other practice, followed as late as the tenth and twelfth century, of carrying the Gospel book in the Palm Sunday procession to take the place of Christ.

In the later Middle Ages the processional character of this act was emphasized in many places by having a cross-bearer precede the group. The cushion for the book was probably also carried in the procession. This stately escort of the Gospel book at a high Mass is sometimes reflected in the action of private Mass, when the priest himself transfers the Mass book for the Gospel. At Le Mans it was even the custom for the priest to carry the Gospel book to the altar at a high Mass, and only then to turn it over to the deacon.

That Christ Himself is honored in the Gospel book is also revealed in the *acclamations* that are uttered. Here we have another of those dramatic elements which the Roman Mass gradually acquired in the countries of the North. The deacon greets the people and receives their greeting in return. Then he announces the pericope and the cry is heard: *Gloria tibi, Domine.* After the lection the Mass-server answers: *Laus tibi, Christe.* And in one Italian church of the twelfth century use is made of the shout of homage with which the crowds greeted our Lord: *Benedictus qui venit in nomine Domini.* In some isolated instances the deacon himself, at the end of the reading, is saluted by the celebrant with a *Pax tibi.*

If, in these cries, the clergy answer the message of joy rather than the people, still the faithful also take a part in showing honor to the Gospel, at least by their *bodily posture.* From ancient times it has been customary to listen to the Gospel *standing.* The practice prevails generally in the Orient, too, and is provable there as far back as the fourth century. In the West also there is early and manifold evidence of standing at the Gospel. The medieval interpreters place a great deal of weight on the usage and describe it in minute detail. When the deacon's greeting sounds, all stand up and turn to him. Thereupon all the people face east, till the words of our Lord begin. Meanwhile the canes that are used to support oneself are put aside and the people either stand erect (like servants before their Lord) or else slightly bowed. The men are to remove every head covering, even the princely crown. Mention is made, too, of setting aside one's weapons and outer mantle or cloak, as well as gloves. Elsewhere the knights laid their hand on the hilt of their sword, or they drew the sword and held it extended all during the reading [1]—expressions, both, of a willingness to fight for the word of God.

When the Gospel ended it was customary in the Roman stational services for a subdeacon to take the book (not with bare hands, however, but holding it *super planetam*), and to bring it around to the attending clergy to be kissed before it was returned again to its casket, sealed and brought back to its place of safekeeping.

---

[1] Some student fraternities have taken over the custom of drawing their swords at the Gospel; such is the custom at the University Church in Innsbruck on solemn occasions. A custom having a similar aim is that of waving banners, as is done by certain Catholic organizations.

In countries of the North the people were, for a time, permitted to share in this *veneration of the Gospel book*. Later the right was limited to those who received an order requiring some kind of anointing, such as priests, bishops and kings. And from there on it was usually handed only to clerics to be kissed, and the celebrant used to do so with the book opened, just as it is customary nowadays, while the rest of the choir did so with the book closed. Gradually, however, since the thirteenth century, the custom of having the clergy kiss the book disappeared, although it was still to be found in some places as late as the eighteenth century. According to present-day practice even the deacon no longer kisses the book, but only the celebrating priest or (but only in his stead) an attending higher prelate, even at a private Mass. And while doing so the priest says: "May our sins be blotted out through the reading of the Gospel." Similar formulas have attended the kissing of the Gospel since around the year 1000. And traces of the original meaning of reverent and grateful greeting are to be seen in a formula from that early period: "Hail, words of the Gospel, which fill the whole world."

In contrast to this sharp retrenchment of the kissing of the book, the use of incense—again in the northern countries—has been on the increase. Originally the censer was merely carried in the procession of the book to the ambo; no special incensing took place. Then later it was to be carried up the ambo with the deacon, if there was room. In fact a second *thuribulum* was probably employed. Now the fragrant smoke emanating from the censer and swirling around the Gospel book gains a special value; everyone wants to be touched by it, to be blessed by the blessing of this consecrated incense, and therefore after the reading the censer is carried through the crowd. This usage is, significantly, mentioned first by the same witness who testifies to the ceremony of handing the book to the people to be kissed. The practice was curtailed and only the celebrant was incensed, but even then this incensation retained its special meaning (already mentioned), different from others, until it, too, was gradually lost. The incensing of the book before the start of the reading is mentioned since the eleventh century. This has been retained and was, in fact, at one time even duplicated after the reading—another instance of the new (and yet basically ancient) concept of honoring the Gospel. It is only in the Mass for the Dead that the kissing of book and hand is omitted, and so also this incensing.

The desire to grasp the sacred word of God and to secure its blessing (a desire that proved transiently effective in the case of the incensing), also found a lasting expression in another symbol—*the sign of the Cross*. In the ninth century for the first time do we come across this practice of the faithful signing a cross on their foreheads after the deacon greets them. Then we hear of another custom, the deacon and all those present imprinting the cross on forehead and breast after the words *Sequentia sancti evangelii*. About the eleventh century mention is made of forehead, mouth and breast, and since that time also of the signing of the book. At the end of the Gospel it was the custom for all those present to sign themselves with the cross once more. The original idea of this signing of oneself is probably indicated in the scriptural text frequently cited in this connection, the quotation about the wicked enemy who is anxious to take the seed of the word of God away from the hearts of the hearers. This, in any case, makes the sign of the Cross at the close intelligible, since it is practically as ancient as the other at the beginning. This opening act, which alone has continued to exist, indeed has grown somewhat, was at first explained in a similar sense. And it is a "blessing" of oneself, that is true. But another explanation takes over by degrees; an ever-increasing stress is placed on the readiness to acknowledge God's word with courage in the sense of St. Paul's assertion: I am not ashamed of this Gospel. Probably it was in this sense that the signing of the forehead grew into a triple signing of forehead, lips and breast, and in addition, the signing of the book. The meaning is this: For the word which Christ brought and which is set down in this book we are willing to stand up with a mind that is open; we are ready to confess it with our mouth; and above all we are determined to safeguard it faithfully in our hearts.

Pursuing this conception of *a blessing* with which we ought to prepare for the Gospel, Amalar remarks that the deacon who is about to scatter the seed of the Gospel stands in need of a "greater blessing." The simple word of blessing which, according to the first Roman *Ordo*, the pope pronounces over the deacon, is soon broadened out into formulas that reproduce or resemble the one we use today. Then too, the deacon formally begs for the blessing with *Iube, domne, benedicere*. Since the eleventh century there appears, either before or after the celebrant pronounces the blessing, another prayer by which the deacon prepares himself, our *Munda cor meum*. But it was far from common even as late as the sixteenth century, and in the Dominican use is lacking even today. Elsewhere the deacon recites the psalm verse: "O Lord, open Thou our lips, and our mouths shall show forth Thy praise." In the *Ordo Missæ* of John Burchard (1502) the *Munda cor meum*, with the petition for the blessing and the blessing, both unchanged, were taken over into the private Mass just as we have them today.

Thus the same thought of a proper preparation is disclosed: Pure must be the heart and chaste the lips of him who is to set forth the word of God, as the Lord Himself had declared in His message to Isaias when the seraph had touched the seer's lips with the glowing coal; lips that were to pronounce the word of God; and the heart, too, because this pronouncement was not to be a mere mechanical movement but an intellectual and intelligent speech, because the messenger of the glad tidings (and this holds also for one who only reads the message to the assembly) must first take the lesson to heart before he conveys it to the congregation.

7. *The Homily*

The sermon, which (together with its embellishments) is delivered in the vernacular after the Gospel, is currently regarded as an interpolation in the course of the liturgy rather than as a step forward in its progress. As a matter of fact, however, it belongs to the earliest constituent parts, indeed to the pre-Christian elements of the liturgy. The Sabbath Bible reading in the synagogue, which according to rigid custom had to be followed by a clarifying explanation, was for our Lord the main opportunity for preaching the word of God to receptive hearers and to proclaim His kingdom. At Antioch in Pisidia Paul and Barnabas, in similar circumstances, were ordered by the rulers of the synagogue to direct "a word of encouragement" to the assembly (Acts 13:15).

It stands to reason, therefore, that in Christian worship the homily was similarly joined at the very start to the reading of the Scriptures. *Indeed, the homily appears almost as an indispensable part of public worship, which took place, of course, only on Sundays.* The Bishop who presided over the community-worship would himself address the congregation after the reading. This was a particular duty of his. Still the priests also were allowed to preach; thus we have the numerous homilies of an Origen, or those of Hippolytus of Rome or later those of Jerome, and—from Antioch—those of Chrysostom. In the fourth century it was the general custom in the East, when several priests were present at the divine service, that each one would preach after the reading; and finally, as a rule the bishop himself.

In other places, the presbyters were not allowed to preach at public gatherings, whereas for the work of catechizing no grade of Orders was required at all. Thus, after the fall of Arius, preaching was forbidden to priests in Alexandria; likewise in North Africa, where the prohibition was not cancelled till the time of St. Augustine, who himself was permitted to preach when only a priest. A similar practice obtained for a long time in Rome and in Italy. In fact under Pope Celestine a letter of disapproval was sent out from Rome to the bishops of Provence where a contrary custom was in vogue. Sozomen made it known that in his day, as he thought, no preaching whatsoever was done in Rome. As a matter of fact there is no provision for preaching in the ancient Roman *Ordines*, which (of course) record primarily only the divine service for the major stations. Still the homiletic works of a Leo the Great and of a Gregory the Great prove that this was not altogether a period of absolute silence. From the beginning of the Middle Ages, at any rate, there was in general a strong return to the preaching of the word of God.

THE PREACHER

But if in Christian antiquity the preaching to the assembled congregation was chiefly restricted to the bishop, there resulted from this the clear and indubitable expression of his teaching authority. Furthermore such a restriction was quite necessary because of the none-too-high ability of the priests. But the restriction was carried through without considerable harm in the well-established provinces of North Africa and middle Italy, where every little town had its own bishopric. In Gaul the case was quite different. There the Council of Vaison (529), at the urgent request of St. Cæsarius, expressly gave the priests in the city and in the country the right to preach; and in case the priest was hindered by sickness, the deacons were to read from the homilies of the Fathers. In fact the ancient commentary on the Gallican Mass has the homily follow the Gospel in the ordinary course of the service; there, apparently, the mere reading of the "homilies of the saints" was practically on a par with the real sermon. In regard to this latter it was the duty of the preacher (stressed by the author of the *Expositio*) above all to find, by his own efforts, the proper medium between the language of the people and the pretensions of the more highly educated. And even when the homilies of the Fathers were read, they had to be rendered more or less freely in the language of the people. The Carolingian Reform-Synods of 813 expressly demanded the translation of the homilies into the people's tongue. The requirements of the clergy were supplied by various collections of homilies, such as were prepared for reading at monastic choir prayer (as, for example, those of Paul Warnefried), or others that offered an explanation of the Epistle and Gospels intended directly for the laymen's service. In this modest form the homily must have been used quite regularly in the following centuries even in the country—at least in Germany—in such a way, at any rate, that it shared the Sunday pulpit along with the repetition of the elementary Christian truths taken from the Symbol and the Our Father. The crest of the Middle Ages, and the appearance of the mendicant Orders, brought a new blossoming, if not of the homily, then surely of the sermon in general.

Although it would be an exaggeration to say that all church preaching should be limited to the framework of the Mass or perhaps even the homily, still there was from olden times a definite and restrictive pattern for the spiritual talk that followed on the reading, a pattern exacted by the circumstances in which it appeared. The talk was to be about the word of God that had been read from the Sacred Scriptures, it was not to stifle it but to apply it to the present day. Therefore the talk is basically a *homily*—the application of the Scripture just read. To this day, in the ordination of the Lector, his office is still designated as: to read for the preacher (*legere ei qui prædicat*).[1] This neither is nor was the spot to unfold the entire preaching of the Church. The homily was the living word of the Church taken up into the liturgy as proof of the higher world in which it lives and into which it enters after being renewed by the sacred mysteries.

Hence also the trend to make visible the hierarchical structure of the Church in the person of the homilist. Hence, too, the guarding as much as possible of the liturgical structure even in its outward appearance. As a rule the Bishop talks from his *cathedra*, and, as an expression of his authority, he is seated, or else standing on the steps that lead to the *cathedra*. A preacher like Chrysostom of course mounts the ambo for the convenience of his audience. According to a rule of the Egyptian Church, the bishop—but not the priest—holds the Gospel book in his hand.

The revival of the sermon during the height of the Middle Ages involved a separation from the liturgy, and also a departure from its homiletic character. It leaves the confines of the Mass in the form of a mission sermon of the new Orders. Even the stand of the preacher is moved into the body of the church, though it takes with it the old name: in French, for example, it takes the name of the *cathedra* (*chaire*; cf. the German *Predigtstuhl*), and in German the name is derived from the ambo as an extension of the chancel (*Kanzel*), but the English word "pulpit" is a mere descriptive term (from Lt. *pulpitum*, a platform or scaffold). Its site on the Gospel side still shows its connection with the reading of the Gospel. On the other hand, the very high pulpit towering over the heads of the listeners is apparently the result of the impassioned oratorical form of the sermon, a condition that also contributed to the fact that now the preacher generally speaks standing.

Although the teacher was seated, the audience (according to the prevailing custom of the ancient Church) was obliged to hear the lecture while standing. Augustine felt that such a rule was quite a strain during long delivery and therefore he praised the custom followed in other places where the people were seated. Cæsarius of Arles permitted the more feeble people to sit during the sermon or the readings, though they

---

[1] The *Pontificale Romanum* gives the bishop his choice between this wording and *legere ea quae prædicat*. But the sources seem to bear out *legere ei qui prædicat* as the original and primary meaning.

probably used the floor for this. Only the clerics were provided quite generally with seats in those early days. The faithful helped themselves with canes on which to lean. Only in modern times in our countries did the laity obtain pews, perhaps copying the Protestant churches.

As a simple homily, the address of the celebrant could follow upon the reading of the Gospel without any further intermediary or any special prayer-introduction. The preacher addressed the people at the beginning and end of his sermon with the usual greeting and began his delivery. Toward the end of the Middle Ages, however, it was the practice for the preacher to begin with an *Ave Maria* while everybody knelt. The custom is possibly traceable to the mendicant preachers. It is prescribed in the *Cæremoniale episcoporum* and seems to have been in use for a long time within the Mass. Alongside of the *Ave*, however, the *Veni, Sancte Spiritus* or the Lord's Prayer was also permitted.

Together with the prayer-introduction in this or that form, there was often also a special song to introduce the sermon, taken over from the independent sermon and adapted here to the sermon that followed the readings at Mass. The patterns that thus arise remind us of the preparatory prayers or songs which precede the readings in the oriental liturgies. And contrariwise, the independent Sunday parochial sermon at times had a very rich prayer ending, the basis of which was borrowed for its connection with the Mass or more precisely (as we shall see), taken from the old "Prayer of the Faithful."

8. The Credo

On Sundays and on certain feast days the last lesson (or the homily, as the case may be) is followed by the *Credo* as a sort of re-enforced echo. Although it is but a supplement on these days, still it gets such a performance at solemn service that both in duration and in musical splendor it often surpasses all the other portions of the Mass. It is precisely in this role of the *Credo* at the high Mass that a contrast is marked out—despite its import, the *Credo* offers the great masters of music only a simple and rather unpoetic verbal text. In addition, this text is stylized as the profession of an individual (*Credo, Confiteor*), exactly like other professions of faith. All the more reason to ask, why this formula of profession of faith secured the singular honor of being used at the celebration of Mass.

Our symbol was not composed just for the Mass. It first appears in the acts of the Council of Chalcedon (451) as the profession of "the 150 holy fathers who were assembled in Constantinople." As time passed the symbol was taken as a compilation summing up the belief proclaimed at the preceding councils of Nicea (325) and Constantinople (381); this is borne out by the current name of Nicene or Niceno-Constantinopolitan Creed. Not that its wording was immediately formulated by these councils. The symbol drawn up at Nicea, which concludes with the words *Et in Spiritum Sanctum*—only an anathema follows—does not coincide exactly with our *Credo* even in the foregoing parts. In the acts of the Council of Constantinople no symbol whatever was handed down and in the interval till Chalcedon there is never a reference to any such profession of faith drawn up there. The only matter ascribed to the synod at Constantinople is the expansion of the statement regarding the Holy Ghost.

In the Niceno-Constantinopolitan symbol we have the draft of a profession which, of all the various forms in use in the episcopal cities of the East, gained the widest acceptance, particularly after the approval accorded it at the Council of Chalcedon. We can track this draft even a little distance back into the fourth century. We discover it, almost complete, about 374 in Epiphanius, and, in a slightly simpler form, about 350 in Cyril of Jerusalem, who explained it to his candidates for Baptism. *We may therefore see in this basic text of the Niceno-Constantinopolitanum the ancient baptismal symbol of Jerusalem.* Our Mass *Credo* thus had originally the same purpose which our Roman "Apostles' Creed" had, the same purpose which it still serves at present, namely, as a profession of faith before Baptism. That is the reason why even in its original form the Mass Creed, like the Apostles', is set in the singular: *Credo.*

In the two texts mentioned we clearly have the typical instances of the basic form of the profession of faith in West and East. And these in turn give us an inkling of the common design underlying both. In both cases the content of our belief falls into three sections, comprising our belief in God the Creator, in Christ our Lord, and in the goods of salvation. And what is more to the point in a baptismal profession, these three sections are linked with the naming of the three divine Persons. Further, in both of these main forms the second section is enlarged through the inclusion of a more detailed profession of Christ. A peculiarity of the oriental type is that its structure was influenced not only by the command to baptize (Matt. 28:19) but also by a second scripture text, Eph. 4:4, which emphasizes the praise of unity: "one body and one spirit . . . one Lord, one faith, one baptism, one God and Father of all." This is the apparent clue to the stressing of oneness in this symbol: I believe in *one* God . . . in *one* Lord . . . in *one* Catholic and apostolic Church . . . I confess *one* baptism. With a certain pride the contrast is drawn between the division caused by error and

the oneness of God and the oneness of his revelation in Christ, Church
and Sacrament.

THE DESIGN OF THE CREDO

The design of the *Credo* will probably be rendered clearer in the following abstract, in which the texts of the older drafts are also indicated:

> I BELIEVE [1] IN ONE GOD, FATHER ALMIGHTY, MAKER OF HEAVEN AND
> EARTH,
> AND OF ALL THINGS VISIBLE AND INVISIBLE.
> AND IN ONE LORD JESUS CHRIST, THE ONLY-BEGOTTEN SON OF GOD
> WHO WAS BORN OF THE FATHER BEFORE ALL AGES,
> GOD OF GOD, light of light, very God of very God,
> begotten not made,
> being of one substance with the Father,
> THROUGH WHOM ALL THINGS WERE MADE.
> Who because of us men and for our salvation came down from
> heaven and was incarnate of the Holy Spirit of the Virgin Mary
> and WAS MADE MAN.
> HE WAS CRUCIFIED also for us under Pontius Pilate, suffered and was
> buried.
> And ON THE THIRD DAY HE ROSE AGAIN according to the scriptures,
> AND ASCENDED INTO HEAVEN,
> AND SITTETH AT THE RIGHT HAND OF THE FATHER
> AND HE SHALL COME AGAIN WITH GLORY TO JUDGE BOTH THE LIVING
> AND THE DEAD, WHOSE
> KINGDOM
> SHALL HAVE NO END.
> [and I believe]
> IN THE HOLY SPIRIT, the Lord and Giver of life,
> Who proceedeth from the Father AND THE SON, Who with the
> Father and the Son is adored and glorified,
> WHO SPOKE THROUGH THE PROPHETS.
> AND IN ONE HOLY CATHOLIC and apostolic CHURCH.
> I confess ONE BAPTISM UNTO THE REMISSION OF SINS.
> AND I look for THE RESURRECTION of the dead AND THE LIFE of the
> world to come. Amen.

CONTENT

The character of this symbol is distinguished by one trait—its theological clarity. While in our Apostles' Creed the faith is asserted simply

[1] The text as found in Epiphanius is printed in small capitals; the parts already attested
by Cyril of Jerusalem are in smaller letters. No account is taken of those additions in
Epiphanius or Cyril which have not survived in the received version.

and forthrightly, in this by contrast we have a theological and polemical profession aimed at giving orthodoxy a clear exposition. Still, after comparing this with other oriental forms of the symbol, we come to recognize the fact that but a few of the phrases are the result of the struggles of the fourth century. In the christological section these are the words "very God of very God, begotten not made, being of one substance with the Father," words with which the Council of Nicea had countered the heresy of Arius. All the other statements circumscribing the divinity of Christ are found in the baptismal confessions, and even where they are wanting in that of Jerusalem, they are contained in the more ancient one of Eusebius of Cæsarea (d. 340), who for his part was never suspected of having gone too far in any opposition to the Arians. But in contrast to this, all the older baptismal professions contained only one assertion regarding the Holy Ghost: "Who spoke through the prophets." Everything else was occasioned by the struggle against the Macedonians who drew the conclusions inherent in the Arian doctrine of the Logos and denied also the divinity of the Holy Ghost. Still the more complete profession regarding the Holy Ghost in its present-day wording appeared (as we can see above), in the symbol of St. Epiphanius even before the solemn condemnation of this heresy which took place at the Council of Constantinople (381).

Even aside from these additions which were first incorporated in opposition to heresy, there still remains in this Mass *Credo*, compared with the extreme terseness of our Apostles' Creed, a notable wealth of statement which serves not so much to oppose heresy as rather to unfold the contents of our faith. In the very first assertion about "God the Creator of heaven and earth," the creation is described by a second double phrase "of all things visible and invisible."

But in this basic text one point is given special prominence, the divinity of Christ. In its *kerygma*[2] of Christ, our Apostles' Creed also goes into detail regarding the mystery of the person of our Lord whom it introduces as the only-begotten Son of God; He was born of the Virgin Mary, conceived by the Holy Ghost. But these assertions refer immediately to His human nature, even if its wonderful origin suggests His godhead. The oriental *Credo*, however, adverts at once expressly to the eternal divinity of the Logos: "Born of the Father before all ages, God of God, light of light, through whom all things were made." Only the last phrase is taken word for word from St. John (1:3), but in the rest we can detect the tone of his language. The additions which the Nicene Creed here embodies, expressing with inexorable lucidity the uncreated divinity of Christ and His essential unity with the Father, dovetail easily

---

[2] For a fuller treatment of the implications of this term, cf. Johannes Hofinger, *The Art of Teaching Christian Doctrine*, U. of Notre Dame Press (1957), 4–7.

with the rest even stylistically, despite the unavoidable abstractness of the ideas. They round out the profession of faith into a tiny hymn.

The additional assertions which describe the entrance of the Logos into the world and His assumption of a human nature from the Virgin wind up the picture of the mysterious *person* of the Redeemer. One significant feature is the prominence given here to the work of salvation: "for us men and for our salvation came down from heaven." Rightly does this article become the center and turning point of the whole creed. In His mercy God wanted it that way, and so the inconceivable became a reality. We therefore fall upon our knees at the words *Et incarnatus est,* in awe of the mystery.[3] Some of the grandest creations of ecclesiastical music have here made the devout offering of their greatest endeavor, in the effort to help us conceive the meaning of that tremendous descent of the Son of God from heaven to bring peace to earth.

After the mystery of the person of the God-man is thus sketched out, the *Credo* turns to *His work,* which is again clearly designated in two steps: first the lowly path of pain and the cross and the grave (with a stressing of *pro nobis*), then the victorious surge of His Resurrection "according to the Scriptures," which even in the Old Testament had announced the concluding triumph of the Messias, His return to the glory of His Father, His judgment, and His kingdom without end, as these were already foretold in the message of the angel.

The third section of the symbol surveys the *fruit which has become ours as a result of the work of redemption.* In various texts of the ancient Church the first thing mentioned in this connection is the Holy Ghost, who is poured out over the believing congregation. This concept is likewise to be supposed in the basic form of our symbol. That He had already spoken through the prophets was the start of His activity. Its completion is the bestowal of the new life, as is added in the later supplement to the older text of the symbol. This supplement also takes into account His divinity; He is the Lord. He proceeds from the Father and from the Son. Rightfully is He given in the doxology the same adoration and the same honor as the other two. The series of predications seems to have been dictated mainly by certain formal considerations, as the Greek text indicates more clearly.

After the mention of the Holy Ghost there follows in nearly all the creeds—and here, too—*the mention of the Church* which is inspired and vitalized by His activity. It is one, as God is one, and as Christ is one. This one Church, to which we pledge ourselves, is holy, because it is filled by the Holy Ghost; it is catholic, because it stands open to all peoples; it is apostolic, because it rests on the foundation of the Apostles. The Church transfers its own life to its children by means of the sacra-

---

[3] This genuflection certainly goes back to the 11th century.

ments. Baptism, mentioned in the creed, stands for all the others which are based on it. In fact Confirmation and the Eucharist are linked with it. Its wonderful efficacy in taking away sin was mentioned by our Lord Himself amongst the basic elements of the glad tidings. A prospect of our final transformation to the likeness of the Risen One in the resurrection from the dead and in the life of eons to come—with this the creed concludes. The outpouring of the Spirit, holy Church, sacrament, glorious resurrection—that is the way by which the new creation and the new creature reach their perfection.

USE OF THE CREDO

This symbol was in use at Constantinople as a baptismal creed formula. Here on Good Friday it was also pronounced at public worship while the bishop catechized the candidates for Baptism. The same historian who mentions this also records that Timotheus, the Patriarch of this city (511–517), a man whose thinking was tainted with Monophysitism, was the first to order the symbol recited at every Mass. He did this in order to put his Catholic predecessors to shame and to emphasize his own zeal for the truth. This example was soon copied everywhere in the Orient. Thus the symbol attained a place in every Mass in all the oriental liturgies. Usually it was the Niceno-Constantinopolitan that was thus taken up, but not without a number of rather significant variants. However, it is not placed right after the Gospel, but only after the Prayer of the Faithful and the Great Entry, either before or after the kiss of peace—a location that makes it less a conclusion to the fore-Mass than rather a foundation and start for the sacrifice. Since the symbol was restricted by the *disciplina arcani*, it is not by chance that the dismissal of the catechumens (the formula for which has retained its ancient place in most rites of the East) had to precede.

The symbol is, as a rule, spoken by the people—thus in the Egyptian liturgies and mostly also in the Byzantine. Or it is spoken by a representative of the people. But it is never said by the priest, and it is never sung. In most of the oriental liturgies—but not in all—the communion of all the faithful is given expression by means of the plural form: we believe, we profess. It is also usually heralded by a call from the deacon.

In the same century in which the Niceno-Constantinopolitanum was for the first time admitted into the Mass in the Orient, it appears also in a similar employ in Spain, a portion of whose coastline was under Byzantine domination. When in 589 King Reccared and his Visigoths renounced Arianism, they made their profession of faith in this creed and it was then ordered said by all the people at every Mass right before the *Pater noster* so that, before the Body and Blood of the Lord were received, the hearts of all might be purified by faith. Thus the symbol here shares in the function of the *Pater noster* as a prayer of preparation for Communion; this was the position it also held, in passing, in the Byzantine Mass, and still holds today in the rite of Communion for the sick.

Two centuries later the creed also makes an appearance in France, just about the time that a reaction was setting in against the last offshoot of christological error, the Adoptionism of the Spanish bishops Elipandus and Felix who had been condemned at various synods since 792. It must have been about this time that Charlemagne introduced the symbol in his palace chapel at Aachen. Various indications point to the theory that the custom came to the Irish from the Spaniards, and was by them carried to the Anglo-Saxons and so, through Alcuin, the custom reached Aachen. In Aachen the symbol was sung after the Gospel. Charlemagne obtained the consent of Pope Leo III to his innovation, perhaps with the subsequent restriction to leave out the *Filioque*. But the custom took long to spread. Of the Carolingian sources of the ninth century a few mention it, others appear to know nothing about it. Not till the next century did it become general in the North. When the emperor Henry II came to Rome in 1014 he was surprised that at Rome the *Credo* was lacking in the Mass. The Roman clerics explained to him that the Roman Church had never been disturbed by error and therefore had no reason to profess the *Credo* so often. However the pope, Benedict VIII, gave in to the emperor's importunings. Still an instruction must have issued from Rome, restricting the *Credo* to Sundays and to those feasts of which mention is made in the symbol. As such the feasts of our Lord from Christmas to Pentecost are named, those of the Blessed Virgin, of the Apostles, of All Saints and the Dedication of a Church. The principle of selection, namely, "of those mentioned in the creed," recurs regularly in the liturgical commentators of the twelfth and thirteenth centuries. Gradually, however, other regulations were adopted till, with Burchard of Strassburg, the present-day rule came into being, according to which only the feasts of martyrs, virgins and confessors are without a *Credo*. Of the confessors, the Doctors of the Church—whose number, before Pius V, was restricted to the "Four great Doctors" (Ambrose, Jerome, Augustine and Gregory the Great)—took a place next to the Apostles as outstanding heralds of the faith to whom a *Credo* was due. And even the feast days of the other saints had the creed when they were celebrated with special solemnity. The *Credo* was thus conceived simply as a means of enhancing the festivity.

Our *Credo* was therefore originally a profession of faith at Baptism; one vestige of this, in the draft of the creed as we know it, is the singular in the formula: *credo*. Just as before Baptism, so here, too, it is the individual who professes his faith. But it is also a profession influenced by

the war against the christological heresies. Because of these its statements
were augmented, and it was set up as a barrier against them even in the
celebration of Mass, first of all in those lands which had become the
battleground. By the subsequent restriction to certain days—days which
show a certain internal relation to the contents of the symbol—a middle
way was found between the early almost belligerent affirmation of the
right belief and the calm inwardness of prayer to almighty God—a solution which in a certain sense bespeaks the peace which the Roman
Church has continued to maintain, ever vigilant for the purity of faith,
yet never permitting the movement of prayer and worship to be disturbed by loud protests against heresy. Thus the creed, the profession of
faith, is simply the conclusion of the reading service, the joyous "yes"
of the faithful to the message they have received. Even when viewed
in its systematic setting, the creed is an organic extension of the line
begun in the readings. Just as the sermon is joined to the lessons on certain occasions to further the teaching of God's word through His
Church, so on appointed days the catechetic and theological formulation
of that teaching is likewise annexed. And so the profession of faith forms
a solemn entrance-gate to the Mass of the Faithful.

The *Credo* was introduced into the Mass as the avowal of the whole
believing congregation. Necessarily, then, it ought to be spoken by the
whole congregation. In the East this was as a general rule always maintained, and at the start also in Spain. In France, too, the same idea was
kept in mind—the priest intoned the creed while standing at the center
of the altar; and the people carried it through to the end. The Mass commentators of the ninth century also ascribe the *Credo* to the people, and
even at a much later time it continued in many places to be entrusted
to them.

When one considers how much trouble must have been taken during
the era of the Carolingian reform to teach the people to recite the simple
Apostles' Creed in the vernacular, it is easy to imagine what results were
achieved with the much longer—and still Latin!—*Credo* in the Mass. A
practicable way out—a solution which agrees with that followed sometimes in the Orient—was to have the faithful recite the symbol they
knew. This seems to have been tried in northern France during the
twelfth century, but whether or not the vernacular was used is not certain. At any rate the attempt was not very widespread at that time,
though nowadays the practice is again being introduced in many places
in the dialogue Mass.

The difficulty of having the people recite the *Credo* was all the
greater when—contrary to the practice usual in the Orient—the words
were to be sung. True, *Credo*-songs played a conspicuous role in vernacular singing, but right now we are concerned with the Latin text of

the symbol. It is not surprising to find that even in the tenth century the performance of the *Credo* was turned over to the clergy who formed the choir at high Mass. This transfer was especially easy since the *Credo* was at that time apparently considered a substitute for the sermon. But the choir was then retained even independently of this.

Even so the chant at first remained in the simplest forms of a syllabic recitation. In addition, in many churches objection was raised to performing the *Credo* in two choruses, since everyone had to profess the entire creed. In contrast to the other chants of the Ordinary the manuscripts and even the early printed copies seldom contain more than a single tune, the ancient recitative. The Gregorian melodies remained generally plain; the melodies included in the present *Graduale Vaticanum* show this clearly. How different, once the *Credo* was set to polyphony. Often it became the show-piece amongst the chants of the Ordinary. In fact, because of its broad presentation and because of the musical unfolding of its inexhaustible contents, it has attained such an importance in the full course of the Mass that it leaves the eucharistic prayer (which, in its design, is much akin to it) quite in shadow. For the sacerdotal eucharistic prayer has much the same aim: to survey, in the form of a thanksgiving, the achievements of the divine plan of salvation which we grasp by faith. So true is this that words like *prædicatio, contestatio* appear as names for this prayer, names which could only be applied to a profession of faith; just as, contrariwise, the profession of faith itself is sometimes designated an eucharistia. And so true is this, that the older formulations of the eucharistic prayer are distinguished in little from a profession of faith. Because the text of the prayer of thanksgiving is kept plain and simple in the Roman Mass, the *Credo* has taken on an even greater importance. In the reawakening of all those concepts of our faith which center on Christ's life-work, in that reawakening with which every celebration of the Eucharist must begin, that reawakening which is the prime purpose of the whole reading service, that reawakening to which the anamnesis after the consecration recurs in a short and hurried word—in that reawakening the *Credo* has become a main element.

On the other hand, in tracing this tremendous growth of the *Credo* we encounter—very early, at that—the phenomena that manifest fatigue, the attempts to counterbalance the musical expansion by cutting down the text. It is an abuse that is to be found frequently enough even today where small choirs try to emulate bigger and more capable groups; in fact, it is an abuse that is almost unavoidable when small choruses pretend to do a many-voiced *Credo* that is beyond their power. But it is a practice that the Congregation of Sacred Rites has repeatedly condemned (SRC 3827 ad II). In any case the plain recitation of the creed by the whole congregation, as is done in the dialogue Mass, is far more in harmony with the original design of the *Credo* and with its place in the plan of the Mass-liturgy, far more in harmony than such and similar residue of a musical culture that is past.

9. The Dismissals

With the *Credo*, which we have for the moment surveyed, we have strictly speaking gone out of the sphere of the Mass of the Cathechumens; for the symbol is a hallowed formula, matter only for the faithful. However, it got its place at a time when there was no longer a question of the *disciplina arcani*, and one merely felt its close, intimate connection with the Gospel. But now, as we return to that early period during which there still existed a sharp boundary between the Mass of the Catechumens and the Mass of the Faithful, we must direct our attention to those forms which were attached to that boundary-line, and of which several remnants still exist.

It was always self-evident and (thanks be to God) still is for the most part even today, that a Christian instruction, a catechesis and a common reading from the Bible are concluded with a prayer. Therefore prayer had also to follow the readings and the instructions of the fore-Mass. And all the less could people forgo a special prayer when the fore-Mass was felt to be an independent entity. Actually the prayer of the entire congregation at this spot we find already attested in the oldest accounts. The prayer that was supposed to be said here, however, coincided with the dismissal of those whose presence at the further course of the holy sacrifice did not seem permissible. For the instructional service did not form a part of the introduction into the Christian world of faith for the catechumens alone; heretics as well as pagans were admitted as guests in the hope that many would in this way find the path to the faith. After the instructional service, however, they had to leave the congregation. The celebration of the Eucharist was the exclusive privilege of the children of the house. This conception was not a result of the *disciplina arcani*, which first came into existence in the third century and was in full force for only a comparatively short time; rather it was the simple expression of a sound Christian feeling, that at least the most sacred possession of the Church ought not be presented to the eyes and ears of all. This conception did not lose ground till the beginning of modern times, as a result of the conditions of a divided Christendom.

Then the question arose, whether these participants of the fore-Mass who were not of the same class as the rest, should be given a part in the community prayer, or whether they were to be dismissed beforehand. When the catechumens had their usual instruction this had to be concluded with a prayer, according to a third-century law. But a prayer said together with the faithful—that was to be avoided. Their common prayer would be looked upon as a strange, coarse and debasing admixture in the prayer of the Church—an idea which somehow continued effectual even later on. Nevertheless several solutions were possible. These participants could be let go after the readings without prayer or any further ado, or they could be permitted to say a certain prayer right at the beginning of the series of community prayers that followed, or they could be allowed to stay at least till that part of the prayer of the Church where, according to an established procedure, the faithful would pray for them and their own act of prayer could then be inserted here.

The first solution, a rather cold one, seems to have been employed in early times.

In the prime of the catechumenate at Antioch, the second solution was taken as a basis. It was so arranged that when the readings and sermon were over, the people were summoned to pray for those who had to leave, that is, to add their Kyrie eleison to the series of supplications which the deacon pronounced for them and during which these persons lay stretched on the floor. Then they were summoned to rise and bow for the blessing which the bishop in solemn prayer bestowed on them. Only then were they asked to leave. During St. Chrysostom's time an independent prayer-act of this sort was devoted to the catechumens, the energumens and the public penitents. The Apostolic Constitutions (belonging to the same area) inserted before the public penitents, as a particular class, the candidates for Baptism who were undergoing their last preparation. Each one of these groups, when it had received the blessing of the celebrant, in the manner previously stated, was summoned by a call from the deacon to leave. After all these had been dismissed the doors were closed and the formal Prayer of the Faithful in the narrower sense followed.

However, in the majority of the liturgies with which we are familiar, the third solution was chosen, namely the insertion of a procedure like the above in the place where prayers were usually said for these respective groups. Moreover, outside the Syrian ambit, only catechumens and penitents were taken into consideration already at an earlier period, and in many provinces of the Church, even of the East, and almost commonly in the West, only the catechumens came under consideration, since as a rule public penitents (who after all were baptized) were permitted to remain during the sacrifice. True, they were only allowed to remain there as mute spectators, and not till at the end of Mass was a blessing (at least for a time) devoted to them.

RITES OF DISMISSAL

The rite of this dismissal was of a form similar to the one at Antioch, although it did not always possess such solemn pageantry as there. It was essential that a blessing with prayer be imparted to the group concerned; this was often done by the celebrant's laying his hands on each one individually. With this was conjoined the deacon's cry for dismissal: Go, catechumens! In this consisted the *missa catechumenorum*.

With the disappearance of the catechumenate the corresponding dismissals had naturally to be omitted or at least contracted. In the Byzantine Mass alone not only is the cry of dismissal retained—and this is a fourfold phrase!—but even the prayer for the catechumens (as a second prayer after the Gospel) is still continued today. In the West and particularly in the sphere of the Roman liturgy, as we shall see more in detail, even the prayer of the congregation in this place has been sharply curtailed. In Rome it had completely disappeared, even in an early period, perhaps at a time when there were still catechumens. So the prayer for them, too, was dropped in the ordinary service.

Elsewhere corresponding forms survived somewhat longer. As a matter of fact a formal dismissal of the catechumens right after the reading service, in which the celebrating bishop had a share, is reported in Milan, Gaul, Spain, and North Africa. The *Expositio* of the Gallican liturgy (a work of the seventh century) still makes particular mention of a prayer for the people, and of one for the catechumens after the readings and the sermon. Both prayers were performed by "Levites" and priests; that is, in form of a litany-like alternating prayer and a collect following. The deacon's voice directed the catechumens and finally called upon them to go. The Upper-Italian churches had a similar rite for dismissing the catechumens with prayer. It was employed with certain individual acts of preparation for Baptism. That it was also used at the end of Mass we know to be true only about Milan, where the twelfth-century documents still prescribe the rite for the Sundays in Lent.

Even in the various acts of preparation for Baptism, Rome did not have any such solemn dismissal. The scrutinies which the candidates for Baptism had to undergo during the course of Lent did indeed contain exorcisms, layings-on of hands, and priestly blessings. But even (for instance) after the solemn sharing of Gospel, symbol and Our Father, in the great scrutinium of the "opening of the ears," the conclusion did not contain any further blessing, but simply the cry of the deacon: "Let the catechumens depart." This manner of dismissal was used in cathedrals along with the complete rite of the scrutinies until the very end of the Middle Ages; within the Mass on the days during Lent it occurred at first before the Gospel then, from the great scrutinium on, after it, but only on the few occasions which were kept for this. For it seems that according to Roman regulations the catechumens, as a closed group, did not appear regularly at the usual divine service even in more ancient times. Formulas similar to the previously mentioned Roman ones were also used in other churches in requesting withdrawal.[1]

A somewhat enlarged cry for dismissal was customary on solemn occasions in various parts of Italy. It was used not only on Holy Saturday before the consecration of the baptismal water, but also (at least in Milan, it would seem) within the Mass, namely, when the bishop confided the *Credo* to the candidates for Baptism, after the Gospel on the evening before Palm Sunday. In this case it is meant for the sacred text of the symbol which came under the *disciplina arcani*. The sixfold cry of the deacon, which was solemnly sung like our *Ite missa est* and the individual phrases of which were repeated by a second deacon or a subdeacon, was as follows:

> If anyone is a catechumen, let him leave!
> If anyone is a heretic, let him leave!
> If anyone is a Jew, let him leave!
> If anyone is a pagan, let him leave!
> If anyone is an Arian, let him leave!
> Let anyone who has no business here leave!

Considering the wide circulation of this last formula, from Milan and Aquileia to Beneventum and Bari, it is not difficult to conclude that Rome was, if not the point of origin, at least a point of intersection. Still the formula must have gone out of use here quite early, because Roman documents make no mention of it.

10. The General Prayer of the Church

Just as the readings of the fore-Mass were everywhere the most excellent form of the reading service, so the prayer which followed upon it—apart from the *eucharistia*—was from ancient times regarded as the most excellent prayer, *the* prayer, simply, of the Church. Its importance became clear already in the earliest accounts. After the sermon by the bishop (here is the description of Sunday service as given by Justin) "we all stand up and recite prayers." These prayers of the assembled brethren are the first in which the neophyte takes part. In them prayer

---

[1] The dismissal of the catechumens and that of the penitents are separate entities occurring at different times, the latter taking place at the end of Mass, not here. This should dispel the doubts of A. King, *Liturgy of the Roman Church*, London (1957), 264, that "Jungmann is mistaken in identifying the Lenten *orationes super populum*, of which there are several in the Leonine Sacramentary, with the blessing over the penitents." One might also point out that it is customary to give a reference when calling into question the findings of another!—REV.

is said "for ourselves, for the neophyte, and for all others everywhere." Prayer "after the delivery of the homily" is a common term in the third and fourth century in Egypt. Later on we meet the prayer after the readings in all the liturgies of the East. In the West it is plainly indicated by Hippolytus; besides, Cyprian clearly refers to it when he speaks of the *Communis oratio*. In Augustine's time a large number of sermons ended with the formula: "Turn to the Lord," that is to say, common prayer followed upon the sermon, and during it, as was always customary, the congregation turned towards the East. In the beginning this prayer was antiphonally recited by celebrant and congregation, a practice that remained in the Roman liturgy and partly in the Egyptian. The bishop led, by first inviting to prayer; then recited his own portion and the congregation answered. Then as time went on, the deacon, who at first only announced short directions, began to take a more prominent place in most liturgies. By the end of the fourth century he took over the invitation to prayer, the announcing of the special intentions which combined into a litany (*ektene* or *synapte*) and to which the congregation answered with the *Kyrie eleison* or some other similar invocation; only then did the celebrant start to pray.

FORMS OF THE GENERAL PRAYER

In the Roman liturgy, in which the older and simpler form was preserved, this general prayer is still in use once a year, on Good Friday. Even in the eighth century this practice was still customary also at least on the Wednesday of Holy Week. It is a well-grounded hypothesis that in these Good Friday prayers, whose echo goes back to the first century,[1] we have the general prayer of the Roman Church in the exact wording in which it was performed after the readings and the homily in the Roman congregation at their regular services since the third century.[2] The petitions that are here offered in nine parts: for the church, for the pope, for the assembled clergy, for the ruler, for the catechumens, for all who are in straits and in danger, for the heretics and schismatics, for the Jews and for the heathens, show up, except for the last two mentioned, and for occasional different groupings, in the general church prayer of other liturgies.

Still in the eastern liturgies, and especially in the litanies introduced by the deacon, which correspond to the invitations to prayer in the Roman Good Friday prayers, numerous other petitions are mentioned, and here

[1] Cf. the Epistle of St. Clement of Rome to the Corinthians, c. 59–61.

[2] For the great antiquity of the Good Friday orations preserved today and already extant in the oldest sacramentaries, Baumstark, *Missale Romanum*, 20 f., refers to the naming of *confessores* after the series of clerics: the prayer belongs to the period of persecution, when those who suffered for the faith were given the honors and rights of clerics; cf. Hippolytus, *Trad. Ap.* (Dix, 18 f.).

they are answered by a supplication of the people. Peace on earth, prosperity in the field, the country or the city or the monastery, the sick, the poor, widows and orphans, travelers, benefactors of the poor and of the Church, eternal rest for the dead, forgiveness for sinners, an untroubled life, a Christian death—these are the intentions recommended to prayer. In the Egyptian liturgies the proper rising of the Nile and beneficial rains are not forgotten. The respective prayers of the celebrant are mostly on more general terms. They follow the pattern of invocations spoken by deacon and people, but bunch several of them together and thus give the course of the prayer its divisions. Usually three such parts are noticed. In Egypt the ending of the general prayer said after the dismissal of the catechumens, "the Prayer of the Faithful"—the only portion that has survived—still retains the name of "the three". In it prayer is offered for the peace of the Church, for the bishop and clergy, for the entire Church and for the worshippers present. Opposed to this, the Byzantine liturgy distinguishes only a first and a second prayer of the faithful, the contents of which very early underwent quite a process of change.

In the other eastern liturgies, the retrogressive evolution ended up with only one such prayer form, made up of the diaconal litany and the celebrant's prayer, similar in structure to the type handed down from older times, though with richer developments. Finally, the East also has the one instance to prove that almost the last trace of the former general prayer of the Church has disappeared.

This is also the case in our Roman Mass as we know it since the sixth century. After the Gospel or the *Credo*, it is true, the priest addresses himself to the congregation with the usual greeting, and adds the invitation to pray: *Oremus.* But he himself then reads out of the missal the text of the offertory which the choir immediately begins. Nor is any form of prayer anywhere indicated for the congregation.[3] In the oldest sacramentaries and *ordos*, which hand down this isolated invocation, no other prayer follows except the *oratio super oblata*, our *secreta. There is nothing to keep us from recognizing in the secret the corresponding prayer of the priest.* For the *oratio super oblata* was at that time spoken, as we shall see, in a loud voice just like the other orations. Likewise it is patterned as a prayer said in the name of the congregation, just as the other orations are, and therefore it requires, no less than these, an introductory invitation to pray and a greeting. Both these elements are present at the offertory, only separated from the oration by a pause. But even the pause involves nothing surprising. It is a time for the prayer by the people, though not announced by a *Flectamus genua*, since in the stricter confines of the sacrifice a bending of the knee, according to

[3] The silent prayers of the Offertory do not come into consideration as an explanation of the isolated *Oremus*, since they are all much more recent.

ancient modes, is not to be thought of. That is the explanation for the lone *Oremus.*

The only thing standing in the way of our recognizing in this formula the ancient concluding oration of the faithful is that in content the prayer is simply and indubitably an *oratio super oblata.* But this need not surprise us. For even in the Byzantine liturgy we noted the same process of change, indeed in two instances at least, namely, in the "first" and the "second" prayer of the faithful. But while here prior to the dismissal of the catechumens a first section of the general prayer of the Church remained unshortened, viz., the fervent *ektene* with the corresponding prayer of the priest, nothing corresponding to it was kept in the Roman liturgy. This seeming disregard of the Roman Mass for the general prayer of the Church ties in with the fact that in its place some substitution was or would be made: in the intercessory prayers that meanwhile found entrance within the canon, and also in the *Kyrie*-litany which begins to emerge at the start of the Mass simultaneously with the disappearance of the prayer of the Church. Probably the general prayer of the Church no longer had (if it ever had) the same extent in connection with the sacrifice which it showed when it was the conclusion of an independent prayer service. And therefore very probably the offertory procession was inserted a long time ago in the pause after the last *Oremus*, and correspondingly also the content of the oration was newly devised. What preceded was at last naturally dropped.

Nevertheless there are traces still to be found of the foregoing prayer of the Church. With a certain regularity the Gelasian Sacramentary—and partly also the Leonine—has an addition to the present-day pattern of one oration (our collect) preceding the *oratio super oblata* (our secret); instead we find not one but two, both having the same form and both of a similar general character. Several conjectures have been made about this twofold prayer. We will be nearest to the truth if we assume that the second oration was to be said after the Gospel, and if we see in it a parallel with the *oratio super sindonem*, which follows the Gospel in the Milanese Mass. Even in the earlier Roman liturgy we occasionally find examples of an *oratio post evangelium*, innovations such as could arise at a time which no longer coupled the secret with the *Oremus*, but which had a living realization that a real closing prayer should follow the readings. Still such an intermediary oration did not survive. The secret in the Roman Missal remained the only formula in which, in place of the former general prayer of the Church between readings and sacrifice, the priest takes up the prayer according to the style and language of the orations. And when in it the *preces populi* are often explicitly mentioned alongside of the *oblationes* which are presented to God, we can see here the traces of the prayer of the faithful which formed a lower level over which was laid the thought of the offertory.

SPECIAL EVOLUTION

Besides all this we still have to dwell on a special evolution of the old prayer of the faithful, a development in the territory of the early Gallican liturgy, within the frame of the Roman Mass, though not in the Roman Missal. Gallican traditions here proved very tenacious.

In the year 517 a council of Lyons mentions the prayer of the people. What this was we learn more precisely when the exposition of the Gallican Mass in the seventh century speaks of prayers after the homily which the Levites solemnly recited for the people and in which the priests made intercession for the sins of the people. There is reference here apparently to a single litany spoken by the deacon or deacons with a collect following *post precem*. Under this name, the contemporary Gothic Missal also actually contained a corresponding formula for the priest for Christmas and Easter services. Likewise examples of the litany of the people are preserved in certain texts in which the Gallican material has been fitted to the Roman: in the Irish Stowe Missal, where each of the petitions is followed, after the Gallican manner, by the people's response, "We pray Thee, O Lord; hear and have mercy"; *or* "Grant it to us, O Lord, grant it to us," and in the Freiburg Pontifical of the ninth century, where the schema of the litany of All Saints forms the groundwork.

When in the eighth century the Frankish Church turned to using the Roman liturgy and found in the newly received forms no palpable traces of the erstwhile general prayer of the Church, there must have been some repercussions also here in Frankish territory in regard to this prayer. For what now appear are either remnants of an old tradition or even products obviously created in an untimely attempt to achieve new forms.

It was a matter of preserving old relics in those various cases in which, after the readings and the sermon, we find the people repeating the *Kyrie eleison*. But the meaning of this isolated *Kyrie eleison*, still found today in the Milanese liturgy, was unclear even in the height of the Middle Ages. The people repeated the cry of *Kyrie*, not only after the clergy had recited the symbol but even during its recitation, and it was explained as signifying among other things a praise of God for the faith received. Then here and there the *Kyrie* turned into a *Leis*, the German hymn which is to be found in many places since the twelfth century at the close of the sermon. But alongside of all this, new forms sprang up, the basic pattern of which is seen in Regino of Prüm (d. 915). On Sundays and feast days after the sermon the priest is to recommend to the faithful a general prayer for various needs: for the rulers, for the heads of the churches, for peace, against plagues, for the sick, and for the departed. The people were to recite quietly an Our Father each time, while the priest recited the corresponding Latin oration. The votive Masses of the Gelasian Sacramentary offered the priest a sufficient supply of such orations. Other orations survived from the Gallican liturgy, as the Leofric Missal indicates.

In many French-speaking dioceses the tradition of Regino has been preserved to this day with remarkable purity in the so-called *prières du prône*. Their wording, while keeping to the basic structure, varies in different places. A form very widespread today has the following outline: After an introductory reference to the Sunday and feast-day offering, there is mention first of a list of prayer intentions: for Church and clergy, for secular rulers, for benefactors, for the soldiers of the parish, for the sick and for sinners. Here follows a *Pater* and *Ave* recited in common, or—what must have been the original—Psalm 122, a silent *Pater noster* and, after the corresponding versicles, the Latin oration. Then follows a second invitation to prayer, this time for the departed. Psalm 129 is recited, the *Requiem æternam*, and again the corresponding oration. Then follow the announcements for the coming week.

On German soil, on the contrary, no such well-adorned form was able to unfold. Of course one can still see a trace of the forms of the older traditions in a German formula of the twelfth century in which a long drawn-out invitation to prayer is divided into two parts: for the living and for the dead, and closes both times with the command to raise a "cry." But for the rest the practice we find from this time on, is that the priest mentions a fairly long list of prayer intentions after the sermon, which usually begin with the temporal and spiritual rulers, but outside of that follows no strict order. Selection, grouping and wording are much interchanged. Even in the same diocese differing practices occur. The participation of the laity was limited to a high degree and tended gradually to disappear entirely. Maybe in the beginning there was a *Kyrie eleison* by the parish after each part. Nevertheless we meet such a chant usually at the end of the entire list. But this too faded out. Towards the end of the Middle Ages we note the practice of inviting the faithful to recite an *Ave*, or a *Pater* and *Ave* after each part. Later a single *Pater* and *Ave* was recited at the end, or once more all noticeable prayer activity of the faithful drops out.

In these circumstances it was indeed a step forward when St. Peter Canisius in 1556–57 wrapped the long list of the current prayer intentions into one single all-embracing and theologically excellent prayer, and began to spread this around. He found sympathy almost everywhere for this idea. His composition prevails to this day as the "general prayer" of the German dioceses; more than this, it has in many places taken the spot in the divine service which belonged to the ancient general prayer:

after the sermon, where Sunday after Sunday it is said by the entire congregation in chorus, and in places, in fact, it has for a long time been said within the Mass itself.

11. Further Adjuncts to the Sermon

Alongside the General Prayer of the Church, other texts in the course of time were also adjoined to the end of the sermon, but no particular order of succession was ever made standard for them. Some of these have come and gone like the wind, others have at least left a permanent mark. The chief of these additions are the announcements, the formulas for *popular catechesis*, and the *"open confession."*

First of all, the end of the sermon was always considered a good spot— though not the only one—to make the announcements to the people, telling them of the future plans for worship or of other matters of interest to the congregation. Pope Leo the Great (to cite one example) at the end of his Embertide sermon always reminded his hearers of the fast days during the coming Ember week and invited them to attend the vigil on the eve of the next Sunday. The practice during the late Middle Ages was much the same, detailed explanation being given of the sanctoral calendar for the week following. Indeed the custom is still maintained to a great extent at the present.

Secondly, this spot right after the homily, or perhaps even in its place, was usually selected for a modest form of popular catechesis, in accordance with the decrees of Charlemagne. The heart of this catechetical instruction consisted of the Our Father and the Apostles' Creed. These formulas had to be explained or at least recited with the people. Often in the course of the Middle Ages the prescription was inculcated anew. Later, from the thirteenth century on, the Ave Maria and the Ten Commandments were added to the materials for catechism, besides the seven sacraments, and at least several times a year other lists or enumerations, as built up in the systematic instruction of the later Middle Ages, and finally "Acts of Faith, Hope and Charity" with other allied formulas.

Insofar as prayer-texts were concerned, the saying of these formulas was on the borderline between an impressive repetition and real praying. General prayer and popular catechesis were therefore often intermixed and combined. Here, too, French tradition has maintained a fixed arrangement with clear limits right down to the present.

"OPEN CONFESSION"

Sometime after the year 1000 another act of purification put in an appearance, connected loosely either with the Prayer of the Church or with the catechetical texts. This act, which was to precede all further prayer and the start of the sacrifice itself, was called the "Open Confession" (*Offene Schuld*). It is an expanded *Confiteor* said in the vernacular. The German texts for this are amongst the most ancient monuments of the German language. At first (since the ninth century) they served patently for the sacramental confession of individuals. But just as the profession of faith in its original singular form was transferred from the baptismal rite into public worship, so now the formula of acknowledging our sin was transferred from the sacrament of Penance. In this instance, however, the complete sacramental rite was originally united with the formula, at least in a limited way, even at Holy Mass. For after the tenth century it became customary to include all the faithful congregated in church in the rite of the reconciliation of penitents on Holy Thursday. And soon this grew into the practice of granting a similar benefit to the faithful also on other days. Already by the middle of the eleventh century it was the custom in Rhenish churches for the preacher after every sermon to make the faithful raise their hands and confess their faults. Then they pronounced over them the then customary formula of sacramental absolution, a variant of our *Indulgentiam*—to which the *Misereatur* was soon prefixed.

Of course it was well known even then that this type of general absolution, without a special individual confession, was not in itself enough for mortal sins; in fact this was inculcated very emphatically. But the practice was so highly treasured that it continued for long even after the sacramental character was denied it (in the period of Scholasticism), and it was no longer performed with sacramental intent. It is even practiced today to some extent, but usually only at the end of the Sunday sermon preached outside Mass.

But it is also retained in the solemn pontifical Mass, in the course of which our rite was already taken for granted as a fixed constituent as early as the twelfth century, and is still, in a way, taken for granted even today. At present it is merely a substitute for the sacramental absolution after the announcement of the indulgences, and the formula of blessing is superadded to that of absolution.

What we have here in substance is an attempt—only halfway successful—to find for the faithful here at the start of the sacrifice a counterpart to that preparation and purification which was provided for the celebrant and his assistants at the beginning of the fore-Mass in the *Confiteor* and the prayers accompanying it. Thus an idea which had once been realized in the primitive Church once more strove to take tangible shape.

Part Four

I. THE OFFERTORY

1. The Offertory Procession of the Faithful

When the lessons have been concluded with the prayer of those assembled, and when all who are not fully competent members of the congregation have departed, it is possible to proceed to the main event in the celebration, the renewal of Christ's institution. The Master had inaugurated the eucharistic mystery under the tokens of bread and wine—bread, such as was to be found on the table of the Last Supper, and the cup which stood before Him, these He took and changed into the heavenly gift. Bread and wine must therefore be ready at hand when the celebration of the Mass is to begin.

This readying of bread and wine need not, of course, be a ritual action. It might be taken care of, some way or other, by anyone before the beginning of the ceremonies. In the most ancient accounts, in fact, we find no traces of a special stressing of this preparatory activity. As long as the Eucharist was joined to the fraternal meal there was scarcely any occasion for such special stress, because the gifts were already on the table. Even in Justin's description the matter is recounted simply and impersonally: bread is brought in, and wine and water. No particular formalities are observed, no symbolism introduced into the movement. This ties in with the strict aloofness which the nascent Church in the first two centuries showed towards material matters, preferring to emphasize, in opposition to pagan and Jewish sacrificial customs, the spiritual nature of the Christian cult. Passing over the earthly bread and wine, the Church's attention focused on the spiritual, not to say heavenly, gift which proceeds from her *Eucharistia,* and on the thanksgiving which pours out heavenward from the hearts of men—a worship which is indeed "in spirit and in truth."

But near the end of the second century we begin to see a trend away from this severe attitude. To oppose the repudiation of matter, which was a doctrine of the growing Hellenistic Gnosis, it was necessary to stress the value of the earthly creation, even in divine worship. The peril then no longer lay in the materialism of heathen sacrificial practices, but in the spiritualism of a doctrine that hovered just on the borderline of Christianity.

So the Eucharist also appeared in a new light. The heavenly gift had an earthly origin; it was from the "firstlings of creation" that it proceeded. In Irenæus, as we saw, this point was emphasized for the first time. The approach towards God, this movement in which the Lord's body and blood were offered up, begins to include the presentation of material gifts which were thus drawn into the liturgical activity. In Tertullian we see the faithful bringing their gifts, and their action is described as an *offerre* directed to God. Similarly, in Hippolytus of Rome not only are the bread and wine (brought in by the deacons before the *eucharistia* of the bishop) called "oblation," but the consecrated gifts are designated "the oblation of holy Church." In another place, describing the liturgy of Baptism, we see that the faithful—at least the newly baptized—"offer up" their gifts for the Eucharist.

By the time we reach Cyprian it has already become a general rule that the faithful should present gifts at the eucharistic solemnity. This is evident from Cyprian's scolding a rich woman for her lack of charity in failing to bring a gift. Apparently the individual worshiper was bound not only to contribute to the community poor box (*corban*) but also to make an offering for the altar, and from Cyprian's words it is quite clear that this offering was nothing more nor less than the bread and wine of the sacrifice.[1]

The evolution must have been such that the offerings which had always been made for the needs of the Church and the poor were gradually drawn more closely into the liturgical pattern. The tie-in with the eucharistic celebration was all the easier since it had been customary to think of every gift to the Church and the poor as a gift to God, or even to designate it as an offering, an oblation. Thus, such gifts of Christian charity were joined to the offering of the Eucharist. It was, then, but a step to connect the offering made by the faithful with the ritual preparation of the gifts for the eucharistic sacrifice—a step which would be taken naturally in an age which was liturgically alive. Thus we find in almost all the liturgies since the fourth century an offering (in some form or other) of gifts directed towards the Eucharist. As a passing custom it was practically universal in the Church. In the Orient, it is true, only fragmentary vestiges have survived. There the connection with the gift-offering at Mass was not very close. At any rate this holds true of the Antiochene-Byzantine area.

---

[1] Cyprian, *De opere et eleemos.*, c. 15 (CSEL, III, 384).

VARIOUS FORMS

The offerings could be made, for instance, before the beginning of the service, being placed in a side-room specially designated for this purpose. Thence the things necessary for the Eucharist were transferred to the altar at the beginning of the sacrifice. The ceremonial accompanying this transfer, first seen in the work of pseudo-Dionysius, expanded gradually into the Great Entrance which takes the place of our offertory and is a climax in the Byzantine liturgy. Preceded by torches and incense, the deacon and priest carry the host and the chalice, reverently covered, from the *prothesis* through the nave of the church and back into the sanctuary. Meanwhile, in the procession the King of all, surrounded by hosts of angels unseen, is greeted and honored in song. Similar forms of a ceremonial transfer of the sacrificial gifts are to be found in other liturgies of this cycle, or at least they can be reconstructed from the vestiges that remain.

In the Gallo-Frankish Church the same had been in use for a long time in a fully-developed form. Obviously, with an elaborate form such as this, an offering on the part of the people within the Mass itself was entirely out of the question. But this does not mean that they made no offering at all. By no means.

For it is precisely from the Gallic Church of this period that we have clear evidence of the part the people took in this, among other things a directive of the National Council of Macon (585), in which the offering of the faithful—consisting of bread and wine—is re-emphasized, with special reference to the fact that the usage was traditional. The faithful made their offering before the beginning of the service in the place set aside for this purpose. Similar arrangements must be presupposed in the Orient, too, wherever there is mention of offerings by the people.

In the ancient Milanese and Roman liturgies, and probably also in the North African, the offering of the faithful was very closely bound up with the eucharistic sacrifice. From the last of these, the North African liturgy, we get our oldest accounts of the offering of the faithful, and the customs connected with it are quite fully expounded, especially in St. Augustine. In Africa it was possible to bring one's offerings to the altar day after day, as Monica was wont to do. The priest himself received what was offered by the people, and in turn he offered these things to God. Thus the offering and oblation of the gifts was built into the very structure of the Mass. This is also certified by the report of the singing of psalms which was introduced at this time "before the oblation" as well as at the communion.

How the offertory was conducted at the papal stational service in seventh century Rome, we know in fullest detail. Here the gifts were not brought by the people to the altar, but were collected by the celebrant and his retinue. After the Gospel the pope and his assistants first approached the nobility and received from them, according to their rank, their offerings of bread, while the archdeacon who followed accepted the wine (which was presented in special flasks or cruets and poured it into a large chalice which was held by a subdeacon who, in turn, emptied this into a still larger vessel. In the same manner the pope handed the breads to a subdeacon accompanying him, who laid them in a large cloth (perhaps a linen sack) held by two acolytes. One of the bishops, assisted by a deacon, then took over and continued to collect the offerings. Meanwhile, the pope left the men's side, and moved to the *confessio* where on feast days he received the offerings of the higher court officials; then he proceeded to the women's side to receive the gifts of the ladies of the nobility. It was then the duty of the archdeacon to prepare the bread offerings on the altar, with the help of subdeacons who handed him the breads which had been collected. He laid out as much as seemed to be needed for the Communion of the people. After this was done the pope himself took up the bread gifts of the assisting clergy and laid on the altar his own offering, which consisted of two breads which the *subdiaconus oblationarius* had brought along. For the chalice, only the offering presented by the pope himself and his group was used, or perhaps a little was taken out of the large vessel containing the wine offered by the people, and this was poured into the "holy chalice." After the water, offered by the singing-boys, was commingled with the wine, the chalice was placed on the altar, to the right of the bread offered by the pope.

The general outlines of this oblation rite are still to be discerned some five hundred years later.

Of the many gifts which were thus gathered, we can readily understand that only a small portion could be used for the altar. What was done with the rest? Where, first of all, was it kept during the service? Amongst the gold and silver objects which the Latern basilica acquired from Constantine, the *Liber pontificalis* lists "seven altars of purest gold." There was but one altar in any one church, as we know full well. These, then, must have been tables to hold the offertory gifts. The fact that they were seven coincides with the fact that there were seven deacons who were called upon "to bestow their care upon tables" as once the deacons did in Jerusalem. On these tables, which were set up somewhere in the forepart of the basilica,[2] the gifts of bread and wine were laid as an oblation to God.[3] Then, insofar as the needs of the clergy did not require

---

[2] Th. Klauser gives it as his opinion that there is a connection between this and the origin of the transepts in the Constantinian basilicas. Room had to be made for setting up each table.

[3] This harmonizes with the fact that the formulas of the *oratio super oblata* in the *Sacramentarium Leonianum*, as well as in our own missal, for that matter, repeatedly

them, they were set aside primarily for the poor, whose care was amongst the chief duties of the deacons.

In other churches of the West, and more especially in the Roman liturgy after it was transplanted to Frankish countries, the oblation was metamorphosed into an offertory procession of the faithful. After the *Credo* a line was formed, which wended its way to the altar. First came the men, then the women; the priests and deacons joined in after them, with the archdeacon bringing up the rear. Frankish interpreters compared the procession to the parade of the multitude that went out to meet and acclaim our Lord on Palm Sunday.

Here, too, bread and wine form the offertory gift of the faithful. The English Synod of Cealychythe (Chelsea, 787) stresses the prescription that the offering should be bread, not cake. As a rule the bread was carried to the altar in a little white cloth; but mention is made also of woven baskets. The celebrant and his assistants went down to meet the offerers at the spot dictated by custom. We learn that the gifts were placed on a large paten carried by an acolyte. But even when they were offered up at the altar they were no longer set down on the altar itself, but "behind the altar." For even when they still consisted of bread and wine, they were no longer intended for consecration. The reception of Communion had sunk to such a minimum that the bread offered by the faithful was superfluous. Besides, usually only unleavened bread was used for the altar, and this was generally procured in some other way; in the years to follow, special regulations were made regarding its preparation. Nevertheless, the offertory procession survived for quite some time, or rather, to put it more correctly, an outgrowth and development of it now put in an appearance almost everywhere.

MATERIAL GIFTS

Granting the principle that, besides the Eucharist, material gifts also could be presented to God, it was not long before the offerings consisted of objects other than bread and wine. From the era of Constantine we have the mosaic from the floor of the large double church excavated at Aquileia; here is the representation of an offertory procession in which men and women are bringing not only bread and wine, but also grapes, flowers, and a bird. For that reason, it became necessary from early times to make regulations specifying in what manner these offerings could be made. A synod of Hippo in 393 says categorically: "At the Sacrament of

---

mention a plurality of altars on which the offerings of the people are laid: *tua, Domine, muneribus altaria cumulamus*. On the other hand, in the formulas of the post-communion the *mensa* is referred to exclusively in the singular.

the Body and Blood of Christ nothing is to be offered except bread and wine mixed with water." About the same time the Apostolic Canons stipulate: "When a bishop or priest, contrary to the institutions of the Lord about the sacrifice at the altar, offers up something else: honey or milk, or, in place of [the right kind], wine turned to vinegar, or fowl, or any type of beast or vegetable, in opposition to the mandate, he should be deposed. Aside from ears of wheat and grapes in season and oil for the lamps and incense, nothing should be brought to the altar at the time of the sacrifice. All other fruits should (as firstlings) be sent to the bishop or the priests at their home and not to the altar; it is clear that the bishop and priests distribute these too among the deacons and the other clergy." These ordinances were repeated and expanded also in the West during the ensuing centuries. Amongst the objects meriting the honor of being allowed to be brought to the altar, there appear, in addition to the oil for the lamps, especially wax and candles. Even at the present time, during the Mass of ordination, the newly ordained bring the bishop a lighted candle, which is presented to him.

Next we hear that in many churches "precious ecclesiastical furnishings" destined for the church were laid on the altar at the offertory procession on great feasts. Even the transfer of immovable property was often executed by handing over a deed or voucher at the offertory. From the eleventh century on, the offering of money began to come to the fore. Peter Damian tells, as something still out of the ordinary, that two prominent ladies offered goldpieces at his Mass. But more and more the offering of bread and wine was made by the clerics alone, and in monastic churches by the monks. Only in unusual circumstances was the presentation of the bread and wine by lay people continued, as, for instance, at the coronation of Kings, or at the consecration of virgins, perhaps also on certain great feasts and, in some instances, at the burial services for the dead. So, since the twelfth century, in explaining the offertory, the enumeration of offerings usually begins with gold: Some offer gold, like the Wise Men from the East, others silver, like the widow in the Temple, still others something else; only after that are bread and wine mentioned as gifts of the clerics, who have always formed the last in the ranks of offerers. In later writings, there is no mention at all of bread and wine in this connection. Only at an episcopal consecration does the Roman liturgy still contain a vestige of this practice: the newly consecrated bishop presents two altar breads, two small casks of wine, and two candles. And at a papal Mass, on the occasion of a solemn canonization, an offering is made of two breads, two barrels of wine and water, five candles, and three cages containing pigeons, turtle-doves, and other birds.

Shortly after this it was pointed out that clerics do not generally have an obligation to make an offering. Other means had long since been devised of procuring the elements of bread and wine, while in the offertory procession the chief concern was a domestic one, to obtain support for the clergy. This offering served, as they said, "to insure the priests' having something to eat." And since money gradually superseded almost all other gifts, and since many objects were already excluded from the offertory proper because of the holiness of the place, there was soon no distinction at all, in intent and disposition, between free-will offerings and those made according to strict ecclesiastical prescription. And inversely, the latter offerings were all the more consciously drawn into the offertory procession and all the more plainly considered as gifts made to God. Even the presentation of the tithes was designated as an *offerre*. Under the concept of oblation were listed all the products of rural industry and all objects of ecclesiastical and domestic use; and in regard to all of these, insofar as it was practicable, an effort was made to integrate them, in some way, with the offertory procession.[4]

Besides, one of the features of the older Gallican rite recurs again—offering up all sorts of things for the altar *before* the services. Because of the richness of such gifts, it so happened that—especially when the churches were privately owned—the landlord would lay hands on the offerings and even demand the majority for himself, claiming that he was already taking care of the church and its priests. As early as 572 the Synod of Braga had ordained that no bishop was to consecrate a church which some landlord had built in order to snatch half the oblations. The struggle against these and similar claims went on for centuries. It even affected the altar oblation proper, which was now grounded on a much wider basis and whose ecclesiastical disposition, in its more ancient modest range, had hardly been imperiled.

TIME OF PROCESSION

In the interval during which the ancient offering of bread and wine was being displaced by the other objects at the offertory procession—the ninth and the tenth centuries—the effort was made to establish a strict distinction between the former offering and the latter. Only bread and wine are to be offered up according to the traditional form at the offertory of the Mass, while candles and the rest are to be presented before Mass or before the Gospel. As a matter of fact, the ensuing years witness a great deal of hesitancy regarding the proper place for this remodeled offertory procession. In Bavarian country parishes an offertory procession before the Gospel has survived right down to the present. An offer-

---

[4] At a First Mass in the diocese of Eichstätt during the 15th century it was customary for all the people to take part in an offertory procession in which they presented not only money and natural products but also all sorts of household goods like cooking utensils and bedding as an endowment for the new priest.

tory procession at the *Kyrie eleison* was also a common practice which continued for a long time. In Spain it was customary, even in earlier times, to offer money at the Communion procession, a custom which also existed elsewhere or was formed anew. And again there was repeated occasion for sharp prohibitions against simoniacal dealings. Later, in Spain, we meet with an offertory procession inserted between the priest's offering of bread and wine and the washing of his hands. This is done in the Mozarabic liturgy, and even in the Roman liturgy this addition is admitted to a certain extent. The author of the *Micrologus* denounces this arrangement as inverted. As a rule, the offertory, even in its new dress, assumes its old place after the *Oremus*, while the *offertorium* is being sung, its gladsome tone spurring one on to joyful giving. It is presupposed as taking place in this spot in the Mass *ordo* of Burchard of Strassburg, printed in 1502, and here, too, it is to be found wherever the old custom still survives.

OTHER CUSTOMS

Burchard's *ordo,* which always notes the rubrics with great exactness, also describes the rite for the priest in these circumstances. After he has read the offertory from the missal, he goes to the Epistle side, takes the maniple from his arm and extends it to each of the offerers to be kissed, at the same time blessing them with a special formula. The same rite is presupposed in Spanish Mass books of the fifteenth and sixteenth centuries. In Spain the rite is an ancient tradition, and here, too, it has survived to this day, with the exception of the blessing which had to be sacrificed in 1881 as the result of a decree of the Congregation of Sacred Rites. The main outlines of the rite are also to be found elsewhere up to very recent times. In many places, instead of the maniple or the stole, the offerer (after handing over his gift) kissed the hand of the celebrant, or, in other places, the corporal or even an extended paten. Sometimes the offerer accompanied his gift with a word of blessing. According to a Mass *ordo* of the fifteenth century the priest was finally to bless the people with the words: "May you receive a hundredfold and possess life everlasting, in the name of the Father . . . ."

A very festive rite of offertory procession is still in use at the solemn papal Mass which is celebrated on the occasion of a canonization. The offerers step up to the pope's throne in three groups, each led by a cardinal. In each group two noblemen precede the cardinal and two other people follow—the four gift-bearers. The gifts borne by the nobles, two heavy candles, two breads, two cruets of wine and water, are handed to the Holy Father by the respective cardinal; in doing so he kisses the pope's hand and stole, and his Holiness in turn blesses the gifts and turns them over to his master of ceremonies. The other gifts (candles, cages with birds) are handed over by the bearers to the cardinal procurator; the latter holds them out to the pope for his blessing.

However, the general attitude of the later Roman liturgy towards the offertory procession, the attitude of reserve and even avoidance, has led to the very singular result that the celebrant as a rule takes no notice of the procession even when it still occurs.[5] This conduct is to be found even earlier in the declining years of the Middle Ages. In such cases the people brought their gifts and laid them in a plate or box standing near the altar. In other instances two places were set apart—perhaps for two different purposes—one on the Gospel side, the other on the Epistle; the faithful presented part of their gift at the first location, circled the altar (where this was possible), and then made their second offering at the second place.

Since the third century, then, it very quickly became a fixed rule that the faithful should offer their gifts at a common eucharistic celebration, but because of the close connection with the performance of the sacred mystery it was from the very start recognized as a right restricted to those who were full members of the Church, just like the reception of the Sacrament. In the Syrian Didascalia there is a long discussion outlining the duty of the bishops and deacons to watch out from whom they accept a gift; the gifts of all who openly lived in sin were to be refused, whether they were the unchaste or thiefs or usurers or even Roman officials who had stained their hands with blood. Similar regulations recur more than once in the ensuing years in both the East and the West. At the beginning of the sixth century the *Statuta Ecclesiæ antiqua,* which stem from the neighborhood of Arles, insist that nothing is to be accepted from dissenting brethren. Penitents, too, were deprived of this right, and it was not restored to them until their reconciliation. Similarly, the gifts of those Christians who lived at enmity were refused. As late as the fifteenth century a preacher, Gottschalk Hollen, made principles of this sort his own.

On the other hand, the congregation was expected to make an offering every Sunday, and the wish for even a daily oblation found utterance. In monasteries, after the reform of Benedict of Aniane (d. 821), a daily offering was actually incorporated into the order of service. But the Sunday offering was an ancient custom, and is still kept up here and there even at the present.[6]

---

[5] But even as cautious a rubricist as B. Gavanti thinks that the present rubrics do not require so narrow an interpretation; where it is the custom the priest could present his hand to be kissed (except at Masses for the dead); therefore he could at least pause. Gavanti-Merati, II, 7, 5 q.

[6] Through my own occasional inquiries I have found that the Sunday offertory procession, in which the whole congregation takes part, is still customary along the northern borders of the Alps, especially in many parishes of Vorarlberg and Upper Bavaria, but also in the vicinity of Schneidemühl. The proceeds belong to the church.

OCCASION FOR THE PROCESSION

After the change from natural goods to money had set in, and the obvious symbolism of the offering of bread and wine had given way before more practical economic considerations, the Sunday oblation seems to have lost favor. In fact it could be pointed out that the necessary income of the Church was assured for the most part by fixed possessions and by taxes which were definitely prescribed. Still, it did seem right that the symbolic activity of the offertory procession should be kept up, at least within modest limits. The Roman reform synod of 1059 deplored the neglect of the oblations (understood here in a somewhat wider sense) and threatened the refusal of Communion. In 1078 Pope Gregory VII reaffirmed the old obligation: "that every Christian procure something to offer to God at Mass (*missarum sollemnia*)," pointing to Exodus 23:15 and ancient tradition as his endorsement. But no special day was mentioned. Actually, since the eleventh century it had become more and more customary to hold the offertory procession on certain specified feast days, and even to regard it as obligatory on such days. The number of these days fluctuated at first. In the later Middle Ages they were usually the greater feasts, Christmas, Easter and Pentecost, to which was added All Saints or the Assumption, or the feast of the dedication of the church, or the church's patronal feast. In the many source documents in which arrangements are made for the proper carrying out of the offering, frequent reference is therefore made to the offering of the "four or five festivities," of the four-time offering or simply the "four offertories." Even in the course of the Catholic Reform during the sixteenth and seventeenth centuries an effort was made to retain these offertory processions or to revive them. But they seem to have disappeared more completely, even, than the old Sunday offerings. Why these efforts at restoration miscarried is not easy to understand; the main reason, perhaps, lay in the opposition to feast day offertory processions which had become entangled in the financial overgrowths of the late Middle Ages, an opposition which, after the Council of Trent, outweighed the desire to restore the ancient symbolical rite.

But in addition to the prescribed processions of the great feast days, the Middle Ages introduced numerous free-will oblations on those occasions when certain specific groups gathered at the Mass: at funeral Masses and the succeeding memorial Masses for the dead, at weddings, at the departure of pilgrims, and the anniversary feasts of guilds and fraternities. It is precisely on such occasions that the offertory procession is often retained in country places right down to the present. Of even greater import were the oblations at Votive Masses which an individual or a family ordered to be celebrated for special intentions: for the sick, for friends, for a good harvest, in honor of a saint, in manifold dangers. Generally the persons concerned made an offering, as the *secreta* and the special *Hanc igitur* formulas in many cases indicate. Besides, the faithful who might be present could always bring their oblation to the altar and thus join more closely in the sacrifice. In this way arose the "daily oblations of the faithful" of which medieval documents make mention.

MASS STIPEND

But then it was here precisely that the close connection between participation and presentation broke down—between a sharing in the sacrifice and the offering of gifts during that sacrifice. Just as had long been the case in regard to foundations whereby, through the gift of a larger sum, the repeated celebration of Mass was guaranteed for a period of time, so now, even for individual Masses, the custom grew of quietly handing the priest a gift beforehand, without thereby prejudicing the right of other offerers. The latter could still, as ever, take part at the regular offertory procession or even, for their part, secure a special share in the Mass by their own private gifts. At the same time, however, the Mass stipend properly so-called makes its appearance—an honorarium paid in advance to obligate the priest to celebrate exclusively for the intention of the donor. For this negotiation the ordinary term employed was *comparatio missæ, missam comparare*. But the system of stipends was not adopted wholeheartedly at once, for as long as the notions were not made clear and precise enough, scrupulous hesitation and opposition were not wanting.

At the Council of Trent, where one of the chief concerns was the removal of abuses regarding ecclesiastical monetary matters, this question of stipends came to the fore. But in the end the Council did nothing more than issue a general admonition to the bishops, and this in turn was amplified by subsequent canonical legislation. In this later amplification the rift between gift and oblation was obviously made even wider, for according to more recent decisions it is no longer forbidden to accept a stipend from non-Catholics, even from heathens who can in no wise become offerers of the oblation of the Church. Of course this does not prevent at least the stipend of the faithful—viewed in the light of ecclesiastical tradition—from continuing to be the gift to God which, like the bread and wine, is directed immediately to the sacrifice of the New Covenant. The priest accepts it with the obligation of consummating the sacrifice for the benefit of the donor, and with the right to use for his own support whatever money is not required for the expense of celebration. The faithful, however, were always to be aware of the priesthood that is theirs through baptism and confirmation, and were therefore to regard their offering of the stipend as only the start of their participation in the sacrifice, much as the Christians of an earlier era did when they not only brought their gifts to the altar but also continued to follow the celebration and partook of the Body of the Lord as a return gift.

The ancient offering of the faithful survives also in another metamorphosis, the offertory collection. There is no reason why this should not be permitted to serve a more than merely utilitarian purpose, no reason why it should not be given a deeper spirit and a more vivid form than it ordinarily presents—a spirit, by harking back to the living roots of this contribution which is primarily intended as a gift to God and which is destined for the earthly recipient only through and over the altar; a form, by confining the collection to the time of the offertory and clothing the activity with dignified and appropriate ceremonial. Even though this is a collection and not an offertory procession, the basic idea of a genuine oblation is not excluded any more than it was at the rite in vogue in the stational services of the city of Rome.

2. The Offertory Chant

The entrance of the clergy at the start of Mass was made to the accompaniment of the introit sung by the *schola cantorum*. It was then but a natural application of the same principle that suggested that the "procession" of the people at the offertory and communion—both interruptions during the audible part of the Mass—should be enlivened and enriched by psalmodic song.

That this was the meaning and purpose of the offertory chant was well understood all during the Middle Ages. The chanting was called by the same name that was given to the presentation of the oblation gifts: *offertorium, offerenda.* Even in the Middle Ages the commentators stressed this connection: the chant (they said in substance) should signify the jubilance of heart with which the faithful proffer their gifts, for (as they quoted) "God loves the cheerful giver."

When all the gifts had been presented, a signal was given the singers to conclude their chanting. And whenever the *oratio super oblata* was not immediately pronounced aloud—as had been customary in the early Middle Ages—complete quiet set in, a conscious silence which foreshadowed the beginning of the priestly activity of oblation, although only preparatory actions immediately followed—actions like washing the hands, incensing, silent prayer. This silence was also made the object of special commentary and explanation. Not till the turn of the medieval epoch, when an understanding of this silence vanished, and when in addition—as the result of the disappearance of even the feast-day procession—the chant was reduced to the antiphon as we have it at present, only then did the masters of polyphony turn their attention on greater feasts to this song—in contrast to introit and communion—and by their art they lengthened and extended it to cover the other rites which are at present comprehended under the term offertory; thus the offertory song became a connecting link with the preface.

The earliest accounts of an offertory chant come from North Africa. It seems to have been introduced there in the time of St. Augustine, first at Carthage, later at Hippo through Augustine's own efforts. In a review of his own literary activity the saint mentions that he wrote a work, now lost, taking issue with a certain Hilarius who had opposed the practice, then recently introduced, of singing psalms during the offering of the gifts and at the communion. At Rome, too, the practice must have gained an entry very early, perhaps about the same time. Nevertheless, on Holy Saturday the offertory chant is missing, as are the other chants of the *schola*, for this Mass retains the features of a more ancient usage. However, to all appearances Rome had but a modest store of offertory chants even in the sixth century, as we can gauge from the Milanese Mass, which has preserved its antique form to the present, and in which the offertory chants give every indication of having been borrowed from Rome. In the Roman Mass itself, however, this modest store was later richly augmented by Gregory the Great and his successors.

FORMS OF THE CHANT

At first the offertory chant probably had the same antiphonal design as the chant at the introit: the *schola*, divided into two choirs, sang a psalm alternately, with an antiphon as prelude. The psalm varied from celebration to celebration, taking into account, as far as possible, the church year with its festivals and seasons.

It is a striking fact that at a very early period the antiphonal performance of the offertory was abandoned and a responsorial style substituted for it. Even the ancient substructure of Roman offertories preserved at Milan, as mentioned above, had this responsorial design. Among these, for instance, is the offertory which the present Roman Missal assigns to the eleventh Sunday after Pentecost (also used on Ash Wednesday); in the oldest sources it has the following form:

> *Exaltabo te, Domine, quoniam suscepisti me, nec delectasti inimicos meos super me.* [*Refrain:*] *Domine clamavi ad te et sanasti me.*
> ℣. *Domine abstraxisti ab inferis animam meam, salvasti me a descendentibus in lacum* [*Refrain:*] *Domine clamavi ad te et sanasti me.*

℣. *Ego autem dixi in mea abundantia: non movebor in æternum.*
Domine in voluntate tua præstitisti decori meo virtutem.
[Refrain:] Domine, clamavi [ad te et sanasti me].

Here, just as in the chants interpolated before the Gospel, a refrain is repeated several times. In line with this, the verse (as found in the oldest manuscripts with neums) is treated as a solo and consequently provided with the greatest melodic richness. A few of the manuscripts devoted to the solo chants therefore contain the verse of the offertory while merely indicating the texts that pertain to the choir, namely, the initial section and the refrain. Apparently the *Gloria Patri* was not appended to these verses.

And now we may well ask how this remarkable development came about. It is almost certain that the main consideration was to give the offertory chant a certain lengthiness, in view (obviously) of the people's procession. True, this extra length could also have been achieved by having the psalm sung antiphonally right down to the end, and then repeating the antiphon which stands at the start. Perhaps the responsorial form was chosen to make it easier for the singers to take part in the offertory procession. Besides, the main point in singing at all was not so much to render the text of a complete psalm, but rather to achieve a festive mood, which could be done more readily by musical means. This resulted, therefore, in a shortening of the psalm, along with a corresponding compensation both by the enrichment of the melody of the verse sung as a solo, and by the repetition of the antiphon or a part thereof, after the manner of a refrain. This refrain could, of course, have been turned over to the people, but by this time there was obviously little interest in such participation of the people in responsorial chanting, at least in the greater stational services. We already noted in the history of the intervenient chants how early the art of the special singers preponderated even in responsorial song. *So the refrain at the offertory was from the very start reserved to the singing choir.*

It is in this responsorial form that the offertory chant regularly appears in the choral books of the early Middle Ages. The number of psalm verses fluctuates between one and four. That is patently more than in the other Mass chants. The extension must be explained, as already indicated, by the length of the offertory procession. Whereas at the introit only a single group, the clergy, wended through the church, and whereas the reception of Communion, for which the communion chant was intended, had become since the close of the ancient era nearly everywhere a rare and slight affair, the whole congregation continued to take part in the offertory procession Sunday after Sunday till at least the year 1000. Not till the eleventh century was there any noticeable drop in the regularity of this procession; after that it was gradually limited to the greater festivals. And, as a matter of fact, it is in the eleventh century that the offertory verses begin to disappear from many manuscripts. By the following century this omission has become a general rule, although exceptions are to be found till the very end of the Middle Ages. The portion which had originally been the antiphon was considered sufficient. In the Missal of Pius V only the Mass for the Dead retained a verse, and with it a refrain: *Hostias et preces* and *Quam olim Abrahæ;* this fits in once again with the fact that *it was precisely at the Requiem that the offertory procession continued in use.* On the other hand, the Milanese Mass has retained the offertory verse even to the present, and similarly the Mozarabic Mass.

As already pointed out, the offertory was always performed by a choral group. And because their singing prevented the choristers from personally taking part in the offertory procession, their place was taken by one of the members; at Rome it was the *archiparaphonista* whose duty it was to offer the water. Since in the churches of the later Middle Ages the singing choir usually represented a part of the clerical choir, it was really only a nominal difference when sometimes the *clerus* was mentioned and sometimes the *chorus.* A reminiscence of the fact that the offertory was a chant sung by the choir survived in some of the Mass *ordos* of the Middle Ages where the texts were appointed to be recited at the high Mass, not only by the celebrant alone, but by the deacon and subdeacon along with him.

As for the texts of the offertory, they are taken as a rule from Holy Scripture; for the most part, in fact, from the Psalms, as the psalmodic origin of the chant would naturally imply. One would expect that the texts chosen would be expressive of the idea of oblation and so suggest the meaning of the offertory procession. But actually this is only the *exceptional* case: examples of this sort are found in the offertory of the Dedication of a Church: "With honesty of intent I have made all these offerings gladly"; on Epiphany: "The kings of Tharsis and the islands shall offer gifts"; on Pentecost: ". . . kings shall offer Thee gifts"; on Corpus Christi: "The priests of the Lord offer incense and loaves to God." The offertory of the Mass for the Dead also belongs to this class; notice the verse: "We offer sacrifices and prayers of praise to Thee, O Lord." But most of the texts have a very general character or dwell on the theme of the feast being celebrated. This is true also of the verses which once were appended here; they regularly belonged to the same psalm or the same scriptural text as the initial verse. As a matter of fact, a reference to what was happening at the offertory procession was superfluous so long as the practice itself was alive. The chief purpose then was not, as it is in our present-day Mass chants, to explain what was already plain enough in itself; the chief thing was to give it a religious dedication.

3. The Matter for the Sacrifice

TYPE OF BREAD

The fate which befell the offertory procession was dependent, to a large extent, on the requirements regarding the condition of the elements for the sacrifice. There can be little doubt that the bread used by Christ our Lord at the Last Supper was the unleavened bread prescribed for the paschal meal, a bread made of fine wheat flour. But the very way the accounts read readily indicates that no importance was attached to the particular paschal practice of using unleavened bread; what our Lord took into his hands is simply called *artos*, a word which could designate not only the unleavened bread used at the paschal feast but also the leavened kind which was otherwise in use among Jews as well as pagans. The latter kind was therefore from earliest times considered at least licit for the Eucharist. Thus it was all the less difficult for the faithful to be able to make an offering of the bread for the altar; they just took bread from their domestic supply and brought it for divine service. Both literary accounts and pictorial illustrations show us that the shape of the eucharistic bread did not differ from the shape of bread used for domestic purposes. The only distinction, if distinction it was, consisted in this, that the finest and best formed loaves were selected, as was only natural. In two mosaics at Ravenna, in which the eucharistic altar is shown, the bread appears in the form of a chaplet or crown, that is, twisted like a braid and then wound into a circlet about four inches across. This is the *corona* referred to by St. Gregory the Great; being an outstanding product of the baker's skill, it is known to us since the third century. Or sometimes the center hole of the crown was filled in, and so the bread had the form of a disk. Perhaps the form most frequently used was a round loaf divided into four parts by a cross-notch (*panis quadratus, panis decussatus*); its form easily lent itself to a Christian explanation, and so was even considered indispensable, although the shape had been developed merely for a very practical reason—easier breaking—and for precisely this reason had been in common use even in pre-Christian culture. Along with this there was a practice, already known in ancient times, of stamping the bread with a symbol or inscription. A breadstamp from the fourth or fifth century shows a superimposed XP symbol; however, there is no proof that a bread so inscribed was intended precisely for the Eucharist. Still, in the years that followed, many of the Oriental rites formed the practice of using just such stamps or irons, although their use for leavened bread (which was less firm) was not a matter of course. In most of these instances the stamp consisted of a repetition of the Cross in various patterns. In the eucharistic stamp of the Byzantine rite the somewhat larger round bread is impressed with a square which is divided into four fields by the Cross, and on these are distributed the symbols of the inscription: ʼI (ησοῦς) X (ριστὸς) νιχᾳ— "Jesus Christ victor."

In the West, various ordinances appeared from the ninth century on, all demanding the exclusive use of unleavened bread for the Eucharist. A growing solicitude for the Blessed Sacrament and a desire to employ only the best and whitest bread, along with various scriptural considerations—all favored this development. Still, the new custom did not come into exclusive vogue until the middle of the eleventh century. Particularly in Rome it was not universally accepted till after the general infiltration of various usages from the North. In the Orient there were few objections to this usage during olden times. Not till the discussions that led to the schism of 1054 did it become one of the chief objections against the Latins. At the Council of Florence (1439), however, it was definitely established that the Sacrament could be confected "in unleavened or leavened bread." Therefore, as we well know, the various groups of Orientals who are united with Rome continue to use the type of bread traditional among them.

MAKING OF THE BREAD

Reverence for the Blessed Sacrament, however, soon took a new turn both in the East and in the West, namely, in the effort to remove the bread destined for the altar farther and farther from the sphere of the merely profane. In the Orient the making of the breads was committed as a rule only to clerics; in any case—according to present practice— women are excluded. The baking is done in a church building to the accompaniment of prayer, and as far as possible on the day of the celebration itself. Among the East Syrians there is a special rite, divided into two parts: the preparation of the dough, and the baking, both encircled with many prayers and psalms; this rite is considered a portion of the Mass-liturgy. Among the Abyssinians each church has for the same purpose a little side building called *beth-lechem* ("House of Bread"), from which three freshly-baked breads are borne to the altar in solemn procession at the beginning of service.

In the West, too, the making of bread was for a time given a liturgical form, particularly within the ambit of the Cluniac reform movement. According to the customs of the monastery of Hirsau in the Black Forest (eleventh century), the wheat had to be selected kernel for kernel; the mill on which it was to be ground had to be cleaned, then hung about with curtains; the monk who supervised the milling had to don alb and humeral. The same vesture was worn by the four monks to whom the baking of the hosts was confided; at least three of these monks were to be in deacon's orders or even higher rank. While working they were to keep strict silence, so that their breath might not touch the bread. According to the instructions in other monasteries, on the other hand, the monks were to combine their work with the singing of psalms according to a precise plan. It might be added that such a solemn act did not take place every day, but only a few times in the year. Recalling the instructions regarding the Old Testament bread of proposition, the desire was expressed that even outside the monasteries only the priest should prepare and bake the host; in France this order was in many instances faithfully followed even as late as the eighteenth century. Elsewhere, at an earlier period, it was thought sufficient if there was some guarantee that the pertinent ecclesiastical prescriptions were fully carried out by the persons entrusted with the operation. As a result, the preparation of the hosts was done mostly in the houses of religious, more especially in convents of women.

THE HOST

The drift away from selecting the bread destined for the altar just from the gifts of the faithful, and towards providing for it carefully in some other way is to be noticed occasionally even at an early period. But with the substitution of unleavened bread the exclusion of the faithful became a matter of course. At first the thin disks of the unleavened wheat bread were made in a larger size and were brought thus to the altar where they were broken up for the Communion of the people. But since this Communion came under consideration almost only on the greatest feast days, it soon became the practice, even in the twelfth century, to shape the priest's host in the more modest size it has today, "in the form of a denarius." This form was then retained even on Communion days, and in order to avoid breaking up the species the custom grew of preparing the "particles" for the Communion of the faithful ahead of time. And since the thin cakes from which the hosts were cut had to be baked in a metal form, the altar-bread irons, it was not hard to impress at least the large hosts with some sort of decorative stamp. At first this was simply the traditional Cross; soon this became the figure of the Crucified or some other image of Christ, and since there was never any general regulation in this regard, many other representations made their appearance in later years, not to mention various inscriptions and legends which are found quite early.

The term we now employ for the wafers desined for the Eucharist is the proleptic expression "hosts." The word *hostia* was originally used only for a living thing, the sacrificial victim that was "slaughtered" (*hostio = ferio*, I strike, I kill). It could therefore be understood in the first instance only of Christ, who had become for us a *hostia* (*cf.* Eph. 5:2), a sacrificial Lamb. More ancient is the use of the word *oblata* for

the bread offered up. In other liturgies, too, we find for the still uncon-
secrated elements a similar use of names which signify the offering, the
sacrifice. The exact parallel to the transfer of meaning which we have in
the word "host" is found in the Byzantine liturgy where the piece of
bread selected in the *proskomide* and destined for the consecration is
called "Lamb."

In regard to the second element, the wine, there are also a number of
questions that had to find their solution in the course of history. But only
in small part do they concern the constitution of the wine itself. In the
Orient, red wine was preferred, and occasionally this was also the case
in the West since thus any accidental confusion with the water was more
surely avoided. But there was at no time any regulation that was universally obligatory. When, later on, the use of the purificator became
general, that is, since the sixteenth century, white wine has been commonly preferred because it leaves fewer traces in the linen.

In some few districts of the Orient where wine is hard to get—especially among the Copts and Abyssinians—a substitute was and is created
by softening dried grapes (raisins, that is) in water and then pressing
them out; this process is permitted even among Catholics, with the pro-
viso that at least the start of fermentation is awaited.

MIXTURE OF THE WINE

Much more profound were the discussions regarding the mixture of
the wine. According to ancient rule some water must be mingled with
the wine. This was not, indeed, a native Palestinian custom, but a Greek
practice which was observed in Palestine in Christ's time. As early as
the second century this admixture for the Eucharist is expressly mentioned. Later, under pressure of Gnostic circles that rejected all wine-
drinking, there was a trend here and there to replace the wine entirely
by water. In one of his detailed writings Cyprian repudiated such a procedure which was practiced by some ignorant people, declaring it
contrary to the institution of Jesus. On the other hand, it was he who
emphasized the symbolic sense of the commingling. Just as the wine receives the water in itself, so has Christ taken to Himself us and our sins.
Therefore, the mixing of the water with the wine symbolizes the intimate union of the faithful with Him to whom they have bound themselves in faith; and this union is so firm that nothing can sever it, just as
the water can no longer be separated from the wine. From this, Cyprian
concludes: "When someone offers only wine, then the blood of Christ
begins to exist without us; but when it is only water, then the people
begin to exist without Christ." [1] These words were often repeated and
extended all through the Middle ages. Along with this symbolism,

[1] Cyprian, *Ep.*, 63, ad Cæcilium (Corpus Scriptorum Eccles. Lat., 3, 701-717).

another made an early appearance—the reference to the blood and water which flowed from Christ's side on Calvary. But in the foreground was always the symbolism of Christ's union with His Church. This was intensified by the statement in the Apocalypse (17:15), that in the water the peoples are represented. The jubilant nations, who are represented by the singers, offer it up. As a picture of the people who still need expiation, it is blessed, while the wine as a rule is not. In the course of the Middle Ages the little ceremony was made the basis for theological reflections: the commingling of the water shows pointedly that in the Mass not only is Christ offered up, but the Church too; still this can be done only by the priest who is not separated from the Church. Precisely because of this symbolism, wherein he perceived the handiwork of God being belittled by human admixture, Luther declared the commingling of the water unfitting inasmuch as it was indicative of our oneness with Christ. Therefore the Council of Trent explicitly defended the practice and threatened its rejection with an anathema.

In the Orient, too, there were some stubborn battles over the droplet of water. Behind the reference to the blood and water from Christ's side, which was also the usual conception here, the Orientals found a theological symbolism that took a somewhat different turn. Matching the acuteness of the christological strife in the Orient, the wine and water were made to represent the divine and human natures in Christ. The Armenians, whose ranks were penetrated by a radical Monophysitism (which taught that after the Incarnation there could be question of only one nature in Christ, namely, the divine), eliminated the admixture of water as early as the sixth century, at any rate surely before 632. In spite of some waverings, they held to their position, even though, in their repeated efforts to unite with Byzantium and with Rome, this point always formed a block.

The exclusion of leaven, too, was given a similar theological signification by the Armenians. "The Chalcedonian error of the two natures" and the practice of "tainting [the Sacrament] by the fermenting of the bread and by [the admixture of] water" are occasionally mentioned in Armenian sources in one and the same breath. Because of this theological background the Catholic Armenians have taken up the use of water with the wine.

In the Roman liturgy of today the water that is added is only a small amount in comparison with the wine, but in the liturgies of the Orient it forms, and has formed, a goodly portion of the contents of the chalice. Amongst the Syrian Jacobites it has been the practice from olden times to add an equal quantity of water to the wine, and this practice corresponds to what was customary in the surroundings of the nascent Church. But in the Occident, too, there is the instance of the synod of Tribur (895), which required that the chalice contain two-thirds wine and one-third water, and even in the thirteenth century it was considered sufficient to insist that more wine be taken than water. But after that there is a definite shrinking of the minimum required by the symbolism, and at the same time the spoon appears, to make it easier to avoid exceeding the minimum.[2]

4. Laying the Offerings on the Altar
The Accompanying Prayers

When the offerings of bread and wine are ready as required, there is still the problem of fitting them into a richly developed liturgy, there is still the question of how and by whom they are to be deposited on the altar, how they are to be disposed there, and particularly whether and how, in these moments before the ancient traditional *Eucharistia*, they are to be drawn by word and gesture into the sacrificial action.

The older Roman liturgy provided only for the well-regulated external activity,[1] and for the single prayer, the *oratio super oblata*, which, however, was said in the name of the whole assembly in a loud voice. When transferred to Frankish territory the external action was soon modified in several ways (principally by being coupled with the offertory procession, which itself was altered through the years), and was enriched by other preparatory acts, like the incensation and the washing of the hands. In addition, each step of the activity was joined by a significant word, spoken by the *liturgus* not aloud, but only softly to himself. Even the prayer itself acquired further addition. This showed the same half-private character and tried especially to connect individual desires with the offering. Moreover, all this liturgical growth in the Frankish realm was not regulated from one appointed center, but emanated rather from different points and criss-crossed in the most diverse ways over all the lands of Christendom. As a result the Mass books of the later Middle Ages contain at the oblation a veritable jungle of new prayers and texts. The diversity and multiplicity of these formulas and their grouping is so great that a classification appears well-nigh impossible. Nevertheless, if we want to get a closer understanding of the form of the oblation rite as it appears in the Roman Missal—comparatively scant though it be—we may not by-pass this jungle entirely.

[2] The spoon is not mentioned in the Roman missal, but its use was approved by the SRC, Feb. 6, 1858 (n. 3064 ad 4). It is commonly used in Spain and Ireland; but elsewhere, e.g., Italy, is even at present entirely unknown.

[1] For a better understanding of this chapter, it is necessary to distinguish two purposes in the offertory ceremonials: (1) the provision of the elements of bread and wine, and (2) a ritual presentation of these elements at the sacrifice, arranging them on the altar and commending them to God.

The point of view which prevails today, in which the worth and importance of the *Eucharistia* is once more discovered and which is swayed but little by the novel medieval customs, makes it appear that the *offertorium* grew out of the fact that the offertory procession had vanished in the course of the Middle Ages and the vacancy which thus arose had to be filled out by these ceremonies and prayers. Besides, according to this conception, these prayers are ascribed in the first instance to the private Masses which were then coming to the fore, and which seemed to be especially adapted to such an enrichment. These are the two assertions that are repeated even by great authorities; but these opinions are in urgent need of investigation. We shall therefore try to follow, in rough outline at least, the development of the forms from their beginnings.

The first thing we notice—right within the framework of the old Roman oblation scheme—*is the quiet praying of the celebrant*, even before he says the *secreta*. The eighth-century Frankish *Capitulare ecclesiastici Ordinis* prescribes that at a solemn high Mass, after the offerings of the faithful and the clergy have been arranged on the altar, the celebrant take his own offering in hand and lift hands and eyes to God in silent prayer. This is also indicated in the other Roman *ordines*. The fact that the celebrant turned to the surrounding clergy to ask for their prayers is also mentioned here.

The first brief *wording* of such an offering prayer is presented in the Sacramentary of Amiens. The heart of this prayer appears to be the humble offering of the gifts already prepared, which are designated as offerings of the faithful and therefore presuppose an offertory procession.

The next thing we specially note in these more ancient oblation prayers and the practices connected with them, is that about the year 1000 they have grown tremendously, and that they are especially extended at the start of the oblation, before the chalice is brought to the altar. They have an essentially intercessory character; the offering is done "for" (*pro*) certain specified purposes and persons. This is evidently the consequence of recollections of the Gallican liturgy. The trend can be traced even in Amalar. In his explanation of the *offerenda* he cites Old Testament requirements and then names a series of requests "for which we should offer sacrifices": for the fulfillment of vows which were made in affliction, for the expiation of our sins, for the royal house, for the ecclesiastical estates, for peace. His younger contemporary, Walafrid Strabo (d. 849), feels compelled to combat the opinion that a special offering and a special petition must be made for each intention, and that it was not possible to beg "for many things under one petition." Along with this another factor, reverence for certain mysteries of faith, found expression both in the prayers themselves and in the *manner in which the oblations were distributed on the altar.* Indeed we encounter this trend about the same time in the East as well as in the West. While in the older Roman *ordines* little importance was attached to the manner of composing the oblations on the altar, in the Carolingian territory we hear of two crosses which the priest is to build out of the oblations and place next to the chalice. Even as late as 1100 some missals from the orbit of Monte Cassino demand that the oblations be arranged in the form of a cross. In Spain, around 845, a Bishop Ildefons gives even more detailed directions: whereas on ordinary days only one bread is laid out, on Sundays five breads are to be taken and arranged crosswise; on Christmas and some other feast days seventeen breads, of which five are to form a cross, the other twelve a circle around the chalice; on Easter and Whitsunday forty-five breads, for which a combined cross-form is sketched. Even in the eleventh century the Trier *Liber officiorum* takes a stand against those who insist that, for the sake of the number three, three *oblatæ* are always to be consecrated. Besides a regard for the Communion of the faithful, such efforts indicate also the tendency to give symbolical expression to certain offertory-motifs or at least to give prominence to symbolic numbers.

PRAYERS

In the Orient the effort was made to indicate symbolically certain mysteries of the faith as well as the most important petitions by the arrangement of the bread oblation, but this never caught on in the West. But for that very reason these latter have stretched to greater proportions in the prayers. Around the same year 1000 we see the bishop at a solemn high Mass stepping to the altar after the offertory procession of the people and clerics, and pronouncing a whole series, more or less long, of offertory prayers in which the most important requests are set forth. And all are formed according to one scheme that plainly displays Gallican features, though previously there were some tentative efforts to model them more or less strictly on the pattern of prayer in the Roman canon. They begin with the phrase "Receive, Holy Trinity, (*Suscipe sancta Trinitas*) this oblation which I offer to Thee . . . ;" then the request is named and continued with an *ut*-clause; the conclusion can be either Gallican or Roman. The formula is met as early as the ninth century in Northern France, either as a single prayer or as a series of prayers in multiple variation. In the Mass *ordines* of the succeeding years it appears in use for the most diverse purposes; for the celebrant himself, for the congregation and its benefactors, for the King and the Christian people, for various persons amongst the living, for the sick, for the dead. At the top is usually the formula which has been retained till now and which, in imitation of the canon of the Mass, presents as the first intention of the offertory the remembrance of the mystery of redemption, with which is linked the commemoration of the saints.

In some Mass books since the eleventh century as many as thirteen formulas of this type are found one after the other. They were appointed to be said by the celebrant when, after the offertory procession, the bread-oblation had been arranged on the altar by the deacon, and very likely after his own oblation was added, but before the chalice was brought to the altar.

But soon other influences began to be felt, influences that resulted from the transformation of the offertory procession. The offertory procession survived above all at the great feast day high Masses which the rubrics of the Mass books usually spoke of, but the offerings made at it were no longer brought to the altar. The bread-oblation consisted mostly of just the thin host which the priest himself offered as his own gift. Therefore, before starting these prayers the celebrant had to await this gift. And in view of its smallness, it is quite understandable that he would also wait till the chalice was prepared; this, as we shall see in a moment, was usually handed to the celebrant along with the paten. The series of offertory prayers therefore moves back to a later position. In fact there must even have been some question whether the prayers were not actually to be postponed till after all the other preparatory activities, which had meanwhile often gained a place in this spot—the hand-washing, the incensation—and so inserted immediately before the petition for prayer (*Orate fratres*) which had long since found a secure place; it would thus serve as the last personal concurrence in the official priestly act, the sacrificial work of the canon of the Mass, which was then usually thought of as starting with the *secreta*.

About the same time another trend was to be noticed, a trend towards limiting the number of these prayers. Bernold of Constance (d. 1100) appears as advocate for this limitation, praising, as he does, those who were content with a single formula in which they commended to God both living and dead. The formula which he means, and which he suggests the priest should say "bowed before the altar," follows the traditional type: *Suscipe sancta Trinitas*. It is the prayer we still recite with bowed head just before the *Orate fratres*, therefore at the later spot as indicated above; formerly this prayer was found at the very top of the list of formulas.

In this place, just before the *Orate fratres*, and said by itself in this bowed attitude, the prayer is to be found even in an earlier period, and in Italy itself, as a component part of the Roman offertory plan there developing. Not till later does it appear at the same place in various countries outside Italy.

In contrast to the present-day wording, the formula regularly showed two expansions, particularly in the older texts. The list of redemptive mysteries commemorated—a list transferred from the canon: Passion, Resurrection, Ascension—was usually enlarged to read: ". . . in memory of the Incarnation, Nativity, Passion, Resurrection, and Ascension of Our Lord Jesus Christ." The mention of saints was made, as a rule, according to the formula: "and in honor of Thy saints who have enjoyed Thy pleasure from the beginning of the world and whose feast is celebrated today (their names here) and (others to be mentioned). In one group of texts, however, the first expansion was soon dropped. In the second expansion, other additions were made; here and there even in the eleventh century the name of the Blessed Virgin was added; a little later, and at first outside Rome, the names of the Princes of the Apostles were inserted; lastly, the Baptist. In place of this comprehensive expansion, however, a simple *istorum* was inserted, especially in the later Mass books.

As for the other contents of the formula, there seems to have been but little concern over the *ut*-clause in which the prayer is continued, and this corresponds exactly with its origin as a formula of commemoration. The clause appears to have been appended only to round out the form: May the sacrifice bring honor to the saints, and to us salvation and the efficacy of their intercession. The function of the formula as a substitute for all other versions and as an epitome of all other offertory intentions is thus only imperfectly expressed.

Elsewhere an oration of the same type, *Suscipe sancta Trinitas*, continued to be connected with the presentations of the offerings, while before the *Orate fratres* another prayer appeared, spoken likewise in the bowed posture of these oblation prayers; the prayer is that of Azarias (Dan. 3:39 f.): *In spiritu humilitatis*. This formula appeared quite early as a rival to formulas of the *Suscipe sancta Trinitas* type. In the Norman-English liturgy it actually won out and appears there as the concluding oblation prayer just before *Orate fratres*. This is true likewise in the liturgies of many religious orders, whereas in the Roman-Italian plan it is found very early, to be sure, but usually it appears as in today's design, immediately after the offering of the chalice. Thus we have in our present-day arrangement two prayers which, even by the bodily posture with which they are said, give an indication that they are meant to anticipate the oblation prayers of the canon.

Another point to remark in this connection is that even in the more recent texts where these prayers are employed as accompaniment to the external act of offering, yet the endeavor is made to join the bowed posture with the gesture of offering. With a demeanor that is quite courteous—forms of social intercourse do recur often enough in divine worship—the gifts are presented to the Almighty while *In spiritu humilitatis* or *Suscipe sancta Trinitas* is said.

Not much later in origin is a second rank of text elements, but these are much more intimately connected with the external rite and essentially directed to the purpose of explaining the visible activity. We can therefore understand them best if we combine our study of them with an exposition of the outer activity itself.

READYING OF THE ALTAR

First of all, the altar has to be readied. At a high Mass even today, immediately before the offertory—or during the *Credo* if there is one—the corporal enclosed in the burse is carried by the deacon to the altar and there spread out, while otherwise the priest carries it to the altar when he comes in, and spreads it out before Mass. This corporal is nowadays reduced to a very modest size; only at a solemn papal Mass does it cover the entire width of the altar, and in this case it is laid out over the altar by a (Cardinal) deacon and the subdeacon at the start of the offering of gifts. This was the practice already in the Roman services of the eighth century.[2] In the Middle Ages this action was frequently accompanied with prayer.

PRESENTATION OF THE GIFTS

When the altar is ready, the gifts can be brought to the altar and properly arranged. For this, too, there was a well-balanced plan in the Roman stational services: the archdeacon, assisted by the subdeacons, selects the oblation from amongst the gifts offered by the people and disposes it on the altar; the pope puts the bread-offering of the clerics and his own next to it; the archdeacon then places the chalice beside the bread offering of the pope. All this without a word being spoken. But such silence was intolerable to the Frankish liturgical concept. In the rite as we find it in the North about the year 1000, a rite developed upon the groundwork of the Roman arrangement as adapted in the Frankish realm, we see how fully this supposed deficiency was provided for. The greatest wealth is supplied in the so-called *Missa Illyrica*, even if we take no account of the overgrowth of apologiæ which we here encounter both at the start of the offering and again in the course of it.

Even at the presentation of the gifts during the offertory procession,

[2] Whereas in the early centuries only the altar coverings made of precious stuffs—from which our antependium derives—remained on the altar outside divine service, by the 7th century it was customary to leave cloths made of linen on the altar continually. A trace of the more ancient practice is to be seen even today on Good Friday when the altar cloths are put on the altar only before the Prayer of the Faithful. Among these was the *palla corporalis* (so called because it came into contact with the body of Christ), our present-day corporal; it is so folded that after the host-breads and the chalice were set on the altar it could be used as a covering over them. But since the later Middle Ages a special pall for the chalice was prepared.

each of the donors is to pronounce a little phrase, the recipient responding each time with a counter-phrase. Then when the deacon accepts from the subdeacon the bread-oblation intended for the celebrating bishop, this act is to be accompanied by a blessing: "May thy sacrifice be acceptable to almighty God and all His saints." When he hands it to the bishop, the latter receives it with a similar blessing, and the deacon meanwhile in his turn pronounces a blessing, and with it offers up the gift to God. Then the bishop himself offers up the gift to God, either with a similar blessing, which comprises approximately the first half of our present-day *Suscipe, sancte Pater*, or with some other suitable formula; and then follows the long series of oblation prayers which were spoken of in a previous paragraph.

Similar is the procedure when this series of prayers is finished and the chalice is brought over to the celebrant. As a rule this is a chalice already filled, at least with wine. The deacon hands it to the celebrant with a prayer composed of several combined psalm verses. Thereupon the celebrant offers it up with the oblation prayer that is customary today, *Offerimus*, or with some like formula. Still, even here there are early examples where the celebrant simply accepts the chalice with a psalm verse or even—as a parallel to the host—with a blessing as a response.

Later on, the procedure was compressed more tightly or more plainly coordinated. After the bread-oblation began to consist mostly of the thin host of the priest (a change which is matched by the change in the size of the paten—now small and flattened), it became more and more the custom for the deacon to bring over the entire offering as a unit: the chalice with the wine, and lying upon it the paten with the host. In this more recent, more developed rite, the deacon addresses the celebrant with the psalm verse (49:14): "Offer to God a sacrifice of praise and render thy vows to the Most High." The celebrant answers him with a different psalm verse (115:4 [13]): "I shall take the chalice of salvation, and I will call upon the name of the Lord." However, other formulas were also in use. Then the priest lifts chalice and paten just as they were handed to him and pronounces a brief oblation for both together. In the Dominican liturgy it is a version of the *Suscipe, sancta Trinitas*, short but enriched as to contents; similarly for the most part in England, often also in France, where the same oblation rite had a wide influence.

But in other places the oblation rite was soon broken up further. At first, indeed, the paten and host were regularly laid on the chalice. Sometimes a blessing was pronounced over them. Then, however, the priest took first the paten and, with an accompanying prayer, offered up the host; only then did he offer up the chalice, unless this was still committed to the deacon to do.

For such a double oblation there were already a number of precedents in the earlier stage of the offertory rite, when the chalice was still handed to the celebrant separately. In the *Missa Illyrica* there is even the beginning of the late Roman formula for the offering of the paten: *Suscipe, sancte Pater*, and the complete formula for the chalice: *Offerimus*, both enchased by other texts. Still, even this double accompaniment did not seem to have had the import of a real prayer, at least not that of a priestly oration. Especially with the chalice a simple and brief blessing was frequently thought sufficient. But little by little the details of the later Roman offertory plan, already present in essentials in the *Missa Illyrica*, became more evident, particularly in Italian Mass *ordines* from the eleventh and twelfth centuries on. The psalm verses that accompanied the handling of the chalice disappear. Alongside a short oblation passage which was often used alone, the otherwise infrequent *Suscipe, sancte Pater* (in its full form) now appears for the offering of the host. After the admixture of the water there follows the offering of the chalice with the formula *Offerimus*. But for a long time it was not a general rule that the celebrant raise paten and chalice above the altar, although in some scattered instances this had been done even in very early times. Add to these, besides, the invocation of the *sanctificator*, the two prayers, *In spiritu humilitatis* and *Suscipe, sancta Trinitas*, which were to be said bowed, and were thus somewhat independent.

It is not entirely an accident that the formula for the paten retains the singular number which predominates in these medieval oblation texts, while the formula for the chalice, *Offerimus*, is couched in the plural. For the latter is found not only put in the mouth of the priest, but instead in that of the deacon, who places the chalice on the altar and accompanies this with these words, which he would then be saying in the celebrant's name. Soon, however, there is an insistence on the fact that the deacon keeps the chalice with wine, which he has carried to the altar, and offers it up, and then arranges it on the altar, but the conclusion is drawn precisely from the *Offerimus*, that in reality the priest is acting through the deacon and that the priest must therefore pronounce the *Offerimus* or at least say it with the deacon. This latter arrangement has in a sense persisted, with the deacon touching the chalice and supporting the priest's arm, and pronouncing the words with the priest, but it is the priest, and not the deacon, who is now considered the chief offerer of the chalice. Thus, in the present-day solemn Mass, there is still a vestige of that older order in which the deacon was entrusted with the chalice, that older relationship which is given utterance in the legend where St. Lawrence says to Pope Xystus: "Never allow thyself to get into the habit of offering the sacrifice without a minister to whom thou hast entrusted the distribution of the blood of the Lord."

A change which was to be found quite early in the rite of the Roman curia, and was then confirmed by the reform of Pius V, consisted in this, that the preparation of the chalice, or in the first instance at least, the admixture of the water, was transferred to the altar and was thus incorporated into the oblation rite. According to the customs prevalent outside Italy this was all taken care of, as a rule, at some earlier moment, after the Epistle, or already at the beginning of Mass;[3] even in Masses celebrated without levites. But according to the rule that was henceforth followed, the subdeacon at a high Mass, after the *Oremus*, brings up the paten with the host, but along with it only an empty chalice or a chalice containing wine alone, hands these to the deacon, and then, without special formality, pours (wine and) water into the chalice. The act of conveying the gifts to the altar—an act of some liturgical significance—thus suffers a certain impoverishment, even at a high Mass where, after the disappearance of the offertory procession, it might still have been continued.

The attempt had been made, time and again, to keep, at least at high Mass, *the symbolism inherent in the impressive transfer of the gifts.* Durandus still mentions the practice of having a subdeacon bring to the altar the paten and chalice along with the corporal, to be followed by two singers, one carrying the host in a little cloth, and a cruet of wine; the other, a cruet of water which the subdeacon uses for mingling with the wine. The usage did not take root. Still, there is an expression of great reverence in the very way chalice and paten have been handled these many centuries. When the gifts were to be carried over to the altar, the cleric whose duty it was to see to this, following an ancient ordinance, threw a veil around his shoulders, and touched the sacred vessels only through this medium.

Another practice on the increase was one prescribing that the deacon, too, when handing the chalice and paten to the priest, do this with the help of his maniple. Even in the most ancient Roman *ordines* when the deacon put the chalice in its place, and likewise when he lifted it aloft at the end of the canon, he used a special cloth for this, the *offertorium;* and the paten, too, was held by the cleric entrusted with it, by means of a veil—called by such names as *sindo, linteum*—until he handed it back before the *fractio.* This concealing of the paten was then transferred to the non-solemn Mass.

There is also an early mention of the kissing of the hand when paten and chalice are handed to the celebrant. The sign of the Cross over the altar, which the celebrant makes with both the paten and the chalice

---

[3] The practice is still customary in today's Dominican rite; as soon as the priest reaches the altar, ready for Mass, he uncovers the chalice, pours wine into it and, with a blessing, water, and covers it again. The offertory itself begins with the oblatory lifting of chalice and paten.

after the oblation is somewhat more recent, but it had its forerunners even in early times.

SYMBOLISM OF THE WATER

After the preparation of the chalice was thus transferred once more to the altar, texts to accompany this action also begin to come to our notice. It stood to reason, for instance, that in the Roman liturgy as accommodated to Frankish tradition, the admixture of water, whose symbolism had so early and so generally become the object of profound consideration, would not long remain without accompanying words. That type of oblation rite which we first encounter in various scattered points along the northern border of the Carolingian realm, and then in the eleventh century in the Italian sphere affected by the Cluniac movement, presents a definite form for this, one which has been retained more or less in the Roman Mass of the present day. This form is as follows: the water is put into the chalice at the altar itself, either before or even after the offering of the chalice; and meanwhile is said the oration, *Deus qui humanæ substantiæ*, an ancient Roman Christmas oration amplified by a reference "through the mystery of this water and wine" and by the solemn invocation of Christ's name before the concluding formula.

Thus the Christmas thought, which hardly ever came under discussion in this connection in the literature of the foregoing centuries, the thought of man's participation in the divinity through the Incarnation of the Son of God, suddenly comes into prominence. It is a concept which presupposes and, to some extent, comprises both the oriental interpretation of the admixture rite, the human and divine natures of Christ, and the western interpretation, our own union with Christ.

Much oftener, however, we come across a very different formula, even in Italian Mass *ordines*. This formula derives from the symbolism of the water-and-blood, and outside of Italy it appears, along with the mixing rite connected with it, but not in the offertory itself (though there are exceptions). Rather it occurs right after the Epistle, or even at the start of Mass, where it is said by the deacon. The reference to the blood and water from the side of Christ must have been very much a favorite; it did, of course, come within the compass of the ordinary allegorism which explained the Mass in terms of Christ's Passion. The notion was kept alive also by a widely-used oblation formula which was spoken over the chalice instead of one of the other formulas mentioned earlier; but more especially by the regulation that the chalice was to stand on the altar to the right of the host "as if it were about to receive the blood of the Lord," an interpretation which is indeed more recent than the custom upon which it is founded, but which recurs, along with the regulation itself, in nearly all the commentaries on the Mass of the later Middle

Ages. It was not generally discarded, until the basis for it was removed by the Missal of Pius V.

BLESSING THE WATER

If the symbolism of the water was thus to be emphasized, at the same time the water was also to be blessed. This is done at the present time by a sign of the Cross which is coupled with the words "through the mystery of this water and wine" and which is omitted at a Requiem Mass because all formal blessings therein are bestowed only on the dead. In the oldest Roman *ordines*, as we have already seen, the act of pouring the water into the chalice was done in the form of a cross. In medieval missals this blessing was not infrequently accented even more forcefully. Perhaps it was as much for the sake of this blessing as for a greater emphasis on the symbolism that the addition of the water was reserved to the priest; at any rate the mixing of the water had to take place at the altar, with the result that the pouring of the wine was likewise transferred to the altar.

For the blessing itself various formulas were handed down. According to English Mass books, the celebrant said the following over the water: "May this water be blessed by Him from whose side there went forth blood and water, in the name of the Father . . . or simply— apparently the original way—"In the name of the Father and of the Son and of the Holy Spirit." Most often such a blessing, coupled with the sign of the Cross, was appended to the formula which was designed to explain the commixture, or it was even combined with it into a single formula.

BENEDICTION FORMULAS

The later Middle Ages was a thriving era for blessings. All the products of nature and all the objects of human use were recipients of the Church's benedictions. No wonder, then, that a blessing was bestowed here at the oblation not only on the water, but also on all the other gifts which were destined for so exalted a purpose. Thus we come to a final layer of texts that were built up in the medieval oblation rite, a series of benediction formulas of which one, the *Veni, sanctificator*, has secured a permanent place in the Roman Missal. Since for the most part these blessings take the form of an invocation, calling down God's blessing, the power of the divine Spirit, or simply the Holy Ghost, we can also talk of epikletic formulas.[4]

[4] However, it would be misleading to talk here precisely of the epiklesis, as Gihr, 569 ff., does, for the formularies are not within the canon, and the blessing is only preparatory in character.

The simplest form is the one mentioned in a previous paragraph: the name of the triune God is mentioned at the preparatory action. In the Carthusian rite the priest sets the chalice (with the paten resting upon it) on the altar with the words: *In nomine Patris . . . Amen.* Or the same trinitarian formula stands at the start of the whole oblation rite, or is correlated to the various parts of the action; or, above all, it is tied in with other epikletic formulas, where, however, as an introductory it is often replaced—especially in earlier times—by the formula "In the name of Our Lord Jesus Christ." After the year 1000 a double formula frequently appears, a double petition for a blessing connected with the action of depositing the bread-oblation and the chalice. However, neither of the formulas held their ground, but on the contrary were supplanted by a third, which had put in an appearance early in the ninth century in the Irish Stowe Missal and which is still found in the present-day *Missale Romanum*, namely, the prayer *Veni, sanctificator*, which was but sparsely spread in Italy before the appearance of the *Missale Romanæ Curiæ*. Whereas in Italian Mass *ordines* it usually stands in the same spot it occupies at present and amid similar surroundings, in German *ordines* it regularly followed the two *Sanctifica* formulas as a sort of recapitulation, thus accentuating its significance as a blessing. But it was also used in these ways. In some few Mass *ordines* the *Veni, sanctificator* introduces the offertory. According to an *ordo* which circulated widely on both sides of the English Channel, it concluded the entire rite, coming in just before the *Orate fratres*. On the other hand, other formulations of the invocation of heaven's power and grace seldom proved even relatively permanent.

In the territory just indicated, another phenomenon should be recorded because it throws some light on the frame of mind in which this epikletic formula was spoken. Towards the end of the Middle Ages both in Normandy and England—and elsewhere, too—we encounter not only one of the invocation formulas mentioned above, but also the hymn *Veni Creator*. The wording of the formula *Veni, sanctificator* does not necessarily force us to refer the invocation to the Holy Spirit, and thus to include in the series of offertory prayers and of the Mass prayers in general a form of address alien to them. Still, in view of the fact just noticed, there can hardly be any doubt that the invocation was often so understood in the Middle Ages. In fact, in some instances the address to the Holy Ghost is explicitly included in the *Veni, sanctificator*. Notice, finally, that the various texts that accompany the oblation ritual—exclusive of the oblation prayers themselves—do not pretend to have the character or the import of orations and are therefore couched in the freer forms of simple invocations and blessings.

5. The Incensation

After the gifts have been deposited on the altar, there follows at high Mass yet another ceremony, the incensation. Today, and already in the *Missale Romanæ Curiæ*, it has been so thoroughly incorporated into the course of the offertory, that, besides the washing of hands, there is still another oblation act to follow, whereas in other places, and according to the original plan, it formed the conclusion, coming immediately before the *Orate fratres*. The incensation at the conclusion of the offertory is first mentioned by Amalar; but in a special preface to his work, written about 832 after his trip to Rome, he indicates that this custom of incensation was unknown in Rome. For that reason it was long contested even in the North, until the date when it at last found entry into Rome itself. In Roman usage incense was burned in fixed braziers; in addition, incense was carried about at the entrance procession, at the procession with the Gospel book, and at the recession; but there was no real incensation. *Incensation is therefore a fruit of Carolingian liturgical development.* In particular, the incensing at the offertory which we are talking about became far more prominent than the incensations at the beginning of Mass and at the Gospel. And this prominence has been retained in our current liturgy, as is seen in the fact that it is richest in prayers and that the incensing of persons is most developed.

The outline of the present-day form is already encountered in the eleventh century. The Mass *ordo* of Séez has the incensation of the gifts, of the altar, and of those standing around, along with all the prayers that are customary today, while several more recent Mass *ordines* are content with one or the other of these formulas. We thus meet here first of all a prayer for the moment the incense is being put into the censer: "Through the intercession of Blessed Gabriel the Archangel,"[1] with a petition to bless the incense and to receive it "for a sweet savor"; a further prayer accompanying the incensation: *Incensum istud*, which continues with the psalm verse, "Let my prayer, O Lord, arise as incense in Thy sight"; and finally the formula which is now spoken by the celebrant when he puts the censer back into the hands of the deacon: "May the Lord enkindle within us the fire of His love, and the flame of everlasting charity," a prayer which the Mass *ordines* of the eleventh and twelfth centuries appointed to be said by each individual who received the incensation.

[1] The allusion to Michael in the present-day version seems somewhat curious. It was perhaps Michael's office as defender of the Church that brought about the abandonment of the clear scriptural reference to Gabriel (Luke 1:11, 18 f.). There is a certain justification for handling the matter so freely in the fact that the angel in the Apoc. 8:3–4, who stands beside the heavenly altar with the censer of gold in his hand, is without a name and could therefore as well be Michael as anyone else.

SIGNIFICANCE OF THE INCENSE

These words give us a clue to the meaning then attributed to this incensation, a significance similar to what we saw on earlier occasions: the incense is something dedicated to God, something holy, in which, by a sort of communion, we want to be associated. The glowing coal and the smoke arising from it draw the mind to the very highest thing that we can beg of God as answer to our gift-offerings—the fire of divine love. This symbolism we may still apply today to the incensing of the participants. The liturgical texts under consideration avoid using the concept of offering, sacrifice, oblation, in express reference to the incense. The only thing asked for is that the incense might ascend to God and God's mercy might descend to us. The verses of Psalm 140 present the soaring clouds of incense as an illustration of the prayer which we send up to God. The incense is never designated as a formal sacrifice, not even a simple gift. In earlier times, however, even in the West, less care was expended to stay within such strict limits. Amalar calls the activity "an offering of incense upon the altar" and manifestly puts it parallel to the Old Testament offering of incense. Already a century earlier the same thought appears in a letter which announces to St. Boniface a shipment of some incense. In the liturgy itself the idea found expression in the prayers accompanying the incensation in the Sacramentary of St. Denis about the middle of the eleventh century; these prayers, which differ sharply from the usual tradition, beg that God may accept this incense as he accepted the gift of the holy men of the Old Covenant. These are the prayers whose Eastern origin, namely, in the Greek liturgy of St. James, has been recognized for some time. In this Eastern sphere both the use and the religious evaluation of incense were strongly developed very early. In the West-Syrian Liturgy mention was made of a three-fold sacrifice completed at each holy Mass—the sacrifice of Melchisedech in the presentation of the bread and wine at the beginning of the celebration, the sacrifice of Aaron in the incensation, and the sacrifice of Christ.

As a matter of fact there is little to reproach in the use of such language as soon as we establish the plain dogma that in the New Testament the one essential sacrifice for the worship of the Church—uniquely essential because God has so ordained it—is the Eucharist. We can symbolize our abasement before God both by word and by signs, even by gifts of our own selection, and few gifts are so expressive as the incense which is consumed in the charcoal, and then rises skyward in fragrant clouds. In the West, however, incense prayers of this kind were soon dislodged. Obviously the singleness of the Christian sacrifice—which was not diminished by extending the concept of offering to the bread and wine—ought not to be unnecessarily obscured in the prayer-language of the liturgy. Even the symbolic action of lifting the incense up towards God before the incensation of the gifts was dropped. The use of incense even within the offertory was thus only a complement, not an independent gift to almighty God. Wherefore the first swings of the censer are for the gifts of bread and wine which are incensed three times cross-wise, three times in a circle. It is the fullest expression of blessing and consecration and in this way really a re-enforcement of the *Veni, sanctificator*. The incense here, just as the further incensing of the altar and the congregation, is intended to envelop the gifts in the holy atmosphere of prayer which "arises as incense in Thy sight"; thus it is intended to symbolically represent and to fortify the primary action at the altar.

In the manner of performing the incensation only a *few variations* need be mentioned. In some cases the celebrant himself performs only the incensation of the sacrificial gifts and perhaps the altar front, leaving the rest to the deacon, who circles the altar. Otherwise, the encircling of the altar is also accented. But although it remained as at least a liturgical norm at the consecration of the altar, at the offertory it gave way before the actualities of Gothic altar-building, so that as a rule it is now omitted even where structural conditions would allow it. However, even in the present-day manner of incensing the altar, the original conception is still plainly to be recognized. According to current custom, the incensation of the altar is always followed by the incensation of the celebrant, and at the offertory also by the incensation of the choir by the deacon, the manner and exact seriation of which, especially for the various circumstances of a great cathedral, are determined by numerous decrees of the Congregation of Sacred Rites; and finally by the incensation of the deacon, of the lower assistants, and of the people by the thurifer.

6. The Washing of the Hands

After the sacrificial gifts are laid ready on the altar, and after the incensation, if there is any, there follows the washing of the hands. Its meaning today in the spot it occupies is no longer plainly to be seen. Evidently the action, which now consists of nothing more than wetting the fingertips, has some symbolic significance. But even so we would like to know why it takes place just here and now.

It is natural that we handle precious things only with hands that are clean. Or to put it more generally, a person approaches a festive or sacred activity only after he has cleansed himself from the grime of the workday and besides has donned festive attire. Thus we find in the liturgy, besides the vesting in liturgical garments, also a washing of hands. In Christian antiquity there is repeated evidence [1] of the established custom

[1] Hippolytus, for instance. Cf. *Apostolic Tradition*, Dix, 65.

of washing the hands before giving oneself to prayer. Domestic devotion was also ruled by this law. We are, therefore, not surprised to find a washing of hands expressly mentioned in the liturgy at a very early date. At Jerusalem in the fourth century, the Mass of the Faithful began with the deacon's administering the water to the celebrant and the surrounding presbyters, and from the very start the symbolic meaning of the act was stressed. Similar was the custom in the Antiochene church. We generally come upon this same washing of the hands likewise in the oriental liturgies of the following era. As a rule it comes right after the gifts have been carried over to the altar. The rite received a notable extension in the Ethiopian Mass: after the priest has unveiled the gifts on the altar, he washes his hands but does not dry them at once; instead he turns and sprinkles the water clinging to his fingers towards the people with a threatening word of warning to those unworthy ones who might want to draw nigh to the Lord's table.

There were attempts, too, to extend to the people either the washing itself or at least some token of it that referred admonishingly to the purity of the interior man. In the atrium of the ancient Christian basilica stood the fount or well which was understood precisely in this sense, and even at the entrance of our own churches there is the holy-water stoup for the people to sprinkle themselves. But since Carolingian times the parish high Mass on Sundays begins with the sprinkling of holy water over the assembled congregation, a custom explained by the very words which are linked with it: *Asperges me*—"Thou shalt sprinkle me with hyssop, O Lord, and I shall be cleansed." The symbolism of purity and purification has obviously been from the very start the guiding factor for the ablutions in the liturgy. This is made clear in the oriental liturgies where the washing of the hands at the prescribed time was never, or hardly anywhere, based on the fact that the offerings were received just previously, for this was done before the beginning of Mass. It is simply an act of reverence after the Great Entrance, connected with the actual entrance into the sanctuary.

It is significant that even in the Western Mass we find the washing of the hands precisely in that place where the holy circle is entered; and because it is a multiple circle, we encounter this hand-washing at divers points: first when we penetrate the outermost circle, and last when we stand at the very threshold of the innermost sanctuary. Even in the earlier medieval sources a hand-washing before vesting is found as a constituent of the Mass pattern, and even today it is still presupposed, though with mitigated importance, in the hand-washing in the sacristy.

However, we come upon some isolated instances of hand-washing immediately before the consecration. The ring encircling the consecration is the canon. Since the canon has been considered as beginning with the *Te igitur*, there are to be found some cases of a hand-washing just before the *Te igitur*. Originally it was the deacon who washed his hands here, since he would assist in the elevation of the chalice at the end of the canon, or else it was the deacons who had to help with the fraction; but towards the end of the Middle Ages this hand-washing had to a great extent become the priest's, especially in German territory.

"SYMBOLIC CHARACTER"

But the hand-washing that came into special prominence was the more ancient one at the beginning of the sacrifice-Mass in connection with the offertory. This, too, *bears first of all a symbolic character*. According to the oldest sources, the pope at the Roman stational service first washed his hands right after the *Oremus*. Then he received the gifts of the nobility. Returning to his throne, he again washed his hands, and only then did he go to the altar and receive the gifts of the clerics. In other accounts this second washing alone is mentioned, but it takes place before the reception of the clerical oblation and is therefore governed not so much by practical motives, but rather by symbolical ones. It is an expression of reverence at the threshold of the Holy of Holies. The same arrangement is to be found in various localities throughout the entire Middle Ages, insofar as a hand-washing is provided for in the course of the Mass. It is found at the start of the offertory, fixed in such a way that any preoccupation with the gift-offerings can hardly come into consideration as a basis of explanation. This is particularly plain in the rite of the Franciscans, who generally did not permit the oblations of the faithful at Mass; they, too, began the offertory with the washing of the hands.

At the same time, however, there also appear various arrangements of the Mass in which the hand-washing is set to follow the offertory procession of the faithful; without detracting from any other symbolic interpretation, they establish the principle that by this hand-washing the priest must cleanse his hands "from the touching of common hands and earthly bread." Sometimes it still precedes the arranging of the gifts on the altar, and in some instances even the incensing is designed to follow.

It is easy to understand how the next step would be taken; the incensation would be made to precede, and this would be done for greater cleanliness. According to one monastic instruction, the priest should now take care not to grasp anything with the fingers that would touch the Body of the Lord. This hand-washing often stands side by side with the first more ancient one which is done before the offertory, as is still the case in the present-day pontifical rite. But in the following years the older one was dropped, and only the more recent one remained. In the rite of the Carthusians, however, the hand-washing has retained its position in the more ancient spot.

Since the Frankish era the fundamental symbolic thought of the hand-washing is regularly expressed in the words which accompany it. The *Lavabo*, which is literally a protestation of the Psalmist's innocence, and which becomes in our mouth an expression of a longing for purity and a worthy service at the altar, was associated with this hand-washing at quite an early period, but its earliest association was with the washing done at the vesting. Usually the only portion used was the one verse, Psalm 25:6, or the two verses 6 and 7. Later, the rest of the psalm was appended, but this was done without any special consideration of the contents, which have no intimate relation to the washing. Medieval arrangements of the Mass often added more appropriate texts to the verses mentioned, both for the hand-washing at the start of Mass and for this one here. In the ambit of Monte Cassino, in the eleventh and twelfth centuries, an oration was added to the *Lavabo*. Late Mass *ordines* in northern France supplement the *Lavabo* with a threefold *Kyrie eleison* and *Pater noster*. Often, too, some such complementary oration appears as the only accompanying text. All the elements that go to make up a well-arranged ceremonial are thus brought together.

How strongly the symbolic sense of the hand-washing is emphasized can be seen in a monastic Mass-*ordo* of Rouen; according to this, the celebrant's *Lavabo* is answered by the abbot with the *Misereatur*. Thus the hand-washing is turned into a formal act of absolution.

However, the hand-washing is occasionally found even at a later time without any formula, and oftener still there is no mention of it whatever in the course of the Mass. In the case of late medieval arrangements of non-solemn Mass, the explanation for this lack is to be found in the practical motivation of the hand-washing, since there would be no question of it when there was neither offertory procession nor incensation. In the Missal of Pius V, however, the hand-washing was retained for every Mass, high or low. This shows that the symbolic meaning of the rite still remained in the foreground; only the position it occupies in the Mass is reminiscent of the other and later concept of its purpose as a precaution before handling the sacred Host and chalice during the canon.

7. *Orate Fratres*

One of the few fixed points which recur unchanged in all the medieval oblation rites is a petition found near the end of the rite, a petition by the priest for the prayer of the bystanders. According to the eighth century Roman pontifical rite as adapted to Frankish circumstances, such a ceremony occurred right after the celebrant had added his own gift to the oblation of the faithful and the clergy; he then turned around and, stretching out his arms, asked the other priests to pray for him. No response is indicated. As is the case today, *oratio super oblata* followed, and it is significant that this prayer was here spoken for the first time in a hushed voice, so that it appears to form some sort of unit with the canon.

The petition for prayer thus occurs at the moment when the presentation and arrangement of the gifts is completed, and the priest at the head of the congregation and in its name is about to draw near to God with those gifts. The ceremony has its parallel, perhaps even its model, in the Eastern liturgies. Here, too, the original meaning seems to be the same. For the Western rite we have the early opinion of Amalar to the same effect. It anticipates the *Sursum corda* and endeavors to summon, so to say, all the forces of prayer. The priest feels very strongly that he is exalted above the people—a matter the early medieval Church was fully conscious of—and even in his sacrificial prayer he realizes he stands alone before God as the people's mediator.

AID OF PRAYER

The same idea may be gleaned from the fact that even in the earliest examples where the wording is included—and thence throughout the Middle Ages—the petition for prayer almost always retains a personal character "Pray for me." Instances where this *pro me* is wanting do appear in some of the oldest sources, but on the other hand the personal note recurs in diverse forms: "for me" or "for me, the sinner." At any rate the next clause, which is seldom missing, stresses the idea that the aid of prayer is being asked for the priest's own sacrifice, which is likewise the sacrifice of the congregation, so that it might be acceptable. The usual version reads: "that my sacrifice and likewise yours be acceptable to God."

The original conception is finally abandoned when in England and in Normandy, in special formulas for Masses for the Dead, prayer is asked only for the dead.

To whom is the petition directed? In the most ancient example cited above it is addressed to the priests standing around. The statements of the succeeding era, beginning with Amalar, mention the people without exception. In the second Roman *ordo* (a product of Frankish territory), the bishop first gives the *schola* a signal to stop singing; then it continues: "and turning to the people, he says: Pray (etc.)." He therefore addresses himself to the whole assembly in a distinctly audible voice. In some isolated instances provision is even made for the priest to prefix a *Dominus vobiscum*. Little, therefore, is lacking to make this address match those addresses which the priest sings at the service. In fact, in the Mozarabic liturgy the corresponding "Assist me, Brethren" is actually sung. In the Roman liturgy, however, it never came to this. The *Dominus vobiscum* was merely spoken softly—the directions for this are remarkably discordant—but then disappeared again.

"TO THE PEOPLE"

The further development adhered to the direction that the priest turn to the people; in at leasat half the cases this is expressly stated. Before this, he kisses the altar, as became the rule later on for all such occasions when the priest turns to the people. But he speaks the words in a subdued voice, as is indicated at various times.

The fact that the priest, in turning towards the people here, completes the turn—a procedure differing from that at the *Dominus vobiscum*—might incline one to look upon this as a similar stressing of the address to the people, but in reality there is a different explanation.

The real reason is probably that the priest turns to where the book is from which he is to read. Formerly the book frequently stood farther from the center of the altar than it does now. In fact, this is made clear, for instance, by the *Ordinarium O.P.* of 1256. According to this order the priest during the secreta stands between the book and the chalice and not simply in the middle, and therefore here too the priest is expected to make a complete turn.

But that the people, and not merely the clerics, are addressed seems evident from the very form of the address as found in those non-monastic documents of the Middle Ages, outside Italy and Spain, which connect an explicit address to the formula; here the words "brothers and sisters" appear quite consistently. In earlier sources, it is true, the address is usually made to the "brothers" alone, and it is quite possible that the word specifies not the entire community of the faithful, as it did in ancient times, but only the clergy.

But the unrestricted addition of "sisters" corroborates the belief that the medieval liturgists were in agreement with us in extending the word to include everyone, men and women, in the same way that St. Paul did when he addressed the whole community with the title "brethren."

The present-day wording of the formula used by the priest first appears in Italian Mass *ordines* of the twelfth century and after.

In the oldest witnesses to our petition for prayer, no provision is made for any answer. Even much later, right down to the present, there are isolated *ordines* where no response follows. The petition is interpreted simply as a request for the prayer of each individual. But already in the Carolingian period, answers of a kind were advised. Amalar heard it said that the people ought to pronounce three verses for the priest, namely verses 3–5 from Psalm 19. These verses, or also the first three verses of the psalm, or at least the one or other verse of the same psalm, recur nearly everywhere during the following centuries in the answer to the *Orate fratres*, seldom alone, however, but usually in combination with other formulas of intercession, which in their turn often occur all by themselves.

Aside from the psalm verses, the most widespread were the *Suscipiat* formulas, but these appeared in various versions and usually as the continuation of some other text which was conjoined. The version familiar to us, which appeared but seldom outside Italy, had become the only formula current in Italy since the eleventh century, and thus reached the *Missale Romanum*.

As is evident from the statements above, the answer is committed, time and again, to the people. This assignment to the people occurs in some individual instances right on to the end of the Middle Ages. At least in those cases where brothers and sisters are addressed, it can hardly cause astonishment. At other times, both in early and late texts, the *circumstantes* (lit., those standing about), or the clergy or the choir are named. It is noteworthy that in a group of Mass-orders of the 11–12th century the answer should be given by each one (*a singulis*). It is curious that the text is not to be said aloud, but is to be regarded as an aid to private prayer. Silent prayer by the individual was evidently presupposed from the very start wherever the books did not contain an answer; and even where texts were then presented, they were at first probably intended for a similar purpose. The later rule was probably that the answer be given by the choir of clerics in common, since its Latin form and considerable length was too much for the people to master. There is one extreme case of an *ordo* of Sarum in England, where at a Mass for the Dead the special answer is united with the chant of the offertory. When the priest has softly spoken the "Pray, brothers and sisters, for the faithful departed," the clergy answer by singing the last verse of the offertory chant: *Requiem æternam*—"Eternal rest grant unto them, O Lord, and may Thy perpetual light shine upon them, Which Thou didst promise once to Abraham and his seed."

8. The Secret

In the liturgy of the city of Rome in the early Middle Ages, the collecting and depositing of the offertory gifts was not accompanied by any prayer at all, but simply by the singing of the offertory. Not till the external activity had come to an end did the celebrant once more take up the phrases of the *oratio super oblata*, the present-day secret. Just as the entrance procession was concluded with the collect, and the communion with the post-communion, so the oblation was concluded with this oration which appears, like the others, in all the Roman sacramentaries and, like them, varies according to the Church year, and agrees with them in structure and design. Like them, it is spoken in the prayer posture of the *orantes*, and was likewise at one time (as is self-evident) pronounced in a loud voice. Even today the final words *Per omnia sæcula sæculorum*, like the *Oremus* at the start, which belongs to it, are sung aloud. In the Milanese Mass the practice has been retained even at present of saying the whole *oratio super oblata* aloud.

SILENT RECITATION

The first point to clear up is the puzzling problem of how the *oratio super oblata* came to be said silently. The earliest evidence of the quiet recitation of this prayer appears in the middle of the eighth century in Frankish territory, in the tradition of the *Capitulare ecclesiastici Ordinis*. We are thus led to the opinion that the name *secreta* appeared in the North and that it was here created to indicate that the pertinent oration was to be spoken softly.[1] From then on, the quiet recitation of this prayer was taken for granted in the Frankish realm, and the custom became common. In fact, the practice was brought into line with this same *secreta*, which was likewise commonly employed. The name *secreta* does indeed appear as a heading even in one portion of the Roman tradition, the earliest evidence being the older Gelasian Sacramentary. But the question is whether its use is not to be traced entirely to the influx of the Gallic liturgy. The cardinal argument for this is the manuscript evidence that at least fifty years before this first Roman witness to its use, it is found in a source of the Gallic liturgy, namely, the Missal of Bobbio, and with every indication of a non-Roman origin. We then find we are forced to a second conclusion, that it was in Gallic territory that this low speaking was first employed for the Roman *Oratio super oblata*, just as was the case somewhat later in regard to the canon. For this low pronouncement of a liturgical text is as much in contradiction to ancient Roman usage as it is in harmony with the tendency of the Gallo-Frankish liturgy. Here, in fact, it is that all the silent prayers come to light which have since filled out the offertory.

In the formation of the practice, reminiscences of the Gallic liturgy and, in the last analysis, some suggestions from the Orient must have been at work. The place of the Roman offertory was taken in the Gallican Mass by the offertory procession at which a holy silence was advised. At any rate, silent prayer at this point is an ancient tradition in the sister-liturgy, the Mozarabic. And silent prayer, especially in the form of *apologiæ*, as well as of incense prayers, and (by no means lastly) oblation prayers, must have become customary in the Gallican Mass, in connection with the offertory procession. Otherwise, the elements of

---

[1] Ever since Bossuet it has come to be generally accepted—without historical evidence—that the word *secreta* means actually *oratio ad secretionem* or "prayer at the sorting out of the sacrificial gifts." Then, if we so desired, we might designate the prayer as *oratio super secreta*.

this sort which had forced their way here into the Roman Mass as early as the ninth century, are not understandable. We have already had occasion to ascertain that precisely at this point oriental models had an influence in the Frankish realm, where we have even encountered word-for-word borrowings from the Greek Liturgy of St. James, *i.e.*, from the liturgy of the center of pilgrimage, Jerusalem. For here we also came upon the pictorial model: the solemn entrance of the Great King (proleptically honored in the gift-offerings) amid the resounding lines of the Cherubic hymn, which demands silence while the priest performs silent prayer. The tendency to perform the prayer at the oblation softly must have been given even further force in the East, since in 565 Justinian felt compelled to issue a special ordinance against it. It is quite possible that recollections from pagan antiquity were still operative here.

That the *secreta*, as it is now usually called, possessed a greater importance in comparison with the other offertory prayers, somehow remained in the consciousness even in the new Frankish arrangement of the offertory. In a few isolated instances it was realized that the secret was conjoined to the foregoing *Oremus*, or it was given a new introduction befitting an oration. The *Statuta antiqua* of the Carthusians stipulate that the priest repeats the *Oremus*, both before the first and before the second secret, but they insist (obviously in opposition to a contrary practice then in process of forming) that no *Domine exaudi* be prefaced. As a matter of fact, this versicle too is found more than once since the thirteenth century prefixed to the secret. Elsewhere the *Orate Fratres* was made equivalent of the *Oremus* and, as we saw, the *Dominus vobiscum* was consistently prefixed to it. All these were attempts at remodeling in line with a late medieval conception of the canon, which was considered as starting with the secret, and in fact as forming a unit with it, a single *secreta*.

CONTENT

But if we want to find the real meaning of our oration, that is, the meaning consonant with its origin, we must look, as we have said, not forwards but backwards. The secret is the prayer which concludes the offering and depositing of the material gifts and which explains their significance by transmuting them into the language of prayer. The creation of such a prayer must be considered a natural result, if not a matter of course, once the material gift itself was regarded as an oblation to God and, by the inclusion of the people in it, its symbolic meaning was emphasized. Thus we find already in the oldest Roman sacramentary, the *Leonianum*, precisely those traits clearly marked which still, even at the present time, distinguish the secret. No matter how the formula varies, the same thought consistently recurs in different words: We offer God gifts, *dona, munera, oblationem;* less frequently—and then obviously only to diversify the expression—*hostias, sacrificium.* They are in the first instance earthly gifts, as is occasionally pointed out in due form in one formula, which we still use today on Thursday of First Passion Week: "O Lord our God, who in these elements which Thou hast created for the support of our weakness, hast commended gifts to be appointed and dedicated to Thy name, grant, we beseech Thee, that they may be made the support of our present life and may become a sacrament for all eternity." Or the attention is called with unconstrained assurance to the heap of gifts offered up: "We heap our gifts upon Thy altars, O Lord . . . ." But the gifts represent no independent sacrifice; they are offered up only to be merged into the sacrifice of Christ. At times, even in the secret, the prayer touches upon this disposition of the gifts: "May the gifts we offer be consecrated to Thee, O Lord . . . ." Still, such an extension of the thought, although corresponding to a general law of development, is less frequent in the older texts, particularly in the *Leonianum,* than in later ones and those of the present time, just as on the other hand the complete absence of the thought of sacrifice has always, from the beginning until now, continued to be an exception.

However, the sacrificial oblation does indeed appear in divers modifications. Besides the "we offer" and "we immolate" there stands the "receive, look graciously upon" or—often on feast days—the reference to the merits of the saints or to the redemptive mystery being celebrated, which may recommend our gifts to God: "May the prayer of the blessed apostle Peter commend to Thee, we beseech Thee, O Lord, the prayers and sacrifices of Thy Church." Or prayer is said for the right disposition to offer the sacrifice worthily or, inversely, even for the fruit of the sacrifice already offered up, with the sacrifice itself being named only *in obliquo.* Sometimes we even get a momentary glimpse of the whole composite of sacrifice and sacrificial symbol, as in the wonderful secret on Pentecost Monday: "We beseech Thee, O Lord, mercifully sanctify these gifts, and having received the oblation of this spiritual victim, make us to be an eternal gift worthy of Thee." Mostly, however, the petition that is linked with the oblation—the secret is indeed formulated as an *oratio,* that is, a prayer of petition—is kept very general: as our gift mounts up, so may God's blessing come down upon us. Thus there is frequent mention of the mystical exchange, of the "most holy *commercia,*" which are consummated in the sacred celebration.

In the whole tradition of the Roman sacramentaries two points are strictly maintained; the secret is always formulated in the plural as a prayer of the congregation: "we offer, we immolate our gifts, the oblations of Thy people"; and it is directed to God and concluded with *Per Dominum.* Even the Missal of Pius V contains not one exception to this rule. As a matter of fact, if that ancient law already cited of prayer being directed to the Father at the altar should have been maintained anywhere in liturgical prayer it was here where there was question not of receiving the sacrifice instituted by Christ, but of offering it up to the heavenly Father. Of course, it is still conformable to Catholic dogma to direct the oblation to Christ Himself. The first exception of this sort in the *Missale Romanum* is found in the secret for the feast of St. Anthony of Padua, which was prescribed for the Church universal by Pope Sixtus V. Later on, a few other cases were added right down to most recent times.

For a long time it has been the rule that at each Mass there should be as many secrets—and then also post-communions—as there are collects. This rule is not entirely self-evident since in the formulas for the secret —which revolves more strictly around its own theme and seldom adds a relative predication to the word of address—the content varies but little and the influence of the Church year is slight, aside from the fact that on saints' feasts the intercession of the saints is usually bracketed with the oblation. Thus, the superaddition of several formulas at times simply amounts to a repetition of the same thought. Still, the rule was inculcated with increasing positiveness, evidently because it conformed to a sense of symmetry.

PUBLIC PERFORMANCE

The concluding words of the last secret, *Per omnia sæcula sæculorum,* are spoken in a loud voice. That at least the words of a prayer destined for public performance should be said aloud is a law which we see followed in other places too: at the conclusion of the canon and the final words of the embolism. In both cases the same phrase is in question, *Per omnia sæcula sæculorum.* The Our Father is also often handled in the same way outside of Mass. In the oriental liturgies, the silent praying of the priestly orations occupies a much larger space, especially owing to the convergence of the priestly prayer with the alternate prayer of deacon and people which used to precede it; as a result, the so-called ἐκφώνησις [2] plays a grand role. It is generally more extensive than its occidental counterpart, comprising as a rule a complete doxology, so that the people's *Amen* retains a meaning as an affirmation of the latter. Our *Per omnia sæcula sæculorum* demands a complement in the foregoing prayer of the priest. This is not difficult, inasmuch as the course of the priestly prayers remains essentially constant in all three instances. Looked upon formally, this loud-spoken *Per omnia sæcula sæculorum* refers back once more to the *Oremus* that stands at the beginning and draws all that comes in between into a unit. For what comes in between is actually an *orare*, with this difference, that the words have been reinforced by the external symbol. Remigius of Auxerre (d. *c.* 908) still had

[2] The singing aloud of the final phrase of a silently sung prayer.—REV.

a vital sense of just this reality, for he explains the seemingly isolated *Oremus* by claiming it to be an invitation to the faithful to be mindful of the oblation by joining to it their inmost offering so that their gift might be agreeable to the Lord. In the same sense a large number of ancient formulas of the secret speak expressly not only of the sacrificial gifts, but at the same time of the prayers of the people: "We offer Thee, O Lord, prayers and gifts."[3] The repeated occurrence of such formulas in the Mass formularies that bear the stamp of greatest antiquity forces the conclusion that the mention of prayer refers basically to that prayer which the *Oremus* had ushered in.

9. The Oblation Rites as a Unit

In view of the perplexing plenitude of forms and formulas which we have seen building up in the offertory during the course of centuries, there is ample ground for inquiring just how, in the light of what we have learned, are we to evaluate the completed structure. More particularly, how should we regard as a whole the series of texts which, as a result of the medieval development, now stand in our *Missale Romanum*? And how can we give this whole its fullest significance in the course of our celebration of Mass?

There is, first of all, no denying that here we have an anticipation of the thought of the canon, and therefore a certain duplication. True, it was not till the late Middle Ages that the term "little (or lesser) canon" was applied to the offertory rites, but the idea long stood unexpressed behind the new formation. In the liturgical thinking of the Middle Ages the wording of the Great Prayer of the Mass had only a small role to play. It was couched in a language whose Roman stamp continued to be strange and foreign to the newer nations, no matter how hard they tried to speak Latin and think Catholic. The canon, and this understood more and more as starting with the *secreta* and continuing through its entire course, was taken as the hallowed consecration text, to be given out objectively and faithfully just as it was, but hardly appeared to be a medium for expressing one's own thought or one's own prayer needs.

So the opportunity was soon taken, in connection with the preparation of the gifts, to get these personal matters into the rite. Basically, however, it was the olden concepts that came to the fore: oblation, prayer for acceptance, intercession; even the wording was taken in great part from the Roman canon and the texts of the *oratio super oblata*. But some new points also put in an appearance. The oblation was made "for" certain intentions; today, however, these are to be found only in a few

[3] Cf. also the formulas Holy Saturday to Easter Tuesday.—REV.

phrases. The oblation of the "spotless sacrifice" was rasied out of the dusty shadows of personal sinfulness; this, too, in contrast to the frequency it had once upon a time amid a profusion of *apologiæ*, is now mentioned only in the first offertory prayer. Besides, the personal activity of the priest is now more to the fore. The priest speaks in the singular, a mode of expression consonant with the new position of the priest, who feels himself more sharply detached from the people. Still, in some passages the singular was again restricted.

On the other hand, in the response to the *Orate fratres* provision was also made, at least in principle, for the prayer of the people, a prayer that represents intercession for the priest himself. There was also a break-up that took place in the formation of a separate oblation for each of the sacrificial elements. The tendency to coordinate the two oblations that had developed out of the original oblation phrases, and to arrange them together in marked symmetry did indeed make some headway, but never succeeded entirely. But if the oblation service was broadened out in extent, it also disintegrated in another way, for the presentation and offering was supplemented by the epikletic pleas for power from above. This double movement is well disclosed in the present-day ceremonial when, after the individual offering of the paten and the chalice, there follows first the humble petition for acceptance, *In spiritu humilitatis*, in which expression is given with biblical force to the more profound meaning of all external oblation, the personal surrender of one's heart and the interior readiness for sacrifice; but then comes a cry for the sanctifying power from above, which can give our earthly gift its proper dedication.

Considered from the viewpoint of language and style, the Roman oration spoken at the commingling of the water with the wine stands in definite contrast to the remaining prayers, which are not formulated with such exactness and which, because of their close connection with the individual activity, manifest no rigorous line of thought. On the other hand, a closer resemblance to the form of the prayer of the canon (such as might have existed had the prayers each ended with *Per Christum*) did not gain general acceptance.

All in all, the offertory prayers of our present-day *Ordo Missæ* can be considered a needless anticipation of the canon only if we pivot our attention on the *Missa lecta* where the dominant and recessive elements of the service are all evened out, and if consequently we bestow on these prayers as much weight as on the pithy phrases of the canon. These prayers do not pretend to be an anticipation of the canon, but rather a suggestion of its various motives. Indeed they are generally not even "prayers" in the full sense, but predominantly accompanying phrases to match the external action. They were never intended—excepting in part the *Orate fratres*—to be recited publicly before the congregation, and thus make no pretense at furthering the dramatic performance of the Mass.

To some extent it is different with regard to the ancient *oratio super oblata*, which is, too, in its own way, actually an anticipation of the concept of sacrifice. From it, too, the proper arrangement of the medieval texts must derive. The *oratio super oblata* endeavors to underline the one step taken during the entire oblation rite: the provisional offering of the material gifts. Even these material gifts of bread and wine can be symbols of our interior surrender. So, just as they were brought to the altar by the faithful, in an external rite, they are now offered up to God by the Church in prayer, but at the same time the attention focuses on the veritable gift which will issue from the material ones. These latter, then, receive thereby a preliminary dedication, a "pre-consecration," similar to the preparatory consecration received by other requisites of divine worship, church and altar, chalice and paten, candles and altar-linens. There is no reason why we cannot include the more recent oblation prayers in this function of the secret; thus they will best fit into the course of the Mass.

If the first prayer includes a phrase, "this immaculate host," in reference to the bread, this may have been intended by the medieval composer for the Holy Eucharist. But objectively we can refer the phrase just as well to the simple earthly bread, and with the same right that we apply the words of the canon, "holy sacrifice, immaculate host" to the sacrifice of Melchisedech. Something like this holds true also for the words "chalice of salvation" in the formula for the chalice. Even on this threshold of the sacrifice our chalice is at least as holy and wholesome as the thanksgiving cup of the singer in Psalm 115, from whom the words are borrowed. Of course it is self-evident that when we say these prayers the higher destiny of our gifts is always kept in view.

Seen thus as a complete unit, we have no reason to deplore the development of the liturgical structure as we have it in the offertory, not at least if we are ready to acknowledge in the Mass not only an activity on God's part, but also an act of a human being who is called by God and who hastens with his earthly gifts to meet his Creator.

II. THE CANON ACTIONIS

1. The Canon Actionis *or the Eucharistic Prayer as a Whole*

In our study of the history of the Mass we have come to recognize that the core of the Mass and the inner area within which Christ's institution is fulfilled is plainly and simply the *Eucharistia*. A thanksgiving prayer rises from the congregation and is borne up to God by the priest; it shifts into the words of consecration, and then into the oblation of the sacred gifts, and this oblation, in turn, concludes with a solemn word of praise. Although the fabric thus formed continues to survive unbroken in our present Mass, it is difficult for anyone not initiated into the history of the Mass to recognize the outlines of such a plan in the text of today. In the "preface," the prayer of thanksgiving is presented as an isolated unit, a preparatory item to be followed by the canon. The canon itself, however, with the exception of the words of consecration, appears to be nothing more than a loosely arranged succession of oblations, prayers of intercession and a reverential citation of apostles and martyrs of early Christianity. Still greater is the divergence from this plan when we turn our attention to the external presentation. At the *Sanctus* the audible performance breaks off, and all the rest is done in utter stillness, with only the altar boy's bell to give warning of the elevation of the sacred species, and again the silence resumes. At a high Mass this quiet is overlaid with the singing of the *Sanctus* and the *Benedictus.* Then the torchbearers appear in procession and range in front of the altar as for a grand reception; those assisting in choir fall on their knees; the *Hosanna* resounds in jubilant worship of Him who cometh in the name of the Lord. The God-ward movement of the great prayer of thanksgiving has been replaced by a reverse movement, turning upon the descent of the sacred mystery, and it is the impetus of this movement which has determined to a large extent the present pattern of the ancient *Eucharistia.*

It will therefore be our task to trace the various elements of this central portion of our Mass to their sources and to show more clearly the underlying ancient plan. We have already mentioned the decisive theological factor: the movement in the eucharistic teaching which led to a lessening regard for the oblation which we ourselves offer up and in which we offer ourselves as members of the Body of Christ, and a greater attention to the act of transubstantiation in which the divine omnipotence becomes operative in the midst of us, bringing Christ to us under the appearances of bread and wine. This theological movement left its mark in various additions and appendages to the eucharistic prayer in the Roman Mass, and thus the work of recasting it was started. The most notable modification was the break at the *Te igitur* which led to splitting off the preface and to a new make-up of the canon that now followed.

CONCEPTS OF THE "EUCHARISTIA"

In all the ancient liturgies the eucharistic prayer is composed as a unit and also titled as a unit. The original name *Eucharistia* was soon replaced by other designations, but these, too, kept the entire canon in view as a single whole. Nearly everywhere in the Orient the substitute for *eucharistia* was found in the word "anaphora," which brings to the fore the notion of sacrifice. In the older Western liturgies, too, there were similar designations which emphasize the sacrifice: "prayer of oblation, action of the sacrifice." But here in the West the names more widely distributed were others that referred immediately only to the accompanying prayer, and either named it in a very general way as a prayer: *oratio, prex,* or else, like the word *Eucharistia* designated its contents as divine praise, above all *prædicatio*—terms which we can represent to a certain extent by "Great Prayer" and "Eucharistic Prayer." Another designation, the word *actio,* defined the section beginning here as a sacred activity; "entering this action" (says a sixth-century source) the people should sing the *Sanctus* along with the priest. This name is also found in several of the most ancient sacramentary manuscripts in the heading over the dialogue that introduces the preface: *Incipit canon actionis.*—Here begins the canon of the action. The text beginning with the words *Sursum corda* is thus designated as the norm, the fixed groundwork for the sacred activity that follows. Later the word *canon* was used all by itself in the same sense.

Even as late as the turn of the eighth century the preface was still included in the conception of the canon. Thus it is directed that the Easter candle should be consecrated "in a chant such as the canon." Even more plainly in a later writing we read that the subdeacon takes the paten "in the middle of the canon, that is when the *Te igitur* is said." Thus the unity of the Great Prayer was also preserved in the concept of "canon." The canon began with what we call the preface, and even the external ritual at the solemn pontifical functions signalized this spot as a beginning.

Later on, however, a splitting of this original unity occurred, and preface and canon appear as separate parts thereof. This split proceeded from the Gallic liturgies. For here the eucharistic prayer, or rather all the praying in the course of the sacrifice-Mass, was from the start a series of individual prayers. The *oratio sexta,* to which Isidore assigns the consecration without further distinction, reached from the end of the *Sanctus*-chant to the *Pater noster.* This scheme derived from Isidore was the one which Frankish commentators of the eighth and ninth centuries applied to the Roman liturgy. Here, too, the Fifth Oration would have to conclude with the *Sanctus,* and the consecratory Sixth Oration would begin at that point. What went ahead was the *præfatio,* that is, in the new language that evolved from the Gallic liturgy, the proem and introduction to the Great Prayer. In the Gregorian Sacramentary the word *præfatio* was to be seen as a heading for the *Vere dignum* formulas. Without hesitation its meaning was confined to the unit that preceded the *Sanctus.* And in consequence, the canon was understood as comprising what followed, namely, the prayer beginning with *Te igitur.*

Despite the prevailing opposition of the Roman books, this notion appeared to be corroborated by a remark in the first Roman *ordo* where, after the mention of the *Sanctus*-chant, the rubric continues: "When this is finished, the Pontiff stands erect and continues the canon alone"; the canon (it seems to imply) is a sanctuary into which the priest enters alone.

The sanctity of this inner chamber, which must be kept closed to the people, is matched by the silence reigning in it. The canon becomes a prayer spoken by the priest in so low a tone that even the bystanders cannot hear it. The transition to this is to be noticed very evidently about the middle of the eighth century in the Frankish revision of the *Capitulare ecclesiatici Ordinis;* here, after the *Sanctus,* we read that he (celebrant) starts to sing in a different tone and melody, so as to be heard only by those standing around the altar. At first the canon was said merely in a subdued tone, whereas the secret had become a completely silent prayer. But about the turn of the eighth century various authentic reports begin to make mention of an absolute silence also for the canon. In a later Carolingian revision of the first Roman *ordo,* the rubric cited above is reworded as follows: "the Pontiff alone stands erect and silently begins the canon."

In the period that followed, the quiet recitation of the canon became the established rule, but this is not to say that before Pius V the rule was everywhere taken in the sense of a fully inaudible recitation. That the canon, however, was a holy of holies which the priest alone could tread, was a concept that was continually developed and consolidated. Other reasons for silently reciting the canon pointed in the same direction; the sacred words must not be profaned, lest we call down God's punishment upon our heads. The same thought is put in a positive way when it is emphasized that the canon must be reserved to the priest alone.

The splitting-off of the preface was also marked out very plainly in the set-up of the Mass book. At the beginning of the eighth century, in Cod. Reg. 316, which gives us the older *Gelasianum,* the *Te igitur* follows right after the last *Hosanna* without a break, indeed without even starting a new line, even though the manuscript is definitely an artistic one; other manuscripts, however, of the same century already show the break.

The cleavage was displayed in several ways. The "T" of *Te igitur* was expanded into an initial. Then the initial was revamped into a picture of the Crucified. At first this was done only in isolated instances, but since the tenth century it became more and more the normal thing. Since the twelfth century the picture was frequently separated from the text and became a special canon-plate; a new initial "T" was then introduced at the start of the text and this, in turn, was not seldom treated as a decorative figure. Along with this there was another tradition of long standing, the artistic transfiguration of the start of the preface, the first words of which (*Vere dignum*) were displayed, as a rule, with two artistically ornamented letters *V D*, usually converted into the form ⅋. Since the ninth century the rounding of this figure was utilized more and more by miniaturists as a space for the *Maiestas Domini*. But towards end of the Middle Ages the preface-symbol disappeared, and with it the special beginning of the Great Prayer. The only picture our missal has is one before the *Te igitur*, so that even the book-making art marks the beginning of the canon as something entirely new. In the manuscripts the greatest care is often expended on the text of the canon. Not infrequently it is written in gold or silver lettering on purple parchment. Even today the Mass books usually print this part in a large (48-point) type which typographers call "canon."

In the course of centuries, the close of the canon was set at various places. The conclusion at the doxology is still presupposed in the third Roman *ordo*, and basically even in the present-day rubrics. On the other hand, our missals extend the page-heading *canon actionis* and the large print to the Last Gospel. Since the ninth century the conclusion of the canon has varied, shifting between these two points, particularly in accord with the various theories regarding the consecration prayer and those rites by which the sacrifice is completed, or the representation of Christ's Passion is concluded. The end of the canon was set after the *Pater noster*, after the embolism, at the *Agnus Dei*, or after the Communion. Other particulars of the external rite were also determined in accordance with these same theories, like the extent of the silence during the canon, the duration of the time assistants stayed on their knees, etc. We will have occasion later to speak about these different regulations. But there can be no doubt that in the original construction of the Mass-liturgy the principal portion of the Mass ended at the *Amen* before the *Pater noster*.

The pre-Carolingian Roman liturgy had, as we have said, no thought at all of the division into preface and canon which we are considering. Not only was the entire eucharistic prayer comprised under the word *canon*, but even the word *præfatio* to all appearances had the same meaning. It was the solemn prayer which ascended to God before the whole assembly. In this sense the word was already current in ancient sacral language,[1] and we find it being employed in a similar sense as a liturgical

---

[1] There are phrases like *præfari divos* (Virgil), *præfari Vestam* (Ovid), *fausta vota præfari* (Apuleius); *præfatio* was precisely the prayer which was joined with the sacrifice (Suetonius). Even in common parlance the word was used in the sense of a public announcement, a proclamation. The same spatial significance is here attached to the *præ* as in the *prælectio, præsidium;* it designates an action that is performed *in the presence* of someone, and not one that precedes another in point of time. However, in the Gallican liturgy *præfatio* was used in the sense of a preparatory announcement for the invitation to prayer.

term in Christian usage. Thus it became, by preference, the name for the Great Prayer of the Mass.

DELIVERY

If, in arguing as we do, we are on the right track, then the name only confirms what we have been forced to conclude from other considerations, namely, that *the whole prayer was said in a loud voice*. If anywhere, then surely here, the solemn recitation must have become even at an early period a kind of speech-song. Since the sixth century there are witnesses to the song-like performance of the Mass-prayers, and obviously these must be referred above all to the eucharistic prayer. This does not mean, of course, that originally the whole eucharistic prayer was sung to the tune of the preface. A great deal of it, indeed, must have been chanted.[2] But we must conclude that after the *Sanctus* a mere recitative—the simple reading tone—predominated from time immemorial. This, indeed, corresponded to the character of the prayer-text which no longer displayed the sublime accent of the hymn of thanksgiving, but rather the quiet current of petition, of oblation and the biblical account; but even here in each case it might be presumed that at least the closing doxology (and not merely the *Per omnia sæcula sæculorum*) returned once more to the solemn tone.

It was in the preface that the altar chant found its richest development as the years passed. The recitative here was not merely provided with proper cadences, but at the start and end of each sentence it took on psalmodic forms and evolved partially into a simple melody. But the step to a full song was never completed. The very seriousness of the meeting with almighty God, who seems to be right before the priest during the Great Prayer, was without doubt what hindered this step. On the other hand, the performance of the preface was never so strictly objective that all mood and emotion were excluded. Music history definitely proves that even the chants at the altar, and especially the preface, were caught up in the stream of Gregorian vitality.

The unity and exclusiveness of the Great Prayer of the Roman Mass, made up of preface and canon together, is indeed none too great, even if we disregard its external delivery, its appearance in the book or its double name, and confine our attention solely to the contents. Besides the oblations, there are the intercessory prayers, which occupy a large space. In turn, these intercessory prayers are broken up into individual prayers, one part of them being placed before the consecration, the other part after. The original basic idea of the *eucharistia* is retained clear and distinct only in the initial prayer, the preface.

[2] That seems to be the sense of the expression mentioned above: "in a chant such as the canon."

This breaking-up of the contents of the eucharistic prayer had already begun at a very early period. Aside from a few phrases, the whole text of today's canon is found already in the fifth century, and the notion which had much to do with producing this dissolution, namely, the recital within the *mysteria*, and not before, of the names of those who had offered the gifts, is found even in Innocent I. In the Orient, the intercessory prayers, in a very elaborate form, obtained an entrance into the inner circle of the Great Prayer as early as the fourth century. The evolution seems to have followed this pattern: By degrees the viewpoint changed, and the celebration was no longer looked upon as an altogether spiritual *eucharistia*; over and above this there was the offering of the gifts, the *anaphora*, the *oblatio* (according to the current designation), and this, too, had to be clearly kept in view; naturally, then, there developed a provision for putting this oblation of gifts forward in an intercessory sense, a thing not easily done in a "thanksgiving prayer." Or, putting it a different way, there was a growing trend to relocate the intercessory prayers which had been said from time past right after the readings, linking them more closely with the gifts. This connection was certainly closest when the intercessory prayers were included in the very inner circle of the oblation prayers.

The driving force could well have been the closely related notion that our prayers would be all the more efficacious the nearer they were drawn to the Holy of Holies, thereby attracting to themselves the power of the Sacrament Itself. Even today, a person asking help is advised to place his needs before God at the consecration. Thus the importunate friend could seek to gain access even into the sanctuary of the Great Prayer. In the Orient the damage done to the prayer by this insertion took place in only one spot, either after the consecration (as in the liturgies of the Syrian and Byzantine domains), or before the consecration, in fact before the *Sanctus* (as in the Egyptian liturgies). But in the West the effect was greater because the prayer of thanks had always been so much more terse (and when the *præfatio communis* became the normal text, it was actually reduced to a mere minimum), and because, on the other hand, the intercessory prayers were inserted finally in two different places, before the consecration and after.

2. *The Introductory Dialogue*

Whereas generally the priestly prayer is preceded only by the customary greeting and the invitation *Oremus*, the Great Prayer displays its higher importance in the increased formality of its introduction. After the greeting there is an invitation not simply to a prayer, to an *oratio*, but to a prayer of thanks, an *Eucharistia: Gratias agamus Domino Deo nostro*. And this formal invitation is preceded by still another: *Sursum corda*. In both instances the people are not ignored, as they are with a mere *Oremus*, but are given a special concurrent response: *Habemus ad Dominum. Dignum et iustum est.*

In this introductory dialogue we have a most ancient Christian tradition. Cyprian already comments on the *Sursum corda* and sees in these words the expression of the mood in which the Christian should properly begin every prayer: every fleshly and worldly thought should be suppressed, and the mind bent solely upon the Lord. Augustine takes occasion, time after time, to speak of the *Sursum corda*. For him the words are the expression of a Christian attitude, much the same as St. Paul's admonition to those who have risen with Christ: "seek the things which are above"; our Head is in heaven, and therefore our hearts must also be with Him. It is through God's grace that they are with Him, and the gladsome consciousness of this, as expressed in the common response of the faithful, "We have [our hearts] with the Lord" is basically the factor which, according to St. Augustine, urges the priest on to the *Gratias agamus*. Of course our thoughts cannot always be on God, but certainly they should be so at least in this sublime hour.

The precise origin of this preliminary *Sursum corda* is not known. On the other hand, *Gratias agamus* is already found as an introduction to the prayer of thanks in the Jewish order of prayer. Likewise the response to the invitation to prayer by a *Dignum et iustum est* was current there. And in ancient culture too, acclamations of this kind played a grand role. It was considered the proper thing for the lawfully assembled people to endorse an important decision, an election, or the taking of office or *leitourgia* by means of an acclamation. And there are evidences that besides the formula most used, "he is worthy" or "it is worthy" (ἄξιος) there were phrases like "it is fair, it is just"; or "it is fitting, it is right" (*Dignum est, iustum est*).

An acclamation of this kind accorded well with the make-up of the Church and the nature of her worship. It is the ecclesiastical assembly that desires to praise God; but its organ, duly authorized from above, is the priest or bishop at its head. Only through him can and will she act, confirming this by her endorsement. But for his part, too, the priest does not wish to appear before God as an isolated petitioner, but rather only as speaker for the congregation. Thus, by means of a dialogue at the great moment when the eucharistic prayer is to begin and the sacrifice is about to be performed, the well-ordered community that is at work secures an expressional outlet. At the same time there is a manifestation of how self-evident and becoming is the action which the Christian congregation has undertaken.

Granted such a line of thought, it would appear to be obvious that the responses mentioned were actually spoken by the people. In fact, in the evidence already presented, this matter is made clear enough.

One peculiarity in the ritual of this introductory dialogue is the fact that the *priest does not turn to the people* when greeting them, as he does otherwise. In the Roman Mass he continues to face the altar. Here, too, we have an example of the more delicate sense of form which ancient culture possessed, for once the sacred action is inaugurated, once this God-ward activity has begun, it would be improper to turn away. At any rate, on this depended the decision as to what precisely was considered the opening of the sacred action, whether at the beginning of the *Eucharistia* itself, as was evidently the case in the Byzantine liturgy, or rather at the presentation of the gifts, as is apparently presupposed in our Mass. This ancient sense of form is also manifested in the accompanying gestures: the summons to lift up the heart is accompanied by the priest's lifting of his hands, and they then remain outstretched in the attitude of the *orantes*, the prayer-attitude of the ancient Church.

In this section of the Roman Mass *the heritage of the ancient Church* has been preserved with special fidelity also in regard to the simple form of the text, which still retains the dialogue, almost word for word as found in Hippolytus. There are none of those additions or expansions which in other liturgies partly disguise the concise exclamations. Here as elsewhere the greeting is confined to the words *Dominus vobiscum*. In the Orient, only Egypt shows a similar simple form of greeting for the opening of the dialogue: "The Lord be with you all," while the other liturgies employ some modification and extension of the solemn triple blessing of the Apostle in II Cor. 13:13. Even the *Sursum corda* has elsewhere undergone enlargements and likewise, though less extensively, the *Gratias agamus* along with its response. In the latter case, where the exclamation announces the theme of the Great Prayer that follows, the changes that have been introduced here and there are all the more characteristic. The West Syrian liturgy of St. James emphasizes the motif of the awesome: "Let us say thanks to the Lord with fear, and adore Him with trembling." The East Syrian Mass brings to the fore the notion of sacrifice which is concealed in the thanksgiving: "The sacrifice is offered up to God, the Lord of all," whereupon the usual answer follows: "It is meet and just." The Mozarabic liturgy connects with this exclamation a trinitarian confession, just as the Byzantine does with the response of the people.

The kiss of peace, too, which, in the oriental liturgies precedes the dialogue, *resp.*, the deacon's warnings, either immediately or mediately, evidently had the same function of an assurance that all were ready for the sacred action.

The Roman liturgy has no such monitory pause at this juncture. The deacon's function is scarcely developed at all, and the kiss of peace is deferred to a different place. Conversely, the dialogue that introduces the prayer of thanks is today so closely interwoven with what precedes that there is no evident break-off. After his silent preparation of the gifts, the priest begins by saying aloud: *Per omnia sæcula sæculorum*, the concluding words of the *secreta* and therefore a part of the offertory. Thus the *Dominus vobiscum* does not sound at all like a start, but rather like a continuation. Such was the case already in the eighth century. Still, at that time there was a conscious knowledge that the real beginning started with the *Dominus vobiscum*, several of the Carolingian commentaries commencing with these words. Some of the oldest manuscripts which contain the canon leave out the *Dominus vobiscum*—taking it for granted —and introduce the canon with the words *Sursum corda*. It is possible to admit that at least the solemn melody did not start till the *Dominus vobiscum*.

3. *The Preface*

The prayer ushered in with the preface is *the* prayer of the Church, her Great Prayer. It is an attempt to create with human words a worthy framework and more especially a fitting adit for the holy mystery which will be accomplished in our midst and which we are privileged to present to God. There are two ranges of ideas which here press for expression: first, the primitive consciousness that we owe God, our Creator and Lord, adoration and praise, the basic acts of all religion and worship; and second, the Christian acknowledgment that we who have been elected and honored by the wonderful vocation which is ours through Christ, can do nothing less than thank Him again and again. The *eucharistia* is the only proper response to the glad tidings brought us by Christ. For what we have here received is something far beyond anything that our human nature might expect from its Creator as a fitting endowment. Gratitude is also called for by the vision of earthly creation, the vision of all that nature provides for men. This gratitude for the benefits of the natural order is to be found remarkably amplified in a number of examples from the early Christian period, both within the eucharistic prayer and outside it. Later, the theme is less common. It is particularly infrequent in the Roman liturgy, though even here it is not entirely absent. But there is a new note and a new urgency in the gratitude with regard to the Christian economy of salvation. The Epistles of St. Paul, which almost invariably begin with a word of thanksgiving, are the first manifestations of this.

CONTENT

In this connection it is hard to decide whether the liturgical *eucharistia* in its pre-Greek beginnings (as they are to be found in the *Berachah*) possessed this evident preponderance of thanksgiving over the general expression of praise or of adoration. This last objective has indeed always been an important factor in the eucharistic prayer, especially after the *Sanctus* was included; it is its expansion into the realm of the universal and metaphysical. Petition, too, is included along with the thanksgiving, at first tentatively, later even in a relatively developed form. But it is equally evident from the earliest sources that in principle, and aside from certain more recent marginal developments, the keynote of the *eucharistia* that now begins has always been thanksgiving.

Besides the character of the Christian dispensation, there was another element that helped bring this about. The Lord had given the Sacrament to his disciples with the command: "Do this for a memory of me." Accordingly, all the liturgies include this commemoration in some form or other in the *anamnesis* after the words of consecration. But in this place they all turn more or less hurriedly to the offering of the gifts just hallowed, as the very nature of the case demands. So the proper place for this concept, a place where it can expand, is not here after the transubstantiation, but rather *before* the words of consecration, for the consecration can be inserted suitably only in a space filled by the thankful remembrance of the Lord. And this concept is most adequately expressed when it is something more than a thoughtful recalling of memories from the past, when it is rather enveloped in prayer before God. It then becomes an act of gratitude, a prayer of thanks for the great thing that has been given us in Christ. "To thank" is after all etymologically nothing less than "to think" about benefits received, and not thoughtlessly to ignore them.

As the central theme of his remembrance, St. Paul already mentions the death of our Lord, the work of redemption (1 Cor. 11:26). And this continued to be, far and wide, the cardinal object of the *eucharistia*, and as such was conscientiously retained. We should remember what the action is really a remembrance of; we should remember what is represented in the action as a memorial. The Mass is not a sacrifice reposing on its own self; it is a sacrifice only insofar as it is at the same time a memorial of the sacrifice already consummated, which brought us redemption. Therefore, it is at the same time a thanksgiving, and demands of us such a thanksgiving. When the fundamental mysteries of the Christian economy are focused in this way in a prayer of thanks that rises to God in the sight of the congregation, the prayer itself becomes a most effective expression of a consciousness of their faith and their acknowledgment of it. Thus, in the most ancient tradition the *eucharistia* appears at the same time as another more exalted form of the profession of faith.

Gratitude for the advent of the Lord, for His Passion and death, for His Resurrection and Ascension, for all that He has done to procure our salvation—these are the themes that form the object of thanksgiving in the prefaces of the Roman liturgy as they range through the course of the year. It is a peculiarity of the occidental liturgies that their prayer, including the Great Prayer, varies with the progress of the year, and, in consequence, the mysteries of faith are kept in view only one portion at a time. Other liturgies, especially the liturgies of the East (taken as a whole), do not have this variety. They do have variations in the formularies, often in great profusion; take the West Syrian liturgy, for example, or the Ethiopian. But each formula of the anaphora surveys the whole field of the Christian economy in a new way. This was likewise the principle which governed the *eucharistia* of the early Church. There was only one further rule, that the preface at a Sunday or a feast-day assembly should be longer and more solemn than at the celebration at the graves of the martyrs, since these latter celebrations naturally drew a smaller congregation and were not fully public in character. In the course of centuries, however, the custom of constantly reshaping the prayer of thanks, along with the effort to say something new for each occasion, must have resulted in the formation of many a version that touched only the periphery of the theme peculiar to the prayer. Traces of such a tendency can be found even in the oldest examples.[1] And those centrifugal forces must have been all the more powerful when every festal ceremony not only gave occasion for a new version but seemed to demand a new theme, one more consonant with the feast itself. This was the case from the very start in the liturgies of the West, and especially in the Latin liturgy of Rome. The most ancient collection of Roman Mass formularies, the *Sacramentarium Leonianum*, has a proper preface for each Mass; thus, although it is quite incomplete, the sacramentary has 267 prefaces! Even the older *Gelasianum* still furnishes 54 prefaces, the later *Gelasianum* in the St. Gall manuscript, 186.

The lion's share of such prefaces fell to the feasts of martyrs. A special theme on such days, the obvious one, was derived from the martyr's victory-in-death. When in the preface of martyrs only the fundamental concept of their bloody witness to Christ was emphasized, the result was a prayer of thanks that stayed pretty close to the basic theme of our salvation.

At other times the victorious struggle of the martyr or even his intercessory power after his victory stands as an independent theme of

---

[1] To some extent the formulary in the *Euchologion* of Serapion belongs here, above I, 23.

thanksgiving. Sometimes, however, a panegyric on the hero is developed in formal outline, and becomes at last a more or less expanded recounting of the history of the saint's suffering. It is not to be wondered at that among the five prefaces which the *Leonianum* contains for the feast of St. Cecelia, one or another should have succumbed to this last danger. Rather is it astonishing to find that, of the twenty prefaces provided in the several Mass formularies for the feast of the apostles Peter and Paul, almost all are still concerned with the theological and Christological contents of the apostolic office.

DRASTIC REFORM

In this oldest of sacramentaries, even Mass-formularies lacking a distinctively festal character are sometimes found with a preface whose contents are far different from the original conception of a eucharistic prayer, for example, when it is used as a tirade against objectionable adversaries or as an exhortation to lead a moral life. Such curiosities as these must lead sooner or later to a reaction. Phenomena of the sort described must finally have induced that drastic reform which is revealed in the Gregorian Sacramentary. In the genuine portions of this sacramentary as sent by Adrian I to Charlemagne, there are only fourteen prefaces counting the *præfatio communis*. Of these, a number—those for extraordinary occasions and for the two saints' feasts which were still favored—were later discontinued in Frankish territory, so that the grand wealth of ancient Rome tradition was reduced to seven formulas. But this poverty was somewhat augmented in the centuries to follow, that same Frankish territory contributing the preface of the Holy Cross, of the Holy Trinity, and of Lent. These ten prefaces—or rather, since the *præfatio communis* was not counted in, the total was usually reckoned as nine—were the only ones considered admissible in the Decretals first mentioned by Burchard of Worms, and by him ascribed to Pelagius II (d. 590); from here they were incorporated in the *Corpus Iuris Canonici*. Finally, to this sparse group was added the Marian preface, prescribed by Urban II at the Synod of Piacenza in 1095, although it is itself of an earlier date.

Many medieval churches, however, were not content with this scarcity. Even in the appendix which Alcuin attached to the Gregorian Sacramentary coming from Rome, there was included, among other things, a special section containing a large number of prefaces, stemming for the most part from old Roman tradition. Up to the eleventh century and even beyond, the Mass books frequently preserved some heritage, large or small, of this tradition. The Leofric Missal (11th century), which originated in the Rhineland, still has a special preface for every Mass-formulary. Similarly, several sacramentaries from France. But in the end the victory was won by the canon which was promoted by

Burchard, and which after that was repeated by all commentators on the liturgy. Even in the Middle Ages, however, the victory was not an absolute one. For saints who were singularly venerated—John the Baptist, Augustine, Jerome, Francis, Roch, Christopher—special prefaces again came into use, but because of the unhistorical contents they provoked the antagonism of various reforming circles at the time of the Council of Trent, and so most of them had again to be dropped. Only in certain orders and in the *proprium* of this or that diocese were special prefaces retained or even brought into use anew. But not till most recent times did the Roman Missal itself experience an enrichment of this sort, after the canon of eleven prefaces had held firm for almost eight hundred years. And this enrichment actually involved, on the whole, a development of the central concept of the prayer of thanks. In 1919 the prefaces for the Requiem Mass and for St. Joseph were introduced; in 1925 there followed the preface for the feast of Christ the King, in 1928 the preface for the Mass of the Sacred Heart.

A remarkable thing in the medieval canon of prefaces is *the absence of any special preface for Sundays*. In the older Roman sacramentary tradition such was not the case. Prefaces for Sunday appear in the newer *Gelasianum* and in the Alcuin appendix. Within the festal cycles, in Advent, after Epiphany, during Lent, and after Easter, they adhere to the theme suggested by the festal cycle.

In the neutral period after Pentecost several formulas appear that depart from the character of the prayer of thanks and either take in the features of a prayer of petition after the manner of a collect or are at least content with a very general theme of praise of God's goodness.

Several formulas, however, present very prominently the cardinal theme of the *eucharistia*, which we must expect above all on Sundays just as we expected it on Easter; a sample of this is concise and to the point:

> It is truely fitting . . . . Through Christ our Lord. For it is He who overcame the devil and restored mankind and the world to paradise, and threw open the doors of life to those who believe. Through whom, etc.

It may well be that the tenacious retention of the special Sunday concepts precisely in Frankish territory is a result of the fact that, even in the ninth century, the Sunday was here called "The day of the Lord's Resurrection," and was consciously celebrated as such. But in the eleventh century the prescription supposedly written by Pelagius II finally prevailed everywhere, and thus evidently the *præfatio communis* was at first used on Sundays, since it had already acquired this role at Rome perhaps as early as the sixth century, and generally took the lead among all the prefaces. Since the thirteenth century, however, the Trinity preface began to be used for Sundays.[2] But it was not prescribed by Rome till 1759.

Among the prefaces in use today, two appear to escape the ordinary scheme for prefaces: the Trinity preface (which presents a profession of belief in the mystery of the Trinity rather than a prayer of thanks) and the preface of the Apostles. There is, to be sure, no reason for supposing that this latter is addressed to Christ, since there is no precedent for such a supposition in the whole Roman sacramentary tradition. But starting with the very introductory phrases, the thanksgiving in this preface is transformed into a prayer of petition, though it is possible to discover in the continuation echoes of the thanksgiving that was heralded by the *Gratias agamus*. We have here a distortion of the original text. The original is found in the *Leonianum* where the preface presupposes the entire normal introduction, starting with a word of thanks and concluding with *Per Christum* (thus obviously assuming the usual mode of address to God the Father).[3] It might be added that even in the *Leonianum* the preface

[2] We might well ask how it came about that the Preface of the Trinity came to be used rather than the more kerygmatic ones of an earlier period. The understanding of this development has been one of Father Jungmann's most valuable contributions to our present understanding of the liturgy and so it does not seem out of place to summarize it briefly here. Obviously, Father Jungmann's thesis should not be judged on the basis of the following summary, but on his original writings on the subject which we shall note below.

The development began with the Church's reaction to Arianism which, as we know, denied the divinity of Christ. The Christian manner of praying to the Father through the Son, together with the whole idea of Christ as Mediator between God and men, were used by the Arians to support their claim that Christ is subordinated to the Father. The Church naturally reacted by stressing Christ's divinity, and this process slowly in the course of time shoved the original concept of Christ's mediatorship to the background. It was this process which produced, among other things, the prayers beginning "O Lord Jesus Christ . . . who liveth and reigneth etc." And of course, when Christ's mediatorship sank to the background in the popular mind, He came to be considered almost exclusively under the aspect of the Second Person of the Trinity, that is to say, under the aspect of His divinity. Instead of Christ as Head of the Church, as the Dispenser of Grace—our life in Him—instead of the Good Shepherd whose sheep are the Church, He became more "Christ our God," the appearance of the Godhead among men, and the terrible Judge who is to come again (cf. *Dies Irae*). While none of these ideas is theologically erroneous, nonetheless, their effect was perhaps a bit unfortunate. (In some nonliturgical texts, we find such extremes as "Christ our Father," and in one almost amusing instance, "Dear Father Jesus, Father of Your Mother)."

With Christ now firmly established as the Second Person of the Trinity, it was only natural that the Trinity *as such* should come to the fore. Trinitarian thought and theology flowered and naturally found expression in the liturgy—*Lex credendi est lex orandi*. It was this whole process which in the final analysis gave us the Preface of the Trinity. Cf. Jungmann, "Die Abwehr des germanischen Arianismus," in *Zeitschrift für katholische Theologie*, 69 (1947) 36–99; also *Die Frohbotschaft und unsere Glaubensverkundigung*, Regensburg, 1936, 67 f.—REV.

[3] *Vere dignum . . . gratias agere . . . æterne Deus suppliciter exorantes ut gregem tuum, pastor æterne, non deseras . . . pastores, per (Christum Dominum nostrum, per quem . . .).* It has been pointed out that the unusual text of the Preface of the Apostles (*gregem tuum pastor aeterne . . .*) is taken from a Prayer over the People (*Oratio super populum*) from the Leonine Sacramentary, which explains its intercessory character.

(aside from the introductory phrases) not infrequently takes on the features of a petition.

BASIC SCHEMA

The basic schema of the Roman preface is to be seen in the *præfatio communis*. Without being commonplace, it embraces only the barest outline of the prayer of thanks. The reason for giving thanks is no longer expounded, but is included in the fact that the thanksgiving is offered *per Christum Dominum nostrum*. The reason is thus presented in the fact that the vast distance separating man from God has been bridged, that we have the access and the trusty password "through Christ our Lord." In the other prefaces this schema is either repeated word for word, as in the prefaces for Lent and Passiontide where, after the word *Deus*, the corresponding expansion is inserted and then the preface continues with *per Christum Dominum nostrum, per quem*, and similarly in the prefaces for the Blessed Virgin and St. Joseph where the expansion begins with the words *per quem*. Or else the Christological expansion is included after the word *Deus*, but in such a way that the *Sanctus* is introduced at once with the phrase *Et ideo*, as in the prefaces for Christmas, Epiphany, the Sacred Heart, and Christ the King. In the Easter preface the introduction itself is also altered somewhat. Or again the expansion occurs only after the phrase *Per Christum Dominum nostrum*, as in the preface for Ascension, for Masses for the Dead and (with a freer conclusion) for Pentecost. In every instance the name of the Saviour comes in the middle. The original arrangement was, no doubt, the introduction of our Lord as a mediator of our prayer of thanks. The delineation of the Christ-mystery in other versions would be taken as merely a variant or substitute. And so, the absence of the name of Christ in the Trinity preface and in the present version of the preface of Apostles is really a more recent and secondary phenomenon.

It is necessary to consider more minutely certain details in this ever-recurring basic schema. Every Roman preface begins, and has for a long time begun, with a declaration of the propriety, we might even say the obligation, of giving thanks: *Vere dignum et iustum est, æquum et salutare*. This phrasing is not to be found in the *eucharistia* of Hippolytus, but it is the reiteration of the yet more ancient response to the priest's *Gratias agamus: Dignum et iustum est*. In nearly all the liturgies this or similar resumption of the people's acclamation has prevailed. Thus the priest, too, declares that what the congregation offers up to God is simply a service due. Regarding the content of this service, only the cardinal thought is expressed: it is gratitude, but gratitude which embraces all the powers of our soul, gratitude measured by that love we owe to God—with our whole heart and our whole soul and all our strength—gratitude that must in essence be paid always and everywhere. Other liturgies intensify the word "thanksgiving" by adding a long series of expressions all designating the praise and worship of God.

The address to God which at present is divided as follows: "Holy Lord, Father almighty, everlasting God" (*Domine sancte, Pater omnipotens, æterne Deus*) must originally have been arranged in this way: "Lord, holy Father, almighty and everlasting God" (*Domine, sancte Pater, omnipotens æterne Deus*). Both the "Lord" and the "Almighty and everlasting God" are usual forms of address in the Roman liturgy. *Sancte Pater* evidently corresponds to the *clementissime Pater* which follows later. The solemnity of this address, grouping as it does various popular titles for God, underlines once again the importance of the moment.

Our thanks and worship we do not bring to God directly as just any group of human petitioners; we offer it rather as a congregation of the redeemed, through Him who is our Redeemer and our Head, through Christ, our Lord. In the festal prefaces this step disappears in favor of a jubilant celebration of the festal theme; since this theme always has reference to a mystery of Christ, it is unnecessary to add that we praise God through Him.

Finally, our praise is joined to the praise of the heavenly choirs. In ancient Christendom a favorite way of representing the salvation which is ours in Christ was to show that it associates us with the blessed spirits of heaven and that by its means we are able to take the place of the fallen angels. "The scene of your approach now is Mount Sion, is the heavenly Jerusalem, the city of the living God; here are gathered thousands upon thousands of angels, here is the assembly of those first-born sons whose names are written in heaven." [4] Thus even in this life, as children of the Jerusalem which is above, and especially when we are assembled for the celebration of the New Covenant, we may join our voices to the songs of praise raised by the hosts of heaven. At first the preface lets us listen, so to speak, to these songs of praise. One thing that surprises us here is that these songs, too—as the *præfatio communis* puts it—are offered up through Christ: *per quem maiestatem tuam laudant angeli . . .* "through whom the angels praise Thy majesty . . . ." But why should we be surprised? He is set "high above all princedoms and powers and virtues and dominations, and every name that is known, not in this world only, but in the world to come" (Eph. 1:21 f.). "All the angels and powers and princedoms [are] made subject under His feet" (I Pet. 3:22). In Christ "all that is in heaven, all that is on earth [is] summed up" (Eph. 1:10). The concept is therefore thoroughly biblical, although the Scholastics were wont to add that the angels cannot bear the same relationship to Christ as do men who were redeemed by Him. Thus even

---

[4] Hebr. 12:22 f.; cf. also the conception of the parable of the Good Shepherd (Luke 15: 4–7), which is almost universal among the Fathers. According to this, the Son of God left the ninety-nine sheep, the angels of heaven, to seek the one lost sheep, lost man, and to bring him back happily to the fold.

in the concise *præfatio communis* the second part is dominated by the Christ-theme: Christ appears before our gaze as the King of the triumphant Church.

The Bible also furnished the materials for the detailed description of the choirs of angels and their activity. The *præfatio communis* presents the lengthiest enumeration of their names: "angels, dominations, powers, heavens, heavenly hosts, seraphim." A shorter series is associated with the concluding formula *Et ideo*, but here two other groups are recorded, Archangels and Thrones. The Trinity preface, in spite of its terse arrangement, adds the Cherubim to the list. The Pentecost preface summarizes the whole series in the phrase "hosts above and angelic powers," much as the *Et ideo* formula mentions last of all "all the hosts (militia) of the heavenly army." All bow in reverence before God's majesty, they sing out their song "in one voice," they cry out "without end"—two phrases adapted from the earthly custom of the acclamation and applied to the description of the heavenly liturgy.

It is in this heavenly liturgy, which is described with even greater emphasis in the texts of the oriental anaphora, that we are bidden to take part. Placing on our lips a humble plea, the *præfatio communis* has us enter the circle of the heavenly spirits: "With whom we pray Thee, join our voices also," and intone with them the triple *Sanctus*.

4. Sanctus *and* Benedictus

The *Sanctus* is the continuation of the preface. So true is this that the oldest melody of the *Sanctus*[1] is simply a continuation of the ferial melody of the preface. But because the *Sanctus* is here more than a mere citation from the account of the Prophet Isaias, because it is intended to do more than recall to our mind that the seraphim sang this hymn, but is rather a reminder that the earthly church should take part in the heavenly singing, the *Sanctus* takes on its own independent importance. All the people join in singing the *Sanctus*—that was taken for granted in ancient Christian times, and to some extent still is in the Orient.

Even in the West as late as 530 the *Liber pontificalis* indicates that Pope Sixtus I ordered that the people should sing the *Sanctus*. Perhaps it was already necessary at that time to recall to memory the tradition which was to be found implicit in the text itself, for then as now it read: "with these, we pray, join our voices also." As a matter of fact the singing at Rome, as described in the Roman *ordines* for feast-day service, was transferred to a group of clerics.

---

[1] In Mass XVIII of the Vatican edition of the *Graduale Romanum*, the Mass appointed for week-days in Advent and Lent. It also coincides with the melody for the Requiem Mass.

In the land of the Franks, however, provision continued to be made for the people to sing the *Sanctus* as of yore. Thus the *Capitulare ecclesiastici Ordinis* still mentions the people. In fact, the reform decrees of the Carolingian period did not have to insist that the people sing the *Sanctus*, but instead had to demand that the celebrating priest go along with the singing to its finish and only then continue with *Te igitur*.

Being music for the people, the *Sanctus* retained its traditional simple melody, which hardly goes beyond a mere recitative. This explains why one Carolingian music writer about 830, in enumerating the songs of the Mass, makes no mention whatever of the *Sanctus*. There is evidence that the *Sanctus* continued to be sung by priest and people together even in the twelfth century; it is so described in Hildebert and Honorius. An intermediate step before its complete disappearance as a people's chant was to be found in northern countries where it was assigned to the clergy assisting in choir. There is a relic of this in the present-day prescription that at high Mass the deacon and the subdeacon recite the *Sanctus* together with the celebrant. The transfer of the *Sanctus* from the people to the special singing choir goes hand in hand with the composition of the more recent *Sanctus* melodies and is finally complete when polyphonic music came into its own in the Gothic period. It is significant that the text of the *Sanctus*—basically little more than a simple outcry of praise, an acclamation—was altered for a time to suit the newer settings, and like the other chants it was expanded by the addition of tropes.

Honorius also stresses the point that the *organ*—a very primitive instrument still—was joined to the chanting of people and clergy. The sound of the organ is likewise emphasized by later commentators. In the compendious liturgical manual of Durandus the *Sanctus* is the only place where any mention is made of the organ. It therefore has here a more conspicuous function than the usual one of accompanying the singing. It has the same purpose as the Psalmist's sounding of many instruments— an expression of joy. It is not unlikely that originally the ringing of the altar bell—a triple ring, to correspond to the triple *Sanctus*—was also intended for the same purpose.[2]

---

[2] The reports about the bell signal that begin to appear in the 13th century pertain almost exclusively to the elevation of the Sacred Species at the consecration, that was, of course, introduced at the time. Nevertheless, even before the *Missale* of Pius V, testimony for a signal with the bell at the *Sanctus* is not entirely lacking. The inventories of the English churches made under Edward VI (d. 1553) frequently record the Sanctus bells. The signal of the bell at the *Sanctus* was a preliminary warning of the approach of the consecration. That, however, need not have been its full purpose. While the little hand-bell may have been introduced to signal the consecration and was then extended also to the *Sanctus*, its primary purpose was not to give a signal, since the singing of the hymn itself was already sufficient for the purpose, but rather for much the same object we have in mind today when at a solemn *Te Deum*, or, as was done for ages, at the *Gloria* when it is resumed on Holy Saturday, every available instrument is sounded. The latter custom is attested in the *Ordo ecclesiæ Lateranensis* (middle of the 12th century).

ORIGINS OF THE SANCTUS

The origins of the *Sanctus* in Christian liturgy are not fully clear. There is no *Sanctus* in the eucharistic prayer of Hippolytus of Rome. On the other hand, even as early as the turn of the first century, it appears to have been part of the prayers of the Christian community right in Rome itself. For it is very surprising that Clement of Rome should not only cite the song itself from the vision of Isaias (Isaias 6:3) but also introduce it with the passage from Daniel 7:10, just as is done later in most of the liturgies of the Orient:

> *Let us consider the vast multitude of His angels, and see how they stand in readiness to minister to His will. For the Scripture says: "Ten thousand thousand stood ready before Him, and a thousand thousand ministered to Him, and cried out: Holy, Holy, Holy is the Lord of Hosts; the whole creation is replete with His splendor." And so we, too, being dutifully assembled with one accord, should as with one voice, cry out to Him earnestly, so that we may participate in His great and glorious promises.*[3]

The triple *Sanctus* is to be found likewise in all the other liturgies known to us, starting with the *Euchologion* of Serapion and the Clementine liturgy. It is then but a step to assume that the *Sanctus* had been sung already in the primitive Church. Perhaps the synagogue served as a model and so concurred in some way in establishing its use.

Be that as it may, this hymn, derived from the prophet's vision, so sparing in words, yet so powerful and weighty, fits best of all in the structure of the eucharistic prayer, especially in the setting mentioned. All of God's benefits and the manifestations of His favor, for which we must give thanks, are after all only revelations of His inmost being, His holiness, which is all light and brilliance, inviolable and without stain, before which creation can only bow in deepest reverence. Wherefore the first phrase taught us by our Lord in His own prayer is "hallowed be Thy name." That the cry resounds three times must have but increased the joy the Christians had in this song, for even when a trinitarian meaning was not expressly attached to the triple "Holy," still there was inherent in it an echo of this most profound of Christian mysteries.

It is surprising, indeed, that the text of the Triple Sanctus, despite its brevity, shows some variations from the basic biblical text and also from that used in the synagogue. The basic text as found in the Vulgate reads as follows: "Holy, holy, holy, Lord God of hosts, all the earth is full of

---

[3] Clement of Rome, *Ad Corinth.*, c. 34; see J. A. Kleist, *The Epistles of St. Clement of Rome and St. Ignatius of Antioch* (Ancient Christian Writers, 1; Westminster, 1946), 30. This, however, is not clearly a reference to the Eucharistic prayer.

His glory." [4] Even here the word God is an addition, already to be found in the Old Latin version. The liturgical text leaves the word *sabaoth* untranslated. God is the Lord of "armies," of "hosts." This refers not only to the hosts of angels but to the "whole multitude" of beings which God had made in the six days of creation. With this the appended clause agrees, for it makes the angels assert that the glory of God fills the whole earth. The liturgical text changes the cry into a form of address, Thy glory, thus reinforcing its character as a prayer.

More important is the addition in the song of the word "heaven": heaven and earth; this is true of all the Christian liturgies, and only of them. This peculiarity is in line with the introduction to the *Sanctus* where all the Christian liturgies have likewise acquired a rather imposing augment. No longer is it the Temple of Jerusalem that resounds with the triple *Sanctus*, nor is it only the seraphim who cry out one to another; heaven has become the scene, and all the choirs of heavenly spirits, the *militia cælestis exercitus*, are united in the singing. *Socia exultatione* they sing their song of praise, and their cry is without end.

Even more impressive is the picture presented in this same spot by the oriental liturgies, like the Egyptian anaphora of St. Mark where the curtain is drawn aside to reveal a thousand times a thousand and ten thousand times ten thousand angels and choirs of archangels standing in God's presence, and the six-winged cherubim calling to each other in this hymn of victory "with untiring mouth and never-ceasing praises of God" and "singing, calling, praising, sounding and speaking" the song "before Thy great glory."

These changes cannot have been fortuitous, even though they could hardly have resulted from any conscious plan. The enlargement of the picture corresponds to the breakdown of the national narrowness of Judaism and of its cult which was conjoined to the Temple. "The glory of the Lord" which had once dwelt in the Temple, had, in a manner new and unparalleled, pitched its tent on earth in the Incarnation of the Son of God (John 1:14). Now, however, no longer to be confined by the boundaries of one country, but to be a light to enlighten all people and—more completely after the Ascension—to be the Head beneath which earth and heaven should be conjoined. From this Head the Spirit should be poured out over the entire world as a new revelation of divine grace and of divine glory. Since the exaltation of the God-man therefore, the proper locale for the praise of God has been the heavenly Jerusalem where the earthly Church has its true home and towards which it makes its pilgrimage. Part of the value of the Church's liturgy is that it is already a participation in the never-ending song of praise of the City of God.

[4] *Sanctus, sanctus, sanctus Dominus Deus exercituum, plena est omnis terra gloria eius.*

NEW TESTAMENT MOTIF

The New Testament motif that bursts forth in the angelic hymn has found even fuller expression in the appended *Benedictus,* with its two enclosing *Hosanna's.* Here, too, the praise resounds "to Him who sits on the throne, and to the Lamb" (Apoc. 5:13). It seems that it was in Gallic territory that the *Benedictus* was first annexed to the *Sanctus.*[5] At any rate the thought that must have been determining was this, that the glory of the Lord, which fills heaven and earth, did not begin to shine in its fullest splendor till the Son of God came to us in the form of flesh. Therefore, even in Bethlehem His coming was heralded by the *Gloria* of the angels' song, and therefore the crowds welcomed Him to Jerusalem in the phrase of the Psalm as He "who comes in the name of the Lord."

In the basic text from the Gospel the words *qui venit* must certainly be taken in the present tense: the people greeted one who was just coming. But one could well inquire whether the liturgical text is to be understood in the preterite (perfect) tense: *qui vēnit.* Naturally the question is independent of the position occupied by the *Benedictus,* whether before or after the consecration, for in either instance the praise must be referred to one who once came down to our midst in His Incarnation. Still, the change of meaning could be unnecessary. Christ is still always "coming." We still continue to pray for the coming of His kingdom, and even at Christmastide when we recall His *adventus* our mind turns as much to the future as it does to the past. Thus, too, His nearness in the Sacrament is a continuous coming which will attain its crown only on the last day.

Although in the *Missale Romanum* the *Sanctus* and the *Benedictus* appear together as a single song, the *Cæremoniale episcoporum* which appeared in 1600 presumes that the *Benedictus* will not be sung till after the consecration. In recent times, this rule has been raised to a general directive.[6] This is obviously an attempt to accommodate to the canon a polyphonic style of song wherein the richer melody of the *Sanctus* (to which the first *Hosanna* is attached in a thoroughly acceptable manner) stretches out to the consecration, while the *Benedictus,* along with the

[5] While the *Benedictus* can be verified in the Orient only since the 8th century, it must already have been customary in the Roman Mass at least in the 7th century; for it appears in most MSS. of the Roman Canon, though not in all.

[6] However, an editorial in *Worship,* XXXI:X (Nov. 1957) informs us as follows: "Two Belgian liturgical reviews, *Paroisse et Liturgie* (1957. No. 5, pp. 433 f.) and *Tijdschrift voor Liturgie* (1957, No. 3, pp. 239 f.) report that according to private communications from members of the Sacred Congregation of Rites, that body in plenary council decided that it would no longer insist on the separation of the *Sanctus* and *Benedictus* in a sung Mass, but since the matter was not of major moment, it would not be made the object of a special decree." As a matter of fact, in many places in Europe the singing of the *Sanctus and Benedictus* together is to all intents and purposes an established practice. Even such noted rubricists as J. B. Umberg, S.J., have acquiesced.—REV.

second *Hosanna,* fills out the rest of the canon. In other words, the silence of the canon is completely surrendered in a Mass celebrated with singing, and space is given over not indeed to the loud praying of the priest, but to the singing of the choir, which thus does essentially little more than continue the dominant note of the Great Prayer—thanksgiving and praise—and unfolds it musically to the ear of the participant over the entire canon.

Suiting his action to the character of this double song—a song of adoration—and to the words "with lowly praise" in the usual introduction to it, the priest (and the two levites with him when the occasion demands) says the Triple Sanctus with head bowed. The practice is rather expected and certainly very ancient. According to old Roman tradition the assistants at a high Mass held this position—which they took, according to another rule, at the words *adorant dominationes*—till the end of the canon. Only the celebrant returned to an upright position when the song was finished, and continued the prayer. According to the present-day usage as laid down in the *Missale Romanum,* he stands erect as soon as he begins the *Benedictus.* This is probably due to the fact that during the *Benedictus* he signs himself with the sign of the Cross, of which mention is made as early as the eleventh century. A sign of the Cross and a blessing also accompany the song, in some fashion or other, in the oriental liturgies.

5. *Various Practices during the Canon*

The Triple *Sanctus* finished, it was originally the custom in Rome for the celebrating priest to continue the performance of the Great Prayer in a loud voice but—we must presume—as a simple recitation, without any melody. Once the Roman Mass was transplanted to Frankish territory, however, the picture was altered, and our present *ritus* is broadly stamped with the new customs that sprang up here. "The Pontiff alone rises and silently begins the canon." This phrase, which crystallizes the Carolingian revision of the older norm found in the first Roman *ordo,* can be considered the basic pattern followed in transforming and re-shaping the rite in the inmost part of the celebration of Mass.

The priest enters the sanctuary of the canon alone. Up till now the people have thronged around him, their songs at times accompanying him in the fore-Mass. But the songs have become less frequent, and after the steep ascent of the Great Prayer they have come to an end in the Triple *Sanctus.* A sacred stillness reigns; silence is a worthy preparation for God's approach. Like the High-priest of the Old Testament, who once a year was permitted to enter the Holy of Holies with the blood of a sacrificial animal (Hebr. 9:7), the priest now separates from the people and makes his way before the all-holy God in order to offer up the sacrifice to Him. In the early medieval Mass he did not do so without first acknowledging his unworthiness in a humble apology, or begging prayerfully for God's help. Sometimes a hand-washing was prescribed. The whole assembly knelt down or, when this was forbidden because of the Sunday or feast day, remained bowed. In many churches of the eleventh and twelfth centuries the choir of clerics surrounding the altar, taking up the *Orate*-plea of the priest, began to recite psalms for him in a loud voice. A formal office of accompanying prayers of petition, akin to the oriental *ektene*, was for a time employed as an outward veil to cover the silent prayer of the celebrant. No surprise, then, that there were even attempts to hide completely the visible activities of the priest from the congregation.[1]

On the other hand, more recent rules, still in force at the present, prescribe that at a pontifical function a procession of clerics should appear with burning tapers and range symmetrically in front of the altar. The result of consecration practices which meantime came into being, this procession functions as a preparation for the reception of the great King. In some churches another practice was added: namely, two clerics to right and left of the altar continually swinging censers from this moment till the Communion. Outside pontifical functions at least two wax tapers (torches) are to be lighted at a high Mass right after the preface. In the same sense another custom grew in many places since the thirteenth century, the custom of lighting the so-called *Sanctus* candle at every Mass. This custom was elevated to a rubric in the *Missale Romanum*, but by contrary custom the rule has lost its force.

Through such rites, without doubt, there was awakened during the Mass in the later Middle Ages a lively reverence for the mystery that took place at the consecration like a new epiphany of the God-man. On the other hand, no one any longer thought of following the priest's prayers, which indeed were now only whispered quietly, and whose ideas turned in a very different direction. In fact, they were in essence for the priest exclusively, and were not supposed to be accessible to lay folk.

EXTERNAL RITES

The only part of the liturgy of the canon that was open to the faithful was the external action of the priest, and, until the elevation of the spe-

---

[1] Still, even in these instances, clearly not many, it was a symbolical concealment since a real concealment of the priest is excluded, at least since the 13th century, by the very fact that he held up the Host to view. Even earlier there is evidence of various altar curtains, but they were hung rather on the sides and were for the sake of ornamentation, especially on altars covered with a ciborium or canopy, where the veils would be fastened between the pillars right and left.

cies became customary in the thirteenth century, this consisted in little more than the extension of the arms, bowing, kissing the altar, and making signs of the Cross over the gifts. We must therefore cast a glance at these external rites, inasmuch as they reappear several times in the course of the canon.

It is taken for granted that the basic attitude of the priest during this most ancient traditional prayer should continue to be the same as that of the preface, the traditional stance of the *orantes*. This same posture was originally taken also by the surrounding clergy, and perhaps also by the faithful, until for them bowing or kneeling became the predominant rule. Only the priest continues to remain standing with arms extended. In the Middle Ages it was often customary for him to stretch his arms out wide in the form of a cross, at least after the consecration, as is still the practice with the Dominicans, amongst others. Then at the *Supplices te rogamus* it was usual to cross them in front of the breast. Both these postures are evident references to the Crucified, whom an older Christendom was accustomed to see in the very attitude of the *orantes*, although no special emphasis was laid on this.

The reverential bowing—the posture stipulated by the Roman *ordines* for the surrounding clergy all through the canon—was originally shared by the celebrant, as we have seen, only at the *Sanctus*. Then he also bowed after the consecration when he began the humble petition for acceptance, at the *Supra quæ* or, as at present, at least at the *Supplices*, and he held this pose to the end of the petition. The textual analogy of the introductory petition for acceptance in the *Te igitur* must have led to a similar bowing right after the *Sanctus*, while pronouncing the words: "We pray and beseech Thee to accept . . . these gifts." While this practice of bowing was stabilized already in the thirteenth century, the preparatory gestures of extending, lifting and joining the hands, and in general also the concluding kiss of the altar were at this same period still unknown.

When the priest straightens up from this first bow after the *Sanctus*, he makes three *signs of the Cross* over the sacrificial gifts. These are the first signs of the Cross within the canon, and likewise the oldest. First evidence for them is found at the beginning of the eighth century. Other crosses follow during the *Quam oblationem*, in the account of the institution, in the *Unde et memores*, in the *Per quem hæc omnia*. These, too, from indications in the manuscripts, came into use in the eighth century, and we are made aware of the headway they achieved when we read in a letter of Pope Zachary to St. Boniface, dated November 4, 751, that he had acceded to the latter's request to mark in the *rotulus* he had sent him through Lullus the passages in the canon where the crosses were to be made. In the ninth century were added the crosses during the closing doxology. The second Roman *ordo*, in a detailed exposition, makes mention of these "six orders (*ordines*) of crosses." Aside from those in the concluding doxology, these crosses were, in general, in the same number as at present. The only crosses that are of a somewhat later date are those in the *Supplices te rogamus* and—in a later passage—at the *Pax Domini*.

The significance of these signs of the Cross in the canon formed since the tenth century one of the main themes in the medieval commentaries on the Mass. It is plain that the sign of the Cross should point to the sacrifice of the Cross which is being made present sacramentally. Nowadays it is taken for granted that the sign of the Cross also signifies a blessing; one meaning of "to bless" is to make the sign of the Cross. Although in the Church of the first thousand years the laying-on of hands was generally the form used for blessing, still this form seems to have been superseded more and more by the sign of the Cross, especially in Gallic territory. In some passages, indeed, it is quite apparent that the cross is meant as a blessing, being linked with words that signify just that: the double *benedixit* at the consecration, the words *benedictam, adscriptam, ratam,* and *sanctificas, vivificas, benedicis.*

But it also appears in other passages. Brinktrine maintains that the sign of the Cross in the canon was intended from most ancient times not only to emphasize the notion of blessing and sanctifying, but also to underline certain significant words. This latter intention (he holds) must be granted in the case of the two crosses that accompany the words *ut nobis corpus et sanguis fiat* just before the consecration, and likewise the five crosses right after the consecration, at "pure host, holy host, immaculate host, holy bread of eternal life, chalice of perpetual salvation." To these would naturally be added at least the crosses over the consecrated gifts in the *Supplices,* at the words *corpus et sanguinem.* The use of the signs of the Cross over the consecrated gifts has often been commented on with some astonishment, because the first thought that strikes one is that these are blessings. A blessing is obviously out of place here. Yet it may be questioned whether it is enough to explain them as underlining certain words. Why precisely are these words emphasized? They are certainly not the most sacred words that appear in the canon.

We must remind ourselves that the solemn prose style that dominates the Roman canon is the type of speech that was cultivated in the schools of rhetoric in the decadent Roman empire. The oratorical phrase implies also the oratorical gesture. The oratorical phrase that touches on some object in the view of the listener implies a gesture directing the attention to that object, a principle that governs every vital speech and therefore likewise the prayer which was naturally and originally eloquent. Although such things, because taken for granted, are seldom mentioned in liturgical works, still there are some examples, and not only in oriental liturgy, but in the Roman as well. We must conclude that these gestures were subsequently—that is, since the eighth century—stylized into a sign of the Cross. For such a process of transformation there is no lack of examples and parallels.[2]

If, with this in mind, we con the text of the canon, we actually find that every time the gifts are mentioned the sign of the Cross is also indicated, with the exception of the *Hanc igitur oblationem*, where the hands are spread out over the gifts, and possibly the phrase *qui tibi offerunt hoc sacrificium laudis*, in which the sacrifice is mentioned in passing. In fact, we have a document, the *Admonitio synodalis* of the ninth century, that may perhaps permit us to see the transition very plainly. *The conclusion is thus forced upon us that the original gesture within the canon was a demonstrative one, and as such was not mentioned in the liturgical text.* And this would hold not only for the three passages cited above, but also at least for the *Te igitur* where the petition for acceptance is mentioned for the first time in the canon: "that Thou wouldst deign to receive and bless these gifts, these offerings, these holy and unblemished sacrifices." The "bless" would then be the occasion for a change, a transformation into the sign of the Cross, while in the other passages the pointing gesture would still be retained, and as such would not be mentioned.

Looking yet more closely at the significance of this pointing gesture, we are forced to remark the following: Since we are concerned with the offering up of gifts which we cannot transfer to an invisible God except by means of interpretative words and gestures, the gesture of pointing would become a gesture of oblation whenever it accompanied the plea for acceptance ("we beseech Thee to accept; we offer to Thy most excellent majesty"). This is not the only gesture used to give visible expression to the oblation. Mention has already been made of bowing which is tied in with the plea for acceptance. Extending the hands over the gifts embodies the same symbolism. Recall that we came upon a prescription in Hippolytus of Rome, ordering the bishop to say the eucharistic prayer extending his hands over the gifts. This extension of hands, which represents the same thought, but with greater emphasis, never became a permanent gesture or one that accompanied the entire eucharistic prayer. Only at the *Hanc igitur* did it remain until the present day, or rather once more come into use. It was also used for a time at *Supra quæ propitio*. For the rest, the hands were left free for the ordi-

---

[2] Attention is especially to be called to the transformation of the laying-on of hands as a form of blessing into the sign of the cross over the object to be blessed. Thus, in the *Indulgentiam* before the sacramental absolution we still have a trace of the imposition of hands, as it was formerly united with the formula, whereas outside of confession only the sign of the cross is conjoined to the formula.

nary posture of the *orantes*, signifying our striving God-ward. Only when the phrase calls for it are the hands used to indicate the gifts that should belong to God. Seen from this vantage point, it is not at all unreasonable that the gesture of pointing—still always valid—should be combined with a sign of the Cross, and thus our offering of Christ on the Cross. These demonstrative signs of the Cross are therefore merely another expression of our will humbly to offer up to God the gifts that lie on the altar, and in this sense they rank with the laying-on of hands over the gifts, the bowing that accompanies the petition for acceptance, and the elevation of chalice and host connected with the closing doxology.

6. Te igitur. *The Plea for Acceptance* [1]

Te igitur, clementissime Pater, per Jesum Christum, Filium tuum, Dominum nostrum, supplices rogamus ac petimus, uti accepta habeas et benedicas, hæc dona, hæc munera, hæc sancta sacrificia illibata, in primis, quæ tibi offerimus pro Ecclesia tua sancta catholica: quam pacificare, custodire, adunare et regere digneris toto orbe terrarum: una cum Papa nostro N. et Antistite nostro N. et omnibus orthodoxis, atque catholicæ et apostolicæ fidei cultoribus.

Therefore, most merciful Father, we humbly beg and entreat Thee through Jesus Christ, Thy Son, our Lord, to accept and bless these gifts, these communal offerings, these holy and spotless sacrifices which we offer to Thee in the first place for Thy holy Catholic Church: that Thou wouldst grant her peace, protection, unity and governance throughout the world: together with Thy servant N. our Pope, N. our Bishop, and all true shepherds of the catholic and apostolic faith.

The first prayer that we meet in the text of the canon after the *Sanctus* is an offering of the gifts in the solemn yet suppliant form of a plea for gracious acceptance. Such an offering, at least in this position, is not self-explanatory. It is on the same footing as the offertory, or more precisely the *oratio super oblata*, the offering up even of the earthly gifts, which is distinctive of the Roman Mass. In other liturgies such an offering, as well as the insertion of the intercessions after the *Sanctus*, is unknown. Instead, they build a short span from the *Sanctus* to the words of institution, either by developing the Christological theme of the prayer of thanks, as in the West Syrian and the Byzantine formularies; or by continuing in a free fashion the words of praise, as often happens in the *Post-Sanctus* of the Gallic liturgies; or, finally, by attaching an epiklesis to the *Pleni sunt cæli*, as the Egyptian liturgies do.

[1] To facilitate understanding of the coming sections on the canon, the Reviser has judged it best to add to them both the Latin text of the canon as well as an English rendition which expresses as closely as possible the conclusions Father Jungmann sets forth in the coming pages. In order to accomplish this, it will be necessary to depart slightly in one or two places from the textual order as found in our present *Missale Romanum.*—Rev.

TRANSITION

The transition from the *Sanctus* to this offering in the *Te igitur* has been considered rather abrupt, and the word *igitur*, which seems to mark the connection externally, has been found unintelligible. Even up to the very present the word has been given various and varied interpretations. But obviously its only purpose is to link the action which is beginning to unfold in the plea for acceptance with the foregoing thanksgiving of the preface, by which it was, in substance, already set in motion. It is the same *igitur* which forms the transition between the first section of the Holy Saturday *Exultet* with the oblation that follows, only in our case the juncture is even closer and more natural. We must try to remember how closely conjoined in ancient Christian thought were the concepts of thanksgiving and offering. What up to the third century was prevailingly styled a thanksgiving: *eucharistia* was thereafter usually called an offering, *oblatio*. The Mass is a thanksgiving which culminates in the offering of a holy gift; it is an offering which is so spiritual that it appears to be only a thanksgiving. The expressions, "sacrifice of praise" and "spiritual oblation," stress within the Roman canon itself this spirituality of the sacrifice. On the other hand, we must not see in the *Gratias agamus* simply an invitation to give thanks by word only. By a Christian *gratias agere* is meant, an *eucharistia*, a thanksgiving which terminates sacrificially in the self-oblation of Christ. Therefore it was possible occasionally to enlarge the *Gratias agamus* in the sense of an oblation, just as the expression of thanks within the preface was associated with paraphrases of the notion of sacrifice. This latter proceeding is to be found in extra-Roman liturgies as well as in the Roman. The intermixture of expressions of thanks and sacrifice is particularly noticeable in the second portion of an *eucharistia* cited among the Arian fragments, a piece bearing evident resemblances to the *Te igitur*.

In a word, the *Te igitur* and its plea for acceptance merely take up the thread of thought begun in the preface, putting it in a definite form, with an eye on the gifts.

In accord with this resumption of the thought after the slight pause in the *Sanctus*, both the term of address and the formula of mediation are repeated. The address, however, is no longer in the solemn, three-section form as found in the beginning of the preface, but merely a simple phrase, *clementissime Pater*, corresponding to the second section, *sancte Pater*. This confident term, otherwise scarcely to be met, is probably inspired by the nearness of the grace-laden mystery. Regarding the formula of mediation, the remarkable thing here is that it appears not at the end of a prayer or of a segment of prayer, as it otherwise always does, but at the beginning. Here it is plainly a supplement to the *rogamus ac petimus:* we carry our petitions before God's throne through our advocate and mediator Jesus Christ. The union of the faithful with the exalted Christ is here so vividly clear that it enters into the prayer even without the impetus of a closing formula.

The plea for acceptance is a reverently reserved form of offering, as the word *supplices* and the deep bow that accompanies it likewise indicate. The gifts are not yet dedicated, but we realize that they must be accepted just as they must be dedicated or consecrated; hence the words: "that Thou wouldst receive and bless." In this petition for a blessing, taken strictly, is contained a plea for the transformation. It is, then, the start of an *epiklesis*, much like those found in some *secreta* formulas, or like the *Quam oblationem* where the epiklesis will appear more formally and extensively. It is significant that in the Georgian liturgy of St. Peter, which represents in its core a tenth-century translation of the Roman canon, a real epiklesis is inserted in this spot. The gifts themselves are indicated by a threefold designation: "these gifts, these offerings, these holy and unblemished sacrifices." We cannot put too much store in this tri-membered expression. In the formulas of the secret prayer all three terms are used to designate the same thing, namely the material gifts. In our passage they are merely juxtaposed in order to emphasize the expression, in accordance with a stylistic law that also operates elsewhere in the canon. A certain gradation, however, is plainly discernible; first the gifts are just called *dona*, gifts such as we are accustomed in some way or other to exchange from man to man; as *munera* they appear a result of a more fixed arrangement, as a public service; and finally as *sacrificia* they are labeled as the sacred tribute dedicated to God.[2]

It is not improbable that in the first version of the Roman canon, in the form it had till about the end of the fourth century, the plea for an acceptance of the gifts, as here outlined, was followed at once by the *Quam oblationem* and the consecration. This design was then disrupted by the interjection of the intercessory prayers.

7. *General Intercessory Prayers*

About the end of the fourth century intercessory prayers began to be inserted into the Great Prayer even in Rome, just as had become customary in the Orient perhaps since the beginning of the same century.

[2] Even the expression *sancta sacrificia illibata* no more requires the accomplished consecration than the addition of the words *sanctum sacrificium, immaculatam hostiam* in regard to the sacrifice of Melchisedech demanded for the latter a sacramental sanctification. *Illibata* refers to the natural lack of blemish that was always demanded in a sacrificial offering. At all events the thought that the consecration would soon take place may well have been a contributing factor in bringing this notion of holiness to the fore.

As we have already seen in Justin's account, intercessory prayers were conjoined to the eucharistic celebration, but they preceded the *eucharistia* and formed the conclusion of the service of prayer and reading. It is in this very same place that we have located the "General Prayer of the Church," even down to the present time, although here a process of contraction set in quite early. As a result, the core of the intercessory prayer, in the Roman liturgy as well as in others, was transferred to the inner sanctuary of the eucharistic prayer. Only the Gallic liturgies withstood this development, so that to the last—and in the Mozarabic Mass right down to the present—the intercessions remained standing outside the gates of the eucharistic prayer, in the portion of the Mass given over to preparing the gifts. In the Roman Mass the intercessions, as we know them at the present, were remodeled in the course of the fifth century and built into the canon between the *Sanctus* and the prayer for the consecration in the *Quam oblationem*, and the corresponding remembrance of the dead was then added after the consecration.

PRAYERS OF THE CHURCH

If we may perceive in the Solemn Orations of Good Friday the General Prayer of the Church as it appeared in the primitive Roman liturgy, we are struck by the strong contrast between these ancient intercessions and the newer type constructed within the canon. The only echoes of the former type that really occur are the prayers for the Church (*pro ecclesia sancta Dei*), for the Pope (*pro beatissimo papa nostro*), and for the rulers of the Church (*pro omnibus episcopis*). The prayer for the Church in the Canon is more strikingly similar to the Good Friday prayers since, in both, petition is made for peace, protection, and unity for the Church throughout the world (*toto orbe terrarum*).

The explanation lies in the fact that, as Innocent I tells us, the chief concern was the mention of the names within the canon, that therefore the main stress was on the *Memento;* and, on the other hand, the General Prayer for the Church still continued in use. Besides this, the prayer for the emperor appears to have actually had its place here in the fifth century. The prayer for the cathechumens, of whom there were but few, would naturally have been considered no longer so opportune as to require a place in the canon. The prayer for heretics, Jews, and pagans, however, as it appeared in the Solemn Orations, was somewhat of a specialty of Rome, in comparison with the other liturgies; it therefore continued to be restricted to the Solemn Orations. These Solemn Orations seem not to have been excluded entirely from the ordinary service until a suitable substitute appeared in the *Kyrie* litany. The *deprecatio Gelasii,* which we took as evidence for this inference, includes in its seventeen petitions all nine titles of the Solemn Orations.

In the canon the pertinent names ought to have been spoken simply with a brief accompanying phrase. The framework provided for this is the *Memento*, with the short preliminary piece beginning with the words *in primis*. Somewhat later the *Communicantes* sprouted from the same root, and lastly the *Hanc igitur* took its place alongside as an independent structure. If the rights of the individual should thus be acknowledged in the very sanctuary of the liturgy, then it is only right and proper that at the head of the list of names should appear the first name of the Christian community and the community itself. The sacrifice which we offer up humbly to God, and which should, in the first instance, be our thanks and our tribute to our Creator and Father, will also draw down upon us God's protection and grace precisely because it is a sacrifice and because it is this sacrifice. May it be of avail above all for the whole Catholic Church! The prayer for the whole Church was a matter very close to the heart of the primitive Christians. Well known are the prayers of the *Didache* (9,4; 10,5). When Bishop Polycarp of Smyrna (d. 155–156), upon being arrested, begged for a little time to pray, he prayed aloud "for all whom he had known and for the whole Catholic Church, spread over the world," as we are told in the Martyrdom of Polycarp (8,1; cf. 5,1).

Only two attributes are joined to the mention of the Church, but in them its entire greatness is made manifest. The Church is *holy*; it is the assembly of those who are sanctified in water and in the Holy Spirit. *Sancte* is the earliest of the adjectives customarily attached to the mention of the Church. And it is *Catholic*; according to God's plan of grace, the Church is appointed for all peoples, and at the time this word was inserted into the canon it could be said triumphantly that it was actually spread to all peoples, *toto orbe terrarum*—an expression that merely serves to underscore the *Catholica*. What we petition for the Church is peace (*pacificare*), or putting it negatively, defense from every threat of danger (*custodire*), so that she might bring forth rich fruit, so that the leaven of the divine power within her might penetrate every level of human society. For the Church internally we follow the example of the Master Himself (John 17:21) by asking above all for unity: that she might continue to be guarded against division and error, that she might be held together through love, the bond of the one family of God (*adunare*), and that the Spirit of God Himself might lead and govern her (*regere*).

This leads on to the mention of those through whom the Spirit of God wills to direct the Church and hold it together as a visible society. In other rites, too, since earliest times, we find that at the start of the intercessory prayer the mention of the Church is followed at once by that name which visibly represents the leadership of the Church. Often the view does not extend beyond the bishop. In the Roman canon the words in this passage that represent the traditional basic text are the words "together with Thy servant our Pope" (*una cum famulo tuo papa nostro illo*), whereupon the *Memento* follows at once. But outside of Rome these words were soon expanded in various ways. In the Frankish realm during the sixth century the title *papa* could, for example, mean any bishop; therefore we find various clarifying additions that univocally designate the Roman pontiff. More and more since the sixth century the naming of the pope in the intercessory prayer became a fixed rule in the churches of the West. In Milan and Ravenna the custom existed already about 500. In the year 519 two bishops from an episcopal city of Epirus tell about it. In the year 529, at the urgent insistence of St. Cæsarius of Arles, the practice was prescribed by the Council of Vaison for that section. Pope Pelagius (d. 561) desired the Bishops of Tuscany to mention his name at Mass. At Constantinople, too, during the sixth century the name of the pope was mentioned in the diptychs, and since the time of Justinian it was put in the first place.

In Italian manuscripts especially, up to the eleventh century, the pope is often named alone. But outside of Rome the name of the bishop could not long be omitted. That name appears with increasing regularity, usually with the wording: "together with our bishop" (*et antistite nostro illo*). The further supplement: *et omnibus orthodoxis atque catholicæ et apostolicæ fidei cultoribus*, is also found first outside Rome, in Gallic territory, and this at a surprisingly early date.

Who are meant by the *orthodoxi*? The word could designate simply those who were sound and solid in doctrine, the Catholic Christians. The same meaning is conveyed by the complementary phrase, *catholicæ et apostolicæ fidei cultores*, a phrase appended in conformity with a stylistic law of the canon which prefers twin-type expressions. The only difference is that the latter phrase designates in the first place those who esteem the Catholic and apostolic faith and who consciously profess it. The first-named *cultores fidei* are obviously, then, the shepherds of the Church, the bishops. A confirmatory argument to show that they, and not simply the faithful, are meant by the double expression, is found in the construction *una cum*, which would otherwise be meaningless; may God, we say, protect the Church (which is composed of the faithful as a unit), along with the pope and all those who, as faithful pastors, have a part in her governance. But in more recent times, when the tautology that arose in connection with *Ecclesia tua* was no longer sensed, the expression was taken to refer to all the faithful; it was opposed as superfluous, for example, by Micrologus, adducing the rather poor argument, among others, that the *Memento* followed.

The civil authorities, for whom St. Paul, even in the time of Nero, earnestly desired the prayer of the faithful community (1 Tim. 2:2), get no mention in the Mass of the city of Rome. This is understandable, considering the time from which the oldest extant manuscripts derive, for then the pope was, in point of fact at least, the civil lord of the "Papal" State. Hardly a shadow of the eastern Roman Empire was any longer noticeable. In the preceding centuries, on the contrary, prayer for the emperor was decidedly a part of the canon. In the Milanese form of the Roman canon, representing a text taken over from Rome perhaps already before Gregory the Great, the prayer for the ruler is still to be found, and this is true also in other isolated instances. When the Roman Empire was revived in the year 800, the mention of the emperor occurs at first only in some few examples. A more frequent occurrence is not noticed till the eleventh century and by this time, because of the trouble arising over investiture, it was again challenged, as erasures and deletions in the text of the canon frequently show. In general, however, it was retained. Commentators on the Mass since the twelfth century refer to it without question. The formula is either: "(together with) our Emperor," or—at first with the same meaning—"with our King." Later, both emperor and king are mentioned together or—an indication of the growing sense of territorialism—the "our King" is understood of the king alone as the ruler of the land.

The *Missale secundum usum Romanæ Curiæ* of the thirteenth century, which originated in an atmosphere of ecclesiastico-political strife, mentions only pope and bishop. Because of its general acceptance, and because of the Missal of Pius V which was founded on it, mention of the civil ruler was generally discontinued. It was only by way of privilege that the monarch was mentioned in the canon; this custom prevailed in Spain in former times, and since 1761 in Austria, with the latter custom continuing till 1918. In the framework of the formula (together with), which can comprise only the heads of Catholic Christendom, the naming of the ruler is possible only in a Christian state. For the rest, the great needs of the political order are expressed in the preceding *pacificare*, which necessarily implies a condition of ecclesiastical life tranquil and undisturbed.

8. *The* Memento *of the Living*

Memento, Domine, famulorum famularumque tuarum N. et N. et omnium circumstantium, quorum tibi fides cognita est et nota devotio, pro quibus tibi offerimus: vel qui tibi offerunt hoc sacrificium laudis, pro se suisque omnibus: pro redemptione animarum suarum, pro spe salutis et incolumitatis suæ.

Remember, O Lord, N. and N. and all here present whose faith and devotion are known to Thee and who offer to Thee this sacrifice of praise—or for whom we offer—both for themselves and for all their intentions: for the redemption of their souls, and for the hope of their salvation and preservation.

DIPTYCHS

The decisive factor which brought about in the Roman Mass the interruptions in the Great Prayer and the insertion of the intercessions was, as we learn from the letter of Pope Innocent I, the desire to mention the names of those offering within the sacred mysteries. The precise setting for this mention of names is the prayer that follows, *Memento Domine*, along with the *Communicantes*.[1] In the intercessory prayer of oriental liturgies the same words (i.e., *Memento, Domine*) are used to introduce a whole series of petitions commending to God various groups of the faithful; these were at one time closely linked with the names from the *diptychs* (lit., twofold double tablet). In ecclesiastical life, especially in oriental Christendom, the diptychs have played a major role since the fourth century.

In ancient times they served as a sort of announcement book, and, because of their beautiful design, were presented as gifts by aristocratic people. In Church circles they were used for a list of names, even if, as was often the case, they were of purely secular origin. The covers were often inlaid on the outside with plates of precious metal or ivory and adorned with sculptured ornaments. Many of these precious ecclesiastical diptych tablets, among them some that date back to the Roman Consuls, were later used as covers for liturgical books and were thus preserved.

Most prominent in the Orient were the diptychs of the dead, but besides these there were also special diptychs of the living, at least in Constantinople. In the East Syrian Rite the reading of the diptychs, the comprehensive "book of the living and the dead," is still done today by the deacon, at this place, on Sundays and feast days. In the Byzantine Mass mentioning the deceased by name is done silently by the priest, as happens in our *Memento*. Seemingly as early as the start of the sixth century, the diptychs for both the living and the dead were read out in a loud voice within the intercessory prayer that followed the consecration. Regarding the diptychs of the dead, we know that they contained the names of prominent personages, above all in ecclesiastical life, but also in civil life, arranged in specified series starting with those of former bishops of the imperial city. The insertion or omission of a name could thus at times cause a popular uproar, as happened at the beginning of the fifth century in the case of the name of St. John Chrysostom, for the inclusion of a name in the diptychs indicated the attitude of the ecclesiastical community towards the person involved and its acknowledgment

[1] The interrelation of the two formulas will occupy our attention again later on. That they belong together seems clear from the fact that the *Per Christum* comes only at the end of the second formula. On the other hand, there does not seem to be sufficient reason to take the *Te igitur*, which likewise lacks the concluding formula, into the same close relationship. For here the *Per Jesum Christum* is already woven into the beginning of the formula.

of his orthodoxy. Therefore, in oriental diptychs since the sixth century, we sometimes find at the top of the list, along with the "patriarchs, prophets, apostles and martyrs," mention of the fathers of the first councils, above all the "318 orthodox fathers" of Nicea.

In the West, and particularly in the Roman liturgy, the listing of the names of the living takes the lead. Regarding the dead, there is, as we shall see, no mention at this moment in public worship. This fits in with what we have already pointed to as the starting-point of the list, namely the offering of the sacrificial gifts of the faithful. Their offerings were to be commended to God by a special prayer, which is precisely what happened in the *oratio super oblata*. Besides this, there was within the canon an additional plea that God might be mindful of those "who offer to Thee this sacrifice of praise." In this connection the names of the officers were read aloud. This much information can be gathered from the exposition of Pope Innocent I, but the account is so sketchy that we are left without any details of how it was done. There were probably only selected names, for obviously it was neither feasible nor reasonable to publish the names of all those who participated in the Sunday service. On the other hand, it stood to reason that where the Mass was celebrated for the benefit of such and such group, as was the case in votive Masses for certain needs or certain occasions, the names involved would be read out. In some instances this would be carried over to public service. The older *Gelasianum* presents an illustrative example on the third Sunday of Lent, on the occasion of the first *scrutinium electorum*. It reads as follows:

> Within the canon, there shall be a pause where it says: "Remember Thy servants who shall sponsor Thine elect at the bestowal of Thy holy grace at Baptism as well as of all Thy servants here present [*omnium circumadstantium*]. And the names shall be recited of those men and women who will sponsor those being baptized. And then the celebrant shall continue: 'whose faith and devotion are known to Thee," (etc.).

While the priest is silent, another cleric reads aloud the names of the godparents or sponsors. At the ordinary service the only names mentioned would probably have been those which merited marked prominence for having given a special oblation over and above the liturgical offering of bread and wine. This can be gathered from a somewhat testy remark of the hermit of Bethlehem, who had probably heard about the new practice at Rome: "In order that . . . they might get their glory publicly, the deacon reads out in church the names of those who are offering: Mrs. So-and-So offers such and such a thing. Mr. Somebody

Else promises to give this or that. And they delight in the applause of the people." [2]

A reading similar to that at Rome is evidenced beyond doubt in the domain of the Gallic liturgy, and here it is the offerers who are expressly named. The Gallican Mass of the seventh century—and likewise the Mozarabic—includes a special priestly oration *Post nomina* after the offertory procession and the introductory prayer. The wording of this oration is often linked to the reading of the names that just took place, then launches into a prayer of intercession for living and dead. The reading itself, however, includes under the notion of *offerentes* not only those present, above all the clergy assembled here, but also all whose society is valued while the sacrifice is being offered up. Even the dead are embodied in this circle of offerers, either because those offering the sacrifice do so "for" them, that is, as their representatives, or that they "remember" them in the oblation. In the Mozarabic Mass this reading, which precedes the oration *Post nomina*, has been retained to the present.

It is noteworthy that not till the second sentence in the Mozarabic formula is the word *offerunt* applied to those present, while in the first sentence it is ascribed in honorary fashion to the representatives of the grand ecclesiastical communion. It is probably to be presumed that originally the names of the persons in office—the leading bishops in Spain and the pope—were pronounced. In the course of time this mention of names was omitted in favor of the bare formula, either because it was deemed unimportant or because it was found too bothersome.

Something like this must also have occurred in the Roman canon where the oldest extant manuscripts in general no longer have any indication whatever of an explicit listing of names after the words: Remember, O Lord, Thy servants. But since the formula obviously implies it, the indication for such an insert was later restored, some way or other, even soon after the Roman Mass was transplanted to Frankish soil. In his *Admonitio Generalis* of 789 Charlemagne decreed: The names should not be publicly read at some earlier part of the Mass (as in the Gallican rite), but during the canon. The express direction is then found variously in the Mass books.

Since the canon began to be said in a low tone, this reading of names could no longer be loud and public. According to one eleventh century account, the names were whispered into the priest's ear on those occasions when he had assistants around him. In another instance the names

---

[2] The custom in many American Negro churches of clapping, applauding, shouting *amen*, etc., is not as foreign to earlier forms of Christian worship as we might at first think. The pilgrim Aetheria mentions that, in Jerusalem in the fourth century, the sound of the people applauding the bishop's words could be heard outside even when the doors were closed. And when the older liturgical sources tell us that the celebrant or the deacon "cried out" something and the people "shouted" their reply, we may be sure they did exactly that.—REV.

were pronounced by the priest himself. Many Mass books, therefore, even indicate certain names right in the text of the canon, at least as a marginal notation, perhaps by reason of foundations. Or a corresponding general formula was inserted, embracing those names that had a right to be mentioned. Sometimes the register of names was laid on the altar and merely a reference introduced into the *Memento,* a practice similar to one still in use at present in the West Syrian rite.

Since the eleventh century these insert formulas, bearing a general character and often joined to the reference mentioned, grew transiently to memorable proportions, encompassing not only the *Memento* itself, but also the preceding intercessory plea for pope and bishop. Often, too, a self-recommendation was added at the start.

But very early a contrary tendency arose, leading in the course of the centuries to a complete suppression of all such additions. Only names were allowed to be inserted, or generally only a silent commemoration was permitted at this moment, and in this the faithful were probably invited to take part.

In the Missal of Pius V the indication of a mention of names and the corresponding pause have been retained. But no rule is prescribed regarding the choice of names. It is in line with the original intent and with the context that at a Mass said for a stipend the one who in this way became an *offerens* should be especially remembered here.

"CIRCUM ADSTANTES"

But in the text of the *Memento* itself the circle is broadened. Into it are drawn all those present, since they did come to church in order to honor God by this communal oblation. They are called *circumstantes* or, in the more ancient texts, *circum adstantes.* During the first thousand years, standing was the principal posture even during the canon. Note, however, that the *circum* is not to be construed as though the faithful had ever completely surrounded the altar. Rather the picture intended is what is suggested by the structure of the old Roman basilicas, where the altar stood between the presbytery and the nave, so that the faithful —especially if there was a transept—could form a semicircle or "open ring" around the altar.

About those mentioned by name and about the group of *circum adstantes,* a two-membered clause originally had two things to say. One phrase regarded their general state of soul, namely: their faith and their devotion is well known to Thee. The other phrase took notice of their activity: they offer up to Thee a sacrifice of praise; this is further described and defined. The original text, like the text of the first prayer after the consecration, ascribes to the faithful the offering of the sacrifice, without any special restriction "who offer to Thee this sacrifice of praise" (*qui tibi offerunt hoc sacrificium laudis*). They are not idle spectators, even less a profane crowd; rather they are all together sharers in that sacred action with which we stand before Thee, O God. But in more recent times, when by reason of language and spatial arrangement the celebration of the priest is markedly withdrawn from the people, who can follow the service only at a certain distance, this unrestricted expression apparently looked too bold, and so the words, "or for whom we offer to Thee" (*pro quibus tibi offerimus vel*) were prefixed. This insertion made its first appearance in several manuscripts of the Gregorian Sacramentary prepared by Alcuin, and after the tenth century speedily became almost universal, not, however, without encountering some opposition. The point made by this phrase was that the priest at the altar (surrounded by his assistants) was primarily the one who offered the sacrifice. It is possible that a contributing factor was to be found in the consideration that in this period, when foundations and stipends were gaining headway, those whose names were to be recalled at the *Memento* were often not present at the Mass, so that the priest was also their representative even in a narrower sense. Still, as a rule the original concept continued to stand unimpaired.

The sacrificial activity of the faithful is next more clearly defined according to its purpose. They offer up the sacrifice for themselves and for their dear ones; the bonds of family have a rightful place in prayer. They offer their sacrifice that thus they might "redeem (purchase) their souls." According to Christ's own words, no price can be high enough to make such a purchase, and yet this will surely do. They want to redeem their souls,[3] that is, they want to gain the welfare and health that they as Christians may dare to hope for—as the clarifying clause puts it— "for the hope of their salvation and preservation" (*pro spe salutis et incolumitatis suæ*). In this phrase the word *salus* can be taken for the salvation of the soul, as Christian usage employs the word, while *incolumitas* at least includes the notion of bodily health and security.

The *Memento* closes with the words "and who render their vows to Thee, eternal God living and true" (*tibique reddunt vota sua æterno Deo vivo et vero*), thus tacking a second phrase to the words "who offer to Thee this sacrifice of praise." One might possibly expect to find in this a continuation of the thought, but this is rather hard to establish. Although *vota* can have other meanings, *reddere vota* is without doubt either the dutiful gift of something commended to God (as is the case in many passages in the Latin rendering of the Old Testament), or it is, as here, simply the giving of a gift to God, taking into account a previ-

---

[3] "Pro redemptione animarum suarum." With this phrase was connected the idea that one could buy his way out of sin by giving gifts. The same thought applies to "pro se suisque, etc." While it is true that such expressions were found in pre-Christian pagan rites, they are obviously meant in a completely Christian sense here. Cf. Daniel 4:24.

ous obligation; it is the offering up of a sacrifice, but with a sharp underscoring of the thought inherent in every sacrifice, that the work is one that is due.

In the clause doubled in this way we have a clear imitation of Psalm 49:14: "Offer to God a sacrifice of praise and render thy vows to the Most High" (*Immola Deo sacrificium laudis et redde Altissimo vota tua*). The only addition is the solemn invocation of God's name, likewise formed on a scriptural quotation, and emphasized by prefacing the word *æterno*. It dawns on one's consciousness that in the sacrifice one is face to face with the eternal, living, true God.

All in all, however, there seems to be something very curious in the twin phrase in this passage, for the poetic parallelism of the two members, as it is found in the quotation from the Psalm, is not to be found here. We are tempted to conclude that the detailed description of the sacrifice of the faithful as outlined here was inserted only belatedly, and that the original text ran as follows: [4] "Remember, O Lord, Thy servants who offer to Thee this sacrifice of praise and who offer this sacrifice due to Thee, eternal God living and true." This conclusion is corroborated by the Mozarabic citation from the Roman canon already referred to. But how is it possible that the first member should have been supplemented as we find it today, while the second member, widely separated from it, should have remained unaltered?

This first surprise is joined by a second. In all the oldest texts of the Roman canon, without exception, the suffix—*que* is missing at the beginning of the second member; invariably it reads: . . . *incolumitatis suæ tibi reddunt vota sua.* . . . Grammatical carelessness of this type, copied century after century, must indeed be serious cause for wonder, particularly in a text of the Roman canon which, taken all in all, is otherwise smooth.

Both problems are solved at one blow if we put a period after the words *incolumitatis suæ*, and then begin with a new sentence: *Tibi reddunt vota sua æterno Deo vivo et vero communicantes . . . .*[5] These words take up the *tibi offerunt sacrificium laudis* with a different wording in order to append to it the idea of the grand Communion. Thus, communion with the saints was originally claimed principally for the faithful, just as was the offering of the sacrifice. But, influenced by the different atmosphere of the Frankish church, both claims were at the same time obscured, not, however, to such an extent that the ancient

[4] *Memento Domine famulorum famularumque tuarum, qui tibi offerunt hoc sacrificium laudis et tibi reddunt vota sua æterno Deo vivo et vero.*

[5] In other words, the *Memento* would run as follows: "Who offer to Thee this sacrifice of praise, for themselves, . . . for the hope of their salvation and preservation.

"They now render their vows to Thee, eternal God living and true, in communion with and in venerable commemoration of, first, the glorious ever Virgin Mary Mother of, etc. . . .".

thought should not be offered as the most natural interpretation of the text. In other words, we feel justified in considering and explaining the phrase *tibi reddunt*, etc., as a part of the *Communicantes* text.

9. Communicantes

Tibique reddunt vota sua, æterno Deo vivo et vero, communicantes, et memoriam venerantes, in primis gloriosæ semper Virginis Mariæ, Genetricis Dei et Domini nostri Jesu Christi: sed et beatorum Apostolorum ac Martyrum tuorum Petri et Pauli, Andreæ, Jacobi, Joannis, Thomæ, Jacobi, Philippi, Bartholomæi, Matthæi, Simonis et Thaddæi: Lini, Cleti, Clementis, Xysti, Cornelii, Cypriani, Laurentii, Chrysogoni, Joannis et Pauli, Cosmæ et Damiani, et omnium sanctorum tuorum; quorum meritis precibusque concedas, ut in omnibus protectionis tuæ muniamur auxilio. Per eumdem Christum Dominum nostrum. Amen.	And now they offer this sacrifice due unto Thee, eternal God living and true, in holy fellowship and venerable memory first of the glorious and ever virgin Mary, Mother of God and Our Lord Jesus Christ, and also of Thy blessed apostles and martyrs Peter and Paul, Andrew, James, John, Thomas, James, Philip, Bartholomew, Matthew, Simon and Thaddeus, Linus, Cletus, Clement, Sixtus, Cornelius, Cyprian, Lawrence, Chrysogonus, John and Paul, Cosmas and Damian, and of all Thy saints; and do Thou grant that through their prayers and merits we may in all things dwell secure under Thy protection. Through the same Christ Our Lord. Amen.

The *Communicantes* that follows is not, as it now stands, a grammatically complete sentence. The first question therefore regarding it naturally is: what is it connected with? Other links have been propounded, but the one that appears most natural is that suggested to us by the text just studied, a proposal that was already made years ago by Suarez. Just as by origin the *Communicantes* is a continuation of the *Memento*, so also its content is a reinforcement of the plea in that *Memento:* Remember all of them, for the congregation which now stands before Thee with its sacrifice does not stand solitary, since it belongs to the great nation of the redeemed, whose foremost ranks have already entered into Thy glory. Once again is made manifest that bond with the Church Triumphant which had already been vividly recalled in a different way by the singing of the *Sanctus*.

COMRADESHIP WITH THE SAINTS

The emphasis here is on the word *communicantes*, on the comradeship with the saints whose names are about to be mentioned. At the same time, however, we become aware of the distance that separates us and so, by the subsequent words, "and venerating the memory," this comradeship is altered into a look of awe and respect. It is this second phrase that governs the following grammatical construction, which would otherwise have run as follows: *communicantes in primis cum*. But this in no way weakens the basic idea of stressing the communion. We have already seen how in the oriental liturgies the reading of the diptychs was correlated since the fifth century with the concept of ecclesiastical communion, and how this thought was logically developed into a consciousness of communion with the saints in heaven. But communion is not mentioned in a direct form; the mention of those who "from the beginning have been pleasing to God" is simply appended to the listing of other names or groups of those who have departed from the earthly congregation. Often the same formula is used to frame both the sections. "We offer up this sacrifice also for . . ." or ". . . in pious memory of . . ." or "Remember also . . ." "Deign to remember . . . ." In fact at one stage, when theological thinking was less clarified, we even find the formal petition that God may give them "peace" applied also to the saints.

But in all these instances the main stress is laid on emphasizing the communion. Thus, too, the *memoriam venerantes* is to be construed. That we are correct in drawing on the oriental diptych practice to illustrate this portion of the ecclesiastical prayer is confirmed not only by the fact that the *Communicantes* must have been introduced into the canon about the same time that this practice was in full flower in the East, when Roman popes were corresponding with the Orient regarding questions of the diptychs, but even more immediately by the wording of the *Communicantes* itself, wherein a model from the area of the Syrian liturgy was evidently of some influence.

Thus, for all the insistence on the concept of communion, the beginning and the end present a slight anomaly. For the one singled out to head the list of saints is one who had the incomparable dignity of being Mother of God and ever virgin. And at the end of the list the relation we bear to the saints in general is indicated with greater exactness by the humble prayer that their intercession might avail us. By such clarifying phrases the ancient formula, accidentally left unchanged, the formula of an offering "for" all of them, was rectified along the lines of the principle already expounded by St. Augustine for the naming of the saints at the altar, namely: instead of our praying for a martyr, he should pray for us.

The list of names in the present-day Roman canon here consists of two well-balanced groups of twelve names, twelve apostles and twelve martyrs, led by the Queen of all saints; similarly, the second list in the *Nobis quoque peccatoribus* comprises twin groups of that other sacred number, the number seven: seven male martyrs and seven female, led by him whom the Lord himself had termed the greatest of those born of woman (Matthew 11:11). Thus a double choir of saints is arrayed, much in the same way as Christian art had sought to represent it. The venerable antiquity of the lists is clearly manifested by the fact that, besides the biblical names, only those saints are included who were honored at Rome as martyrs; the cult of confessors, whose beginnings are surely to be found in the fourth century, has not yet left a mark here. The honor of being mentioned in the Great Prayer of the sacrifice is reserved to those heroes of the faith who had faced the struggle of suffering along with Christ.

THE SAINTS

Upon closer scrutiny the *Communicantes* list reveals a well-planned arrangement. The twelve martyrs are aligned in hierarchical order. First come six bishops, five of them popes, and then a non-Roman, Cyprian, contemporary of St. Cornelius (who is therefore the only one taken out of chronological order so as to be set side by side with Cyprian). Among the other six martyrs, the first two are clerics. Lawrence and Chrysogonus; then follow the laymen, John and Paul, Cosmas and Damian. Clearly we have here the work of a systematic hand. In the sacred precincts of the Great Prayer, so to say, a properly chosen representation from the choirs of martyrs ought to appear. This is the one conception that we can make our own even at the present; the one thought that can reconcile us with the catalogue of saints in the canon, in spite of its weaknesses, even though two thousand years of Church history and the extension of the horizon beyond that of a city-liturgy into a world-liturgy has presented us with numberless other names to choose from. To this double series of twelve names from the early ages of Christianity and from the life of the Roman Mother-Church we are pleased to grant the privilege to be named at the altar as representatives of the Church Triumphant.

It is obvious, no doubt, that the list of saints in the *Communicantes*—and something similar must be said later about the second list—is not a first draft. In some oriental anaphoras the list of saints named in the prayer of intercession has been kept at a minimum. In the Roman canon as it was when transferred to Milan, perhaps in the sixth century, some names found in our present-day list are missing, namely, those of Popes Linus and Cletus, and the names included are not yet presented in the nice order they now possess.

The original list must have comprised those saints who enjoyed a special cult at Rome at the time of the introduction of the *Communicantes*. Around the turn of the fifth century these were: Mary, Peter and Paul, Xystus and Lawrence, Cornelius and Cyprian. Soon after the Council of Ephesus devotion to the Blessed Virgin in the Eternal City had acquired a magnificent center through the consecration of the renovated Liberian basilica in her honor, S. Maria Maggiore, under Sixtus III (432–440). The development of the cultus of the Princes of the Apostles, Peter and Paul, is attested not only by the most ancient sacramentaries with their Mass formularies for their feasts, but above all by the graves of the apostles, which had acquired beautiful buildings already in Constantine's time. Pope Xystus (or, as his name was later spelled, Sixtus), the second of that name, was seized in the cemetery of Callistus in 258, during the persecution of Valerian, and summarily executed. He was followed in martyrdom a few days later by his deacon, Lawrence. The memorial days for both of them, which were celebrated yearly on the sixth and tenth of August, belong to the oldest Martyr feasts of Rome. Pope Cornelius, of an old Roman family, died in exile after a short reign (251–253); his remains were shortly after returned to Rome. His grave is the first of the papal tombs to bear a Latin inscription: *Cornelius Martyr ep.* Bishop Cyprian of Carthage, who had corresponded with Cornelius, was one of the great figures of the third Christian century; he suffered martyrdom a few years later (258). His memorial day was celebrated at Rome already in the fourth century, and the oldest sacramentaries present Cornelius and Cyprian together on the fourteenth of September.

The twelve apostles as a group were venerated at Rome as early as the fifth century. Still the full listing of their names cannot have been included in the canon till later. For this list displays a very curious dissimilarity to both the biblical list and to all other known catalogues. It is closest to that in Matthew 10:2–4, but is distinguished from it (aside from the insertion of St. Paul and the reversal of the last two names, as found likewise in Luke and the Acts of the Apostles) by the fact that the sons of Zebedee are followed at once by Thomas, James and Philip. These last two take the ninth and the fifth place in all the biblical catalogues. A special cult of the Apostle Thomas is attested since the days of Pope Symmachus (498–514), who had erected an *oratorium Sancti Thomæ.* A similar *cultus* for Philip and James is found since the time of Pelagius I and John III (556–574), when the great Basilica of the Apostles was built in their honor. Of the preceding names in the list, the apostles John and Andrew had their sanctuaries in Rome already in the fifth century. James the Greater appears originally to have been celebrated at Rome along with his brother John on the feast of December 27, for which there is evidence a bit later. But evidence for a *cultus* of the other apostles that follow is wanting. So it is probable that the list of apostles in the canon consisted at first of the names of Peter, Paul, Andrew (James?), and John, and that in the course of the sixth century Thomas, James and Philip were added, and finally the remainder, until the number twelve was filled out. Something like that must also have occurred in the list of martyrs.

In the course of the same century there was an increase of devotion to

Pope Clement, who was being glorified by an extensive literature; to Chrysogonus, the martyr whose history is interwoven with legend and who was identified with a like-named founder of one of the Roman titular churches; for John and Paul, whom one legend assumed to have been Roman martyrs of the time of Julian the Apostate; for the two physicians and martyrs so highly venerated in the Orient, Cosmas and Damian, who were invoked as liberal helpers in cases of sickness. Thus the list must have grown during the sixth century more or less of itself. The redactor who put the list in the order we have today, to fill out the number twelve for the martyrs as for the apostles must have inserted the two first successors of St. Peter, Linus and Cletus, who are otherwise seldom mentioned. This redactor, whose work must have been done about the turn of the sixth century, can have been no other than Pope Gregory the Great. Due to the circumstance that the Roman Church in the period of the persecutions, unlike the Church in North Africa, kept no acts of the Martyrs, and so gave ample play for the development of legend, there is considerable doubt about the last five names in the series of martyrs, so that from the viewpoint of historical truth little more can be established than the names.

In the centuries following there was no feeling that the list as found in the Roman canon was closed once and for all. While keeping the twice twelve saints, there was nothing to hinder the addition of names of other prominent figures, in keeping with the altering features of ecclesiastical life. Thus the oldest Frankish manuscripts tack on not only the two great saints of Gaul, Hilary and Martin, but also the Doctors of the Church then already in high honor: (Ambrose), Augustine, Gregory, Jerome, along with the father of Western monasticism, Benedict.

Sometimes additions were made of regional saints or of patrons of the particular diocese or church. Thus, in the environs of Fulda, Boniface was attached to the list of martyrs. The names thus added in many manuscripts have become important indexes in establishing their origin. Often enough the number of additional names became unbearably long; thus in one eleventh-century manuscript of Rouen twenty-three names are annexed.

One expedient for satisfying local requirements without lengthening the list unduly was intimated by Pope Gregory III (731–741) when he prescribed for the monks of an oratory of St. Peter's, endowed with a wealth of relics, an addition to the *Communicantes* as follows: "celebrating the feast day (*diem natalitium*) of Thy holy martyrs and confessors, of those perfect just ones whose solemnity is today celebrated in the presence of Thy glory, whose merits and prayers (*quorum meritis precibusque*) ...." As a matter of fact, this or a similar addition is found in numerous medieval Mass books, mostly (it is true) as a further enrichment of the already longish formula, especially as a means of including the special saints of the day. But in the meantime there arose a determined opposition to the unnatural embellishment of the *Communicantes* formula, until at last all such frills disappeared altogether.

A different type of addition, however, has continued down to our own day, the most ancient addition to the *Communicantes* that we know of, namely the announcement of the day's mystery on Christmas, Epiphany, Maundy Thursday, Easter, Ascension and Pentecost. The addition on these six days is provided consistently in the old sacramentaries. Besides, the pre-Gregorian sacramentaries have an extra formula for the vigil of Pentecost, and the *Leonianum* has a further formula for two of the days mentioned that differs from the one in use at present. These additions were therefore in existence by the middle of the sixth century. It was just about this time that they appear to be cited in a message addressed to Bishop Profuturus of Braga by Pope Vigilius, in which the pontiff stresses the fact that the Roman eucharistic prayer is otherwise unchangeable.

But in spite of their venerable age, and in spite of the masterly commentary on the festal mystery which they supply, we are unable to account these formulas as organic continuations of the text of the canon. They jumble still further the word *communicantes* (already disjointed by the words *memoriam venerantes* and formed into a sort of anacoluthon), and separate it entirely from the names of the saints to which it naturally belongs. Viewed in their relationships to other forms, these inserts are of a piece with the prefaces of the *Leonianum*, which, after becoming a plaything for composers of novelties, departed consciously or unconsciously from the basic concept of the eucharistic prayer and therefore earnestly invited reform. If these festal inserts in the *Communicantes* escaped such reform, it is probably because they go back in substance to the very basic concept of all eucharistic solemnity. Also, perhaps, because we have grown accustomed to giving the word *communicantes* a broader meaning, so that the line of thought on these days might be paraphrased somewhat in this fashion.

They render Thee their gifts as members of the sacred congregation, in remembrance of the mystery of redemption which we recall this day, and in respectful regard for these saints. The insert would thus have become a sort of anamnesis.

In reference to these inserts, the words *Infra actionem* have been left in the Roman Missal within the canon, just before the *Communicantes*, the same words which, in accord with their strict meaning, are to be found as a heading above the text of the insert formula which is usually located after the prefaces. These words signify that the text is to be inserted "within the action." This title, *Infra actionem*, derives from the Gelasian Sacramentaries, where it generally stands just before the *Communicantes* formulas to be inserted, and also before the *Hanc igitur* formulas. Many of the manuscripts of this group of sacramentaries like-wise disclose a special caption just before the *Sursum corda*, namely: *Incipit canon actionis.*

The *Communicantes* brings to a close the first section of the interces-sory prayer. Externally this is manifested by the concluding formula, *Per Christum Dominum nostrum*, which thus appears for the first time in the canon. Our intercessory prayers and commendations, like all our prayers, should be offered up only "through Christ our Lord." We are conscious of this especially in the preliminary conclusion of our plead-ing. The same *Per Christum Dominum nostrum* then reappears after the *Hanc igitur*, after the *Supplices*, after the *Memento etiam* and after the *Nobis quoque*. Like a sign-post marking the line of our prayer, the formula is found today after successive stages all through the canon. While in all these places the formula is part and parcel of the oldest canon text to come down to us (although only as a secondary augmenta-tion), its first appearance is in the preface: . . . *gratias agere per Christum Dominum nostrum.* Here it strikes no definitely *conclusive* note, but rather, like the close of the *Nobis quoque*, it is at once expanded by means of a relative clause. In the remaining four passages, where this expansion is omitted, the post-Carolingian Middle Ages seemed more and more to expect that the *Per Christum Dominum nostrum* must be fol-lowed by an *Amen*. In the manuscripts this *Amen* appears for the first time in the ninth century, and after that with ever-increasing frequency, till by the twelfth century its insertion in all these passages became the prevailing rule, although even at the close of the Middle Ages there were some outstanding exceptions. Since the *Amen* at the close of the canon—the only place where of old it was spoken by all the people—had lost its uniqueness, it became merely an indispensable sign of the end of the prayer and thus had to be added to the Christological formula.

Later on, in the neo-Gallican movement, this *Amen* which had passed into the Missal of Pius V played a new role. In some dioceses the faithful had to recite it in a loud voice. It was thought that by so doing, a custom of the ancient Church was being revived.

10. Hanc igitur

Hanc igitur oblationem servitutis nostræ, sed et cunctæ familiæ tuæ, quæsumus, Domine, ut placatus accipias: diesque nos-tros in tua pace disponas, atque ab æterna damnatione nos eripi, et in electorum tu-orum iubeas grege numerari. Per Christum Dominum nostrum. Amen.

We therefore beseech Thee, O Lord, to accept this offering of our service and of all Thy household: that our days may be ordered in Thy peace, and at Thy bidding we may be delivered from eternal damna-tion and numbered among the flock of Thine elect. Through Christ Our Lord. Amen.

By the closing formula *Per Christum Dominum nostrum*, the *Hanc igitur* also labels itself as an independent prayer that did not belong to the original draft of the canon but was inserted only later on. The meaning of the words appears, at first sight, obvious and unequivocal, leaving little to be explained. The only problem that seems to require further elucidation is why this prayer, in its present form, should have been inserted just here. Is the prayer nothing more than a plea for the acceptance of the sacrificial gifts, as it is captioned in some translations? But such a plea has already been made and is here simply repeated in different words. One would scarcely have inserted an independent prayer just for this purpose. Or maybe the stress is on the contents of the petitions appended? But then why are these petitions included precisely in this place? It is around this prayer that the various theories regarding the canon have been developed, and a summary consideration has forced the conclusion that in this prayer we have "perhaps the most difficult prayer in the Mass," as Fortescue puts it.

As regards its history, it is known, first of all, that the *Hanc igitur* (which all textual evidence shows to have belonged to the traditional wording of the Roman canon) did not acquire its present-day form before Gregory the Great, who (as the *Liber pontificalis* recounts) added the last words. Even the earlier form of the prayer is not merely a matter of hypothesis. True, it is nowhere found, as we might be led to expect from this account, in a form which merely omits the Gregorian addition: *Hanc igitur oblationem . . . quæsumus Domine ut placatus accipias.* But in the pre-Gregorian sacramentaries there are certainly a considerable number of formulas in which these or similar initial words are connected to a lengthy complementary clause and fitted to the respective Mass-formularies in much the same way as the present-day basic formula is provided with special supplements for certain occasions like Holy Saturday, Easter, Pentecost, and the consecration of a bishop. Incidentally we thus discover that the account in the *Liber pontificalis* is not quite exact, since the additional phrase of Gregory proves to be not entirely new, and, on the other hand, in the most ancient texts the preceding initial phrases do not recur at all with the same wording, so that here, too, a crystallizing process must have occurred.

In general, the formula shows great variability, both in the subordinate clause and in the main clause. Only the first few words, *Hanc igitur oblationem*, commonly remain unaltered. But in most cases the oblation was in some way more exactly defined in the subordinate clause, the determination having in view those who offer it up. As a rule, it was defined as an oblation which "we" offer up for someone; but it was also described as the oblation of one person which we, in turn, offer up for a second person, or as the oblation of one person which he offers up for a second, or even as an oblation which the priest offers up.

SPECIAL INTENTION

Even more pronounced was the variation in the main clause, which was regularly annexed. It appears that generally there was no basic scheme, but that one of the alternate texts was chosen at random and inserted, these texts being augmented at pleasure. In this main clause mention was made of the special intention which was connected with the particular celebration. Such an intention did not come into consideration for every Mass. The Mass on Sundays and feast days, for example, is not, and never was, for a special intention, but was simply the Mass of the congregation. This tallies with the fact that in pre-Gregorian sacramentaries the *Hanc igitur* does not appertain to the Sunday Mass or feast-day Mass as such, but to the Mass for special occasions and to the Votive Mass, as is especially plain from the evidence of the older *Gelasianum*,[1] and is also confirmed by the *Leonianum*.

This also tallies with the form the *Hanc igitur* takes, and more particularly with the manner in which certain persons or groups of persons are introduced in it. These, whether named or not, appear either as offerers themselves or—and this especially often—as those for whom the Mass is offered; or else mention is made of persons for both functions. An offering *for* someone turns out to be plainly a characteristic of the *Hanc igitur* formula. It finds expression in the formulas for the Masses for the Dead and in the Mass of the scrutinies of candidates for Baptism, both cases where those involved cannot themselves make the offering. Certain Votive Masses from the very nature of the case fit in here. But neophytes also, although possessing all the rights of full Christians, do not appear as offerers themselves, and the same is true of newly-ordained deacons and priests, and of the bride at a Nuptial Mass. We discover here a fine piece of ancient Christian etiquette. It must have been accounted an honor to relieve those concerned of their duty of offering on this their great day, and to make the offering "for" them, in their stead and for their benefit.

Further investigation finally brings to light the fact that the mention of those for whom the offering is made is missing in the *Hanc igitur* only where these persons are the same as the offerers, the sacrifice being offered for oneself and one's own intentions. It is only in such cases that the offerer alone is mentioned, and even then he is mentioned not as such, but rather as one expecting the fruits of the sacrifice. Especially instruc-

---

1 This Sacramentary of the 6th century is divided into three books: (1) Proprium de tempore; (2) Proprium sanctorum; (3) Masses for different purposes and occasions. In the whole Sacramentary there are 41 *Hanc igitur* formulas, and yet the fomula is missing entirely in the second book. In the first book it is generally missing, e.g., on all days of Lent, and appears only, outside of Maundy Thursday, on such days when within the festal celebration a particular group of the faithful come forward and thus provide a special motive. In the third book not all but many votive Masses have a *Hanc igitur* formula.

tive is the case of the Mass of the scrutinies already cited, where the candidates for Baptism are, in the main, the only ones mentioned in the *Hanc igitur*. As already pointed out regarding this Mass, at the *Memento* for the living the names of the sponsors were read out, and these could of course be offerers. Now at the *Hanc igitur* there follows the names of the children who are ready for Baptism, for whom the sacrifice is offered up. Even if in other cases there is no evidence of such a distribution of names, and even if time and again in the *Hanc igitur* itself those who offer and those for whom the offering is made are both mentioned one after the other, still this case makes it plain enough that the *accent of the* Hanc igitur *is placed on naming the ones for whom Mass is offered and on the special intentions*. Thus there exists a certain external parallel to the *Memento* for the living, insofar as in either instance definite persons are mentioned and names are read out. But there is more here than simply a doubling of the framework for such a listing of names. The real matter is a determination of the aim of our action, the intention of the particular celebration which is aptly included here. It was a very thoughtful plan, one that lies close to the human heart, to use this climactic moment of the sacred action not only to join the little congregation with the large society of the earthly and heavenly Church (as had been done in the preceding prayers), but to add thereto a list of names and petitions to be specially recommended to the divine favor and thus to "join" a personal offering to that which would soon be made on the altar.

In view of the marked distinctiveness and almost unlimited changeableness of the *Hanc igitur* formula, it must not always have been easy for the celebrant to find a satisfactory form to include the names of all the offerers and all those for whose benefit the offering was made, or to define all the various intentions. Interested ears would be cocked to catch every word, and woe if he missed something. The difficulty grew with the ever-increasing development of the Votive Masses which we discover in the *Gelasianum* in the sixth century. The desire of the faithful to have their earthly intentions—often all too earthly—included in the sacred sacrifice must not infrequently have become a source of deep embarrassment. It is the same difficulty encountered everywhere by present-day pastors trying to incorporate all the intentions that have been recommended to their prayers, from ailing pets to menacing school exams. So it is not hard to understand why Gregory the Great put an end to all this variety by one unswerving directive. Henceforth, only a broad and general recommendation would be made at the altar. The various offerers and recipients would be eliminated in favor of the great Christian community of clergy and people which includes every special group. "(Graciously accept) this oblation of Thy servants as well as of all Thy people." All offer for all. And in place of the variety of individual petitions, we have the enduring and common interests of the community in which all particular requests are included. First, the universal plea for a peaceful life on earth: "That Thou wouldst order our days in Thy peace"; and the all-conclusive plea for our eternal welfare: "that Thou wouldst snatch us from eternal damnation and bid us be numbered among the flock of Thine elect." We may also assume that it was Gregory who directed that the prayer be said in this form at every Mass.

Only in a very few Mass formularies was the right to a special formula subsequently permitted to remain. In the missal of today it is only in the two baptismal Masses of Easter and Pentecost, and (surprisingly) in the Mass of Maundy Thursday.[1] Besides these, the *Pontificale Romanum* retains a special *Hanc igitur* for the consecration of a bishop. The Gregorian Sacramentary of Hadrian I still exhibits additional formulas—traditional ones—for the ordination of a priest, for the Nuptial Mass and for the burial of bishops.

The *Hanc igitur* formulas still in use are so constructed that the basic Gregorian form is retained even on these special days, a supplementary phrase derived from the ancient wording being incorporated into it. On the other hand, Gregory the Great himself appears to have retained for these special formulas only the conclusion of his common text, not utilizing the continuation of the introductory words in all cases.

Furthermore, outside of Rome not only did a certain amount of the older *Hanc igitur* formulas survive for a time, due to Alcuin's supplement to Gregory's Sacramentary, but actually in the milieu of the Gallic liturgies there was a whole new growth of formulas, as we can see from examples in Gallican and Irish Sacramentaries, and from the formation of new formulas even in the Carolingian period. But the Roman Church adhered to Gregory's reform. The formulation of the particular intention for each celebration was excluded, thus to an extent shunting the formula away from its original and proper intent. But the loss was more than compensated for by the fact that the perpetual intentions of all Christendom were firmly fixed therein. This is above all the decisive request for endless glory which we can gain only by persevering prayer, and for which we therefore humbly beg, day after day, right before the sacred moment of consecration.

There was but one further change in the *Hanc igitur*, namely in the contours of the external rite. Because the sacrificial note was emphasized in the prayer, it was quite natural to employ the same bowed posture that was attached in other places to prayers of offering. For this bow there are various evidences throughout the course of the Middle Ages. But since the close of the Middle Ages the present-day rubric of holding

---

[1] Perhaps the "law of retaining the ancient in seasons of high liturgical worth" (Baumstark) was especially effective here as in so many instances during the Holy Week liturgy. Still, the formula may originally have been intended for the penitents, who were permitted to offer their gifts again for the first time.

the hands outstretched over the offerings gradually prevailed, unless objection was taken to every sort of accompanying rite.[2] The present rite was originally a pointing gesture, occasioned by the word *hanc*. The gesture indicates the gifts we wish to offer God and thus is the natural oblation rite we have come upon before. But the meaning of the offering is not thereby more distinctly defined. In the Old Testament the same rite of laying the hands over the sacrificial victim is prescribed for various types of offering—for burnt offering and peace offering, and more particularly for a sacrifice with propitiatory character, pre-eminently the sacrifice of the scape-goat on the great Day of Atonement. Still there is no real reason to interpret the gesture precisely in this last sense, as long as the accompanying text gives no hint of it.

11. Quam oblationem

Quam oblationem tu, Deus, in omnibus, quæsumus, benedictam, adscriptam, ratam, rationabilem, acceptabilemque facere digneris: ut nobis corpus, et sanguis fiat dilectissimi Filii tui, Domini nostri Jesu Christi.

We beseech Thee, O God, deign to make this offering in every way blessed and dedicated, approved, spiritual, and acceptable: that it may become for us the Body and Blood of Thy most beloved Son, Our Lord, Jesus Christ.

The last prayer before the account of the institution forms with it a grammatical unit. It is like an up-beat before the full measure, a final swell in human words before the introduction of the imposing phrases of the sacred account, which are attached by means of a simple relative pronoun. For this introductory prayer of our canon we have the early testimony of St. Ambrose, both for the prayer itself and for its introductory character, since when he cites it his chief concern is with the words of Christ which it introduces. In the *eucharistia* of Hippolytus a preliminary of this kind is still lacking. There the account of the institution simply follows the words of praise regarding the redemption in the course of the prayer of thanksgiving. But meditation on the work of the divine omnipotence and favor which is about to be performed must have induced the notion of prefacing it with a formal prayer, much in the same way as we pray for our daily bread before we sit down to eat it.

The prayer *Quam oblationem* is the plea for the final hallowing of the earthly gift and, in the last analysis, a plea "that it may become for us the Body and Blood of Thy most beloved Son, our Lord Jesus Christ." The main thought is clear, but the expression is not very sharply stamped. The present-day wording of the prayer is already to be found in the Sacramentary of Gregory the Great, but it differs considerably from the

[2] Which was the case with the Dominicans.

earlier form presented by Ambrose. The old traditional formulations are not fitted together into the newer framework very smoothly. In Ambrose we read: "Make for us an approved, a spiritual, and an acceptable oblation which is the figure of the Body and Blood of Our Lord Jesus Christ." [1] Here the meaning is quite plain; an appeal is made that God may turn the gift into a perfect offering, which is Christ's Body and Blood. The expressions *adscripta*,[2] etc., here describe the sacrificial gift in its already altered state.

We may explain the present-day text in a similar sense. In the introductory phrase only the *fac* has been changed to *facere digneris* and the word *benedictam* added, in no way altering the meaning. The four-member expression has been changed into five, thus giving still greater force to the guarded legal terminology of the Romans which is here in evidence. In the second clause a noteworthy addition, evoked doubtlessly by the nearness of the great, grace-filled event, is the emotional word joined to the mention of our Saviour, the word *dilectissimi*, all the more remarkable because of the contrast to the legal language of the preceding phrase. Of greater importance, however, is the fact that, after the ambiguous *figura* was dropped, the *quod est* should be turned into *ut fiat*. Thus, according to the grammatical formulation now presented, the change into the Body and Blood of Christ is no longer contained amongst the properties of the sacrificial gift expected from God, but appears instead as the result of it (or as a goal to which that divine operation is ordered). Still it is possible to consider this result as being provided in the divine operation itself and would only be detached from it conceptually as the desired consequence. Make this gift (we seem to say) into a perfect oblation in such a way that it becomes the Body and Blood of our Lord.

ANCIENT MEANING

The attempt to wrest the ancient meaning out of the later wording is given special impetus by one expression which has survived in the first clause. Along with the other qualifications, our oblation gift should be *rationabilis*. Even in the Vulgate the word *rationabile* corresponds to the Greek *logikon: spiritual, spiritualized, immaterial. Oblatio rationabilis = logike thusia* is an exact description of the spiritual sacrifice proper to Christianity, a sacrifice lifted high above the realm of matter. In the Roman canon as quoted by Ambrose, the same word reappears after the consecration begged for a divinely effected exaltation and spiritualizing in the sense just indicated: "We offer to Thee this immaculate host, this

---

[1] Fac nobis hanc oblationem adscriptam, ratam, rationabilem, acceptabilem, quod figura est corporis et sanguinis Domini nostri Jesu Christi.
[2] We might do better in this section if we retain the Latin terminology.—REV.

spiritual (*rationabilem*) host . . . ." Thus, too, the prayer before the consecration begged for a divinely effected exaltation and spiritualizing of our sacrifice beyond blood and earthly taint. The other terms from the Roman legal language merely attempted to define this plea more exactly within the given context. *Adscriptam*, for instance, applied to citizens and soldiers, indicated that they were entered in the lists, and so here, too, it means recognized and accepted. The meaning of the word *rationabilis* certainly seems to have undergone a radical change between Ambrose and Gregory the Great. To some extent in the usage of Leo the Great, and completely in Gregory, *rationabilis* has lost the meaning assigned to it by the Christian cult and now signifies more or less what is suited to the reason. It is certainly possible that this loss of understanding for the root meaning of the word had an influence on our text and was partially responsible for the transformation of the next sentence into an *ut*-sentence. Thus the *facere digneris* along with the five adjectives would only be a sort of first stage onto which God might raise the gift in order that it might become worthy of the final consecration. But this meaning is not completely evident and at any rate we are not tied down to it. Nor are we forced to conclude that the word *rationabilis*, whose original meaning was kept alive at least through the Vulgate, also suffered that same loss of meaning within the hallowed reaches of the liturgy. It is no secret that words used in the liturgy often have a different meaning there than in ordinary speech (e.g., He descended into *hell*). Thus, if one seeks the meaning of such words, he must seek the *original* meaning. So it is with *rationabilis*.

EPIKLESIS

The goal of our petition is still the consecration, or more exactly the transformation of our sacrificial gift,[3] even though it is modestly pushed to the background in favor of the preparatory step. The formula thus represents the plea for consecration or—viewing the matter technically— the epiklesis of the Roman Mass. This is therefore the proper place to make a comparative study of what is generally called in other liturgies an epiklesis.

At two points in the Mass the sacramental world intrudes into the liturgical activity of the Church: at the consecration and at the Communion. God Himself is operative, giving us invisible grace by means of visible sacramental signs. Man can do nothing here except place the signs

---

[3] This *nobis* which appears already in the Ambrosian text is not without meaning. It is inserted to point out that the object is not merely Christ's presence as such, something that might have been sufficient for a later form of piety, but His presence as our sacrificial offering, in which our sacrifice is completed and into which He desires that we ourselves be finally taken up.

and—early reflection had soon deemed this proper—beg for the divine operation. Just how this appeal will be worded depends on the mode of theological thought, whether to call upon God in a formal request for this operation, or (more in line with pre-Christian forms of expression) to implore the assistance of divine power. Both of these modes of approach were designated in Christian antiquity as *epiklesis*, because in both cases God's name is invoked and God's power is elicited. The earliest record of an epiklesis is found in reference to Baptism, in the consecration of the baptismal water, but there is also early mention of it in reference to the Eucharist.

Coming now to particulars, it could be sufficient simply and bluntly to implore God for the hallowing of the gift and for its salutary and fruitful enjoyment, as actually happens in the Roman Mass at the *Quam oblationem* and the *Supplices*. Or one could attempt to define and designate the divine power by name. Christian terms which could be considered include: the Spirit of God, the power or the grace of God or His blessing, the Wisdom or the Word of God, the Holy Ghost; one could even think of an angel of God. In the early Christian era there was no hard and fast rule in this regard. In Greek, where *logos* and *pneuma* appear with the meaning "spirit," where in the theological consideration of the matter the idea was emphasized that God had created and accomplished everything through the Logos, it was natural that mention should be made oftener of the Logos as the power by which the gift is sanctified.[4] In the *Mystagogic Catecheses*, with which (according to the prevailing opinion) Cyril of Jerusalem concluded his baptismal instructions in the year 348, we find the earliest record of the basic form of that epiklesis which became typical of the oriental liturgies: "Then . . . we call on the good God to send the Holy Ghost upon the gifts, so that He might change the bread into the Body of Christ and the wine into the Blood of Christ." This epiklesis, taken in the narrow sense as a plea to God to send the Holy Spirit, thereafter appears first in the liturgies in the region of Syria; when it does appear it is found *after* the words of institution and the anamnesis and oblation prayer that follow. Its object is that the Holy Ghost might "make" the gifts into Christ's Body and Blood or "manifest" them as such. Thus they might have a salutary effect on the recipients. In the last sense, as a plea to the Holy Ghost to let the Communion strengthen the recipients in their faith, an epiklesis is to be found at the same point even in the *eucharistia* of Hippolytus. But there is no reference here to the transformation of the gifts. The oriental liturgies, too, must have had originally in place of the epiklesis only a petition for the salutary effects of Communion, from which a more general plea for blessing, with special reference to the transubstantiation, could easily have developed.

[4] Cf. Serapion.

Besides this consecratory epiklesis, which emerged from Syria, and which was pronounced *after* the words of consecration, there was another in the Church of Egypt which *preceded* the words of consecration. The basic form of this reads as follows: Heaven and earth are full of Thy glory; fill this gift, too, with Thy blessing. It was not till later that the Egyptian liturgy of St. Mark also adopted the Syro-Byzantine epiklesis.

Thus the consecratory epiklesis following the words of institution became, by degrees, *a distinctive feature of the entire Eastern Church*, and in the dissident churches was given a theological interpretation consonant with the wording of the prayer. But viewed in the light of tradition it represents the fourth-century custom of only one of the three great patriarchates, namely, that of Antioch, while in the other two, Alexandria and Rome, the traditional practice, going back at least to the same early period, involved an invocation of the divine power *before* the words of institution. The fact that more and more emphasis was given to the invocation of the Holy Ghost coincides with a basic trend of oriental theology, a trend noticed at a very early stage; for Eastern theologians are wont to consider the Holy Ghost as "the executor and accomplisher of every divine work," and in general their theological thinking is built more strongly on the mystery of the Trinity.

However, there is no solid and unimpeachable evidence in the original sources of the Roman liturgy that the Roman Mass also at one time had an epiklesis of the Holy Ghost as a plea for the consecration. The pertinent remark in a letter of Pope Gelasius I is indeed striking but not unequivocal. At any rate, an epiklesis of this sort did not belong to the older tradition in Rome, and later the simple ancient form of the plea for the blessing of the gift before the consecration remained as decisive as the plea after the consecration for the fulfillment of the blessing in all who received the gift of the altar.

This blessing was given further outward expression by means of the gestures, the first three of the five attributes of the sacrificial gifts being each accompanied by a sign of the Cross, to which were added two demonstrative signs of the Cross at the mention of the Body and Blood of our Lord.

12. The Consecration: The Account of Institution

Qui pridie quam pateretur, accepit panem in sanctas ac venerabiles manus suas, et elevatis oculis in cælum ad te Deum Patrem suum omnipotentem, tibi gratias agens, benedixit, fregit, deditque discipulis suis, dicens: Accipite, et manducate ex hoc omnes. Hoc est enim corpus meum.

Who, on the day before He suffered, took bread into His holy and venerable hands, and lifting up His eyes to heaven, to Thee O God, His almighty Father, gave thanks unto Thee, blessed it, broke it, and gave it to His disciples, saying: All take and eat of this. For this is My Body.

Simili modo postquam cenatum est, accipiens hunc præclarum calicem in sanctas ac venerabiles manus suas: item tibi gratias agens, benedixit, deditque discipulis suis, dicens: Accipite, et bibite ex eo omnes. Hic est enim calix sanguinis mei, novi et æterni testamenti: mysterium fidei: qui pro vobis et pro multis effundetur in remissionem peccatorum.

In like manner, after He had supped, taking this wondrous chalice into His holy and venerable hands, He again gave thanks unto Thee, blessed it and gave it to His disciples, saying: All take and drink of this. For this is the chalice of My Blood, of the new and eternal covenant: Mystery of Faith: which shall be shed for you and for many unto the remission of sins.

Hæc quotiescumque feceritis, in mei memoriam facietis.

As often as you shall do these things, you shall do them in memory of me.

In all the known liturgies the core of the *eucharistia*, and therefore of the Mass, is formed by the narrative of institution and the words of consecration. Our very first observation in this regard is the remarkable fact that the texts of the account of institution, among them in particular the most ancient (whether as handed down or as reconstructed by comparative studies), are never simply a Scripture text restated. *They go back to pre-biblical tradition.* Here we face an outgrowth of the fact that the Eucharist was celebrated long before the evangelists and St. Paul set out to record the Gospel story. Even the glaring discrepancies in the biblical texts themselves regarding this very point are explained by this fact. For in them we evidently find segments from the liturgical life of the first generation of Christians.

Later on, because liturgical texts were still very fluid, the account of the institution was developed along three different lines. First of all, the two sections on the bread and the chalice were refashioned to gain greater symmetry. Such a symmetrical conformation, undoubtedly introduced in the interest of a well-balanced audible performance, is seen already in the phrases of the rather simple account of the institution as recorded by Hippolytus: "This is My Body which is broken for you— This is My Blood which is shed for you." The parallelism was even more advanced in a liturgy a good hundred years after, namely, the Liturgy of Serapion, where the single account has been broken up into two independent parallel accounts separated by a prayer. The trend reached a crest before the middle of the fifth century in the basic form of the main oriental liturgies, the anaphoras of St. Mark, St. James and St. Basil. Then came the second phase, wherein symmetry was abandoned in favor of a word-for-word dependence on the biblical accounts. Some expressions from the Scriptures were interwoven bit by bit with the traditional text. And finally, along with these, a third phenomenon appeared, the effort to refit the phrases in decorative fashion, to underscore certain theological concepts,[1] and to make more room for a reverential participation. In

---

[1] Of this type are the terms found in oriental liturgies where, besides the intention "for the forgiveness of sins," we find other paraphrases of the purpose of Christ's gift, "as an

addition, elements of local table etiquette[2] or elements from the customs of worship[3] were frequently re-projected into the biblical account.

ANCIENT CHARACTER

Viewed against such a background, the account of the institution in our Roman Mass displays a relatively ancient character. The trend towards parallelism and biblicism has made great progress, but further transformation has remained within modest limits. The parallelism is manifested in the double occurrence of the ornamental phrase, "in Thy holy and venerable hands"; further, in the words, "giving thanks to Thee, He blessed (it) and gave it to His disciples, saying: take . . . ," of which only "giving thanks, (He) gave it, saying" are biblical, and only "He gave it, saying" are found in parallel in the scriptural text (of Matthew and Mark); and lastly in the words, *ex hoc omnes* and *enim*, both found in Matthew 26:28, but with reference only to the chalice.

The inclusion of the biblical wording is almost complete. Of the entire stock in the various biblical accounts, only one text-phrase is missing in our canon, aside from the command to "do this in remembrance of me" which is found in Paul-Luke right after the institution of the bread, and the remark in Mark 14:23, "and they all drank from it." However, this missing phrase, namely the words added to "This is My Body" in the Paul-Luke report: "which is given for you," is an amazingly significant omission. Its absence is all the more remarkable because it already appeared (in the form: "which is broken [*resp.* for many] for you") in both of the older texts of the Roman tradition. So it must have been expunged some time between the fourth and the seventh centuries, for a reason unknown to us. On the other hand, in the oldest known text of the Roman Mass, the one in Hippolytus, almost half the biblical text is wanting. In reference to the bread, the words "He blessed, broke, and gave to His disciples" are missing. In reference to the chalice, the words "After He had supped," "giving thanks," "all of you drink of this" are omitted, as well as the words "for" and "many" from Matthew, and the expressions "chalice," "New Testament" and "unto the remission of sins." About midway between the text of Hippolytus and our present canon is the text recorded by Ambrose, insofar as it still shows none of the additions regarding the chalice.

---

atonement of transgressions," "for eternal life," "for the life of the world," "for those who believe in me." Also the attributes given to the hands of our Lord, and the word *consecrans* are the result of theological reflection.

[2] Oriental liturgies often mention the mingling and also the tasting. The idea that the Lord as host drank from the chalice first of all was already advanced by Irenæus; that He also partook of the bread was frequently mentioned by the Syrians.

[3] In this category are included the raising of the eyes and the making of the sign of the cross (*benedixit*) over the gift-offerings.

Another surprising thing in our Roman canon is the beginning of the words over the chalice:, "This is the chalice of My Blood of the new (and eternal) Testament." To the simple formula of the older Roman tradition, "This is My Blood," the "chalice" of Paul-Luke has been added. And following the model of Matthew-Mark, the notion of a covenant has been included.

Even though these additions make the formula somewhat cumbersome from the viewpoint of grammar, still there is a double reward, for the mention of the chalice directly characterizes the Blood of our Lord as a drink, and the mention of the covenant opens up a broader vista of the work of redemption, accomplished (in fulfillment of the Old Testament figure) by the Blood of our Lord. Furthermore, it is a *testamentum*, a "covenant," a new divine economy binding heaven and earth together.

The further transformation of our Roman text of the institution was very limited. The time is given in the words, "the day before He suffered." This manner of chronicling the time is as characteristic of the occidental texts as the Pauline expression, "On the night when He was betrayed," is, in general, of the oriental ones. In the interest of theological precision, the latter text is often augmented by a reference to the voluntariness of the Passion. Similarly there is in the occidental text a special addition which emphasizes the redemptive quality of Christ's Passion: "Who on the day before He suffered for our salvation and the salvation of all men." This addition is used at present only on Maundy Thursday, but in Gallic texts it is also employed on other occasions.

In all probability it was formerly a part of the everyday text, and may originally have been incorporated to underscore the all-embracing character of the redemption as a protest against the gloomy predestinationism rampant in the fifth and sixth centuries.

EXPRESSIONS OF REVERENCE AND AWE

An opening for an expression of reverence and awe was found by augmenting the word "He took" with "into His holy and venerable hands." The same motif appeared even earlier in oriental texts, and especially in Egypt reached even richer expanses, but as a rule this occurred only in reference to the bread because with it was to be joined an offering gesture which suited the bread: The Lord (it reads) takes the bread *upon* His holy hands, *looks up* to His heavenly Father, or *shows* it to Him.

Our Roman text also makes mention of looking up: "lifting up His eyes," and the reason for its introduction here is probably the same, the idea of oblation. It does not derive from the biblical account of the Last Supper, but is borrowed, as in some of the liturgies of the Orient, from other passages of the New Testament. Moreover, the attitude of prayer, which also dominates the account and gives it the note of worship, is emphasized by the form regarding the heavenly Father—not a mere mention of Him, but a formal address: "to Thee, God, His almighty Father."

The solemn wording of this mention of God somehow re-echoes the solemn address at the beginning of the preface. Then, in mentioning the chalice, the pathos hitherto suppressed breaks through in a single word: "taking this wondrous Chalice."[4] That expression, "wondrous Chalice," is plucked from Psalm 22:5. And again it is quite natural to make mention of the venerable hands, since the meal ritual included raising the cup on high.

The most striking phenomenon in the Roman text is the augmentation of the words of consecration said over the chalice. The mention of the New Testament is turned into an acknowledgment of its everlasting duration: "new and eternal Covenant." And then, in the middle of the sacred text, stand the enigmatic words so frequently discussed: *mysterium fidei*. Unfortunately the popular explanation (that the words were originally spoken by the deacon to reveal to the congregation what had been performed at the altar, which was screened from view by curtains) is poetry, not history. The phrase is found inserted in the earliest texts of the sacramentaries, and mentioned even in the seventh century. It is missing only in some later sources.

MYSTERIUM FIDEI

Regarding the meaning of the words *mysterium fidei*, there is absolutely no agreement. A distant parallel is to be found in the *Apostolic Constitutions*, where our Lord is made to say at the consecration of the bread: "This is the mystery of the New Testament, take of it, eat, it is My Body." Just as here the *mysterium* is referred to the bread in the form of a predicate, so in the canon of our Mass it is referred to the chalice in the form of an apposition. It has been proposed that the words be taken as relating more closely to what precedes, so that in our text we should read: "new (and eternal) Covenant mystery (of faith)." But such a rendering can hardly be upheld, particularly because of the word *fidei* that follows, but also because the whole phrase dependent on the word *mysterium* would then become a man-made insertion into the consecrating words of our Lord. *Mysterium fidei* is an independent expansion, superadded to the whole self-sufficient complex that precedes.

What is meant by the words *mysterium fidei*? Christian antiquity

[4] The root idea seems to be "inebriating Chalice." Cf. Jean Danielou, *The Bible and the Liturgy*, Notre Dame (1956), 183 ff. The author says in part, 184, "The Eucharist produces spiritual effects analogous to those of wine, that is to say, spiritual joy, forgetfulness of the things of earth, ecstasy. . . . The inebriation given by the Eucharist is a 'sober inebriation' . . . ." This idea, as the author shows, is found already in Cyprian, Ambrose and others.—Rev.

would not have referred them so much to the obscurity of what is here hidden from the senses, but accessible (in part) only to (subjective) faith. Rather it would have taken them as a reference to the grace-laden *sacramentum* in which the entire (objective) faith, the whole divine order of salvation is comprised. The chalice of the New Testament is the life-giving symbol of truth, the sanctuary of our belief.

How or when or why this insertion was made, or what external event occasioned it, cannot readily be ascertained.

The sacred account concludes with the command to repeat what Christ had done. The text is taken basically from St. Paul; however, the entire Roman tradition, from Hippolytus on, has substituted for the Pauline phrase "'whenever you drink it," the phrase "whenever you do this." In some form or other our Lord's injunction is mentioned in almost all the liturgical formularies. Where it is missing, it is presupposed. It is in the very nature of the Christian liturgy of the Mass that the account of the institution of the Blessed Sacrament should not be recited as a merely historical record, as are other portions of the Gospels. Indeed, the words of the account are spoken over the bread and a chalice, and, in accord with our Lord's word, are uttered precisely in order to repeat Christ's action. This repetition, is, in fact, accomplished in all its essentials by rehearsing the words of the account of the institution.

13. The Consecration: The Accompanying Actions

A rehearsal of the sacred narrative is included in the Lord's injunction to do what He had done—that comes clearly to light in the actions accompanying the words as they are said at Mass.

As the priest mentions the Lord's actions, one after the other, he suits his own actions to the words in dramatic fashion. He speaks the words at a table on which bread and wine stand ready. He takes the bread into his hands, as also the chalice; the gesture of presentation that seems to lie hid in this "taking"[1] was and is made even plainer by this acting it out.[2] Praying, he lifts his eyes to heaven, "unto Thee, God, His almighty Father." At the words *gratias agens* he bows, just as he had done in reverence at the *gratias agimus* and *gratias agamus* that he himself had

---

[1] It is likely that in the "taking" mentioned above and in the gesture of raising the bread aloft connected with it in the oriental liturgies, we have a survival of a Palestinian table custom, a custom the Lord Himself observed. Likewise the taking and raising of the cup must have been done as one movement.

[2] In the Roman liturgy, too, before the elevating of the consecrated host came into vogue as a means of presenting it to the view of the people, the taking and raising at this point was understood as an oblation.

spoken earlier in the Mass. At the *benedixit*, by way of giving to an older biblical expression a more modern interpretation, he makes the sign of the Cross. The West Syrians and the Copts go even further, and acting out the *fregit*, crack the host without however separating the parts. This imitating of the actions, which expresses as clearly as possible the priest's desire of fulfilling here and now the Lord's commission to do as He had done, is lacking in the East only in the Byzantine rite, and even there it would seem to have existed at one time.

As the *dedit discipulis suis* is realized fully only in the Communion, and the *fregit* is usually carried out only at the fraction before Communion, so the *gratias agens* in its wider sense has already been anticipated, and the *accepit* has been already portrayed in an earlier passage. But the heart of the process is renewed at this very instant. The narrative of what once took place passes into the actuality of the present happening. There is a wonderful identification of Christ and the priest. In the person of the priest, Christ Himself stands at the altar, and picks up the bread, and lifts up, in the words of Psalm 22:5, *hunc præclarum calicem*—"this inebriating chalice." Through this mode of speech clear expression is given to the fact that it is Christ Himself who is now active, and that it is by virtue of power deriving from Him that the transubstantiation which follows takes place.

Numerous usages in oriental rites are understandable only from this same viewpoint. Thus, for example, the fact that the whole eucharistic prayer (aside from the *Sanctus,* which is sung in common) is spoken softly by the priest up to this passage, and then the words "take and eat, this is My body," and the corresponding words over the chalice are spoken in a loud voice; in fact, they are chanted in a solemn melody. And this is done over the bread held in the hands, and over the chalice grasped by the hands. In the West-Syrian anaphora of St. James the people answer *Amen* both times the priest says the words of consecration. This was already an established custom in the ninth century, when Moses bar Kepha was vainly tilting against it, for he rightly saw in the custom an acknowledgment of the completed transubstantiation, for which he contended the epiklesis was still requisite. This *Amen* is found also in the Byzantine and the Armenian Masses. In the present-day Ethiopian liturgy the *Amen* is repeated three times on each occasion, and followed by acts of faith. In the Coptic liturgy the dramatic element is heightened by inserting the *Amens* between the phrases of the introductory words of the priest: "He took bread . . . and gave thanks"— *Amen;* "blessed it"—*Amen;* "consecrated it"—*Amen.* And after the words of consecration in each instance comes a profession of faith in Greek, "We believe and confess and profess," and therefore a tradition from as early as the sixth century at least.

RITUAL DEDUCTIONS

In comparison with these we must confess that the Roman liturgy of the first millenary lacked the impulse to direct the attention at once to the completion of the sacramental process, or to draw ritual deductions from it. Only in the eleventh century do we begin to find, hand in hand with an increased care for everything connected with the Sacrament, the first signs of a new attitude. According to the Cluniac Customary, written about 1068 by the monk Bernhard, the priest at the consecration should hold the host "with the first four fingers washed for this purpose." After the consecration, even when praying with outstretched arms, some priests began to hold those fingers which had "touched" the Lord's Body, pressed together, others even began this at the ablution of the fingers at the offertory. In one form or another the idea soon became a general rule. Even in the twelfth century, however, the special tokens of honor towards the Sacrament which began to appear were at first found not in this precise connection but rather in other parts of the Mass.

Now, however, the people entered to dominate the scene. A religious movement swept over the faithful, prompting them, now that they hardly presumed to receive Communion, at least to look at the sacred species with their bodily eyes. This impulse to see fastened upon the precise moment when the priest picked up the host and blessed it, as he was about to pronounce over it the words of consecration. The presentation of the Host by elevating it a little, which we find more clearly expressed in the oriental rites, had also become more pronounced in the Roman Mass. Towards the end of the twelfth century stories were in circulation of visions imparted at this very moment: the Host shone like the sun; a tiny child appeared in the priest's hands as he was about to bless the host.

In some places the priest was accustomed to replace the host upon the altar after making the sign of the Cross over it, and only then to recite the words of consecration; in other places, on the contrary, he would hold it aloft as he spoke these words. Thus the people were not to be blamed if, without making any further distinction, they reverenced the host as soon as they were able to see it.

To forestall this impropriety, the bishop of Paris in 1210 ordered that the priests should hold the host breast-high, before the consecration, and only *after* the consecration should they lift it high enough to be seen by all. This is the first authentic instance of that elevation of the Host which is so familiar to us.

The custom spread rapidly. A regulation of the year 1210 appears to have prescribed it for the Cistercians; for the Carthusians it was ordered in 1222. From then until the middle of the century it was mentioned in various synods as a usage already in vogue. At the same time, and on till the fourteenth and fifteenth centuries, other synods continued in various ways to oppose any elevation before the consecration, "lest" (as a London synod of 1215 put it) "a creature be adored instead of the Creator." The great theologians of Scholasticism speak of the elevation of the Host as a general practice of the Church.[3]

But that does not mean that there was a similar elevation of the chalice. The elevation of the chalice is found, indeed, even as early as the thirteenth century, but the usage was rare and exceptional. However, it forced its way through, but only slowly, especially outside of France. Even the printed Roman Missals of 1500, 1507, and 1526 make no mention of it. Various difficulties stood in the way of a rapid spread of the rite, especially the danger of spilling the contents of the chalice. Then there was the fact that the chalice used to be covered with the back part of the corporal folded up over it.[4] But particularly cogent was the objection that in seeing the chalice one does not "see" the Precious Blood. For this last reason, even where the elevation of the chalice took place, it was little more than a mere suggestion: the chalice was merely lifted up to about the level of the eyes. Not till the Missal of Pius V was the second elevation made to correspond with that of the Host.

The desire of gazing upon the Lord's Body was the driving force which, since the twelfth century, brought about this intrusion of a very notable innovation into the canon which for ages had been regarded as an inviolable sanctuary. The oblatory elevation before the words of consecration lost its importance, and the displaying of the Host after the words, instead became the new pivot and center of the canon of the Mass. From the intrusion of this new element a further development had to follow. It was basically only a pious idea to regard seeing the Host, ("contacting" the species with the organs of sight), as a participation in the Sacrament and its streams of grace, and even to value it as a sort of Communion. But it was a logical conclusion that, the moment the consecration took place, all honor and reverence are owing to the Lord's Body and Blood. This conclusion, as we have seen, was actually realized in oriental rites. So any further regulation of the new usage had to be directed to keeping this desire to gaze on the Host within proper limits and to working out suitable terms for honoring It. This, then, was substantially what was done.

---

[3] The elevation of the Host therefore has a different function than the genuflections at the consecration. The preceding paragraph should make it quite clear that we are not here discussing "gestures of reverence." This fact alone renders superfluous the remark of S. J. P. van Dijk and J. H. Walker, *The Myth of the Aumbry*, London (1957), 77 n. 3, that Fr. Jungmann looked in the wrong place for "gestures of reverence."—Rev.
[4] Thus, a second corporal, or the pall that later developed from it, was required to be able to elevate the covered chalice.

The longing to look at the Host soon received ecclesiastical approval and support in several ways. This we see not only in the ruling that the Body of our Lord should be lifted high enough to enable the faithful to see It—to "show" It to the people, as our present-day rubric puts it: *Ostendit populo*. There was even a tendency to emphasize this "showing" by lingering a moment while elevating the Host, or by turning to right and left. But a stop was soon put to such efforts, since they involved too large a break in the course of the action.[5] But then we hear of another custom, especially in French and English churches, the custom of drawing a dark curtain behind the altar in order to make the white Host stand out clearly against the background. The consecration candle, from which in many places the *Sanctus* candle developed, was originally intended to be lighted and lifted aloft by the deacon or the Mass-server at the early Mass, when it was still dark, "that the Body of Christ . . . may be seen." We hear of admonitions directed to the thurifer not to let the clouds of incense obscure the view of the species. In monastic churches the doors of the choir, which were ordinarily kept closed, were opened at the consecration. The signal of the bell at the elevation was likewise introduced for similar reasons. The first evidence for such a practice comes from churches in Cologne as early as 1201. It makes its appearance first as a signal accompanying the elevation of the Host, and then the corresponding elevation of the chalice. Soon we hear of the signal's being anticipated, when the priest makes the sign of the Cross over the Host and the chalice. Further, the bell was used not only to direct the attention to the moment of the "showing," but also to call the people in to worship the Sacrament. So by the end of the thirteenth century the signal with the little bell was augmented by a signal from the large church bell, so that those who were absent, busy at home or in the field, might pause at this moment, turn towards the church and adore our Lord in the Blessed Sacrament.

It was self-evident from the start that honor should be paid to the Sacrament when It was elevated, all the more so when heresy had made an assault on faith in the Eucharist. Clergy and faithful were to kneel down—this was the admonition of the first decrees and synods that dealt with the new consecration practices. Or at least a humble bow was ordered, as in a regulation of Honorius III in the year 1219, and in several later decrees. Especially canons in various cathedral churches continued for a long time to follow their age-old practice of bowing: at Chartres this was done as late as the eighteenth century. Here and there, too, the wish was expressed or even insisted on, that while kneeling the

[5] It is only in the papal Mass that the turning to the right and left at the elevation has been retained until the present time.

arms be stretched out and the hands raised. But merely kneeling was the general rule. According to the thirteenth Roman *ordo*, which was written under Gregory X (d. 1276), the choir of clerics was to remain stretched out on the floor "until the priest receives the Body and Blood" (unless, because of a feast day or a festal season, standing was prescribed). According to the choir rules now in effect, where the influence of the ancient custom of standing bowed during the canon is at work alongside the newer attitude of special honor for the Blessed Sacrament, the choir usually kneels down at the *Te igitur*. Among the people, too, the idea of looking at the Sacrament was in many ways curbed, so that they knelt not only during the consecration but, where possible, from the *Sanctus* on, and remained on their knees till the Communion. After the close of the Middle Ages the desire to honor the Sacrament, which led to this kneeling, had gained the ascendancy over the desire to see, so far, indeed, that by the beginning of the twentieth century it even became customary in almost all countries to bow the head while kneeling at the consecration. Even at the elevation hardly a thought was given to looking up at the Host, and this was not changed until Pius X, in 1907, gave a new incentive by granting an indulgence to those who, while contemplating the sacred Host, recited the prayer "My Lord and my God."

It would be quite natural to expect the celebrant also to participate in giving these signs of reverence to the Blessed Sacrament. Yet for a long time the only token thus given was a slight bow made to our Lord's Body after the words of consecration, just before elevating It. Here and there the practice grew of kissing the Host; this was during the thirteenth century, the time which witnessed the multiplication of the altar kisses. But these well-intentioned efforts were countered at once by various prohibitions, subsequently repeated. Our form of genuflection—falling on one knee and then rising at once—was not at that time recognized as a religious practice, and therefore was not used at this moment. To kneel on both knees during the consecration was demanded early of deacon and subdeacon, but appears to have been impracticable for the priest, although the insertion of a lengthy payer—as was sometimes done after the *Pater noster*—seems to have been thought desirable. The first evidence of a short genuflection made by the priest at the consecration is found in Henry of Hesse (d. 1397), who was teaching theology at Vienna. Still, even in the fifteenth century the simple bow was still prevalent, and provision is made for it even in some of the Mass ordinaries of the sixteenth century. In Roman Mass books the genuflection appears from 1498 on, and from the start the arrangement is the one we have today, with a genuflection before and after the elevation of the species. It was made definitive in 1570 by the Missal of Pius V.

While the priest genuflects, the Mass-server grasps the edge of the chasuble. Because of the shape which the chasuble has commonly assumed since the close of the Middle Ages, the precise sense of this little ceremony is no longer evident. Nowadays it gives the general impression of being a gesture of readiness, not at all out of keeping with the sacredness of the moment. The explanation usually offered is that the chasuble is lifted so the celebrant might not be impeded when genuflecting, and this might be understandable on the supposition that—as was the case in the last years of the Middle Ages—the chasuble used to reach in back down to the heels. But at that time this reason was not actually given, but instead a very different one, the same reason still found in the Roman Missal. According to this, the server should take hold of the edge of the *planeta*, "lest it hinder the celebrant when he raises his arms." This explanation, it must be granted, is even less obvious today than the other. But that it is the true one can be deduced from the fact that the same gesture had already been prescribed for the deacon long before there was any thought of a genuflection. And in the thirteenth century it was definitely in order. For then they still commonly used the bell-shaped chasuble, and when the arms were raised, the back part, being pulled away by the uplifted arms, presented a very ugly picture unless there was a helping hand to hold it neat. With the return of the ample chasuble the old ceremony is again regaining its full meaning, so that it is once more intelligible.

There remains yet another question: Should our worship of the Blessed Sacrament be manifested by prayers and songs? Prayers spoken aloud and songs during the consecration are not things that would explain themselves. The rule of silence during the canon had indeed been violated often enough in the thirteenth century, but it had not yet lost all its force. At all events, the celebrating priest was permitted to say special prayers, but only in a subdued tone. Such an action was not at all strange in medieval times. True, the *apologiæ* which had cropped out everywhere between the various prayers had for the most part disappeared from the Mass books by the thirteenth century, and the injunctions, like those of Bernold of Constance, forbidding any and all insertions into the canon, did not remain ineffective. But a short ejaculatory prayer right after the consecration still appeared admissible and was actually recommended and practiced by many, although others again absolutely prohibited any such interpolation, even before the appearance of the Missal of Pius V.

But the faithful, at any rate, were admonished to pray, at first using prayers which they would recite quietly to themselves. About 1215 William of Auxerre, in his *Summa aurea*, mentions such prayers and asserts: "Many petitions are heard while one is actually looking at the

Body of Christ." According to Berthold of Regensburg, the faithful ought at this moment to pray for three things: for forgiveness of sin, for a contrite reception of the last sacraments, and for eternal beatitude. As outward expression of their prayer, the faithful might strike their breast or sign themselves with the sign of the Cross. The only vocal prayers commonly recommended were the usual formulas, or else a simple greeting or invocation. One such salutation which recurs in various versions, both Latin and vernacular, in many prayer books towards the end of the medieval era is the formula: "Hail Salvation of the world, Word of the Father, true Host." Such pieces as *Adoro te devote, Anima Christi*, and *Ave verum corpus* also served to salute the Blessed Sacrament at the elevation.

Well-shaped texts of this sort were naturally an open invitation for common recitation and singing, even if they were not intended for this from the start. By the end of the Middle Ages a solemn salutation of the Blessed Sacrament at the elevation formed part of the ceremony of high Mass. According to a Strassburg statute of 1450, the antiphon *O sacrum convivium*, with versicle and oration, was to be sung on certain occasions "at the elevation, immediately after the *Benedictus*." A decree issued in 1512 by Louis XII of France ordained that at the daily high Mass in Notre Dame in Paris the *O salutaris hostia* was to be sung *in elevatione corporis Christi* between the *Sanctus* and *Benedictus*. A Paris foundation of 1521 presupposes the *Ave verum*. Other songs, too, are mentioned for the same occasion. We must admit that these songs are all, in general, truly artistic works which fit into the setting with theological propriety. The break in the God-ward motion of the prayer and oblation made by the ceremony of elevating the sacred species and showing them to the people is intelligently shaped and filled out by these hymnic salutations, the product reminding one of a similar creation on Maundy Thursday where, after the holy oils are blessed, a greeting of veneration is likewise offered them.

Soon after the expiration of the Middle Ages, and with them, of the Gothic spirit, there was a rapid decline in the simple desire to contemplate the sacred Host at the moment of the consecration. That meant the disappearance, too, of the hymns which had been sung in honor of the Blessed Sacrament. The elevation ceremony was maintained, but was conducted in utter silence. Often even the organ was silenced, although the decrees still in force would permit a soft playing of the instrument. The only perceptible sound was the server's little bell. The faithful venerated the sacred species, but did so in silent prayer. Still there were some countries which maintained the old practice of saying certain designated prayers aloud, as for instance in Ireland, where we find the curious expression, "All praise to Thee, Lord Jesus, white and red."

14. Unde et memores

Unde et memores, Domine, nos servi tui, sed et plebs tua sancta, eiusdem Christi Filii tui, Domini nostri, tam beatæ passionis, nec non ab inferis resurrectionis, sed et in cælos gloriosæ ascensionis: offerimus præclaræ maiestati tuæ de tuis donis ac datis, hostiam puram, hostiam sanctam, hostiam immaculatam, Panem sanctum vitæ æternæ, et Calicem salutis perpetuæ.

Wherefore, O Lord, making memory of the blessed passion of this same Christ, Thy Son, our Lord, of His resurrection from the grave and glorious ascension into heaven, we Thy servants together with Thy holy people offer unto Thy supreme majesty from the gifts Thou hast bestowed upon us, a pure, a holy, and an unblemished Victim, the holy bread of everlasting life and the chalice of eternal salvation.

In reciting the account of the institution, the priest simply relates what then took place, and only the actions which are coupled with the words, and the veneration which follows upon them, make it clear that the scene is being re-enacted. But once the Great Prayer is resumed after the consecration, the very first thing done is to interpret the mystery thus accomplished. The link with the preceding account is made by the word *Unde*, harking back to our Saviour's injunction which closes the account. Now what is it we are doing at the altar in conformity with this injunction?

In almost all the liturgies two ideas are used to define the mystery, the two being placed side by side and contrasted in various ways. The mystery is a *commemoration* or *anamnesis;* and it is an *oblation*, a sacrifice. In some few instances the oblation is mentioned first, as in the Armenian Mass, where, after pronouncing the words of institution, the priest pursues and expands the thought of the command to do what Christ had done. As a rule, however, the remembrance is mentioned first, but in participial form, so that, though it is first, yet the main stress will be on the oblation, expressed by means of a verb like *offerimus*.

For both ideas the connection with the command of our Lord is the same: we come before Thee, O God—and these are the basic thoughts—with a grateful memorial of the redemptive work of Christ *and* offer up to Thee His Body and Blood. And both ideas contain an objective element as well as a subjective one. What we hold here in our hands is a memorial and an oblation. But memorial as well as oblation must be realized within ourselves as our own remembrance and our offering. Then, and only then, can a "worship in spirit and truth" in the fullest sense arise to God from our hands.

COMMEMORATION

The *memorial* is usually referred to here in just a short phrase. This is only natural, for the whole Prayer of Thanksgiving is, in substance, a memorial prayer, particularly the Christological portion. In fact, even the readings in the fore-Mass, especially the Gospel, have as their aim to revive the memory of our Lord, His word and His work. The whole purpose of the yearly round of Church feasts is, basically, nothing other than an enlargement of that recollection, making room for an ever-increasing store of memories. The basic theme of the Church year, too, is precisely the *passio Domini*, the redemption accomplished by Christ's death and Resurrection. In the anamnesis this theme is treated very briefly, but its contents are not analyzed as a subjective memory, since it is taken for granted that the soul is already alive to everything contained therein. All that is stated here is that in the sacramental operation the divine charge to do this "in remembrance of Me" (Luke 22:19; 1 Cor. 11:24 f.) is being fulfilled, and that, moreover, we are thus doing what Paul had demanded in more detail, namely, to "proclaim the death of the Lord" (1 Cor. 11.26). Nevertheless, the concept of Christ's sacrificial death does undergo a certain development, for related—or shall we say component—concepts are disclosed in much the same way as in the ancient professions of faith. *The death of the Lord is His victory, it is His triumph over death.* The Gallic Mass appears to have mentioned originally only the Passion. Even in Hippolytus the Resurrection is already added: "Making memory therefore of His death and resurrection." In Ambrose's text of the canon there is the further addition of the Ascension, and the *passio*—or rather, the triplet beginning with it—is characterized by the word *gloriosissima*.

The text of our present-day anamnesis follows the same lines. The adjective *gloriosa* has been transferred to the Ascension, while the *passio* has acquired the attribute *tam beata;* we surely have reason for hailing the Passion as blessed, since it is the root of our salvation. The later Middle Ages sought to emphasize the memory of the Cross also in the outward gesture, by reciting the anamnesis prayer, and sometimes also the *Supra quæ*, with outstretched arms.

In most of the oriental formulas the anamnesis underwent an extended evolution, but in the chief liturgies this did not go beyond a development of the theme of redemption. The three steps, Passion, Resurrection and Ascension, continue as the permanent threesome around which every added thing is marshalled. Thus to the Passion is added, for example, "the life-giving Cross and the three-days' stay in the tomb" (in the Byzantine Liturgy of St. James). And after the Ascension, is added in both these cases—and similarly in most of the others—the sitting at the right hand of the Father and "the glorious and awesome second coming." It is the description of the second coming which bursts the limitations of the anamnesis as such, particularly in West-Syrian formulas, as (for instance) in the fourth-century addition: "when He comes with glory and power to judge the living and the dead and to reward everyone according to his deeds," a description which grows ever richer and more fearsome and which, in the Greek anaphora of St. James, is supplemented by a plea for mercy. Later West-Syrian formulas even tacked on other events in Christ's life. Similarly, His birth is mentioned also in the Occident, but this is not found till long after, in late Carolingian Mass books.

The mention of various phases in the work of redemption which are to be kept in remembrance is often matched in oriental liturgies by a well-rounded expansion of the words incorporating Christ's injunction to do as He had done. At first only the words of St. Paul are put on Christ's lips. But then the addition is made of the Resurrection, or of the Resurrection and Ascension, especially in Egyptian liturgies: "As often as you eat this bread . . . you shall manifest My death and profess My Resurrection and Ascension, until I come." Similar formations made their way into the area of the Gallic liturgies.

The remembrance should be realized not only in and by the priest, but also in and by the entire congregation assembled. In the Roman Mass this is brought out by the fact that the subject of the anamnesis is defined as "We Thy servants together with Thy holy people"—*nos servi tui, sed et plebs tua sancta*. In Egypt, at an early date, it was revealed even more vividly; a solemn outcry of the people, corresponding to the expanded phrases of our Lord's injunction to do as He had done, followed immediately after it as a sort of response to it, and was then followed by the priest's prayer. Even today the Coptic Mass retains this anamnesis cry of the people, and since it still employs the Greek tongue it is evidently a heritage of at least the sixth century.

THE OBLATION

The second point that is expressed in the *Unde et memores* and then taken up and developed in the following prayers, is the *oblation* or offering. Here we have the central sacrificial prayer of the entire Mass, the foremost liturgical expression of the fact that the Mass is actually a sacrifice. In this connection it is to be noted that there is reference here exclusively to a sacrifice offered up by the Church. Christ, the high-priest, remains wholly in the background. It is only in the ceremonies of the consecration, when the priest all at once starts to present our Lord's actions step by step, acting as "another Christ" in reciting the words of transubstantiation—only here is the veil momentarily withdrawn from the profound depths of this mystery. But now it is once more the Church, the attendant congregation, that speaks and acts. And it is the Church *in concreto*, manifest plainly in its membership; it is the congregation composed of the "servants" of God and the "holy people," which has already appeared as the subject of the remembrance in the anamnesis. To show how aware the Church is of what she is, we must point to the significant words here used, *plebs sancta*, words which bring to the fore the sacerdotal dignity of the people of God in the sense implied by 1 Peter 2:5, 9.

In the Roman Mass just a few impressive words are used for the oblation. In Hippolytus the terseness here as well as in the anamnesis borders on the extreme: "Making memory therefore of His death and resurrection, we offer to Thee this bread and chalice." In the present Roman canon the expression has hardly blossomed out beyond this, and it is not till the concluding words, the five-part description of the sacrificial gifts, that the phrasing is caught up in the enveloping praise: "We offer to Thy supreme majesty from those gifts Thou hast bestowed upon us a pure, a holy and an unblemished Victim . . ." By the use of the words "Thy majesty" (which we encountered already in the preface) as a term of address, we are brought face to face with the divine greatness before which man crumbles into nothingness. In accordance with this consideration, the gifts which we undertake to present to Him must be regarded as already His own; they are "from the gifts Thou hast bestowed upon us." This is a biblical concept (1 Paral. 29:14) that reappears time and again in different forms on foundation inscriptions of Christian antiquity. Where the pagan founder of a sanctuary or a memorial, conscious of his own largess, has the words *de suo fecit* carved on the stone, the Christian benefactor humbly acknowledges that all he has given was granted him by God; his gift is *ex donis Dei*. Thus, too, every sacrificial gift which we can proffer to God is already "a gift and a present" which He had loaned us. And this is surely true in an eminent way of the gift on our altars. Another concept that might be a contributing factor here is the one proposed by Irenæus in his opposition to Gnosticism; with regard to the material components of our sacrifice, he argues that we do not offer up an uncreated being, but rather we sacrifice to the Lord of creation something that He himself has created.

Next the gifts themselves are given mention, just as they are found in our hands, and the mention turns into a short hymn on the Blessed Sacrament. First, the sacrament is described in three phrases which stress the spotless purity and holiness of the sacrifice: *hostiam puram, hostiam sanctam, hostiam immaculatam*. Our sacrifice is not like that of the heathens or even that of the Jews, who could offer God only a material and bloody sacrifice; ours is spiritualized and therefore clean. Its positive content is next suggested, first of all by the word *hostia*, which originally implied a living being. The subsequent words also continue the same line of thought, for they are a two-part expression (corresponding to the double form of the sacrificial gifts) proclaiming the preciousness of these gifts, pointing to the results of partaking of them, the everlasting life towards which they tend: "the holy bread of everlasting life and the chalice of eternal salvation."

In the *eucharistia* of Hippolytus the awareness that the possibility of offering such gifts is the greatest grace suggested the inclusion of a word of thanks at the close of the oblation: "giving thanks to Thee because Thou hast found us worthy to stand before Thee and to minister unto Thee." Some formularies in the East also contain a thanksgiving in the same position. And either then, or else right after the oblation, they make a transition to the epiklesis. The Roman Mass, on the contrary, lingers on the main theme, the oblation, without going into these subsidiary ideas.

15. Supra quæ *and* Supplices

Supra quæ propitio ac sereno vultu respicere digneris: et accepta habere, sicuti accepta habere dignatus es munera pueri tui iusti Abel, et sacrificium patriarchæ nostri Abrahæ: et quod tibi obtulit summus sacerdos tuus Melchisedech, sanctum sacrificium, immaculatam hostiam.

Deign therefore to look upon these offerings with a gracious and kindly countenance and to accept them as Thou once accepted the offerings of Thy just servant Abel, the sacrifice of our patriarch Abraham, and that which Thy high priest Melchisedech offered to Thee, a holy sacrifice, an unblemished victim.

Supplices te rogamus, omnipotens Deus: iube hæc perferri per manus sancti Angeli tui in sublime altare tuum, in conspectu divinæ majestatis tuæ: ut quotquot ex hac altaris participatione sacrosanctum Filii tui Corpus, et Sanguinem sumpserimus, omni benedictione cælesti et gratia repleamur. Per eundem Christum Dominum nostrum. Amen.

We humbly beseech Thee, Almighty God, bid these offerings to be borne by the hands of Thy holy Angel to Thine altar on high, before Thy divine majesty: so that as many of us as shall receive the most holy Body and Blood of Thy Son from this sharing of the altar may be filled with all heavenly benediction and grace. Through the same Christ our Lord. Amen.

For man—and even for the ecclesiastical congregation—to offer God gifts, no matter how holy these might be, is certainly the utmost daring. For this reason the oblation is expressed in yet another manner, in words that endeavor to show that it is nothing less than a grace of God to expect the acceptance of the gifts from our hands.

All we can do is make the offering; *offerimus*. It is up to God to cast a favorable glance upon our offering (*respicere*) and to consider it with approval (*accepta habere*). Continuing in this figurative language, we add that it also pertains to God to have our gifts carried up to His heavenly altar of sacrifice. The line of thinking manifested in these words follows easily and naturally from what precedes, and it therefore belongs to the most ancient portion of even the non-Roman liturgy. And yet it gives occasion for more than one problem.

The first thing that strikes us is the fact that these prayers linger wholly over the external performance of the sacrifice, tracing each step of it prayerfully. They are concerned that the symbol be properly executed and also acknowledged by God. But regarding what is symbolized, that sacrificial sentiment from which our action must proceed, that spirit of sacrifice which rightly plays so great a role (perhaps not yet sufficiently stressed) in our present-day religious thinking and in our pastoral monitions regarding attendance at Holy Mass, the wholehearted subjection of the creature to the Creator, the ever-growing conformity of our will with that of almighty God, the resolute surge of our mind towards that mind "which was in Christ Jesus"—all this is here given no special consideration. But this should in no way astonish us. After all, in view of the sacrificial activity of the community, such a state of mind in the individual is taken for granted; it is presupposed, if not as something already acquired, then surely as something to be sought. Expression must be given not to the subjective striving (which varies from soul to soul), but to the objective act which is valid for all.

A further surprise is the fact that even after the gifts have been consecrated and changed there should still be a plea for acceptance. For there is question here really of the most sacred gifts, of the sacrificial oblation which Christ Himself makes through the ministry of His priests. Certainly there can be no thought of pleading for its acceptance, since it is antecedently valid in full. On the contrary, all the sacrifices which are cited from the Old Testament, those of Abel and Abraham and Melchisedech, are only earthly shadows of its heavenly grandeur.

As a matter of fact, the Reformers who raised their voices against the Mass and canon also pounced on this point, that the priest undertook to play the part of mediator between Christ and God. Right down to our own day, therefore, modern commentaries on the Mass have assumed a tone of apology when explaining this passage. But if we reflect for a moment that the sacrifice of the New Law, being an act of official worship, is essentially placed in the hands of the Church, which in turn relies on the sacrifice of Christ, then it becomes clear at once that we possess therein, despite the solemnity of its essential core, only an external symbol by which the Church—or more immediately, the congregation— honors God. And God can really receive it from her hands as a gift of homage only when at least the lowest degree of an internal will to give on the part of the participants accompanies and quickens the external offering. In this sense, then, it would be quite understandable that the harsh words of the prophets, in which God rejects the purely external and soulless offerings of His people, would refer with equal weight to the sacrifice of the New Law, were it offered by unworthy sacerdotal hands. Besides, in such a case little more would remain of this holiest of sacrifices than a new *hic et nunc* of Christ's sacrifice long since accomplished, a *hic et nunc* which is without its salvific meaning, since, contrary to its purpose, it is no longer the expression of a willing Christian mind, no longer has its roots in the earth, but hovers aimlessly in the air.[1]

Since corruptible and sinful man can never be sufficiently worthy of the great and holy God this humble plea for God's gracious glance is in any case well-grounded. Joined to it is a confident reference to the illustrative figures of the Old Testament, whose sacrifice had won God's pleasure. The outstanding types from the Old Dispensation are reviewed to encourage the soul, and a certain pride takes possession of our hearts as we link our action with the action of these biblical saints. Three figures are selected: innocent Abel, who made a sacrifice of the firstlings of his flock (Genesis: 4:4) and himself succumbed to his brother's hate —our gift is "the Lamb of God," the first-born of all creation, who turned His death, suffered at the hands of His own people, into a sacrifice of redemption. Next, Abraham who, as ancestor of all "who are of faith," is called "our patriarch," the hero of obedience to God, ready to make a sacrifice of his very son, but receiving him back alive (cf. Hebrews, 11:19)—our sacrifice, too, the most perfect expression of obedience unto death, has risen again and returned to life. Finally, Melchisedech who, as priest of the most high God, offers up bread and wine—our oblation also is taken from bread and wine. May God (such is our prayer) look down upon our oblation with the same pleasure as He looked upon the oblation of these men; "The Lord looked upon Abel and upon his gifts," as we read concerning the first of them: on Abel, and on his offering, the Lord looked with favor. That prayer of ours will be fulfilled if the oblation proceeds from an intention pure as theirs, and if the temper of our own hearts accords in some measure with the incomparable holiness of our sacrifice.

This comparative view of the Christian sacrifice in conjunction with the sacrifices of the Old Law, and in particular with those specially mentioned, was not alien to Christian antiquity. In fact, this consideration of the Old Testament as the antecedent shadow of the New was as self-evident to primitive Christianity as was the concept of the continuity of the history of grace. Abraham's sacrifice was one of the favorite subjects of ancient Christian iconography, and at least since the fourth century it appears predominantly as a type of the sacrifice of the Cross, and therefore, mediately at least, as a type of the eucharistic sacrifice. But there is immediate reference to the Eucharist in the representation of the three types mentioned in the canon found in the two large mosaics in the choir of San Vitale in Ravenna. One of these shows Abel and Melchisedech, the former bringing a lamb, the latter bread and wine to the altar. The other pictures Abraham in two different scenes, in one case at the point

---

[1] This extreme case is, however, not entirely present even in an unworthy celebration of the priest, not so long as at least one participant takes part with proper dispositions.

of sacrificing his son, in the other as host to the three mysterious strangers. It may be that the wording of the Roman canon itself gave an impetus to these portrayals at Ravenna, but the mention of Abel and Abraham (to whom Melchisedech was perhaps joined originally) in an Egyptian offertory prayer brings us back to a much earlier period when Rome and Egypt had a liturgical practice in common.

In the Roman canon the name of Melchisedech is followed by a further clarifying phrase: "holy sacrifice, unblemished victim." This is an addition which the *Liber pontificalis* attributes to Leo the Great. Older commentators frequently understood this addition as an attribute of the Christian sacrifice, as though meant in apposition to (*Supra quæ*, with the words in between, *sicuti . . . Melchisedech*, construed as parenthetical) but the purport of the words demands rather a connection with the sacrifice of Melchisedech. For this reason there is no accompanying sign of the Cross. True, to us nowadays such an addition might appear superfluous. But it was otherwise in the fifth century, when anti-materialist heresies were still causing trouble, when in particular the use of wine was still exposed to Manichean attacks, and the disuse of the chalice at Communion roused a suspicion of Manichean sentiment.

SUPPLICES

The oblation is set forth in a third way, in the *Supplices*. A gift is fully accepted not when it has drawn to itself a friendly glance, but when it is actually taken into the recipient's possession. In a daring illustration this final phase of human gift-giving is transferred to our sacrificial gift and to God to whom we offer it. The Apocalypse, 8:3–5, tells of an altar in heaven on which the angel deposits incense and the prayers of the saints: "And there was given to him [the angel] much incense, that he should offer of the prayers of all the saints, upon the golden altar which is before the throne of God." This is but a figure of spiritual activity, just as it is only a figure to speak of the throne of God. But the figure serves as a device in the third prayer, where the offering of our sacrifice is now to be set forth as a petition for its final acceptance.

The wording of the older version in Ambrose shows clearly that we are dealing with a plea for acceptance: "We ask and pray that Thou receive this offering on Thine altar on high through the hands of Thine angels, as Thou didst deign to receive . . ." In our current text the figure, as against the reality, is even more sharply delineated. The prayer begs for the sending of a holy angel to carry the gifts to the heavenly altar which is erected before the face of the divine majesty. Such a mode of expression, speaking of the heavenly altar, is to be found in various places in the Eastern liturgies since early times.

In the Roman liturgy, where the *Supplices* in the canon is the only instance of the use of this figure, medieval commentators ascribed a very wide significance to the heavenly altar in the performance of the sacrifice. This is correlated for the most part with the incomplete sacramental theology of the time. Remigius of Auxerre considered that after the Body and Blood of Christ were made present by the words of institution, a second act was necessary by which the Body of Christ on earth, sacramentally present in many different places, was drawn into unity with the glorified *corpus Domini* in heaven. This action was petitioned and consummated in the *Supplices*. The Cistercian abbot, Isaac of Stella, writing in 1165, also viewed the *Supplices* as completing our sacrifice, but in a different way. In the first step, which he likened to the altar of holocausts in the ancient Temple, we have offered up, with contrite hearts, bread and wine as tokens of our own lives; in the second step, which was compared to the golden altar of incense, we have offered up the Body and Blood of the Lord; in the third step, which corresponded to the Holy of Holies, our sacrifice was borne up by angel hands to be united to the glorified Christ in heaven, and thus was completed. Just as the clouds of incense—another commentator takes up the theme—in which the high-priest stepped before the Ark of the Covenant on the great Day of Atonement, obscured his vision, so the earthly eyes of the priest can no longer at this point recognize anything; all that is left is to beg the angels to bear the sacrifice up before God's countenance. Other theologians of this period also found that in this transfer of the gifts to the heavenly altar a real activity is connoted, in which the sacrifice attains its completion. By the *Supplices* this activity is petitioned. Thus, under the influence, no doubt, of the Gallic liturgy, the prayer became a sort of epiklesis; and actually there is a plea that the power of God might touch our sacrificial gift, but in reverse order, not by the descent of the Spirit, but by the ascent of the gift.

Closely allied to this in some way is the belief that in the "angel" something more is to be seen than just a created angel. It is Christ Himself who, as *magni consilii angelus* (Is. 9:6), takes our sacrifice and bears it away to the altar celestial. This idea was repeated by several commentators, especially around the twelfth century, and even in our own time it has been broached in the thesis which postulates a heavenly sacrifice into which our earthly sacrifice is merged. Finally, taking the view that the *Supplices* is a consecratory epiklesis, as would appear by an external comparison with oriental and Gallic Mass formulas, the angel carrying the sacrifice aloft has been identified as the Holy Ghost.

Since all these meanings are founded on certain assumptions which, to say the least, are very questionable, there is no good reason for departing from the natural sense of the word, which is supported by the reading in Ambrose (*angelorum*) and by parallel passages in oriental liturgies; as the prayers of the faithful are deposited on the heavenly altar by the angel of the Apocalypse, so may the same be done by the holy angel with our sacrifice. Without doubt this means that there is some participation of the angelic world in our oblation. But that can no longer be surprising, after the *Sanctus* that was sung by earth and heaven conjointly. Well known are Chrysostom's descriptions of the "awesome mystery," with the altar surrounded by angels. Gregory the Great pictures the hour of the sacrifice, with the heavens opening and choirs of angels coming down. It is also in accord with the solidarity of the Christian order of salvation that the angels who (of course) have a very different relationship to man's redemption, should yet in some way take part in the sacrifice of redemption. But to try to define this participation in more detail or to single out the participating angels by name would be unbecoming curiosity.

FRUITFUL RECEPTION

The second half of the *Supplices* takes a new turn; bringing our sacrifice up to the heavenly altar should give rise to a *fruitful reception* of the holy gift by the assembled congregation—such is the prayer we take up. Our view thus turns away to the concluding act in the celebration of the Eucharist, the Communion. Criticism in the past generation saw in this re-orientation a break in the thought which offered an opportunity for bold theorizing. Actually, however, although there is progress in the thought, it is a thoroughly natural and uninterrupted transition, as we can see by comparison with the *eucharistia* of Hippolytus, where the oblation likewise turns shortly to a Communion plea. Besides, we could regard this prayer in either case, both in Hippolytus and in the present Roman canon, as an epiklesis. But it is not a consecration but a *communion epiklesis* and so (to look at the heart of the matter) there is nothing significant about the fact that the invocation of the Holy Ghost is missing in our *Supplices*, though found in Hippolytus. The Communion is the second great event which the celebration of the Eucharist comprises, the second intervention of God in the activity of the Church. The Christian sacrifice is so constituted that, from the very beginning, the congregation making the oblation is invited to the sacrificial meal. As soon, then, as the oblation is completed, the expectant gaze is turned without further ado to the sacrificial repast, and it is quite seemly that this expectation should become a humble prayer.

Next, the idea that all who wish can receive the Body and Blood of the Lord is introduced as something taken for granted. We receive this double gift *ex hac altaris participatione*, from this sharing of the altar. If the gifts of today's sacrifice, our very own, are carried up to the heavenly altar, i.e., are accepted by God, then this sharing, the association thus established in God's heavenly table upon which our gifts rest, grants us the possibility of receiving the Body and Blood of the Lord truly as God's table guests, and thus procuring not only the external appearance of the mystery, but also its inmost power. More simple was the thought as transmitted in the text of the Irish and Milanese canons, where we read: *ex hoc altari sanctificationis*—"from this altar of sanctification," thus signifying the earthly altar on which the gifts were hallowed. Still the greater simplicity of the thought is no guarantee of its originality. It is not likely that the word "altar" would be used in one and the same breath to signify first the heavenly and then the earthly altar. Rather it must be said that in the metaphorical language of our prayer the earthly altar wholly disappears from view and is absorbed, so to say, in the heavenly one which alone has validity.

What we ask for is that the reception may be for our good, so that we may be filled with every heavenly benediction and every grace. The "heavenly benediction" again corresponds to the heavenly altar. In the restrained enthusiasm of expression there are echoes of phrases from the introductory paragraph of the Epistle to the Ephesians (1:3).

Whereas the preceding prayers had but few ceremonial accompaniments—at present simply the crosses at *hostiam puram*, etc.—the *Supplices* once more brings movement into the bodily bearing of the priest. Bowing the body, which (according to olden custom) was usually linked with the humble oblation and therefore was at one time begun here at the *Supra quæ*, is at present required at *Supplices te rogamus*. Here it is a practice of long standing. To the profound bow is added a kiss of the altar. This kiss is probably suggested by the *Supplices*, as an expression of deep, reverent petition. The mention of the holy gifts that follows again occasions the demonstrative gesture, added here in the form of two crosses at *corpus et sanguinem*. There are indications of this gesture here and there even in Carolingian texts, but it spread only very slowly and is still missing even in manuscripts of the thirteenth century. In like manner, the priest's signing himself at *omni benedictione cælesti*—a gesture that conveyed even by action the notion of pleading for heavenly blessing—did not become prevalent till towards the end of the Middle Ages. Therefore, to consider the crossing of the gifts as a manifestation of our hope to transfer the blessing from them to ourselves is only a secondary interpretation, although not inadmissible.

After the oblation has been completed and the Communion plea has been pronounced, at once, according to the most ancient pattern, the conclusion of the *eucharistia* follows, with a solemn doxology and the *Amen* of the people. In our Roman Mass, however, we find here only an anticipated *Per Christum Dominum nostrum*, which is repeated again after each of the two insertions that follow. Our prayer rises aloft to

God through our high-priest when His servant at the altar, as His representative, has spoken the words of consecration.

16. The Memento *of the Dead*

Memento etiam, Domine, famulorum famularumque tuarum N. et N., qui nos præcesserunt cum signo fidei, et dormiunt in somno pacis.

Ipsis, Domine, et omnibus in Christo quiescentibus locum refrigerii, lucis et pacis, ut indulgeas, deprecamur. Per eundem Christum Dominum nostrum. Amen.

Remember also, O Lord, Thy servants N. and N. who have gone before us with the sign of faith and who rest in the sleep of peace.

To them, O Lord, and to all who rest in Christ, we beseech Thee to grant a place of comfort, light, and peace. Through Christ Our Lord. Amen.

The first of three inserts which precede the doxology in the present Roman canon is the *Memento* of the dead. That this is an insertion of a later date is evident on several grounds. First of all, there is nothing corresponding to it in the *eucharistia* of the primitive age. Secondly, it is missing in a considerable portion of older manuscripts, e.g., in the sacramentary which Pope Hadrian I had sent to Charlemagne; indeed it is wanting in some text-sources here and there as late as the eleventh century. And even where it appears, it is sometimes wedged into other spots than its present location. This sporadic appearance of the remembrance of the dead can hardly be explained on the supposition that at one time it was placed on a special tablet, the *diptychon*, for if that were the case similar vestiges would be found in the *Memento* of the living. Rather the explanation is to be sought in a fact which is sustained by several accounts of the Mass, namely, that the *Memento* of the dead for a long time had no place in the Mass on Sundays and feasts, that is to say, in public service properly so called. Since the turn of the fifth century a general remembrance of the dead had a place in the *Kyrie* litany. But a special mention within the canon itself was probably regarded as a peculiarity of the Mass which was offered in some way for the dead; it was looked upon as something concerning only the group of relatives rather than the full community. Its standing was similar to that of the pre-Gregorian *Hanc igitur*, which in many cases, in fact, was revamped and inserted for the dead. In some documents which introduced the *Memento* of the dead into the canon there is a definite rubric limiting it to weekdays only and barring it on Sundays and feasts. This old rule had not entirely vanished from memory even as late as the fourteenth century. The Mass commentary of Melk, from the year 1366, testifies to the practice of some priests of omitting the *Memento* of the dead on Sunday; even the author himself is inclined to give his approval, although he is unable to allege any authentic decisions in its favor.

On the other hand, the oldest extant texts of our Mass book do contain the *Memento* for the dead. The Irish tradition of the canon, including the Bobbio Missal which was written about 700, contains it. In the case of the Bobbio Missal the presence of this *Memento* is not surprising, at least in the light of what was just explained above. For the Bobbio Missal is one of the first Mass books in which the needs of the private monastic Masses were given prime consideration. In this book the Roman canon is found within a Mass formula captioned *missa Romensis cottidiana*, hence one not intended for Sunday. Therefore, in Rome even at an early period the *Memento* must have formed part of the *missa cotidiana*, which even then was most frequently devoted to the dead.

But there remains one striking fact, namely, that the remembrance of the dead was inserted here and not in connection with the intercessory prayers before the consecration, where it might have been yoked with the remembrance of the living or with the recollection of the saints in heaven, or where a permanent *Hanc igitur* formula might have performed the same function. This is all the more true if we are to regard the *Nobis quoque* not as a part of the intercessory prayer, but as a special independent prayer, so that the *Memento* must be looked upon as isolated, as a segregated part of that block of prayers which were inserted before the consecration.

It is true that in the Orient—except Egypt—the memorial of the dead is not only actually linked with the other intercessions after the consecration, but its location in this spot is emphasized and justified by argument. Thus we read in the *Mystagogic Catecheses* of Jerusalem: "Then we remember also those who have fallen asleep, first the patriarchs and prophets . . . and in general all who have fallen asleep amongst us, because we believe it is of the greatest value for the souls for whom the prayer is offered while the holy and tremendous sacrifice lies before us." The same idea appears in Chrysostom: "When . . . that awe-inspiring sacrifice lies displayed on the altar, how shall we not prevail with God by our entreaties for them [the dead]?" Preceding the *Memento* both in the Liturgy of St. James at Jerusalem and in the Byzantine liturgy, we have the petition for a fruitful reception of the Eucharist by the congregation. Perhaps we have to suppose that the thought of the Sacrament of union more or less consciously concurred in placing the remembrance of the dead right here; the sacramental proof of their membership in the communion of saints is no longer theirs to have, but a substitute for it would be offered if the living would remember them at this moment. It is this idea precisely which Augustine suggests when he remarks that the dead are remembered at the altar "in the communion of the body of Christ," because they are certainly not separated from the Church.

A corroboration of this opinion worth noting is to be found in the oldest Egyptian formulary, that of Serapion. Although the main traditional liturgies of Egypt generally place the intercession before the consecration, this most ancient text commemorates the dead likewise after the consecration, attaching this commemoration immediately to a somewhat expanded petition for a fruitful communion, as follows:

> . . . and grant that all who participate might receive a medicine of life for curing every sickness and for strengthening every forward step and every virtue, not unto damnation, O God of truth, and not unto denunciation and shame. For we have called upon Thee, the uncreated, through Thy only-begotten in the Holy Ghost, that this people might find mercy and might be granted improvement; may angels be sent to assist the people to annihilate the evil one and to fortify the Church. We also cry out for all who have fallen asleep, who are also remembered. [Then, after the reading of the names:] Sanctify these souls, for thou knowest them all. Sanctify all who have died in the Lord, and number them among Thy holy troops and give them place and dwelling in Thy kingdom.

Although the phrasing is quite different, yet there is a close kinship in the structure and in the train of ideas between this commemoration of the dead and the Roman *Memento*. In both cases there is the immediate attachment to the petition for Communion, the division of the remembrance into two parts, the reading of the names between these two parts, whereupon the prayer turns towards "all who rest in Christ" and closes with a picture of the life to come, conceived in local terms. This is not mere coincidence, but the result of a common tradition, as we can gather from those closer relationships between Egyptian and Roman liturgy which were established above. But whereas in Egypt the *Memento* of the dead later on disappeared from this position, at Rome it was retained except at Sunday service, and then later on it became general.

In regard to the wording, the word *etiam* in the introduction immediately arrests our attention. Usually this *etiam* is regarded as a coupling which establishes the connection with the *Memento* of the living, which is supposed at one time to have followed immediately. The Egyptian parallel just quoted shows that this supposition is unnecessary. The line of ideas is rather as follows: When we are being filled "with every heavenly blessing" through the power of the Sacrament, we think also of those who can no longer have a part in the Sacrament. And the idea is extended: Even if they can no longer eat the hallowed bread, yet they have gone into the beyond with the seal of faith, *præcesserunt cum signo fidei*.

This *signum fidei* is not just a "sign of faith" in an indefinite and general sense; it is the seal which in Baptism is impressed upon the profession of faith; thus it is Baptism itself. Baptism is the completion, the sacramental authentication or "sealing" of faith. At the same time it is the mark with which Christ has stamped those who are His own, and it is therefore both a guarantee against the perils of darkness and a proud badge of the Christian confessor. The *signum fidei* gives assurance of entrance into life everlasting provided that it is preserved inviolate. In any case, those for whom we petition have not disowned their Baptism; the seal of Christ is shining on their souls. It is indeed for this reason that the burial places of Christians in the catacombs and the primitive Christian sarcophagi are decorated with the allegorical symbols of Baptism. In that age of adult baptism the reference to this sacrament on the Christian grave was as natural an expression of Christian hope as in our own day the reception of the last sacraments is. It is quite in keeping with our changed circumstances to regard those sacraments in general by whose reception the preservation of our Baptism is made manifest, as the sacramental seal of faith, the *signum fidei* with which our brethren have departed this life.

The intercession here made for the dead is primarily for those who have departed this life as Christians. This coincides with the practice of the Church, which even from oldest times has offered the sacrifice only for those who have remained in communion with her, and who thus have a right to her treasuries of grace. Only those, at any rate, can be mentioned by name. But then the circle is widened: "all who rest in Christ," so that all are included who are waiting their final purification, since there is none among them who could have attained his salvation except "in Christ."

In this short sentence the other phrases, too, echo the first Christian centuries as closely as do the words *signum fidei*. Thus *præcessit in pace* or *præcessit nos in pace—*"he (or she) has gone before us in peace" is an expression which also occurs in the grave inscriptions. Following our Lord's example, the Church of old was wont to call the death of the just, from which they would arise after a short while, a sleep. And it is a sleep of peace, not only because the struggle and strife of earthly life are past, but also because only in death is that peace which Christ willed to bring finally secured. *Et dormiunt in somno pacis.* "Who rest in the sleep of peace." Countless are the inscriptions which employ the word peace: *requiescit in pace, in somno pacis, præcessit in somno pacis.* An inscription from the year 397, at St. Praxedes' in Rome, begins: *Dulcis et inno- ces hic dormit Severianus XP in somno pacis. Qui vixit annos p.m.L, cuius spiritus in luce Domini susceptus est.*

The deceased faithful are resting in Christ in the same sense that Holy Writ speaks of "the dead who are in Christ" (1 Thess. 4:17) and of those "who die in the Lord" (Apoc. 14:13). They are forever joined to Christ's Body, forever inspired by His life. But those for whom we pray have not yet attained the consummation. The dust of their earthly pilgrimage still clings to their feet. They have not yet been allowed to enter "a place of comfort, light and peace." In the torrid lands of the South the word *refrigerium* was early employed as a designation of the state of those blessed who have been granted "coolness." The word light, which is universally regarded as the epitome of joy, is given still greater prominence by the images used in the Apocalypse 21:23 f.; 22:5.

MENTION OF NAMES

The mention of personal names in the commemoration of the dead, as in that of the living, is also an ancient practice. An evidence of this is found in the text of the Irish tradition of the Roman canon. The celebrating priest at a Mass for certain deceased persons would insert their names in place of the word *nomina* or else after *in somno pacis*. But the other textual form, with *famulorum famularumque*, as we have it in the tradition of the Roman canon outside the Irish, had no such indication for the insertion of names. The first case of the use of *ill. et ill.* (equivalent to the present *N. et N.*) is presented in the group of sacramentaries which goes back to Alcuin, who had inserted the remembrance of the dead into the Hadrianic Sacramentary as a permanent part. It was about this time that the custom began of saying the canon half-aloud or even silently; hence no surprise would be caused by such a catalogueing of names, if it actually occurred," or by the appearance of the *Memento* itself on Sundays and feasts.

Nevertheless there is evidence, even in the pre-Carolingian Roman liturgy, of the custom of formally reciting the names of the dead with the aid of diptychs (except on Sundays and feast days). The reading was done by the deacon, and in this case as a rule not in the place where the *N. et N.* now stands, but between the two sentences of the prayer, in the same place where today silent prayer is suggested.

Until late in the Middle Ages we not infrequently find the rubric here: "Here the names of the dead are recited." Less often we find the heading *Super diptycia* placed above the *Memento etiam*. Insofar as this recitation of names found a place in public services, it must have been occupied, like its counterpart, the reading of the diptychs in the Orient, with the names of outstanding personalities and special benefactors. The deacon's role in this could not have lasted very long. Soon interpolated formulas, more or less comprehensive, were developed, so that the priest himself could combine them with the recitation of the names, or could even substitute them for the latter, unless perhaps a detailed catalogue or recitation of names of the dead with a similar formula was already joined to the remembrance of the living. Finally, instead of all these interpolations, there remained a personal recollection by the priest according to his own judgment, just as at the *Memento* of the living. But for this, as was also the case with the *Memento* of the dead, special formulas were worked out.

Just as the *Memento* for the living became a basis for all sorts of additions, so the *Memento* for the dead, too, served as the groundwork to which a variety of interpolations could be affixed. For example, an *apologia* was widely used in this connection, inserted generally before the *Memento*. Insertions of this type had already appeared within the preceding *Supplices*, or even in front of it. Ancient and widespread was a rubric which enjoined a pause for personal prayer after the words *Supplices te rogamus*. The obtrusion of personal intentions had thus been inaugurated very early.

The conclusion of the remembrance of the dead is also *Per Christum Dominum nostrum*. In this instance, the phrase is accompanied by a bow on the part of the priest. That is unusual. Many explanations have been offered. Some suggest that the bow is meant for the preceding *deprecamur*, or for the humble self-accusation of the following *Nobis quoque peccatoribus*, or else that it is intended for the word *Christus*. The last postulate can appeal to several parallels since the fifteenth century. But why, then, is this the only place that the bow is prescribed? We should rather seek our explanation in the allegorical treatment of the Mass-liturgy, the same sort of thinking that led the later Middle Ages to give a symbolic representation of the Crucified by means of the outstretched arms after the consecration, and the crossed hands at the *Supplices*. Toward the end of the canon some externalization had to be made of the moment when the dying Redeemer bowed His head.

17. Nobis quoque

Nobis quoque peccatoribus famulis tuis, de multitudine miserationum tuarum sperantibus, partem aliquam et societatem donare digneris, cum tuis sanctis Apostolis et Martyribus: cum Ioanne, Stephano, Matthia, Barnaba, Ignatio, Alexandro, Marcellino, Petro, Felicitate, Perpetua, Agatha, Lucia, Agnete, Cæcilia, Anastasia, et omnibus sanctis tuis: intra quorum nos consortium, non æstimator meriti, sed veniæ, quæsumus, largitor admitte. Per eundem Christum Dominum nostrum.

And also to us Thy sinful servants, trusting in Thy boundless mercy, graciously grant unto us some part and fellowship with Thy holy Apostles and Martyrs: with John, Stephen, Matthias, Barnabas, Ignatius, Alexander, Marcellinus, Peter, Felicity, Perpetua, Agatha, Lucy, Agnes, Caecilia, Anastasia, and with all Thy saints: we beseech Thee to admit us into their company, not weighing our merits, but freely granting us forgiveness. Through Christ Our Lord.

In the present-day text of the Roman canon, the *Nobis quoque*, the last of the large prayers of the canon, is appended to the remembrance of the dead without giving the least impression of a skip or break. After we have prayed for the dead, that they may attain the place of light and peace, we pray also for ourselves, that we may obtain a part with the saints of heaven. But simple and natural though this thought transition appears at first, still upon closer study we encounter several problems. Why is this prayer put here at all? Has not its main theme already been expressed in the *Supplices*, with the appeal for "every heavenly blessing?" The problem grows even more vexing when we turn our attention to the history of the text, for we discover that the remembrance of the dead did not even belong to the permanent parts of the canon, whereas the *Nobis quoque* is found in all our text sources and must therefore have followed immediately after the *Supplices*.

The most obvious conclusion would then be that our prayer arose as a continuation of the *Supplices* and is to be explained as such, and this opinion, despite the difficulties already hinted at, has been maintained even in most recent times. There is indeed a forward step in the thought of the second prayer, since the petition is not only for blessing and grace from heaven, but for eternal bliss itself in the company of apostles and martyrs. Besides, it is possible to point to oriental parallels which likewise extend the plea for the fruits of Communion into a plea for heavenly happiness, and thus pursue the biblical concept of a bond between the Eucharist and heavenly life (John 6:48–51). In one case, in fact, the wording reminds one of the phrases of our *Nobis quoque*.

On the other hand, it is certainly very surprising that an imposing construction like the *Nobis quoque*, an independent sentence, well-rounded in its phrases, should be set up for the simple continuation of a thought which was already expressed in substance, when it would have been more than sufficient to follow up the words "we may be filled with all heavenly benediction and grace" with a phrase like "and may attain life everlasting." That this should have been the original pattern seems almost excluded by the fact that the *Supplices*, unlike the prayers that precede it, has the concluding formula *Per Christum Dominum nostrum*. Add to this the puzzling *quoque*, which is understandable on the supposition that the remembrance of the dead precedes, and a prayer is included "also" for us as for the dead; but remove the remembrance of the dead and the word *quoque* loses its point of reference, since "we" have already been named as recipients of the favor petitioned in the *Supplices*.

"SINFUL SERVANTS"

But it is possible—and perhaps necessary—to take a different view, in which the *quoque* receives a satisfactory meaning. Is it so sure that the same group of persons is referred to in both the *Supplices* and the *Nobis quoque*? The terms *nos peccatores*, or more correctly *nos peccatores famuli tui*, "us, thy sinful servants," could *per se* designate the whole congregation assembled, as many commentators suppose either by their silence or even expressly. But amongst all the designations for the congregation represented by the priest in prayer—we possess thousands of examples in the sacramentaries—this would be the only case of the kind. On the contrary, *peccator* had been used as a term of self-designation, especially as the self-designation of the clergy. At the close of his work on Baptism, Tertullian begs "that when you pray, remember also *Tertulliani peccatoris*." For centuries, it was the practice in clerical circles to add the word *peccator* to one's signature. Therefore here, too, the *clergy* must be meant by the *peccatores famuli*—the celebrating priest and his assistants. If this be true, then the addition of a *quoque*, even right after the *Supplices*, takes on an acceptable meaning; *quoque* then signifies something like "and especially." To the prayer for all, we priests now add a particular appeal for ourselves, poor sinners.

Such a recommendation of self, pleading for one's own person, combined at the same time with the acknowledgment of one's own unworthiness, was part of the intercessory prayer already in the fourth century, at least in the Orient. In the Syrian Liturgy of St. James it is inserted at the very beginning, while in Egypt it appears near the end of the intercessions. In the Alexandrian Greek Liturgy of St. Mark it consists of two members: "Remember, O Lord, in grace and mercy also us, thy sinful and unworthy servants, and blot out our sins, good and loving God; remember, Lord, also me, thy lowly and sinful and unworthy servant . . ." The similarity of expression is astonishing. In view of the connection—already verified more than once—between Egypt especially and Rome, this similarity can hardly be accidental. Thus we are forced to accept in the Roman Mass, too, the meaning which is unequivocally given in the oriental text, the meaning of self-recommendation. Moreover, this was the meaning given the *Nobis quoque* by medieval commentators.

In this way we make room for the possibility that the *Nobis quoque* was originally attached to the *Supplices*. But the fact is not therefore assured—not at all. It would be certainly very surprising to find this solitary instance where, in order to admit this recommendation of self, the oblation prayers would be concluded before the close of the canon and another special prayer would be introduced at once. Such a fresh start might be brought about more easily if the remembrance of the dead were inserted first and if then the *Nobis quoque* followed as a sort of embolism. To be sure, we would then be forced to admit that both prayers were at first alien to the Sunday and feast-day Mass. Then, about the turn of the sixth century, when the original number of the saints' names in the *Nobis quoque* began to be expanded into the present well-ordered double series and the list set consciously side by side with the series in the *Communicantes*, this parallel would have furnished a reason for including the *Nobis quoque* in the canon as a permanent part.

Related evidences in Egypt also lend a color of probability to such a connection with the remembrance of the dead. For it is worthy of note that there too a prayer which is remarkably reminiscent of the "some part and fellowship with Thy holy apostles and martyrs" in our Roman formula is frequently attached to the remembrance of the dead, not indeed as a self-recommendation on the part of the clergy, but as a petition for the congregation. This appears in the fourth century.

In the papyrus fragment of the anaphora of St. Mark which comes from this period, we read near the end of the intercession: "[1] Give peace to the souls of the deceased, [2] remember those [for whom] we keep a memorial on this day, [3] and those whose names we speak and whose names we do not speak, [4] [above all] our very faithful fathers and bishops everywhere, [5] and permit us to take part and lot, [6] with [the assembly] of the holy prophets, apostles, and martyrs."

This wording recurs in later Egyptian texts, but with amplifications and several inversions. We might mention in passing that as a matter of fact the West-Syrian Mass is also familiar with similar expansions of the remembrance of the dead. Thus it is not impossible that the prayers added to the *Memento* of the dead in the Roman canon simply began: *Nobis quoque partem et societatem donare digneris cum tuis sanctis apostolis et martyribus* . . . However, on the evidence of the oriental parallels cited at the start, it seems clear that contemporaneously a self-recommendation was added to the preceding intercessory prayer, and the plea itself was restricted to the narrower circle of the clergy by means of the words *peccatoribus famulis*.

With the prayer certain names were probably linked from the very beginning. It is a striking fact that the first two names in the Roman prayer, John and Stephen, also appear in Egypt, in the corresponding prayer of the Coptic Mass; although the precise point of insertion here is slightly different and the name of Mother of God precedes. It is very probable that at an early period these two or three names were added to the wording as it appears in the papyrus fragment already quoted, and that the remembrance of the dead, along with the appendage thus expanded, belonged to the ancient fund of prayers which the Roman and Alexandrian churches had in common as early as the fourth century. The general designation, "with Thy holy apostles and martyrs," is Roman and corresponds to the "of Thy blessed apostles and martyrs" in the *Communicantes*. But then, feeling that the very first of the names that followed was beyond the announced group of apostles and martyrs, a new start was made by inserting a preposition, *cum Joanne*, another indication that a series of special names had already been supplied beforehand.

THE SAINTS

As long as the emphasis was put on the remembrance as such, only a few names could possibly be brought forward for mention with the holy apostles and martyrs. Even here the earliest saints to be considered were those who already enjoyed a devotion at Rome. But then, in the period when the veneration of martyrs flourished so vigorously, there was a rapid growth in the list here, just as there was in the *Communicantes*. Of the saints in the *Nobis quoque* list, besides the Baptist and Stephen, those who had such honor paid them around the end of the fifth century were the following Roman martyrs: Peter and Marcellinus, whose grave on the Via Lavicana had been decorated with verses by Pope Damasus, and whose feast on June 2 was contained in the sacramentaries; Agnes, over whose grave on the Via Nomentana a basilica had already been erected by Emperor Constantine's daughter Constantia; Cecilia, whose grave in the catacomb of Callistus had been honored at a very early date, but whose veneration at any rate reached a peak about the turn of the fourth century (this was when a new basilica was built and dedicated to her at the old Titulus Cæciliæ in Trastevere, and thus in the end, foundress and martyr became identified); further, a Roman lady, Felicity, over whose grave Pope Boniface I (d. 422) had built an oratory, and whose feast was celebrated in the oldest sacramentaries—as it is at present—on November 23. Here again as in the case of the *Communicantes*, the list of saints in the Milanese Mass offers a confirmation of what we have established. The Roman martyrs are there set down plainly in their historical sequence; they show the following succession: Peter, Marcellinus, Agnes, Cecilia, and Felicity; and only after that some other names follow.

Of the rest of the names in the Roman *Nobis quoque*, an Alexander is mentioned at least three times in the fourth-century Roman lists of martyrs. For two who bore this name there is also an annual commemoration in the sacramentaries, although they enjoyed no other special veneration. The Alexander in the canon appears to be the Alexander of the group of seven martyrs, who for a long time have been commemorated on July 10, and whom later legends linked with St. Felicity, as seven brothers; since the sixth century, Alexander stood out in this group. Of the two women martyrs of Sicily, Agatha and Lucy, the former was honored at Rome in the fifth century, when the Goth Ricimer built a church in her honor, and the latter about the sixth century; although both had surely been venerated previously in their native cities of Catania and Syracuse. The rich possessions of the Roman church in Sicily probably led to this transfer of cult. To Felicity the name of Perpetua was added. Perhaps the name of the Roman martyr drew after itself the name of the great African lady whose *Passio*, one of the most precious documents in the history of the martyrs, was known even at Rome at quite an early date. But that the names in the list are not to be referred to both the African martyrs, Perpetua and her slave Felicity, is clearly deduced from the way they are mentioned, for if they did they would certainly have been left in their usual order. Anastasia is the martyr of Sirmium whose body was brought to Constantinople in 460, and whose veneration had probably received an impetus in Rome during the period of Byzantine domination.

Regarding the two Sicilian martyrs, a trustworthy account expressly tells us that Gregory the Great placed their names in the canon. Nor can the rest of the names in this later layer have come into the canon much earlier than this. Regarding Alexander and Agatha, we might think of Pope Symmachus (498–514), who had provided funds for the memorial places of both, as he had also done for Agnes and Felicity. On the other hand, Matthias and Barnabas, who appear as representatives of the "holy apostles," evidently did not acquire this role until the twelve Apostles had all found a place in the *Communicantes* series. To these two saints no particular veneration was paid in the liturgy of the city of Rome during the first millenary, and the same is true of Ignatius, martyr-bishop of Antioch, in spite of his connection with the city of Rome. Still, in view of the manuscript evidence, their insertion into the canon cannot have been substantially later. So everything points to Gregory the Great as having undertaken the final revision here as in the *Communicantes*. Duplication of the names was avoided, but the same principles regarding the disposition of names held in both instances: at the top of the list an outstanding name, John the Baptist; then a double column of seven (the scriptural number)—seven men and seven women; among the men the hierarchical order once more: first the apostles, then the martyr-bishop Ignatius, then Alexander, who is designated by the legend as a priest (or bishop); likewise the pair of martyrs who are otherwise generally named in this order, Peter and Marcellinus, but in line with the legend are reversed according to their hierarchical standing: Marcellinus the priest and Peter the exorcist. Amongst the women a certain territorial division is recognizable. In the first pair, the names of the two African women seem to have been decisive; then follow the two martyrs from Sicily, Agatha and Lucy, then the two Roman maidens, Agnes and Cecilia, and finally the oriental Anastasia.

As is already clear from what has been said, those named (with the exception of the biblical characters, of Ignatius, the bishop of Antioch and author of seven letters [d.c. 107], and of the African lady Perpetua [d. 202–3]) are all martyrs of whom little is known beyond their name, the place of their confession and—through the annual commemoration of their death—perhaps the day of their death; no year, no history of their suffering, no biographical details. Not till later did legend sketch out a picture. These are properly the true representatives of the unknown heroes of the first Christian centuries who, because of their glorious death for Christ, continued to live on in the minds and hearts of men. But their death for Christ was likewise their triumph with Christ, and that is enough to have their names serve as symbols of that blessed lot which we beg God we, along with our own departed, might share at least to some extent.

As in the case of the *Communicantes*, the list of the *Nobis quoque* was enlarged during the Middle Ages by the addition of favorite medieval names, particularly at the end of the list. But as a rule these additions stayed within modest bounds.

GENERAL FEATURES

The parallelism with the *Communicantes* and its series of saints extends also to the general features of both prayers. In both cases the prayer represents a continuation of the *Memento*, in such wise that a certain connection with the saints in heaven is represented. But the connection is different in the two cases. After the *Memento* of the living, the assembled congregation, looking up humbly to the saints, offers up its sacrifice in common with them; the only connection here is that already established by association in the one kingdom of God. After the *Memento* of the dead the concept is raised a degree and the plea is for a final participation in the blessedness of the elect. Being about to eat the bread of life everlasting, we have prayed for the dead that God might be mindful of them and vouchsafe them entry into the place of light and peace. And it is this place of light and peace, viewed as the home of the saints, that we beg also for ourselves, *nobis quoque peccatoribus famulis tuis*.

Regarding the rest of the wording of the prayer, the only thing to notice is that the note of modest retirement and humble self-accusation which was struck by the word *peccatores* sets the tone of the whole prayer. The petition is spoken only with the utmost trust in the fullness of divine mercy, and the only object sought is that God may grant "some part," and even this not as a reward of present merit, but solely because He is the giver of grace (cf. Psalm 129:3–4). All this is quite in keeping in a prayer spoken before the people for one's own person, whereas in a prayer said in the name of the congregation it would sound rather unusual.

The words *Nobis quoque peccatoribus* are lifted out of the quiet of the canon, for the priest says them audibly, meanwhile striking his breast. There is scattered evidence of this striking of the breast as early as the twelfth century, and soon thereafter it became a general practice. In some places, since the thirteenth century, there is mention even of a triple striking of the breast.

And the custom of saying the first words aloud goes back even further. We hear of it already in the ninth century, and since that time it has become and remained an almost universal usage. However, there is no account at all prior to this of such a practice, which would be explained on the assumption that the whole canon was said aloud, and thus the words were already perceptible. But why is it that precisely these words are given special prominence? What passes at present as the reason for emphasizing these words is of no importance. The real and adequate reason must be sought in the circumstances of the past. The survival of the practice is a typical case of the great endurance of liturgical customs even when the basis for them has long since been removed—in fact, when that basis was in existence only a short time.

In the Roman *Ordines* of the seventh century the plan supposed that the subdeacons, who, at the start of the preface, had ranged themselves in a row opposite the celebrant on the other side of the free-standing altar, and who during the canon bowed profoundly, would straighten up at the *Nobis quoque* and go to their assigned places so that they might be ready to assist in the fraction of the bread as soon as the canon was over. This rule, which naturally had no meaning except at the grand pontifical services, was retained even when, at the end of the eighth century, it became customary to recite the canon in a low tone. So, to give the subdeacons the signal when the time came, the celebrant had to say these words in an audible voice. This relationship between the two was still to be seen in the Roman *Ordines* at the end of the tenth century. Once admitted, the custom stayed, even though, in accordance with the Romano-Frankish liturgy, the subdeacons usually did not have to change their places till after the closing doxology, and even though later on, in consequence of the introduction of unleavened bread and lastly of the small particles, the fraction became unnecessary and the assistance of the subdeacons superfluous. Its survival was sustained by the allegorical interpretation which saw in it the confession of the centurion beneath the Cross, and thus the practice was transferred not only to the simple high Mass celebrated without assistants, but even to the private Mass.

This also makes it easier to understand the striking of the breast. The medieval interpreters since the thirteenth century explicitly cited, along with the centurion's outcry, the statement in Luke 13:48 that all the people went home beating their breasts. And finally this throws light on the puzzling bow of the head at the words just before this, in the conclusion of the *Memento:* this becomes the moment when our Lord bowed His head and died.

18. Concluding Doxologies

Per quem hæc omnia, Domine, semper bona creas, sanctificas, vivificas, benedicis et præstas nobis.

Through Whom, O Lord, all these gifts are ever created as good, sanctified, vivified, blessed and bestowed upon us.

Per Ipsum, et cum Ipso, et in Ipso, est tibi Deo Patri omnipotenti, in unitate Spiritus Sancti, omnis honor, et gloria. Per omnia sæcula sæculorum. Amen.

Through Him, with Him, and in Him, is to Thee, God Father almighty all honor and glory in the communion of the Holy Spirit. World without end. Amen.

The canon closes with two formulas, both of which give the impression of a summary and a conclusion, the second formula quite plainly, since it is a true doxology (*omnis honor et gloria*), and even the first, with a wording (*hæc omnia*) that suggests a recapitulation. Neither of these formulas are prayers in the usual sense of petition or oblation, as were the foregoing formulas; rather they display the traits of a commendatory statement, a "predication": Thou workest, it is. Thus, even a superficial examination of the first formula reveals the same character of a doxology which is patent in the second. In its wording, however, the first presents a picture of God's gifts streaming down from heaven through Christ's mediatorship, while the second brings into relief how, through Him, all honor and glory surge from creation up to God. The *admirabile commercium* which has just been given reality once again on the altar, thus gains expression in the very words of the canon and gives them their worthy crowning.

If we turn now to study the first of these two formulas, *Per quem hæc omnia*, we are confronted with certain obscurities. We do not see at first glance just where the emphasis is placed. Nor is it clear what idea this word of praise is unraveling, whether the creative work and the blessing of God, or perhaps the activity of Christ (with which the nexus is made to the preceding *Nobis quoque*). In any case, the *Per Christum Dominum nostrum* is seized upon as the opportunity for appraising, in retrospect, the divine grace which has again come and is coming to us in this hour "through Christ." He is the invisible high-priest who has exercised His office anew and is exercising it; through Him, God has sanctified these gifts once more and is now ready to distribute them—for reference has already been made to receiving "from this sharing of the altar." Now it is our task to see how these striking ideas are to be expounded in detail.

EXACT MEANING

In order to make clear the exact meaning of the words, we must first of all note the important fact that in the earlier stage of the Roman canon, and for that matter right on to the late Middle Ages and even after, a blessing of natural products was on occasion inserted in this spot. In the oldest sacramentaries we find a blessing of water, milk and honey on the occasion of solemn Baptism, and a blessing of fresh grapes on the feast of St. Xystus (Aug. 6). The "Easter lamb" was also blessed at this point on Easter Sunday. In the declining Middle Ages the blessing of other gifts of nature, which was customary on certain occasions, was sometimes inserted here: the blessing of bread, wine, fruits, and seeds on the feast of St. Blase; of bread on the feast of St. Agatha; of fodder for cattle on St. Stephen's, of wine on the feast of St. John the Evangelist.

To this day the consecration by the bishop of the oil for the sick on Holy Thursday has continued in this location. In all these cases the prayer ends with the mention of Christ's name and then, without any concluding formula of its own, continues with our *Per quem hæc omnia*, which thus plainly forms a unit with the respective prayers of blessing.

The question, therefore, that presses for an answer is, whether the *Per quem hæc omnia* is nothing else than the unchanging conclusion of the more or less variable prayer of blessing, perhaps because the latter was part of the plan of the canon, perhaps because both formulas originally arose as occasional inserts. Recently the question has been answered in the affirmative, particularly by Duchesne, who stresses the point that without such a prayer of blessing there would be a hiatus between our formula and what precedes it in the canon, and moreover that the word *omnia* in particular could hardly be understood simply of the consecrated sacrificial gifts.

A further point in favor of such an opinion is presented in the *Church Order* of Hippolytus of Rome. Here, as we have already seen, mention is made of that custom, then very vigorous and alive, of which the blessing of water, milk, and honey is only a later relic. But in addition, right after the text of the *Eucharistia*, we find a rubric which tells about the blessing of natural products: If someone brings oil, the bishop should pronounce a prayer of thanksgiving similar to that for bread and wine, with the proper changes, and the same if someone brings cheese or olives. For both cases a short prayer-text is offered, to suggest the spiritual meaning of the natural gift, and a Trinitarian doxology is presented to be used for the conclusion. These blessings apparently were independent liturgical creations, having only an extrinsic connection with the Mass. But perhaps they had been attached thus to the Mass even at an early period. At any rate, in the Egyptian Mass they were incorporated into the canon. At least in this case the same thing happened which (as we saw) occurred everywhere in regard to the intercessory prayers which were placed just before the Sacrifice-Mass and then later were drawn into it. The blessings, too, which followed after the Mass proper were at last brought into the narrower compass of the canon. The same process obviously occurred also in the Roman Mass. This is shown by the remarkable agreement, sometimes word for word, between the basic text in Hippolytus and that in the Latin liturgy of Rome for the blessing of oil, and also for the blessing of grapes, *resp.*, new fruits. They represent a direct continuation of the practice found in Hippolytus.

Therefore, the evolution must actually have been such that first the blessings of produce were inserted before the end of the canon, then later our *Per quem hæc omnia* was developed. The insertion of the blessing took place at this precise point because of the desire to link the ecclesiastical blessings with the great blessing which Christ Himself had instituted and in which He (and God through Him) grants to earthly gifts the highest hallowing and fullness of grace. This interconnection is brought out strikingly by the closing phrase: *Per quem hæc omnia*—the Eucharistic gifts are thus included—*semper bona creas*. By taking up again the antithesis against Gnosticism and Manichæism, our retrospective mediation leads to a statement of praise, proclaiming that the gifts which lie before us, sanctified, are God-created, and that God always has done well in His creative labors, and continues to do so. This He does through the Logos, through whom all things came into being, and through Him who Himself became man and a member of our earthly cosmos, He also hallows all things. The Incarnation itself was the grand consecration of creation. But a new wave of blessing pours out over creation whenever the Church makes use of the power of sanctification granted her by her founder. The words *vivificas* and *benedicis* are probably thought of only as re-enforcing the *sanctificas*. Sanctification is a herald of that new and everlasting life in which earthly creation has a share; indeed, the consecration of bread and wine has filled these figures, these species, with the noblest, the highest life. Lastly, the word *benedicis* receives the cardinal stress. It was a blessing that was inserted, and this word makes the tie-in with it. In the chief formulas this blessing takes the following shape: "Bless, O Lord, these new fruits . . ." In other words the preceding activity, the completion of the *Eucharistia*, was also such a blessing, only of an incomparably higher kind. Already in the *Te igitur* the petition had been made "to accept and bless" just as we find it in the *Quam oblationem* and not seldom even anticipated in the *Oratio super oblata*. The finale is presented by the words *præstas nobis*, with the suggestion that every hallowing and blessing which proceeds from Christ has but one aim, namely, to enrich us. Communion, for which we are now preparing ourselves, is only the most wondrous example of this.

So we see that the words of the Per quem hæc omnia *got their full meaning in connection with the preceding prayer of blessing, and that they obviously owe to it their origin in the form we have at present.* On the other hand, taking into consideration what we have said so often, that because of the consecrated gifts the connection with earthly creation is never lost sight of, we could still leave the words in the text of the canon even without any such blessing preceding them, regarding them merely as a glorification of our Redeemer. In this case, however, the word *omnia* would lose some of its significance, since only the species of bread and wine are before us. The words are the counterpart of the plea for the consecration in the *Quam oblationem;* they are a thanksgiving for the consecration, a "thank you" to God and to our high-priest through whom he does all and through whom He grants all. They are a doxological acknowledgment that every grace comes to us through Christ, and thus they form a preliminary to the greater doxology that follows, wherein we acknowledge further that all praise and glory return to God through Christ our Lord.

PER IPSUM

It is an old rule of public prayer that such a prayer should close with praise of God and thus revert to the grand function of all prayer, in which the creature bows before his Creator. Even the prayers in the *Didache* have this structure, and in oriental liturgies there is scarcely one prayer of the priest to be found which does not end in a solemn doxology: "For Thou art a kind and loving God and we offer up praise to Thee, the Father and the Son and the Holy Ghost, now and always and unto all eternity"—thus we read in the Byzantine liturgy. In the Roman liturgy, as in the rest of Christendom, this has been the rule for a long time in regard to the Psalms, where the *Gloria Patri* regularly forms the final verse. The closing formula of the priestly prayer, on the contrary, is somewhat less rigid in construction, bringing the mediatorship of our Redeemer to the fore usually in such a way that a doxological reference to His eternal dominion is worked into the formula. Only the main prayer of all liturgy, the Great Prayer of the Mass, has retained a formula of praise in the Roman style, a formula where simplicity and grandeur are combined most felicitously. The present form is that already found in the earliest tradition of the canon. An indication of its antique structure is the fact that it not only includes a praise of God, but insists that this praise is offered through Christ, a turn of thought which was lost in most of the oriental liturgies in consequence of the Arian turmoil, lost not only in this passage, but generally in all prayer-endings.

As a matter of fact, the closing doxology of the Roman canon is closely akin to that which marks the end of the *Eucharistia* in Hippolytus. The connection is made apparent by setting the two side by side (with a slight transposition in the present text of the canon).

Per ipsum et cum ipso et in ipso	*Per quem*
est tibi	*tibi*
omnis honor et gloria	*gloria et honor*
Deo Patri omnipotenti	*Patri et Filio cum Sancto Spiritu*
in unitate Spiritus Sancti	*in sancta Ecclesia tua*
per omnia sæcula sæculorum.	*et nunc et in sæcula sæculorum.*

The chief difference is that the Trinitarian names, which in Hippolytus are grouped together in the address, in our present canon, in accordance with the Christian economy of salvation, are fitted stepwise into the very structure of the encomium itself. The "unity of the Holy Ghost" in the modern Mass is only another way of saying the "holy Church," as in the Hippolytan text. The Church is brought to unity and *communion* in the Holy Ghost: *Sancto Spiritu congregata,* and is sanctified by His indwelling. She *is* the unity of the Holy Ghost. From her arises all honor and glory to God the Father almighty. And it arises "through Him," for Christ is the Head of redeemed mankind, yea, of all creation, which is summed up in Him (Eph. 1:10). He is her high-priest, standing before the Father. Therefore, "through Him" is more clearly defined by "with Him" and "in Him." He is not standing before His Father as a lone petitioner, as He had been during His earthly pilgrimage when He spent quiet nights on the mountain praying alone; now His redeemed are around Him. They have learnt how they can, with Him, praise the Father who is in heaven. In truth they are in Him, taken up into the living union of His Body and therefore drawn into the fervent glow of His prayer, so that they are really in a position to worship the Father "in spirit and in truth." "In Him" and "in the communion of the Holy Spirit" therefore designate one and the same all-encompassing well-spring whence arises the glorification of the Father. It may be considered in relation to Christ since the redeemed comprise His Mystical Body, or in relation to the Spirit whose breath inspires them.

It is not by chance that this encomium stands at the end of the Eucharistic prayer, nor is it by chance that it has the indicative form (*est*) instead of the subjunctive or "wishing" form. Here, where the Church is gathered, right in front of the altar on which the Sacrament reposes, gathered indeed to offer the Body and Blood of Christ in reverence— here God does actually receive all honor and glory. In this moment the word of Malachias (1:11) is fulfilled: The name of the Lord is great among the peoples.

ACCOMPANYING RITES

This connnection is represented also in the rite. The priest grasps the chalice and Host and lifts them aloft. This is the so-called "little elevation"—little not because it is of less importance or because it is the remnant of a larger one, but because it does not, like its younger sister, the "big elevation," consist in showing the holy gifts to the people, but only in raising them up to God as an oblation. By its very nature this elevation can be a symbolic one, as we have already found on various other occasions, even though at the same time it must always be a visible one.

At present, this elevation occurs only during the words "all honor and glory." Here we have a certain contraction. Its history is a long one.

It is in the seventh-century liturgy of the city of Rome that we first find the original and full form of the rite in unimpaired clarity. The assisting archdeacon, who at *Per quem hæc omnia* had raised himself erect from his bowed position, at the words *Per ipsum,* with hands covered with a linen cloth, grasps the chalice, and raises it up while the pope at the same time picks up the bread, that is, the two consecrated breads from his own oblation, and raises them to the height of the chalice brim, and while touching the latter with them, finishes the doxology. But gradually the rite was obscured and interrupted by the intrusion of the sign of the cross which gradually grew more prominent. At first, and until the eleventh century, only the three signs of the cross are mentioned, those made over Host and chalice at the words *sanctificas, vivificas, benedicis*, which do not yet disturb the procedure at the doxology. But then appear, here and there, the crosses made with the Host at *Per ipsum et cum ipso et in ipso*, and these became a more general practice after the year 1000. In the beginning, there were but two, later on regularly three as nowadays. Finally, since the eleventh century, a fourth appears, and not much later a fifth came into general use, those, namely, which now are tied in with the words *Deo Patri* and *in unitate Spiritus Sancti*.

While the meaning of the crosses that accompany the words of blessing is clear—they are not, of course, an exercise of the power of blessing, but they do illustrate the statement contained in *sanctificas, vivificas* and *benedicis*—there is no directly convincing explanation of those which are joined to the doxology, not even in the sphere of their origin. The circumstances do, to some small degree, explain the triple cross made at the thrice-repeated *ipse;* here we probably have a strengthening and stylizing of the demonstrative or "pointing" gesture which is inherent in the elevation itself, and thus receives added stress at the word *ipse*.

More obscure, however, is the origin of the last crosses. They go back to certain symbolic considerations. Obviously, the starting point hinged on the old rubric which enjoined that the priest was to touch with the Host the chalice lifted by the deacon. This puzzling action of touching the chalice with the Host, originally intended, no doubt, to express the connection between the two species, invited further elaborations. The chalice was touched in all four directions. The resulting sign of the cross signified that the Crucified is desirous of drawing mankind to Himself from all the four winds. If we add this fourth cross to the three made at *Per ipsum*, we again have the number four—another representation of the four corners of the earth. This system of four crosses was certainly widespread until the Missal of Pius V. In the thirteenth century a four-part sentence from Augustine on God's infinity was linked with the ceremony [1] and given some circulation; in its turn, this had an influence on the rite of the four crosses. In accord with the catch-words: *Deus infra omnia non depressus*, at least the fourth cross had to be made at the base of the chalice.

[1] Hugo of S. Cher cites it as a reason for his localizing of the signs of the cross, in the form: *Deus est extra omnia non exclusus . . . super omnia non elatus . . . intra omnia non inclusus . . . infra omnia non depressus.*

The rubric of touching the chalice is also the starting-point for a second explanation, which in turn led to the five crosses. The rubric enjoined touching the chalice "from the side"—*a latere*. At a time which was able to discover everywhere reminiscences of the Passion of Christ, particularly near the close of the canon, this phrase, *a latere*, must have been a reminder of the wound in our Lord's side, and consequently of the five wounds. To complete the representation of the five wounds, two more crosses had to be added to the three already in use. These two complementary crosses appear in the manuscripts since the end of the eleventh century. It is precisely in this period that we come upon explicit witnesses to the explanation about the five wounds, and we hear of differences of opinion as to the manner of executing the last sign of the cross in order to represent the wound in the side more closely. Since, according to a widespread custom, the chalice stood to the right of the Host, there was a double reason for making at least the last cross at the side of the chalice. Thus it was kept until finally the law of symmetry won the upper hand over the symbolism.

All that we have said so far forces the conclusion that in the later Middle Ages the old rite which accompanied the closing doxology, a simple rite indeed, had been overwhelmed by this luxuriant growth of crosses. There is some consolation in the fact that the number of crosses, now increased to five, in the last analysis serves to emphasize the naming of Christ (*ipse*) all the more by a reference to the mystery of the Cross in which finally "all honor and glory" mounts to God.

In the Middle Ages, however, the rite which originally accompanied the doxology was often entirely absorbed by the signs of the cross. Or else it was turned into a demonstrative rite which then in many cases was ejected from its original position (for example, we will meet the old ceremony again at the *Pater noster*). When there was no deacon to help along, the elevation of the chalice had to be postponed until after the celebrant was through with the signs of the cross, that is, until the closing words of the doxology. And soon even at high Mass the assistance of the deacon shrank into insignificance, until at last he did no more than support the celebrant's arm or concur in touching the foot of the chalice. And on the other hand, this service of the deacon, in accordance with court etiquette, was finished off with a kiss on the celebrant's shoulder.

Later, however, this mark of subservience was allowed to disappear. So even in the eleventh century, when the present full number of crosses first appears, the rule was that the priest lifted the chalice only when he said the words *Per omnia sæcula sæculorum*. This was the prevailing practice during the height of the Middle Ages, was adopted by the old monastic liturgies, and did not cease till the Missal of Pius V. The advantage of this practice was that the rite of elevation was joined to the final words of the canon, the words spoken aloud, and immediately answered by the time-honored *Amen*, so that it retained its importance and made a clear impression on one's consciousness. It was only later that the present method appeared, which joined the elevation with the words *omnis honor et gloria*, and the final words *Per omnia sæcula sæculorum* were not spoken till the chalice and Host had been replaced in their proper position. This practice did not become general in Rome till the fifteenth century. Through it, the elevation of the gifts marked the very climax of the doxology. But there was certainly a double disadvantage in the fact that the final words were not joined to the rite, but were separated from it—by the action of replacing the chalice and Host, as well as by the genuflection, added since the fifteenth-sixteenth century. First of all, the elevation was once more overshadowed. And secondly, the detached words *Per omnia sæcula sæculorum*, which by the prominence given them should signalize the conclusion of the canon, now appear to be joined to the *Oremus* that introduces the *Pater noster* as though they were an inaugural piece. In some localities, e.g., in France, it was customary to signalize the *omnis honor et gloria* along with its accompanying rite by ringing the altar bell. The altar missal, prepared by the Abbey of Maria Laach in 1931, has sought to recapture some of its original importance for the whole closing doxology by artistic designing, and particularly by the size of its lettering.

The importance of these words is shared also by the *Amen* in which, according to age-old custom, all the people now join to affirm and corroborate what had been said and done. We have already seen what significance was attached to this *Amen* in ancient times. In the third century we hear a voice enumerating in one breath the several privileges of the people: to listen to the eucharistic prayer, to join in answering *Amen*, to stand at the table and stretch out their hands for the reception of the sacred food. This *Amen* is the people's signature. It was to permit the *Amen* to be shouted aloud that, even in Carolingian times, these final words were not included in the silence which prevailed throughout the rest of the canon.

III. THE COMMUNION CYCLE

1. The Beginnings of a Communion Cycle

It is not essential to the notion of sacrifice that the offerers should be invited afterwards to be God's guests at table. But the Sacrifice of Christendom was so instituted, for it is a family celebration, the celebration of the family of God, namely, those who belong to Christ and who, because of Baptism, are bound to Him by ties of most intimate fellowship. Thus they stand before God, a holy people. The *communio sanctorum*, which is holy Church, has to be made manifest in the *sacra communio* of the Sacrament.[1] It has always been regarded as a requirement of every Mass celebration that at least the celebrating priest must receive Communion, and every contrary practice has been condemned, time and again, as an abuse.

In the biblical texts the meal feature of the Eucharist was so much in evidence that Its sacrificial nature has had to be proved. True, even in the nascent Church the oblation was manifestly more than a mere introduction to the meal. It was a first step, to be followed at once by the second step, the meal. Or rather, both formed so complete a unit that participation in one appeared unthinkable without sharing also in the other. There is a clear relationship between this and the fact that those who were unworthy of the Sacrament—not only the unbaptized but often also the penitents—were excluded at the very beginning of the Sacrifice-Mass, and that even before the start of the Prayer of Thanksgiving there was another warning by the deacon directed to all those who were not clean of heart. Coming to particulars, in the oriental rites even at present the kiss of peace comes at the very beginning of the Sacrifice-Mass, whereas the western form of the ceremony was relocated in the course of time. In all rites, however, a series of prayers and practices eventually developed around the Communion, as preparation and sequel to it.

According to the oldest accounts, the Communion simply formed the conclusion of the eucharistic service, with no special prayers to accompany it. The preparation consisted in the thankful oblation to God. But already in the fourth century, in the ambit of the Greek Church, we meet with several arrangements of the Mass where the Communion is preceded by at least a prayer of the celebrant begging for a worthy reception, or even by a special prayer as a blessing of the recipients, and after the Communion there follows at least a thanksgiving prayer. Other details of the later oriental order of Communion are also to be noticed in the same documents, in particular the invocation, "*Holy things to holy ones*," which the priest pronounces after the preparatory prayer, and the psalm chant which accompanies the Communion. Likewise, before the end of the fourth century there appeared in certain Greek sources the prayer which soon became a permanent part of the preparation for Communion in all Mass-liturgies, a prayer which indeed forms the very center of that preparation, namely, the *Pater Noster*.

---

[1] The word *communio* therefore, even in its application to the Sacrament, denotes in its primary sense not the "union" of the individual with Christ—for then it would have to be *co-unio*—but rather the sublime Good that holds together the society of the faithful.

2. Pater noster

In the Latin area, too, there is evidence since the fourth century of the use of the *Pater noster* at the celebration of the Eucharist. Augustine mentions it time after time. In regard to the Roman Mass there is, indeed, no direct testimony outside the tradition of the canon itself, but it would surely have been remarkable if the Our Father had not by that time come into use at Rome, too. Only in Spain is there any evidence of fluctuation even at a later period, since the IV Council of Toledo (633) had to insist that the Lord's Prayer was to be said every day and not merely on Sunday.

LOCATION

In the Roman Mass the *Pater noster* stands at the beginning of the preparation for Communion. This is not a categorical position, and as a matter of fact in other liturgies there is a different arrangement. In the non-Byzantine liturgies of the East, as a rule, at least the fraction of the species precedes the Our Father. Even in the non-Roman rites of the West the fraction comes before the *Pater noster*. Thus the gifts are first readied for distribution, the table is set, and only after that does the prayer begin.

The present arrangement of the Roman Mass in this regard goes back to Gregory the Great. As he himself relates, he had been accused of introducing Greek practices; in particular, it was charged that he wanted the Lord's Prayer said right after the canon. In his letter to Bishop John of Syracuse the pontiff defends himself by saying in effect:

The Mass of the Apostles consisted simply in this, that they consecrated with the *oratio oblationis;* everything else is a later addition. If some other prayer is to be said over the consecrated gifts, certainly the first prayer to be considered, before any human composition, is the Lord's Prayer. Since Gregory's time this prayer, the Our Father, is said right after the canon, and therefore *super oblationem,* that is, over the sacrificial gifts still lying upon the altar, whereas formerly the prayer was not said till immediately before the Communion, after the consecrated breads had been removed from the altar and broken. It might be that Gregory was impelled to make this change by the practice among the Greeks as he had got to know it in Constantinople. But Gregory went beyond his model. Whereas in Byzantium, as in nearly all the rites of the East, the new prayer-group which starts after the closing doxology of the canon is preceded not only by a renewed invitation to prayer, but also, prior to this, by another greeting of the people, the Roman arrangement omits every such salutation and is satisfied with a simple *Oremus*. This call to prayer, therefore, still comes under the *Dominus vobiscum* and *Sursum corda* of the Great Prayer, the *Eucharistia*. Thus the connection with the canon is quite close. By these means the weighty words which constitute the Our Father are emphasized all the more. The priest pronounces the prayer at the altar in the same fashion as he did the canon. Indeed, the first part of the Lord's Prayer actually forms, to a certain extent, a sort of summary and recapitulation of the preceding eucharistic prayer. The *sanctificetur* is a synopsis of the triple *Sanctus*; the *adveniat regnum tuum* is a kind of epitome of the two epiklesis prayers: *Quam oblationem* and *Supplices*; and the *fiat voluntas tua* sets forth the basic idea regarding obedience from which all sacrifice must proceed. The spirit and disposition in which our Lord Himself had offered up His sacrifice and which we must draw from our co-performance of it, could hardly have been expressed more cogently.

But it would be a mistake to think that the Our Father in this new location right after the canon had acquired an essentially different function and given up its purpose as a preparation for Communion, or even to suppose that Gregory had intended something of the sort when making the new arrangement. The pope's own account of his action gives no hint of such a thing. The canon remains an absolute unit (and therefore it concludes with a doxology), and the Our Father remains a Communion prayer, as it is in all liturgies, only with a closer nexus to the canon than in other rites.

COMMUNION PRAYER

In the life of the ancient Church the Our Father had a close connection with the Communion, even aside from the Mass-liturgy; this is shown by the treatment of the petition for bread in the commentaries on the Our Father, and also in other pertinent remarks of the Fathers. Beginning with Tertullian, the Latin Fathers generally correlate this petition to the Eucharist. The same is done by some of the Greeks. This is certainly very remarkable in regard to a text whose literal meaning obviously signifies the material bread; it seems to presuppose that the faithful were accustomed to recite the Our Father at the reception of Communion, even before it appears in liturgical monuments as part of the liturgy. This would have been done at the daily house Communion, but also at Communion in church in connection with the Eucharist. The first prayer that the neophytes said in the bosom of the congregation before their first Communion appears to have been the Our Father, even in earliest times, and at least on this occasion it must have been recited by all in common and aloud. In the earliest commentaries on the Mass which mention the Our Father—the *Mystagogic Catecheses* of Jerusalem and the exposition of the Bishop of Milan—the petition for bread is emphatically explained in a sacramental sense; it was therefore also recited in this sense. Ambrose attaches long additions to the passages in question, in which he exhorts to daily reception.

A thing that clearly shows that the Our Father was looked upon as a Communion prayer in the Roman liturgy of the Middle Ages as well as in the extra-Roman liturgies of the West and those of the East, is the fact that it also makes an appearance among the preparatory prayers—in fact, as the most important of them—even where only the Communion is celebrated. That is the case in the Good Friday service and in most rites of Communion for the sick.

The enthusiasm for the grandeur of the prayer is proclaimed in a restrained way in the introductory words of our Roman Mass. For a man of dust and ashes a certain boldness (*audemus*) is implied in making his own a prayer such as this, in which he approaches God as a child does its father. That reference to boldness we have already encountered in the liturgies of the East. In the Fathers it recurs very frequently when they talk about the Our Father. We can better understand the reverence for the Lord's Prayer which is thus manifested, and which is surely appropriate, if we recall that in those days it was not only kept secret from the pagans but was even withheld from the catechumens until shortly before the time when, by Baptism, they became children of the heavenly Father. But even the baptized must always remain conscious of the immense distance separating them from God. Nevertheless, God's Son Himself had put these words on our lips and it was He who ordered us to recite them. It was salutary counsel, it was indeed a divine instruction. The attitude and spirit which this prayer embodies is fitting at this hour when we have in our hands the offering with which the Son Himself met His heavenly Father and meets Him still.

But besides the petition for bread there is another passage in the Our Father which receives special stress in its use at Mass. This is the petition for the forgiveness of sins. Even Optatus of Mileve gives this petition prominence above all. Augustine refers to its presence in the Our Father, and asks impressively: "Why is it spoken before the reception of Christ's Body and Blood? For the following reason: If perchance, in consequence of human frailty, our thought seized on something indecent, if our tongue spoke something unjust, if our eye was turned to something unseemly, if our ear listened complacently to something unnecessary . . . it is blotted out by the Lord's Prayer in the passage: Forgive us our debts, so that we may approach in peace and so that we may not eat or drink what we receive unto judgment." For Augustine, the Our Father is like washing the face before going to the altar. For that reason it was the practice at Hippo for all, priest and faithful, to strike their breast while pronouncing the words, *dimitte nobis debita nostra.*

EMBOLISM

That the Roman Mass also gave special importance to the final petitions introduced by these words, is shown by the supplement, the so-called *embolism*, (*embole*—interpolation) which has its counterpart in all the liturgies except the Byzantine.

In the extra-Byzantine liturgies of the East, this supplement regularly accentuates not only the last petition, but the last two, sometimes by just repeating the words, sometimes by a marked expansion. Thus, in the anaphora of St. James, the priest continues: "(Yea, Lord, our God), lead us not into a temptation which we are not able to bear, (but with the temptation grant also the issue, so that we may be able to remain steadfast, and) deliver us from the evil," thereupon a doxology follows as in all oriental texts. Thus the continuation of the petition for forgiveness is taken up and, with an eye on the future, a plea is made for preservation especially from that evil which would bar us from approaching the sacred repast.

The same is also to be found where (as in the West) only the last petition is taken up. In the Gallic Liturgy the formula in question was again subjected to the variations of the Mass-formulary. Its basic outline, however, for all the various additions made to it, was mostly the same as that which appears in the simplest form in a Sunday Mass of the *Missale Gothicum;* it reads: "Deliver us from evil, Almighty God, and keep us in goodness. Who livest and reignest." Nor is the Roman form of the embolism to be judged different. That its plea to be freed "from all evil" is concerned above all with evil in the moral order is clearly seen from the added words: "past, present, and to come." Only moral evils, even when they are "past," still lie heavy on the soul. Therefore, in the word *past* there is a renewed stressing of the petition for forgiveness, just as in the *future* there is an echo of the petition to be safeguarded from overly hard trial. Then, on the positive side, an all-comprehensive good is included in the petition, the same good already mentioned in the *Hanc igitur* formula: "Graciously grant us peace in our times." Our human wants are all of equal value for the kingdom of God. If a proper peace surround us within and without, then, as we hope, a double result will be more easily forthcoming: we will remain free from sin and will be protected against every disturbance and error. This will then be the correct disposition to have in order to eat the heavenly bread with benefit.

Just as we are accustomed to find it in the orations of Roman saints' feasts, the petition is strengthened by reference to the intercession of heavenly helpers. Here, besides the Mother of God and the protectors of the Roman community, Peter and Paul, the Apostle Andrew is also mentioned. Of course Andrew is mentioned in the *Communicantes* list, being named right after the Princes of the Apostles, just as in the two biblical catalogues (Matthew 10:2; Luke 6:14) his name stands right after Peter's. But it is surely unusual to find his name mentioned right after theirs, all by itself. It is well known that the New Rome on the Bosporus, in rivalry with the old Rome on the Tiber, had early laid claim to the Apostle Andrew, Peter's brother, and "first called" of the Twelve, as its founder. This accounts also for the honor paid to the apostle at Rome; the prominence given to him—after Peter and Paul, of course—was halfway in opposition to Byzantium, halfway as a gesture of concord. That we are on the right track in our conclusion is shown by a related occurrence among the prefaces of the *Gregorianum*, where special prefaces are provided for only two saints besides the Princes of the Apostles—Anastasia, who was likewise highly revered in Byzantium, and Andrew. Some have thought that the addition of *atque Andrea* was due to Gregory the Great who, before his election as pope, had founded a monastery in honor of St. Andrew and had been abbot there. But the addition could have been made earlier than this, since even in the fifth century there was at Rome not only this somewhat uneasy relationship to Byzantium, but even an explicit devotion to the Apostle Andrew. The Middle Ages not seldom added other names here, and this was done even in later times, since the *Micrologus* offered the liberty just for this passage. But in the end they were satisfied with the supplementary phrase, *cum* (later: *et*) *omnibus sanctis*, which was wanting originally, but which appeared here and there even in early manuscripts.

The conclusion is formed by the ordinary formula *Per Dominum nostrum*. This acts as a close not only for the embolism itself, but also for the *Pater noster* which is merely extended into the embolism. Thus it is an exact parallel to the doxology which, in most oriental liturgies, follows in the same location after the Our Father or its supplement, as the case may be. By this formula we give expression to the fact that even in the Lord's Prayer we direct our petition to the heavenly Father through Christ, just as with His encouragement we pronounced it.

If the Our Father at Mass was designed to serve as a preparation of the assembled people for the reception of Holy Communion, this had to be made clear also in *the manner of performance*. Actually, the Lord's Prayer was frequently said at Mass by all the people, and in any case it was always said aloud. This might not be entirely expected in ancient Christendom, since the Our Father still remained under the discipline of the secret. Thus a loud rehearsal of the Our Father was excluded from the fore-Mass. True to the command to guard it as a sacred mystery and not even to write it down, it would seem that outside of Mass it was only said quietly, just as the symbol was said only quietly outside of Baptism. Within the Mass, where only those could be present who were full citizens of God's kingdom, there was nothing to hinder its being said aloud.

The only question was, by whom was it to be said: whether, like the *Sanctus,* by all the assembly or, like the other prayers of the *Ordo missæ,* by the celebrant in the name of the faithful. Since the prayer was intended as a preparation for everyone to receive the Sacrament, it certainly was appropriate that everyone—the whole people—should take part immediately in the Lord's Prayer, especially since it was certainly quite familiar to everyone.

This solution was the one that became standard in the Orient. Everywhere the rubrics assigned the Our Father to the people, except in the Armenian Mass, where clerics were to sing it with arms outstretched. However, in the Byzantine Mass, too, it became customary for the choir to say it, but always as representative of the people. In the old Gallican Liturgy also, the Our Father was pronounced by all the people in common, but in the remainder of the West, by the celebrating priest. This was the method already followed in Augustine's African Church, although with provision for both a vital interest and ritual participation by the people. In the old Spanish Mass this participation was manifested by responding *Amen* to every section of the prayer.

Even in the Roman Mass there is not wanting an indication that the Our Father belongs to the people. It is apportioned between priest and people, although in rather unequal parts. Whereas the old sacramentaries and most of the *ordines* contain no reference to this division of the text, and Gregory the Great, in his frequently quoted letter, says tersely that at Rome, in contrast to the practice of the Greeks, the Lord's Prayer is said "by the priest alone," yet we find the responsorial method in the *Capitulare ecclesiastici Ordinis,* therefore at the very latest in the eighth century; the Our Father is concluded "by all answering: but deliver us from evil." Basically, therefore, the people say the Our Father along with the celebrant. *It is the people's Communion prayer.*[1]

In the mouth of the priest the rendition of the Lord's Prayer takes on the distinction of a special *musical form,* reminiscent of the chant of the preface. Manuscript evidence of our *Pater noster* melodies is not to be found before the peak of the Middle Ages, but on intrinsic grounds, particularly in view of the characteristic cadences, the origin of the melodies is put as early as the fifth to the seventh century. Of the two melodies, the more elaborate one is the earlier. Perhaps even in the days of Gregory the Great this tune served to accent the value of this great prayer.

As is self-evident, the loud rendition of the prayer was continued through the appended embolism. But in the Roman Mass this was done not in the solemn melody of the *Pater noster,* but in a simple recitative

[1] The reformed order for the Communion Service on Good Friday demonstrates this by the prominence it accords the prayer itself as well as by insisting that it should be said by the priest and people together "since," as the rubric tells us, "it is a prayer for communion."—REV.

tone, like that which we inferred regarding the canon at the *Te igitur*. This manner of performance has been retained till now in the Milanese rite and in the rite of Lyons, as well as in our own Good Friday liturgy. But about the year 1000 the Roman Mass changed to a quiet recitation of the embolism, except for Good Friday. It seems that the factor that led to this change was the consideration that the embolism was still within that portion of the Mass which represented the Passion of Christ. The termination of the Passion was the Resurrection, which since the sixth century was increasingly considered as symbolized in the ceremony of commingling, while the fraction that preceded it continued to be referred to the Passion. This whole section—the canon in the medieval sense, also called the *secreta*—would as far as possible continue in silence. The silence was indeed interrupted by the preface and the *Pater noster*, for which chant was prescribed long before, but thus a more mysterious image was created, a triple silence, during the *secreta*, from the *Te igitur* to the *Pater noster*, and during the embolism, which seemed to refer to the three days of rest in the tomb.

An *Amen* appears after the *Sed libera nos a malo*, first in Alcuin's recension of the sacramentary, then by degrees generally. It must have been taken over from the Vulgate edition of the Our Father in the Bible; there is no *Amen* in the original Greek. The question next came up, who was to say this *Amen*. Sometimes it was added to the people's response, and then it was said out loud. But finally, probably because of the growing practice in the Roman liturgy of leaving the *Sed libera nos a malo*, when said aloud, without an *Amen*, it was shifted to the priest, who says it softly before beginning his quiet embolism.

In the later Middle Ages the *Pater noster* was attended by certain *external rites*, not counting those which today are associated with the embolism. Widespread was the custom of combining with the Lord's Prayer the elevation of chalice and Host, which had been separated from the closing doxology by the signs of the Cross. Various methods were used; sometimes chalice and Host were lifted only during the words "Thy will be done," sometimes all through the first three petitions, up to the words "on earth as it is in heaven." Whereas in these two cases the doxological import of the ceremony still remained clearly visible, this was less so when, as happened elsewhere, the elevation was continued during the whole *Pater noster*. Probably quite consciously a new sense was given to the action. Just as in the case of the elevation at *omnis honor et gloria*, where, at the end of the Middle Ages, even the rubric sometimes directed the change, so here, too, the oblatory elevation was turned instead into a "showing" to the people, as at the consecration. This new signification is even more sharply projected when, as happened in some places, the elevation was linked to the words *Panem nostrum:* here (it seemed to indicate) is the bread which we are asking for. In some places, especially in northern France, a practice akin to this arose, namely, that the cleric who held the paten, or the subdeacon to whom he gave it, held it up high, "as a sign of the approaching Communion," as we read in one place. On the other hand, since the thirteenth century the doxological gesture which accompanied the *per omnia sæcula sæculorum* of the doxology at the end of the canon, was sometimes duplicated at the end of the embolism, the chalice and the little particle of Host being raised when the same words were repeated.

In some churches, a considerable emphasis was put on the *bodily posture* to be taken during the *Pater noster*. On days that did not have a festal character, a *prostratio* was expected of the people. A Mass *ordo* of Bec even demanded the *prostratio* of the celebrant in the embolism.

This is bracketed with the fact that at the height of the Middle Ages, *prayers for help* were often inserted here during times of stress. At first this was done right after the embolism, but later, when the connection of the embolism with the *Pater noster* was no longer so strongly realized, the prayers were inserted between the *Pater noster* and the embolism. Since the Lord's Prayer was less and less conceived as a Communion prayer, this universal prayer of Christendom became the starting point for adding a special prayer in times of need. In 1040 the *consuetudines* of Farfa laid down the rule: After the *Pater noster* a crucifix, Gospel book, and relics are to be set out in front of the altar, the clergy are to throw themselves on the floor and recite Psalm 73: "O God, hast Thou altogether abandoned us," with the corresponding prayer, while the priest at the altar remains silent. In 1194, during the high tide of the Crusades, the Cistercians introduced at this same spot Psalm 78: "O God, the heathen have broken into thy inheritance," as a prayer for the Holy Land. In the reform of the Mass book in the sixteenth century, these and other similar additions were allowed to drop, but in some places the custom still continued for some time longer.

3. Preparatory Activities

In different liturgies, especially those of the East, the reception and distribution of Communion is preceded by a series of preparatory acts and prayers. In the Roman liturgy these acts and prayers either never developed or were reduced to very modest forms and compressed between the embolism and the more immediate Communion prayers.

Among the preparatory acts regarding the Sacrament itself, the oldest and most important one, the one that therefore reappears in all the liturgies, is the *fraction*, or the breaking of the consecrated bread. This is but a continuation of an action which, according to all four New Testament accounts, our Lord Himself performed at the Last Supper: He took the bread, broke it, and gave it to His disciples. The Breaking of the Bread is, in fact, the oldest name used for the celebration of the Eucharist. The more immediate occasion for the breaking or fraction was the necessity of dividing the whole breads for the Communion of the congregation, and, in any case, for the purpose of having a particle to keep for the rite of commingling which followed. The example of the breaking of the bread in the supper room and in the primitive Church must surely have been the factor which determined that the rite would continue not as a *cutting* of the bread, as might easily have been, but as a "breaking"; in other words, this is what determined and determines the choice of a form of bread which could be broken, so that there would be question only of a "breaking" of bread.

In its ritual form, the fraction which was designed to prepare the particles for the Communion of the congregation continued along simple lines. In the oriental rites it appears to have been done generally by the celebrant himself. Probably in view of greater Communion days, when more time was required, rather lengthy prayer-texts are in part provided to accompany the rite.

But the fraction which served for symbolism and which culminates in the commingling of the two species is much more elaborate. There are three parts: first, the fraction itself, performed on the Host intended for the celebrant, which is divided into from two to four portions; then the crossing (*consignatio*), very detailed, especially in the Syrian Liturgy, the particle of Host being crossed either over the chalice or in the chalice; finally, the commingling, in which a particle is dropped into the chalice. We shall attempt to explain this rite farther on. Fifth century witnesses from Syria mention the symbolic meaning even at this date, that is, the unity of the Bread and Wine of the same Sacrament. The same interpretation is assigned to the signs of the cross. Likewise, certain corresponding texts which accompany the commingling in some of the rites emphasize this point of unification in the sacrifice.

Of the rites which developed in the various liturgies between canon and Communion, only the fraction and commingling gained any special importance in the Roman Mass.

4. The Fraction

In the Roman Mass since Gregory the Great, as in the Byzantine Mass, the fraction does not take place till after the *Pater noster* and its embolism have been recited. Years ago on great feast days, when all the people partook of Holy Communion, it must have been a very important activity, which was then carefully regulated, and which led, towards the end of the seventh century, to the introduction of a special chant, the *Agnus Dei*.

The older Roman *ordines* have carefully outlined the proceedings. After the *Pax Domini* was said and the kiss of peace given, the pope took the two Host-breads, now consecrated, which he had himself presented, and after breaking off a small piece, which remained at the altar, laid the two breads on the large paten held out for him by the deacon; then he made his way to his *cathedra*, the deacon following with the paten. Now acolytes stepped up to the altar, taking their stations at both sides of it. They had scarfs over their shoulders, for they were about to bear a precious burden. They all carried linen bags which, with the subdeacons' help, they held open and ready, and in which the archdeacon placed the breads which lay on the altar. Then they divided to right and left among the bishops and priests who, at a sign from the pope, began the fraction. At the same time, deacons also began the fraction over the pope's paten.

PATEN

This paten was very large; for that reason the first *ordo* stated in one place that two subdeacons brought it over, and obviously it was also held by them during the fraction. In the larger Roman basilicas there was no dearth of such large patens made of gold and silver. One is inclined to wonder why patens were not used in place of the linen bags. As a matter of fact, in the Mass *ordines* of the later Carolingian-Ottoian period, patens or (at least optionally) chalices were used in their stead. But then, all of a sudden, the paten loses its function. The introduction of un-leavened bread was followed, perhaps not everywhere at once, but cer-tainly not too much later, by the introduction of the small hosts, which changed the whole rite of the fraction as performed up till then, and so likewise rendered the use of the paten superfluous. In the Romano-Ger-man Pontifical which originated at Mainz about 950 there is a plan for the bishop's Mass which gives us a glimpse of the new procedure. The subdeacons took their usual place right after the concluding doxology of the canon, and the deacons right after the *Pater noster*, since their function at the fraction dropped out. The archdeacon took the paten as he had always done, but simply handed it to the bishop after the *propitius pacem*, and nothing special was done with it as far as we can see. The Gallic episcopal blessing and the kiss of peace followed at once. However, the paten reappeared again at the Communion, along with the chalice held by an acolyte. From the paten the bishop, as the first to re-ceive, took his Communion; the particles had therefore been deposited on it. But a hundred years later, in the Mass *ordo* of John of Avranches (d. 1079), this last use has also disappeared. The paten now is used only as a resting-place for the large Host during its fraction, and then till the Communion. Its use no longer extends beyond the altar. And all this agrees with the fact that precisely in the eleventh century the patent shrinks in size. It now becomes a rule that its diameter should be about the same as the height of the chalice (at first very low), and soon, in fact, that it should not even reach that dimension.

Subsequently the paten gained further use when the custom grew of putting the host on it even at the offertory (as we have seen), and thus making the offering, and this, in turn, especially at private Mass, led to the practice of bringing chalice and paten together to the altar, and further, to fitting the patent to the cup of the chalice, so that it could lie smoothly on the chalice, a rule which was already in effect in the tenth century.

So if the newer form of paten has little in common with the vessel of the same name in the first ten centuries, still reminiscences of the ritual handling of the latter have been transferred to it. At a high Mass it does not remain lying on the altar after the offertory, even though this contracted paten would not be in the way on the altar, which meanwhile had been enlarged; but instead, the subdeacon takes it and holds it, covering it with the ends of the humeral veil, until he returns it to the altar near the end of the *Pater noster*. This is a survival of the function of the acolyte of the seventh-century papal liturgy, who appeared at the beginning of the preface, carrying the paten which he had brought from the *secretarium*, and which he held to his breast under the folds of a cloth thrown over his shoulders, until *medio canone* he turned it over to others; then near the end of the embolism it was carried over to be used at the fraction. It would not be necessary to presume that the undoubtedly remarkable reverence in handling the paten which the earliest *ordines* prescribe was due to some more profound reason, as though a particle of the Eucharist which, as the *sancta*, was displayed at the entrance procession, was still lying on it. Both the fact that the paten is brought in at the start of the Sacrifice-Mass and that it is carried with covered hands correspond wholly with the usual manner of handling holy objects.

The reverent attentions towards the paten were not only retained even after the disappearance of its prime use at the fraction, they were even increased. The kiss which had long been given it by the deacon was sometimes offered also by others, above all by the celebrant himself. Since the twelfth century there was added a sign of the Cross made over himself by the celebrant with the paten, sometimes after the kiss, more usually before it, as is customary at present.

In the later Middle Ages the ceremony of blessing which thus originated was elaborated even further and sometimes brought to the very verge of superstition. Instead of one cross there were several. Or the mouth and eyes were touched with the paten; or first the Host was touched with the paten; or else the Host was touched once, the chalice three times. All these excrescences were set aside by the Missal of Pius V.

According to the present Mass book, the paten is kissed right after it is used to make the sign of the Cross, and while the final words of the embolism are still being recited the celebrant genuflects, takes up the Sacred Host and begins the fraction. But this no longer takes place over the paten, but over the chalice, so that no tiny particle might be lost.

Thus, according to the present arrangement, the fraction is anticipated, taking place not after, but before the *Pax Domini*. We will come back to this later. The use of the paten during the fraction, which is stressed even at present in the *Pontificale*, is now only suggested by the fact that the Host rests on the paten before the fraction, and the separated portions are deposited on it afterwards.

At present the Sacred Host is broken into three parts. Here, too, we have a survival of ancient memories. According to the Roman *ordines*, the pope, after the kiss of peace, broke off a part of his own host-bread "from the right side," and this was left on the altar. Then, at his Communion, he again separated a small piece from the Host, and put it in the chalice with the words *Fiat commixtio et consecratio . . .* Although the fraction for practical purposes, namely for apportioning in the Communion of the people, which before was so prominent, had since disappeared, still fractions occasioned by symbolic considerations continued on. This is abundantly clear in regard to the second fraction by the very formula already cited, a formula for the commingling. But it holds even more immediately true of the first fraction. Even several hundred years later the priest was still ordered to break the host "from the right side"; the particle thus removed was then used for the commingling. A second particle was broken off for his own Communion. The third portion remained, as of old, on the altar, but it was now preserved as *viaticum* or it was also used for the communicants. These three parts were already stipulated by Amalar, and even for him they have their symbolic meaning; the particle mixed with the Sacred Blood refers to the Body of Christ at the Resurrection; the particle for the celebrant's own Communion refers to the Body of Christ on earth, the earthly Church; the particle intended for the sick refers to Christ's Body in the grave. This reference to the *corpus Christi triforme* often recurs in the following centuries, although it is not the only explanation given. But then it is readjusted so that the three parts refer to three phases of the Church as militant, suffering, and triumphant; this combination became a constituent element of the Mass commentaries of the later Middle Ages and found its way into popular sermons. The crystallization caused by these symbolic considerations must then have been the reason that this tripartition of the Host continued even after it had become the practice for the priest to use small Hosts for the distribution of Communion, in particular for the Communion of the sick. Actually, however, a division into two would have sufficed both to preserve the rite which inhered in the fraction itself and to obtain a particle for the *mixtio*.

5. The Commingling [1]

In the present-day Roman liturgy the fraction is followed at once by the commingling: the separated particle is dropped into the chalice with an accompanying prayer that had been used in a similar way already in the papal Mass of the eighth century. Thus in the present-day ceremony of the commingling there is a survival of that ceremony in which the celebrating pope, just before his Communion, broke off a particle from his own Host and dropped it into the chalice. But the Roman liturgy of that time also had a commingling at the same spot in which we have it today. Originally, this rite was only in the non-papal liturgy of the churches in the environs of Rome. By an acolyte, the bishop sent the priests of the vicinity a particle of the Eucharist as an expression of ecclesiastical unity, as a token that they belonged to his *communio*. This particle was called the *fermentum*. The priests dropped it into the chalice at this part of the Mass. The practice is ancient indeed. It answered to that awareness, so keen in the ancient Church, that the Eucharist was the *sacramentum unitatis*, that this Sacrament held the Church together, and that all the people of God subject to a bishop should, if it were possible, be gathered around that bishop's altar and receive the Sacrament from his table of sacrifice.

In France, the *fermentum* was unknown. However, the Frankish editor of a widely used Roman Ordo saw that in the ordinary Mass of a priest a commingling always took place at the *Pax Domini*, whereas in the papal Mass things were done differently. In any case, he concluded that a fraction must take place beforehand since a first commingling had to take place *before* the *Pax Domini*, and a second, as the First Roman Ordo clearly demonstrated, before the Communion.

Naturally, one or the other of these was soon dropped, although for a time there was some confusion and hesitancy as to which one should be retained. It was not long before the first of the two gained the upper hand. Symbolism was probably a determining factor in this decision, because thus the commingling, which was to represent the Body of

[1] This chapter has been newly edited by Father Jungmann himself, especially for this edition. The re-editing was necessitated chiefly because of the important findings of the Dutch liturgist Johann Peter de Jong with reference to the rite of commingling. We refer here to his last published word on the subject: "Le rite de la commixtion dans la Messe Romaine dans ses rapports avec les liturgies syriennes": *Archiv für Liturgiewissenschaft* 4 (1956) 245–278; 5 (1957) 33–79.—REV.

Christ returned to life, preceded the peace greeting of the *Pax Domini;* for indeed our Lord first rose from the dead, and only then did He bring peace to heaven and earth.

Here we find a symbolic interpretation for the old practice which came about with the combining of the two commingling rites. What was the original meaning of the second commingling rite which took place at the Communion? A careful examination of the evidence in the *Ordines* as well as in the Oriental rites has recently shed some light on a previously little known area.

We find ourselves confronted with a twofold origin. First there was the Roman (and general) practice which was linked with the reception of Holy Communion under both species. In the early Church it was thought to be of real importance that the faithful receive the Wine as well as the Bread, and of course they found themselves face to face with the difficulties that are bound to accompany the practice. For the most part (with the exception of Egypt) the early Christians wanted to avoid consecrating more than one chalice. So the solution was adopted of taking other vessels of plain wine and "sanctifying" them. That is to say, they somehow "consecrated" them either by pouring some of the Precious Blood into them or by dipping one of the consecrated particles into them, "mixing it in." Or sometimes both were done. But the last mentioned practice seems to be what is referred to in the *Ordo Romanus Primus.*

According to this *Ordo*, the Pope returns to his cathedra after the fraction. The consecrated Bread is then brought to him on a paten. He consumes part of it and drops the rest into the chalice while he says the commingling prayer. Then he drinks of the Precious Blood. What now follows is especially noteworthy. The Archdeacon also receives part of the Precious Blood, and after the Communion of the bishops and priests, pours the rest together (it seems) with the Particle into another chalice with wine. From this the people will receive their Communion, and should there not be enough, more will be added.

As we learn from the *Ordo* of St. Amand, there could even be more such chalices and each priest had to take one of them, make the sign of the cross with a consecrated Particle over it, and drop the Particle into the chalice. It was certainly a rite of this kind which is referred to in the legend of St. Lawrence as described by St. Ambrose where Lawrence is described as the holy deacon to whom was entrusted "the consecration of the Blood of the Lord."

THE SYMBOLISM

But this explanation does not alone suffice. For this commingling was also carried out in the chalice of the priest which held the Precious Blood.

And the priest accompanies it even today with the words: *fiat accipientibus nobis in vitam æternam*—"may there be accomplished (this commingling and consecration) for life everlasting to us who receive it." Why is this rite here as well?

Here symbolism had a part to play, a symbolism which came from the Orient from the Syrian liturgy. With the Syrians, at least since the fifth century (Theodore of Mopsuestia), there was a great enthusiasm for the idea that at the words of consecration the *death* of the Lord was represented, especially in the *separation* of the Body and Blood. But in the Communion we should receive the food of immortality; therefore, the *Resurrection* must also be expressed by the sacramental species. This took place by *reuniting* the Body and Blood. The Sacred Host was sprinkled in the form of a cross with a few drops of the Precious Blood and a Particle was mixed with the Chalice. Thus there was expressed in this rite the idea that the Blood and with it the soul returned to the Body in the resurrection. This also corresponds to the formula with which the rite was accompanied: "It is united and sanctified and completed in the name of the Father and of the Son and of the Holy Spirit."

The accompanying formula in our Roman Mass also reminds us of this oriental parallel. Since the words were not intended to be spoken aloud, they are not mentioned in the older sacramentaries but are rather to be found in the *Ordines* and run as follows: *Fiat commixtio et consecratio corporis et sanguinis D.N.J.C. accipientibus nobis in vitam æternam. Amen.* "May there be accomplished the commingling and consecration of the Body and Blood of Our Lord Jesus Christ for life everlasting to us who receive it." We may certainly assume that in Rome a similar formula served to accompany and illustrate the commingling of the Particle of the Blood with the wine of the different Communion chalices. Still, the words "us who receive it" in the form that has come down to us remain strange on the part of the priest, who certainly receives the Precious Blood from the altar chalice itself and not from one of the secondary Communion chalices. The commingling must have had a meaning of its own independent of the "sanctifying" of the secondary chalices. It must now have had the same meaning it had in the Syrian liturgy: the symbolic expression of the unity of the Body and Blood of the Lord, in other words, the representation of the Resurrection. The carrying over of such a practice from Syria to Rome could easily have been achieved especially at that time when a number of popes came from Syria.

The above-mentioned formula which was said at the commingling continued in use, unchanged, especially in Italian Mass books. In the preparation of the reform of the missal at the Council of Trent, theological doubts were raised against this formula, for on the face of it, its meaning—leaving aside the word *consecratio* for a moment—clearly was: let there be a commixture of our Lord's Body and Blood, (let it bring) us recipients to life everlasting. Thus, the formula could be construed as though, in consequence of it, the Body and Blood of Christ would be united to each other only after the commingling, and not already at the consecration of the two species, so that the Utraquists had grounds for arguing that Communion under one kind was insufficient. So the change to the present reading was proposed: *Hæc commixtio . . . fiat accipientibus nobis in vitam æternam*, here there is no longer any possible question of a commingling taking place beyond the visible performance; it is now merely the expression of a wish that this external ceremonial commingling may avail us for salvation. It has been established that this is the only change in the Tridentine Missal that was aimed at the Reformers. The word *consecratio*, which stayed in the text in spite of the objections brought against it, and in spite of the fact that it was missing in some medieval texts here and there, must be rendered by "hallowing" in the sense that through the commingling a sacred token or symbol is effected in the sacramental species and mediately in the Body and Blood of Christ a symbol of the Resurrection.

Elsewhere, in Carolingian territory, at least since the ninth century, a second formula was rife. This one presented, in a somewhat more verbose vein, the thoughts that were stressed in the Missal of Pius V. It was in general use in Northern France and in England till the reform of the missal, and in the Dominican rite is used even at present. It runs as follows: "May this most sacred commingling of the Body and Blood of Our Lord Jesus Christ be for all who receive it salvation (*salus*) of mind and body and a salutary preparation for obtaining eternal life."

The thought of the Resurrection, which, among the Syrians, had been linked first with the Fraction and then with the commingling, was associated with the latter also by the Carolingian commentators on the liturgy. It was even stressed by the fact that the rite of commingling (as we said above) was inserted not immediately before the Communion, but already before the *Pax Domini*. So the idea of the Resurrection in this relationship remained as an element in the explanation of the Mass all through the Middle Ages and even down to the present. On the other hand, the fraction was not until somewhat more recent times linked to the Passion of Christ, as signifying Christ's death, a signification on which later theologians, even post-Tridentine ones, placed a great deal of importance.

It must have been the attitude of Amalar which ultimately decided the anticipation of the commingling ceremony. According to him, this ceremony, along with the accompanying phrase, ought to be placed before the *Pax Domini*, in the short pause after the conclusion of the embolism during which the fraction of the Host and the crossing of the chalice would already have occurred; for it was not till after His Resurrection that our Lord appeared to His disciples and saluted them with His greeting of peace. Thereafter only the partition of the Host was anticipated, being linked with the concluding formula, *Per Dominum*, in lieu of a pause. The crossing then was joined to the *Pax Domini*, for this latter was by degrees interpreted as a formula of blessing.

However, only in one portion of the post-Carolingian Mass plans did this commingling follow immediately; but it was this arrangement that was adopted in Italy and therefore also the one definitely fixed in the Missal of Pius V.

By far the greater portion of the Carolingian Mass plans contained a different arrangement. True, they did not hold to the original Roman pattern, where the commingling was linked to the Communion itself or, at any rate, followed the kiss of peace. But the commingling often occurred after the *Agnus Dei* in those churches where it had already become customary for the priest to recite it. And so the priests kept the sacred particle in their hands during the *Agnus Dei* with the purpose (as Durandus says) of making their prayer more efficacious since they were holding the Lord Himself in their hands. In this case, then, we have a secondary reshifting which likewise rests on Amalar's solution and which in the main has disappeared since 1570.

Since Amalar had indicated for the rite of commingling a place at the *Pax Domini*, the very spot where, according to the practice of the ancient Church, the space-encircling unifying force of the Eucharist had been represented by the admixture of the *fermentum*, our modest rite had gained an additional significance beyond its original meaning of representing the intrinsic unity of the Sacrament under two kinds and the Resurrection, borrowing from the farther-reaching significance of its sister rite the symbolism of Communion of church with church. The accompanying *Pax Domini* could easily add support to these latter ideas. On the other hand, the rite of fraction and commingling, as now in use in the Roman Mass, has lost some of its importance, since it does not occupy a place in the pause mentioned above and, as a consequence, appears simply as an accompaniment to the close of the embolism and the *Pax Domini*, texts which have no immediate relevance to the rite. Thus few celebrants will find it possible to keep in mind the significance of the venerable rite. And for the other participants, the rite has hardly any purpose at all, since it is perceptible only to those close to the altar. Besides, the ancient song that formerly accompanied the fraction, the *Agnus Dei*, did not follow the change of position of the rite as we have it now, but continued to occupy the position of the older fraction, as we shall see. Scarcely anywhere else has the transparency of the liturgical procedure suffered so much by later contraction and compression as here in the purlieu of the fraction and commingling, although the elements of the ancient tradition have been faithfully preserved.

6. Pax Domini *and the Kiss of Peace*

Whether we study the development of the Roman Communion rite or confine our attention to the external picture of the Mass as it is today (where the *Pax Domini* is taken up right after the close of the embolism), we must deal with the kiss of peace. *For the* Pax Domini *was regarded as a signal and an invitation to the faithful to exchange the kiss of peace with each other.* Nowhere is this indicated in any explicit rubric, but it follows from parallels in the African liturgy and from the actual procedure outlined in the oldest *ordines*. Even in documentary sources of the tenth century the fact that the *Pax Domini* is omitted on Good Friday was explained by the fact that the kiss, given by those present to one another, was omitted. The arrangement of the present-day high Mass, where the kiss of peace is not given till after the *Agnus Dei* and another prayer for peace are said, is (as we shall see) the result of more recent developments.

By placing the kiss of peace just before the Communion, the Roman Mass (along with the African already mentioned) assumes a position apart, for all the other liturgies have it at the beginning of the Sacrifice-Mass. The original place of the kiss of peace was, in reality, *at the end of the service of reading and prayers* rather than at the start of the Sacrifice-Mass. According to the ancient Christian conception, it formed the seal and pledge of the prayers that preceded it. But after the service of readings and prayers had been joined to the celebration of the Eucharist, regard for our Lord's admonition (Matthew 5:23 f.) about the proper dispositions in one who wishes to make an offering would probably have led to placing the kiss of peace (as guarantee of fraternal sentiment) closer to the moment when one is "bringing his gift before the altar."

KISS OF PEACE AND COMMUNION

At a very early date the Roman liturgy went a step further. In opposition to the practice which the Bishop of Gubbio had in view, of announcing the kiss of peace "before carrying out the mysteries," Pope Innocent I, in his reply in 416, insisted that it was not to be proclaimed till after the completion of the entire sacrifice; for, he asserted, the people ought by means of it to make known their assent to all that had gone before. Here again attention is immediately drawn to its function as a seal and guarantee. But ultimately (when, as a result of Gregory the Great's rearrangement, the *Pater noster* was placed directly after the close of the canon and there was no proclamation of the kiss of peace until after the embolism), it was quite natural that the kiss appear as an illustration of the "as we forgive those." Perhaps it was this phrase which first drew it towards the conclusion of the *Pater noster*.

As a matter of fact, even in Gregory the Great's time the kiss of peace was regarded as a natural preparation for Communion. A group of monks, threatened by shipwreck, gave each other the kiss of peace and then received the Sacrament which they carried with them. The same opinion predominated at this period also outside the area of the Roman liturgy. Sophronius (d. 638) pictures St. Mary of Egypt giving the kiss of peace to the aged monk who brings her the Mysteries, whereupon she receives the Body of the Lord.

In the Carolingian area also the same succession (of kiss of peace and distribution of Communion) is found both at Communion of the sick and at public service. Indeed the kiss is often restricted to the communicants. The *canones* of Theodore of Canterbury, in one version (eighth century), contain the rule: "Whoever does not communicate should not receive the [kiss of] peace nor the kiss in church." The rule was also known in the Carolingian Church, but there, alongside the severe regulation, a milder interpretation also appeared, which did not make restriction so narrow. Nevertheless, at least in monasteries, it was still the rule even in the year 1000 that on Communion days, and only on these, the brethren received the *pax*. This was true in England as well as on the continent. The kiss of peace was a pre-condition for Communion,[1] or at least a fitting preparation for it, and in reverse, the deacon and subdeacon at high Mass, who were to receive the pax were for a long time obliged also to receive Holy Communion. In fact, amongst the Cistercians there was a regulation even for private Mass that the server receive *pax* and Communion each time, until in 1437 Eugene IV rescinded this obligation of the server as dangerous. But even so, the connnection between kiss of peace and Communion survived for a long time.

Elsewhere the kiss of peace gradually became a sort of substitute for Communion. Not only was the kiss exchanged at the altar, but all the people participated. The ancient way of exchanging the kiss of peace would not entail the disturbance and confusion in the service that we would be led to expect today, for then the kiss was not continued from person to person, but merely exchanged between neighbors.

The first Roman *ordo* says explicitly: When the *Pax Domini* has been spoken, the archdeacon gives the kiss of peace to the first bishop, "and then the others [give it] in order and then the people." At the given

---

[1] A remnant of it is a custom still much in use today, that the communicant kiss the ring of the bishop administering Communion, or as the *Cæremoniale Episcoporum*, II, 29, 5 declares, the hand. Although a kissing of the hand just before receiving Communion was customary in the ancient church, still the present-day use seems to be derived from the mutual Kiss of Peace that was exchanged at the altar, or at least was inspired by it. The transition to the kissing of the hand on the part of one receiving Communion is evident in John of Avranches (d. 1079).

signal, therefore, those in the nave of the church greeted each other with the kiss. But many of the later manuscripts of this *ordo* have introduced an inconspicuous but very important change: "and then *to* the others in order and then *to* the people." Thus the kiss of peace is made to proceed from the altar and, like a message or even like a gift which comes from the Sacrament, is handed on "to the others and to the people." The new rule is clearly expressed in a plan for Mass, which is placed at the beginning of the tenth-century Romano-German Pontifical and its derivatives: "the presbyter receives the [kiss of] peace from the bishop and gives it to the others."

With this in view it was only natural that the kiss of peace was no longer received from the deacon but from the celebrant himself, and even he "received" it. Therefore he first kissed the altar: "having kissed the altar, he gives the [kiss of] peace to him standing by." Even this was not fully satisfactory, and efforts were made to indicate even more plainly the source from which the peace was to be derived. According to a pontifical from lower Italy, about 1100, the celebrant kissed first the altar, then the book, and finally the Sacred Host, before he offered the deacon the kiss of peace. Elsewhere, as in France, as a rule only the Host was kissed. In England, however, during the thirteenth century this custom was stopped as being less seemly. Here, and in part also in France, it was customary to kiss instead the brim of the chalice and in addition generally the corporal or the paten, while in Germany the prevailing practice was to kiss the altar and the book. Altar and crucifix are also mentioned for this.

The participation of the people continued for several centuries, especially after the kiss of peace was everywhere extended beyond the circle of communicants, and in particular when it was brought from the altar. Therefore the old rule which is found in earlier Christian sources was repeated, namely, that men may give the kiss of peace only to men, and women to women. This rule was very easy to keep when—as was usually the case—the old ordinance regarding the separation of the sexes was still observed.

Nevertheless we feel it would always have been somewhat risky to employ a token of the deepest confidence, such as the kiss is, only in the tiny circle of a young community borne up by high idealism, but even as a permanent institution in public assembly. Of course conditions of ancient culture must be taken into account. Still, in all Christian liturgies in the course of time a certain stylizing was effected, in which only a discreet indication of the former kiss remained. Aside from the Byzantine liturgy (where the kiss is executed in this restrained form only by the celebrant and deacon, and by no one else) this symbolic gesture has been retained also for the people in all the rites of the East. Among the East Syrians it is customary for each one to clasp the hands of his neighbor and kiss them. Among the Maronites the faithful clasp the neighbor's fingers with their own, then kiss the latter. Even more reserved are the Copts, who merely bow to their neighbor and then touch his hand, and the Armenians who are—partly—satisfied with a mere bow.

STYLIZING

Such a stylizing is also found in the present Roman liturgy in the kiss of peace given within the ranks of the clergy at high Mass, the only time it is still practiced. Here it is a light embrace. A different stylization for the kiss of peace in the whole congregation had its origin in England, where the finer touch had also been shown in regard to the kissing of the Host. This is the kiss of peace given by means of the *osculatorium*, a plaque (often richly ornamented) called a pax-board or pax-brede.[2] It put in a first appearance after 1248 in English diocesan statutes, then gradually spread to the continent where, however, the earlier manner of communicating the kiss long remained in vogue. Charles V, in his efforts for reform, had also determined on the renewal of the kiss of peace, wherever the practice had died out, with the employment of the pax-board. The kiss of peace with the *instrumentum pacis* is also provided in the Missal of Pius V of 1570 and in the *Cæremoniale episcoporum* of 1600. In this way it can, at high Mass, be communicated also to the laity. Outside of high Mass, both at the *missa cantata* and the low Mass, this is the only manner of giving the kiss of peace that is considered, both for the clergy of all ranks and for the laity. Thus, the kiss of peace, like the incensation at solemn services, could in the last few centuries be regarded most often as a privilege of persons of rank. But precisely this restriction was the occasion for unedifying disputes about precedence (for the principle of handing it on from person to person involved a certain order or gradation), which was in direct contradiction to the very meaning of the ceremony. For these and similar reasons, the kiss of peace even with the pax-board was impracticable and, except on certain extraordinary occasions and in a few areas here and there, could continue only in various religious groups.

Today the kiss of peace is preceded not only by the *Pax Domini*, but also by a *special prayer for peace* which, however, is separated from the announcement (the *Pax Domini*) by the commingling formula and by the *Agnus Dei*, which is now also said by the priest. Even as late as the ninth century the Carolingian source documents present the kiss of

---

[2] The pax-tablet, called of old in England the Pax-board (Pax-brede), consisted of a small tablet of wood or ivory or metal (even gold or silver) upon which was graven or painted the figure of Our Lord or of a saint or sometimes symbolic figures, and usually encased in a frame with a handle at the back so that it could stand on the altar during Mass.

peace as given right after the *Pax Domini*. Frequently the *Agnus Dei* was still only sung by the choir without being said by the priest, and therefore did not form any interruption before the kiss.

A prayer for peace before the *pax* is still missing even in some late medieval Mass plans. Only the commingling formula had to be inserted after the *Pax Domini*, since the latter, of course, was coupled with the preceding triple crossing.

Our prayer for peace, *Domine Jesu Christe qui dixisti*, made its appearance since the eleventh century, first of all in German territory. It replaced an older prayer for peace. From then on it recurred regularly, even in Italian Mass plans, and thus was introduced into the Missal of Pius V. It is the first formal prayer in the *Ordo missæ* addressed to Christ. This address to Christ which is already found, in a different way, in the *Agnus Dei*, and which has here been continued obviously in view of the Communion about to be received, is retained also in the following Communion prayers.

This prayer for peace is a prayer for the priest in preparation for giving the *pax*. It presupposes the kiss of peace, which starts here at the altar and thence is continued through the church. Therefore, the priest begs the Lord—in view of the promise He made (John 14:27)—not to look upon his sins, but rather upon the confident attitude of the people gathered in church; to disregard the unworthiness of His representative and grant peace and concord through this sacred symbol of a kiss. The prayer, therefore, gains its full meaning only when supported by the performance of the rite.

When the kiss of peace was omitted, the *Pax Domini* no longer had to be omitted with it, but perhaps this prayer would be left out. However, since the *pax* is almost generally omitted, except at high Mass, the prayer, in which the priest pleads for peace and concord for the Church, offers a substitute for it. Other formularies of such a prayer never made much headway.

Even in Carolingian times the kiss of peace was still given without any accompanying greeting aside from the *Pax Domini*. But after the practice began of letting the kiss proceed from the altar, it became customary for the priest to combine it with a special blessing. The oldest version of such a blessing—which, however, became rarer later in the Middle Ages —still regarded the kiss of peace as a preparation for Communion: "Have the bond of peace and charity, that you may be disposed to receive the most sacred mysteries." Those who handed on the kiss and those who received it were to say together: "May the peace of Christ and the Church abound in our hearts." In other cases this phrase is featured at least as the response of the *ministri*, or it is put into the mouth of the celebrant, usually in combination with the aforementioned prayer, and with the variation: "in your hearts." But the simpler *Pax tecum*, the greeting which we heard from the lips of our Saviour Himself, with the answer of the recipient, *Et cum spiritu tuo*, comes more and more into use.

7. Agnus Dei

MEANING

After the answer to the *Pax Domini* has been given, the choir (according to present custom) at once begins the singing of the *Agnus Dei*. The chant is continued while the priest quietly recites the *Agnus Dei* and the following prayers, and while he receives Communion, so that we get the impression that here we have a Communion song. On the other hand, the final petition, *dona nobis pacem*, seems to suggest some relation between the chant and the wish expressed in the *Pax Domini*. What is really the original meaning of the *Agnus Dei*?

Regarding the introduction of the *Agnus Dei* into the Roman Mass, the *Liber pontificalis* has this to tell: Pope Sergius I (687–701) had decreed "that during the fraction of the Body of the Lord, '*Agnus Dei qui tollis peccata mundi miserere nobis*' should be sung by the clergy and people." The older Roman *ordines* direct that, after the archdeacon has distributed the consecrated breads to the acolytes so that the fraction can begin, he should give a signal to the singers for the start of the *Agnus Dei*, which is coupled with the fraction.

So the *Agnus Dei* was a chant to accompany the fraction designed to fill out the interval after the *Pax Domini*, which was given over to the activity of breaking the breads. The one occasion when it is not used for this is on Holy Saturday, a custom which goes back to times immemorial.[1] Otherwise, it continued to have the character of a fraction chant until the fraction itself was rendered superfluous by the introduction of unleavened bread and small particles. It is surprising to read that Sergius I was the one who introduced the song; indeed, that statement has been contested in various ways. However, the *Agnus Dei* could not have had a place in the Roman Mass very much earlier. Even if it was not brought into Rome by Sergius himself, a Syrian by descent, still it was during the later seventh century, in the train of that great inrush of Greek clerics from the Eastern lands overrun by Islam, above all Syria; for it is manifestly an element from the Eastern liturgy. In the East it had become the practice since the sixth century to regard the breaking of the species of bread as a reference to our Lord's Passion and death. In the East, too,

---

[1] The reason generally alleged for the omission, namely the great antiquity of the Easter Vigil Mass, is not entirely pertinent. Rather the same reason holds as was alleged for the omission of the *Kyrie* in the same Mass; the *Agnus Dei* was already sung in the litany.

since an even earlier date, the sacrificial gifts had been designated as the "Lamb," an expression occasioned, no doubt, by St. John's Apocalypse. And here, finally, especially in the liturgy of the West Syrians, liturgical texts—some of them coming from this earlier period—are found which have a reference to the Sacrament and are especially used during the fraction, and these texts speak of the Lamb of God who taketh away the sins of the world.

HYMN OF GREETING

From all that has been said we can see at once that the address to the Lamb of God patently does not refer to Christ simply, but rather to Christ present in the Eucharist as a sacrificial offering; in the same way, just before the distribution of Communion, when the priest holds the Sacrament upraised before the faithful with the words, *Ecce Agnus Dei*, it is the sacramental Christ who is meant. In the liturgy of the City of Rome during the first thousand years this would perhaps be rather strange and unexpected if the prayer under scrutiny were a formal oration said by the priest and not rather a hymnic element intended first of all for the congregation, for in its whole rather imposing store of prayers there is scarcely even one exception to the rule that the prayers be addressed to God. Among the prayers apportioned to the congregation, however, the Roman Mass had long appropriated the *Kyrie eleison;* now, for the same purpose, it took over the *Agnus Dei*. In the interval between consecration and Communion this hymn represents a reverential and, at the same time, humble greeting of Him who has been made present under the form of bread. We might compare it to what occurred some five hundred years later when, under the impulse of a new wave of eucharistic devotion, the silence of the consecration and the elevation of the bread was broken by the introduction of hymns which were engendered not only by the Latin genius but by a new attitude towards the Sacrament—hymns like *Ave verum corpus* and *O Salutaris hostia*. An indication of the close kinship between these two scenes is to be found in the fact that the beginnings of the more recent rites of adoration before the Blessed Sacrament were introduced in the twelfth century at the *Agnus Dei*, and then gradually transferred to the elevation. On the other hand, the note of reverence and adoration at the *Agnus Dei* was later on frequently fortified by the priest not putting the two halves of the Host back on the altar after the fraction, but continuing to hold them raised over the chalice till the Communion or else—according to a widespread custom—holding the particle intended for the commingling over the chalice during the *Agnus Dei*.

According to the *Liber pontificalis*, the *Agnus Dei* was sung by clergy and people. That the priest also said it—at least in some localities—is extremely unlikely. References here and there which seem to point to such a practice do not stand up under closer investigation. Most of the older sacramentaries, which as a rule present only the prayer texts of the celebrant, do not contain the *Agnus Dei*. And that is true down to the eleventh century. Only then does it begin to appear regularly in the sacramentaries, with all indications that the priest is also to say it. On the contrary, the older sources often expressly mention the singing by the people or by the clergy around the altar. The members of the *chorus* or the *clerus* (which is the same thing) would naturally have been the chief performers in most cases, and therefore even at an early period they alone are mentioned.

A refinement, in keeping with the grand pontifical liturgy, is the direction in the first Roman *ordo* which delegates the *Agnus Dei* to the *schola*. That does not mean, of course, that the *schola* alone was to undertake the singing, as was the case later. It could well mean that the *schola* was to intone it and to alternate with the rest of the clergy and the people, as in the *litania*, the stylistic structure of which is either the repetition of the entire invocation or else the final petition in each phrase, *miserere nobis*. In any case, outside the papal stational services the *Agnus Dei* was largely a popular chant. Therefore the oldest melody to which it was sung, the one still used at freial and Requiem Masses, is very simple. Not till the eleventh and twelfth centuries were newer and richer melodies added, an indication that the simple hymn had been transferred to the choir. Soon after this we begin to read reports that the priest at the altar also says the *Agnus Dei*.

The *Agnus Dei early lost its original purpose*, since the fraction was gradually abandoned after the ninth-tenth century. Up to this time the *Agnus Dei* actually appears as an accompaniment of this function. But about this time it also appears in other positions, as the song accompanying the *pax* or simply as a Communion song. When, in some instances even later, the fraction was still customary, the *Agnus Dei* was no longer intrinsically connected with it.

WORDING

As regards the wording—based on the testimonial of the Baptist (John 1:29)—the first thing that occasions surprise is the vocative form *agnus*. This is in keeping with a grammatical rule which is in effect in many languages: from a feeling of reverence, religious terms are apt to be handled as indeclinable. For the biblical *peccatum* is substituted a plural, *peccata*, which is substantially contained in it. And as in other similar cases, only one all-inclusive petition—according to strict Roman usage—is joined to the invocation, namely, *miserere nobis*.

Originally the one simple verse was repeated as often as necessary, just as the *Kyrie eleison* or the *Christe eleison*, as the case might be, could be repeated as often as one pleased. But when the time period necessitated by the fraction fell out, the song itself (which no one wanted to drop) gradually assumed the hallowed number three. The earliest testimonies to this change begin even in the ninth century. Thus a hymn developed, short in its wording but impressive in its import, capable (especially within the limits in which it appears) of being compared to the hymns of the Apocalypse. The Lamb that is our sacrifice and will become our food, in which the paschal lamb of the Old Testament has found its fulfillment, is the triumphant Lamb of the end of the world, that opens the books of mankind's fate. And as from the heavenly Church the canticles of thanksgiving sung by the elect resound to His praise, so also a plea rises aloft from the assembly of the redeemed who still wander through the pilgrimage of life. All this is made even plainer if we take into account the symbolic reference to our Lord's Passion and Resurrection which followed at the fraction and commingling.

Originally the same plea, *miserere nobis*, was sung unchanged at every repetition, as is still done in the Lateran Basilica. But here and there even in the tenth century, and with increasing frequency in the eleventh, a substitution was made in the third place (except often on Holy Thursday), by singing *dona nobis pacem*.[2] The first occasion for this change was probably the transfer of the song to accompany the Kiss of Peace. Periods of external distress, which recur so often, would then probably have led to the retention of this petition for peace. Indeed, the whole *Agnus Dei* was regarded as a prayer for peace, and the plea for external peace was thus appended to the affirmation of inward peace which was inherent in the ceremony of the kiss of peace, or else a special prayer to obtain peace was added to the *dona nobis pacem*, as the Salzburg synod of 1281 decreed for a certain period, or—as an echo from the period of the Crusades—a prayer for the deliverance of the Holy Land was added, as is attested in England. One change of the *miserere* soon led to another. In the Requiem Mass, as early as the eleventh century, the words *dona eis requiem* are substituted, and in the third place *requiem sempiternam*.

Another indication of the effort to give the *Agnus Dei* special importance is seen in the prescription that it is to be sung or said "not continually but *interpolate* and with prayer conjoined to it." Thus it often happened, and still does among the Carthusians, that only one *Agnus Dei* was sung after the *Pax Domini*, the second and third not being taken up till after the Communion. Thus, insofar as a Communion of the assistants or of the people followed, the *Agnus Dei* became even more of a Communion song, with the *communio* of the Proper of the Mass added as sequel.

---

[2] On Holy Thursday, we have since 1955 the threefold *Miserere nobis*.

Like so many other chants of the Mass, the *Agnus Dei* also was over-spread with tropes, especially in the later *Middle Ages*. These tropes are a good index of the notions that were at that time associated with the *Agnus Dei*.

8. Concluding Rites before the Communion

In many sacramentaries of the earlier Middle Ages the Mass *ordo* closes with the *Agnus Dei*, if it has not already ended with the *Pax Domini*. This should not be surprising, for according to the older system the only thing that followed in the way of priestly prayers was the post-communion (after the communion), which, being a variable text, did not really belong to the *ordo* of the Mass.

At the same time—to follow the conceptions of this and the following period further—the *Agnus Dei* formed the conclusion of the canon, the point at which the priest once more emerged from the sanctuary of the sacrificial and commemorative celebration. Since for a long time the *Te igitur* was not to be started till after the *Sanctus* and *Benedictus* had been sung, the *Agnus Dei* was the first song after the beginning of the canon—prescinding from the closing formulas and the *Pater noster* of the priest—to break through the stillness. Even as late as 1549 a synod of Trier objected to the practice of singing any antiphons at all after the consecration till this moment of the Mass; the organ, too, was supposed to be silent till the *Agnus Dei*, and all were to be on their knees or stretched out on the floor, meditating *silenter* on the Passion of Christ.

But even in an earlier period the portion of the Mass where the *Agnus Dei* was inserted marked the end of the Mass in a different and more profound sense. When general participation in Communion was no longer taken for granted, it would seem that no one at first expected the non-communicants to remain during the Communion. In the Gallic liturgy the solemn blessing after the *Pater noster* formed an ostensible termination, you might say, a sort of formal dismissal of the faithful who were not communicating, and it was actually so understood. In Rome the forms were much plainer, but the views were the same. In the sixth century it had already become a time-honored practice for the deacon to call out before Communion: "If anyone is not going to Communion, let him get out of the way!" In practice this meant that they had to leave. For, in view of the Roman manner of distributing Communion, which was done not before the altar to those who came up, but in the nave of the church to all present, any other solution was difficult.

A further step in this arrangement is found in other Roman sources of the seventh and eighth centuries. After the *Pax Domini* the announcements were made regarding the next stational service, pertinent feasts of martyrs, fast days and other ecclesiastical affairs, the time set aside for these announcements being either before the Communion in general or (after the celebrant had communicated) before the Communion of the congregation, that is, before the *Agnus Dei*, insofar as this had become a Communion song.

In Rome, just as in the area of the Gallic liturgy, only those remained at the Communion who were really going to receive. Efforts to get a stricter idea under way and to insist on the presence of all the people also at Communion first cropped up in Spain. This idea then took hold all through the land of the Franks in conjunction with the adoption of the Roman liturgy. In the Gelasian Sacramentaries, which were substituted for the Gallican since the turn of the seventh century, both a text and a suitable location were wanting for the accustomed Gallic blessing after the *Pater noster*. But on many days a prayer *super populum* was provided after the post-communion, and besides, as an appendix to the canon of the Mass, a special selection of other formulas of such a blessing were offered under the title: "Blessings over the people." The Gallic benedictions after the *Pater noster* were kept in part, but only at pontifical Mass. All the more eagerly, then, must these benedictions have been adopted. As a natural result the old direction, in these new circumstances, was taken to mean that the people were to remain, according to the Roman pattern, till this last prayer of blessing, therefore also during the Communion. This interpretation of the law became so firmly established in the course of the century that it could not be dislodged even with the ultimate adoption of the Gregorian Sacramentary which began about 785, even though here the *oratio super populum* was no longer to be found during the Lenten season.

9. Communion of the Priest: Preparatory Prayers

In the early Church, because the concept of the Mass as a sacred repast, a meal, the Lord's Supper, was so much to the fore, it was taken for granted that the Mass would culminate in the reception of the Sacrament by all the participants. In Justin's time this was so much a matter of course that the deacons, as he remarked in both of his accounts, even brought some of the hallowed gift to the absent. A fixed order was followed in arranging the reception, as we discover somewhat later: the leader (bishop or priest) of the assembly was the first to receive "so that it may be made clear that he has offered the sacrifice for all, according to the established order of priestly service," as Theodore of Mopsuestia remarks (*Sermones catecheticæ*, VI). Next came the other members of the clergy, in order of their ecclesiastical rank; and finally the people.

Even in the most ancient Roman *ordines*, the Communion of the assembled congregation, at least at the stational services, formed a natural termination, which appeared like the exact counterpart of the offering of the gifts by the congregation at the start of the Sacrifice-Mass. Here, too, the pope himself received the Sacrament first; he took the bread and partook from the chalice held by the archdeacon. Then he distributed the Body of the Lord to the bishops and priests, and started off the distribution to the people by stepping down (followed by the archdeacon with the chalice), first to the noble men and then over to the noble ladies, to give them the Sacrament.

In the fuller development of the Mass liturgy, as it proceeded eventually on Frankish soil, the Communion of the celebrant assumed a more prominent position, to such an extent, in fact, that as time went on it alone began to be considered an integral part of the liturgy. Its rite was regulated more and more, and encompassed by special prayers which the priest was to say softly to himself. Even here the comparison to the offertory is marked, for in the offertory, too, a similar evolution took place, although in a somewhat different rhythm. But neither in the offertory nor in the Communion was the original design destroyed by this development; it is still clearly manifest at present. So just as the offertory activity of the congregation is still recalled in the offertory chant which grew around it, and still finds its conclusion in the *oratio super oblata* that marks the close, so the Communion chant which was designed to accompany the Communion of the people has been retained throughout all the changes in the ceremony, and so too until now—and especially in our own day—the Communion cycle closes with a community prayer (corresponding to the oration mentioned above), called the post-communion.

INTRODUCTORY PRAYERS

The Communion of the priest is at present introduced by two lengthy prayers in oration style, subjoined to the prayer for peace, and it is accompanied by a series of shorter prayer-phrases which continue even after the consumption of the Precious Blood. This cycle of silent prayers —like the parallel structure around the offertory—was added to the Roman Mass in the area of the Gallo-Frankish Church. Like the former, they are mainly shoots that grew from the still living roots of the abandoned Gallican liturgy. But to a higher degree even than the prayers at the offertory, they are private prayers, as the "I"-form which is their very basis clearly betrays. We will also have occasion to establish that they were all originally designed to serve for the devotion of the other communicants as well. This is not strange. The oriental lit-urgies, too, have the priest prepare himself for Communion by private prayer, and at least the Byzantine has him make a private thanksgiving at once after Communion. The prevailing address to Christ and the partly unusual concluding formulas are also in keeping with the non-Roman origin of these prayers.

The oldest texts are again found in the Sacramentary of Amiens, which belongs to the ninth century. It presents two preparatory prayers, the first of which is the one that is still used at present as the first prayer: *Domine Jesu Christe, Fili Dei vivi*. But it is clear that we do not here have the beginnings of all later Communion prayers, but only one sample of such creations, for the first prayer here shows one isolated variant, while the other prayer apparently does not generally recur in the later transmission of such texts.

Our second preparatory prayer, *Perceptio*, also is met already in the tenth century, in two books stemming from the northeast portion of the Carolingian domain, and in both cases it precedes its companion formula. In contrast to our first prayer, this formula as a rule makes men-tion only of the Body of our Lord, as it does at present. For this reason it was in later times preferred for the Good Friday Communion, where only the species of bread was received.

Often (as was the case already in the Sacramentary of Fulda) these two formulas are accompanied by a third which is addressed to God the Father. This prayer frequently took the place of the others. But even at its first appearance it presented itself not as a component of liturgical prayer, but as a private prayer.

A series of other formulations of a prayer of preparation appear here and there, but never gain widespread use. Some of them, like the prayers already mentioned, are marked entirely by a tone of humble petition. Others have a hymnic character.

However, some Mass books even in the tenth and the eleventh cen-turies did not take up any of these new Communion prayers. On the other hand, Bernold of Constance tells of many prayers which some associate with the kiss of peace and the Communion. And he agrees with other custodians of a good tradition in maintaining that one ought to lose no time over such *privatæ orationes* which are in use *non ex ordine*, but "from the tradition of religious clergy (*religiosorum*)," and that one ought to be satisfied with the one oration *Domine Jesu Christe, qui ex voluntate Patris*, which is to be said bowed. As a matter of fact, this prayer usually appeared all alone. How much a favorite it was is attested also by the different variants.

But the eagerness for an increase of such prayers was even stronger. Some wanted first a prayer addressed to God the Father, and only then one addressed to the Son. Finally, the wish was expressed that a prayer should be added addressed to the Holy Ghost, or at any rate one for the grace of the Holy Ghost. Or else free rein should be given to the private devotion of the celebrant. Even in the sixteenth century there were those who upheld this opinion and put it into practice. In the Mass plans of Middle Italy, where the monasteries had obviously borrowed their prayer material from the sister establishments of the North, the two prayers come to the fore side by side with increasing frequency since the eleventh century. But the first of them, *Domine Jesu Christe*, in these and other uses very frequently follows the reception of Communion; this is true less often of the second formula, *Perceptio*.

In these arrangements of the prayers is revealed the attitude towards the Sacrament which prevailed even at the height of the Middle Ages, an attitude which was concerned less with a special preparation of the soul as such, but rather with the production of the *opus operatum* which is to be sought from God. Since the last years of the eleventh century the two formulas appear at one or another time in Italy in the present-day arrangement, and even outside Italy the same arrangement had made its way before Pius V.

In the arrangement as we have it now, the two prayers serve as a final preparation for the reception of the Sacrament. Prescinding from the Great Prayer itself, there was already a first preparation in the Lord's Prayer, in which we asked the heavenly Father for the sacred bread. In this second step we turn our prayer to Christ, a course which is undoubtedly to be expected even in liturgical prayer. But all the same, even in this we do not lose sight of the gift character of the Sacrament. In other words, our prayer is directed not to Christ as present under the form of bread, but always to Christ who "liveth and reigneth" in heavenly majesty and who, "by this, His most holy Body and Blood," will deliver us from sin and sorrow. The idea of the heavenly Christ and his heavenly existence is so strong that it is not eclipsed even by the sacramental nearness. In the *Agnus Dei* the latter could flash momentarily. But the mood which prevails in the popular devotion since the late Middle Ages, and which has found an outlet in the Fourth Book of the *Imitatio Christi*, and in subsequent prayerbook literature—that mood here was stopped short and not permitted to turn the reception of Communion into a meditative visit to the Blessed Sacrament. Instead, a complete view of the Christian world of faith is maintained and not even in the moment of reception is it forsaken in favor of a partial view.

This complete view is unfolded in a wonderful way, briefly, concisely, in the very first Communion prayer, *Domine Jesu Christe*. As someone has rightly said, a whole theology is contained in this one prayer. We can also say that in it the grand concepts of the anamnesis once more come to life. Grand, indeed. Before our mind's eye appears again the picture of Him whose Body and Blood will soon be our nourishment. At the very start of the prayer our gaze is fixed on the Christ whom we in this solemn moment call—as Peter did (Matt. 16:16) —the Son of the living God. Then our look takes in His momentous work of renewing and reviving the world (*vivificasti*), that work which will be continued in one tiny point in the approaching sacramental reception. Our look takes in the well-spring of this work in the grace-laden decree of the heavenly Father and in the obedience unto death of the Son; it takes in the completion of that work in the operation of the Holy Spirit. Grand, too, is the plea which we now direct to the Lord, confiding in His most holy Body and Blood which He has vouchsafed to us as a sacrifice and which He wills to grant us as a repast; the things we ask are things of magnitude: deliverance from all sin, the strength to be true to His commandments, and—the same petition which we made in the instant before the consecration—the grace of final perseverance, so that we may never be separated from Him. Here, in bold strokes, the whole pattern of Christianity is presented to view.

The second prayer, *Perceptio*, recalling the Apostle's earnest words about an unworthy reception (1 Cor. 11:29), seizes upon one negative point in the first prayer, the curbing of sin. Whoever dares to receive (*præsumo*) may not be conscious of any grave fault; he that eats unworthily, eats the judgment unto himself. But who is really worthy? All that each and everyone can do is raise a humble prayer for the Lord's leniency (*pro tua pietate*). The positive side of the petition blends the objects that are stipulated as the effect of the Sacrament and numerous formulas of the post-communion: protection of soul and body and the cure of our manifold weakness. Even if the body is not the direct subject of grace, yet it is the recipient of the sacramental tokens and is destined to secure those rays of grace which issue from the spiritual center of man's essence.

10. *Communion of the Priest: Ritual Procedure*

As before the priest's Communion, so also during it, the old liturgy had no accompanying prayers. In some individual places this situation lasted a long time, even when some preparatory prayers had been admitted.

The conduct of the Communion itself was one of utmost simplicity, even if not the same everywhere. Any previous genuflection here or elsewhere was unknown till very late in the Middle Ages. The priest simply retained the posture he had, until now. He uncovered the chalice, then conveyed first the Host and next the chalice to his mouth. A previous sign of the Cross with the Host appears here and there since the

thirteenth century. According to the system still observed by the Dominicans, the priest held the two halves of the Host just as they were
at the fraction, in the left hand, while the right rested on the node of
the chalice. In this case the reception of the Host was—and is—done with
the left hand, and then the chalice was taken up at once. But elsewhere
the practice of making a sign of the Cross over himself with the Body
of the Lord before the reception entailed an increasing employment
of the right hand, even when it was not already in use. When—as at the
grand pontifical service—the Communion of the celebrant did not take
place at the altar, care was exercised in olden times that he should be
facing East, as at solemn prayer.

Even in later texts, when at times mention is made of a meditative
pause either before or after the reception by the priest, still a further
direction is given that the priest must take the sacred meal quickly, as
did the Israelites at the exodus, and he may not, by his own private devotion, keep the participants waiting.

THREE MOTIFS

Regarding the accompanying prayers at the priest's Communion, the
texts of the earlier Middle Ages give indications of three motifs in their
introduction. The first was the desire to give proper expression to the
veneration of the Sacrament. It is the same desire from which proceeded
the *Agnus Dei*, and later the elevation and salutation of the Sacrament
right after the consecration. The texts composed for this we find in the
earliest and purest form in the Missal of Troyes written about 1050,
where no other type of text is given.

And just as the salutation—sometimes even to the wording—was used
since the thirteenth century for the veneration of the Sacrament at the
consecration; so, in reverse, the forms which were created for the consecration were later used also before Communion.

The second motif consists of short scriptural passages which were
suited to accompany the Communion. There was above all Psalm 115:
3 f. (12 f.) which presented the phrase "I will take the chalice of the
Lord" as a happy accompaniment for the reception of the chalice, but
also the words "What shall I render to the Lord" as an expression of
awed thankfulness for the Communion. As a matter of fact, we find it
used already since the beginning of the eleventh century in its present-
day length and in the place it occupies today, and even, as now, continued with the phrase from Psalm 17:4, "With praise I shall call upon
the Lord and I shall be saved from my enemies." Here, too, it is preceded by a phrase composed as a parallel for the reception of the bread:
"I shall take the heavenly bread and call upon the name of the Lord."
Here, of course, the scriptural passage is farther removed from its literal

meaning than it was in its first and more ancient use at the offering of the chalice. In the psalm the singer speaks out his resolve to make a thank-offering for his delivery from a great peril and in so doing (as was probably part of the ritual of a thank-offering) to raise the cup to praise God. But here the cup which we intend to pick up itself contains the welfare and therefore the reason for thanksgiving, and next to the cup lies the bread from heaven. At this moment both of them are not so much gifts we offer up to God as rather that sacred repast to which we are now invited. But since we eat of this meal, it behooves us, as it behooved the psalmist, to praise the Lord because, as His guests at table, we are delivered from every earthly peril and safeguarded even if—as it added from Psalm 17:4—our enemies beset us on all sides.

In later years this combination of psalm passages appears in more or less complete form in most of the German Mass plans and also in the majority of the Italian—here since the eleventh century—while in France it is less frequent. In Normandy and England it is absolutely unknown. Sometimes, to be sure, only portions are used, or a different order is chosen, or a different method of interweaving them with the other texts. In Spain the "heavenly bread" is occasionally continued with the phrase from Psalm 77:25 about the bread of angels. Again the last words before the reception of Communion are formed from Psalm 50:11 f. or Psalm 50:11–14, the celebrant striking his breast as he recites the verses. Here we have the same penitential concept that is behind the prescriptions of our ritual, which lays down that at Communion for the sick the Psalm *Miserere* is to be recited on the way. It presupposes somewhat the same spiritual experience that agitated the soul of the Apostle Peter at the miraculous draught of fishes; the nearness of the Son of God draws from our lips the anguished cry: "Depart from me, O Lord, for I am a sinful man" (Luke 5:8).

Especially in later times, similar exclamations, in which an acknowledgment of sinfulness is combined with confidence in God's mercy, are frequently extracted from the New Testament, to be used at the moment of Communion. Thus, there is the exclamation of the prodigal son: "Father I have sinned . . . ." (Luke 15:18 f.). But other phrases that express only unreserved trust also find a place, phrases like the last prayer of the dying Saviour (Luke 23:46): "Father, into Thy hands I commend my spirit."

However, the oldest of such phrases, combining both humility and confidence, is the *Domine non sum dignus* of the centurion of Capharnaum (Matthew 8:8). It had already been used since the tenth century as a reinforcement of longer prayers preceding the reception. Then it was thought sufficient to use only a shortened version, substituting for the clause beginning with *sed tantum*—which could not be used directly —some other scriptural saying. There is no mention here of any repetition of the phrase. But at the same time in Italy the practice began of using the words of the centurion as they are, repeating them three times, either with no change at all, or by using only the first half, or finally inserting *anima mea* in place of *puer meus* in the second half of the phrase, just as is done nowadays. Outside Italy this shorter *Domine non sum dignus* is seldom found before Pius V; it is most frequent in German Mass plans. Even in Italy its ascendancy was only gradual. And striking the breast while saying the words seems to have come into vogue quite late.

How closely associated the centurion's words are with the reception of Communion is seen in the fact that they were used also in oriental liturgies. In the Ethiopian Mass *ordo* the words form the beginning of a lengthy Communion prayer, and the Byzantine liturgy contains amongst its semi-liturgical Communion prayers also some with the same beginning. Even the Fathers had already shifted the centurion's phrase to the reception of Holy Communion.

Although in the broad perspectives of liturgical prayer the notion of a visit is not one of the fundamental ideas in the contemplation of the Eucharist, still, in this biblical phrase, it is taken up for an instant as a relevant simile. And there is nothing to hinder our considering the *Agnus Dei* as a background, or to find in the *Domine* an echo of the title by which the Lamb is addressed in St. John's revelations according to the Vulgate (Apoc. 5:19), that Lamb who, together with Him who sits on the throne, receives the adoration of the four living creatures and the four-and-twenty elders. Not only His coming, but even the word which we beg of Him (*dic verbo*) brings health to the sick—and every recipient acknowledges himself sick in soul. However, by not declining the visit (as did the humble centurion), but instead longingly awaiting it, we alter the sense of the plea. We think now not of the word that substitutes for His visit, but of the word that prepares us for it.

A third motif of words to accompany the reception of the Sacrament —in this case to accompany it immediately—are the formulas for the distribution which came into use in the early Middle Ages, at first for Communion of the sick. These formulas were simply turned into formulas for reception, usually with only a change of "you" and "your soul" to "me" and "my soul." An early and as yet isolated example is once again offered by the Sacramentary of Amiens, which presents, after the two preparatory prayers, a single formula under the heading *Alia*. This formula, meant for the double reception, reads as follows: "May the Body and Blood of Our Lord Jesus Christ avail unto the remission of all [my] sins and life everlasting *in sæcula sæculorum*." Both the reserve discernible here and the effort here seen to enrich the expression is found in the Sacramentary of St. Thierry (end of the tenth century) which offers only a formula for the chalice Communion, probably out of consideration for the fact that the longer prefatory prayers immediately precede the reception of the Host. Some Mass books even after the year 1000 still contain no sumption formula. English Mass arrangements avoided them even in the later Middle Ages, and the Carthusians even at the present have none.

But in general they crop up everywhere, usually for Host and chalice separately, and sometimes accompanied by a third formula which originally was an independent chalice formula. Very frequently the second formula has the wording *Corpus et sanguis*, in view of the particle included at the commingling; this was partially the practice in Normandy and England. As a rule, the formulas are spoken before the sumption, as is the present-day practice. Still, even in the late Middle Ages examples are to be found where they follow the sumption.

The formulas present almost the same picture which we will encounter in the formulas for the distribution. Within the basic framework there is the greatest variation, so that even in the Mass *ordo* the identical version of the formula for both Host and chalice is studiously avoided.

11. Communion of the Faithful: Frequency

As we have already seen, the Communion of the celebrating priest is generally followed by the Communion of the rest of the congregation. This is in accord both with the original practice and also with the established plan of the Roman Mass. This pattern, which in our own day has again come to be taken for granted more and more, was subjected, during the course of centuries, to several fluctuations and violent upheavals. These fluctuations and upheavals have had their effect upon the liturgical design of the people's Communion. They also led to the result that in the explanation of the Mass, even down to the present, the Communion of the people was sometimes treated as a sort of foreign element that did not belong to the structure of the Mass-liturgy and could therefore be disregarded.

Up to the fourth century it was not only a rule that the faithful communicated at every Mass; but Communion was even more frequent than the celebration of Mass, which was usually restricted to the Sunday. On Sunday, the consecrated bread could be received not only to be eaten there and then, but also to be taken home. There it was to be carefully preserved so that it could be eaten day after day before every other food. This practice actually continued in Egypt even much longer, and we find in particular the monks and hermits of the desert, who generally attended the celebration of the Eucharist on Saturdays and Sundays, making good use of the custom. Often they did not partake of the Eucharist till the ninth hour, when they began their spare meal. In those days, and even later, it was customary to take the Eucharist along on journeys of greater length. But in general, after the Church had finally gained freedom and peace, the reception of the Sacrament was restricted to the divine services which had meanwhile increased in frequency. About the fourth century, therefore, Communion of all the faithful present was generally an integral part of the regular course of the eucharistic celebration.

But then, with unexpected rapidity, the frequency of reception, at least in some countries, took a sharp drop. Already Chrysostom, among the Greeks, complained: "In vain do we stand before the altar; there is no one to partake." In Gaul, too, the Synod of Agde (506) found it necessary to insist on Communion three times a year, on Christmas, Easter, and Pentecost, as a minimum. And this demand was repeated time and time again till the very height of the Middle Ages, sometimes with the addition of Maundy Thursday. In the Carolingian reform the attempt was made to re-introduce Communion every Sunday, especially on the Sundays of Lent, but the result was at best temporary. From the eighth century onward, the actuality seems generally not to have gone beyond what the Lateran Council of 1215 established as a new minimum: Communion at Easter.

It was only in monasteries that the Sunday Communion continued to be the rule in the early Middle Ages, and among the Cluniacs and Cistercians even later. But the lay brothers had to be content with a much more restricted quantity; for example, in a monastery as zealous for reform as Camaldoli, the lay brothers received only four times a year. A similar rule was in force in the military orders and quite generally also in convents of women.

TWO HINDRANCES

How could the eagerness to receive the Sacrament reach such a low state? And how could it continue even through a period we are accustomed to regard as the flowering period of ecclesiastical life, the central Middle Ages? Obviously the reason could not have been the lukewarmness or coldness of Christians so often remarked upon, and admittedly on the increase since the earlier years of the Church. Otherwise, this regression would have been halted at least at the gates of the many monasteries which were borne on the crest of religious enthusiasm. Certainly the mass of those in the Roman Empire who, after Constantine, were converts for external reasons only, and who, therefore, were believers only externally, must have had a debilitating effect on religious life. So too among the Germanic tribes that were but superficially missionized, a profound understanding of the sacramental life unfolded very slowly. But it is certainly surprising that this regression should be most noticeable in those countries where the *struggle against Arianism had led to a one-sided stressing of the divinity in Christ* and in the process had brought about a religious attitude which in turn produced in those very same countries—namely, in the Greek Orient and in the milieu of the Gallic liturgy—corresponding modifications of liturgical prayer and a novel form of language in respect to the Eucharist. The humanity in Christ, Christ's mediatorship which draws us to Him, receded into the shadows. The *tremendous distance* that separates us from God and the saints gained greater and greater power over the Christian mind in spite of the strong hold which traditional teaching had. It became customary to speak of the awesome table of the Lord, of the *mysterium tremendum.* No wonder, then, that people hardly dared approach. Where the upheavals in the structure of liturgical prayer were least violent, namely in Rome, the ancient traditions of a frequent Communion, naturally connected with the celebration of the sacrifice, continued the longest.

Since the early Middle Ages an additional hindrance to frequent Communion developed: *the change of the penitential discipline.* In contrast to the unrestricted—perhaps often too unrestricted—manner of an older Christendom, the *probet se ipsum homo* of the Apostle (1 Cor. 11:28) was soon explained not merely as demanding a preliminary sacramental confession for "criminal sins" but, with increasing positiveness since the tenth century, as requiring sacramental confession before each and every reception of Communion. But in the Middle Ages, with the prevailing parish restrictions and the often insufficient organization of the cure of souls, not only was there no willingness, but to a great extent even no possibility, to confess and thus to communicate frequently. In addition, various cases of exclusion from the Sacrament were established in the spirit of the Old Testament purification laws, especially for married people and women. And on the other hand, greater and greater requirements were set down for the preparation. A synod of Coventry in 1237 desired a previous fast of half a week for lay people. Elsewhere, six days' abstinence from flesh meat was required. Whoever had not already acquired a high degree of perfection and was not supported by devotion of the most definite sort should, like the centurion, consider himself unworthy, rather than, like Zacchæus, have the Lord often lodge with him. For people said to themselves—and herein a genuinely religious judgment of the problem is once more revealed—"from the frequent celebration a low esteem is sure to develop, but from the infrequent celebration grows reverence for the Sacrament."

The eucharistic wave that passed over Christendom from the end of the twelfth century on, did indeed magnify the *cult* of the Sacrament, *but not the frequency of its reception.* On the contrary, the notion grew that frequent gazing upon the Eucharist could in some way replace the sacramental reception. The idea of spiritual communion developed. With an appeal to the Augustinian *Crede et manducasti,* this form of piety, when one turned with loving faith to Christ, contemplated His Passion with profoundest love, devoutly assisted at Holy Mass or looked up at the Sacred Host, was explained as a work scarcely less valuable than sacramental Communion itself. In the later Middle Ages, the desire for sacramental Communion was regarded as a requisite for such a spiritual communion, in fact as its essential mark. At a time when frequent Communion was made almost impossible by exaggerated requirements, this desire must really have been a genuine one for many people.

OFFERING UP

A certain justification for the existing practice of infrequent Communion was found in the Middle Ages in the thought that the priest surely communicates and does so as representative of the entire community. This idea of a representative activity is brought out time and again, and there was even a tendency to put the idea into effect in other instances. A Trier synod of 1227 had to prohibit the practice of priests receiving the Body of the Lord in place of the sick. Even the faithful—especially in convents of women—began somehow to practice such a representative Communion—Communion in place of someone else. Thus in the thirteenth century there are evidences of the practice of receiving or, to use a better term, "offering up" Communion for others, especially for the dead. So even this practice is one of the fruits of the infrequent Communion during these centuries.

Towards the end of the Middle Ages, other forces came into play, forces aimed at favoring and promoting a more frequent reception of the Eucharist. These new aims were decidedly encouraged at the Council of Trent and finally gained a complete triumph through the action of Pius X.

So, in the two thousand years of the Church's history, we see two viewpoints, the most opposite imaginable, enjoying the field: on the one hand, the undiscerning confidence that he who by Baptism was implanted in Christ and accepted into the Kingdom of God, should also be allowed to regard the bread of heaven as his daily food; on the other hand, that feeling of reserve and timidity that looked more to human weakness than to the grace-made dignity of the Christian, and which hindered even the pious from often approaching the holy mystery.

Aside from the state of grace, another condition was stipulated even in early days both for the priest and for the faithful: to remain *fasting* before the reception of the Sacrament. This requirement was already silently fulfilled in the ancient practice of taking the Sacrament "before every other food." But by the end of the fourth century this condition was more or less explicitly imposed, although some few exceptions were still granted, especially on Maundy Thursday, when the pattern suggested by the Last Supper was to be copied. All through the Middle Ages the precept of fasting was not only strictly adhered to with regard to Holy Communion, but was even repeatedly prescribed for attendance at Mass (as in a synod of Brixen as late as 1453), or at least it was counseled for Mass. It has been left to our own day to make bigger inroads into the law of strict eucharistic fast. Various concessions had already been made in favor of the sick, the military, and those working night hours, when on the feast of the Epiphany, 1953, Pope Pius XII, in a special Apostolic Constitution, restated the basic principles governing the law, and promulgated for the whole world certain mitigations dictated by the changed conditions of modern society. And, finally, we have the most far-reaching reform of all, the *Motu Proprio* of March 19, 1957, which has brought the Lord's Table even closer to the faithful of our times.

12. Communion of the Faithful: Preparatory Prayers

As long as the Mass, throughout its course, remained a common celebration of both priest and people, there was no reason to think of other prayers for the Communion of the faithful than those they said with the priest, and the priest with them. The Mass itself moved on towards the sacred repast. This was true also of the ancient Roman Mass, in spite of the special poverty which its prayer-plan shows in the area of the Communion.

But when, during the Carolingian epoch, the Roman Mass was transplanted to the land of the Franks, it was apparent that the Frankish clergymen did not feel at home in its rhythm. The result: attempts to readjust and build up the prayers, particularly in the Communion cycle. Even the faithful—in that thin layer of people who had mastered Latin—took an attitude towards the antique severity of the Roman Mass that could hardly have been more favorable than that of the clerics. So it is no surprise to learn that a large portion of the priest's new Communion prayers—those that he begins to recite in a low tone as he inserts them in his Mass *ordo*—are prayers of the *faithful*, or at least of the assisting and participating clerics and monks. The prayers which are still in use at the present, all of them, appear in this double role. The convergence is here more complete than in the parallel occurrence in the oblation cycle.

The prayer to God the Father that usually occupies the first place, *Domine sancte Pater*, we encounter first in the prayer book of Charles the Bald. Also the prayer *Domine Jesu Christe, fili Dei vivi* appears about the same time in private collections of prayers, amongst others in one version of the "Communion Devotions of Monte Cassino" (written during the closing years of the eleventh century), where it is used as a prayer after Communion. It is also inserted in the Mass plan of the Alsatian monastery of Gregorienmünster (eleventh century), with the rubric: "When we go to receive the Body and Blood of the Lord, we say"; it was therefore a prayer for communicants. The same is true of the prayer *Perceptio corporis*. In one instance it appears as a second formula, introduced by the word *Item*, under the heading: "Let this prayer be said by the individual communicants." For the prayers that follow in our order of Communion, parallels are to be found in the Missal of St. Lawrence in Liége (first half of the eleventh century). The *Domine non sum dignus* was already recommended to lay people since the eleventh century. As a matter of fact, it is found in the "Communion Devotions of Monte Cassino" cited above, as the last of the prayers spoken before Communion, and since the thirteenth century the custom began in monasteries of reciting it in common before Communion.

The "Communion Devotions of Monte Cassino" gives us a good picture of the manner in which zealous monks prepared themselves for Communion. The *Ordo ad accipiendum corpus Domini* begins with Psalms 50, 15 and 38. *Kyrie*, *Pater noster*, and *Credo* follow, and then, in a free version, formulas of the *Confiteor* and *Misereatur*. After several versicles come the Communion prayers proper, addressed in turn first to God the Father, then to the Son, and then to the Holy Ghost. Next follows the centurion's protestation, said three times. After the reception of the Sacrament the Communicant says three times: "The Word was made flesh and dwelt among us," and then the doxology, "Praise, glory, and thanksgiving be to Thee, O Blessed Trinity." Among the prayers that follow we find, besides the *Domine Jesu Christe Fili* already mentioned, the prayer *Corpus tuum Domine quod sumpsi*. A few other formulas present variations on the prayer for the purifying and strengthening effect of the Sacrament.

It is astonishing that this group of prayers, which since the end of the Carolingian era had been transferred from the private sphere into the liturgical prayers even of the priest, after a few centuries played no special role in private Communion devotions. While the prayers in the priest's Mass *ordo* became more and more fixed, private piety in the pre-Gothic period took a new direction. By the eleventh century we encounter the salutations of the Blessed Sacrament which even found a place in the Mass books and which reached their climax in the elevation of the Sacred Host at the consecration. In connection with these a new mode of speech gradually broke through. No more is the Body and

Blood of Christ kept in view, but simply Christ, who is desired and greeted as the guest of our souls. The fundamental tone is produced not by the phrase "Who eats My flesh and drinks My blood" (John 6:53 ff.) but by that other phrase "who eats me" (John 6:58). As a result, the contemplation of Christ's Passion, which had been brought to the fore in the allegorical explanations of the Mass, and (in general) the reminiscent preoccupation with our Lord's life and suffering, had their effect on the preparation for Communion.

SPECIAL SERIES OF PRAYERS

It is against this background that we must evaluate the appearance, towards the end of the Middle Ages, of a special series of prayers within the Mass for the case when Communion was to be distributed to the faithful. And as time went on, the rite thus inserted into the Mass became more and more identical with that used when Communion was distributed outside of Mass, as was necessary at least for the Communion of the sick and dying. This development had been preceded by substantially the reverse procedure. For the oldest rites for the Communion of the sick which we know of transported, as far as possible, the Communion part of the Mass into the sick room. The *Pater noster* was said, with its introduction and its embolism, the kiss of peace was given with a formula corresponding to the *Pax Domini*, and then the Sacrament was presented to the sick.

After the eleventh century, however, this rite for the Communion of the sick grew less common. It was broken up and various other elements assumed a more prominent role in it, especially a confession of sin and a profession of faith. Of course a confession of sin was long a part of the correct preparation for Communion, in fact fundamentally it was a part of it from the very beginning. But it did not always come right before the reception of the Sacrament. In the prayer book of Charles the Bald the imperial petitioner is admonished: "Sins must be confessed secretly before God, before you offer your oblation or communicate." To be sure, at the Communion of the sick these requirements were of necessity drawn closer together. As one twelfth-century source puts it, the sick person should recite "his Confiteor," after which the *Misereatur* follows, along with the *Indulgentiam* (embodying the absolution) and the rest of the Communion rite.

Already in the sources of the eighth and ninth centuries there is evidence here and there of a profession of faith made by the sick, usually in the form of the Apostles' Creed. However, it never became a general practice. But when, in the eleventh and twelfth centuries, it was drawn into closer relation with the Communion, it again appears.

Both elements were then transferred to the order of Communion at

Mass. The liturgies of the religious orders in the twelfth and thirteenth centuries usually indicate the *Confiteor* before the Communion of the brethren. Soon, in the form of the *culpa* or "open confession," it gained entrance into the parish churches, where it was generally recited by the entire congregation. Since the thirteenth century we sometimes find, in some form or other, a profession of faith in the truth of the Sacrament, made before the Communion of the Mass. It appears in the form of a question by the priest and an answer by the people, especially after the Reformers began to attack the Sacrament.

A very happy method of making such a profession of faith was found when, in place of the questions about faith and the knowledge of faith, the more quiet and harmonious form we have in our *Ecce Agnus Dei* appeared. By its pertinent and pregnant designation of the Blessed Sacrament as the Lamb of God it takes up the message of the *Agnus Dei* chant which preceded. It can surely be put on a par with the *Sancta sanctis* ("Holy things to holy ones") of old. The earliest witness to the use of these words before Communion seems to be the Synod of Aix (1585), where they were prescribed along with the accompanying *ritus*. In order to attain their purpose as an acknowledgment of belief in the Eucharist they were often—even to very recent times—spoken in the vernacular, just as was done earlier with regard to the questions about faith, and even as was done with the *Domine non sum dignus* following. Quite a number of synods and diocesan rituals, even in the eighteenth century and later, both in Germany and France, expressly ordered this use of the vernacular. Then this group of formulas, *Confiteor* with the accompanying words of absolution, *Ecce Agnus Dei*, and *Domine non sum dignus*, were introduced into the order of Communion in the Roman Ritual of 1614. There it was naturally given in Latin, and insofar as the Roman Ritual took the place of the diocesan rituals, this resulted in the exclusion of the vernacular. Now the *Confiteor* is to be recited by the Mass-server in the name of the people, and the *Domine non sum dignus* is to be said by the priest.

The acceptance of these prayers into the Roman Missal was a matter of course. From what we have said we see that it was entirely in keeping with long usage. However, in our day, when we have learned to follow the procedure of the Mass from start to finish, we find the *Confiteor* especially a rather unnecessary repetition,[1] since, even without considering the community type of Mass, every attempt to participate at the sacrifice demands from the very beginning the humble acknowledgment

[1] In the reformed Holy Week, we have a clear instance of the conscious avoiding of repeating the *Confiteor*. It is only said once on Holy Thursday, and that is at the beginning of Mass, at the foot of the altar. On Good Friday, it is said only before the Communion. (We here abstract from the origins of the prostration before the altar which we still have on Good Friday at the beginning of the Liturgical Action).—Rev.

of sin. At the Communion of the ordination Mass, the *Ecce Agnus Dei* and the *Domine non sum dignus* are wanting, and at the Communion of newly-ordained priests the *Confiteor* also is omitted.

That these interpolations before the dispensing of Holy Communion could so easily succeed in gaining general acceptance during the last years of the Middle Ages is linked in some way with the fact that even from ancient times it was customary on occasion to stop momentarily at this place and use the sacred moment for important explanations. It is already recounted of Novatian that he exacted from his followers an oath of fealty before he let them approach for Communion. In the early Middle Ages similar demands and explanations were customary when Communion was dispensed at a Mass which had been preceded by an ordeal. From this, it was but a short step to consider the religious profession as a kind of sacred oath which was sealed with the reception of the Sacrament. An example of this sort is seen in French Franciscan circles in the year 1331. In the Society of Jesus it became an established institution to take the vows a moment before receiving the Sacrament, an example which has been imitated in many later congregations.

13. Communion of the Faithful: Ritual Shape

Regarding the problem of the *place* to be occupied by the faithful when receiving Holy Communion, there have been various solutions in the course of time. When all or a great part of those present communicated, the manner described in the Roman *ordines* had certain advantages: the faithful remain in their place, and the clergy bring them the Sacrament. In other localities, as early as the fourth century, the faithful went up to the altar. In Gaul that was the old traditional practice. The gates which separated the sanctuary (and consequently the place of the clergy) from the people were left open at this time; the faithful ascended the steps to the altar, a right which the Synod of Tours (567) expressly ratified, and which was not curtailed till the Carolingian period. After that it still remained at least the privilege of monks, and frequently also of nuns. It was seldom granted to the laity to receive at the main altar, as was the case with the Augustinian Canons according to a rule confirmed in 1116 for the foundation of Ravenna. Usually lay people received Communion at a side altar where the Sacrament had been placed beforehand, or where a special Mass was said. This was especially the case where (as frequently happened since the Romanesque period in churches with many priests) the choir was separated from the nave of the church by a high wall, the so-called screen. Here Communion was usually given at a transept-altar erected outside the screen.

In the North African Church of ancient times, and elsewhere, too, the method adopted was for the faithful to approach the rail which surrounded the altar. Augustine warned the guilty who had lost their right to Communion not to approach "lest they be sent away from the rail (*de cancellis*)." A similar custom must have existed in the Orient. During the Carolingian era, too, we find mention made of these rails. These rails, however, were not so low as those of today; they reached as high as the chest. Consequently, the faithful were able to receive standing.

Since the thirteenth century it was customary here and there to spread a cloth (held by two acolytes) for those communicants kneeling at the altar. Later on, in the sixteenth century, this cloth began to be laid over a table or a bench which had been placed before the communicants between the nave and the *presbyterium*. This was found very convenient for an orderly coming and going. Various synods now laid down prescriptions along these lines. However, in place of table or bench, solid rails of wood or stone gradually came into use, but they were calculated for kneeling and hence were made lower—our Communion rail, which since the seventeenth century has almost everywhere taken the place of the former screen.

When the faithful go to Communion we say nowadays: They approach the Lord's table. This had never meant the Communion rail or any of its forerunners, but from the very beginning it always meant only the altar-table, the *mensa Domini* at which the Sacrament was confected, and from which it was distributed. Nevertheless, it still remains a splendid task for the church-architect so to arrange and align the structure mentioned as to trace the connection with the holy table which we actually approach when we kneel at the Communion rail.

POSTURE AND REVERENCE

That the Body of the Lord should be received kneeling is a custom which slowly and gradually gained the ascendancy in the West between the eleventh and the sixteenth centuries. Prior to that, it was the practice, as we have said, to stand while communicating.

The changes of bodily bearing are mirrored, amongst others, in the picturizations of the Last Supper. While the exegete must surely conclude from the accounts at hand that the disciples received the divine bread in the same posture which they had assumed during the meal, art, delving into the very core of the matter, has preferred to sketch the event in accordance with contemporary Communion rites. A Gospel codex of Rossano, which originated in Egypt about the year 500, pictures our Lord standing while giving His disciples, also standing, Communion under the form of bread. In reverse, the Evangeliary of Bernard of Hildesheim (d. 1024) shows the apostle Judas receiving the

Eucharist kneeling. That this practice, however, had not yet become common everywhere can be seen from the statutes of the various religious orders in the eleventh, twelfth, and thirteenth centuries, which expressly prescribe it. For parochial churches in several dioceses it was not till much later that its introduction was recommended. Thus we read in a Paderborn memorandum-book printed in 1602 that the custom was to be introduced there "where it can be done conveniently." In the rite of the Roman Curia, on the other hand, it had become so firmly rooted as early as the fourteenth century that, as today, outside of the celebrant, only the bishop stood when receiving Communion at his consecration Mass.

For evident reasons the standing position was the rule for the chalice Communion, and this position was retained also for the ablution wine.

Apropos of the Communion which was received standing, the question arises, whether in this case there was not perhaps some sign of adoration or reverence connected with the reception. For the period which witnessed anew the increase in that eucharistic devotion which brought with it the change to reception while kneeling, signs of veneration could naturally be taken for granted. St. Hildegard had her nuns approach Communion dressed in white, adorned like brides, with a crown which displayed on the forehead the picture of the *Agnus Dei*. About the same time, when the Canons of the Lateran went to Communion they all wore the cope. In Cluny, they were still speaking of the custom practiced by the Fathers of approaching with bare feet. Reverence was also shown by bodily movement. The *Consuetudines* of Cluny, written down by Udalricus about 1080, demand a genuflection before receiving.[1] Elsewhere it was customary to kiss the floor or the priest's foot. A threefold inclination was already prescribed in the rule of St. Columban (d. 615).

St. Augustine seems to have had something similar in mind when he remarked that no one partook of this Flesh "unless he shall first have adored It," but we find nothing further about a bodily gesture except that the faithful were to approach with their hands joined. According to Theodore of Mopsuestia the communicant should draw near with lowered eyes, both hands extended, and at the same time he should speak a word of adoration, since he is to receive the Body of the King.

A clear picture of the procedure at Communion in the fourth century is given us in the *Mystagogic Catecheses* of Jerusalem:

> When you approach, do not go stretching out your open hands or having your fingers spread out, but make the left hand into a throne

[1] For the question of reverences at the reception of Holy Communion, Rubric No. 29 of the reformed Ordo for Holy Thursday is certainly of some importance. Here we find a genuflection prescribed for clerics and servers *before* receiving Communion, but not afterwards. There is no mention at all of genuflections for the faithful.

for the right which shall receive the King, and then cup your open hand and take the Body of Christ, reciting the *Amen*. Then sanctify with all care your eyes by touching the Sacred Body, and receive It. But be careful that no particles fall, for what you lose would be to you as if you had lost some of your members. Tell me, if anybody had given you gold dust, would you not hold fast to it with all care, and watch lest some of it fall and be lost to you? Must you not then be even more careful with that which is more precious than gold and diamonds, so that no particles are lost? Then, after you have partaken of the Body of Christ, approach the chalice with the Blood without stretching out your hands, but bowed, in a position of worship and reverence, and repeat the *Amen* and sanctify yourself by receiving the Blood of Christ. Should your lips still be moist, then touch them with your hands and sanctify your eyes and your forehead and the other senses. Then tarry in prayer and thank God who has made you worthy of such mysteries.

Most of the details found in the picture presented above are corroborated for the period of Christian antiquity not only by the texts cited before and by pictures and drawings, but also in many other sources: the giving of the Eucharist into the hand of the communicant, the placing of both hands together open and in cruciform, the blessing of the senses with the sacramental species, the admonition to take great care in handling them, and the immediate reception of the eucharistic bread before proceeding to partake of the chalice. However, there are a few sources which advise the communicant to remain in prayer momentarily before the reception; one should keep in mind the power of Him whose Body is held in one's hands, acknowledge one's own sinfulness and unworthiness, and praise the Lord *qui tale dedit tali*. A prayer for this moment, first attested in the fifth century, is still in use in Egypt today. Only after this prayer had been said was the Body of the Lord received. In the West, too, the customary manner of receiving Communion in early medieval times was similar to this. We see this more plainly in the Communion of clerics by whom the practice of taking the Communion in the hands was retained longest. At the papal Mass in the eighth and ninth centuries, after the bishops and priests had received the Body of the Lord, they went to the left side of the altar, placed their hands with the Sacrament on the altar and communicated; the deacons did the same on the right side of the altar. The practice was not much different even in the pontifical Mass of the tenth century.

The laity intending to receive Communion were expected to wash their hands beforehand. It is not clear, however, if this washing of the hands was demanded only as needed or if it represented a settled ritual prescription: the latter seems probable, for it was customary since ancient times to wash the hands before prayer. Be that as it may, in the plans for the great basilicas, a fountain was placed in the fore-court. That it was not intended merely as an ornament is seen clearly from the fact that in front of St. Peter's Basilica in Rome, behind the splendid Constantinian fountain, a second, more modest one was erected by Pope Symmachus in order to satisfy the need. In Gaul, the women were not permitted to receive the Body of the Lord in their bare hands, but were obliged to cover them with a white cloth.

Before receiving the eucharistic bread the faithful often kissed the hand of the one giving them Communion. Even today the Byzantine deacon does the same before taking the sacred bread.

In giving the Eucharist into the hands the danger arose that the Eucharist was sometimes misused. Spanish synods found it necessary to decree that whoever receives the Eucharist and does not eat It should be considered as *sacrilegus*.

Even stronger than this worry about possible misuse was the influence of the growing respect for the Eucharist. Both together led to the practice of placing the Sacred Host in the mouth. Even though there may be some isolated instances of this practice in earlier times, the method dates substantially from the ninth century.

The change of custom is contemporaneous with the transition from leavened to unleavened bread, and is probably related to it. The delicate pieces of thin wafer almost invited this method of distribution, since, unlike the pieces of unleavened bread formerly used, they easily adhered to the moist tongue. At the synod of Rouen a further rule was established that at high Mass the priest was to give the Eucharist into the hands of the deacon and subdeacon as *ministri altaris*. During the tenth and eleventh centuries this right was narrowed down to priests and deacons. Then it disappeared entirely, although there are isolated accounts still of the laity taking the Sacrament into their own hand.

This manner of distributing the Sacrament removed the worry about the recipient's clean hands, and also the greater worry that small particles of the sacred bread would be lost or that something had to be done about purifying the fingers, as had become the custom for the priest. The Communion cloth later introduced and, since 1929, the Communion paten or plate are expressions of further increased care in the direction mentioned.

COMMUNION OF THE CHALICE

Giving the chalice to the Christian people lasted longer than giving the eucharistic bread into the hand. Naturally, with regard to the chalice, there was even greater insistence in the warning not to spill anything, but even with the best will in the world it was often of no avail.

However, for centuries the Communion of the chalice continued un-changed for the laity, and even today such a Communion takes place in the Liturgy of the East Syrians and the Abyssinians. All drank from the same chalice, which was either the consecration chalice or a special dis-tribution chalice, originally called *calix ministerialis* in Rome. When necessary, several such chalices were used.

But with the use of a special Communion chalice they soon found an-other solution, a solution which in a certain measure lessened the danger of irreverence towards the sacred contents. A small amount of the Pre-cious Blood was poured into a chalice which contained other non-conse-crated wine, a custom which must have been known in early times in the Orient, as we have seen. Perhaps the Council of Laodicea had something like this in view when it forbade the deacon to "bless the chalice." At any rate, this custom is to be found in the Roman *ordines* since the sev-enth century. As we saw above, the acolytes held vessels of wine in readiness, into which, after the Communion of the celebrant, a part of the Precious Blood from the *calix sanctus* (which alone was allowed to be consecrated) was poured. This mixture could still be called *sanguis Dominicus*, as a recension of a Roman *ordo* remarks, "because even non-consecrated wine mixed with the Blood of the Lord is in every respect sanctified." In the same manner the Communion chalice was provided for in monastic *Consuetudines* up to the twelfth century: before the contents of the consecrated chalice given to the brethren were used up, it was permitted to add wine for the remaining communicants. As we have already had occasion to see, the "sanctification" of the wine by touching the particle of the Holy Host to it was another practice, espe-cially in the case of Communion for the sick.

The Roman *ordines* bring to our attention a second prescription: the faithful are not permitted to drink directly from the chalice, but by means of a tube or reed, also called *calamus* or *fistula*. For the Com-munion of the faithful at the stational services a number of these tubes was kept on hand. They also seem to have served for the clergy, for besides the silver there are also golden ones. The use of the tube spread everywhere from Rome; it even frequently remained in use in taking the ablution wine after the Communion chalice had been abrogated.

In some places outside of Rome a third way was practiced: the Sacra-ment was given to the faithful in the form of consecrated bread which had been dipped into the Precious Blood and so was soaked with it (*intinctio*). This method was first attested by the Third Synod of Braga (675) which discountenanced it, just as happened later at the synod of Clermont (1096). However, it must have been widely spread in north-ern countries, especially as a method of making it possible to give Com-munion under both species to the sick. In most of the rites of the East and especially in the Byzantine rite this is at present the ordinary way Communion is dispensed to the faithful.[2]

Since the twelfth century the chalice Communion was discontinued more and more in the West. Developments in dogma which led to a clearer understanding that *per concomitantiam* the entire Christ is present under both species seemed to have been decisive in bringing this about. The command of Christ, "Eat and drink," could be regarded as fulfilled by the priest who stands at the altar as head of the congregation. In fact Communion under one species was not unknown even in earlier times. Communion was given to infants and young children after Baptism under the form of wine. Occasionally, too, this was done in the case of those mortally sick. In Communion at home, of course, only the form of bread was generally under consideration.

At the time the *Summa theologica* of St. Thomas (d. 1274) was being completed, the chalice Communion had not as yet disappeared everywhere, for the author mentions the practice of not giving the Precious Blood to the people and of having the priest alone consume it, and he qualifies the practice merely as the well-founded custom of some churches.[3] On special occasions the lay chalice was still retained in the fourteenth century and even later, as at the coronation of emperors and kings, and at the Easter-Sunday Mass at the *Capella papalis*, where anyone was permitted to communicate in this way. Also in some monasteries of the old orders the chalice Communion was still retained for a long time, in part even beyond the Middle Ages. A certain reminder of this is seen in the ablution chalice which remained customary in part until the last centuries.

When the chalice Communion was already practically forgotten, it was seized upon by hostile groups and made a symbol of their movement. Thereupon, after first being forbidden, the lay chalice was granted in 1433 for Bohemia. After the Council of Trent, the use of the chalice was granted for Germany, under certain specified conditions, but after some unhappy experiences the concession was withdrawn, for Bavaria in 1571, for Austria in 1584, and for Bohemia and in general in 1621.

According to ancient tradition it was the *deacon* who passed the chalice at solemn services. Evidences for this are found as early as the third century. In the Roman liturgy this arrangement is clearly witnessed by the Roman *Ordines* and their offshoots. In the oldest descriptions, those in Justin, it was the principal task of the deacons to distribute the Eucharist, and likewise to bring it to the absent. Of this office of theirs a remnant is found even today. At the ordination to diaconate the bishop calls

---

[2] The particles that have been dipped into the chalice and thus moistened with the Precious Blood are taken out by means of a small spoon and placed in the mouth. Among the Armenians this is done without the small spoon.

[3] St. Thomas, *Summa theol.*, III, 80, 12: *In quibusdam ecclesiis . . . .*

the deacons *comministri et cooperatores corporis et sanguinis Domini,* and the *Codex Iuris Canonici* still describes the deacon as *minister extraordinarius sacræ communionis.*

The connection between the office of deacon and the Sacrament was, for that matter, even closer during the Middle Ages, since it was taken for granted that at solemn high Mass he should communicate himself, a right that is still his among the Greeks and Armenians, and which the subdeacon also enjoyed. In this connection the Communion chalice also survived, especially in many French monasteries. At St. Denis, even as late as 1760, the deacon and subdeacon received under both species on all Sundays and feast days during the high Mass at which they served. In other places, in old foundations and cathedrals, the same custom was still observed at least as late as the twelfth century.

ACCOMPANYING WORDS

The distribution of the Sacrament was accompanied with corresponding words even in the early Christian era. The ordinary form of distribution was Σῶμα Χριστοῦ, *Corpus Christi.* This had the significance of a profession, as the Arabic *Testamentum Domini* explicitly indicates when it describes the formula: "The priest shall give testimony to each one who partakes of the Bread of Thanksgiving that it is the Body of Christ." Hence special stress was laid upon the recipient's answer of *Amen.* The same was repeated with the chalice, where, however, the formula was often expanded: "Blood of Christ received unto life." Also when giving the species of bread, expanded formulas were in use at an early period. Such expanded versions are also seen in the later oriental liturgies. Reverential epithets were added, as in the Greek liturgy of St. Mark: "The holy Body (Precious Blood) of Our Lord and God and Saviour Jesus Christ." Besides this, where possible, the recipient was even mentioned by name, and when the occasion demanded, with his ecclesiastical title, as in the Byzantine Mass, where, as also with the Syrians, the wish was added: "For the forgiveness of his sins and unto eternal life." Or the profession character of the formula was underlined, as with the Coptic: "This is in truth the Body and Blood of Emmanuel, our Lord," whereupon the communicant answered: "Amen. I believe."

In the liturgy of the city of Rome in the early Middle Ages the old tradition of handing out the sacramental species with a corresponding phrase seems to have been broken. Not only are the sacramentaries silent about this, but also the *ordines* which faithfully give us the words for the commingling, *Fiat commixtio,* which are about on a par. What later appears among the Franks is not the ancient profession, "The Body of Christ," which demands the actualizing *Amen* of the communicant, but instead is a blessing which is said, in general, only by the priest. Perhaps we have a link which represents the connection with the old form of distribution; according to some sources the newly-baptized child was given the Sacrament with the words: "The Body of Our Lord Jesus Christ unto life everlasting."

The basic form of this blessing, from which the later formularies branch off and which reaches back to the eighth century, seems to have been as follows: "May the Body and Blood of Our Lord Jesus Christ preserve thee unto life everlasting."

We meet similar forms after the ninth century also at the distribution at Mass. And these formulas of distribution are found in many different shapes. This is all the more worthy of remark because the sumption formulas were not so frequent even as late as the eleventh century, and because, on the other hand, the Communion of the faithful since that time has been given less consideration in the Mass plans. Although these distribution formulas all are built upon the schema mentioned above, no value was laid upon keeping to any special text. In fact, the fashion seems to have been to try for variety.

The Missal of Troyes, which was written about 1050, gives us three versions. The somewhat older Mass of Flaccius Illyricus gives three different versions, one for the Communion of the priest and the deacon, one for the rest of the clergy, and one for the people. A special prayer with which the priest introduced the giving of the Sacrament to the faithful is encountered in sources of the eleventh and twelfth centuries.

A more detailed enumeration of the different versions in which the formula appears would be without value, for there seems to be hardly any difference in the meaning, and no expansions worth mentioning appear. Every member of the traditional schema has its variants. It is almost astounding that from the midst of this confusion the seemingly oldest wording was finally chosen: in ordinary use with *custodiat animam tuam*, and at the ordination of subdeacon and deacon with the simple *custodiat te*.

14. The Communion Chant

It is so natural that the distribution of Communion should be accompanied by song, particularly when a large crowd is to receive and the divine service is somewhat solemn, that even in our own day, when the original Communion chant no longer seems sufficient, other substitutes are pressed into use. Among the three ancient *schola* songs of the Roman Mass, introit, offertory and communion, *the oldest without doubt is the communion.*

We first come upon a Communion song in the liturgies of the fourth century. Here it appears at first as a responsorial song, hence one in which the people responded in the ancient Christian manner of congregational singing, answering verse for verse, with an unchanging refrain, as the precentor chanted a psalm. At least Chrysostom mentions that the "confirmed"—he is therefore treating about the very core of the eucharistic celebration—responded constantly with the verse "The eyes of all look hopefully to Thee and Thou givest them their food in due time." Evidently Psalm 144 was being sung. A similar participation of the people was presupposed for Psalm 33, since Jerome remarks: "Each day when we are filled with the heavenly bread, we say, 'Taste and see how sweet the Lord is.' "

We meet with this Psalm 33 as a Communion song almost everywhere in ancient Christendom. There is evidence of the use either of the whole psalm, or of the ninth verse already cited, as in the Liturgy of Jerusalem and other places, or else of the sixth verse, with which Augustine repeatedly directs the faithful to the table of the Lord. In various forms, or in combination with the other psalms or with hymns, we encounter these two psalm verses in future times among the Communion songs of the West, just as Psalm 33 is also found at different parts of the Mass in the Orient.

In a special version this psalm survives in the Mozarabic liturgy, where the so-called *antiphona ad accedentes*, used during the greater part of the year, reads as follows:

> "Taste and see how sweet the Lord is,
> alleluia, alleluia, alleluia.
> I shall bless the Lord at all times,
> Always shall His praise be upon my lips,
> alleluia, alleluia, alleluia.
> The Lord shall save the souls of His
> servants and He will not abandon all who
> trust in Him, alleluia, alleluia, alleluia.
> Glory and honor to the Father, and the
> Son, and the Holy Spirit for ever and
> ever. Amen. Alleluia . . . ."

The pendent *Alleluia* at the end of every verse is evidently the response with which the faithful were accustomed to answer. The oriental liturgies also show traces of this responsorial use of the *alleluia* in their *Communion* songs; this is especially plain in the Armenian rite which also uses the alleluiatic Psalm 148, and in the Coptic which employs the alleluiatic Psalm 150.

So, whereas in the ancient period the communicants themselves as a rule took part in this song, we find in the later sources immediately available of both Eastern and Western liturgies, that this Communion song or one of the Communion songs was turned over to the choir. Hand in hand with this, we find, besides the enriching of the melodies, an increased use of other texts; among others they used hymns of their own composition.

FURTHER DEVELOPMENT

The Roman liturgy at first clung to the chanting of psalms, but in such a way that the Communion psalm changed according to the ecclesiastical year. As the first Roman *ordo* prescribed, the *schola* was to intone the *antiphona ad communionem* as soon as the pope began to distribute Communion in the *senatorium*. Then came the psalmody until all the people had communicated. When the archdeacon saw that nearly everyone had received, he gave the *schola* a sign for the *Gloria Patri*, after which the verse was again repeated. The communion was therefore an antiphonal song of the *schola cantorum* similar to the introit, consisting of a psalm sung alternately by two semi-choruses, and with a pre-verse which was repeated at the end.

The introduction of this antiphonal manner of singing at the Communion, as at the offertory, took place in North Africa in St. Augustine's time, and could not have been much later in Rome. The absence of the Communion song on Holy Saturday recalls the time before the introduction of the chant.

Whereas at the offertory the responsorial form replaced the antiphonal, at the Communion the antiphonal manner of singing continued unchanged for centuries. It was thought important that the song should actually accompany the distribution of Communion. A Carolingian explanation of the Mass remarks that during the Communion "soft melody should touch the ear [of the faithful] so that hearing this sound they would busy themselves less with distracting thoughts and . . . their hearts would be moved to humble love for that which they receive." The oldest manuscripts of the Mass song-book, which belong to the eighth-ninth century, give us the same picture for the communion as for the introit: the antiphon (the same which today forms the entire communion in the Roman Missal) is intoned; thereupon follow the initial words of the psalm, or else, in those many cases in which the introit psalm is simply to be repeated, the remark: *Psalm. ut supra*.

In a few scattered Frankish manuscripts we find something similar to what we discovered in regard to the introit, namely, a second psalm verse, under the heading *Ad repet.*, the function of which has hitherto been a riddle. But the riddle is solved if we hark back to the *trecanum*, the Communion song of the Gallican liturgy. Here we have what proves to be a remnant from the Gallican liturgy, so strongly Trinitarian in character, where, in the interweaving of antiphon, psalm verse and *Gloria Patri*, this extra verse served to round out the picture of the circumincession of the three divine Persons.

Other expansions of the *communio* also put in an appearance, especially by the repetition of the antiphon. Apropos of this, it seems that during the ninth century the subdeacons formed a sort of counter-choir to the *schola* of chanters. And then, according to Carolingian prescription, all the people were to join in at the *Gloria Patri*.

Although the development of the Communion song thus ran parallel in part to the introit, yet, in contrast to the latter, the psalm began to be dropped very soon. The psalm begins to be missed in the manuscripts during the tenth century, and by the twelfth century it is found only very seldom. The remarks of the exponents of the liturgy correspond; Bernold of Constance still mentions the addition of the psalm with the *Gloria Patri* but with the quiet limitation, "if it should be necessary." The embellishment by tropes which started in the tenth century, fell into decay even before it could be properly developed. When we take into consideration the ability of liturgical creations to survive, then this phenomenon more or less matches the fact that in the Carolingian reform, which faithfully copied the practices of the city of Rome, Sunday Communion was once again on the increase, but when this slowed down the grounds for a Communion song also crumbled. All that remained was the antiphon, which in the thirteenth century gets the name *communio*.

In reality the Communion chant should ordinarily have been dropped, since it was meant to accompany the Communion of the people, not that of the priest. Thus it was not incorrect to regard the *communio* as more or less a symbol of the Communion of the people, which should have taken place, and therefore to put it after the Communion of the priest. But then a further step was taken, and it was looked upon as a thanksgiving "after the saving food"; it was even called *antiphona post communionem*, or simply *postcommunio*. Finally came a new development when, even if Communion was distributed to the faithful, the Communion song was not intoned till after the Communion was over, just as is generally done with the Communion verse in our own day.

Meanwhile the *Agnus Dei* had become the real Communion song. This held true at least for the Communion of the priest, to which, during the high Middle Ages, the extra distribution of Communion could be added without much of a pause being necessary. But on great Communion days other songs were soon added, excepting always Good Friday and Holy Saturday, when Communion was received in profound silence. Thus, towards the end of the ninth century there appears in the Pontifical of Poitiers for Easter Sunday a festive antiphon with the heading: *Ante communionem*, which was in use on such occasions during the entire Middle Ages and beyond, especially in many French churches.

In other places, *a part of the choir Office* was inserted. In the Cathedral of Soissons around 1130 the canons sang Sext on Easter Sunday during the Communion of the faithful. In a Hungarian cathedral of the eleventh-twelfth century of this same day it was Vespers that was said, and care was taken that its close would coincide with the *Ite missa est* of the deacon. According to John of Avranches (d. 1097) Vespers was to be inserted on Holy Thursday during the Communion, since its closing oration was identical with the post-communion.[1] Other songs, psalms, hymns or antiphons which seemed suitable were also used, either according to strict regulation or according to choice, which is in line with our present-day practice, even aside from the fact that even on festive occasions the greater proportion of Communions are given at the early Masses, which are *missæ lectæ* where Communion songs even in the vernacular can be freely developed.

On the other hand, the Communion verse became solidly anchored in the Roman Mass by the practice of having the priest read it from the missal. This custom was already to be found long ago at private Masses even though for a long time it was not universal. For the Mass celebrated with chant it seems not to have become very common until quite late, since the corresponding direction is still missing in most of the Mass plans even of the late Middle Ages.

Even if the Communion song as it stands in the Roman Missal is but a tiny part of what was originally intended, it must be stated that even the original plan of this song in the Roman Mass represented the result of an evolution that was markedly peripheral. The principle of psalmody was kept, but there was no tendency to prefer one of the Communion psalms, or even the "praise" and alleluia psalms.

There was no intention to establish at this point a Communion song in the narrower sense, but instead, much as in the case of the other songs in the Roman Mass, to set up an ecclesiastical song of a general character which could present the festal thoughts as the occasion demanded. From all this it can be seen how far the Roman Mass was from evolving a special Communion devotion.

Even in regard to the prayers in the part of the Mass around Communion, we have already shown that the early medieval Roman Mass *ordo*, in comparison with other liturgies, displayed the utmost poverty.

So when we consider only the Communion antiphons of the present time we find that on the Sundays after Pentecost verses are simply taken from the psalms in order of the psalter, from Psalm 9 to 118. On the ferias of Quadragesima, if we except the later formulas of Thursday, Psalms 1 to 26 are used in regular progression from Ash Wednesday to Palm Sunday.

[1] In the rubrics for the restored Easter Vigil an abbreviated form of Lauds is inserted in the Mass after Communion.

If the antiphon was taken from the Book of Psalms, then the corresponding psalm followed. In the other cases, the psalm used was the introit psalm, which could have but little relevance to Communion. However, for festive seasons and on feast days some reference to the thought of the day was sought. This draws closer again to the ideas connected with Communion. Thus, on the Sundays after Easter, we can listen to our Lord challenging Thomas: "Bring thy hand and find the place of the nails," or the call of the Good Shepherd. In Advent we can hear the prophet's cry: "Behold the Lord shall come and all His holy ones with Him." And besides, even our missal contains a small number of Mass formularies whose creators obviously had in mind to give a more eucharistic touch to the Communion verse. We refer to the Masses for the Thursdays of Lent, which originated in the eighth century. For the second and third Thursdays phrases are taken from our Lord's promise of the Eucharist (John 6:52; 6:57); according to one tradition these verses were linked with the Communion Psalm 33.

15. *Silent Prayer after the Reception*

After the priest has received and distributed Communion, several actions in the interest of good order still remain, especially the ablutions, which he again accompanies with silent prayer. In the very nature of things this prayer is not concerned with the performance of the actions, in themselves of no importance, but with that which has just happened, namely the Holy Communion. The prayers are similar both in origin and in character to the preceding prayers that prepared for and accompanied the Communion. And here again we discover that originally these prayers were intended for the faithful as well as for the priest; both found nourishment for their personal devotion from the same source.

QUOD ORE SUMPSIMUS

The first prayer, *Quod ore sumpsimus*, which is found already in the oldest sacramentaries, we also encounter in the prayer book of Charles the Bald, where it bears the superscription: *Oratio post communionem;* this version reads: "What I have received with my mouth, O Lord, may I take into my heart, that the Body and Blood of Our Lord Jesus Christ may serve me as an eternal healing." Later on, we find it as the prayer for communicating clerics. Since it is evident that this prayer is spoken by the priest not with a loud voice, but softly, it is to be considered here as his personal prayer, as a private prayer coming before the *post-communio*. We find it in the majority of medieval Mass plans, as a rule in the plural form of the original text, and not seldom also with the closing formula, *Per Christum D. n.*, which has been dropped from the text of the Roman Missal. In a twofold antithesis the plea is made that the internal efficacy of the Sacrament might tally with this sacramental reception in time.

CORPUS TUUM DOMINE

Our second prayer after Communion, namely, the *Corpus tuum Domine*, which (in keeping with its origin in the Gallic liturgy) displays a somewhat different character, also served for the private devotion of the faithful. It is found in the "Communion Devotions of Monte Cassino" at the end of the eleventh century. It also appears as early as the tenth century as a fixed part of many Mass arrangements, and, in contrast to the other formula we considered above, it appears here in the singular, the very trait of private prayer. Among the earliest witnesses is, significantly, a Mass *ordo* from nearby Subiaco, to which we can add other Benedictine *Ordines* and also others from Italy, especially the Franciscan Missal which was to be decisive for the later development. This prayer also gained a wide though not general acceptance elsewhere. In France, even the original plural form was retained for some time, partly in conjunction with a different version of the second part, going back perhaps to a Mozarabic origin. Frequently this prayer also showed other more or less marked expansions or variations. Sometimes, too, instead of the Gallican mode of address to Christ, it had the ordinary form of address, "May the Body of Our Lord Jesus Christ which I have received . . . ," so that the "Through Christ" could also be added at the close. But such changes did not become common.

In regard to its contents, this prayer goes a step beyond the preceding one. It does not feature the contrast between the outer sign and the inner efficacy; instead, the Sacrament Itself appears almost as the grace: through that which It contains, It is so pure and so holy that in a certain sense It need only remain in us in order to push aside and burn up all stain of sin.

Besides these two formulas, which were seldom found together in earlier times, and even then not often in the order they have today, a great number of other prayers and texts on which the priest could nourish his devotion after the reception of the Sacrament were current during the Middle Ages. We have remarked before that the prayers *Domine Jesu Christe Fili* and *Perceptio*, which precede the reception and which in another manner beg for the efficacy of the Sacrament, frequently also had a place after the reception.

OTHER FORMULAS

Frequently other formulas of the post-communion type, or even actual post-communion texts were used. The Mass *ordo* of a Parisian manuscript has as many as thirteen orations following Communion.

Here we must also reckon the *Agimus tibi gratias* that appears occasionally during the late Middle Ages. Even earlier a *Gratias tibi ago*, one of the treasures of private prayer, was widespread. Its apparently original form is found in the Missal of Remiremont in the twelfth century. It runs as follows:

> I give Thee thanks, Lord, God the Father almighty, who hast deigned to fill me a sinner with the Body and Blood of Our Lord Jesus Christ. And I beg Thee that this Holy Communion work in me as a weapon of faith, as a shield of good will to repel all the snares of the devil from my heart and my work. And grant that it may cleanse me that I may enter in where there is the True Light and the Joy of the Just.

That this version goes back to even earlier days is seen from the fact that the "Communion Devotions of Monte Cassino," dating back to the eleventh century, present a form of the prayer more than twice this length, and this, in turn, after further expansions, found its way into our missal in the section *Gratiarum actio post missam* under the title *Oratio S. Thomæ Aquinatis*.

In many instances during the Middle Ages a prayer such as these was followed by the canticle *Nunc dimittis* as a further expression of joyful thanks. Without doubt it fits the occasion perfectly. It is also used in the Byzantine liturgy as part of the conclusion of Mass. With a remarkable feeling for form, the *Kyrie* and *Pater noster* were used to bridge the passage from the *Gloria Patri* at the end of the canticle to the post-communion which was used as a conclusion, or else a special concluding oration was added. With the latter, this complex of prayers belongs to a Communion devotion dating back, seemingly, at least, to the twelfth century.

In the same spirit of tarrying meditatively over the great mystery of divine condescension, we often find in the same place the sentence from St. John, "The Word was made flesh and dwelt among us," or the antiphon *O sacrum convivium*, to which Swedish missals add the versicle *Panem de cælo* and the oration of the Blessed Sacrament. More frequently the Marian encomium, "Thou, Daughter, hast been blessed by the Lord, for through thee we have partaken of the Fruit of Life" appears, or else a passage from the Passion of St. Agnes. Other texts appear only occasionally.

The prayers which thus serve to nourish and support the devotion of the priest after the reception of Communion as a rule coincide, in whole or in part, with the movements the priest makes while cleansing and arranging the vessels which have come in contact with the Sacrament. We must now turn our attention to both of these, the reservation and the ablutions.

16. Reservation. Ablutions [1]

It is almost self-evident that some sort of preservation of the Sacrament after the celebration of the Eucharist was necessary from the start, since It had to be on hand for the sick. This preservation was nothing very special in itself, because the faithful were permitted to keep the Body of the Lord in their homes. But the question arose, what should be done when, after the needs of the communicants have been fulfilled, a large portion of the sacred species should be left over. According to the custom of Antioch during the fourth century, the deacons were obliged to take the particles remaining after the Communion of the faithful into the sacristy at once; what happened after that is not mentioned. But from various isolated ordinances of that period we can gather that the case when a large amount of the consecrated gifts remained after the Communion posed quite a problem. The Sahidic ecclesiastical *canones* warned the responsible clerics not to place too much bread and wine on the altar, so that the punishment meted out to the sons of Heli for their disrespect to the sacrifice might not fall upon them. In some places, basing their action on Leviticus 8:32, they burned what was left. In other places it was thought more seemly to bury the remainder in the ground. Seldom was there the possibility of doing what was done at the pilgrim church in Jerusalem, where the remaining particles were used for Communion on the following day. Elsewhere, innocent children were called in on certain days and given the sacred species, or else—a practice that was certainly more natural and obvious—the clerics themselves partook of the remaining particles at the end of the divine service.

Reservation was thought of only for the sake of the sick. The amount of time which seemed admissible for the preservation of the species for this purpose was measured in various ways. It is the Byzantine custom even today to consecrate the Sacrament for the sick for the whole year on Maundy Thursday. This practice was already known to the West

[1] For an interesting discussion of various aspects of the question of reservation, cf. S. van Dijk and J. Walker, *The Myth of the Aumbry*. Notes on Medieval Reservation Practice and Eucharistic Devotion, London (1957).—Rev.

Syrians in the seventh century, and by the year 1000 had also become established in England. In the West, the custom was rapidly overthrown, and was also attacked in the East. Among the Uniate congregations it has long since disappeared. In England about the year 1000 Abbot Aelfric of Eynsham struck at the practice by insisting that the Hosts reserved for the sick must be renewed every week or two, and this regulation was generally retained during the centuries that followed. Among the Carthusians during the thirteenth century the renewal of the species was molded into the structure of the Sunday high Mass, and the same happened in other places also. In Soissons every Sunday at the priest's Communion the deacon was supposed to bring the vessel (containing the Blessed Sacrament) which hung over the altar to the celebrant, who put in a new Host and consumed the old.

All through the Middle Ages reservation was considered only in relation to the sick. Hence, in the pertinent decrees we find mention made of only one or two Hosts. All the rest of the faithful communicated with the priest at Mass and partook of the Hosts which had just been consecrated. The one exception was Good Friday, which was, until near the end of the Middle Ages, a favorite Communion day; following the oriental model, Communion then took place within the *missa præsanctificatorum*, using Hosts consecrated the day before. On other occasions the practice of purposely consecrating and reserving a large number of Hosts for later distribution was unknown all during the Middle Ages.

But even in early times it was unheard of that Communion was distributed after Mass. In the Byzantine Mass of the Greeks this is the ordinary practice. On the other hand, wherever (as in Rome and Gaul) the non-communicants left the church before Communion, there was no reason why, even on great Communion days, the distribution of the Sacrament should not take place within the Mass. This was true at least till the eighth century. But a changed attitude is noticed already in the Carolingian reform. True, it was presumed that the faithful would remain only until after the priestly blessing, but this was now identified with the final prayers of the newly-accepted Roman Mass. The result was soon seen. Not only on occasions here and there, but even on the greater Communion days, Communion was distributed after Mass at least to a great number of communicants. Evidences for such a usage begin to grow more numerous since the twelfth century. In the year 1256 the *Ordinarium* of the Dominicans directs the priest, that in general, when people are present who are waiting for the end of the Mass, the Communion should then be postponed "until after Mass," but this should not be done on Maundy Thursday. Still, Communion remained united with the Mass.

A certain perplexity in regard to the exact time when the faithful were to receive is seen even earlier. Therfore, some exponents of the liturgy insisted that the right moment for it was before the post-communion, because the latter presupposes the Communion of the faithful. Even the Roman Ritual, which first appeared in 1614, proposes the same reason in a pertinent admonition, but then, with a genuine regard for the cure of souls, it leaves room for distributing Communion before or after Mass *ex rationabili causa*.

After the Council of Trent, the tendency to separate the Communion from the Mass moved forward by leaps and bounds, since the appreciation of the liturgical pattern did not keep step with the zeal for the sacramental life. At first, this held true only for Communion on greater feasts and for general Communions, but later it spread to other occasions also, so that by the time the eighteenth century had faded into the nineteenth, Communion outside of Mass had become the general rule. But during our own century a reverse movement has gradually gained ground. Moreover, an increasing number of voices are being heard in favor of using for Communion substantially only those Hosts which were consecrated at the same Mass, so that the connection between sacrifice and repast might again gain its full, natural expression. This aspiration has been heartily praised and encouraged by Pius XII.[1]

ABLUTION RITE

When the Communion is ended and the remaining sacred particles have been reserved there follows what we might designate by the comprehensive term, the ablution rite.

We are accustomed nowadays to think in this connection only of the washing of the fingertips that touched the Body of the Lord, and of the purification of the chalice, which should be freed from the remains of the Precious Blood by twice pouring wine (and water) into it. But even the Roman Missal of the present day designates something else as the first act of this rite when, speaking about the first ablution after Communion, it uses these words: "he purifies himself." [2] The ablution of the mouth is, in fact, the most ancient part of the ablution rite. While for everything else we do not hear of any express prescriptions until much later, we find Chrysostom already advocating, and himself carrying out, the practice of taking a bit of water after Communion, or eating a piece of bread, so that whatever remained of the sacred species might not be ejected from the mouth along with the spittle. This practice was previously unknown in Constantinople, and was one of the charges leveled against the saint. A similar practice is still in vogue amongst the Copts even today; after Communion they take a swallow of water which

---

[1] In the Encyclical *Mediator Dei*, N.C.W.C. Edition, 121–122.
[2] *Ritus serv.*, X, 5; also in the text of the *Ordo missæ*.

they call "the water of covering" because by it the Sacrament will be "covered." In the West, too, the *Regula Magistri* in the same sense permits the reader at table to take a drink of wine before the reading on Communion days "because of the spittle of the sacrament," and the Rule of St. Benedict has a similar ordinance.

Although in the beginning of the Middle Ages the custom was not generally widespread, still it was mentioned repeatedly. Two examples can be cited from the life of Louis the Pious (d. 840), who took a drink immediately after Communion; the first time it was offered him by Alcuin himself, on a pilgrimage in Tours; and the second time on his deathbed. And it was not entirely unknown even in the Roman pontifical liturgy. At Monte Gargano, after the faithful had communicated they were accustomed to drink from a certain well next to the church.

If we thus see greater stress put on this cleansing of the mouth than we would expect, we must remember that before the change from leavened to unleavened bread the Sacred Host had to be chewed.

Nevertheless, the custom continued and, in fact, burgeoned out after the aforementioned change of matter. It is the time when all our ideas about reverence for the Blessed Sacrament were beginning to blossom. In 1165 Beleth favored the custom; he would have liked to see it introduced everywhere, at least at Easter. It had been the practice in monasteries even before this. We come upon a first mention of it in the prescriptions of William of Hirsau (d. 1091). Also among the Cistercians it was customary for the *sacrista* to offer wine to every communicant when he had left the altar after having received Holy Communion under both kinds. We see the same thing being done in other orders after the chalice was no longer received, with the express admonition: "to diligently cleanse the mouth lest any particle of the Host remain between the teeth."

The reason given naturally held good for the priest as well as for the rest of the communicants. But since the thirteenth century the custom of giving the faithful wine after Communion became more and more general. The practice then amalgamated with the last remnants of the practice of the lay chalice in which, in fact, only wine that had been mixed with a little of the Precious Blood or "consecrated" by contact with a particle, was presented. Hence, the transition went in part unnoticed. The new practice was merely an enfeebled continuation of the other. But in some instances the modification was brought to the attention of the faithful.

The reform synods of the sixteenth century often demanded that the drink be given not from a chalice, but from a vessel differently shaped, so as not to occasion any wrong conception. With this special restriction the practice is still found imbedded in the Roman Missal. (*Ritus servandus*, X, 6.) For the same reason, the vessel was not to be presented by the priest. To keep the custom intact and to ensure themselves that there was sufficient wine ready for the feast days, many foundations were established for this purpose almost everywhere towards the end of the Middle Ages and the beginning of the modern era. Even today there are survivals of this last reminiscence of the communion chalice, which in turn had absorbed the old custom of the ablution of the mouth.

As at the ablution of the mouth, or the purification, so even more at what we call the ablution in a narrower sense, namely, the cleansing of the chalice and the fingertips that have come in contact with the Body of the Lord, the earliest standard set was the feeling of the individual liturgus. Whatever was thought proper was done as a rule after divine service, as is usually the case in the oriental rites even today. First of all, there is the cleansing of the chalice. The older Roman *Ordines* do not as yet contain any special provisions in this regard. It is not till the ninth and tenth centuries that we find any express directions about this in the West. The purification of the chalice was handed over to the deacon or the subdeacon, if they were present; otherwise, the priest himself had to take over the task. There must have been a special place in the sacristy or next to the altar where the water used for this purpose was poured out.

Here mention is still made only of water, but we find that even in the eleventh century monastic prescriptions called for wine for the purification. It was considered praiseworthy to wash the vessel not only once, but three times, as was customary amongst the Premonstratensians, and as is particularly recorded about Blessed Herman Joseph (d. 1241).

Later, the purification of the chalice was combined with the purification of the tips of the fingers. Seldom is there mention of a special purification of the paten. A washing of the fingers after the sacrifice is already mentioned in the life of Bishop Bonitus of Clermont (d. 709), of whom it is related that the sick made efforts to obtain some of this ablution water. The same is recounted about a certain monk from Monte Cassino around the year 1050. The first Roman *Ordo* also speaks of the washing of the hands of the pope as soon as all had communicated. Similarly, in the tenth century in the sixth Roman *Ordo*, which was intended primarily for Germany. This is nothing else than the hand-washing which is still customary in the pontifical rite, but which at that time and in many places, even as late as the twelfth and thirteenth centuries, was considered a sufficient ablution; the only direction stressed in regard to it was that the water was to be poured out in some fitting place. Meanwhile, however, especially in monasteries, even greater care was exercised in regard to this ablution. The fingers were first cleansed with wine, using either another chalice or else the Mass chalice. After this, the fingers were washed with water at the *piscina* set up near the altar, or in some other manner, and then were dried. Only then was the ablution wine taken from the chalice. Thereafter, wine was again poured into the chalice, *i.e.*, the Mass chalice for certain, and then drunk.

A special ablution of the mouth, consequently, became superfluous, since it was bound up with the ablution of the chalice. While, as we have said, it was thought satisfactory in some places to use only wine to cleanse the chalice, it was generally considered necessary, for obvious reasons, to use water too, at least for the fingers, and thus to adhere to the traditional method of washing the hands. The *Ordinarium* of the Dominicans, introduced in 1256, contains for the first time, at least for the occasion when no *piscina* was to be had, the advice to wash the fingers with water over the chalice, and then to drink this water along with the wine that had been previously used for cleansing the fingers. This manner of procedure was propagated only gradually, but finally became normal. In the pontifical *ritus* of today it has been added to the ancient manner of washing the hands.

However, until the very end of the Middle Ages there was no uniform practice in these matters. According to Gabriel Biel, for instance, it was left to the choice of the priest to have the ablution of the fingers either right after the Communion or only after Mass. On the other hand, English Mass books of that same period gave very careful and circumstantial rules in this regard, although varying in details.

A custom had been spread in Germany since the fourteenth century which reminds us of the blessing of the senses with the Eucharist which had been in vogue a thousand years earlier. After the ablution of the fingers, the eyes were touched, and these words uttered: "The Lord made clay from spittle and spread it over my eyes, and I went and washed, and I saw and believed in God." It was a custom which could easily have led to superstition and abuse, but it later disappeared.

Special prayers were not generally composed for the ablution. The prayers which today accompany the ablution are (as we see from their history) only outwardly connected with it.

It is remarkable that the oriental rites—even those outside the union—in spite of their greater indifference in regard to the care of the Blessed Sacrament, have also come to have a special ablution rite which, at least in some points, is quite close to our western one. Amongst the Syrians as early as the sixth century we find an ordinance which demands that the water used in purifying the sacred vessels should be poured out in a decent place. Amongst the West-Syrian Jacobites the rite of ablution is even more detailed and framed with many prayers, and includes, besides the washing of the vessels, a repeated ablution of the fingers and a wiping of the chalice with a sponge. A sponge is also one of the appurtenances of the Byzantine liturgy. The Copts also have several traditional ablutions.

17. *The Post-Communion*

Even the earliest expositions of the liturgy, after speaking about the Communion to which all the faithful are invited, do not forget to admonish them to make a thanksgiving. Basing himself on Timothy 2:1, Augustine distinguishes four sections of the Mass; as the last of these he places the *gratiarum actio*, the thanksgiving after Communion. Chrysostom thrusts sharply at those who cannot wait for the thanksgiving canticles, but, like Judas, hurry away instead of singing a hymn of praise with the Lord and His true disciples.

THANKSGIVING IN COMMON

There is question, first of all, of a thanksgiving said in common in the church—that is what we must naturally expect. We find this in early times in the liturgies of the Orient, and regularly as follows: after a prayer of thanksgiving, generally composed of several members, another such prayer of blessing follows, whereupon the faithful are dismissed. Sometimes the hymns accompanying the Communion are so prolonged that they seem to be the first part of the thanksgiving. Before the actual prayer of thanksgiving, according to the *Apostolic Constitutions*, the deacon invites the faithful to prayer: "After we have received the Precious Body and the Precious Blood of Christ, we want to give thanks to Him who has made us worthy to partake of these sacred mysteries, and we wish to plead that it shall not redound to our fault but to our salvation, to the weal of soul and body, to the preservation of piety, to the remission of sin, to life everlasting." At this, all arise and the bishop recites a comprehensive prayer in which thanksgiving merges into a renewed plea for all the intentions of the congregation and for all classes and ranks of the Church. Similarly, this call to prayer by the deacon recurs later on also, but in other places it has developed in various ways. In the Greek Liturgy of St. James it begins with a solemn praise of Christ, and then, as in all Greek liturgies, it unfolds into a short litany to which the people respond in the usual manner with *Kyrie eleison*. In the Ethiopian Mass, after the deacon's call to prayer, there is an exchange of prayers between priest and people, in which the latter reply three times to the priest's recitation of Psalm 144: 1, 2, 21: "Our Father who art in heaven, lead us not into temptation." In all cases, the close is essentially formed by the thanksgiving prayer of the celebrant of which —in the Greek liturgies at any rate—only the closing doxology is now spoken in a loud voice and in the Byzantine liturgy this doxology is all that has survived. On the other hand, the priest's prayer of thanksgiving in the West-Syrian Mass is assimilated to the eucharistic prayer by tak-

ing up and amplifying the introductory formula: "It is worthy and right
and meet . . . ." In the Gallican liturgy, too, the thanksgiving consists
of a lengthy call to prayer, and the priestly oration.

Here again the Roman liturgy is distinguished by the special scanti-
ness of its prayer language. Originally it also had a double close consisting of a prayer of thanksgiving and a prayer of blessing. This prayer of
thanksgiving, usually captioned *Ad complendum* or *Ad completa* in the
Gregorian Sacramentaries, and *Post communionem* in the Gelasian, with
its ever-varying formulas belongs to the very substance of the Roman
Sacramentary, just like the collect and the *secreta*. The post-communion
is also formed exactly like them. And hence, like them, it displays the
outlines of a prayer of petition. Like them, in its older forms it turns
without exception to God through Christ, and so closes with the formula, *Per Dominum*, which in many medieval churches gained special
stressing at this point by being recited in the middle of the altar.

The parallelism of the post-communion to the two earlier orations is
broadened by reason of the surroundings in which it appears. The opening, the offertory and the communion represent three liturgical structures of closely corresponding patterns. In each case there is outward
activity united with a certain local movement: the entrance, the offertory procession and the march to the Communion. In each case—and
originally only at these three points—the choir of singers is busied with
the antiphonal singing of the palms. In each case—and again almost only
here—there is an introductory series of silent prayers with which the
celebrant nurtures his devotion. So again, in each case the singing and
the praying come to a close with an oration which is preceded, mediately or immediately, by the liturgical greeting and the *Oremus*. And
the oration itself has been formed according to the same stylistic rules.

In this instance the *Dominus vobiscum* and the *Oremus* immediately
precede the prayer, for although the entire Communion cycle must be
hidden in an atmosphere of prayer, even prayer of the faithful, yet the
prayer here demanded is not a prayer of public and ecclesiastical character as in the *oratio communis* which is united with the offertory. How
close a bond was judged to exist between the *post-communio* and the
Communion cycle (and hence with the Sacrifice-Mass) can be seen
from the fact that, as the later versions of the Roman *Ordo* note, the
pope did not turn to the people at the *Dominus vobiscum* but stood
before the altar facing East, the same attitude he assumes at the beginning of the preface when he is not to turn away any more from the
gifts of sacrifice on the altar. This prescription, however, was not retained for any length of time, since it had to be conceded that the sacrifice had already been completed. But for the same reason the *Flectamus
genua* was never said before this oration, for surely it belongs at least
to the culmination of the prayers grouped about the Eucharist.

THEME OF THE POST-COMMUNION

Considering the contents, the theme of the *post-communio* is given by the communion just finished; and it is *always the Communion of the assembled congregation that is thought of, not that of the priest alone.* This rule of form was followed even in those formulas that go back only to the times when a congregational Communion was exceptional.

Relatively few formulas appear which have no connection with the Communion and present merely an oration of a more general character—a consideration of the celebration of the day or some special needs. The rule is that the prayer begin with a grateful glance at the gifts received. The reception of the sacrament is represented either as an item in the delineation of the petitioner: "Filled with heavenly food and drink," or as a starting-point of the effect prayed for: "May this Communion cleanse us, Through the working of this mystery"; or else it is simply represented as a fact, either in the ablative form, or as an independent clause or else it is worked into the course of thought in some other way.

If we combine all the various details in these approaches to the mention of the Sacrament, we acquire an excellent picture of Christian revelation regarding the Eucharist and Communion. What we have received is called a holy gift, a heavenly banquet, spiritual nourishment, an efficacious mystery, the Holy Body and Precious Blood. Just as in the preceding prayers of the Roman Mass, the Person of our Lord is not brought to the fore as such, wherefore there is no special impetus here to address ourselves to Christ directly. The picture that is constantly presented is a picture of the sacrifice as a whole, the sacrifice that we have offered to God along with Christ, the sacrifice in which we take part, and the petition which we direct to the Father "through Our Lord." It is the same way of looking at the Sacrament which in our own day is at the bottom of the admonition in the Roman Ritual when it advises the faithful to remain in prayer for some time after Communion, "giving thanks to God for such a singular gift." As a matter of fact, our thanks to God is best expressed in such a manner, even though the word "thanks" itself seldom appears, for in such words we "think of" that which God has granted.

Next, to give the picture that distinctive mark which it gets by pointing to the sacramental effects of Communion, the wording of the post-communion shifts to the petition. What we expect and implore from our partaking of the Body and Blood of Christ is the progress and final triumph of its redemptive efficacy in us: "that that which we carry out in holy devotion, we may have as certain redemption, that we may be numbered among His members Whose Body and Blood we have received." As part of this, deliverance from both internal and external obstacles enters in: "and may we be cleansed from our hidden faults and be freed from the snares of our enemies." Our bodily welfare is also mentioned time and again in the constant recurrence of the antithesis of body and soul, present and future, internal and external. But the essential effect is inward. The Sacrament must not only heal and strengthen us; it must above all increase love in our hearts, as it is the Sacrament of fellowship: "that those whom Thou hast filled with one heavenly Bread may be of one heart according to Thy holiness." We know, however, that our own free effort is co-decisive in this matter. Hence, looking at the Sacrament, we entreat "that Thou wouldst grant to those whom Thou hast refreshed with Thy Sacraments, that they may serve Thee worthily with a life well pleasing to Thee." An ideal of Christian living flashes out when, after the reception of the Sacrament, we ask that we may never slip away from it: "that we may always live in our sharing in it," and that we may always remain grateful for it. The final fruit, however, that this Sacrament must give us is life eternal, as our Lord Himself has promised. What occurs at the altar remains in the world of symbol and sacrament, but we desire the full actuality: "that we who carry out its cult may enjoy its effect." What we have received was grand, but it was only a pledge and first payment; boldly we desire "that we may receive still greater blessings." Apropos of this, it is most generally the thought of the feast which determines what special effect is emphasized in our petition. Sometimes, too, expression is given to our consciousness that the sacrament is not the only source of grace, that faith and the profession of faith also enter in and should lead us to salvation. On the feasts of saints the plea is generally changed only insofar as the effect of grace is petitioned, but there also the intercession of the saint sometimes appears alongside the efficacy of the Sacrament.

In Rome it seems that for a short time the constant variation of the post-communion was given up. The fourth Roman *ordo* has the pope after the Communion chant recite with a loud voice, *Dominus vobiscum*, and then the one oration, *Quod ore sumpsimus*, which in Rome at that time was not yet one of the private Communion prayers. In its double progression, from the food of the body to that of the spirit, and from the gift in time to the remedy which is effective in eternity, this formula in typical fashion marks the upward progress which we ought to bring to completion on the strength of this Sacrament.

IV. CLOSE OF THE MASS

1. *The* Oratio super Populum

With the prayer of the thanksgiving after communion the service comes to an end and the assembly can disperse. However, the ancients with their sense of form and order could not have been satisfied for very long with a formless dispersal. Hence a certain procedure took shape. In addition there was a second, still stronger influence and that was the consciousness of the Christian communities of their fellowship, tied together in Christ and united anew precisely at the divine service. Even though they separated, they were still bound to one another by means of those spiritual influences which were alive in the Church. We need not be surprised, then, that they wished to see these influences again become operative before their leaving one another. To the formal declaration of the close of the service, therefore, was united a last blessing, with which the Church sent her children out into the world. In the course of centuries this blessing took on various forms, dwindled away and was built up anew, was doubled and tripled, shifted over into the final thanksgivings and petitions which then ended up in private prayer. And so at the end of Mass there was once again a development of various forms, and it is these we want to consider more closely.

PRAYER OF BLESSING

The first closing act we come upon is a prayer of blessing by which the celebrating priest calls down God's help and protection upon the people as they go back to their work. A remnant of this is seen in the *oratio super populum* during Lent. This prayer, generally described as a prayer of inclination (or bowing), is an exact parallel to those prayers at the end of the fore-Mass which we found variously used to bless those who had to leave the divine service after listening to the readings. As in that case, so here also the prayer is preceded by a call from the deacon admonishing the people to bow before the Lord to receive the blessing. Then follows the prayer of the celebrant in the form of an oration which is answered with *Amen.* In this shape the prayer appears as a fixed part of the Mass in the ancient Roman liturgy as well as in the Egyptian and Syrian liturgies of the Orient; and since we find it in the earliest sources for these liturgies, as also in other sources of the fourth century, we can conclude that the tradition goes back at least to the third century.

In Egypt, the admonition of the deacon is exactly the same cry as in our Roman liturgy: *Humiliate capita vestra Deo* "Bow your heads to God." In the Orient the prayer is most generally much developed. In the West-Syrian liturgy every anaphora has its own blessing prayer. In the oldest one, the anaphora of St. James, we read: "God, great and wonderful, look down upon Thy servants who have bowed their necks before Thee, stretch out Thy strong hand filled with blessings and bless Thy people, protect Thy inheritance, so that we may praise Thee now and forevermore . . . ." It is characteristic of this blessing that the personal object is not designated as "us," as if the celebrant includes himself, but instead it is "Thy servants," "Thy people," *populus tuus, ecclesia tua, familia, tua*, etc. This stylistic law has been observed almost without exception in the corresponding formulas of the Leonianum, while in the Gregorianum, to which the *Super populum* formulas of the Roman Missal go back, the law governs only a portion of the prayers. A further distinction of the prayer with which the faithful were dismissed lies in this, that the gifts petitioned—protection in peril, spiritual and corporal welfare, preservation from sin—were all implored not as in other orations, in a general way, but for the whole indefinite future: *semper, iugiter, perpetua protectione*, etc., much as we conclude the formula of blessing which we have at present: *Benedictio . . . descendat super vos et maneat semper*. That temporal wants are not seldom given mention here is understandable, considering the place these prayers occupy, the frontier between the Church and the world. However, in the formulas of the Gelasian Sacramentaries, in contrast to those in the Leonianum, a certain spiritualization of the petitions has taken place. How highly the Roman people valued this blessing can be seen from an event in the year 538. Pope Vigilius had conducted the stational service on the feast of St. Cecilia in the church of that saint and had just given out Communion; then suddenly an envoy of the emperor arrived to take the pope into custody and lead him to Byzantium. The people followed him to the ship and demanded "that they might receive the prayer from him." The pope recited the oration, all the people answered *Amen*, and the ship got under way.

One thing that seems strange about the *oratio super populum* which is still retained today is that it is only to be found in the Lenten season. That was exactly the case already in the Mass book of Gregory the Great, whereas in the Leonianum it is found in every formulary of the Mass, and in the Gelasian books it is at least scattered throughout the year. Beginning with Amalar and down to our own time there have been various attempts to explain why the *oratio super populum* is confined to Lent: Quadragesima was said to be a time of greater spiritual combat, which therefore required more blessings; this oration of blessing was a substitute for Communion (for one was expected to receive daily at least in this season), a prayer dedicated to the non-communicants; or a substitute for the *eulogiæ* which one received at other times, or the oration was originally used only as the oration at Vespers and not till later on was it taken into the Mass, which in Lent was celebrated after Vespers. Finally an important fact is noted, a fact we have already verified elsewhere in the history of the liturgy, that especially in Lent an older tradition still continues to survive.

This point without question deserves consideration. It is possible that the old blessing of the people, the *oratio super populum* as it is still called at present, could have been preserved in Quadragesima just as a series of venerable customs have been retained in the last days of Holy Week. But it will still be a mystery why the most celebrated days of Lent, the Sundays, form an exception, and why the series is broken off already at the Wednesday in Holy Week.

Here it will be necessary to consider the institutions of *public ecclesiastical penance* in the closing years of Christian antiquity. Not long after the end of the fifth century public penance must have been limited at Rome to the time of Quadragesima, in contradistinction to the former system of having it all through the year. Only Sundays, even in Quadragesima, were never regarded as actual days of penance. The end of the time of penance for the penitents was Holy Thursday, the day they were reconciled. The penance therefore embraced those very days to which, in our missal as well as in the Gregorian Sacramentary, an *oratio super populum* is assigned. But if we want to be more exact, we must point out that Quadragesima at the time of Gregory the Great began only with the first Sunday of Lent, so that the time of public penance opened the following Monday. In addition, the Thursdays of Lent and the Saturday before Palm Sunday were aliturgical; that is, they did not as yet have any Mass, and consequently no *oratio super populum*. So if we do not count these days on which the blessing was added only later with the further development of Quadragesima, we find that the *oratio super populum* on the remaining days in the Sacramentary of Gregory the Great displays two peculiarities. In comparison with the older sacramentaries it consists of entirely new formulas, evidence therefore of a reorganization. And in no case—as occasionally happened otherwise—does it presuppose a Communion on the part of the recipients of the blessing, which is again understandable if we keep the penitents above all in mind. But another circumstance forces us to come to the same conclusion. The history of penance shows not only that in Rome, just as elsewhere in the closing years of Christian antiquity, there was an *ordo pænitentium*, but also that the penitents during their time of penance were obliged to receive regularly the blessing of their bishop—of which there is no trace in the rich liturgical sources if the *oratio super populum* is not regarded as such. All this forces us to the conclusion that Gregory the Great, in the new arrangement of the *oratio super populum* seen in his Sacramentary, took into account the conditions of the penitential discipline. During the year he permitted the oration of blessing to be dropped; it had already been missing sporadically in the Gelasian formularies, without any clear principle apparent for its use or non-use. But during Quadragesima he retained it, since during that time the penitents at least were obliged to receive a blessing on each occasion. True, the *oratio super populum* was still what the name implied, a blessing of all the people, who were to spend these forty days, especially in that age of constant and dire need, as a time of penance and prayer, and the words of this blessing and petition remained, as before, broad and general, embracing all temporal and spiritual wants; but the core of the penitential assembly was formed by the public sinners, who perhaps at that time had still to step forward at the call of the deacon, kneel, and receive the imposition of hands, then remain in deep prostration with the rest of the faithful while the pope pronounced the oration of blessing.

However, this function of the *oratio super populum* in the discipline of penance seems not to have been continued for long. Among those formulas which were entered in the Gregorianum in the seventh and eighth centuries we again find, as already remarked, those which speak of the Communion of the recipients of the blessing. The Frankish commentators make absolutely no mention about any relation to public penance, wherefore even its limitation to the Lenten season was in some instances broken through. And it could not be otherwise, because the Gregorian Sacramentary—which was originally intended for the pontifical service, where alone the blessing of the penitents came into question—was now used in the ordinary divine service. Since then the *oratio super populum* has again become simply an oration of blessing which is kept during the holy season of Lent as a piece of ancient tradition. Soon, in fact, it was not even regarded as a blessing at all, since no one except the celebrant paid any attention to the admonition to bow the head. So when a missal from Huesca in 1505, although not daring to suppress the oration, did however direct that it be said *submissa voce*, thus relegating it to a secondary position, we cannot quarrel about the consistency of such a measure.

2. The Dismissal

Just as at the close of the fore-Mass, once the prayer of blessing had been said over those who were told to leave, there follows (at least according to some of the sources) a formal dismissal, so all the more there probably must always have been such a dismissal at the end of the entire service. One cannot expect much more than the word with which the one presiding at every well-ordered assembly ordinarily announces the close, especially when the farewell blessing has just preceded. Such announcement of the conclusion was common in ancient culture, at times even using the word *missa*. In Christian usage the corresponding formula often acquired a religious or a biblical cast. In Milan, the invitation to leave was one still used today on certain occasions, "Let us proceed in peace," with the answer of the people, "In Christ's name."

ITE MISSA EST, BENEDICAMUS DOMINO

Our form of dismissal, *Ite missa est*, in contrast to all these is more laconic, but true to the essential genius of the Roman liturgy. While the *Ite* has an exact parallel in the Egyptian liturgy, the *missa est* added thereto is somewhat unique. Here the word *missa* still has its original meaning: dismissal, conclusion. When it was incorporated into the formula, it must have been so widely used with this meaning that it became in particular a technical expression for the conclusion of an assembly, because otherwise a phrase like *finis est* would rather have been employed. The word had this meaning at least as far back as the fourth century, while, on the other hand, this meaning was no longer current even in the early Middle Ages. So even if the first literary evidence for the *Ite missa est* is found in the Roman *ordines*, we will not be blundering if we hold that this formula is as old as the Latin Mass itself. A corroborating argument is found in the fact that similar formulas were prevalent in the everyday social life of the Romans. After a funeral the assembled mourners were dismissed with the word *Ilicet = Ire licet*. According to the bronze tablets of Iguvium (Gubbio in Umbria) from the last century before Christ, the conjoined blessing of the people and cursing of the strangers closed with the cry: *Itote Iguvini*. Other formulas were stipulated for the conclusion of gatherings in political life.

The dismissal in the Roman Mass is given emphasis and at the same time a religious framework by being introduced with the *Dominus vobiscum* and answered by the *Deo gratias* of the people. In substance the *Dominus vobiscum* merely takes the place of the vocative of address which ought otherwise to precede the imperative *Ite*. Even at high Mass this *Dominus vobiscum* is pronounced by the celebrant, so that the deacon appears only as his organ when he announces the dismissal. The *Deo gratias* with which this announcement is answered is an exact parallel to that which the people (according to the liturgical sources of the early Middle Ages) also answered the announcement of the coming feast days. It is therefore only an acknowledgment that the message has been received, but is imbedded in that fundamental Christian sentiment of thanksgiving.

At Rome the *Ite missa est* was originally used at every Mass no matter what its character, and probably also at the end of other services. On the other hand, the *Benedicamus Domino* could have been a concluding formula of the Gallican liturgy. For although there are apparently no signs of it in Roman sources before the year 1000, we find traces of it considerably earlier in Frankish territory. The *Ordo Angilberti*, of about the year 800, in describing the order of Communion on high festivals, mentions that after the completion of Mass, the people left "praising God" and *benedicentes Dominum*. In an *ordo* for the sick from about the same time we read after the giving of Communion: "In the end, after he has said the oration, the priest shall say, *Benedicamus Domino*, and all shall answer, *Deo gratias*. Then it is finished."

In the eleventh century, however, an adjustment was made between these two formulas, such as we have at present: the *Ite missa est* is used whenever there is a *Gloria*; the *Benedicamus Domino* on the other days. But efforts were made to find a deeper reason for this merely outward division. The days with *Ite missa est* are days of a festive character, when the entire populace is assembled, so that the invitation to leave at the end of service has a meaning, while the days with *Benedicamus Domino* are days when only the *religiosi*, the pious whose life is more especially devoted to spiritual service, are present; wherefore the priest, without turning around, urges them, and himself with them, to continue praising God. That this explanation for the present-day arrangement does not reach deep enough is seen from the use of the *Benedicamus Domino*, amongst other times, on the Sundays of Advent and from Septuagesima on. Besides, if people had been so sensitive about the communal character of each celebration, then we would have had to omit many other things, at least at private Mass, for instance, the *Dominus vobiscum*. The *Benedicamus Domino* was as much a formula of departure for the assembled faithful as the *Ite missa est*. Hence, like it, it receives the response *Deo gratias*. But here the dismissal is given a religious turn, just as the acknowledgment of the message receives a religious expression in the *Deo gratias*. However, we must admit that when the lines were drawn for the use of the two formulas, considerations like those referred to above, especially the solemn character of certain festivals, played a part. Also when the divine service was continued, as at the midnight Mass of Christmas, when Lauds followed, or on Maundy Thursday and the vigils of Easter and Pentecost, preference was given to the invitation to praise God, *Benedicamus Domino*. Since the *Ite missa est* was considered an expression of joy, it had to disappear from the Requiem Mass. So we find that since the twelfth century the *Requiescant in pace* begins to supplant it.

When the herald in olden times announced the conclusion of an assembly, he did so with a corresponding raising of his voice. The judge, the official of the state, remembering his dignity, speaks in a moderate tone, but the herald lets his cry resound loudly over the whole assembly. It could not be much different in the case of a dismissal from divine service. As a further step, the *Ite missa est* must soon have been provided with a special singing tone. Already in the tenth century there must have been various melodies which were richly adorned with melismas; for this time also marks the appearance of tropes, the expanding texts which set a syllable to each note of the melody. On the other hand, there seem to have been no tropes for the *Benedicamus Domino* in the Mass.

The *Ite missa est* has kept another sensible expression of its function as a call to the people: just like the greetings, it is pronounced with face turned to the people. Hence this cry has always remained a manifest closing point of the service.

3. Leaving the Altar

In the first Roman *ordo*, when the deacon had sung the *Ite missa est*, the seven torch-bearers and the subdeacon with the censer begin to move and precede the pope to the *secretarium*. The *Ite missa est* was therefore the real conclusion of the Mass. Among the Carthusians even today the priest leaves the altar immediately after these words. There is only a short ceremony, perhaps accidentally omitted from the first Roman *ordo:* the kiss of the altar as a farewell salute, the counterpart of the kiss of greeting at the beginning of Mass.

This or a similar farewell salute is also customary in other liturgies. Amongst the West-Syrian Jacobites we also find the kiss, which is followed by a threefold farewell of highly poetic beauty. It begins: "Remain in peace, holy and divine altar of the Lord. I know not whether I shall return to you again or no. May the Lord grant that I may see you in the church of the First-born in heaven. In this covenant I put my confidence."

In the Roman Mass in the Frankish area an accompanying word was also added to this kiss of the altar, just as was done at the beginning with the kiss of greeting; these are the only kisses of the altar customary at that time. The Sacramentary of Amiens in the ninth century ordains: "When the office (i.e., service) has been finished, the holy altar is kissed with the words: *Placeat tibi sancta Trinitas.*" This prayer, which in the following centuries was used everywhere, although not universally, was of Gallic origin, as is plain from the fact that it is addressed to the Trinity. It is a very natural idea when leaving the table of sacrifice to beg once more for God's gracious glance on that which happened there. Here again the dual meaning of the offering appears: honor to God's majesty, that our actions may find gracious acceptance, and a plea for our own needs and those of others, that they may be graciously heard.

The *Placeat* is the only prayer recited in the middle of the altar after Communion because it is an accompaniment to the act of kissing. Since this is a personal action of the priest, the prayer is kept in the singular. As a counterpart to the *Oramus te Domine* which is attached to the altar kiss at the beginning of Mass and which is likewise a plea for the priest's own person (*peccata mea*), the *Placeat* is also distinguished by the fact that it is recited with a deep bow, the hands resting on the altar, and in a quiet voice. In the Mass books from the eleventh to the thirteenth centuries the *Placeat* is often joined by a second prayer which more clearly shows the relationship to the altar kiss: "By the merits and intercessions of all His saints, may the omnipotent Lord have mercy upon us." This prayer, which as a rule appears only where the kiss of the altar is previously mentioned, obviously parallels the notice of the altar relics in the *Oramus te Domine* at the beginning. Often it was expanded to the form: "By the merits and intercessions of those and all the saints." As a consequence of these additions, the special meaning of the altar kiss as a farewell salute had become somewhat clouded by the end of the Middle Ages.

4. The Closing Blessing of the Priest

At present when the bishop leaves the cathedral after a pontifical high Mass, he passes through the ranks of the faithful, blessing them while they genuflect to receive his benediction. Something similar took place at the close of the Roman stational service, as recounted in the first Roman *ordo*. When the pope had left the altar after the *Ite missa est*, with the thurifer and the seven torch-bearers going on ahead and accompanied by the deacons, the bishops stepped forward and said, "Grant us a blessing, Sir," whereupon the pope answered, "May the Lord bless us." The same was done by the priests, then by the monks. Next the *schola* approached and intoned the same petition and answered with a loud *Amen*. As the entourage advanced, the noble banner-bearers, the light-carriers, the acolytes who had charge of the doors, the cross-bearers and the other officials of the divine service did the same.

Such a blessing on leaving was a very ancient episcopal practice. In the northern countries, even if it was not always the practice, still it became customary at least upon acceptance of the Roman liturgy. It was first of all the privilege of the bishop. It was in the northern countries precisely that old laws—that the simple priest was not allowed to give the blessing at public service—were not forgotten. The Carolingian legal codes stressed this prescription anew because they wished to protect the superior position of the episcopate. But, besides this, a second interpretation was abroad and already partly anchored even in the *canones;* this, too, denied the priest the right to bless even at the final blessing of the Mass, but only if a bishop were present. Accordingly, in the Gallican Mass of the seventh century, there was a practice of a closing priestly blessing after the *Pater noster.*

It was but natural that the defenders of the Gallican tradition and the rights (there included) of the priest should not want to abandon this right of the priest to bless, especially since it was possible as always, to rest their claim upon the desire of the people and their spiritual needs. In the transition to the Roman Mass, i.e., at first to the Gelasian Sacramentaries, a prayer of blessing *super populum* at the end of Mass was to be found in a large portion of the Mass formularies, and this was even preceded by a formal invitation to receive the blessing. At the same time a transfer of the blessing to the real end of the Mass could be welcomed, because the exit of the non-communicants right after the *Pater noster* would have looked almost like a universal flight from the house of God. But when the further transition was made to the Gregorian Sacramentary and only the post-communion remained as the last blessing, many would not see therein a proper substitute and therefore, insofar as the *oratio super populum* was not kept in the ordinary plan of the Mass, they began to fix their attention on the gesture and phrase of blessing as they were prescribed by the Roman *ordines* at the recession from the altar. This manner of blessing must then have become widespread by the end of the eleventh century.

Apropos of this, however, it is surprising that the true liturgical sources do not mention this new closing blessing until considerably later. For the liturgical texts not only of the eleventh century but even those of the twelfth are almost entirely silent about the matter. This is quite understandable because first, the blessing was not given till "after the Mass"—and even today in many churches there are various additamenta "after the Mass" which are not to be found in any liturgical book; and because, secondly, liturgists still regarded the action as not justifiable and would rather not talk about it. But because occasionally even in the later Middle Ages there were *ordines* of the Mass (some which describe the close of the Mass in exact detail) which leave out any reference to a blessing, we are forced to infer that the blessing was really not given in many places. And this is true especially in monastery churches, where many private Masses were said and consequently there was no need of a blessing. In this sense the Dominican *Ordinarium* of 1256 concludes the Mass *ordo* with the remark: "Let a blessing be given according to the custom of the country if it be the custom of the country and if there are strangers present who expect it." The silence especially of the monastic Mass books at the end of the Middle Ages must be understood, as a rule, as implying that the blessing was omitted. The Benedictines, Cistercians, Premonstratensians, and Dominicans did not incorporate the final blessing in their Mass plans until later, and the Carthusians have not done so even to this day.

On the other hand, another final blessing at the Sunday high Mass was to be found precisely in monasteries; namely, a blessing of the reader at table for the coming week.

FORMULAS AND GESTURES

The citation of a special formula of blessing was generally superfluous, because ordinarily the form used was the form common in that particular country, the same as that always in use at private blessings. Consequently, where the texts of blessings are mentioned, we find the most diverse formulations.

However, the connection with the blessing as it was described in the Roman *ordo* and as it became ever more strongly anchored in the episcopal service, remained clearly evident. The liturgical commentators pay more and more attention to this episcopal blessing. As far back as the middle of the twelfth century, even in Rome, this blessing was no longer given on leaving, but imparted from the altar. At the beginning of the fourteenth century we find it in a heightened form. It is the same ceremonial that has become customary at episcopal pontifical Mass and also in the episcopal private Mass. Even in the later Middle Ages this Roman method of imparting the blessing had often become current also outside of Rome and Italy. Thus, the living model of the episcopal rite could gradually have encouraged the sacerdotal blessing, all the more so in northern countries, since the episcopal blessing given in this place—perhaps generally on less festive occasions—did not have the solemn form of the Gallic pontifical blessing, which was always reserved to the bishop. But we also recall at once the simple "May the Lord bless us" of the Roman rubric booklets when, in the accounts of the sacerdotal blessing that now begin to be more plain and outspoken, we find frequent mention made of the priest blessing himself. Or we are reminded of it in the formulas which begin with the same words (and by degrees become more expanded) or which in some other way modestly include the one imparting the blessing. Formulas or variants that employ the word "you" appear comparatively seldom: "May the blessing . . . descend upon and remain with you," and so forth. The formula in use today, "May Almighty God bless you, the Father, the Son, and the Holy Spirit," appears (among other places) at the Synod of Albi (1230).

Here and there, however, the solemnity of the concluding sacerdotal blessing began gradually to increase, taking on forms which, according to modern ideas, belong to the episcopal rite. There are introductory versicles, which have been used even in the thirteenth century as a specialty of the episcopal rite: "May the name of the Lord be blessed" and "Our help is in the name of the Lord." The words of blessing are accompanied not with a single sign of the Cross, but with three or even four—towards the four points of the compass. In pronouncing the blessing a chant tone is used. In all these matters the missal of Pius V and its revision by Clement VIII (1604) have indicated retrenchments and clear restrictions.

On the other hand, the consciousness that there ought to be some difference even in the final blessing between the bishop's way of doing it and the priest's was manifested in various ways also in the Middle Ages. The bishop made the sign of the Cross with his hand, while the priest was to use some blessed object. It had been the custom in some places already in the eleventh century to place relics on the altar during Mass or a particle of the true Cross, and to use these to impart the blessing at the end of Mass. Durandus advises the priest to make this sign of the Cross with a crucifix or with the paten or with the corporal. This manner of giving the sacerdotal blessing, especially with the paten or with the corporal, is frequently attested since the fourteenth century, at first in France, and then also in Germany. The chalice and paten, indeed, generally remained uncovered on the altar till the end of Mass.

While these methods of imparting the final blessing have disappeared, yet one peculiarity which, aside from the words, distinguished it from the sacerdotal blessing otherwise used outside of Mass, has been kept; before giving the blessing the priest raises his eyes and hands towards heaven. This gesture is explained by the medieval allegorism, which saw in this blessing the last blessing of Our Lord before He ascended into heaven when He blessed His disciples, "with His hands lifted up." (Luke 24:50).

The final blessing was sometimes given before kissing the altar and reciting the *Placeat*, sometimes after. In general the determining factor seems to have been the priority of the respective development. In France, where the *Placeat* had been incorporated earlier, the blessing generally followed. On the other hand, in Germany, where the *Placeat* was introduced only later, the blessing was as a rule given before. This latter sequence was for a time the prevailing one also in Rome. It is found even in various editions of the Roman Missal, e.g., in those of 1474, 1530 and 1540. The inversion, as fixed in the missal of Pius V, must have originated from the notion that, if blessing and prayer were to follow the dismissal, then surely the blessing which at one time was itself called a *missa* must necessarily stand at the end. The same feeling lay at the root of the practice in the church of Rouen where, in the dying years of the medieval era, when the final blessing had been magnified into a form of great solemnity, this blessing was placed after the last Gospel. In regard to the formula to be used, for a long time—as we have already said—there was no fixed rule. In the printed editions of the *Missale Romanum* of 1530 and 1540 we find a choice between two forms; they were essentially the ones which had been recommended by Durandus. In the printed editions of 1505, 1509, 1543, 1558, 1560 and 1561 only one of them is given, "May the Father and the Son bless you in the unity of the Holy Spirit." which was eventually displaced in favor of the formula we have at present.

The editions of the Roman missal printed in 1558 and 1560 also presented a special form of blessing for the Mass of the Dead: "May God, the Life of the living, and the Resurrection of the dead, bless you for ever and ever." But here, too, the later *Missale Romanum* asserted the general principle that all blessing of the living should be omitted in Requiem Masses. German missals of the declining Middle Ages introduced in the Mass *ordo* a blessing for the departed, even outside of Masses of the Dead. As in the office the oration and *Benedicamus Domino* are followed by *Fidelium animæ*, so also in the Mass following the post-communion and the dismissal first a blessing for the dead was given and then the blessing of the living.[1] In the Roman missals at Rome this blessing of the dead did not have a place. But the *Requiescant in pace* at Requiem Masses, which seems like a shortened form of this blessing, appears to have sprung from a similar source. But an immediate derivation is not possible because of the time interval—the *Requiescant in pace* appears 300 years earlier.

5. The Last Gospel

It is certainly remarkable that at the close of the Roman Mass a gospel pericope should be read. But if we go back to its origin, we find that this reading harmonizes with the series of dismissal rites and more particularly with the blessings. The prologue of the Gospel according to St. John, with the exalted flight of its ideas and the profundity of its mysteries, was accorded an extraordinary esteem even in the early Church. Augustine quotes the saying of a contemporary of his that this text ought to be placed in gold letters at some prominent place in all the churches.

The prologue of St. John is rightly regarded as a summary of the Gospel, the divine power of which is, in a measure, concentrated there. Just as sacred symbols, words or pictures were used as pledges of divine protection, just as blessings were and still are imparted with holy objects, cross, chalice, paten, or (in the Orient) with *dikirion* and *trikirion*, so in the course of time the beginning of the Gospel of St. John began to be used as an instrument of blessing. It might be that the written words were carried on one's person, or that they were recited or listened to. Naturally it could happen that, in place of that Christian trust in God which, inspired by the sacred word, looks up to Him in humble petition, superstitious and magical practices would creep in. In the year 1022 the synod of Seligenstadt noted that many lay people and especially

[1] In other words, we would find first something like "May the souls of the faithful departed through the mercy of God rest in peace," and then the "May Almighty God bless you, etc."

women placed great store in daily hearing the Gospel *In principio erat Verbum* or special Masses *de s. Trinitate* or *de s. Michaele*. In the future, this was to be allowed only *suo tempore* and insofar as it was asked out of reverence for the Blessed Trinity, and "not for any kind of divination."

But alongside this misuse of the holy text there was still room for the proper and Christian use of it. The beginning of the Gospel of St. John was read in the sick-room before dispensing the last sacraments, or after baptism over the newly baptized child. A particularly favorite use, dating back to the twelfth century, was as a blessing for the weather, just as later the introductions of the four Gospels (for the four points of the compass) were used, and are still used, for the purpose. Just as during the summer—from Holy Cross (May 3) to Holy Cross (Sept. 14)—this blessing in some form or other is given even today, in many dioceses every Sunday, and in some places every day after the parish Mass, so it might have happened that the prologue of St. John, as a pericope of blessing, became more and more a permanent part of the end of Mass. In his explanation of the Mass which appeared about 1505, the Augustinian hermit John Bechofen speaks about the reading of this Gospel as a "laudable custom," and he grounds the custom on the argument that reading or hearing the Gospel is a direct attack on the devil, who is trying to rob us of our union with God and to harm us in soul, body and goods.

The first evidence of the Gospel of St. John at the end of Mass—it is a question here primarily of private Mass—is found in the *Ordinarium* of the Dominicans, which was fixed in 1256: The priest may recite it when unvesting or later, together with the oration *Omnipotens æterne Deus, dirige actus*. This custom must have rapidly found favor in the Dominican order, for members of the order working in the Armenian mission introduced the last Gospel, among other things, into the Armenian Mass, and with such effect indeed, that in spite of the break-down of the union in 1380 it remained in the liturgy even of the schismatics down to the present—an example of missionary latinizing which, to the Middle Ages (which were not renowned for their historical sense), seemed only natural.

In the West, however, it had not become common everywhere even at the close of the Middle Ages. When, in the year 1558, the first general chapter of the Society of Jesus, convened to choose a successor to St. Ignatius, expressed the desire to make the rite of the Mass uniform within the order, the last Gospel was one of the points that still hung in balance even in Rome itself. A last Gospel was indeed decided upon for the order's rite, but it was left free to choose Luke 11:27 f (the pericope which recounts the happy cry of the woman in the crowd: "Blessed is the womb that bore thee"), or the prologue of St. John. On the other hand, the Carthusians have not yet taken the last Gospel into their rite even today, just as they have not inserted the last blessing.

Oftentimes the last Gospel was rounded off liturgically by reciting an oration after it, and as a rule this latter was introduced by a few versicles.

Already in the thirteenth century the prologue of St. John was not commonly regarded as the only possible last Gospel, although this is seldom indicated in earlier sources. But with the increasing possibility of using another Gospel reading, the thought suggested itself with ever greater force that the last Gospel, besides having the character of a final blessing and sacramental, might at the same time be a commemoration in which the main text of a second formulary could be taken up in this place in the Mass. This notion was all the more natural because even in the sixteenth century the *missa sicca* was still current custom. At such a "mass," at which the priest officiated without chasuble, and which was generally added to the regular Mass, the celebrant as a rule read the entire proper text of the second formulary, along with other Mass prayers (except the canon), or else only the Epistle, the Gospel and the *Pater noster*. Then, as the *missa sicca* gradually disappeared after the Council of Trent, it did not involve too great a change to keep at least the proper Gospel of the second formulary as an appendage to the first Mass. It did not take long to make such a proposal. In the missal of Pius V a special addition of this kind was proposed first of all for those formularies of the *proprium de tempore* which were hindered. In 1920, in the new edition of Benedict XV, this was extended to all those Masses which have an *evangelium stricte proprium*, as, for example, the Mass formularies of the Blessed Mother or an apostle. But finally, in the reform of the rubrics in 1955, the use of another last Gospel was confined to the third Mass of Christmas, and Palm Sunday.

CHANGE IN CHARACTER

It cannot be denied that through such directions a progressive change in the character of the last Gospel and a refinement of its function is revealed. The note of blessing draws into the background. It is the content of the pericope, even that of St. John, that comes to the fore. More recent exponents of the Mass no longer mention the benedictional character of the last Gospel; they try to portray the Johannine pericope, with the mystery of the incarnation therein contained, as the real epilogue of the entire Mass, the concluding paragraph by which the Mass is brought back to its "eternal root" or source. The prologue of the "good tidings" has thus become the epilogue of the sacrifice by which those tidings are renewed. Naturally a convincing reason for the necessity of such an epilogue is not forthcoming. In consequence there is something incongruous, something discordant about this last point of the Mass-liturgy. This is shown also by the fact that there is no actual "proclamation" of the Gospel, no public reading of it. True, the Gospel is introduced with the same forms as the Gospel of the fore-Mass, a greeting, an announcement, with an acclamatory response, and the faithful are accustomed to rise and cross themselves with the priest as at the Gospel of the fore-Mass. But this greeting and announcement and acclamation, like the reading itself, are all done only in a semi-audible voice. Evidently, then, these are only imitations designed to create a worthy frame around the priest's reading. In fact, the reading itself has not the formal character of a lesson; it is normally recited by rote, like a sacred text which is always handy. At the end of the Middle Ages, "in many countries," as the *Hortulus animæ* (published at Strassburg in 1503) averred, the Gospel of St. John was recited by all present, a practice which obviously was planned to strengthen its function as a blessing. In the pontifical high Mass the bishop speaks these words while leaving the altar; he merely makes the sign of the cross on the altar, to show that he receives the word of the Gospel from the altar, from Christ, from God.

6. *The Prayers of Leo XIII*

More than once in the course of our study of the Mass-liturgy and its historical development we have come upon this notion of intercessory prayers, and precisely intercessory prayers for the needs of the Church, to be said by the people in common. They had their original place at the end of the readings or lessons, in the General Prayer of the Church. When this General Prayer was dropped from the Roman liturgy at the turn of the fifth century, its popular components acquired a fresh and rich development in the *Kyrie* litany, while the priest's intercessory plea entered more deeply into the innermost sanctuary of the canon. Then, as the *Kyrie* litany was reduced to a manifold repetition of the *Kyrie* invocation and modified into a melodic song for the choir, the need for supplication in times of dire trouble produced anew, since the ninth century, a mode of expression in conjunction with the Lord's Prayer, at first after the embolism, later before it.

And finally, in the later years of the Middle Ages, prayers for wants and peace were injected into other places, especially after the *Dona nobis pacem*. In the latter cases we are dealing only with common prayers to be recited by the clerics assembled in choir, but the *literati* who knew Latin were expected to join in.

The kernel of the prayers which we recite after private Mass had been in use even before Leo XIII. In 1859, when the danger to the Papal States grew ever more serious, Pius IX ordered prayers for the area of his secular dominion. The prescription continued even after the Papal States had fallen. When Leo XIII made his last efforts to set aside the laws of the *Kulturkampf* in Germany and to win back the liberty of the Church, on January 6, 1884, he extended these prayers to the whole Church. Even after the liberty of the Church was essentially won back here, the prayers nevertheless remained. In their new form, as we have it today, they were broadened to include a purpose which undoubtedly must be dear to the heart of the Church at all times: in the oration, among other things, the words "for the conversion of sinners" were added.[1]

Measured by the ceremonial form of the Roman Mass-liturgy, it is indeed striking that these prayers are recited kneeling at the foot of the altar. It had been customary for the priest to give expression to the humble and suppliant petition of such prayers by means of a low bow. But since such a bodily bearing was no longer customary among the faithful, and it is with the faithful that the priest is to say these prayers, nothing was left but this kneeling together, an attitude of prayer for which there were precedents even at the altar. This kneeling position at the end of Mass had been prescribed in the liturgy of the Carthusians long ago, in their *Statuta antiqua* (before 1259); according to this direction the priest, after laying aside his vestments, is to recite the *Pater noster* kneeling at the foot of the altar.

As regards their construction, the prayers of Leo XIII follow in all essentials the laws of form of the Roman liturgy. Whereas earlier examples of similar prayers in need regularly began with psalms, here the more popular element of the Hail Mary was chosen; with the petition which is a part of it, this prayer is recited three times, and then the *Salve Regina*[2] is added to further enforce the tone of supplication. As we know, the effort to give the liturgical celebration a Marian note in the high Middle Ages led to the practice of concluding the canonical office, or at least certain hours of it, with a Marian antiphon. A prayer of praise addressed to the Blessed Virgin was sometimes added also in the Mass, either after Communion or at the close. The *Salve Regina*, too, sometimes formed the close of the *ordo* of the Mass. The versicle "Pray for us, O Holy Mother of God," then leads over to an oration, as is ordinarily done according to traditional usage after a psalm or an antiphon. And the oration gathers together our prayers and formulates our pleading. Here again the old stylistic rules of the Roman method of prayer are at work: in view of the intercession (already sought) of the

---

[1] It should also be pointed out that both Pius XI and Pius XII have designated the prayers as being chiefly for the conversion of Russia. For Pius XII, cf. *Acta Ap. Sedis* 44 (1952). 508.

[2] The *Salve Regina* must have originated in the 11th century in the monastery of Reichenau; for more details about its history see Wm. Martin, "The Salve Regina," *Liturgical Arts*, 16 (1948), 41–48.

Mother of God, with whom are ranged the great protectors of holy Church, we beg of God's grace the internal welfare and the external freedom and growth of the Church, and we close the prayer with "Through Christ Our Lord."

Finally, to this addition other further additions were made, and again we cannot affirm that these additions have any intrinsic relationship to what has gone before. Leo XIII himself, in 1886, when issuing the new form of the oration, added the invocation to the Archangel Michael. There is no question here of a second oration but rather of an isolated invocation, something very unusual in the Roman liturgy.

Another independent composition, of an entirely different character, strikingly in contrast with the final words of the preceding prayer,[3] "cast into hell," is the threefold cry: "Most Sacred Heart of Jesus, have mercy on us," added under Pius X. However, here is not a matter of regulation but of permission granted by the Congregation of Indulgences, dated June 17, 1904. If, however, a certain obligation has arisen in this matter, as it seems it has, it must be derived from the custom that has been established.

The publication of the prayers of Leo XIII included the direction that they be said with the people, but no official text in the vernacular was prescribed. As a result almost every diocese uses its own version. This is true not only in Germany but elsewhere, too.[4] Obviously such a state of things did not help to endear the prayers to either priest or people. Insofar as they had to be added—and they had to be added even on feasts that excluded every commemoration!—these prayers not seldom underwent that same "liturgizing," that same reduction to an exchange between priest and server, that same fusion with the Latin of the rest of the Mass-liturgy that forced other textual elements which were originally conceived in the vernacular—like the phrases before the distribution of Communion—back into a Latin mold.

In France, Italy, and elsewhere for the past few decades another prayer in the vernacular has become customary at the end of Mass and Benediction. This prayer consists of a number of laudatory sentences recited singly by the faithful after the priest. It is called "The Divine Praises." It begins with the praise of God: "Blessed be God," then touches on the most important mysteries of faith in the form suited to the religious thought of the time, and ends with the words, "Blessed be God in his angels and in his saints."[5] In this way the close of the Mass acquires a final harmony which re-echoes in the *Benedicite* of the priest.

[3] In Latin, the final words of the prayer are *infernum detrude*, "cast into hell." As far as the Reviser knows, this is not the case in English translation.—Rev.
[4] On the difficulties of translation see the article by R. E. Brennan, "The Leonine Prayers," *American Ecclesiastical Review*, 125 (1951), 85–94, especially 89 f.
[5] The "Divine Praises" originated in Rome, the work of Fr. Aloysius Felici, S.J., who presumably publicized them in 1797 as a means of combating blasphemy.

7. *Recession*

When all the final obligations have been taken care of, the priest leaves the altar. In the Mass celebrated without levites, the priest—according to present-day practice—himself carries the chalice, with the paten on top and a veil covering it, and the burse with the corporal, back to the sacristy, while the Mass-server as a rule precedes him with the book. At a high Mass the sacred vessels remain on the credence table.

This order, which appears to us so natural, is of relatively recent date. That the chalice and paten should be carried in the manner customary today could not have been considered, as we have seen, until the time when the paten was reduced in size. A German Mass-plan about the year *1000*, in describing the end of the high Mass, directs the subdeacon to carry the (uncovered) chalice, and an acolyte, the paten. But after that both chalice and paten are taken together. However, because even at the close of the Middle Ages our chalice-veil did not yet exist, the priest—according to the Mass-*ordo* of Burchard of Strassburg (*1502*)—placed the chalice and paten in a small bag which he then tied, put the burse with the folded corporal on top of the bag, and carried the two into the sacristy, while the server preceded him (according to this *ordo*) carrying the book, the pillow, the cruets, the box for the hosts, the altar candles and the elevation candle. The present arrangement, therefore, dates back only to the time of Pius V.

ACCOMPANYING TEXTS

At the recession the priest begins the canticle *Benedicite*, the song sung by the three young Hebrews in the Babylonian furnace (Dan. 3:57–88). This, and the prayers that go with it are now found in the Roman missal no longer as part of the text of the *Ordo missæ* but in the *Gratiarum actio post missam* which is prefaced to the missal. The pertinent rubric is therefore today considered as merely directive. On the other hand, medieval Mass books which include this canticle and the other closing prayers that follow it, after they became customary about the year 1000, regularly group them with the preceding texts without indicating any distinction. This song of praise, which was recited at the recession and which from the very start was united with Psalm 150, was on about the same level with the psalm *Judica* which was said at the beginning of Mass, and it was recited or sung by the celebrant, together with the assistants, at the altar, as the oldest witnesses from about the tenth century expressly remark. Even here the psalmody was followed by a number of versicles and the oration *Deus qui tribus pueris*. But, soon after, various expansions begin to appear.

Between the *Benedicite* and Psalm 150, Psalm 116 *Laudate Dominum omnes gentes*, was sometimes inserted, or the ancient hymn *Te decet laus* was appended. Later we find that they sometimes added the *Nunc dimittis*. At the head of the versicles which were subject to a great deal of shifting, we find the *Pater noster* and the *Kyrie*, and as an addition to the oration *Deus qui tribus pueris*, which for centuries has been used even in other circumstances as an adjunct to the canticle of the Three Young Men, we find a second oration, *Actiones nostras*.

Much later, and only occasionally, do we find the oration (in the third place in our day) which refers to the victorious suffering of St. Lawrence. Some have suggested that this rather strange oration is to be traced back to the practice of the pre-Avignon popes, who were accustomed to celebrate daily Mass in the papal chapel of the Lateran's *Sancta sanctorum* dedicated to St. Lawrence. The facts, however, contradict this opinion. The oration from the Mass of St. Lawrence would have been adopted whenever they began to put greater emphasis on the character of the canticle as the song of the three young men in the fiery furnace, with whose fate St. Lawrence's had such a likeness. That was evidently the case after the song was framed with the antiphon *Trium puerorum cantemus hymnum*, which appears for the first time in 1170 in the pontifical of Mainz. For in the medieval texts the Laurentian oration has a different position than in the Roman missal, either immediately after the oration *Deus qui tribus pueris*, or separated only by the oration *Ure igne Sancti Spiritus* which is intrinsically akin to it. These orations were intended to petition help against the most dangerous enemy, the enemy within us. In this tradition the oration *Actiones nostras* was not at first provided.

On the other hand, the versicles which even at present precede the orations endeavor to take up the tone of praise and above all to continue the theme started in the verse *Benedicite, sacerdotes Domini, Domino*, the stirring call to priests whose very first duty it is to hymn the praises of God. Hence such versicles as "The saints shall rejoice in glory." One series of sources, in fact, provides only that part of the canticle itself beginning with the verse cited above. In the concluding orations there was less room for such a tone of joy, since they were prayers of petition.

The idea of a psalmodic song of praise at the end of Mass is so natural that there is hardly any need of a special explanation, more particularly when such a song of praise at the recession (as is the case in the oldest witnesses) is only the counterpart of the psalm of longing which has accompanied the accession to the altar. Indeed, it is surprising that the song of praise at the end did not, like the psalm at the beginning, remain an integral part of the actual liturgy to be recited at the altar.

The canticle *Benedicite* and Psalm 150 are eminently suited to the purpose. In view of what has occurred at the altar, all creation seems to us to resound in wordless jubilee and to sing the praises of Him who has so richly favored the world and mankind.

Then, too, the canonical hours have been drawn on occasionally to prolong the praise of God. In the Lateran basilica during the twelfth century, after the *Ite missa est* of a pontifical high Mass, sext was begun, and only after it was finished did the bishop return to his seat. A similar thing is still done in many cathedrals at the present.

Next comes silent prayer and meditation. It is no discovery of modern piety that the time after Mass and Communion, when the crowd has dispersed and quiet has settled over the church, is a time for the priest—and the same holds for the faithful—to give himself to more than vocal prayer. Monastic Mass-plans of the thirteenth century, after indicating the recessional prayers, add this direction for the priest: "When all is finished, the priest can pray silently as the Lord inspires him." In the spirit of olden prescriptions the canon law at present warns the priest that just as he prepared himself for the sacrifice by prayer, so he ought not to forget to make a proper thanksgiving afterward. This is in accord with a long-established ascetical practice.

For this, of course, the liturgical books can offer nothing else but more prayer texts. In the Roman missal the appendix to the real recessional prayers, the *Orationes pro opportunitate sacerdotis dicendæ*, contains such texts, of which particularly the first, captioned as *Oratio s. Thomæ Aquinatis*, is very old. The prayer following, which is called *Oratio s. Bonaventuræ*, actually comes from the pen of that doctor of the Church. For the rest, the series of prayers here presented has in recent years been enriched in many ways. Missals of the Middle Ages now and again contain at the end an addition of private prayers of a similar sort. But here a distinction between private and public prayer, while not absolutely excluded, is even harder to make than in the present missal, since indeed some of the Mass prayers themselves were still in the stage of private prayers.

When we look farther back and try to get a picture of the first thousand years of the Mass-liturgy, we must admit that generally with the *Ite missa est* not only communal divine service but also personal devotion were terminated, so that the Mass in the Roman liturgy, even when the older oration of blessing was still customary, came to a relatively rapid and abrupt end, and there could be but little talk of a special thanksgiving for all the great things which God had granted in Christ and in His Church. What was momentarily received in the Sacrament was only a sacramental corroboration of the presence of that grace in which our Christian life is imbedded. If the realization of this were revived in the celebration, the work of the entire day could actually become a sufficient thanksgiving for this new hour of grace, as many a *post-communio* sets forth. But with the increasing separation of a gradually fixed Mass-liturgy on the one side and of personal piety, ever seeking new roads, on the other side, and with the growing accentuation of the Eucharist as an all-embracing and all-illuminating gift of God, it was but natural that a *gratiarum actio* should become a requirement even after the *Eucharistia*. The more conscious practice of meditative prayer, which was known to the ancient monks only in the form of the *lectio divina*, was also bound to lead in the same direction. For no moment is so opportune for meditating on what we have received and what we possess, as the moment when the last prayers of Mass have died away. Although we are less shocked than our forebears were when the faithful who have work to do take the *Ite missa est* more or less literally, even when they have been to Communion, still for clerics at least a good solution would be to use the few moments of quiet prayer after the sacred action as an opportunity to allow the spirit of the Eucharist to permeate our innermost soul more and more.

Index

Set up, printed and bound by Benziger Brothers, Inc., New York

Votive Mass: one that takes care of personal
concerns (vota) – special intentions